CHILD ABUSE
AND NEGLECT

CONTEMPORARY PROBLEMS OF CHILDHOOD: A Bibliographic Series
Series Editor: Carol Ann Winchell

THE GIFTED STUDENT: An Annotated Bibliography
Jean Laubenfels

CHILD ABUSE AND NEGLECT

AN ANNOTATED BIBLIOGRAPHY

Beatrice J. Kalisch

Contemporary Problems of Childhood, Number 2

GREENWOOD PRESS
Westport, Connecticut • London, England

Library of Congress Cataloging in Publication Data

Kalisch, Beatrice J., 1943-
    Child abuse and neglect.
    (Contemporary problems of childhood ; no. 2 ISSN 0147
-1082)
    Includes indexes.
    1. Child abuse—Bibliography. 2. Child abuse—
United States—Bibliography. I. Title. II. Series.
Z7164.C5K34   [HV713]   016.3627'1   78-3123
ISBN 0-313-20376-8

Library of Congress Catalog Card Number: 78-3123
ISBN: 0-313-20376-8
ISSN: 0147-1082

First published in 1978

Greenwood Press, Inc.
51 Riverside Avenue, Westport, Connecticut 06880

Printed in the United States of America

10 9 8 7 6 5 4 3 2

To my husband, Philip,
for his support and encouragement

CONTENTS

Series Foreword	xiii
Preface	xv
Introduction	xix

I. INTRODUCTION **3**
  A. GENERAL 3
     1. Comprehensive Studies and Symposiums 3
     2. Brief Summaries 16
     3. Bibliographies 25

  B. HISTORICAL OVERVIEW 26
     1. Attitudes Toward Children 26
     2. Cruelty to Children 29
     3. Child Protective Services 32

  C. DEFINITIONS 36
     1. Child Abuse 36
     2. Child Neglect 39
     3. Institutional and Societal Abuse 42

  D. INCIDENCE 47

  E. DEMOGRAPHIC CHARACTERISTICS 55
     1. Demographic Studies in the United States 55
     2. Demographic Studies in Other Countries 66

II. PREDICTION, DETECTION, AND PREVENTION **71**
  A. PREDICTION 71

  B. DETECTION 76

  C. INVESTIGATING AND REPORTING 79
     1. General Investigations 79

2. The Role of Professionals   80
3. Hospitals, Agencies, and Central Registers   85

D. PREVENTIVE MEASURES   90
1. Protective Programs and Centers   90
2. Health Visitors   100
3. Family Planning   101
4. Adult Education   104
5. Child Care   107
6. Hot-Lines   108

III. *CAUSATIVE FACTORS*   111
A. SOCIOLOGICAL/CULTURAL FACTORS   111
1. Urban Life and Environmental Stress   111
2. Poverty and Social Deprivation   119

B. PSYCHOLOGICAL CAUSES   125
1. Psychological Studies of Abusive Parents   125
2. Psychological Profiles of the Abusive Mother   139

C. DYNAMICS OF PREGNANCY AND THE
NEONATAL PERIOD   144
1. Prenatal Indicators of Abuse   144
2. Parent-to-Infant Bonding Failure   148
3. Infanticide   153

D. FAMILY DYSFUNCTION   158
1. General Factors   158
2. Marital Stress   164
3. Inadequate Parenting Practices   166
4. Discipline and Familial Violence   170
5. The Generational Cycle of Abuse   177
6. The Child's Role in Provoking Abuse   182
7. Drug-Addicted Mothers   185

IV. *MANIFESTATIONS*   187
A. DIAGNOSTIC TECHNIQUES   187

B. ABUSE: PHYSICAL SIGNS   204
1. Subdural Hematomas and Other Head Injuries   204
2. Skeletal Injury   211
3. Internal Trauma   221
4. Visual Problems   225
5. Poisoning   227
6. Other Physical Signs   229

C. ABUSE: PSYCHOLOGICAL EFFECTS 236

D. NEGLECT 243
    1. Physical Effects 243
    2. Psychological Effects 251
    3. Mental Retardation and Learning Problems 259

E. VIOLENCE AND CRIME 264

V. TREATMENT **268**
A. OVERVIEW 268

B. COMMUNITY AND HOSPITAL SERVICES 281
    1. Multidisciplinary Efforts 281
    2. State, City, and County Programs 291
    3. Private Programs 300
    4. Community-Based Teams 303
    5. Hospital-Based Teams 309
    6. Medical Care 314
    7. Nursing Care 325
    8. Social Services 331
    9. Responsibility of the Schools 339

C. SEPARATION AND PLACEMENT 343
    1. Discussion of Procedures 343
    2. Foster Care 346
    3. Institutional Care 349

D. PSYCHOLOGICAL TREATMENT 349
    1. Group Therapy 349
    2. Parents 352
        a. General 352
        b. Psychotherapy 355
        c. Parents Anonymous 360
    3. Children 362
    4. Family Therapy 363

E. FEDERAL PROJECTS AND POLICIES 372

F. EVALUATIONS OF PROGRAMS 375

VI. SEXUAL ABUSE **379**
A. PATTERNS AND CAUSES 379
    1. Incestual Offenders 379
    2. Other Child Molesters 384

B. EFFECTS 385

	1. Incest	385
	2. Other Sexual Molestations	387
C.	DIAGNOSIS AND REPORTING	390
D.	LEGAL PROSECUTION	393
E.	TREATMENT AND PREVENTION	394
	1. Child Care	394
	2. Corrective Measures for the Offender	395
	3. Preventive Measures	396
F.	PORNOGRAPHY	397

VII. LEGAL ISSUES   **399**

A.	THE RIGHTS OF CHILDREN	399
	1. Historical Survey and Present Issues	399
	2. Child vs. Institution	401
B.	LEGISLATION	404
	1. Historical Survey of Child Protection	404
	2. Status of Present Legislation	406
	a. Model Legislation	406
	b. Existing Systems: General	408
	c. Federal Initiatives	414
	(1) Child Abuse Prevention and Treatment Act	414
	(2) Office of Child Development Programs;	
	Other Programs	418
	d. Individual State Initiatives	421
C.	REPORTING AND ENFORCEMENT	426
	1. Reporting Laws	426
	a. Model Reporting Laws	426
	b. Comparisons and Surveys of Reporting Legislation	427
	c. Individual State Laws	434
	2. Enforcement	443
	a. Role of Physician	443
	(1) Responsibilities	443
	(2) Reluctance, Failure to Report	448
	b. Role of Police	454
	c. Role of Other Professionals	455
D.	THE COURTS	457
	1. Bases for Judicial Intervention	457
	2. Judicial Procedures for Intervention	468
	3. Courts and Welfare Agencies	474

E.   PROTECTIVE SERVICES   476

APPENDIX A: Basic Bibliographic Tools   480
APPENDIX B: Selected Organizations Interested in Child
                  Abuse and Neglect   482
APPENDIX C: Child Abuse Prevention and Treatment Act
                  (Text of Public Law 93-247)   483
Author Index   489
Selective Key Word Subject Index   511
List of Journal Abbreviations   523

SERIES FOREWORD

The attention focused on children's problems has become increasingly pronounced in the United States during the last two decades. Particular interest and involvement have been directed toward certain problems: pathological conditions, the handicapped child, the educationally and culturally deprived child, and various behavior disorders. This interest has produced a voluminous body of knowledge. One needs only a cursory perusal through the literature to realize that it has now proliferated into an extensive, but unorganized, number of publications. Through modern technology, masses of material have been flowing from the presses; given this plethora of publication, it is frequently difficult to locate specific materials. A Tower of Babel situation has developed in that some of this valuable information is unknown to the researcher who might wish to be aware of its existence.

The purpose of *Contemporary Problems of Childhood* is to identify, collect, classify, abstract, and index relevant material on the following topics in need of systematic control: the gifted child, child abuse, behavior modification techniques with children, the autistic child, the child with dyslexia, and the hyperkinetic syndrome. Not only have these topics been the subject of academe, but the mass media—magazines, newspapers, and commercial and educational television specials—have recently devoted considerable attention to these problems. To bring some order to this discipline, it was decided to issue a series of volumes, each considering one of these topics and following the format of an earlier volume by this editor, *The Hyperkinetic Child: A Bibliography of Medical, Educational, and Psychological Studies* (Greenwood Press, 1975). Volumes are intended to aid the retrieval of information for educators, psychologists, physicians, researchers, parents, and others interested in etiology, diagnosis, and management.

The volumes in the series are broad in scope, interdisciplinary, comprehensive in coverage, and contain retrospective and current citations. The titles cited mainly reflect developments over the last decade, but some earlier titles of relevance are included. Selection of citations is based on the quality and direct applicability to the topic under consideration. For these publications only English-language sources are selected.

The entries are culled from extensive searches of manual and computerized information sources. Basic indexing and abstracting services, as well as many diverse and widely scattered sources, have been searched. Books, chapters in books, journal articles, conference reports, pamphlets, government documents, dissertations, and proceedings of symposiums are included. Since a bewildering variety of terminology exists for each subject, compilers have attempted to weed out unexplicitly defined topics.

Front matter contains appropriate introductory material: preface, contents, and a "state-of-the-art" message by a specialist in the area. Entries are classified and arranged alphabetically by author under the correct subject heading and appear only once in the bibliography.

Citations include complete and verified bibliographic information: author, title, source, volume, issue number, publisher, place, date, number of pages, and references. An attempt is made to annotate all citations that can be located, giving context, scope, and possible findings and results of the book or article.

Appendixes, author and key-word subject indexes, and journal abbreviations complete each volume.

It is hoped that the documentation provided by *Contemporary Problems of Childhood* will facilitate access to retrospective and current sources of information and help bring bibliographic control to this rapidly expanding body of literature.

Carol A. Winchell
General Editor

PREFACE

PURPOSE

Although instances of child abuse and neglect can be traced back five thousand years to the beginning of man's recorded activities, it was not until the 1870s that the first societies for the prevention of cruelty to children were founded in the United States, and it was 1930 before an American Children's Charter was adopted which promised every child a loving and secure home and public welfare services to protect children from abuse and neglect. Medical recognition of child abuse and neglect was painfully slow. Dr. John Caffey reported in 1946 the unusual coexistence of subdural hematomas (blood on the brain) and new and old fractures in the long bones of infants,[1] and Paul V. Woolley and William A. Evans surmised in 1955 that such injuries were not accidental.[2] Six years later, a 1961 symposium on the battered child, sponsored by the American Academy of Pediatrics, called widespread attention to the problem. It heralded the beginning of a surge of research and writing on the subject of child abuse and neglect that has continued to the present day.

Despite the recent outpouring of literature pertaining to child abuse and neglect, the strong interest in the problem, the multidisciplinary nature of the topic, and the obscurity of early publications all suggest the utility of some form of bibliographic control. This work aims to provide a tool which may assist researchers, human service workers, and lay persons in finding and using the available literature on child abuse and neglect.

COVERAGE

The literature from the late 1800s, when child abuse and neglect was first recognized as a problem in the modern sense, to 1977 is included in this bibliography. Due to the recent mushrooming of materials on child abuse and neglect, however, the vast majority of the publications cited appeared in the 1960s and 1970s. References prior to the 1960s were uncovered under such topics as cruelty to children, child welfare, child development, and protective services.

SCOPE

The broadest possible search was made to incorporate literature from more than a dozen fields of knowledge including sociology, psychology, nursing, social work, medicine, education, law, and child development. Lay persons seeking a general introduction to the subject will find an extensive survey of articles that appeared in popular magazines. The type of publication analyzed and abstracted includes not only books, book chapters, and journal articles, but also government documents, reports of special investigative committees, conference proceedings, doctoral dissertations, and pamphlets. Excluded from this bibliography are foreign language references, newspaper articles, speeches, and unpublished papers.

ARRANGEMENT

The arrangement of entries follows a logical breakdown of the subject of child abuse and neglect, beginning with general surveys, historical studies, attempts at defining the problem, and demographic variables, and ending with legal issues. The Contents identifies the major headings around which the abstracts have been clustered. The Selective Key Word Subject Index is the basic point of departure in identifying all of the abstracts on a given area of interest since each entry appears only once under the most predominant focus of the item. Within each section, arrangement is alphabetical by author. Entry numbers preceding the author's names run consecutively throughout the text.

THE ENTRIES

For books and monographs, the complete citation includes author(s), title, edition, place, publisher, date, pages, inclusive pages of sections appearing as parts of larger works, and presence of bibliography. Journal citations contain author (three are given; et al. is used to indicate additional names), title of the article, journal abbreviation, volume number, issue number (in parentheses), inclusive pages, month, year, and usually the number of references. For dissertations, the user is referred to *Dissertation Abstracts International* with volume number, issue number, pages, and date given. Books and conference proceedings have been verified and entered in the bibliography under the Library of Congress *National Union Catalog: Author List* entry to facilitate retrieval for the user. Annotations are given for all entries except dissertations and several items which could not be located.

APPENDIXES

Appendix A identifies the basic bibliographic tools that were utilized in identifying and verifying the citations in this bibliography. Appendix B lists selected organizations interested in child abuse and neglect while Appendix C contains the text of the federal Child Abuse Prevention and Treatment Act (Public Law 93-247).

INDEXES

The Author Index lists the names of all individuals cited as author, joint author, editor, or compiler, including up to three names per citation. Forenames, middle initials, and surnames are given in most cases. Numbers following the names refer to item numbers in the text.

The Selective Key Word Subject Index alphabetically lists important words in entry titles. The user may find it convenient to use the broader subject arrangement under subcategories in the Contents, or this index may be consulted for more specific aspects of the topic. In general, 1) only unique terms are given— alternate words for child abuse and neglect and other high frequency terms are omitted; 2) phrases are used to put certain words in more meaningful contexts; and 3) *see also* references are used to refer the reader to similar concepts. Numbers following the words refer to item numbers in the text.

The List of Journal Abbreviations lists alphabetically all journals cited in the text. Journal title abbreviations have been formulated according to the rules of the *American National Standard for the Abbreviation of Titles of Periodicals,* and the individual words of the title are abbreviated according to the forms given in the *International List of Periodical Title Word Abbreviations.*

ACKNOWLEDGMENTS

Completion of this project over the past two and one-half years has been facilitated by several persons. A special thanks is tendered to Carol Hart, Debra Konopacki, and Diane Tasca for their very able research assistance. Also acknowledged is the work of Beverly I. McDonald, head, Authority Files Section, Cataloging Services, the Ohio State University Libraries, who served as filer; Noelle Van Pulis, information specialist, Mechanized Information Center, the Ohio State University Libraries, who developed the key word index; Jean Stouder, who typed the final manuscript; and Carol Winchell, series editor, whose general assistance was invaluable. In addition, the contribution of Ray Helfer, M.D., who generously wrote the Introduction to this work, is very much appreciated. Finally, the support and understanding of my husband, Philip, is gratefully recognized.

NOTES

1. John Caffey, "Multiple fractures in the long bones of infants suffering from chronic subdural hematoma," *Am. J. Roentgenol. Radium Ther. Nucl. Med.* 56 (2): 163-73, August, 1946.
2. Paul V. Woolley and Williams A. Evans, "Significance of skeletal lesions in infants resembling those of traumatic origin," *JAMA* 158 (7): 539-43, June 18, 1955.

INTRODUCTION

Putting Child Abuse and
Neglect into Perspective

Sixteen years have passed since Dr. C. Henry Kempe first became incensed over the presence of physically abused children on the pediatric ward at Colorado General Hospital. He proceeded to survey many prosecuting attorneys throughout the United States, only to find a large number of cases of child abuse that had occurred in the preceding year.[1] Shortly thereafter, he coined the term "the battered child" and presented his findings and concerns to the American Academy of Pediatrics.

The concerns of Kempe were preceded by similar, but not well publicized, expressions of alarm from the fields of radiology[2,3] and pathology.[4] Finally in the early 1960s the Children's Bureau became concerned about the plight of children who were physically abused and began to fund research projects designed to ascertain the cause and magnitude of the problem. The results of these studies were published in *The Battered Child*.[5]

The accumulation of data that delineated the underlying pathology seen in families who were caught up in the cycle of child abuse permitted a movement toward therapeutic approaches to this problem. Progress has been made not only in the understanding of the problem of child abuse but also in the therapeutic approaches that are helpful and the method of delivering these services. The studies of the late 1960s and early 1970s expanded upon these therapeutic endeavors and were reported in *Helping the Battered Child and His Family*[6] in 1972.

The Office of Child Development was formed in the early 1970s. Through the diligent efforts of then Senator Walter Mondale, part of its funding was earmarked to include study of the problem of child neglect and abuse. Funds soon became available to augment research and expand treatment programs throughout the country. The need for multidisciplinary diagnostic and treatment teams became evident, and hundreds of articles and publications began to appear in the literature of law, social work, psychology, medicine and other disciplines. A joint and coordinated community effort has been shown to be of critical importance for the implementation of programs to proceed smoothly. A number of endeavors in this area were described in the literature and are recorded in the publications of the Office of Child Development[7] and *Child Abuse and Neglect: The Family and the Community*.[8]

Figure 1

PUTTING ABUSE AND NEGLECT INTO PERSPECTIVE

Classification: Problems with Parent-Child Interaction

Definition: Any *interaction* or *lack of interaction* between a *caregiver* and *child* which results in *non-accidental* harm to the child's *physical* and/or *developmental* state.

RELATED CAUSES (PARENTS):

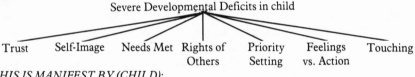

Deficits in ECD★
Mental Illness
Mental Retardation
Fanaticism

±

Serious Personal and/or Ecological Crises such as:
    Physical Illness
    Difficult Child - real or perceived
    Substance Abuse
    Wife Abuse
    Separation from mate
    Legal problems
    Poverty/wealth

★ECD = Early Child Development

THIS RESULTS IN (CHILD):

Severe Developmental Deficits in child

Trust   Self-Image   Needs Met   Rights of Others   Priority Setting   Feelings vs. Action   Touching

THIS IS MANIFEST BY (CHILD):

Physical Abuse	⟷	Run Away	⟷	Delinquency
Physical Neglect		Habit Disorder		Mental Illness
Failure to Thrive		Behavior Disorder		Substance Abuse
Hyperactivity		Physical Illness		Etc.
Learning Disorder	⟷	Retardation	⟷	Etc.

THIS RESULTS IN (ADOLESCENT):

Pre-parent with Serious Deficits

Inability to Cope with Normal Stresses of Adolescence

Bizarre Mate Selection

Problem-solving Pregnancy

THIS IS MANIFEST BY (PARENTS):

See Related Causes Above

CYCLE STARTS OVER

The abstracts that are being published in this book include a summary of the publications that have occurred in this field. This has not been an easy task which Beatrice Kalisch has undertaken. Her work will be greatly appreciated and beneficial to a large number of professionals working in this field.

What has not appeared in the literature is an attempt to place the problem of child abuse and neglect into some order or perspective. Clearly, the physical abuse and overt neglect of small children does *not* occur in isolation to the many other problems that are manifested in the younger generation. This introduction will summarize the author's assessment of how child abuse and neglect can be placed into perspective. Prior to reading the remainder of this introduction, the reader is encouraged to scan Figure 1 which is an overview of this perspective.

CLASSIFICATION

The problem of physical abuse to and/or neglect of children falls within the total framework of "Problems With Parent-Child Interaction (P-C I)." The interactions that occur between parents and children are of critical importance in molding the early developmental experiences of a small child. When these interactions go astray on a consistent basis, a variety of serious problems results. Child abuse and neglect are only two of these major problems.

DEFINITION

Considerable thought has been given to attempts to define this adverse interaction. While the definition that follows is not considered to be one that might be applicable for legislative action, it is, nevertheless, very helpful in developing service and therapeutic programs. The working definition that this author is currently using is as follows:

> Any *interaction* or *lack of interaction* between a *caregiver* and *child* which results in *non-accidental harm* to the child's *physical* and/or *developmental* state.

The seven italicized words or phases are of primary importance. The first two indicate that the problems that children get into are indeed the results of an interaction or lack of interaction between a caregiver and child. The concept of the interaction is important since it is the input of *both* the caregiver and the child that must be considered. The fourth critical phrase is *non-accidental*. Several phrases and words were used in the past to describe what is happening. Words such as *intentional* or *deliberate* were abandoned, since they implied some premeditated plan. *Non-accidental* seems to describe most accurately what actually is happening.

When one considers the use of the word *harm*, it must be placed in conjunction with the last two critical points, that is, *physical* and/or *developmental*. The problems seen when parent-child interaction goes astray must be considered to produce harm, either to the body or to the child's developmental state. The fact that the body is harmed seriously in one child and moderately in another does not necessarily indicate that the harm was more severe in one case as contrasted with the other. The degree of severity truly depends on a combination of effects of both the physical and developmental components.

RELATED CAUSES (PARENTS)

Parents who are having serious difficulty in interacting with their children have at least one or more of the following major problems.

1. Serious deficits in their early child development
2. Mental illness
3. Mental retardation
4. Fanaticism

The problem of deficits in early child development will be discussed in some detail. This is by far the most common of these four problems. On occasion a serious mental illness, such as psychosis or sociopathic personality, is present in these parents. The mentally retarded parent may also have serious problems in parent-child interaction. The latter two categories, that is, mental illness and mental retardation, appear to be seen more commonly now than in the past. This is apparently due to the fact that more mentally ill and retarded adults are living within the community rather than in a restrained institution. This permits them to produce children, for whom they must care, in larger numbers than in the past. *

When one or more of these four basic underlying conditions are coupled with serious physical illness in the parent or child, substance abuse, wife abuse, and/or environmental stress or personal crises, the setting is ripe for the development of a serious problem in parent-child interaction. Consider, if you will, the ecological situation made up of parents with one or more of these four basic deficits, plus certain personal problems and/or environmental stresses. When a child, who must thrive and develop in a reasonably normal fashion, is placed into this setting, serious deficits will result.

DEVELOPMENTAL DEFICITS SEEN IN THE CHILD

Expecting a small child to thrive in the setting described is unrealistic. When a child is indeed placed in this situation over a long period of time, his or her developmental state is placed in serious jeopardy. These issues are discussed in some detail in chapter 3 entitled "The Frozen or Arrested Developmental State"

---

*Parenthetically, when the parent(s) is seriously retarded, mentally ill, and/or fanatical, treatment becomes *most* difficult.

in *Child Abuse and Neglect: The Family and the Community.*[8] Basic developmental concepts are being referred to at this time. These include such things as:

1. Learning to trust others
2. Developing a positive self-image
3. Learning acceptable methods of getting needs met
4. Understanding the rights and responsibilities of others
5. Making decisions and setting priorities
6. Understanding the difference between feelings and actions
7. Being conditioned in a positive way to the sensation of touch and smell
8. Learning how to use eye contact to develop communication with others

There are scores of examples in the developmental literature of serious deficits resulting when the developmental process is insulted by either the presence of repeated adverse stimuli or the absence of positive interaction with the child. The developmental deficits that result, for example, when a child learns that touching hurts, rather than feels good, and that eye contact is fearful, rather than pleasant, are devastating. Add this to the developmental deficit of distrust and terrible self-image, and the result is a very mixed-up child. A child who lives in an environment that can neither nurture him nor provide him with sufficient positive developmental experiences necessary to teach him how to function in a reasonable manner during adolescence and adulthood is in desperate trouble.

The child should be perceived as an individual in a dynamic state of growth and development. What happens to him during these critical years prepares him for adolescence and the adult years. This dynamic state of the child's growth and development is likened to the trajectory of a missile as it moves from Cape Kennedy to Mars. This trajectory must be guided with care if one expects the landing craft to end up on Mars (adulthood) in a condition that will enable it to function satisfactorily.

MANIFESTATIONS SEEN IN THE CHILD

Children reared in the environment described above have serious deficits in their development. These children will become evident to professional workers in a variety of ways. The manifestations of these problems vary, depending on the stage at which the development was seriously insulted and the degree of alertness of the professional working with the child. For example, if an experienced and alert delivery room nurse and/or newborn nursery nurse observes the mother and child interacting in a bizarre fashion, the problem of parent-child interaction might be identified at this time. On the other hand, if there is no alert professional making appropriate observations until the child reaches school, then not only will the manifestation of the problem be different, but its recognition will also have been seriously delayed.

Figure 1 lists a variety of manifestations that result from serious problems in parent-child interaction. The reader should keep in mind that the physical abuse and overt neglect of small children are only two of many manifestations. Learning disorders, hyperactivity, runaway children, and substance abuse are some of the other characteristics these children present to nurses, physicians, school teachers, pre-school teachers, day care workers, court workers, law enforcement officers, and others. The concept should not be interpreted to imply that *all* learning disorder or hyperactive children, for example, are the result of problems in parent-child interaction. It is certainly possible that the problems between parent and child result *after* a child manifests the problem of learning disorder and/or hyperactivity. What *is* intended, however, is that a large number of children who are seen by professionals for many of these problems are indeed the result of primary parent-child interaction difficulties.

The arrows that are depicted in Figure 1 are placed there to demonstrate the interaction that occurs. How common it is for a physician to see a child at age two, for example, with signs of physical abuse and then only a year or two later diagnose failure to thrive in one of this child's siblings. How unfortunate when these same two siblings appear to school teachers four to six years later as learning disorder or hyperactive children. One manifestation of the problem has been substituted for another. These same children may well be seen, in the ensuing years, in an adolescent program for troubled teenagers or the juvenile court.

Children who are reared in an environment that is not conducive to experiencing normal developmental phenomena acquire serious developmental deficits which manifest themselves in a variety of ways.

RESULTS IN YOUNG ADULTS

This process has a devastating effect on the growing and developing child. While these *basic* developmental deficits of distrust, poor self-image, inability to touch or establish eye contact, and others may be hidden or go unnoticed, the manifestations of these deficits are varied in number and seen by many professionals and nonprofessionals alike.

The end result is a young adult or adolescent (or "pre-parent") who is experiencing major problems. These young people have not been prepared to cope with the normal developmental stresses of adolescents. Rather than having the background to help them find their way into adulthood, the foundations necessary for these critical years are truly built on sand. The extra stresses of adolescence are more than they can handle, resulting in serious antisocial behavior and/or interpersonal problems.

These young people are unable to identify mates who are at all helpful. They have not learned the innuendos of positive communications. This results in bizarre mate selection. Gradually their life is perceived as a disaster. The girls, at least, perceive that the solution will come to them in the form of pregnancy and a baby. These pregnancies are "problem-solving pregnancies" which are perceived as one method of finally getting some of their own needs met. Once the baby has been conceived by this confused adolescent who has experienced this multitude of insults to her developmental process, abortion is rarely considered an option. The pregnancy is often wanted. The baby is delivered and finds his way into an environment almost identical to that in which the new parents themselves were reared some years before. The cycle thereby starts once again.

SUMMARY

Problems in parent-child interaction result when the developmentally deficient young adult becomes a parent who has one or more of four major problems (deficits in early child development, mental retardation, mental illness, or fanaticism). To this is added a child or children who find themselves being reared in an environment that produces very serious developmental deficits. These deficits surface in many ways and to different individuals. These childhood experiences produce a very deficient young adult, who then becomes a parent, and the cycle continues. This summary is depicted in Figure 2.

While this review is not intended to discuss treatment programs, one point must be made at this time. The attack point on this cycle that is currently receiving the most interest and funding is "after-the-fact services" offered by a variety of agencies and disciplines. These services occur *after* the child has displayed to a health care provider one or more of the multiple manifestations discussed. The time has now come to realize that the amount of knowledge and understanding is sufficient to begin the attack point much earlier. The problem must be approached in the form of *prevention* rather than after-the-fact services (see chapter 18 in *Child Abuse and Neglect: The Family and the Community*).

INCIDENCE

Before completing this discussion, one further point should be placed in perspective. How common are serious parent-child interaction problems? The total incidence, of course, is not known. If one takes only *two* of the manifestations of this problem, for example, physical abuse and overt neglect, existing figures are most alarming. In 1975, the departments of social services in the United States were asked to evaluate approximately 550,000 cases of suspected child abuse and neglect. *One percent of our children are reported as suspected cases of abuse and neglect every year.* This estimate fails to take into consideration the many other manifestations of problems in the area of parent-child interaction. Most alarming is the fact that the 1 percent figure is cumulative. While agencies and other groups are working with last year's 1 percent of children, trying to get their developmental experiences into some kind of reasonable order, another 1

Figure 2

SUMMARY

Problems in Parent-Child Interaction Result When:

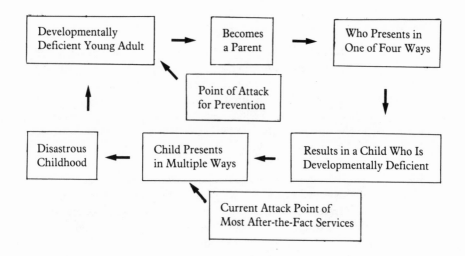

percent of children are reported for the same problem. At the same time, these same agencies are gearing up for next year's 1 percent.

The ultimate result—at least 10 to 15 percent of our teenagers have experienced child abuse or neglect during their developmental years. This is most alarming. Abuse and neglect are not like measles or chicken pox. Once these diseases affect a child, they rarely leave any serious underlying deficits. When a child is abused and neglected, the developmental process is scarred, much like the insult to a growing tree after having been struck by lightning.

The end result—a huge number of young adults have experienced serious developmental insults during their early years. This problem is most disturbing, one that has a long-term effect on the strength and stability of our total society.

A child is a growing, dynamic individual who is most vulnerable to the stimuli received from his or her environment. If these stimuli are consistently adverse, developmental scarring will be permanent. While every effort must be made to upgrade and expand after-the-fact services to give as much assistance to these families as possible, the long-term hope lies in the early recognition of problems, long before the children are born. By working with the pre-parents during their school years and early in their pregnancies, a long-term positive effect on the next generation will result. If we wait for the manifestations of parent-child interactions to appear, the problems will be never ending.

RAY E. HELFER, M.D.
Professor
Department of Human Development
College of Human Medicine
Michigan State University
East Lansing, Michigan

August 1977

NOTES

1. C.H. Kempe, F.N. Silverman, F.B. Steele, W. Droegemuller, and H.D. Silver, "The battered-child syndrome," *JAMA* 181(1):17-24, July 7, 1962.
2. J. Caffey, "Multiple fractures in the long bones of children suffering from chronic subdural hematoma," *Am. J. Roentgenol. Radium Ther. Nucl. Med.* 56(2):163-73, August, 1946.
3. F.N. Silverman, "The Roentgen manifestations of unrecognized skeletal trauma in infants," *Am. J. Roentgenol. Radium Ther. Nucl. Med.* 69(3): 413-27, March, 1953.
4. L. Adelsen, "Slaughter of the innocents," *N. Engl. J. Med.* 264(26):1345-49, June 29, 1961.

5. R.E. Helfer and C.H. Kempe, *The Battered Child* (Chicago: University of Chicago Press, 1968).

6. C.H. Kempe and R.E. Helfer, *Helping the Battered Child and His Family* (Philadelphia: J. B. Lippincott, 1972).

7. Several manuals published by the Office of Child Development. For details, contact U.S. Government Printing Office, HEW, National Center for Child Abuse and Neglect, Post Office Box 1182, Washington, D.C. 20013.

8. R.E. Helfer and C.H. Kempe, *Child Abuse and Neglect: The Family and the Community* (Cambridge, Mass.: Ballinger Publishers, 1976).

SAMPLE BOOK ENTRY

① ②   ③
Helfer, Ray E., and Kempe, C. Henry, eds. *Child abuse and neglect: the family and the community.* Cambridge, Massachusetts: Ballinger, 1976.

④   ⑤   ⑥
438 p.   (Bibliography).

⑦   ⑧

⑨ A compilation of medical, sociological, and legally-oriented essays written by experts active in the prevention, treatment, and management of child abuse and neglect. Several chapters evaluate the complex causes and manifestations of family pathology. Because attitudes toward parenting are learned as a child, the importance of perinatal observation of the family's potential for successful bonding is emphasized. Prenatal mother-child care is an ideal time for assessing high risk babies. Most mothers begin early in pregnancy to prepare for their baby's arrival, both physically at home and emotionally. A potentially abusive mother may exhibit depression, fear, and anxiety in her prenatal check-ups. In the delivery room she will often be a passive patient rather than an active participant in birth. Postnatal observation of the mother and infant may uncover a lack of interest in touching, talking to, and maintaining eye contact with the baby. Problem babies, such as premature infants and those born with a congenital malformation, create special bonding problems, because the child has been hospitalized for a considerable period of time. It is recommended that mother, father, and child be together immediately after birth for a private family session in order that strong parent-child bonds begin to form.

A large section of the book deals with the community's response to the abusive family. The role of the child protection team and special residential treatment programs are discussed. Guidelines for organizing a community sponsored treatment program are given. Any successful program must integrate the following three components: (1) the child protection team, usually affiliated with a hospital, and trained in crisis intervention; (2) long-term therapy and rehabilitation carried on by a social service agency; and (3) education, training, and research conducted by universities and medical schools. An exemplary program plan with explanations on how to administer the technical aspects of planning, budgeting, and directing a child abuse treatment and prevention program is provided. An historical description of the evolution and retraction of children's rights is given from Biblical times, through European history, and up to the present. Today, children's rights are negative rights because they are only enforced when parental behavior does not meet minimum standards. A family court judge argues in one article that children's rights can best be guaranteed when the child is represented by legal counsel at a family court hearing. The role of the court is therapeutic, not punitive. The increased constructive use of the family court is advocated, because the court can support and implement decisions made by the physician or child welfare agency, or suggest its own knowledgeable course of remedial action. Additional chapters analyze the sexual exploitation of children in incest cases and the etiology of, and problems of jurisdiction associated with, child abuse and neglect in the military.

1. Item number
2. Author(s)
3. Title of book
4. Place of publication
5. Publisher
6. Date of publication
7. Number of pages
8. Presence of bibliography
9. Annotation

SAMPLE JOURNAL ENTRY

① ②   ③   ④
31 Silver, Larry B. "Child abuse syndrome: a review." *Med. Times*
        96(8): 803-20, August, 1968.   (57 References).
        ⑤   ⑥   ⑦   ⑧

⑨ A literature review of articles published in social work, legal, and other specialized professional journals. Aspects of child abuse that are covered include definition, history, physical and psychological manifestations, psychological characteristics of the abusive parents, consequences of abuse, reporting legislation, and community approaches to the problem. Literature from all disciplines is included in the hope that such a summary would help the practicing physician to become more alert to the child abuse syndrome and to recognize the contribution that non-medical professions can make in its management.

1. Item number
2. Author(s)
3. Title of article
4. Name of journal (abbreviation)
5. Volume and issue number
6. Inclusive pagination
7. Month and year of publication
8. Number of bibliographical references
9. Annotation

CHILD ABUSE
AND NEGLECT

I

Introduction

A. GENERAL

1. COMPREHENSIVE STUDIES AND SYMPOSIUMS

1 Baher, Edwina; Hyman, Clare; Jones, Carolyn; <u>et al</u>. <u>At risk: an</u>
   <u>account of the work of the Battered Child Research Department,</u>
   <u>NSPCC</u>. London: Routledge & Kegan Paul, 1976. 246p. (Bibliography).
Documents twenty-five cases of non-accidental injury in children under
four years of age during a fifteen month period. Study methodology included interviews with parents, an examination of medical and court
records, and an evaluation of the families' progress under treatment.
Fourteen children suffered severe physical or mental injuries as a sequel
to the battering incident(s). Two children died. In three-fourths of
the cases, the mother was identified as the abusive parent, since she was
an isolated caretaker. Factors precipitating abuse in the sample population included: (1) the abused child's conception was unplanned and un-
welcome; (2) the abused child exhibited persistent health or behavioral
problems from early infancy; (3) additional pregnancies created unbearable stress for the mother; (4) the mother lacked basic childrearing
knowledge; and (5) spouses failed to provide each other with adequate
emotional support. Interviews with the study subjects uncovered that as
children these parents felt rejected and unloved. Most had been raised
under harsh economic circumstances, and 80 percent acknowledged having
been emotionally abused as children. These parents had married early and
most lived in locations isolated from other family members.

All twenty-five children underwent long-term treatment provided by a
social work agency. Six cases were referred to the juvenile court. In
all, thirteen children were transferred to residential nurseries or group
homes for treatment. For the twelve children remaining at home, foster
drop-in mothers were employed to observe the family's progress. A day
nursery offered a protective and therapeutic environment for the children. Rehabilitative treatment for parents was organized in phases. In
the first phase, social workers helped the parents deal with the immediate crisis of the child's hospitalization and possible removal from the
home. The second phase was oriented toward solving the parents' practical
problems. In the third phase, the social worker assumed the role of an
extended family member as she nurtured the parents. The final phase of
treatment involved the careful monitoring of the child's progress once
he was returned home. Twenty children were eventually returned to their
parents.

2 Bell, Gwyneth. "Parents who abuse their children." Can Psychiatr
      Assoc J 18(3): 223-28, June, 1973. (34 References).
Surveys the literature regarding a number of aspects of the child abuse
problem including: (1) the incidence of child abuse in the United States
and Canada; (2) the permanent physical effects on the child; (3) the
thwarted development of the normal maternal role in abuse-prone mothers;
(4) the effect of family background and present environment on abusive
parents; (5) the characteristic features of abuse-prone families; and
(6) the management and prevention of child abuse.

3 Brett, Dawn I. "The battered and abused child syndrome." For a sum-
      mary see: Diss Abstr 27A(12): 4344, June, 1967.

4 Brown, Rowine H. "The battered child syndrome." J Forensic Sci
      21(1): 65-70, January, 1976. (22 References).
At Cook County Hospital, an average of sixty cases of severe child abuse
are seen per year, of which 67.7 percent are three years of age or less.
The death rate of children who are admitted for abuse is approximately
10 percent. Abusers come from all strata of society, but many times their
lives have been filled with stress and frustration. The diagnosis of
child abuse should be considered in any young infant with an injury, any
child with multiple injuries or multiple scars, and any child whose injuries are not consistent with the parents' explanation of what happened
to the child. Treatment depends on the severity of the child's injuries
and the degree of pathology in the family. If the courts become involved
in child abuse cases, difficulties can arise when legal counsel is not
provided to represent the rights of the child, when the court must rely
on circumstantial evidence, and when the physicians involved in the case
are unwilling to testify. Attempts to solve the child abuse problem are
being made: (1) the mass media and professional agencies are alerting
the public to the severity of the problem; (2) interdisciplinary child
abuse teams are being formed in hospitals; (3) Parents Anonymous groups
are being established; (4) day care centers are providing relief for
harassed parents; and (5) children's rights groups are working with the
legislature. But vast improvements in social conditions will also be
necessary before the problem of child abuse will be completely alleviated.

5 Carter, Jan, ed. The maltreated child. Westport, Connecticut:
      Technomic Publishing, 1976. 159p. (Bibliography).
Child abuse is a community problem. As family responsibilities have been
allotted to schools, health clinics, and other social agencies, and as
society's tolerance for child maltreatment has declined, child abuse has
won prominence as a critical medical and social disease. This book aims
to be a handbook for professionals in assisting them to understand and
manage abuse in their individual communities.

Numerous essays explore such factors conducive to abuse as social stress
from isolation to overcrowding, the particular stages of child development during which an infant is more apt to aggravate a parent, and the
inbred reliance in some persons upon physical force. In addition to the
obvious physical and possible mental injuries sustained by a battered
child, delay in mastering language and similar social behaviors are also
consequences of abuse. Aggressive behavior toward children originates
in the parents' own unsatisfactory or strained relationship and, therefore, treatment should be directed toward the restoration of the family's
total health. The aims of treatment should be: (1) to protect the child

from further abuse; (2) to provide an optimal setting for the child's
later development; (3) to assist the parents in communicating and providing for each other's and their children's needs; and (4) to give instruction in childrearing.

Selections written by physicians and social workers address the peculiar
problems faced by each during the course of treatment. While all contributors may favor coordination of services, they disagree in their basic
models of the abusive family and in the preferred manner of treatment.
The physician focuses his attention on treating the child's injuries; the
social worker demonstrates compassion and concern for the parent; the
legal system acts to uphold the law and punish all guilty parties; and
the political activist names society as the culprit and works for social
reform. Cooperation among the different professions is thus contingent
upon open communication and shared efforts in both management and completion of treatment. The juvenile court process is elucidated by discussing the significance of important legislative acts in Britain and
demonstrating their application to questions of liability, protection,
and custody.

6 Castle, Raymond L. "Providing a service." In: Franklin, Alfred
    White, ed. Concerning child abuse. New York: Churchill Living-
    stone, 1975. 113-19. (0 References).
Defines the overall problem of child abuse. It is a misconception that
child abuse is a contemporary problem, occurs primarily in low income
families, and involves seriously disturbed parents. Results of the
Battered Research Project show that the younger the child, the more
likely he is to be injured. An abused child will most likely continue to
receive injury if he remains in the home. Descriptions of the parents
emphasize their need for mothering. Lack of reporting, lack of interagency coordination and communication, problems with the court system,
and the law enforcement attitude toward child abusers inhibit effective
management.

7 Chase, Naomi Feigelson. A child is being beaten: violence against
    children, an American tragedy. New York: Holt, Rinehart and
    Winston, 1975. 225p. (Bibliography).
Accounts of violence against children can be read in myths, classical
writings, biblical stories, and fairy tales. Throughout history, children have been the victims of religious sacrifices, cannibalism, and
infanticide. The industrial revolution wrenched children from their
homes and delivered them to factories and textile mills. In the twentieth
century, childrearing and disciplining practices still follow the primitive and fixed pattern of scolding, slapping, and swatting. Violence
toward children has changed only in method. In modern, isolated nuclear
family settings, child abuse flourishes. Young and immature parents
stuggling with financial and marital problems and unwed mothers receiving
public assistance often cannot cope with anxiety, stress, and failure.
A sick, unresponsive, or troublesome child compounds the tension. To
such desperate parents, violence often seems the only solution.

Physicans, child protection workers, public welfare agencies, lawyers,
and family court judges are all involved in treating children and families plagued with crisis or multigenerational abuse. Sometimes, as in
the case of Roxanne Felumero, these professionals and their agencies do
not cooperate, and a child's life is lost. Family court judges lecture
abusive parents on morals and then prescribe rehabilitative treatment

which is never delivered. Agencies are handicapped by understaffing and bare minimal budgets. As a consequence, children are shuffled back and forth from foster home to institution without ever enjoying the warmth and security of a family. Major reforms at all levels of government must be initiated in order to give the family unit greater support. Women ought to receive instructive and financial help in the role of mothering. Contraceptives and abortion on demand should be made available to all women, including teenagers. Livable housing, medical care, and decent employment should be guaranteed all citizens.

8 Delaney, Donald W. "The physically abused child." World Med J 13(5): 145-47, September-October, 1966. (22 References).
Presents an overview of the subject of child abuse in the United States with historical information, incidence, clinical manifestations, legislator responsibilities, characteristics of abusing parents, and physician responsibilities included. Laws requiring mandatory reporting while protecting the physician from civil liability are advocated.

9 Fontana, Vincent J. The maltreated child: the maltreatment syndrome in children. 2nd ed. Springfield, Illinois: Charles C. Thomas, 1971. 96p. (Bibliography).
Traces the limited and sparsely documented history of the physical maltreatment of children, and the current understanding of such abusive behavior, while repeatedly deploring the fact that accurate statistics reflecting the truly staggering incidence and nature of child abuse are not available and would be difficult to obtain. A detailed list of clinical and roentgenologic manifestations indicative of actual inflicted trauma alert the physician to the possibility of maltreatment and assist him with an accurate diagnosis. This medical diagnosis, coupled with the casework carried out by social services, forms the evidence needed for the courts to take over their legal responsibility to determine what action is needed. Portions of the Penal Code of the State of California and the New York State Child Abuse Law are included as exemplary and illustrative of the difficulties inherent in the enforcement of such provisions. Seven medical case studies of physical maltreatment conclude the book, offering some dramatic insights into the depth of the problem.

10 Friedman, Robert M.; Helfer, Ray E.; Katz, Sanford N.; et al. Four perspectives on the status of child abuse and neglect research. Washington, D.C.: Herner and Company, 1976. 281p. ERIC Document ED 127 764. For ordering information see: Government Reports Announcements and Index 76(12): 30, June 11, 1976.
Child abuse research is reviewed from the perspectives of mental health, medicine, law, and social work. The mental health section contains a discussion of the characteristics of the abused child, the abusing parent, the environment, and theoretical approaches to the problem. Medicine is reviewed in terms of physical effects of abuse, preventive measures, developmental aspects, and the relationship of medicine to sociocultural concerns. Legal aspects dealt with include criminal laws, reporting statutes, jurisdiction, and parents' and childrens' rights. The social work section provides a definition of neglect and predictive behavior.

11 George, James E. "Spare the rod: a survey of the battered-child syndrome." Forensic Sci 2(2): 129-67, May, 1973. (71 References).

Surveys the battered child syndrome, including its history, estimates of the incidence of abuse, characteristics of the abuser as well as the abused, and the circumstances precipitating abuse. Numerous medical case histories illustrate the typical radiologic, dermatologic, and pathologic manifestations of battered children. Medical personnel must be trained to respond to abusing parents with a non-punitive attitude, in order to avoid any risk of discouraging them from seeking help. The medical profession carries with it the responsibility of recognizing abuse and providing care, whereas the legal and social professions are responsible for carrying out protective services, which include rehabilitating the parents. A lengthy discussion of the legal aspects of child abuse, such as reporting legislation, criminal law, juvenile courts, the role of the attorney, and central registries, is included. Kempe's program of "mothering" in Denver, Colorado stands out as one of few successful attempts to transcend the network of social welfare agencies and to provide effective treatment. Protective services represent, both financially and organizationally, the weakest area of progress in handling child abuse. Administrative efficiency and coordinated efforts among social agencies must be accomplished if successful results are to be achieved.

12 Grantmyre, Edward B. "Trauma X -- Wednesday's child." NS Med Bull
     52(1): 29-31, February, 1973. (7 References).
Discusses the battered child syndrome, including the characteristics of abused children and their parents, the importance of radiological findings, the issue of mandatory reporting by physicians, and suggestions for prevention. The role of the physician, particularly his responsibility to report, is emphasized.

13 Harris, Susan B., ed. Child abuse: present and future. Chicago:
     National Committee for Prevention of Child Abuse, 1975. 237p.
     (Bibliography).
Consists of a compilation of addresses by professionals and volunteers active in the field of child abuse presented at the 1974 symposium of the National Committee for the Prevention of Child Abuse. The personality of the abusive parent, situations which produce abuse, the multidisciplinary treatment team, critical research topics, and personal experiences in working with abusive families are discussed. Child abuse is a learned pattern of behavior because it is a person's reaction to his own abnormal upbringing. In homes where violence and force are the only means of discipline, a child learns no other method for releasing tension and anger. Certain living situations encourage child abuse and neglect. Social isolation, poverty, unfit housing, unemployment, and an inadequate education can create familial stress. Problems in interpersonal relations such as a poor husband-wife relationship or an incapacity for nurturing also contribute to this stress. Moreover, the non-egalitarian construct of American society which condones corporal punishment and overlooks the specific rights of children promotes family isolation and its ensuing manifold problems. Primary prevention in the area of child abuse must attack and transform these prevailing societal attitudes and correct the familial causal model. Secondary research should be more pragmatic and immediate, such as implementing effective childrearing education programs, devising screening tests for mothers who visit prenatal clinics, and conducting follow-up investigations of adolescents who were abused as children.

All members of the symposium stress the need for cooperation between private and governmental child protection agencies and for a more generous

and systematic dissemination of information. Multidisciplinary child protection teams which include medical personnel, social workers, psychologists, educators, lawyers, and parents themselves, are the most effective
community-based treatment units. The team is responsible for investigating rehabilitative programs for both parents and children. Because most
abusive families are reluctant to accept outside help, it was stressed
that whatever the parent perceives as his greatest need should be first,
be this housing, employment, child care education, or monetary problems.
Described also was an "A-B-C" assessment plan and its three-fold approach
to working with the antecedents of behavior, the particular abusive behavior, and the consequences to the family. Members of Parents' Anonymous, CALM, and other volunteer groups shared information about the
history and effectiveness of their programs.

14 Helfer, Ray E., and Kempe, C. Henry, eds. The battered child. 2nd ed.
      Chicago: The University of Chicago Press, 1974. 262p. (Bibliog-
      raphy).
This compilation of essays by various professionals involved in the diagnosis, treatment, and management of child abuse represents an early contribution to the body of literature directed at the syndrome. The fully
documented essays, supported by photographs, statistics, and vivid case
histories, provide a large amount of factual knowledge. The chapter on
the history of child abuse presents a multicultural account of discipline,
mutilation, infanticide, abandonment, and how such early religious or
societal customs prefigure the abused child syndrome. The section devoted
to the incidence and demographic characteristics of abuse contains numerous tables and analysis of data.

The physician's protective relationship to the child and his responsibility to explain the medical and legal ramifications of the abusive action
to the parents are discussed. Specific radiographic signs of the syndrome
are illustrated and compared with those of other bone diseases not resulting from abuse. The chapter on the pathology of child abuse outlines
the following procedure for investigating infant deaths resulting from
neglect or abuse: a preliminary investigation of the site of death,
external and internal medical examinations, follow-up questioning of
parents, and the role of the pathologist in court.

In a psychiatric study of abusing parents, the development of aggression
through such factors as a superego conditioned to destroy "bad" things,
unresolved sibling rivalry, an obsessive-compulsive character, and unresolved Oedipal conflicts with excessive guilt are traced. The contributory roles of the non-abusing parent and the child are also probed.
Chapters devoted to the roles and problems encountered by the social
worker, law enforcement agency, and welfare department illustrate the
essential interdisciplinary approach to treatment. The legal aspects of
abuse, including criminal law, juvenile court action, and protective
child welfare services, are investigated. Mandatory reporting laws are
clarified with the help of an appendix which summarizes child abuse
legislation in the fifty states and the Virgin Islands through 1973.
Concluding remarks emphasize the need for trained specialists to conduct
research aimed at the prevention of abuse.

15 ————. Child abuse and neglect: the family and the community.
      Cambridge, Massachusetts: Ballinger, 1976. 438p. (Bibliography).
A compilation of medical, sociological, and legally-oriented essays
written by experts active in the prevention, treatment, and management

of child abuse and neglect. Several chapters evaluate the complex causes
and manifestations of family pathology. Because attitudes toward parenting are learned as a child, the importance of perinatal observation of
the family's potential for successful bonding is emphasized. Prenatal
mother-child care is an ideal time for assessing high risk babies. Most
mothers begin early in pregnancy to prepare for their baby's arrival, both
physically at home and emotionally. A potentially abusive mother may
exhibit depression, fear, and anxiety in her prenatal check-ups. In the
delivery room she will often be a passive patient rather than an active
participant in birth. Postnatal observation of the mother and infant may
uncover a lack of interest in touching, talking to, and maintaining eye
contact with the baby. Problem babies, such as premature infants and
those born with a congenital malformation, create special bonding problems, because the child has been hospitalized for a considerable period
of time. It is recommended that mother, father, and child be together
immediately after birth for a private family session in order that strong
parent-child bonds begin to form.

A large section of the book deals with the community's response to the
abusive family. The role of the child protection team and special residential treatment programs are discussed. Guidelines for organizing a
community sponsored treatment program are given. Any successful program
must integrate the following three components: (1) the child protection
team, usually affiliated with a hospital, and trained in crisis intervention; (2) long-term therapy and rehabilitation carried on by a social
service agency; and (3) education, training, and research conducted by
universities and medical schools. An exemplary program plan with explanations on how to administer the technical aspects of planning, budgeting,
and directing a child abuse treatment and prevention program is provided.
An historical description of the evolution and retraction of children's
rights is given from Biblical times, through European history, and up to
the present. Today, children's rights are negative rights because they
are only enforced when parental behavior does not meet minimum standards.
A family court judge argues in one article that children's rights can
best be guaranteed when the child is represented by legal counsel at a
family court hearing. The role of the court is therapeutic, not punitive. The increased constructive use of the family court is advocated,
because the court can support and implement decisions made by the physician or child welfare agency, or suggest its own knowledgeable course of
remedial action. Additional chapters analyze the sexual exploitation of
children in incest cases and the etiology of, and problems of jurisdiction associated with, child abuse and neglect in the military.

16 Hurt, Maure, Jr. <u>Child abuse and neglect: a report of the status</u>
      <u>of the research</u>. Washington, D.C.: U. S. Government Printing
      Office, 1975. 63p. (Bibliography). (DHEW Publication no. (OHD)
      74-20).

Reports on the status of child abuse research. A growing sensitivity to
the painful subject of abuse has outstripped knowledge about its etiology
and competence to prevent and treat it, although research efforts have
produced important results. The lack of generally accepted definitions
of abuse and neglect contributes to detection and reporting problems,
which, in turn, hinder efforts to establish the incidence of the problem.
Granting Ray Helfer's equation (Kempe and Helfer, 1972) that parent plus
child plus situation equals abuse, the conclusions of various researchers
on the characteristics of these elements of an abuse pattern are summarized. Observations on the physical and psychological effects of abuse

are also presented. A review of reporting and recording issues concludes
that a combination of a hot-line reporting service, a central registry,
and an information campaign to alert the public is a most effective system
for casefinding. The report provides information about a model for public
reporting in Florida. Some reasons for the reluctance of private physicians to report are considered and examples of hospital emergency teams
illustrate the role they may play in the diagnosis and management of abuse
cases. Treatment issues are reviewed with attention to the various levels
of intervention possible, ranging from prevention to remediation. Some
model treatment programs are described. Appendices include a copy of the
Child Abuse Act, abstracts of federally funded projects, and an annotated
bibliography.

17 Kamerman, Sheila B. "Eight countries: cross national perspectives
        on child abuse and neglect." Child Today 4(3): 34-37, May-June,
        1975. (5 References).
Major questions regarding the definition of child abuse and neglect, child
protective legislation, devices for identifying abused children, treatment
programs, and relevant research were posed to social service agencies in
the United States, Canada, France, West Germany, Israel, Poland, and
Yugoslavia. While five of the countries studied have become increasingly
aware of child abuse and neglect, Poland and Yugoslavia consider its
incidence to be slight. All eight countries except Yugoslavia have child
protective legislation, but provisions in the law specifically concerning
child abuse are limited. Except for the United States and Canada, no
other country has found it necessary to develop special programs to identify abused children. The other countries have universal maternal and
child health care programs such as visiting nurses or nationalized health
care clinics which make identification of such children routine. Special
programs for the treatment of child abuse distinct from general family
health care programs are considered unnecessary in most countries.
Formal research and evaluation studies in all countries except the United
States are limited.

18 Leavitt, Jerome E. The battered child: selected readings. Morris-
        town, New Jersey: General Learning Press, 1974. 268p. (Bibliog-
        raphy).
A multidisciplinary collection of forty-six articles, originally published
in medical, law, social work, and psychology journals, discuss the manifestations, treatment, management, and prevention of child abuse. Designed to be used as a college textbook for courses in psychology, nursing, and sociology, it is divided into individual study units which focus
on a particular aspect of the abuse syndrome, such as the identification
of abused children or the legal problems of mandatory reporting, custody,
and criminal prosecution associated with abuse. Each unit is preceded
by an introduction and concluded with summarizing remarks, study questions, and suggestions for further reading. Examples of specific articles
include the identification of the battered child syndrome, the personality
of abusive parents, the role of group therapy in treatment, the use of
homemaker services as an alternative to separation, and suggestions for
the prevention of abuse.

19 Margrain, Susan A. "Review: battered children, their parents, treat-
        ment and prevention." Child Care Health Dev 3(1): 49-63,
        January-February, 1977. (34 References).

Reviews and summarizes the literature on child abuse. Maltreated children are children of either sex under five years old who are often characterized as motionless or without affect. The parents are thought to come from a low socioeconomic background and to commonly be experiencing marital stress and isolation from their community. Personality disorders, emotional strain, and feelings of rejection are also frequent. Management of abuse problems tends to emphasize keeping the family together, a conclusion not always conducive to the welfare of the child. Treatment concentrates on prevention; drawing the parents into the community and changing basic childrearing techniques are recommended measures.

20 Merrill, Edgar J.; Kaufman, Irving; Dodge, Philip R.; et al. Protect-
     ing the battered child. Denver, Colorado: The American Humane
     Association, Children's Division, 1962. 30p.
Contains four papers on different aspects of child abuse. "Physical Abuse of Children -- An Agency Study" shows characteristics of 115 abusing families in Massachusetts. Abusers were typically young parents showing one of three distinct clusters of personality characteristics--hostility, compulsiveness, or passivity. In addition, many of the fathers were disabled to some degree and unable to support their families. The abused children characteristically were under thirteen years of age, with badly impaired relationships with the abusing parents. Usually, they were the only children in the family to be abused. Case studies serve as illustrations. "Psychiatric Implications of Physical Abuse of Children" shows that abusing parents perceive the child as a symbolic figure representing their own disturbances. Parents frequently have a type of schizophrenia that renders them not psychotic but periodically out of control. The concerns of the authorities should be to protect the child in those periods, to help parents become aware of their motives, and to take an authoritative approach to the abusive parent. "Medical Implications of Physical Abuse of Children" shows that although statistics on battered children are numerous, physicians are often slow or unwilling to report child abuse. The article suggests thorough training of medical students in the characteristic symptoms of abuse. Reporting of suspected abuse should be mandatory. "Legal Implications . . . in Physical Abuse of Children" emphasizes legal complexities of abuse cases, stresses the need for social workers and physicians to seek legal consultation, and suggests ways that they can make their cases stronger in court.

21 Nagi, Saad Z. Child treatment in the United States: a cry for help
     and organizational response. Columbus, Ohio: Ohio State University,
     1976. 231p.
Examines the findings from a national survey of programs and individuals concerned with child abuse and neglect. Recommendations for policy makers are offered, based on analysis of the data collected. The current status of knowledge about these problems and techniques for solving them is investigated, and the rights of children and the role of the government in safeguarding these rights are also discussed. Child abuse statistics are estimated, and the various, and often opposing, approaches to the handling of the parents are analyzed.

22 National Conference on Child Abuse, Washington, D.C., 1973. Summary
     report. Washington, D.C.: U. S. Government Printing Office, 1974.
     42p. (DHEW Publication no. (ADM) 74-117).
Reprints the proceedings of a national conference on child abuse held in 1973. Major topics discussed were: legislation, prevention, identifica-

tion, education, and research. Recommendations evolving from the conference included establishment of family and community education relative to
prevention, treatment, and casefinding, and a national center on child
abuse.

23   National Symposium on Child Abuse, 4th, Charleston, S. C., 1973.
     Collected papers . . . to explore on an interdisciplinary basis
     the problems of child abuse and neglect. Denver, Colorado: The
     American Humane Association, Children's Division, 1975. 91p.
     (Bibliography).
A collection of papers presented in 1973 discussing the medical, social,
and legal issues of child abuse. Because abuse is often a symptom of
family problems, it is less important for the physician to determine the
exact circumstances of the abusive event than it is to focus on family
pathology. A multidisciplinary approach to management is emphasized,
along with more community responsibility in establishing services to aid
abused children and to help potential abuse families. A federal official
reported on the focus of current and projected funding, and projects related to the problem of child abuse and neglect. It was noted that legal
involvement was expanding as many state laws were requiring more professional groups to report abuse. It was suggested that laws defining
reportable abuse be less specific so that the potential informant would
have less difficulty in deciding if his report meets the requirements of
the law. In order to assure successful court decisions on behalf of children, health care professionals need to know what legally constitutes a
solid case just as legal professionals need more understanding about the
psychosocial and physical aspects of the abuse problem.

24   National Symposium on Child Abuse, 5th, Boston, 1974. Collected
     papers to examine contemporary issues and therapeutic approaches
     to the problems of child abuse and neglect. Denver, Colorado:
     The American Humane Association, Children's Division, 1976. 151p.
These papers, presented in October, 1974, examine contemporary issues
about child abuse and neglect. Issues in interdisciplinary management
emphasize cooperation and communication between disciplines. The difficulties hampering the identification and treatment of child abuse by
protective services include insufficient resources, inadequate data on
which to make decisions, and insufficient administration. The responsibilities of the attorneys for the parents and for the child in abuse
hearings are discussed in addition to the problems which accompany court
intervention. Other legal concerns of child abuse include the possibility of a national law and a proposed model reporting law. Issues concerning central registries focus on their purpose and misuse by protective
services. Representatives from Children's Protective Services in Boston
share the techniques and results of therapy groups for mothers and
adolescents of abusive families.

25   Oglov, Linda, and Lalonde, Claire. "International conference provides
     analysis of child abuse problems." Can Med Assoc J 117(2):
     170-76, July 23, 1977. (0 References).
Summarizes various talks given at the second world conference of the
International Society on Family Law, held at McGill University, June
13-17, 1977. Some of the topics investigated were: (1) ordinary and
abnormal aggression within the family; (2) primary and secondary prevention of child abuse; (3) protection of family privacy in abuse cases;
(4) inadequacies in medical treatment in family crisis and child abuse

cases; (5) characteristics of abusive parents; (6) psychological causes of child abuse; (7) treatment of the whole family in abuse cases; (8) problems of incest; and (9) causes of sexual abuse of children.

26 Paulson, Morris J., and Blake, Phillip R. "The abused, battered and
       maltreated child: a review." Trauma 9(4): 1-3, December, 1967.
Reviews the literature pertaining to the abused and otherwise maltreated child through October, 1967. Particular concerns are the incidence, identifying symptoms, parental profiles, and preventive measures.

27 Pfundt, Theodore R. "The problem of the battered child." Postgrad
       Med 35(4): 426-31, April, 1964. (12 References).
Outlines the problem of child abuse, using three case histories as examples. One area of concern is the lack of research available about the battered child. Skeletal traumas, sexual assault, and the changing family structure are briefly commented upon. Recommendations regarding the child's protection are made, and the importance of the physician's role in this regard is noted.

28 Rausen, Aaron R. "Symposium on child abuse." Pediatrics 51(4,
       Part 2): 771-812, April, 1973. (0 References).
A transcript of the Symposium on Child Abuse held on June 15, 1971 and sponsored by the New York County Medical Society. The symposium featured eight speakers from the fields of medicine, social work, and law and covered such topics as the history and demography of child abuse, its etiology and diagnosis, the role of the medical community, the role of legislation, the courts and child protective organizations, and various practical approaches to the rehabilitation of the abused child and his family.

29 "Reflections on child abuse and neglect: editorial." Clin Proc
       Child Hosp 30(2): 31-58, February, 1974. (0 References).
Presents the proceedings of a June, 1973 National Conference on Child Abuse, sponsored by the Children's Hospital National Medical Center and the National Institute of Mental Health. The conference was divided into five work groups, each focusing on a single topic germane to child abuse: identification of abused children and problem families, the role of the legal system, rehabilitation of children and parents through public and private agencies, education of the general public and policy-makers, and research priorities in child abuse.

30 Shaffer, Helen B. "Child abuse: search for remedies." Ed Res Rep
       1(18): 343-59, May 12, 1965. (24 References).
Calls attention to the problem of child abuse as of 1965. Particular concerns are the permeation of child abuse through all socioeconomic levels, the characteristic patterns of injury resulting from child abuse, the protection of abused children, and the rehabilitation of abusive parents. Mandatory reporting legislation is called for, along with further study of the issue.

31 Silver, Larry B. "Child abuse syndrome: a review." Med Times
       96(8): 803-20, August, 1968. (57 References).
A literature review of articles published in social work, legal, and other specialized professional journals. Aspects of child abuse that are covered include definition, history, physical and psychological mani-festations, psychological characteristics of the abusive parents, con-

sequences of abuse, reporting legislation, and community approaches to
the problem. Literature from all disciplines is included in the hope
that such a summary would help the practicing physician to become more
alert to the child abuse syndrome and to recognize the contribution that
non-medical professions can make in its management.

32 Stoenner, Herb. Plain talk about child abuse. Denver, Colorado:
      The American Humane Association, Children's Division, 1973. 24p.
      (Bibliography).
Consists of articles originally appearing in the Denver Post which present the basic facts about child abuse. Much of the material for the
article was drawn from an interview with Vincent De Francis, director of
the Children's Division of the American Humane Association. Subjects
discussed include: the common, but inaccurate myths about child abuse,
an historical overview of child protection services, the incidence and
nature of sexual abuse, the emotional trauma suffered by a child when
forced to testify before a criminal court, and recent non-punitive trends
employed when working with abusive families.

33 ten Bensel, Robert W., and Berdie, Jane. "The neglect and abuse of
      children and youth: the scope of the problem and the school's
      role." J Sch Health 46(8): 453-61, October, 1976. (54 Refer-
      ences).
General overview of the historical development of child abuse. Definitions of physical neglect, emotional neglect and abuse, physical and
sexual abuse are included, along with the incidence, characteristics of
abusing persons and abused children, physical findings observed by school
personnel, and consequences of abuse and neglect. Guidelines are given
to increase the school personnel's understanding of the problem and for
developing a school policy and procedures for reporting abuse and dealing
with it. A model for the process of identification and reporting is
given.

34 ten Bensel, Robert W., and King, Kurt J. "Neglect and abuse in chil-
      dren: historical aspects, identification, and management." J
      Dent Child 42(5): 348-58, September-October, 1975. (54 Refer-
      ences).
Discusses the historical aspects of maltreatment to children, the role
of the dentist in the detection of child abuse and neglect, and the procedures and requirements for reporting suspected cases. Violent abuse
and physical neglect have been present in society for centuries. Infanticides, ritualistic murders or surgery, and whipping of children for
disciplinary reasons have been documented in many cultures. Today the
incidence of child abuse and neglect is estimated to be 350 per 100,000
preschool children and 40-120 per 100,000 school-aged children. The death
rate is approximately 10 percent. Characteristics of parents who abuse
their children include: (1) a personal history of being abused or neglected as children; (2) the inability to call on other people to help
them when a crisis arises; (3) an unstable marital relationship; and (4)
unrealistic expectations about the child's capacities. The abused or
neglected child is often different in some way. Hyperactive children,
mentally defective children, unwanted children, or children with other
physical handicaps are abused more frequently than normal children. Abuse
is often precipitated by a single or multiple series of crises in the
family. Manifestations of physical abuse include skin surface injuries;
fractures of the long bones, ribs, and skull; orofacial lesions; central

nervous system damage; and gastrointestinal injuries. When a dentist suspects that a child has been abused or neglected, he should talk to the child or youth about the injuries, discuss the situation with the parents, contact the county child protection agency, and obtain medical attention for the child's injuries. Orofacial trauma is present in up to half of the reported cases of child abuse and consists of bruises, lacerations, burns, and fractures of the teeth and jaws.

35 U.S. National Center for Child Abuse and Neglect. <u>Child abuse and</u>
    <u>neglect: the problem and its management. Volume I: An overview</u>
    <u>of the problem</u>. Washington, D.C.: U.S. Government Printing Office,
    1976. 63p. (Bibliography). (DHEW Publication no. (OHD) 75-30073).
The first of a series of booklets published by the National Center on Child Abuse and Neglect. An overview of child maltreatment is offered. An initial problem in attempting to combat child abuse is the difficulty in distinguishing between abuse and neglect which is necessary to clearly define the conditions which must be reported under present laws. The general characteristics of abused or neglected children and their parents are offered for the purpose of aiding in the identification of the syndrome. Sexual abuse and emotional neglect or abuse are felt to be more difficult to identify than their physical counterparts. Estimates concerning the incidence of the problem vary widely, but it is felt that there are tens of thousands of abused or neglected children in the United States each year. Among the myths that have discouraged proper attention to the problem is the idealization of parenthood and the refusal to believe that a biologic parent could abuse a child. Another common fallacy is that child abuse occurs only among lower socioeconomic groups. The effects of abuse, in terms of the child victim's physical and emotional difficulties, are briefly presented. A psychiatric view of the abusing parent assesses some of the intrapsychic dynamics commonly at work in a pattern of abuse. Typically, the parent feels insufficient love for the child, makes extreme and premature demands on the child, and reacts with excessive criticism and physical punishment when the child fails to meet such demands.

The approach to abuse has been split historically between punishment and rehabilitation. State legislation increasingly emphasizes a therapeutic approach, with social workers rather than police conducting investigations of abuse complaints. A social worker can offer supportive services while the feasibility and usefulness of criminal prosecution is extremely limited. An account of state mandatory child abuse reporting legislation evaluates the law in terms of remaining loopholes in problems. The child protective services system designated to receive and act upon reports of abuse must be given clear and realistic goals to follow. All states should have clearly written and readable laws which can serve to guide both the reporter and the agency charged with responsibility to intervene in the problem family. Various professional disciplines must cooperate and coordinate their services for effective problem-solving.

36 Wright, Logan. "Psychological aspects of the battered child syn-
    drome." <u>South Med Bull</u> 58(3): 14-18, June, 1970. (16 Refer-
    ences).
A general discussion of the phenomenon of child abuse covers the nature and incidence of the problem, its occurrence at all socioeconomic levels (although poor whites are seen as accounting for a disproportionate number of cases), and the permanent effects of the battering upon the

child's physical and emotional development. The common emotional features of the abusive parent are presented. These include psychopathy, depression, and immaturity, usually masked by a fairly normal facade.

37 Young, Leontine R. Wednesday's children: a study of child neglect
      and abuse. New York: McGraw-Hill, 1971. 195p. (Bibliography).
Consists of a two-part study of child abuse and neglect. Part I sketches the profiles of abusive and neglectful families, using a broad, thematic outline to collect data. One hundred and twenty families were selected from the active case files of two public child welfare agencies and one private agency, all located in a large Eastern metropolitan area. Part II attempts to fill in the details of the family profiles and employs a more precise information schedule. The active files of public child welfare departments in seven different localities in the Midwest and Pacific coast regions of the country provided information on 180 families. The study design is detailed in an appendix. The families were divided into four categories according to the severity of neglect or abuse. They were defined as severely neglecting, moderately neglecting, severely abusing, or moderately abusing. Case examples were extrapolated in discussing the behavioral characteristics which seemed common to families in each category. Important differences emerged between abusive and neglecting parents, although poverty, poor housing conditions, sporadic employment, large numbers of children, health problems with inadequate medical care, alcoholism, psychosis, and criminal records were noted in all categories.

Individual and social factors are key aspects of the etiology of child abuse, but a great deal is still unknown about the causes of abuse. In addition, professionals are not sufficiently able to distinguish between those families who can be helped to provide appropriate care for their children and those who are untreatable. While professional understanding of the problem is further developed, the safety of the child should be the first priority of those in positions of responsibility. Biologic parenthood does not guarantee good parenting; the nature of parental rights needs reassessment. Caseworkers need to revise their schemes of intervention. Placement out of the home will often be the only safe course of action. Community awareness and involvement is also a vital dimension of the problem-solving process.

38 Zalba, Serapio R. "The abused child -- I: A survey of the problem."
      Soc Work 11(4): 3-16, October, 1966. (49 References).
Surveys the literature concerning child abuse. After the history, definition, and nature of the phenomenon are reviewed, strategies for managing abuse are discussed at some length. The current state of information regarding the identification, reporting, treatment, and sociolegal disposition of child abuse cases is presented with particular attention to the treatment of the abusive or abuse-prone parent. The roles of physicians and local agencies are emphasized.

2. BRIEF SUMMARIES

39 Allen, Ann F. "Maltreatment syndrome in children." Can Nurse
      62(4): 40-42, April, 1966. (13 References).
Surveys the maltreatment syndrome in children, with analyses of the kinds of trauma, parental characteristics, and preventive methods. Injuries to

children are categorized as (1) accidental; (2) occurring within an unprotected environment; and (3) direct abuse. In determining whether
trauma is an accident or abuse, x-rays are cited as the most useful diagnostic tool. Maltreated children, generally under three years of age,
tend to be singled out for abuse while other siblings are well cared for.
The parents lead isolated lives, have social problems, and are emotionally
unstable and immature. The mother is typically found to be the aggressor.
A history of past legislation is given with the urging that laws be passed
protecting parents, children, and reporting physicians. The importance
of social agencies in prevention is indicated by a case report.

40 Allen, Hugh D.; ten Bensel, Robert W.; Raile, Richard B. "The bat-
      tered child syndrome -- Part IV: Summary." Minn Med 52(3):
      539-40, March, 1969. (0 References).
Summarizes the incidence, early detection, and suggested legislation pertaining to the battered child syndrome.

41 "Assaulted children." Lancet 1(7332): 532-44, March 7, 1964. (12
      References).
Presents a brief overall description of the characteristics of child
abuse. A review of recent findings, a list of clinical features, and
suggestions for procedures to be followed in such cases are included.
Legal and sociological implications regarding abusing parents are also
described.

42 "Battered child syndrome." Time 80(3): 60, July 20, 1962. (0
      References).
Calls attention to a recent American Medical Association Journal report
on the battered child syndrome. Modern theories of childrearing have
not eliminated the serious abuse of children, which may be a more frequent
cause of death than such well-recognized diseases as leukemia or muscular
dystrophy. The physical manifestations of child abuse are distinct
enough to be readily recognized by the physician. The problem is not
confined to parents with psychopathic personalities or of low socioeconomic status. Physicians must learn to overcome their reluctance to
recognize and report this syndrome.

43 Bowley, Agatha H. Children at risk: the basic needs of children in
      the world today. New York: Churchill Livingstone, 1975. 61p.
Outlines the needs and care of children being brought up by immature,
unstable, or inadequate parents, with first-hand accounts of family situations met in child guidance work. Data is based on forty years work with
parents and children in hospitals, clinics, schools, and counseling
centers.

44 Brenneman, George. "Battered child syndrome." Alaska Med 10(4):
      175-78, December, 1968. (26 References).
Designed to call the attention of the medical community in Alaska to the
problem of child abuse. Two characteristic case histories of battered
children precede a brief account of previous literature on the subject.
There are no statistics on the incidence of the problem in Alaska, but
the high degree of morbidity and mortality associated with it is cited
as sufficient to warrant active concern. Diagnostic guidelines, some
common social features of abusing families, and prognostic issues are
discussed. The physician's responsibility is to make the correct diagnosis, to initiate treatment, and to insure that help is obtained

from the appropriate welfare and/or legal agencies. The pros and cons of
mandatory reporting laws are considered, although no recommendations are
made other than the fact that the physician must assert his leadership
in the management of abuse cases.

45 "Child battery: seek and save: consultation." <u>Med World News</u>
      13(22): 21ff., June 1, 1972. (0 References).
Consists of a question and answer symposium on child abuse involving
several experts in the field. Questions are wide ranging and address such
issues as the diagnosis of child abuse, the typical abusive parent, the
pervasiveness of child abuse throughout all levels of society, therapy
for child abusers, and the role of the physician in the identification,
treatment, and prevention of child abuse.

46 "Children in peril." <u>Nation</u> 214(10): 293-94, March 6, 1972. (0
      References).
Examines the topic of child abuse, emphasizing that many times statistics
are distorted, in particular those which involve the lower socioeconomic
groups in the country.

47 Cobe, P. "Winning the battle against child abuse." <u>Forecast Home
      Econ</u> 21: F46, May, 1976.

48 "Cry rises from beaten babies." <u>Life</u> 54(24): 38-39, June, 1963.
      (0 References).
Reviews general facts about child abuse for the lay public. The increased
awareness of abuse cases, the problems of reporting such cases, legal or
otherwise, and the characteristics of battered children and their parents
are discussed, along with a short case study with illustrative x-rays.

49 Currie, J. R. B. "A psychiatric assessment of the battered child
      syndrome." <u>S Afr Med J</u> 44(22): 635-39, May 30, 1970. (24
      References).
Summarizes the literature on the battered child syndrome and illustrates
the findings with several case studies. The parents tend to be under
twenty-five years of age, beset with financial, marital, and social
worries, often have poor impulse control, and pattern themselves after
their own abusive parents. The child, usually under six months of age,
is seen as critical and rejecting. The incidence of abuse is unknown,
and the prognosis is poor. Early diagnosis would enhance opportunities
for prevention and protection.

50 David, Lester. "The shocking price of parental anger." <u>Good House-
      keeping</u> 158(3): 87ff., March, 1964. (0 References).
Emphasizes that child abuse occurs in all communities. Studies reveal
that abusive parents feel threatened or frustrated with their children,
depend extensively on the support of someone else, and are themselves the
products of unloving, possibly abusive families. Because of insufficient
evidence and the need to appear in court, physicians previously were
reluctant to report child abuse cases. However, the telltale syndrome
(specific fractures, bruises) aids physicians in detection. The model
child protection law of the Children's Bureau (HEW) also helps identify
child abuse and protect the child from immediate danger.

51 Dawe, Kathleen E. "Maltreated children at home and overseas." <u>Aust
      Paediatr J</u> 9(4): 177-84, August, 1973. (12 References).

Explores various issues related to child abuse, with recommendations for
the provision of adequate services at the Royal Children's Hospital. The
concept of abuse is not limited to non-accidental physical injuries to the
child, but includes any "lack of capacity on the part of parents to protect and nurture their offspring." The importance of early diagnosis and
recognition of the danger signals which often precede more serious injury
to the child are stressed. Research and projects undertaken by the
University of Colorado Medical Center, Child Protection Team highlight
key concerns, such as the incidence of abuse, characteristics of abusing
parents, and identification of the circumstances likely to give rise to
the problem. A study designed to ascertain whether it is possible to
recognize the potential for abuse and to institute preventive measures is
described, along with alternative modes of treatment for parents.

52   "Dealing with child abusers." Sci Dig 76(4): 70-71, October, 1974.
        (0 References).
Highlights from a panel discussion by various experts involved in managing
child abuse cases in the Indianapolis area are outlined.

53   de Lesseps, Suzanne. "Child abuse." Ed Res Rep 1(4): 67-84,
        January 30, 1976. (24 References).
Presents an overview of the problem of child abuse in terms of community
detection projects, children's rights, and statistics about child abuse.

54   Earl, Howard G. "10,000 children battered and starved. Hundreds
        die: some parents admit guilt -- intensive two-year study of bat-
        tered and maltreated children reveals the true story behind abused
        youngsters." Todays Health 43(8): 24-31, September, 1965. (0
        References).
A photographic essay attempts to alert the public to the pervasiveness
and severity of the problem of child battering. Several actual incidents
are described in which children were grossly injured by their parents.
An interview with the supervising probation officer of the San Francisco
Juvenile Court reviews the types of children who are likely to become
targets of abuse and some characteristics of abusive parents. Diagnostic
questions are presented in lay terms. The essay concludes with the
AMA's recommendations for comprehensive legislation, which would not only
require the reporting of suspected cases of abuse, but would also mandate
the provision of adequate protection for children.

55   Elmer, Elizabeth. "Abused young children seen in hospitals." Soc
        Work 5(4): 98-102, October, 1960. (13 References).
The repugnance felt by society toward child abuse is the chief reason for
the avoidance of systematic study of the problem. Symptoms for medical
recognition and a brief survey of the medical literature are presented.
Both physicians and social workers are subject to feelings which may prevent them from acting upon suspicions of child abuse. A concise history
of cultural attitudes toward childrearing demonstrates the radical changes
which have come about in the past 150 years, during which severe physical
measures instituted against children have come to be deplored. Abusing
families have resisted these cultural changes, and little is known about
them. Numerous questions about the nature and treatment of the problem
of child abuse are raised.

56   Flato, Charles. "Parents who beat children." Saturday Evening Post
        235(35): 30-35, October 6, 1962. (0 References).

A photographic overview of issues relating to child abuse is designed to educate the lay person to the problem. Case histories provide the basis of discussions of incidence, diagnostic techniques, characteristics of abusive parents, legal entanglements typically associated with the problem, and the need for legislative and attitudinal reforms.

57 Fleming, G. M. "Cruelty to children." Br Med J 2(5549): 421-22, May 13, 1967. (11 References).
Outlines the major issues relating to cruelty to children. Cruelty is defined in broad terms to include mental as well as physical abuse, neglect, and deprivation. The article traces the following topics: (1) the reasons physicians often fail to report abuse cases; (2) the extent of the problem, including 1965 nationwide statistics; (3) the physical manifestations typical of abuse; (4) the legal difficulties in proving intentional injury; (5) the personalities of abusing parents; and (6) the procedures for treating the problem, stressing cooperation between physicians and social agencies.

58 Fontana, Vincent J. "The battered child by Ray E. Helfer and C. Henry Kempe: book review." Crime Delinq 16(1): 120-22, 1970.
Review of The Battered Child, by Ray E. Helfer and C. Henry Kempe. The work is found to be a thorough discussion of the medical, social, and legal aspects of child battering. Helfer and Kempe's treatment of the legal problems is particularly praised.

59 ———. "Child abuse -- a tragic problem: guest editorial." Parents Mag 48(3): 20, March, 1973. (0 References).
The incidence, parental characteristics, social effects, and preventive methods of child abuse are suggested.

60 ———. "The neglect and abuse of children." NY State J Med 64(2): 215-24, January 15, 1964. (8 References).
Presents the clinical and social manifestations of child abuse, along with the medical, social, and legal responsibilities essential for prevention. A plea is made for coordinated efforts. Statistics on the incidence of child abuse are included, along with two typical case reports.

61 Gardner, John W. "Abused child." McCalls 94(9): 96-97, 143, September, 1967. (0 References).
Reviews the history and characteristics of child abuse and methods which are being developed for prevention and treatment. Studies undertaken by C. Henry Kempe, Children's Division of The American Humane Society, and the Children's Bureau (HEW) have led to the incipient establishment of a national system of reporting--the state central registries. This research has also raised important issues about parental rights versus the role of society in protecting its children. Adequate social services, research on abusers, and public education are badly needed, in addition to the child abuse legislation which has already been passed.

62 Gelles, Richard J. "Demythologizing child abuse." Fam Coord 25(2): 13-41, April, 1976. (19 References).
Analyzes several predominant myths which cloud the issue of child abuse and, therefore, impede society's ability to understand and handle the problem effectively. Many people believe that child abuse is a new problem which is increasing drastically, while, in fact, it has existed

throughout history. Although child abuse is often considered a single, uniform phenomenon, it is actually a general label for a variety of parental behaviors, including poisonings, physical maltreatment, abandonment, neglect, and others. The abusive parent is frequently believed to be mentally ill. But the "sick" label serves to make the abusive parent a scapegoat in a society which actually condones violence toward children. Finally, the belief that society is doing a good job in preventing and treating child abuse is invalidated by the social stigma attached to the parent being treated, and the narrow client-specific programs that are provided. An eclectic approach is what is really needed to reach the widest range of people who need social services.

63 Gordon, A. "A child is being beaten." Physicians Manage 5(6):
      22-34, June, 1965. (0 References).
Considers the various forms child abuse may assume, the types of parents involved, and the legislative problems which ensue from statutorial attempts to deal with the matter. Existing legislation and widespread publicity have increased sensitivity to the problem, but have not supplied answers to the difficult questions regarding the most beneficial handling of the child and his family environment during and after treatment.

64 Green, Karl M. "The abused child." Md State Med J 15(3): 47-49,
      March, 1966. (13 References).
Presents a general survey of the characteristics of child abuse, a review of the literature and legislation since 1946, and a statistical report of incidence. Clinical characteristics of child abuse include a discrepancy between the presented history of a short illness and the actual physical findings upon examination. X-rays typically show bone injuries, including multiple fractures which have occurred at various times. The problem, however, is not strictly medical in that its prevention depends on protective laws for reporting physicians who must be willing to pursue suspicions. Social agencies are responsible for placement of the child or family treatment. Recognition of the problem is essential for adequate treatment.

65 Heins, Marilyn. "Child abuse -- analysis of a current epidemic."
      Mich Med 68(17): 887-91, September, 1969. (5 References).
A brief account of the history of child abuse up to 1969 is offered. Based upon a sample of cases seen at Detroit General Hospital, the incidence, method of diagnosis, sex and age of the abused child, and the relationship of the abuser to the child are discussed. The physician must recognize and report suspected abuse; and, in addition, he must support proper legislation to establish and maintain child protective services.

66 Helfer, Ray E. "Somewhere a child is crying by Vincent Fontana:
      book review." Compact 8(2): 34-35, March-April, 1974. (0 Refer-
      ences).
Commends the book for the challenge it offers to parents and professionals to understand and help families that live in constant violence. Points out the book's failure to differentiate between family and criminal courts and its seeming advocation of criminal prosecution as a solution to the problem of child abuse.

67 Houston Child Care Council. Houston report on children. Houston,
      Texas: Child Care Council, 1975.

68 Lawton, Henry. "Child abuse: four book reviews." Hist Child Q
      3(4): 606-17, Spring, 1976. (55 References).
Four works on child abuse are reviewed: A Child is Being Beaten: Vio-
lence Against Children, An American Tragedy, by Naomi Feigelson Chase;
Child Abuse: Intervention and Treatment, edited by Nancy B. Ebeling and
Deborah A. Hill; The Little Victims: How America Treats its Children, by
Howard James; and The Myth of the Hyperactive Child and Other Means of
Child Control, by Peter Schrag and Diane Divorky. Chase's book receives
the most negative criticism for its "hysterical" tone and simplistic
middle class bias. Ebeling and Hill's collection of short papers is regarded as a persuasive discussion of family therapy and the need for more
coordination in the prevention and treatment of abuse, but the work
strikes the reviewer as ultimately evading the realities of the problem.
Howard James' work is similarly admired for its intent to raise the
reader's conscience over society's frequently inhumane treatment of
deviant and unwanted children, but is ultimately faulted for its generalizations concerning sweeping reform. The reviewer labels Schrag and
Divorky's study of the control of the hyperactive child by vast and powerful systems as "easily the best" of the four books despite some "fuzzy
thinking." The work traces the chilling implications of the national
faith in perfection for those children who are unable to conform to the
norm. In the name of benevolence, such children are labeled hyperactive
and are drugged and used as test subjects for other forms of behavior
suppression. All four books are regarded by the reviewer as being less
precise and concrete than they should be, and exhibiting tendencies
toward emotionalism which cloud any attempt to analyze or remedy the
situations they present. The problem of child abuse needs to be exposed
in all its full horror and in all its forms, particularly those sanctioned
by American society. This is the reviewer's ultimate concern; his disappointment with most of these books in their failure to come to full
and realistic grips with the situation.

69 LeBourdais, Eleanor. "Look again . . . is it accident or abuse?"
      Can Hosp 49(1): 26-28, January, 1972. (5 References).
Explores child abuse in Canada, including topics such as the reporting of
cases, characteristics of the abusing parent and the abused child, reasons
for reluctance to report, and suggestions for prevention.

70 Mulford, Robert M. "The battered child by Ray E. Helfer and C. Henry
      Kempe: book review." Child Welfare 49(6): 351, June, 1970. (0
      References).
The Battered Child, edited by Ray Helfer and C. Henry Kempe, 1968, is
called by this reviewer "the most comprehensive single volume now available on the subject of the battered child." It is organized in four
parts: history and incidence, medical aspects, psychiatric and social
aspects, and legal aspects. The appendices include a description of a
California pilot study of child abuse incidents, a summary of neglect and
traumatic cases of abuse, and a summary of child abuse legislation in the
United States.

71 Nomura, Fred M. "The battered child 'syndrome.'" Hawaii Med J
      25(5): 387-94, May-June, 1966. (22 References).
Reviews the problems, literature, and characteristics of child abuse.
While the incidence of maltreatment has not been established, abuse is
viewed as the major cause of childhood affliction and death. Abusing
parents are commonly unstable, with serious personality defects and

neuroses. Marital difficulty, premarital conception, and maltreatment
in their own childhoods can also be factors. The child commonly shows
bruises, swellings on the arms or legs and subdural bleeding upon admission. He improves while hospitalized with no new lesions appearing.
Unlike a well-cared-for child, the abused one seems frightened of contact,
especially with his parents. Parents frequently deny abuse and resist
efforts to help them. Close physical and radiological examination are
crucial for diagnosis; repeated injury, and even death, can occur when
abuse is undetected. Once the case has been classified as maltreatment,
it must be reported, hopefully to a protective agency which can work with
the parents and child. Physicians have been reluctant to report because
of disbelief, ignorance, or fear. However, legislation prompted by the
Children's Bureau (HEW) makes reporting mandatory in more and more situations. Legislation is reviewed with the suggestion that reports be submitted to protective agencies rather than to the police.

72 "Quiz: child abuse and neglect." Pediatr Ann 5(3): 130-31, 135,
       March, 1976. (0 References).
Quiz concerning the legal, historical, diagnostic, referral, and treatment
aspects of child abuse and neglect.

73 Sage, Wayne. "Violence in the children's room." Hum Behav 4(7):
       41-47, July, 1975. (0 References).
Child abuse is a social problem that affects everyone and is not just the
individual personal problem of a minority. The warning signals, reasons
for abuse, and methods of treatment are described.

74 Scoville, A. B. "The battered-child syndrome: editorial." J Tenn
       Med Assoc 64(4): 346-47, April, 1971. (3 References).
Offers a brief and general overview of the problem of child abuse. The
most prevalent characteristics of the abusing parent are discussed and
compliance with the reporting laws is urged.

75 Sheils, Merrill; Agrest, Susan; Maier, Frank; et al. "The battered
       children." Newsweek 90(15): 112-13, 115, October 10, 1977. (0
       References).
Presents an overview of the problem of child abuse. Statistics are quoted
from the National Center on Child Abuse and Neglect which reveal that over
one-half million children are abused each year, 2,000 of them fatally.
The common characteristics of abusive parents, such as their social isolation and low tolerance for stress, are discussed. Several therapy programs, including Odyssey Institute in New York (a residential treatment
facility for parents and children), Parents Anonymous, and emergency hot-
lines and homemaker services, are described. Problems with mandatory
reporting and program funding are examined. Recommended preventive measures include parent education programs and greater public awareness of
the problem, coupled with a willingness to intervene on behalf of the
battered child.

76 Simpson, Keith S. "The battered baby problem." S Afr Med J 42(26):
       661-63, July 6, 1968. (0 References).
See abstract of Keith Simpson, "The battered baby problem." R Soc Health
J 87(3): 168-70, May-June, 1967. (Item no. 77).

77 ————. "The battered baby problem." R Soc Health J 87(3): 168-
       70, May-June, 1967. (0 References).

Calls attention to the phenomenon of child abuse, touching on its definition, incidence, victims, perpetrators, injuries, legal questions, and
prevention. Six characteristic features of the battered child syndrome
are identified: (1) victims are usually two to three years old; (2) the
violence is recurrent; (3) the parents or caretakers are usually the
perpetrators; (4) the parents often do not report injuries which result
from battering or they delay in their report; (5) the parents lie about
the injury; and (6) the parents are inadequate, subnormal, or simple.

78 Soman, Shirley C. <u>Let's stop destroying our children</u>. New York:
      Hawthorn Books, 1974. 274p.
Offers an emotional, often sensational account of children maimed or
killed by unsafe consumer products, in preventable home accidents, or by
other persons, interspersed with the plea for a sense of morality in industry and greater concern by legislators and all adults with protecting
children. In detailed, journalistic prose, stories of children killed in
freak accidents on playground equipment or bicycles, in swimming pools,
at summer camps, and at home following household poisonings are cited.
Careful parental supervision of children's activities, along with stricter
control for manufacturers of children's toys and clothing, are urged.

The second section of the book focuses upon the breakdown of the family
and the children who suffer the consequences of neglect, abuse, and abandonment. The courts are blamed for persisting in breaking up the family
in neglect cases rather than providing counseling or homemaker services
which might uphold the integrity of the family unit. Emergency parents,
more foster home placements, and small group homes would provide the
abandoned child with a secure and uninterrupted home environment. The
horrors of children abused in mental institutions, in adult jails after
being arrested for minor offenses, by their parents, and by other children point to an almost universal victimization of children and to
society's failure to provide adequate protection for its children.

A new bill of rights for children with a statute promising each child the
right to be a part of a family who wants him/her is proposed. The efforts
of various state programs in child advocacy and protection, such as the
Office for Children in Massachusetts, are described. A program of action
in behalf of children with provisions for establishing a parent-child
action movement on consumer products, a national housing program for families with children, and a national children's ombudsman office are discussed.

79 Texas. State Department of Public Welfare. <u>Children in danger</u>.
      Austin, Texas: State Department of Public Welfare, 1974.

80 Van Dyke, Vicki. <u>Understanding child abuse</u>. Springfield, Illinois:
      Illinois State Department of Children and Family Services, 1977.
      6p. (Bibliography).
While the frequency of child abuse is not known, reports of abuse have
increased since the Illinois laws were changed, widening the numbers and
categories of people required to report suspected abuse and granting
immunity from civil or criminal liability to those who report. Child
abuse is caused by a combination of several factors: a potentially abusive parent, a child with certain characteristics which seem to invite
abuse, and a crisis which precipitates the abuse. Abusive parents typically have been themselves abused, have disturbed marital relationships,
and have feelings of isolation from other people. The abused child is

often viewed as unresponsive, handicapped, or willful. The precipitating crisis can be large (family death, loss of job) or small (crying baby, broken TV); but whatever the severity, the actual abuse usually occurs during the crisis. Treatment of abuse must be to provide for the child's immediate safety and to improve the home situation. The child may be removed from the home, but the Department of Children and Family Services tries, when possible, to save the home for the child rather than save the child from the home. Some new approaches which have been tried are: Parents Anonymous groups, crisis centers, community awareness programs, day care centers, family counseling, and use of temporary caretakers placed in homes of abandoned children.

81 Venkatadri, P. C. "The battered baby: editorial." Clinician 36(9): 369-70, September, 1972. (0 References).
Briefly reviews the discovery of the battered baby syndrome, along with an enumeration of its manifestations and recommendations for government action to combat it.

82 "'When they're angry . . .'" Newsweek 59(16): 74, April 16, 1962. (0 References).
Notes the fiftieth anniversary of the Children's Bureau (HEW), which intends to give the problem of the battered child top priority. Aspects of the problem are briefly considered, including frequency of occurrence, physician reluctance to report, methods of detection, and characteristics of the abusing parent. A typical case of an abused child admitted to a city hospital emergency room is also described.

3. BIBLIOGRAPHIES

83 "Child abuse and neglect: a bibliography." Res Relat Child 37: 1-16, 1976.
This selective 104-item bibliography on child abuse and neglect updates previous ERIC Clearinghouse on Early Childhood Education bibliographies on the subject. Included are ERIC documents, books, pamphlets, journal articles, and a few additional sources. The rest of the report deals with on-going research projects in the following areas: child growth and development, special groups of children, the child in the family, socioeconomic and cultural factors influencing children, educational factors and service, social services, and health services. Included are indices of investigators, institutions and subjects, and a listing of other abstracting services.

84 Council for Exceptional Children. Information Services and Publica- tions. Child abuse: a selective bibliography. Exceptional child bibliography series no. 601. Reston, Virginia: Council for Exceptional Children, 1975. 17p. ERIC Document ED 102 805.
An annotated bibliography of seventy-five documents and articles on child abuse published between 1963 and 1974. Selected from the computer files of the Council for Exceptional Children's Information Services and the Education Resources Information Center (ERIC), the items chosen for in- clusion in the bibliography were based on user requests. The citations include summaries of the content of the sources, along with descriptions of the subjects covered.

85 ————. Child abuse: a selective bibliography. Exceptional child
     bibliography series no. 601. Reston, Virginia: Council for
     Exceptional Children, 1976. 24p. ERIC Document ED 129 002.
An annotated bibliography of some eighty journal articles and documents
on the subject of child abuse published between 1968 and 1975. Abstracts
include a content summary, bibliographical data, and descriptive words
about the citation. The items included in the bibliography were based on
user requests from the computer files of the Council for Exceptional
Children's Informational Services and the Education Resources Information
Center (ERIC).

86 Davis, Gwendolyn, and Higgins, Judith. "Child abuse: a bibliography."
     SLJ Sch Libr J 23(3): 29-33, November, 1976. (38 References).
An annotated bibliography of child abuse literature of special interest
to teachers and school administrators includes books, pamphlets, journal
articles, films, filmstrips, and posters.

87 Glockner, Mary, and Goodman, Sharon T. "ERIC/ECE." Child Educ
     52(3): 117-18, November, 1975. (8 References).
The ERIC/ECE Clearinghouse on Early Childhood Education is part of ERIC,
a federally funded information network which has microfiche collections
of 500 university libraries and contributes annotations to the Current
Index of Journals in Education. Included are sample ERIC annotations of
books dealing with child abuse.

88 Goldstein, Jeffrey H. "Social and psychological aspects of child
     abuse: a bibliography." Cat Sel Doc Psychol 5: 289, Summer,
     1975.
Cites a 210-item bibliography on the non-medical aspects of child abuse.
The bibliography also includes an introduction and discussion of problems
in research methods.

89 Kline, Donald F., and Hopper, Mark A. Child abuse: an integration
     of the literature and a concept analysis with recommendations for
     educational research. Washington, D.C.: U.S. Department of Health,
     Education, and Welfare, Bureau of Education for the Handicapped,
     Research Projects Branch, 1975. 124p. (Bibliography).
Surveys and evaluates the current state of literature regarding child
abuse, and includes an annotated bibliography and recommendations for
future research priorities. An overwhelming proportion of the items surveyed were confined to the physical identification of child abuse; very
little was said about the psychological effects of abuse on the child.
In addition, it was found that current definitions and theories about
child abuse were very emotional and often confused. It is recommended
that future research approach the questions of the teacher's involvement
and the school's responsibility.

B. HISTORICAL OVERVIEW

1. ATTITUDES TOWARD CHILDREN

90 Aptekar, Herbert. "Infanticide." In: Aptekar, Herbert. Anjea:
     Infanticide, abortion and contraception in savage society. New
     York: William Godwin, 1931. 155-71. (15 References).

Studies the use of infanticide in primitive societies, focusing on its
relation to economic life and to polyandry. No definite conclusions are
reached except that where economic hardship or population pressures exist
and infanticide is practiced, a relationship does exist between the two.
This rule applies as well to the coexistence of polyandry and female infanticide and of polygyny and male infanticide. The interrelationship of
infanticide and cultural forces in primitive societies implies the same
interrelationship between birth control methods and cultural elements in
the western world.

91 deMause, Lloyd. "The evolution of childhood." Hist Child Q 1(4):
      503-75, Spring, 1974. (258 References).
Surveys the historical evolution of parent-child relations, which, it is
proposed, represents the central force for all changes throughout the
history of human experience. History is regarded as a succession of six
major psychogenic changes in human personality brought about by parental
attitudes toward children: (1) in antiquity, infanticide was commonly
practiced and accepted; (2) in the middle ages, the child was abandoned
rather than killed; (3) in the Renaissance, the prevailing parental
attitude was ambivalent, containing both hostility and the desire to mold
the child; (4) in the eighteenth century, the parental attitude was in-
trusive, very concerned with controlling and shaping the child; (5) in
nineteenth and early twentieth centuries, there was less concern over
controlling the child, and more with educating and socializing him; and
(6) finally, in the mid and late twentieth century, the "Helping Mode"
took over, and the child's rights to control his own life with a minimum
of interference was acknowledged.

92 ————. "Our forebearers made childhood a nightmare." Psychol
      Today 8(11): 85-88, April, 1975. (0 References).
Presents an historical survey of parental attitudes toward children. The
incidence of child abuse and infanticide has been high throughout recorded
history, largely because only recently have children begun to be thought
of as fully fledged human beings. The history of child psychology is
short, and recognition of children's rights is preceded by a long and
bloody evolution, which is divided into several periods. In antiquity,
outright infanticide was common; in the medieval period, infanticide took
the less brutal form of abandonment. The Renaissance attitude toward
children was ambivalent, and the shift away from physical harm to more
psychological discipline occurred in the eighteenth and nineteenth
centuries. The twentieth century marks the first acknowledgment of the
damage which parents can do to their children.

93 Frazier, Claude A. "Child abuse: society's symptom of stress."
      Christ Today 21(17): 6-8, June 3, 1977. (0 References).
Discusses child abuse from the Christian standpoint. Physical and emotional abuse are briefly defined. Biblical quotes describe how a parent
should raise his children. The Christian's responsibility in the problem of child abuse is to recognize the problem, support protective and
counseling services, and provide for underprivileged children.

94 Jones, John W. "Position of slaves, women, minors." In: Jones,
      John W. Law and legal theory of the Greeks: an introduction.
      Oxford: Clarendon Press, 1956. 287-88. (8 References).
Describes the Greek practice of exposure of infants, a procedure which
was not widespread until the third century when females and deformed
infants were the primary victims.

95 Kiel, Frank W.   "Forensic science in China -- traditional and contem-
       porary aspects."   J Forensic Sci   15(2): 201-34, April, 1970.
       (113 References).
The functions and procedures of forensic medicine in China from ancient
times to the present are detailed. Some material on infanticide is included. The practice was an old and accepted one in many areas of China;
as late as the nineteenth century, 40 percent of the female infant population in certain regions was eliminated. Female children were the usual
victims since they were generally seen as contributing less to the
patriarchal and patrilineal family than the males. Fathers usually performed the killings, but in some places, the murders involved several
family members. Infanticide has been outlawed in China today, but contemporary forensic pathologists are advised to watch for poisoning and
the insertion of needles as causes of death in infants.

96 Lorence, Bogna W.   "Parents and children in eighteenth-century
       Europe."   Hist Child Q   2(1): 1-30, Summer, 1974. (63 References).
The eighteenth century attitude toward childrearing involved two alternative and opposing mindsets, generally based on class lines. Members of
the upper class affected indifference, the display of emotion being regarded as sentimental and in poor taste. Children were, at best, play
things and parents were responsible mainly to prepare the child to advance
socially. Among the middle class, however, parents were intent on shaping
their children from birth, often out of the religious concern that the
child was born depraved and a constant effort needed to be made for his
salvation. A small minority of people simply enjoyed their children and
believed in giving children greater freedom.

97 Parsons, Elsie C.   "Social factors in birth and child death rates."
       In: Parsons, Elsie C. The family: an ethnographical and histori-
       cal outline with descriptive notes, planned as a text-book for the
       use of college lectures and of directors of home-reading clubs.
       New York: G. P. Putnam's Sons, 1906. 44-59. (15 References).
Discusses the varying attitudes toward the practice of feticide and infanticide in different societies. In some cultures a younger child is
killed when an older child has not yet been weaned; in other, if the
mother dies, the child is buried alive with her. Examples of other tribal
behavior which show a greater reverence for children are given.

98 Payne, George Henry. The child in human progress. New York: B. P.
       Putnam's Sons, 1916. 400p. (Bibliography).
Finding that there was no organized movement until 1874 to defend the
rights of children led to this study of the history of conditions before
that time, examining the physical, domestic, economic, and social existence of the child throughout all nations and all eras. Until recently,
children have typically been considered as the property of the parents,
possessing no rights of their own. Cultures on every continent have
sanctioned infanticide to control population, to ease food shortages, to
render a tribe more mobile, or to destroy "unnatural" births. Parents
might drown, poison, abandon, sacrifice, mutilate, cannibalize their
children, or leave them to die by exposure or live burial. A society's
attitude toward its young is considered a barometer of progress; and the
major religions (Judaism, Mohammedism, and especially Christianity) are
seen as the main forces which awakened humane instincts toward children.
Even after infanticide was discouraged, many cultures continued to sell
or mutilate children for profit or to overwork them in apprenticeships

or in factories. Not until recent centuries did any orphanages, asylums, or protective agencies develop. The famous Mary Ellen case sparked protest against child abuse in America and led to the founding of the Society for the Prevention of Cruelty to Children in 1875.

99 Rice, Mary P. "The battered child." Henry Ford Hosp Med Bull
    12(4): 401-4, December, 1964. (13 References).
Reviews literature concerning child abuse, including brief reports on attitudes in the ancient world, statistics demonstrating incidence, characteristics of parents and their means of abuse, and known and hypothesized causes.

100 Shaheen, Eleanor; Husain, S. A.; Hays, Janice. "Child abuse -- a
    medical emergency." Mo Med 72(9): 532-35, September, 1975. (19
    References).
The history of child abuse, including its definition and incidence, is briefly outlined. Characteristics of the abused and the abuser, along with criteria for diagnosing abuse and neglect, are presented. The Missouri mandatory reporting statute and community resources available in Missouri provide potential for effectively handling abuse and neglect. However, successful management depends on cooperation and open communication among all agencies providing treatment.

101 Thomas, Mason P., Jr. "Child abuse and neglect. I: Historical
    overview, legal matrix, and social perspectives." NC Law Rev 50:
    293-349, February, 1972. (107 References).
Studies the treatment of children by their parents throughout history. Incidents of cruelty are found to be very commonly accepted and acknowledged by the community. The more recent development of concern for more humanitarian treatment is traced through the nineteenth and twentieth centuries, along with the concomitant growth of the body of law devoted to the welfare of children. The post war recognition of the phenomenon of child abuse is discussed in terms of the still inconclusive etiologies for and the statutory response to the problem. The state's shift of emphases from the paternalistic doctrine of parens patriae to explicit concern for the entire family meets with approval.

2. CRUELTY TO CHILDREN

102 Cable, Mary. "The federal child." In: Cable, Mary. The little
    darlings: a history of childrearing in America. New York: Charles
    Scribner's Sons, 1975. 73-76. (0 References).
Reviews former Puritan childrearing practices in America, including the case history of a boy who in 1829 was so severely beaten by his teacher that he died a few days later. The incident caused an outrage, which indicated that society was perhaps beginning to develop a more understanding and humane attitude toward children by the early nineteenth century.

103 Caulfield, Ernest. The infant welfare movement in the eighteenth
    century. New York: Paul B. Hoeber, 1931. 203p. (Bibliography).
Presents a descriptive account of infanticide, child abandonment, and neglect during the eighteenth century. According to the London burial registry for 1741, 40 percent of all deaths were children under five years of age. In many instances, these were abortive or stillborn deaths, frequently the result of improper use of the newly-introduced obstetrical

forceps. When nurse and infant slept in the same bed, a child was often suffocated or crushed. Infants were neglected by fashionable women who refused to nurse their own. Children of poverty stricken mothers were often abandoned on the doorsteps of the wealthy or at parish convents, and some unmarried mothers secretly murdered their infants. Cruelty to children was rampant. Infants were stolen, maimed, and used as accomplices in begging or in circus performing. Despite the widespread disregard for the welfare of children, various philanthropists and physicians struggled to improve maternity practices and to establish charitable asylums for abandoned infants. Such foundling hospitals were, nevertheless, abused by parents who brought in their dying children to save themselves the expense of burial, and by child traffickers who transported unwanted children en masse and for a fee to these hospitals, without regard for delivering their charges alive.

104 Earle, Alice. "Oldtime discipline." In: Earle, Alice. Child
     life in colonial days. New York: Macmillan, 1909. 191-211.
     (0 References).
Describes methods of child discipline used in England and America in colonial times. Children were considered naturally stubborn and proud and in need of "breaking and beating down." Schoolmasters, with the encouragement of parents, rigidly enforced discipline with whips, rods, ferules, switches, leather straps, or clubs. Others disciplined children with a wide diversity of painful or humiliating punishments--gagging, pinching, calling names, making children hold heavy weights, punishing them for another child's offense, and others. Few teachers or parents seemed to believe in disciplining only with love or reason, without physical violence. Servants--child or adult--could expect similarly severe punishments for idleness, rudeness, or disobedience.

105 Green, M. A. "Dr. Scattergood's case books: a 19th century medico-
     legal record." Practitioner 211(265): 679-84, November, 1973.
     (0 References).
Brief biography and discussion of some of the 300 recorded medicolegal cases of Thomas Scattergood, a nineteenth century physician. Several cases of child abuse are outlined, including three of smothering by bed clothes, one of a fifteen-month-old child poisoned by silver nitrate administered by his mother, and one of a child beaten to death by his mother's lover.

106 Hartman, Mary S. "Child-abuse and self-abuse: two Victorian cases."
     Hist Child Q 2(2): 221-48, Fall, 1974. (34 References).
Two bizarre Victorian cases of child abuse are investigated. In the one case, a young girl named Constance Kent was abandoned by her father and left in a convent after the slaying of her three-and-one-half-year-old half brother. It is believed that the father actually killed the boy, but Constance ultimately confessed to the murder. In another case, the five Marsden girls were abused by their French governess who had been charged by their father to cure them of alleged masturbation. The governess beat the girls and starved them, convincing their father that they persisted in their bad habits. The governess was eventually brought to trial, but the Marsden girls had to prove their innocence of masturbation before the governess' treatment of them could be regarded as abusive.

107 Judge, Cliff, and Emmerson, Roma. "Some children at risk in Victoria
     in the 19th century." Med J Aust 1(13): 490-95, March 30, 1974.
     (20 References).

A delineation of the terrible conditions prevalent in Australian reform schools in the late nineteenth century. Admonitory parallels are drawn to the present day situations of some 100,000 at risk children in Australia.

108 McLoughlin, William G. "Evangelical childrearing in the age of Jackson: Francis Wayland's views on when and how to subdue the willfulness of children." J Soc Hist 9(1): 21-39, Fall, 1975. (13 References).

Considers the effects of the harsh parental discipline practiced by American Evangelical Protestants in the early nineteenth century, with particular reference to the history of the Rev. Francis Wayland. Wayland was regarded as an educational authority at the time; the material presented treats his successful and permanently damaging effort to "break the will" of his children (willfulness being regarded as a precursor of sociopathic behavior). This "breaking of the will" was essentially a form of the operant conditioning approach used by animal trainers.

109 Mayhew, Henry. The great world of London. London, 1856. 498p. (Bibliography).

Examines factors of the imprisonment of young boys in London, particularly those at Tothill Fields House of Correction. In poverty areas, the necessity for both parents to work left children without proper supervision and moral instruction, allowing them to mix with criminal elements. However, the imprisonment of large numbers of children for petty crimes did not serve as correction; rather, it introduced them further into a criminal way of life. Indeed, at Tothill Fields, the readmittance of one-half of the child offenders indicated it was used by many of them as a refuge rather than as a correction facility. Figures suggesting that one-fifth of youthful offenders became adult offenders supported the idea that these correctional houses were in some way a training ground for adult criminal life. Attempts at reform through education resulted only in a more literate prison population; industrial training for productive jobs was recommended as a more likely means of prevention.

110 Spargo, John. The bitter cry of the children. New York: Quadrangle Books, 1957. Reprint of 1906 edition. 549p. (Bibliography).

A rhetorical discussion of the plight of the poor and working child at the turn of the century. Poor children, though not intentionally abused by their parents, were often underfed, poorly clothed, and neglected. The high infant mortality rate was, in part, due to a mother's returning to work shortly after giving birth and leaving her child in the care of a young girl who was often only a child herself. In school, the physically neglected child appeared dull and irritable because of hunger. Simple breakfast or lunch programs instituted at the Salvation Army or in the schools were instrumental in teaching the child better eating habits. In the chapter on the working child, descriptions of textile mills, factories, and coal mines provided evidence that child labor was a form of child slavery. Numerous instances of pathos and cruelty to individual children were cited.

111 Trexler, Richard C. "Infanticide in Florence: new sources and first results." Hist Child Q 1(1): 98-116, Summer, 1973. (74 References).

Analyzes the implications of new data from the sixteenth century Florentine orphanage, The Innocenti Asylum. The Asylum's records indicate a

sharp increase in the abandonment of children in the early sixteenth
century. The unlikely preponderance of males in the baptismal records
of the period also suggests that newborn female infants were being murdered. A survey of the history of infanticide and abandonment from the
Greco Roman period to the Renaissance provides the background for this
discussion, and the attitudes of the church and the law toward these
phenomena are presented.

3. CHILD PROTECTIVE SERVICES

112 Bremner, Robert H. "Child protection: a. protection against
         cruelty and neglect." In: Bremner, Robert H., ed. <u>Children and
         youth in America: a documentary history</u>. Boston: Harvard
         University Press, 1970-1974. 185-236. (43 References).
Traces the development of humane societies, child protection legislation,
and immorality laws. The case of Mary Ellen Wilson, rescued by the
Society for the Prevention of Cruelty to Animals, led to the origin of
the Society for the Prevention of Cruelty to Children in 1874. The number of societies grew, focusing on law enforcement and legislation rather
than child welfare services which were left to other agencies. One
result was the widespread institutionalization of children. Immorality
laws, promoted by Anthony Comstock beginning in 1872, waged campaigns
against vices, especially the sale of obscene literature. After 1905,
the moral standards of the motion picture industry also became controversial, and efforts toward self-regulation were made by the industry.

113 ————. "Protection against neglect, abuse, and immorality: a.
         neglect and abuse." In: Bremner, Robert H., ed. <u>Children and
         youth in America: a documentary history</u>. Boston: Harvard
         University Press, 1970-1974. 849-91. (15 References).
A collection of articles from 1933 to 1973 reveals the changing attitudes
and approaches to the problem of child abuse. Interests centering on
protective services for abused children have proposed, over the years,
improvements in the philosophies and administration of existing services
and have called for increased community responsibility and legislation
on reporting child abuse. A national survey of protective services in
1967 indicated that these services exist in every state but do not necessarily meet the needs of abused and neglected children. The specific
case of Mark in Detroit identified the inadequacy of a protected service
which allowed an abandoned child to be placed in a juvenile detention
home. Public and professional awareness of the problem of child abuse
reached a peak in the early 1960's when C. Henry Kempe became alarmed at
the number of his patients who were suffering from willfully inflicted
injuries. This finding later led to a symposium on the battered child
syndrome and stimulated much research and legislation on child abuse,
particularly on how to detect it and procedures for reporting or preventing it. In addition to physical protection for children, the issue of
moral protection has focused on the content of movies and efforts by the
film industry for self-regulation.

114 Chance, William. "The boarding-out system." In: Chance, William.
         <u>Children under the poor law: their education, training and after-
         care</u>. London: Swan Sonnenschein, 1897. 180-236. (159 Refer-
         ences).

Examines different public programs for the care of orphans and deserted children in nineteenth century England. The reform of the Poor Law in 1834 insured pauper children in workhouses and district schools of better care and education. Moreover, these institutionalized children were often treated better than children boarded out to working class families. The defects of the boarding-out system were numerous. A child's basic needs were neglected when the foster parents pocketed for their own use the allowance provided for the child's food and clothing. Underneath their respectable outer attire, many children were filthy and covered with lice and sores. For this reason, bodily inspection of each child, as opposed to a cursory inspection of the premises, was recommended. The inspector was to be a woman and visit the families unannounced. Several cases of physical abuse were detected after female inspectors undressed a child and discovered bruises and scars from previous beatings. In one case, intervention by the Society for Prevention of Cruelty to Children was necessary and the foster parents were subsequently convicted and imprisoned. For the most part, only youngsters under ten years were boarded out; it was found that older children were often regarded as servants by the foster parents. Stricter standards for selecting foster parents, along with more stringent and regular observation of existing foster homes were urged.

115 Folks, Homer. The care of destitute, neglected, and delinquent children. New York: Macmillan, 1902. 251p.
Reports on the public care of destitute, neglected, and delinquent children during the nineteenth century when assistance was provided by local governmental units prior to any all-encompassing federal relief plan. Destitute children were often apprenticed or indentured as servants during the eighteenth century, but in the nineteenth century they were commonly placed in almshouses where they were taught a trade, while a few were boarded out to families. In some instances, destitute children were placed in reformatories, along with juvenile offenders and other morally wayward youths. Neglected children did not receive such systematic care but often went unnoticed in the homes of unfit and violent parents. In 1875, the Society for the Prevention of Cruelty to Children was established in New York City which, along with humane societies founded in other cities, investigated cases of alleged neglect or cruelty to children. These societies were criticized for breaking up families and for institutionalizing children instead of seeking appropriate family placements. Moreover, they did not oversee the subsequent care of the children who they had so dramatically rescued. The newly instituted children's courts are praised for their uniformity in handling cases of neglected or delinquent children and for their greater cooperation with social service agencies. Eighteenth century child care legislation of the various states is traced. It is concluded that the concern of the twentieth century would be whether the state should manage child care institutions or subsidize charitable organizations to do that same work.

116 Gane, E. Marguerite. "A decade of child protection." In: Bossard, James H. S., ed. Children in a depression decade. Philadelphia: The American Academy of Political and Social Science, 1940. 153-58. (6 References).
Presents an historical review of child protective services with special emphasis on the extent and nature of these services in 1939. With the advancement of modern family life, increasingly serious and complex problems with children had developed and child protective services were urged

to readjust to meet the changing needs of children. Social casework was recommended as a type of prevention and treatment method with the potential for making substantial contributions to the welfare of children. In the past, a lack of well-trained caseworkers had restricted the progress of casework in child protection.

117 McDonald, D. I. "The care of destitute children in Australia: beginnings in New South Wales." Med J Aust 1(18): 904-6, May 5, 1973. (20 References).
The Orphans' Schools and Benevolent Asylum was established in New South Wales (Australia) in the nineteenth century to undertake the care and training of poor children. The institutions are seen as reflecting a benevolent intention.

118 Mangold, George B. "The dependent and neglected child." In: Mangold, George B. Child problems. New York: Macmillan, 1910. 293-345. (14 References).
Identifies and outlines the proper care for dependent and neglected children. Different types of dependent children and various causes of their becoming dependent on the state are discussed, and some statistics about the numbers of dependent children in institutions are given. One chapter discusses in detail the guiding principles of child-saving adopted by the 1899 National Conference of Charities and Correction. Most of these principles stem from the belief in the value of the home to the child, whether it be the natural home or a foster home. Several chapters identify and describe the operations of such private agencies for saving children as the Children's Aid Society, the Society for the Prevention of Cruelty to Children, and various institutions or foundling asylums. A final chapter discusses public child-saving agencies, such as the state school systems, the state placing-out system, the county home plan, and the system of public subsidies to private institutions. At the time this book was written, Indiana was the only state which made direct public provision for handling of cruelty cases.

119 Mindlin, Rowland L. "Background to the current interest in child abuse and neglect." Pediatr Ann 5(3): 10-12, 14, March, 1976. (7 References).
Briefly outlines the history of child abuse and what society has done about it over the last 200 years. As early as 1729, orphanages for homeless children were established by religious orders. In 1874, the Society for the Prevention of Cruelty to Children in the United States was founded as a response to a small child's death resulting from starvation and physical maltreatment. Similar societies were established throughout the country during the late 1800's and early 1900's. Then, in the 1930's, the Social Security Act provided funds for public welfare agencies to protect and care for dependent and neglected children. In the 1950's, physicians began to report unexplained fractures and subdural hematomas in infants. They eventually came to the conclusion that many of the injuries were inflicted, not accidental. In 1961, C. Henry Kempe called this phenomenon the battered child syndrome. Children's aid societies began to lobby for mandatory reporting laws, and within five years, all states had them. Interest in the etiology, psychodynamics, methods of management, and legal implications of child abuse increased rapidly. In 1973, Congress passed a bill to establish a National Center on Child Abuse and Neglect and to provide financial support for training, research, and operation of child abuse and neglect programs throughout the country.

120 Oettinger, Katherine B.; Morton, Arthur; Mulford, Robert M. In the
     interest of children -- a century of progress. Denver, Colorado:
     The American Humane Association, Children's Division, 1966. 28p.
     (Bibliography).
Examines the role of society in the protection of children and the history
of child protective services in the United States and England. Although
some people contend that the rights of parents and the privacy of the home
should not be challenged, society must embrace the role of loco parentis
when the safety of the child is at stake. In England, the first society
for the prevention of cruelty to children was established in 1883.
Brutality to children and gross neglect were more common in England at
that time. Today, the importance of mental and emotional factors in the
treatment of the abused child are recognized, and the idea that the child
can best be helped in the setting of his own family has been accepted.
Similar changes in philosophy have occurred in the United States over the
past 100 years. The early child protective societies (established in the
late 1800's) viewed themselves as arms of the law and considered their
major responsibility to be that of law enforcement and child rescue.
Today, the emphasis is on the treatment of the abused or neglected child
and his family in the home if possible. The child abuse statutes of many
states require medical personnel to report suspected cases of abuse or
neglect to child protective rather than law enforcement agencies. The
major function of the child protective movement in 1966 is to increase
public recognition of the problem, establish more adequate services under
public auspices, and encourage research in the area.

121 Patti, Rino J. "Child protection in California, 1850-1966: an
     analysis of public policy." For a summary see: Diss Abstr 28A(7):
     2783, January, 1968.

122 Pfohl, Stephen J. "The 'discovery' of child abuse." Soc Probl
     24(3): 310-23, February, 1977. (53 References).
Traces the history of society's concern for child welfare, which recently
culminated in the formulation of labels such as "battered child syndrome"
to explain the maltreatment of children. It documents social reactions
to abuse from the nineteenth century house of refuge movement, to action
taken by the Society for the Prevention of Cruelty to Children early in
the twentieth century, and to the establishment of juvenile courts.
Society in the first half of the twentieth century showed evidence of increasing concern for child welfare, but at the same time demonstrated a
universally permissive attitude toward the use of physical force in
childrearing. The realization that abuse represented a deviance from the
culturally accepted norm did not come until there was a united, organized
social reaction against abuse stimulated by pediatric radiologists' discoveries. Legislation against abuse, especially laws requiring medical
personnel to report abuse to proper authorities, followed in the wake of
these medical discoveries and the subsequent labeling of abuse as social
deviance.

123 Seed, Philip. "Should any child be placed in care? The forgotten
     great debate, 1841-74." Br J Soc Work 3: 321-30, Autumn, 1973.
     (20 References).
Describes a program of day care for children which flourished in Scotland
in the mid-nineteenth century. The Aberdeen system of industrial schools
was conceived as an alternative to care centers which separated the child
from his family. In the Aberdeen system, the child received meals, educa-

tion, and industrial training at the school, from early morning until
early evening, and then went home to spend the night with his parents.
The importance of family ties was the cornerstone of the Aberdeen philosophy. It is suggested that this lesson from history is applicable to the
present day dilemmas regarding child care. In cases where the choice has
become a matter of leaving the child in an overburdened family, or shunt-
ing him off to live in an institution, the Aberdeen system seems a humane
and preferable alternative. The system's merging of the roles of teacher
and social worker might prove a particularly helpful remedy to the com-
partmentalization and bureaucracy which characterize the modern approach
to institutional child care.

124   ten Bensel, Robert W. "The physician's perspective and role." In:
      National Symposium on Child Abuse, 5th, Boston, 1974. Collected
      papers. Denver, Colorado: The American Humane Association,
      Children's Division, 1976. 16-21. (0 References).
A brief history traces the awareness of child abuse, emphasizing the case
of Mary Ellen in the late 1800's, the work of Wooley, Evans, and Kempe,
and the more recent concerns regarding emotional neglect. Various methods
of neglect and abuse are cited, such as maternal deprivation, burning,
kicking, and shaking. The role of the physician as educator and as advocate of the child is stressed.

C. DEFINITIONS

1. CHILD ABUSE

125   Andrews, John P. "The battered baby syndrome." Ill Med J   122(5):
      494, November, 1962. (0 References).
Sets forth a brief description of the battered baby syndrome. The basic
clinical signs, radiologic indications, and psychiatric aspects of the
problem are discussed. A significant discrepancy between the medical
history and the physician's clinical findings is cited as an important
indicator of child abuse.

126   Bakan, David. "Slaughter of the innocents." J Clin Child Psychol
      2(3): 10-12, Fall, 1973. (0 References).
Argues that child abuse is unnatural behavior which evolves from abnormal
experiences in the abuser's own childhood. Child abuse cannot be
eliminated until children are fully acknowledged as human beings.

127   Buist, Neil R. M. "Violent parents: letter to editor." Lancet
      1(7740): 36, January 1, 1972. (0 References).
In the past, most attention in the area of child abuse has been directed
to the area of physical assault. However, the psychological effects of
abusive parental behavior may be more profound. At times, it becomes difficult to distinguish between those acts which are intended as disciplinary measures and those which are deliberate attempts to injure the child.
A need to reevaluate existing procedures for handling such cases is underlined.

128   Delsordo, James D. "Protective casework for abused children."
      Children 10(6): 213-18, November-December, 1963. (1 Reference).

Cites findings of a study based on eighty cases handled by the Pennsylvania
Society to Protect Children from Cruelty. Five types of cases involving
physical abuse of children are classified: (1) abuse by a mentally ill
parent; (2) overflow abuse; (3) the battered child; (4) disciplinary abuse;
and (5) misplaced abuse. The assessment and management of each type are
outlined and illustrated by typical case examples.

129   Fontana, Vincent J. "To prevent the abuse of the future." Trial
        10(3): 14-18, May-June, 1974. (0 References).
Proposes that the term "battered child syndrome" be replaced by "maltreatment syndrome." The proposed change would broaden the designation so that
it could more accurately refer to the many forms of child abuse currently
recognized and treated. The discussion mentions various behavioral and
physical symptoms of child maltreatment, along with emotional factors
leading to the problem, and opposes the removal of the abused child from
the home without the concomitant rehabilitation of the family environment.

130   Gelles, Richard J. "The social construction of child abuse." Am J
        Orthopsychiatry 45(3): 363-71, April, 1975. (41 References).
Offers a social construction of child abuse, in which child abuse is
viewed as social deviance. Child abuse has proven to be difficult to
define in terms of objective behavior. Nevertheless, defining such terms
as "mental injury" and "negligent treatment," found in the 1973 Child
Abuse Prevention and Treatment Act, would provide a means for labeling
abusers. These definitions are essential for prevention and treatment
strategies. Suggested in this study is a method for identifying abusers
from the rest of society by determining which specific behaviors indicate
a deviance from the norm. The method involves investigating several factors: (1) who does the public labeling of abuse; (2) what definitions
are used; (3) what conditions determine the successful application of
labels; and (4) what are the consequences of labeling. Finally, all of
the systems involved in labeling, preventing, and treating abused children and the abusers need to be integrated within a total open systems
approach.

131   Hopper, Mark A. "A concept analysis of the abused child." For a
        summary see: Diss Abstr Int 37A(10): 6402-3, April, 1977.

132   Kaul, Mohan L. "Physical child abuse and its prevention." Intellect
        105(2381): 270-72, February, 1977. (11 References).
Discusses the definition, scope, manifestations, and causes of child
abuse and describes characteristics of abused children and of abusing
parents. An epidemiological approach to child abuse is favored; that is,
a study of the distribution and the determinants of the "disease" in
hopes of developing preventative measures.

133   Kempe C. Henry. "Report from the Identification Work Group." Clin
        Proc 30(2): 37-38, 1974. (0 References).
Summarizes the Identification Work Group of the National Conference on
Child Abuse. Two definitions of child abuse have been accepted in recognition of the restrictions of mandatory reporting laws: (1) a stringent
legal definition covering children under eighteen who are suffering from
willfully inflicted injuries, sexual abuse, malnutrition, or neglect
which poses the threat of serious physical or emotional damage; and (2)
a more inclusive definition which might be utilized by social service
agencies to identify at risk children without legal action.

134   Kline, Donald F., and Hopper, Mark A. <u>Child abuse: an integration
      of the research related to education of children handicapped as a
      result of child abuse: final report</u>. Logan, Utah: Utah State
      University, Department of Special Education, 1975. 136p. ERIC
      Document ED 107 056.
Presents a concept analysis of child abuse indicating that any person
under eighteen years of age undergoing an injury which was not an accident
inflicted by a caretaker should be designated an abused child. Over 600
annotated bibliographic sources are included.

135   Maurer, Adah. "Corporal punishment." <u>Am Psychol</u> 29(8): 614-26,
      August, 1974. (150 References).
A semantic investigation of the use of the word punishment in popular and
scientific cultures. For the general public, punishment implies pain and
penalty following an act of disobedience. For behaviorists, the word
signifies an attempt to diminish or eliminate certain unwanted behavior.
When scientific definitions are borrowed by the laity, confusion arises
and theoretical findings are dangerously misused. Instances of corporal
punishment in schools touching upon acts of brutality are cited. In
place of both punishment and reward theories, substitution of non-emotive
correctives is suggested; and in lieu of psychological experimentation
with behavior modification, a direct confrontation with ethical judgments
is favored.

136   Newberger, Eli H. "Condensation of 'The myth of the battered child
      syndrome: a compassionate medical view of the protection of chil-
      dren.'" <u>Curr Med Dialog</u> 40(4): 327-34, April, 1973. (9 Refer-
      ences).
This condensation of a paper presented in a panel discussion on child
abuse at the 95th Anniversary Symposium of the American Humane Association
focuses on the often unjust and punitive connotations of the designation
"battered child syndrome." The phrase implies the deliberate infliction
of injury by the parent, while observation of actual cases has suggested
that the parent does not necessarily intend to injure the child. Instead,
the parent is incapable of nurturing the child, often because of environmental conditions which intervention may not be able to remedy. The substitution of a more compassionate designation is recommended, and the
positive experience of working with both abused children and their parents
is cited. The literature advocating more sensitive and selective intervention is reviewed.

137   Ratner, Herbert. "A public health physician views abortion." <u>Child
      Fam</u> 7(1): 38-46, 52, 1968. (39 References).
Condemns the liberalized attitude of the scientific community toward
abortion. It is argued that abortion is a form of intrauterine child
abuse.

138   Salmon, M. A. "The spectrum of abuse in the battered-child syn-
      drome." <u>Injury</u> 2(3): 211-17, January, 1971. (13 References).
The battered child syndrome has become both a clinical and a social
entity. Early definitions spoke primarily of physical abuse of the child,
but emotional factors involving the child and the abusing parent must be
considered as well. Six case histories illustrate the wide range of
problems which may fall within the battered child syndrome definitional
category. Specific questions are suggested to aid the physician in obtaining a history, as well as the physical findings which should alert
his suspicion of abuse.

139 Seaberg, James R. "Physical child abuse: an expanded analysis."
For a summary see: <u>Diss Abstr Int</u> 35A(9): 6239, March, 1975.

140 Welner, Zila; Welner, Amos; Robins, Eli. "Child abuse: a case for
a different approach." <u>Compr Psychiatry</u> 18(4): 363-67, July-
August, 1977. (22 References).
Examines the lack of consensus among recent studies of the etiology of
child abuse and the characteristics of the abusive patient and the child
victim. It is pointed out that literature in the field has been of a
speculative and opinionated nature, owing to the lack of controlled
studies. Disagreement with those researchers who consider child abuse
a universal phenomenon is underlined. Rather than attempt to discriminate
between intentional and accidental abuse, a definition of child abuse
which focuses on all physical injuries in children in some way related to
parental behavior is proposed.

141 Wertham, Frederic. "Battered children and baffled adults." <u>Bull NY</u>
<u>Acad Med</u> 48(7): 887-98, August, 1972. (5 References).
Critically reviews current medical, social, and legal theories about child
abuse. Appraisal of David Gil's report on the battered child syndrome
suggests that its value is to point out the amount of disagreement existing between professionals about every aspect of child abuse and to provoke
public thought on the subject. Viewing each abuse case either as an
isolated incident or as part of a general sociological problem evades
issues such as the recognition of the methods and symptoms of battering.
The tendency toward case management, which excludes legal punishment on
the basis of mental illness, protects the victimizer, not the victim. The
theory that aggression is instinctual and the portrayal of violence by
the mass media are criticized.

142 Yudkin, S. "Battered baby syndrome: letter to editor." <u>Br Med J</u>
2(5493): 980-81, April 16, 1966. (0 References).
States that the battered baby syndrome should be distinguished from other
forms of child neglect and the preliminary investigation of the case
should be confined to the hospital to which the battered child is admitted.
The contention is that other agencies could make valuable contributions
to the investigation, and that the battered child syndrome as a form of
neglect is not clearly distinct from other forms of neglect and maltreatment.

2. CHILD NEGLECT

143 Collins, Seymour. "Neglected children." <u>R Soc Health J</u> 79(6):
743-50, November-December, 1959. (0 References).
Highlights the various forms of child neglect, the circumstances which
occasion it, the various ways in which it is brought to light, and some
means of prevention. Parental neglect of children is most often uninten-
tional. Although cruelty implies an active process, neglect may bring
equal suffering and psychological damage to the child. Factors which
may give rise to the abuse or neglect of children include parent inadequacy, one parent's abandonment of home, the belief that a child is
illegitimate, marital difficulties, poor housing conditions, parental
preoccupation with outside activities, and poverty. Child neglect can
be easily detected by school officials and neighbors, although the interval between detection and action is often large. Cases of neglect are

often brought to the attention of the authorities through the courts, when
either a wife submits a summons against her husband or a child who has
committed an offense is seen in the juvenile court. The education of newly
married couples and other potential parents, who may have highly unrealistic expectations of marriage and parenthood, is strongly recommended. The
law is felt to be adequate to deal with the cases of abuse or neglect which
are brought within its purview.

144 Giovannoni, Jeanne M. "Parental mistreatment: perpetrators and
        victims." J Marriage Fam 33(4): 649-57, November, 1971. (15
        References).
Examines the phenomena of familial violence and maltreatment of children
from a historical and sociological viewpoint. Child maltreatment can be
divided into abusive and neglectful behavior. Too much parental control
leads to abuse, whereas a parent's failure to fulfill his responsibilities
constitutes neglect. Of the two, neglect is more directly a product of
poverty. Only within the last century have provisions been made to care
for neglected children. At first, such children were removed from their
homes and placed in orphanages. In this century, an attempt has been
made to keep the family unit intact and provide community services for
neglectful families. The dynamics of family and agency interaction are
discussed.

145 Henley, Arthur. "The abandoned child." In: Bryant, Clifton D.,
        and Wells, J. Gipson, eds. Deviancy and the family. Philadelphia:
        F. A. Davis, 1973. 199-208. (0 References).
Describes the plight of the abandoned child. The number of abandoned
children is difficult to assess, but as of 1973, there were a quarter of
a million homeless children in the United States. These children, often
dressed in brand new clothes, are found in bus stations, on doorsteps, or
wandering in department stores. They are commonly the victims of broken
homes, and the mother, overwhelmed by responsibilities, abandons them in
despair. Abandoning the child is often less frightening to the parent
than facing state adoption procedures. Although what happens to the child
varies from state to state, in New York he is placed in the Foundling
Hospital or in the care of the Bureau of Child Welfare. He is then filed
with the Missing Persons' Bureau and finally placed in foster care or an
adoptive home. Those who are not adopted become wards of the state. The
lack of clear legal procedures makes it difficult to prosecute abandoning
parents. The rise in mental illness, the changing social pattern, and
urbanization are all seen as reasons for the steady increase in abandonment. The solutions lie in treatment for the parents and in creating a
society which prevents their hopelessness and despair.

146 Polansky, Norman A.; Hally, Carolyn; Polansky, Nancy F. Profile of
        neglect: a survey of the state of knowledge of child neglect.
        Washington, D.C.: Social and Rehabilitation Services, Community
        Services Administration, 1975. 57p. (Bibliography).
A state of the art document for professionals and laymen. Recent concern
with the maltreatment of children has been limited primarily to the abuse
of children. It has not sufficiently questioned and researched the problem of neglected children and the family situations that produce them.
This study was designed specifically to provide detailed, documented information in this area. As its first task, the study systematically distinguishes neglect from abuse. Once the distinction is established, it
devises an operational definition of neglect to be used as a starting

point for casework and legal action. It is termed as a condition imposed upon a child by his caretaker, whereby he experiences avoidable stress and/or fails to receive what is needed for his physical, emotional, and intellectual development. Unfortunately, the prevalence of neglect is unknown. Like many social problems, it is often a chronic condition and difficult to detect. Only a small fraction of neglect cases are ever reported and presently there is no standard procedure for collecting such data. The State of Florida is cited as having the most advanced system of detection, and reports indicate that neglect cases outnumber abuse cases three to one. Judging from such figures, the need for accurate data is imperative.

The causes of neglect are complex and hard to assess. Results, however, indicate that neglecting parents typically have internal, personal problems as well as external, economic problems. Other contributing factors are listed as follows: (1) cultural values and patterns of child caring; (2) the breakdown of the nuclear family; and (3) parental pathology. Neglect also appears to manifest itself to some degree in intergenerational cycles. Most of the current means for detecting the maltreatment of children apply to abuse rather than to neglect. Consequently, new detection procedures and early warning signals must be designed to reflect the definition of neglect. The study lists several parent and child behavioral patterns that have been used to detect abuse and could also signal cases of neglect. More than anything else, the consequences of neglect point to the pressing need for action. Severe emotional disorders, serious neurological and other physical defects, as well as intellectual decrements and radically antisocial behavior have all been documented as direct consequences. They point to the urgent need to prevent and treat the victims of neglect. Standard treatment guidelines that effectively match the diagnosis of a case to the form of intervention necessary to protect the children and counsel the parents are essential. A sketch of intervention, methods, their contributions, complexities, and limitations includes the following treatment approaches: social casework, group techniques, parent-child community programs, mental health centers, day care facilities, and engineered communities.

147 Sutherland, Dorothy. "Child neglect: color me grey." Soc Rehabil Rec 2(7): 18-23, September, 1975. (1 Reference).
Explores the problems involved in defining, treating, and preventing child neglect, based on Norman Polansky's work in the area. While child abuse is something done to someone, neglect is something not done. These parental acts of omission can include failures to provide adequate clothing, health care, or encouragement to attend school. Distinguishing neglect from a mere low quality life style is often difficult. The point at which social services or the courts can justifiably intervene is hazy. Various working definitions of neglect, including statutory definitions, are examined. According to Polansky, the caretaker involved in neglect can be a non-parental figure such as a social agency or the community. He contends that neglect does not have to be limited to intentional behavior, nor must it impose serious long-term damage on the child in order to be considered neglectful.

148 Whiting, Leila. "Defining emotional neglect." Child Today 5(1): 2-5, January-February, 1976. (1 Reference).
Examines a community workshop held in Montgomery County, Maryland which focused on the emotional neglect of children. The problems of distinguishing neglect from cultural differences in styles of discipline, and

applying vague definitions of neglect to specific cases were discussed. The workshop also differentiated between emotional disturbance and emotional neglect by examining the parental response to the situation.   If the parents indicate a concern for the child and take appropriate steps to deal with behavioral symptoms of the child, it is considered a case of emotional disturbance.   If the parents will not acknowledge a problem and resist help that is offered for the child and family, then it is considered a case of emotional neglect.   The way that neglect is defined and reported has important legal implications.

3. INSTITUTIONAL AND SOCIETAL ABUSE

149   Alvy, Kerby T.   "On child abuse: values and analytic approaches."
      J Clin Child Psychol   4(1):   36-37, Spring, 1975.
Maintains that the conventional definition of child abuse as abuse inflicted on a child by an individual must be expanded to include sociocultural abuse, which is authorized by traditional culture-wide assumptions.

150   Amiel, Shirley.   "Child abuse in schools."   Northwest Med   71(11):
      808, November, 1972.   (0 References).
Briefly considers child abuse and neglect by teachers in schools.   Several examples are presented.   It is estimated that 82,500 children are being exposed to seriously maladjusted teachers each year in the State of Washington.   This is not simply an education problem, but a public health problem as well.

151   Bloch, Harry.   "The battered child: letter to editor."   Pediatrics
      39(4):   625, April, 1967.   (1 Reference).
Points out that children can be battered by society as well as by their parents.   Abused children who suffer because of a societal problem like poverty or war should not be taken any less seriously than parental abuse as a form of child abuse to be prevented.

152   ————.   "Dilemma of 'battered child' and 'battered children.'"
      NY State J Med   73(6):   799-802, March 15, 1973.   (33 References).
Distinguishes between the individual child who is abused by a disturbed parent or guardian, and the masses of children who are subject to society's cruelty.   Social institutions which abuse children, such as the use of child sacrifices in religious rites, date back to antiquity. Reform measures, commencing with the early Christians and extending into the twentieth century, are briefly surveyed, with a primary emphasis on British and American history.   Society is hardened to brutality and must take resolute action to correct the multiple causes of cruelty to children.

153   Brown, George W.   "School: child advocate or adversary?"   Clin
      Pediatr   16(5):   439-46, May, 1977.   (4 References).
Points out that schools can subtly abuse children through ignorance and apathy, as well as direct cruelty.   The medical diagnostic labeling of children by teachers in school can be dangerous.   Educators should confine their comments about children with educational problems to descriptive observations such as a child's physical appearance, aptitudes, and talents.   Diagnostic labels (mental retardation, neurosis, or epilepsy) should be determined by a physician.   Other forms of institutional abuse

of children in schools include direct verbal and physical cruelty, confused and inappropriate academic goals, and administrative bungling. Suggestions are made as to how these problems can be eliminated or reduced.

154 Brown, Richard J. "Brain damaged adolescents: their miseducation
     in a rehabilitation center." Am J Orthopsychiatry 42(1): 326-27,
     January, 1972. (0 References).
Digest of a critical report on a therapeutic program for adolescents with
brain damage. The program, devised by a city school system and a voluntary rehabilitation agency, was supposed to offer prevocational training;
actually, if offered little in the way of training and resulted in several
incidents of child abuse. The work given the adolescents was very repetitious and depressing. The report is particularly critical of the agency
which helped to engineer the program; the agency is characterized as
being concerned only with its own good.

155 Children's Defense Fund. Children out of school in America. Cam-
     bridge, Massachusetts: Children's Defense Fund, 1974. 366p.
     (Bibliography).
An investigation was made by the Children's Defense Fund to determine the
number of school age children not receiving an education and to assess
the seriousness of the problem on a national scale. It was found that
most of the out-of-school children somehow deviated from the majority of
the population, either in terms of race, income, age, or physical, mental,
or emotional handicap. These children are not out of school because they
want to be, but because schools have literally excluded them, and states
have contrived reasons for exempting them from their compulsory attendance
laws. On a national scale, the problem of school exclusion is a major
one. Race, poverty, language, and handicap can no longer be tolerated
as barriers that keep children from attending school.

Recommendations to the federal government to substantially improve the
situation include: (1) conducting hearings to determine the extent and
causes of the problem; (2) adopting nationally accepted guidelines for
correcting suspension, discipline, and discrimination policies; and (3)
establishing and enforcing reporting requirements for Department of
Health, Education and Welfare funded programs. A lengthy list of bureaucratic excuses for inaction demonstrates the extent of the obstacles that
must be overcome in order to make progress.

Further recommendations for action are directed toward the schools, which
need to reexamine suspension policies and to retain only those policies
involving violence against person and property. A clear statement of
conditions for emergency exclusions, along with a hearing prior to action,
are defined as part of the school's responsibility. Approaches to curriculum must be diverse and reflect the needs of all children. Furthermore, parental involvement can be fostered by encouraging parents to take
part in selecting school principals. Teachers should be assisted in
learning to react to children with discipline problems. Most importantly,
schools must immediately bring an end to racial discrimination in disciplinary procedures. Twenty-three appendices encompass the state
statistical studies and the methodologies used in compiling the final
report. The report itself relates a wide variety of case reports throughout the text to support its conclusions and recommendations.

156 Denzin, Norman K., ed. Children and their caretakers. New Bruns-
     wick, New Jersey: Transaction Books, 1973. 333p. (Bibliography).

A collection of readings which analyzes the traditional roles of parents, teachers, physicians, and judges as caretakers of America's children while exposing how these authority figures have failed their young. The evolutionary concept of children as political, cultural, economic, and scientific objects is examined. The juvenile court system is criticized for punishing children for offenses which, if they had been committed by adults, would not even be considered misdemeanors. A history of medical and sociological awareness of the battered child syndrome, in addition to a description of the syndrome and a psychological overview of abusive parents, is provided.

157 Duncan, C. "They beat children, don't they?" J Clin Child Psychol 2(3): 13-14, Fall, 1973. (0 References).
Calls attention to institutional violence against children, within the school system, at care centers, in mental institutions, and juvenile jails. It is presently impossible to prevent officially-inflicted violence; the attention of national organizations concerned with child abuse is directed to this problem.

158 Gil, David G. "A holistic perspective on child abuse and its prevention." J Sociol Soc Welfare 2(2): 110-25, Winter, 1974. (6 References).
Advocates a more integrated approach to the problem of child abuse as a means of generating more effective methods of prevention. Such efforts have failed in the past because child abuse has been traditionally studied in a fragmentary manner by different disciplines, and thereby has been divorced from the social context in which it occurs. It is suggested that a holistic approach replace the fragmentary one, so that child abuse can be seen simultaneously on the interpersonal, institutional, and societal levels. A broader definition of child abuse is also proposed which sees child abuse as inflicted deficits on the child's right to develop fully and freely, irrespective of the source of the deficits. Thus, the potential for abusive behavior would be extended beyond the home into society, and prevention of the more broadly defined child abuse could involve fundamental changes in society itself.

159 James, Howard. The little victims: how America treats its children. New York: David McKay, 1975. 374p.
The story of America's unwanted, unloved, and useless children. The author visited hundreds of public institutions, reform schools, and jails throughout the country where he found teenagers and children who had been abused, neglected, ignored, or outright abandoned by their parents. Because these children were different--handicapped, retarded, deaf, or behavioral problem children--they were disposed of in a manner befitting what James calls our system of "hedonistic consumerism:" a seeking for things which provide self-gratification, and disposing of the outdated and the useless.

It is a simple process for a parent to have a child committed to an institution. Overcrowded conditions, inadequate budgets, and understaffing produce warehouses, rather than therapeutic centers, for the retarded and handicapped. In addition to obvious instances of maltreatment and exploitation, the monotony of the day to day existence of institutionalized children is also illustrated. The special plight of deaf children who, despite their normal or superior intelligence, are ridiculed for their inability to function in a language-oriented society, is described.

Normal children are no more privileged or protected than their handicapped peers. Nowadays, although most children live with their parents in what appears to be modern, comfortable homes, they may still be physically, sexually, or emotionally abused. Selections from published studies of the incidence, causes, and effects of child abuse are interspersed with personal narratives of family violence and upheaval told by individual children. Victims of incest frequently run away from home to escape their fathers. But then they are captured, sent to reform schools, and further victimized. Many middle class children are emotionally abused by their parents who criticize them too harshly, or ignore them, leaving them to spend their time with the television set. Many of these children become delinquent, promiscuous, or suicidal. Physically abused children sometimes die as a result of their wounds; but survivors struggle with their frustration, fear, anger, and hatred through adolescence and into a crisis-ridden adulthood where they reenact their childhood traumas upon their own children.

160 Langmeier, Josef, and Matejcek, Z. Psychological deprivation in
     childhood. New York: Wiley, 1975. 496p. (Bibliography).
An exhaustive study focusing on cultural beliefs regarding child care, developmental problems peculiar to institutionalized children, and a review of significant clinical and scholarly literature in the field of psychological deprivation in children. Although many definitions for the phenomenon have been provided, deprivation can best be described as a condition, including one or more of the following factors: a lack of stimuli necessary for normal motor and mental development; unsatisfied needs for love, protection, and communication; extreme loneliness; and separation anxiety.

The two principal deprivation situations--isolation and separation--are compared. Social isolation is an extreme situation, but examples have been found of wolf children and wild children. Separation anxiety is more common in Western culture. Deprivation in the family can have external causes, as in the case of a death, divorce, or the hospitalization or employment of the mother. It can also be of a psychological origin, such as when a parent is mentally retarded or otherwise unable to provide adequate nurturing. Institutional children suffer the most serious form of psychological deprivation. For decades, such children failed to thrive, died young, or reached adulthood without ever having experienced affection and warmth. In this century, the design of institutions for children has changed drastically. The following child care institutions are critically evaluated: nurseries, kindergartens, boarding schools, kibbutzim, and children's hospitals.

Alternatives to traditional child care institutions, such as family-type institutions, parental homes, and foster homes are described. A basic treatment program aimed at combating childhood deprivation include four states of therapy: reactivation, relearning, reattachment, and resocialization. Suggestions for preventing childhood deprivation are: (1) each family must be assured a stable existence; (2) new parents ought to be trained in child care fundamentals; and (3) medical clinics and supplementary family care facilities should be readily available to all families.

161 Plank, Esther L. "Violations of children's rights in the classroom."
     Child Educ 52(3): 73-75, November-December, 1975. (8 References).

Contends that placing unnecessary and excessive pressures on school children is a violation of children's rights and a form of abuse comparable to physical battering or molestation. In spite of efforts to change such practices, educators repeatedly apply pressures on children that prove to be damaging. Two practices that have consistently been part of many school systems for years, have had insidious effects on children, namely, the no talking order and the assumption that first graders should all be ready to read. In order to decrease the pressures upon young school children, teachers need to learn more about the intellectual and emotional development of children and to respect a child's rights in the classroom.

162 Schorr, Alvin L., ed. Children and decent people. New York: Basic
     Books, 1974. 222p. (Bibliography).
Consists of a collection of articles written by American experts in child care dealing with society's abuse and neglect of poor children. The instruments of abuse are the inadequate child care delivery systems which selectively treat poor children, thereby perpetuating socioeconomic class differences. When substitute care for children is needed, non-poor families utilize private boarding schools or the homes of financially stable relatives, while poor families must rely on foster family care. Foster parents are generally upper-lower class and lower-middle class people who have no formal training in child care. They are not given adequate financial assistance to properly care for the children in their custody. In addition, once a child enters the system of foster family care, he may never escape it. Private boarding schools for the wealthy, however, have fewer of these defects.

This discrepancy between the use of services by the poor and non-poor is also evident when institutional placement of children is considered. The overwhelming number of children in public and charitable institutions come from poor and/or minority families, while those children in private educational or treatment institutions are from affluent families. The quality of care in the public institutions is poor, as evidenced by the large ratio of children to caretakers, the lack of formal training and education for the caretakers, and the high degree of regimentation present in the daily lives of the child residents. Public institutions prepare lower income and dependent children for inferior socioeconomic positions and roles in society as adults, which tends to perpetuate an unequitable class system.

This book uncovers the selective or dual nature of other child care delivery systems as well. In the area of health care, poor children use the crowded public facilities and generally receive episodic or crisis care, while rich children use private family physicians and specialists who provide both preventive and crisis health care. Poor children are much more likely to come into contact with the juvenile justice system than are rich children. The non-poor use family day care either in their own home or a neighbor's when the mother works, while the poor are encouraged by welfare agencies to use day care centers that are inconvenient, expensive, and undesirable. In our society, poor children receive poor care, as a direct result of selective and dual child care systems. The only way to change this situation is to have universal programming for all children, rich and poor. These programs, modeled after our system of public education, would include public social and health care services of high quality for everyone, and would guarantee adequate financial support for each child in every American family.

163 Wooden, Ken. Weeping in the playtime of others: America's incar-
       cerated children. New York: McGraw-Hill, 1976. 264p. (Bibliog-
       raphy)
Exposes the physical, mental, and sexual abuses against children committed
in juvenile corrections institutions, county jails, and homes for the
retarded. The diligence of one Texas attorney in working to have some
800 children released from a correctional institution which practiced
cruel and unusual punishment is described. Many youths are incarcerated
for status offenses. It is not unusual for neglected children or girls
fleeing from a forced incestuous relationship at home to be sent to state
training schools. Once imprisoned, these youths are further victimized
and alienated from the world. For many, suicide becomes the only release
from anxiety, shame, and fear. Additional issues, such as the psychological abuse of female delinquents (many incarcerated for sexual acts
alone), the misuse of psychotherapeutic drugs, and the political corruption uncovered during investigation of the CHAMPUS scandal, are also
reported. Recommendations for reforming correctional institutions include:
(1) providing family counseling for all children arrested for minor
offenses; (2) stricter licensing laws for private institutions; and (3)
abolition of the practice of detaining children in county jails with
adult offenders. A children's bill of rights which guarantees each child
a family, an education, freedom, and protection from harm is presented.

D. INCIDENCE

164 Alexander, Jerry. "Protecting the children of life-threatening
       parents." J Clin Child Psychol 3(2): 53-54, Summer, 1974.
Offers a statistical survey of the phenomenon of child abuse, with suggestions aimed at reducing the problem.

165 "Battered child syndrome." America 116(7): 236, February 18, 1967.
       (0 References).
A survey of several hundred physicians across the country revealed the
occurrence of at least 10,000 cases of child abuse each year in the
United States. The results indicate that there is a 50 percent chance
that an abused child will suffer further injury.

166 Berdie, Jane; Baizerman, Michael; Lourie, Ira S. "Violence towards
       youth: themes from a workshop." Child Today 6(2): 7-35, March-
       April, 1977. (17 References).
Reports a 1975 two-day workshop on adolescent and youth abuse and neglect
held at the University of Minnesota. Despite the significance of the
percentage of children aged twelve to eighteen who make up the national
child abuse incidence statistics, society still fails to regard these
adolescents as victims of child abuse. Normal adolescent behavior is
often confusing, annoying, and provocative to adults and may frequently
be interpreted as intentional. This kind of stress on family interactions
can cause parents to apply severe punishment in an attempt to force a
youth into his former less provocative role. However, there is growing
concern that adolescents do not always deserve what they get in terms of
punishment and that violence toward these children has become a problem
of major social significance.

167 Bleiberg, Nina. "The neglected child and the child health confer-
       ence." NY State J Med 65(14): 1880-85, July 15, 1965. (10
       References).

Attempts to determine the approximate magnitude of child neglect in New
York City. In order to gather the data, a questionnaire was distributed
to 200 physicians working with the eighty-eight child health stations
throughout the city. It called for information regarding the child's
family, medical history, and a description of his physical state. Eighteen cases, consisting of eight boys and ten girls, were reported by twelve
physicians. In each case, the family was described as fragmented and in
crisis in spite of outward appearances. Although only brief summaries
typically appear, four cases are noted in detail and focus on the problems professionals face in handling the parents. The study involved
children whose parents had voluntarily brought them in for a check-up,
indicating that countless cases not voluntarily reported by parents must
go undetected. The main conclusion drawn is that medical and social
service professionals must become more astute in detecting cases of neglect and abuse and also see that they receive priority for follow-up
treatments in the health care centers.

168   Chambers, Douglas R. "A coroner's view." In: Franklin, Alfred
       White, ed. Concerning child abuse. New York: Churchill Living-
       stone, 1975. 69-70. (0 References).
The coroner's involvement in cases of child abuse begins when the police
report the death of an infant which was sudden and of unknown cause, violent, or unnatural. In 1971, the registrar-general's statistical review
of England and Wales reported that in the age group of 0-4 years, the
ratio of homicide to accident was 1:2, and in the 5-14 year age group,
the ratio was 1:9. When the violent or unnatural nature of a child's
death is confirmed at postmortem examination, the coroner is required to
present the evidence to the law enforcement agencies.

169   Cohen, Stephan J., and Sussman, Alan. "The incidence of child abuse
       in the United States." Child Welfare 54(6): 432-43, June, 1975.
       (23 References).
Because estimates of the incidence and mortality rates of child abuse and
neglect are variable, it is difficult to determine the appropriate social
response to the problem. Accurate national statistics on the actual incidence of abuse are unavailable for several reasons: (1) although the
reporting of suspected child abuse is mandatory in forty-nine states, the
definition of abuse, the persons required to report, and the procedures
for reporting vary from state to state; (2) many states fail to distinguish between reports of abuse and reports of neglect--among those states
that do maintain separate records, reports of neglect far outnumber those
of abuse; (3) most states do not distinguish between the number of reports
of suspected abuse/neglect and the number of confirmed cases in each
category. Therefore, estimates used as evidence in support of legal or
social programs should be received with some degree of caution.

170   Farn, Kenneth T. "Deaths from non-accidental injuries in childhood:
       letter to editor." Br Med J 3(5979): 370-71, August 9, 1975.
       (3 References).
Defends the validity of the Registrar General's child death statistics
used in child abuse incidence studies. The coroner's verdict as to cause
of death is processed in each case in conjunction with the judicial verdict in order to obtain a formal verdict. This final formal verdict is
then recorded for use in the Registrar General's figures.

171 Fontana, Vincent J. "We must stop the vicious cycle of child abuse."
     Parents Mag 50(12): 8, December, 1975. (6 References).
Cites the epidemic proportions of child abuse and the abuse inherent in
a parental "cold shoulder." To promote supportive services, resources
for concerned parents as well as reading material are listed.

172 Fontana, Vincent J.; Gil, David G.; Meyer, Roger J. "Physical abuse
     of children: letters to editor." Pediatrics 45(3, Part I):
     509-11, March, 1970. (15 References).
Vincent J. Fontana criticizes David G. Gil's report on child abuse as
minimizing the incidence of maltreatment and its effects. Gil denies the
charge and insists that deprivation is a more serious problem in the United
States than abuse. Another physician agrees with Gil's multidisciplinary
community approach.

173 Franklin, Alfred White. "Statistics of child abuse: letter to
     editor." Br Med J 3(5975): 98-99, July 12, 1975. (0 References).
A balanced consideration of the problem of child abuse is urged. Widespread denial of its existence has been replaced by outraged condemnation
of battering parents and by the assumption that someone must be at fault
wherever this problem occurs. The professional and public press has
sought to modify exaggerated notions about abuse, but calm and skilled
investigations into the real dimensions of the problem are needed. Both
the child's need for protection and the integrity of the family unit must
be part of any solution.

174 Gibson, Christine H.; Watson, Jacqueline; Stevenson, W. J. "Battered
     baby syndrome: letter to editor." Med J Aust 2(23): 1073,
     December 8, 1973. (10 References).
Briefly presents the results of a survey which indicates that many abused
children who come into contact with the hospital are not recognized as
battered children.

175 Gil, David G. "Physical abuse of children: findings and implica-
     tions of a nationwide survey." Pediatrics 44(5, Part II): 857-64,
     November, 1969. (23 References).
Enumerates the findings of a nationwide survey of child abuse begun in
1965 by Brandeis University in cooperation with the Children's Bureau
(HEW). One important implication of the study was that the incidence of
maltreatment had been overestimated. Although the reporting rate for
this survey was admittedly low, 6,000 cases reported nationwide in one
year's time was believed not to be epidemic in relation to the total
population size. Social acceptance of varying forms of corporal punishment is listed as a major cause of abuse. Also indicated as causes are
the differences in childrearing practices among varying ethnic and
cultural groups, deviances of the individual family structure from the
norm, environmental stress factors, and environmental chance factors.
Poverty is cited as a major determining factor in abuse cases, and
several recommendations are made concerning increases in family allot-
ments. Reeducating the population about childrearing practices, as well
as legally and socially prohibiting physical punishment, are two additional suggestions for reform.

176 ————. "Violence against children." J Marriage Fam 33(4):
     637-48, November, 1971. (5 References).

Summarizes data regarding the incidence of child abuse in the United
States. A 1968 study analyzed data on 13,000 incidents reported through
legal channels, a representative sample of 1,400 incidents, and interviews with 1,520 adults. Study findings establish the reporting rate in
1968 as 8.4 children per 100,000 population. The rate of actual incidence
is believed to exceed this figure derived only from official reporting
sources, because incidents of minor physical injury in children are often
diagnosed as accidental. A breakdown of the statistics revealed the
following: (1) minority children were over-represented in the incidence
figure; (2) though preadolescent boys and girls were equally abused, most
teenage victims of abuse (particularly sexual abuse) were girls; (3) 60
percent of the cases had a previous history of abuse; and (4) abusive
parents had a lower educational and income level than the general population. Gil proposes that child abuse is a multidimensional phenomenon,
the causes of which can include: strict discipline, environmental stress,
marital problems, the child is unwanted, the parent's anger is displaced
and directed at the child, the parent is an emotional or mental deviant,
or the child's behavior provokes the abuse. Of those surveyed, 60 percent felt that any adult might injure a child. Recommended strategies
for prevention include: (1) changes in the American attitude toward
childrearing; (2) abolition of corporal punishment; (3) family life education and counseling programs; and (4) community based health care units.

177 ————. "Violence against children: letter to editor." Pediatrics
      49(4): 641, April, 1972. (2 References).
Defends the conclusions of his book Violence Against Children (1970)
against Newberger's unfavorable review. Newberger's review had questioned Gil's research procedures. Gil responds that his book discusses
the limitations of his design in its relationship to the data and asserts,
contrary to Newberger, that his studies are sufficient on which to base
hypotheses for further testing.

178 ————. "Violence against children: physical child abuse in the
      United States." In: Bronfenbrenner, Urie, and Mahoney, Maureen
      A. Influences on human development. 2nd ed. Hinsdale, Illinois:
      The Dryden Press, 1975. 190-202. (1 Reference).
Analyzes a nationwide survey of incidence statistics to determine the
forces that cause individuals to use excessive and extreme physical force
against children. Findings point to a typology of seven circumstances of
child abuse: (1) psychological rejection leading to repeated abuse and
battering; (2) disciplinary measures administered during a fit of uncontrolled anger; (3) male caretaker acting out sadistic and sexual
impulses in the mother's temporary absence, sometimes while intoxicated;
(4) mentally or emotionally disturbed caretaker acting under mounting
environmental stress; (5) unusual and offensive behavioral traits of a
child making him susceptible to abuse; (6) female babysitter abusing a
child in her care during mother's absence; and (7) quarrel between caretakers. Recommendations to reduce and to prevent a growing incidence of
abuse are given. Emphasis needs to be shifted from a punitive to a
therapeutic philosophy. The recommendations are detailed in three sets
of proposals aimed at attacking the cultural factors that induce abuse,
such as widespread permissive attitudes in society toward the use of
physical force with children, poverty, and deviance and pathology in
families where normal, social, intellectual, and emotional functioning
have been impaired.

179 Gil, David G., and Noble, John H. Public knowledge, attitudes and
     opinions about physical child abuse in the United States. Waltham,
     Massachusetts: Brandeis University, 1967. 48p. ERIC Document
     ED 014 107.
The general public's level of awareness with respect to child abuse was
studied by means of a survey designed by Brandeis University and administered by the National Opinion Research Center. The survey focused on
personal experience of actual incidents, general knowledge about child
abuse, awareness of facilities and programs to identify and prevent it,
and opinions regarding child abuse and child abusers.

180 ————. "Public knowledge, attitudes, and opinions about physical
     child abuse in the U.S." Child Welfare 48(7): 395-401, July,
     1969. (9 References).
Results of a national survey of 1,520 adults aimed at discerning the
general public's knowledge of and attitude toward child abuse, and at
estimating the incidence of child abuse in the United States. Statistical
findings are broken down according to the age, sex, race, and educational
level of the respondents. The study revealed that 80 percent of adults
had heard of child abuse, with newspapers most frequently cited as their
principal source of knowledge. Approximately 60 percent of the respondents were of the opinion that most parents have the potential to injure
a child intentionally. Less than 25 percent, however, admitted that they
themselves might abuse a child. Presupposing knowledge of an abused child
in their neighborhood, only 7 percent of the respondents would refuse to
get involved in some fashion. Upon actually witnessing a child being
abused, 65 percent of the adults would intervene directly to protect the
child. Most persons demonstrated a sympathetic attitude toward child
abusers; 55 percent, for example, favored placing such cases under the
auspices of a social welfare agency. Nevertheless, only half of the
respondents were aware of child protective agencies in their own communities. After reviewing all data, the study calculated an estimated
upper limit of the incidence of child abuse in the United States as between 2.53 and 4.07 million.

181 Helfer, Ray E. "Physical abuse of children: letter to editor."
     Pediatrics 46(4): 651-52, October, 1970. (2 References).
Strongly contradicts David G. Gil's report on child abuse which cites a
low incidence of maltreatment. The occurrence of child abuse is far
greater than suspected, and continued research in the area is essential
for upgrading childrearing practices and preventing abuse and neglect.

182 Howells, J. G. "Death from non-accidental injuries in childhood:
     letter to editor." Br Med J 3(5984): 651-52, September 13, 1975.
     (3 References).
States various factors that can cause discrepancies in child abuse incidence statistics. Reporting procedures are neither uniform nor followed
consistently by all physicians.

183 Jacobziner, Harold. "Rescuing the battered child." Am J Nurs
     64(6): 92-97, June, 1964. (14 References).
The extent of the problem of child abuse is demonstrated by statistics
obtained from studies performed throughout the country. Characteristics
of abusive parents precede the presentation of two case studies in which
the parents were responsive to treatment. The growing awareness of the
problem is cited, as are the legislative principles developing out of that

awareness. Finally, the role of the physician and nurse in reporting
cases and preventing the syndrome is discussed.

184 Joyner, Edmund N., III. "The battered child." NY Med 26(9): 383-
        85, September, 1970. (0 References).
The phenomenon of child abuse is seen as pervading all strata of American
life and affecting as many as four million children in 1969. The passage
of child abuse legislation by most states is mentioned. The major problems in child abuse management are seen to be the difficulty of coordinating all of the organizations, personnel, and disciplines involved, along
with the reluctance of many physicians to report suspected cases. The
institution of a child abuse committee within each hospital is recommended as a means of educating the staff about child abuse.

185 Light, Richard J. "Abused and neglected children in America: a
        study of alternative policies." Harv Educ Rev 43(4): 556-98,
        November, 1973. (48 References).
A statistical model for estimating national incidence of child abuse from
available empirical data has been developed which indicates that approximately 0.01 percent of all American families physically abuse a child.
Three social policies for dealing with child abuse are analyzed. The
first is a national health screening program for the detection of abused
children. It is emphasized that the diagnostic personnel would need
excellent training so that false negatives (abused children who are not
detected) and false positives (non-abused children who are diagnosed as
abused) could be avoided. The second policy involves the provision of
educational curricula on childrearing for teenagers. It is sometimes
argued that if young parents had more knowledge about different stages of
a child's development, they would not become as overwhelmed by the demands of parenthood. However, this author contends that there is little
evidence to suggest that education in childrearing would lower the rate
of abuse.

The third policy involves the development of profiles of abusing families.
The results of an exploratory data analysis indicated that the employment
status of the father, the type of dwelling unit, the number of persons
under eighteen, and the child's age were the discriminating variables between child abusing and non-abusing families. If a set of new parents
were found by profile analysis to be highly potential child abusers, they
could be offered help through social services on a voluntary basis.

186 Lohner, CDR Thomas. "Child advocacy at Naval Regional Medical
        Center, Portsmouth, Virginia." US Navy Med 68(3): 16-17, March,
        1977. (0 References).
Military populations have a heightened incidence of child abuse and neglect for several reasons, including frequent family separations, isolation
from friends and relatives, high incidence of alcoholism, and limited
health services at military medical centers. A child advocacy committee
was established at one naval medical center to deal with child abuse.
Its purposes were: (1) to define the magnitude of the problem; (2) to
secure trained personnel to work with abused children and their parents;
(3) to process all cases of documented or suspected child abuse; and (4)
to coordinate the activities of medical, social, psychiatric, and law
enforcement agencies. Three case histories are presented to demonstrate
how the committee operates.

187 Lynch, Annette. "Child abuse in the school-age population." J Sch
     Health 45(3): 141-48, March, 1975. (13 References).
A program to improve the management of child abuse and neglect cases by
school personnel was carried out in a large metropolitan school district.
Eight committees composed primarily of school nurses conducted a survey
of the prevalence and types of abuse among school age children, characteristics of the abused child, and methods of handling abuse cases by
school staff. Three to six committee meetings were held for the discussion of child abuse management. A procedure for the reporting of abuse
was developed whereby all school personnel would report suspected cases
to the physician-director of the department, who would then refer the
family to the child welfare agency. Results of the survey demonstrated
that child abuse among school age children is a condition of high prevalence which is often under-reported and often mishandled. A content
analysis of the minutes of the committee meetings revealed a significant
change in attitude toward child abuse over a six month period. Nurses
came to consider the child abuse reporting laws as helpful rather than
punitive, to accept the existence of child abuse rather than denying the
problem, and to understand that society must sometimes intervene in the
family in behalf of the child's welfare rather than respecting the parent's right to discipline or privacy. Recommendations for improvement
in the handling of child abuse cases by school personnel are outlined.

188 Nwako, Festus. "Child abuse syndrome in Nigeria." Int Surg
     59(11-12): 613-15, November-December, 1974. (3 References).
Calls attention to the incidence of child abuse in the representative
African nation of Nigeria. Owing to the efforts of a hospital staff armed
with a knowledge of the syndrome and a high degree of suspicion, fifty
cases of child abuse were detected among 2,462 cases of reported accidental injury during a two year period.

189 "Our children's keepers: editorial." J Can Dent Assoc 37(7):
     245, July, 1971. (0 References).
The regrettably high incidence of child abuse, particularly among poorer
families, is discussed, and some attention is devoted to the role of the
courts and reporting laws.

190 Paul, Shashi D. "Recognition of the entity 'the battered child
     syndrome' in India." Indian J Pediatr 39(289): 58-62, February,
     1972. (12 References).
Reviews the general history and characteristics of child abuse with an
emphasis on findings related to India. In India, children with bruises,
fractures, and/or subdural hematomas whose physical condition does not
coincide with the history presented by parents often go unrecognized as
battered child cases. This lack of recognition, plus the absence of reporting laws, make the incidence of cases in India unknown. X-rays are
excellent for detecting bone injuries and belie the physician's disbelief
and the parent's denial. A dependency petition filed by a welfare agency
undertaking the child's care is recommended to free physician and agency
from direct accusation of the parents. Hospitals need to have at least
one physician experienced with maltreatment on the staff, and physicians
should use every community resource to prevent further abuse of children.

191 Peckham, Catherine S., and Jobling, Megan. "Deaths from non-
     accidental injuries in childhood: letter to editor." Br Med J
     2(5972): 686, June 21, 1975. (0 References).

A critical review of the Registrar General's statistics shows an estimated 750 fatal accidents in children under five from 1968 to 1972, indicating that the figures are perhaps inflated and distorted. Accurate
statistics are imperative for making appropriate policy decisions designed
to create effective child abuse management programs.

192 Pugh, R. J. "Battered babies: letter to editor." Lancet 2(7670):
       466-67, August 29, 1970. (0 References).
Reports the incidence of battered children in a district hospital in
Great Britain and makes predictions for the general populace based on
these findings.

193 "Reporting abuse and neglect." Child Today 6(3): 27-28, May-June,
       1977. (0 References).
Announces the release of a report on the incidence and characteristics of
child abuse and neglect compiled by the Children's Division of the
American Humane Association. The report organizes the statistics and
information under four topics: (1) reporting of child abuse and neglect;
(2) the alleged perpetrators; (3) types of abuse reported; and (4) types
of neglect reported.

194 Ryan, James H. "Child abuse among blacks." Sepia 22(11): 27-30,
       November, 1973. (0 References).
Investigates the increased frequency of child abuse, especially among
black families who were previously believed to be immune to this problem.
Characteristics of battering parents and ways to help them are described.

195 Smith, Selwyn M. "Child abuse syndrome: letter to editor." Br
       Med J 3(5818): 113-14, July 8, 1972. (0 References).
Reveals a high incidence of abuse in a group of children hospitalized for
varying reasons. Indications are that child abuse occurs at all socioeconomic levels and that current British enforcement of laws against
child abuse has not served as a deterrent.

196 Smith, Sona, and Deasy, Patrick. "Child abuse in Ireland -- Part
       I: Does it occur?" J Ir Med Assoc 70(3): 65-69, March 19, 1977.
       (17 References).
Part I of a comprehensive study on child abuse deals specifically with
the incidence of abuse in Ireland. The social worker's case records in
a Dublin hospital between the years 1971 and 1975 were reviewed to ex-
tract those patients with indications of possible child abuse. One
hundred forty-one patients, representing 126 family units, formed the
basis for the report. It was found that child abuse in Ireland accounts
for one in 700 childhood hospital admissions. The infant or toddler has
greater vulnerability to child abuse than the older child, although it
was pointed out that this difference could be due to reporting failures
or to the fact that infants are more fragile than older children. When
more than one case of child abuse was reported in a given family, the
category of abuse (unlikely, suspect, or proven) tended to be constant.
There was a high frequency of abused twins, which identifies them as a
vulnerable group. The place of a child in the family (birth order) or
prematurity and neonatal separation, or death, was not related to child
abuse in this study.

197 Stillman, Angeliki K. "An epidemiological study of child abuse."
       For a summary see: Diss Abstr Int 37B(9): 4410, March, 1977.

198 "Taking it out on the baby: editorial." <u>NZ Med J</u> 66(413): 394, January, 1967. (0 References).
Decrys the persistence of child abuse in New Zealand, and calls for a coordinated attack on the problem.

199 Webb, K. W.; Burt, Marvin R.; Friedman, F. G. A.; <u>et al</u>. <u>Report and plan on recommended approach(es) and methods for determination of national incidence of child abuse and neglect</u>. Washington, D.C.: Department of Health, Education, and Welfare, Office of Child Development, Children's Bureau, 1975. 41p. (Bibliography).
An account of the development of a methodology for ascertaining the incidence of child abuse and child neglect over a period of several years. Some thirteen approaches to the problem are evaluated (including surveys of children, teachers, physicians, ordinary individuals; methods of national health screening; reviews of agency records; and combination of these various approaches). The recommended methodology includes a nomination questionnaire survey and a randomized telephone survey to gather data on child abuse, and questionnaire-structured interviews by social workers to determine the incidence of child neglect.

200 ————. <u>Report and plan on recommended approaches and methods for determination of national incidence of child abuse and neglect, Volume II</u>. Washington, D.C.: Department of Health, Education, and Welfare, Office of Child Development, Children's Bureau, 1975. 218p. (Bibliography).
Describes the methodologies recommended for gathering data on the incidence of child abuse and child neglect. The principal research technique is the citizen survey, with abuse surveys being distinguished from neglect surveys. The creation of questionnaires for these purposes and methods of evaluating the data they elicit are discussed, along with sampling and interview techniques. Cost estimates for national surveys are provided, the total projected cost of the recommended surveys coming to less than $1.5 million.

E. DEMOGRAPHIC CHARACTERISTICS

1. DEMOGRAPHIC STUDIES IN THE UNITED STATES

201 Allen, Hugh D.; Kosciolek, Edward J.; ten Bensel, Robert W.; <u>et al</u>. "The battered child syndrome -- Part II: Social and psychiatric aspects." <u>Minn Med</u> 52(1): 155-56, January, 1969. (0 References).
Emphasizes the social and psychiatric aspects of child abuse, based on observations of Hennepin County (Minnesota) for the years 1963 to 1968 and January, 1968 to June, 1968. Such topics as sources of referral, socioeconomic status, level of education, factors precipitating the abuse, and reporting procedures are briefly explored.

202 Banagale, Raul C., and McIntire, Matilda S. "Child abuse and neglect: a study of cases reported to Douglas County Child Protective Service from 1967-1973." <u>Nebr Med J</u> 60(9): 353-441, September, 1975. (28 References).
The child abuse and neglect cases reported to Douglas County Child Protective Service from 1967 to 1973 were reviewed to determine the incidence, types, extent, and distribution pattern of cases throughout Omaha,

Nebraska. It was found that 25.9 percent of the abused children were
between one and six years of age. More females than males were abused.
The majority of the families of abused children were of lower socioeconomic status. Eighteen percent of the abuse cases and 11.2 percent
of the neglect cases were heard in the juvenile court. Successful family
rehabilitation was noted in 37 percent of the abuse cases and in 30.8
percent of the neglect cases. But parental rights were terminated in
6.4 percent of the abuse and 10 percent of the neglect cases. The precipitating factors of abuse and/or neglect were found to be unemployment,
financial problems, alcoholism, drug addiction, functional mental retardation, psychiatric problems, immature parents, promiscuity, and marital
discord. Only 3 percent of the abuse cases and 0.4 percent of the neglect cases between 1970 and 1973 were reported by private physicians.
The reluctance of physicians to report abuse cases was attributed to:
(1) inability of physicians to suspect abuse in a child with evidence of
trauma or failure to thrive; (2) lack of understanding of his role and
responsibility; (3) unwillingness to accept that a parent could abuse his
own child; (4) fear of legal entanglements and harassment; and (5) the
belief that the child protective agency or the court will not take
appropriate action.

203 Brown, Rowine H. "The battered child." Med Trial Tech Q 20:
       272-81, 1974. (14 References).
Studies 395 cases of child abuse encountered in Cook County, Illinois.
Included are a breakdown of the major injuries suffered and treatment of
the child, along with procedures for the rehabilitation and/or legal
prosecution of the child abuser.

204 "Child abuse." Children 16(5): 205-6, September-October, 1969.
       (0 References).
Statistics are cited from a nationwide survey of child abuse in 1967 and
1968 conducted by David Gil at Brandeis University.

205 Corey, Eleanor J. B.; Miller, Carol L.; Widlak, Frederic W. "Factors
       contributing to child abuse." Nurs Res 24(4): 293-95, July-
       August, 1975. (16 References).
Compares demographic data collected on battered and non-battered children.
Forty-eight children under six were hospitalized between 1965 and 1973
for battering. These children were compared with a random sample of
fifty children hospitalized for other reasons. Comparisons were based on
characteristics such as sex, abuse of siblings, sex of the perpetrator,
and the mother's marital status, as well as on medical history factors
such as prematurity and extended postnatal hospitalization. Significant
differences between abused and non-abused children were negligible in all
areas.

206 Cosgrove, John G. "Management and follow-up of child abuse." J
       Med Soc NJ 69(1): 27-30, January, 1972. (1 Reference).
Analyzes the results of a one year follow-up study of fifteen abused
children and their families. The families were representative of the
community in terms of race, socioeconomic status, and education. The
average age of the abused child was three-years-seven-months. The children sustained injuries to the head, skeletal fractures, burns, malnutrition, and soft tissue trauma. An assessment of the families receiving follow-up treatment revealed that there had been some improvement in
the quality of care in the home. Five children, however, had to be
placed in foster care.

207 De Francis, Vincent. Child abuse -- preview of a nationwide survey.
     Denver, Colorado: The American Humane Association, Children's
     Division, 1963. 18p. (Bibliography).
Presents the findings of a two part project which studied data on child
abuse cases reported in newspapers around the country between January 1,
1962 and December 31, 1972, and community reaction to the problem of child
abuse. Six hundred and sixty-two cases of child abuse are analyzed with
respect to incidence, nature of injuries, age of victims, and identity
of the assailant. The complex motivations leading to abusive behavior
included emotional immaturity, a loss of control, and acute depression.
The second phase of the study pointed out that, inasmuch as three-fourths
of all reports were first directed to a law enforcement agency, the
general community attitude toward child abusers was an indignant and punitive one.

208 Ebbin, Allan J.; Gollub, Michael H.; Stein, Arthur M.; et al.
     "Battered child syndrome at the Los Angeles County General Hos-
     pital." Am J Dis Child 118(4): 660-67, October, 1969. (6
     References).
Report of an in-depth, ex post facto study of fifty battered children
seen at the Los Angeles County General Hospital from April, 1966 through
March, 1967. It was found that a majority of the children were under
two years old; 50 percent had sustained previous injury; almost half had
serious fractures; and the majority had bruises and lacerations. The
families of the battered children were often unstable, with a large proportion of children living with one natural parent who was single or
divorced. Twenty-three children had one parent with a previous criminal
conviction, psychiatric history, or alcoholic problem. The problems in
reporting child abuse cases and deficiencies in the law are discussed.

209 Friedrich, William N. "Epidemiological survey of physical child
     abuse." Tex Med 72(10): 81-84, October, 1976. (9 References).
Harris County child welfare intake reports of physical child abuse for a
seventeen week period during 1974 and 1975 were analyzed. Results indicated that 50 percent of all reports involved children six years old
and younger. Approximately 85 percent of the children had been abused
previously. Abuse was evenly distributed across all lines of race, education level, and socioeconomic status. The abusing families were characterized by a high rate of marital instability and unemployment. Although
the mother was the abusing parent more often than the father, this finding reflects the large number of mother-headed households. Neighbors
were the most frequent reporters of abuse, followed by school personnel,
relatives, friends, and agencies.

210 Gil, David G. Violence against children: physical child abuse in
     the United States. Cambridge, Massachusetts: Harvard University
     Press, 1970. 204p.
Details an epidemiologic study of physical abuse directed against children. The study spanned the years 1967 and 1968 and was based on standardized information received from every state and territory on every
reported incident of child abuse. In addition, a more comprehensive investigation of cases reported in 1967 was conducted in a representative
sample of cities and counties.

The purpose of the study was to obtain knowledge about the nature, dynamics, and scope of physical abuse and its incidence in the total population and in subgroups of society. More specifically, it sought to explore:

(1) public attitudes toward abuse; (2) the characteristics of the victims, perpetrators and families; (3) the circumstances surrounding incidents of abuse; (4) the nature of the injuries received; (5) the health, welfare and legal measures taken by the authorities receiving reports of abuse; and (6) the important associations between these variables. The information was to be shaped into social policy recommendations aimed at the prevention of child abuse. The study's conceptual framework strongly emphasized the sociocultural factors underlying specific incidents of abuse. Individual personality disorders, while important, are necessarily influenced by the cultural context in which they find expression.

There were 5,993 children in the study cohort for 1967 and 6,617 in the cohort for 1968. It was found that over half of the subjects below age twelve were male, while the majority of subjects over age twelve were female. More than three-fourths of the sample were over age two, nearly half were above the age of six, and one-fifth were teenagers. These findings contradicted those of earlier studies which concluded that very young children were the most frequent victims of abuse. One-third of the subjects were non-white, which was attributed both to a bias in the study's reporting sources and to a real, higher incidence of abuse among minority groups, due to conditions of poverty and to differences in child-rearing practices. Religious affiliation was not a factor in abuse incidence. Appraisals of social interaction, and intellectual and physical functioning, showed that the level of deviance in abused children was in excess of that of any group of children. At least half had been previously abused. There was a marked association between physical child abuse and deviance in family structure from the normative nuclear family. Abusing parents were found to have low educational and occupational status, low income, poor housing conditions, and more children than the average family. Parents' backgrounds were examined for psychiatric hospitalizations, juvenile court appearances, criminal records, medical problems, and deviant intellectual and social functioning. As with abused children, it was found that a higher level of deviance existed among abusive parents than among any other group. Analysis of the perpetrators and of the circumstances surrounding abuse acts led to the identification of seven categories of abuse: (1) that caused by the parent's psychological rejection of the child; (2) that resulting from an angry and uncontrolled disciplinary response; (3) male babysitter abuse; (4) abuse resulting from personality deviance and reality stress; (5) child-originated abuse; (6) female babysitter abuse; and (7) abuse resulting from quarrels between caretakers.

The study concluded that the social context in which childrearing occurs does not exclude the use of physical force but that differences do exist between various segments of society. Low socioeconomic groups, for example, tend to approve of corporal punishment more than do middle class groups. Certain conditions are responsible for pushing individual parents or caretakers beyond socially acceptable levels of physical force: (1) environmental chance factors; (2) environmental stress factors; (3) physical, social, intellectual or emotional deviance on the part of the victim or the perpetrator; (4) disturbed family relationships; and (5) various combinations of these elements. The scope of physical abuse is not felt to constitute a major social problem in comparison with more pervasive and insidious problems such as poverty and discrimination, which constantly act to undermine the potential and development of the nation's children. The study recommended widespread educational efforts aimed at changing childrearing philosophies, the elimination of poverty, extensive family planning, family-life education and counseling programs, neighborhood-based national health services, and accessible and effective child-welfare and child-protective services.

211 Gonzalez-Pardo, Lillian, and Thomas, Mary. "Child abuse and neg-
        lect." J Kansas Med Soc 78(2): 65-69, February, 1977. (5
        References).
All child abuse and neglect reports made to Social Rehabilitation Services or juvenile courts throughout the State of Kansas between July, 1972 and December, 1975 were analyzed. The annual incidence rate was 1,756 cases per million population. It was found that bruises and welts occurred in 43 percent of all cases of physical abuse. Seventy percent of the neg-lect cases involved inadequate supervision, poor or unsafe environment, and/or insufficient food, clothing, and hygiene. Eighty-eight percent of the perpetrators of abuse and neglect were the parents of the child. Differences in the pattern and frequency of abuse and/or neglect among the various counties were observed. These differences were attributed to the stability of child protective services, the experience and skill of social workers, environmental conditions, geographical location, the attitude of residents' toward abuse, and the life style of the residents (urban or rural) in each of the counties. Any program designed to deal with the problem of child abuse and neglect should consider the epidemio-logic characteristics of the county in which it will be located to de-termine how the particular area may best be helped.

212 Hartley, Albert I. "Identifying the physically abused child." Tex
        Med 65(3): 50-55, March, 1969. (7 References).
Twenty physically abused children treated at the University of Texas Medical Branch were studied in order to determine patient and family characteristics which indicate a susceptibility to abuse. Findings sug-gest that while the socioeconomic level of the family is not a factor, deviations from the typical nuclear family, such as a single parent or a step-parent, are important. The abused children are most likely to be under three years of age and to be the offspring of a biracial marriage. White girls and black boys are abused most often, as are single children or the youngest of several. The physician treating these cases must con-sider first the safety of the child and the legal protection of the par-ent who may be falsely accused of abuse. Stories told by parents which are at odds with the actual injury are often the first sign that abuse has occurred.

213 Hawaii. State Department of Social Services and Housing. Division
        of Public Welfare. A statistical report on child abuse in Hawaii.
        Honolulu, Hawaii: Hawaii State Department of Social Services and
        Housing, Division of Public Welfare, 1968. 17p.
Presents statistical data on child abuse and child neglect in Hawaii in 1967 and 1968. Data is cross referenced according to geographical dis-tribution, age, sex, religion, time of abuse or neglect, type of injury, and psychosocial factors.

214 ————. A statistical report on child abuse and neglect in Hawaii.
        Honolulu, Hawaii: Hawaii State Department of Social Services and
        Housing, Division of Public Welfare, 1969. 23p.
A statistical report on child abuse and child neglect in Hawaii. The increase in cases is imputed to an increase in the reporting of cases of suspected child abuse/neglect. The cases are broken down into such

categories as sex of child, sex of parent suspected of abuse or neglect, sex of household head, and source of report of the abuse or neglect.

215 ————. A statistical report on child abuse and neglect in Hawaii. Honolulu, Hawaii: Hawaii State Department of Social Services and Housing, Division of Public Welfare, 1971. 17p.
Reports the statistics concerning child abuse and neglect in Hawaii during 1970 to 1971. Reported cases of child abuse doubled in 1970, and half of these cases were confirmed as abuse. The largest reporting source was school authorities, and 72 percent of confirmed cases were reported by persons required to do so. Eighty percent of the children were from two parent families, although a number had step-parents. Natural parents and step-parents were the two largest groups of abusers. Girls were most often the objects of abuse, and welts and bruises were the most common injury. Follow-up indicated that 27 percent of the children were removed from their homes in 1970 and 41 percent in 1971. As with abused children, the number of neglected children reported also doubled in 1970 and increased only slightly in 1971. Two-thirds of the neglect cases were reported by non-professionals, neighbors being the largest reporting source. Often more than one child per family was neglected, and the largest number of these children were in the preschool age group. They most frequently suffered from a lack of supervision by the natural parent, usually the mother. Approximately one-quarter of the neglected children were removed from their homes in 1970 and 40 percent in 1971, figures similar to those for child abuse. In some cases, abuse and neglect occurred simultaneously, and this fact is accounted for in the statistical figures.

216 ————. A statistical report on child abuse and neglect in Hawaii: 1972-1974. Honolulu, Hawaii: Hawaii State Department of Social Services and Housing, Division of Public Welfare, 1974. 42p.
Provides a statistical analysis of child abuse and neglect in Hawaii from 1972 to 1974. During that time, 3,400 children were reported; roughly half for abuse and half for neglect. Persons required to report filed just under half of abuse cases and one-third of neglect cases. Schools reported the highest number of abuse cases and neighbors the highest number of neglect cases. Children under five years of age were the primary victims of abuse, with bruises and welts being the most common injury. Neglected children were most frequently left unattended or unsupervised and were, on the average, aged three to five. Girls were abused more frequently, and boys were more often neglected. The natural parents primarily generated both forms of maltreatment, with fathers the primary abusers and mothers the primary neglecters. Cases often overlapped, as neglect frequently followed abuse. A majority of children remained in their homes following the reporting.

217 "The intricacies of violence against children in American society: editorial." Clin Pediatr 10(10): 557-58, October, 1971. (0 References).
Analyses David Gil's descriptive survey of child abuse. His findings are presented in terms of the following variables: (1) the age, sex, race, and school performance of the child; (2) the sex, race, occupation, educational level, intellectual functioning, and mental health of the abusing parent; (3) the organization of the family unit; and (4) the seriousness of injuries received. Seven major causative factors were categorized, emphasizing the need for comprehensive social action.

218   Johnson, Betty, and Morse, Harold.   The battered child: a study of
        children with inflicted injuries.   Denver, Colorado: Denver Depart-
        ment of Welfare, 1968.   22p.
Presents a follow-up study of a group of 101 battered children who were
under the supervision of the Denver Division of Child Services in 1963.
Statistics are given regarding the age of the children, type and severity
of injuries sustained, the identity of the abusive parent, placement, and
court convictions.   In researching the etiology of the abusive incidents,
it was found that at least 70 percent of the children demonstrated prior
physical or developmental deviation.   The families often lived in rented
housing and underwent financial difficulties and marital conflict at the
time of the abuse incident.   Three years later, and after extensive
treatment, many families showed improvement.   However, 30 percent of the
marriages ended in separation or divorce and 20 percent of the children
suffered subsequent abuse.

219   ————.   "Injured children and their parents."   Children   15(4):
        147-52, July-August, 1968.   (0 References).
A study of the characteristics of 101 abused children and their families
was undertaken by the Denver Welfare Department from 1963 to 1966.   Two-
thirds of the children were severely injured, and seventy-nine removed
from their homes as a result of the abuse.   Twenty-two adult arrests for
child abuse were made, resulting in nine convictions.   The injured children were often found to be below normal in speech development, to have
feeding and toilet training problems, to be undernourished, and to show
signs of emotional disturbance.   An evaluation of the siblings of the
abused children revealed that eleven of them had also been maltreated.
The abusing parents were often anxious, hostile, or depressed.   Poor
economic conditions, limited mobility, and unemployment were common.   It
is recommended that the community approve a multidisciplinary child protective service and provide the resources to effectively alleviate acute
and long-range economic and emotional stress on families with child abuse
problems.

220   Johnson, Clara L.   Child abuse in the Southeast: analysis of 1172
        reported cases.   Athens, Georgia: University of Georgia, Regional
        Institute of Social Welfare Research, 1974.   153p.   (Bibliography).
Investigates the incidence of child abuse and its demographic characteristics, as indicated by 1,172 cases reported in the southeast region of
the United States.   The increase in the number of cases reported reflects
a change in legislation and public awareness rather than a rise in actual
abuse.   The study outlines the variance in the number of cases reported
and those confirmed as abuse according to sex, race, and age.   Parental
characteristics such as age, marital status, education, occupation, and
economic standing are explored.   Circumstances surrounding the injury,
such as a listing of prior abuse, referral source, and the nature of the
injuries are described, and associations between factors are analyzed.

221   Kaplun, David, and Reich, Robert.   "The murdered child and his
        killers."   Am J Psychiatry   133(7):   809-13, July, 1976.   (15
        References).
Reports a study of 112 cases of child homicide occurring in New York
City during 1968 and 1969.   The families of the murdered children lived
in areas of severe poverty.   Twenty-five percent of the families had
teenage mothers, and 73 percent had other children under the age of three.
Severe marital discord was frequent among these families, and a history

of child maltreatment extending to siblings was common. The child victims were usually illegitimate preschoolers, and the assailants were most
often mothers of their paramours. The assailants had backgrounds of
social deviance, narcotics and alcohol addiction, promiscuity, assaultive-
ness, criminal behavior, and psychiatric disorder. Law enforcement
activity subsequent to the murders was minimal: only seventeen suspects
went to trial, and almost all of these were given short sentences on
reduced charges. Follow-up contact with psychiatric, counseling, and
guidance agencies was also negligible. Further research is needed to determine what characteristics of a person or environmental conditions can
identify the potentially abusive situation so that child abuse and homicide can be prevented.

222 Kentucky. Department for Human Resources. Bureau of Social Services.
      Family and Children's Services Branch. Child abuse report: fiscal
      year 1973-74. Frankfurt, Kentucky: Department for Human Resources,
      Bureau of Social Services, Family and Children's Services Branch,
      1974. 8p.
Incidence statistics on child abuse in Kentucky from 1973 to 1974 are
detailed. Since the child abuse laws were passed in 1964, reported abuse
had increased, and in 1973, 832 reports of suspected abuse cases were
submitted. The statistics indicate that the maltreated children were
more often female and the largest percentage, 27 percent, were from five
to nine years old. Twenty percent were victims of repeated abuse. The
types of injuries are listed, with bruises and welts being the most common
manifestation. Parents were the abusers in 66 percent of the cases. They
were most often white and in their twenties. Twenty percent had formerly
been involved in maltreatment cases. While this compilation of characteristics was helpful, a method of determining the incidence of abuse more
exactly was felt to be necessary for effective services.

223 ————. Profile on child abuse, 1974-75. Frankfurt, Kentucky:
      Department for Human Resources, Bureau of Social Services, Family
      and Children's Services Branch, 1975. 14p.
Reports on child abuse in Kentucky from 1974 to 1975. Reported abuse
cases increased 137.6 percent from 1973-1974 to 1974-1975. Additional
public attention accounts for the rise in reports rather than an increase
in abuse itself. The highest percentage of reports, 14.3 percent, came
from anonymous sources. The abusing parties were commonly white parents
under age thirty. Over half the children were females, predominantly
white, and 27.3 percent were five to nine years of age. The most frequent
injuries were bruises and welts. Of the 1977 reported cases, 28.27 percent were confirmed during initial investigation.

224 Lauer, Brian; Ten Broeck, Elsa; Grossman, Moses. "Battered child
      syndrome: review of 130 patients with controls." Pediatrics
      54(1): 67-70, July, 1974. (9 References).
A six year study comparing child abuse with other pediatric admissions
was undertaken at San Francisco General Hospital. Sixty-three percent
of the abused children were under two years of age and the majority were
offspring of young, white, and mobile parents. Total pediatric admissions
remained constant while abuse cases rose steadily, accounting for nearly
3 percent of all pediatric admissions over the final three years of the
study.

225 Lloyd-Still, John D., and Martin, Barbara. "Child abuse in a rural
    setting." Pa Med 79(3): 56-60, March, 1976. (15 References).
Data is presented on characteristics of child abuse as witnessed at the
Milton S. Hershey Medical Center. The data is very similar to that
acquired elsewhere in the country. Failure to thrive due to deliberate
deprivation accounted for only 3 percent of the cases, whereas physically
abused children accounted for 44 percent. Most children were under three
years of age. The Child Protection Team, responsible for the management
of such cases, utilized a very non-punitive approach. It is paramount
that physicians and child welfare departments maintain a cooperative relationship and that prospective physicians be trained in the management of
this condition.

226 Lyons, Michael M. "Pediatric forensic pathology." NY State J Med
    72(3): 816-19, April 1, 1972. (12 References).
Data from the New York Medical Examiner's Office is used in a statistical
report on violent childhood deaths. Most homicides of children are
perpetuated by parents, and the most common causes of death in these cases
are injury by blunt instrument, firearm wound, and drowning. Most cases
of child abuse induced homicide involve victims under the age of four.

227 Michael, Marianne K. "The battered child." Iowa J Soc Work 3(3):
    78-83, 1970. (2 References).
Surveys medical and personal data for twenty-eight cases of the battered
child syndrome reported at a university hospital in a four year period.
Nearly half of the patients were only children, but in seven cases, there
were siblings in the family who had been reported as abuse cases as well.
The median age for the children was eight months, and the median hospital
stay, twenty-four days, doubled that of the average patient. Recommendations are made for the provision of education in family planning and
family life.

228 Ott, John F. "Neglected or physically abused children." J SC Med
    Assoc 60(10): 309-15, October, 1964. (12 References).
Reviews several studies on child abuse. The neglected child is distinguished from the battered child; though unbeaten, he is still emotionally
and physically deprived. Two case reports serve to illustrate both
types. Indications of abuse include the parents' story of sudden illness
at odds with the child's condition of starvation and neglect. In the
case of physical abuse, the appearance of surface lesions and a subdural
hematoma with multiple skeletal fractures should arouse suspicion. The
Merrill study, conducted in 1960 by the Massachusetts Society for the
Prevention of Cruelty to Children, suggests that parents fall into three
categories: hostile, rigid and compulsive, and overly passive. That
report also concluded that 90 percent of abusing families had serious
social problems, and in 50 percent, premarital conception had occurred.
In 86 percent of the cases, both parents were equally abusing. The children were not found to provoke the abuse, although one child was usually
singled out for battering. Other studies indicate that parents showed
little feeling and seemed to lack the ordinary restraint for their aggressive behavior, especially in relation to some unresolved conflict from
their past. Often these parents feared close relationships and responded
to authority more easily than to warmth. They usually denied abusing
their child.

The Massachusetts study also indicated that although 30 percent of abused
children had been seen by physicians, only 9 percent were referred to

agencies. Causes cited were: (1) missed diagnosis; (2) refusal to believe parents could abuse in this way; (3) uncertainty about what to do; and (4) fear of liability. The principles of the model state law proposed by the Children's Bureau (HEW) for the protection of children and reporting physicians are stated in full, and an outline of procedures a physician can follow is clearly delineated.

229 Patterson, Peter H., and Char, Donald. "Child abuse in Hawaii."
     Hawaii Med J 25(1): 395-97, September-October, 1965. (4 References).
Documents the results of a questionnaire distributed to some 300 physicians on the detection and reporting of child abuse in Hawaii. Physicians were asked about the number of incidents of child abuse they had seen, the number they had reported, their actions regarding the cases which they did not report, and their recommendations for dealing with child abuse.

230 Paulson, Morris J., and Blake, Phillip R. "The physically abused
     child: a focus on prevention." Child Welfare 48(2): 86-95,
     February, 1969. (24 References).
A review of the history, definition, incidence, and causes of child abuse reported in the literature. The data from a study of ninety-six battered children seen at a Los Angeles hospital are compared with the findings of previous studies. It was concluded that 90 percent of these cases fit the classic definition of the battered child syndrome. Sixty percent of the children were less than three years old. The data also revealed important personal-social characteristics of the abusing parents. More research is needed in the areas of identification of the potential child abuser so that injury to children can be prevented and parents deficient in child caring practices can be rehabilitated.

231 Schloesser, Patricia T. "The abused child." Bull Menninger Clin
     28(5): 260-68, September, 1964. (7 References).
Discusses child abuse based on the results of a study by Kansas State Department of Health for the year 1962-1963. The study sent questionnaires to 1,000 physicians. Out of the 337 returned, thirty-seven physicians reported a total of fifty cases of child abuse during 1962. The Department also selected information from thirty-five cases from two urban and two rural county health departments, one urban juvenile court, and the Kansas Bureau of Investigation. Out of seventy-one cases, 70 percent of the children were under three years of age and had suffered from fractures, brain injury, starvation, and strangulation. The abusers of younger children were usually mothers, while fathers tended to abuse older children. Parents were usually under twenty-five years of age. Most of the families were white and held low income occupations. For many, extended family and community roots had dissipated with increasing mobility. Included are illustrative case histories and a discussion emphasizing the responsibility of physicians and agencies to report, with special attention to a law which requires the reporting of suspected abuse and which grants immunity from prosecution. Children whose families were referred to public agencies were generally better protected from further injuries.

232 Simons, Betty; Downs, Elinor F.; Hurster, Madeline M.; et al. "Child
     abuse: epidemiologic study of medically reported cases." NY State
     J Med 66(21): 2783-88, November 1, 1966. (11 References).

Presents an epidemiologic study of 313 children registered with the New
York City Child Abuse Registry, 1964 to 1965. The recorded incidence of
cases is not accurate in that only children receiving medical care are
registered. Eighty-seven percent of the children were reported by hospitals, suggesting that private physicians are more comfortable referring
their patients indirectly. The city boroughs with the highest number of
registered cases shared common characteristics of overcrowding, non-white
mothers, low weight newborns, inadequate prenatal care, and a high rate
of infant mortality. It is proposed that either poverty is a factor or
that people from low socioeconomic backgrounds provoke more suspicion and
are easier to report. Although a majority of the parents were married,
many of the marriages were unstable, and one or both of the parents suffered past and/or present psychological difficulties. The results of the
study indicated a broad range of abuse patterns with more multiproblem
families than previously recorded. Classifying abuse may not be so important for prevention as detecting family conditions which lead to abuse.

233 Solomon, Theo. "History and demography of child abuse." Pediatrics
       51(4, Part II): 773-76, April, 1973. (0 References).
Traces the demography and history of child abuse, starting with a discussion of ritualistic or traditionally acceptable infanticide in many
cultures and progressing to contemporary child battering and neglect.
Although there are no means available for obtaining consistent national
statistics on the incidence of child abuse, a chart illustrating a com-
posite demographic representation of the abused child, the abusive parent, and family dynamics is provided. Several additional problems related
to abuse, such as gross neglect, juvenile laws that often engender excessively harsh punishment, and the continual production of defective children's toys, are discussed.

234 Surdock, Pete W., Jr. Report on child abuse and neglect in Montana
       for January 1, 1974 through June 30, 1974. Helena, Montana:
       Montana State Department of Social and Rehabilitative Services,
       1974. 22p.
The incidence of child abuse and neglect in Montana is analyzed. From
January to June, 1974, community services received 367 referrals, 250
of them valid. Physical neglect (43.2 percent), emotional neglect (23.6
percent), and beatings (21.2 percent) were the most frequent types of
abuse. Protective service while remaining in their home was received by
49.6 percent of the children, and 24.4 percent had to be placed temporarily outside the home. Statistics show that victims were typically
school aged (especially adolescent), Caucasian, legitimate, and one of
several siblings. The abusers were usually the natural parents; typically
they had a low income, had less than high school education, and had a
previous record of abuse or neglect. A number of stress factors commonly
seemed to trigger ill-use of children: arguments, job troubles, alcohol,
family breakups, children's disobedience, and health problems were the
most frequent. Statistics on referral sources show that community support
is vital to effective protective services. Most reports of abuse or
neglect came from neighbors, law officers, schools, public social agencies
or relatives.

235 Virginia. Department of Welfare. Bureau of Child Protective Serv-
       ices. Local summary, child abuse and neglect: addendum to annual
       report, 1975-76. Richmond, Virginia: Department of Welfare, Bureau
       of Child Protective Services, 1977.

Presents the results of a statistical survey of the number of child abuse cases reported in Virginia between 1975 and 1976. Included is a break-down by locality, age and sex of the abused child, person or group to whom the offense was reported, relationship of abuser to child, type of abuse, result of abuse, and type of social service agency available in each region. This information was obtained from the Central Registry of the Bureau of Child Protective Services.

236   Wight, Byron W. "The control of child-environment interaction: a conceptual approach to accident occurrence." Pediatrics 44(5, Part II): 799-805, November, 1969. (0 References).
A one year longitudinal study of seventy-seven cases of infant accidents resulting from physical collision with the environment is presented. The investigators sought to determine whether characteristics of family back-ground, of the mother's capacity to supervise the child, of the infant's temperament, and of the mother-child relationship could differentiate be-tween accidents in which the child played an active role (such as crawl-ing and subsequently colliding with a piece of furniture) versus accidents in which the child played a passive role (such as being struck or dropped by a parent or object in the home environment). It was found that fami-lies of infants who were struck were more likely to be non-white and of lower socioeconomic status. They had little education, and few supportive sources available to them. In addition, the families of infants sustain-ing child-passive injuries had more stress than those infants with child-active injuries. The capacity of mothers to supervise their infant's be-havior and the quality of the mother-child relationship were poor among the child-passive accident categories. Infants of the child-active accident group were older, more highly motoric, and more negative in mood than the infants of the child-passive groups. It was discovered during the accident follow-up that every infant sustaining injuries from sus-pected abuse showed a retarded rate of development.

2. DEMOGRAPHIC STUDIES IN OTHER COUNTRIES

237   Baldwin, J. A., and Oliver, J. E. "Epidemiology and family charac-teristics of severely-abused children." Br J Prev Soc Med 29(4): 205-21, December, 1975. (53 References).
Presents a study of thirty-eight cases of severe child abuse occurring between 1965 and 1971 in northeast Wiltshire. An incidence rate of 1 per 1,000 children under four years of age and a death rate of 0.1 per 1,000 were obtained. Many of the abused children were abnormal at birth: 21 percent were premature, 10 percent had congenital defects, and 23 percent were illegitimate. The most common injuries or effects of abuse were fractures, bruises, malnutrition, and persistent or severe emotional trauma. The families of the abused children were characterized by low social class, marital instability, youthfulness, severe psychiat-ric, medical, and social pathology, and a large number of children. These findings are compared with those of other studies of severely abused children.

238   "Battered babies." R Soc Health J 90(5): 282-88, September-October, 1970. (9 References).
Outlines the history, incidence, and background of child abuse and rec-ommends procedures for case management. Although incidence is not known, one study indicates forty deaths occur each year in England and Wales of

infants under one year of age. The younger the child, the more severe
the injury, and the male child is the more likely target. Personality
disorders in the parent, coupled with stressful circumstances, lead to
the abuse. Clinical signs include multiple injuries such as bruises,
fractures, and hematomas. Management must always attend first to the
safety of the child in terms of his present injuries and the possibility
of recurrence. Where agencies are involved, a team approach and the
coordination of information is recommended.

239   Fergusson, David M.; Fleming, Joan; O'Neill, David P.   Child abuse
      in New Zealand: a report on a nationwide survey of the physical
      ill-treatment of children in New Zealand. Wellington, New Zealand:
      A. R. Shearer, 1972. 342p. (Bibliography).
Presents a demographic analysis of child abuse in New Zealand from data
gathered in a nationwide survey conducted by the Child Welfare Division
in 1967. Two hundred and fifty-five cases of alleged or suspected abuse,
the total number of cases brought to the attention of the authorities
that year, were investigated. The survey utilized interviewers who researched the families' case histories, and then questioned the parents
concerning their socioeconomic environment and marital situation while
simultaneously evaluating the parents' psychological makeup.

Survey results treat both the child victims and the parent figures involved in the abusive act. Charts depict the types and severity of
injuries sustained by the children. Sixteen percent of the children suffered serious injury or death. Forty-one percent of the victims were
under five years of age. Although sex distribution was relatively equal
for young children, after age eleven there were more cases of abused
females than males. Sixty-three percent of the 255 instances were classified as episodic abuse, while slightly more than half of them had
previously come to the attention of the child welfare authorities. As a
lower limit, an incidence of 2.57 cases of abuse per 10,000 children in
New Zealand with higher rates in areas with substantial Maori or other
non-European populations is predicted.

Natural or substitute mothers composed 61 percent of the abusing parents.
These women frequently exhibited signs of stress associated with health
problems, pregnancy, and child raising, in addition to symptoms of anxiety,
depression, irritability, and compulsive behavior. Abusing fathers often
had past histories of adverse childhood experiences, juvenile delinquency,
and some criminal prosecutions. Unstable family circumstances characterized the home environment of the abusive families. Twenty-three percent
had changed residences three to seven times prior to the abuse incident.
Half of the abused children were living in homes in which at least one
of the natural parents was absent. Fifty-eight percent of the male heads
of household were employed in semi-skilled or seasonal unskilled work,
and a consequent 35 percent of all families acknowledged having inadequate
finances. In conclusion, these findings are compared with those of other
European and American studies. Appendices include a copy of the survey
form used by the interviewers and illustrative case histories.

240   Fraser, F. Murray; Anderson, John P.; Burns, Kevin; et al.   Child
      abuse in Nova Scotia: a research project about battered and
      maternally deprived children. Halifax, Nova Scotia, 1973. 295p.
      (8 References).
Analyzes the results of a 1971 research study to determine the incidence,
treatment, and management of child abuse and maternal deprivation in Nova

Scotia. The research team examined hospital and court records from the period 1966 to 1970 and identified thirty-five cases of child abuse and twenty-four cases of maternal deprivation. Research uncovered that at the time of the incident, forty-one families were under the supervision of a social welfare agency, public health nurse, or other professional. The majority of parents had received less than a ninth grade education. Abusive families displayed a high rate of urban mobility, whereas deprived children were generally found in private, rural homes.

Part Two of the study contains the statistical results of a survey of 950 professionals concerning their knowledge and attitudes toward child abuse. Proportionate numbers of physicians, social workers, nurses, teachers, lawyers, police officers, clergy, and journalists were interviewed. Ninety-five percent acknowledged an awareness of the problem of child abuse, and 48 percent had been involved in at least one case of child abuse in the previous three year period. Only slightly more than half recognized their legal obligation to report suspected cases of abuse, while 64 percent were ignorant of the immunity clause in the reporting laws.

Numerous recommendations developed from the initial research and the professional survey. The establishment of a province-wide central registry of abuse and neglect cases, the expansion of the jurisdiction of the family court, and the appointment of a child's advocate were urged. Hospitals were encouraged to standardize their records and to permanently retain nurses' notes on patient progress and family interaction. Additional recommendations for basic preventive services in the community included: family life education programs, day care centers, crisis counseling, family planning programs, and neighborhood community centers.

241   Langshaw, W. C. "The battered child." Aust J Forensic Sci 3(2):
        60-70, December, 1970. (6 References).
Discusses a survey of the records of the Department of Child Welfare in New South Wales (Australia). Data on twenty-six cases of child abuse was analyzed in terms of the injuries inflicted, the sex and age of the victims and perpetrators, and the size, financial, social, and emotional status of the families involved. Half of the children were returned to their families, while ten were given over to the custody of the Minister, agencies, or foster homes. Three of the children had died as a result of their injuries. During the same period, social workers increased their visits to families alleged to be negligent, while the number of children removed from the family environment for reasons of negligence declined.

242   McRae, Kenneth N.; Ferguson, Charles A.; Lederman, R. S. "The bat-
        tered child syndrome." Can Med Assoc J 108(7): 859-66, April
        7, 1973. (7 References).
Statistical data on 132 abused children seen at Children's Hospital of Winnipeg from 1957 to 1971 are analyzed. Information is provided about the yearly incidence of abuse, the age of distribution of the child victims, the types of abuse and the presenting medical problems which may conceal abuse. The ways in which the child may unwittingly contribute to a pattern of abuse are considered. The importance of early detection and intervention is stressed in relation to the child's safety. A follow-up of some children revealed a high incidence of permanent brain damage, retardation, and severe disturbance, some of which may have been preventable if strenuous intervention had occurred. A discussion of management issues includes a consideration of the problems involved in child placement.

243 Robertson, B. A., and Hayward, M. A. "Transcultural factors in
    child abuse." S Afr Med J 50(43): 1765-67, October 9, 1976.
    (9 References).

Presents a crosscultural study of fifty-four cases of child abuse seen at
the Red Cross War Memorial Children's Hospital, Cape Town, South Africa.
The low number of abused black children may be due to cultural differences
in childrearing practices or to inadequate reporting of cases. The
larger number of abused white children may reflect their greater access
to child welfare agencies. The black population was found to have a
large number of abused children who were also born out of wedlock, perhaps a factor in the overall greater number of illegitimate babies born
to black parents and also to their lower class position. The white
mothers, often the abusers, seldom admitted abuse, in contrast to the
black mothers who, less often the abuser, related abuse as the cause of
injury. This may reflect the fact that many black mothers work and retain inadequate caretakers. Abuse occurs more often in the lower class;
the upper class, however, can afford reliable caretakers. The study indicated that children temporarily removed from their homes were returned
following their parents' completion of in-patient psychiatric treatment.
Simultaneous care of child and parent is a suggested improvement for the
future.

244 Savage, S. W. "Intelligence and infant mortality in problem fami-
    lies." Br Med J 1(1946): 86-87, January 19, 1946. (0 Refer-
    ences).

A study was conducted to uncover the number of problem mothers in a rural
area, to ascertain their intelligence, to determine the impact of their
children as compared to a normal group, and to compare the number of infant deaths in the problem versus the normal families. Problem families
were classified by type of neglect. Regarding educational position, it
was observed that almost half of the children of problem families were retarded as compared to only 9 percent for the control group. The infant
death rate for the problem group was twice as high as the rate of the
control group. When average and below average intelligence groups from
both problem and normal families were compared, it was found that in
problem families with mothers of average intelligence, about half of the
children were two or more years retarded. This percentage dropped to
seven for the control group. In the below average intelligence group of
problem mothers, 45 percent of the children were retarded two or more
years as compared to 12.3 percent for the control group.

245 Skinner, Angela E., and Castle, Raymond L. Seventy-eight battered
    children: a retrospective study. London, England: National
    Society for the Prevention of Cruelty to Children, Department of
    Battered Child Research, 1969. 21p. (Bibliography).

Analyzes seventy-eight incidents of the battered child syndrome with respect to the victims, the families, and the governmental intervention in
the cases. Most of the incidents occurred in the home, and many of the
abusing parents were found to have histories of emotional problems. The
injuries occurring most frequently involved the soft tissues (77 percent)
and bones (45 percent). Increased public knowledge about child abuse,
new reporting legislation, and greater professional education are recom-

246 Smith, Selwyn, and Noble, Sheila. "Battered children and their
    parents." New Soc 26(580): 393-95, November 15, 1973. (0 Refer-
    ences).

Some demographic aspects of the child abuse problem in England are detailed. Results were based on a study of the records of 134 hospitalized
battered infants. Parents were generally younger than average, unskilled
or semi-skilled members of the working class who exhibited personality
disorders. The deficiency of the present legal apparatus for dealing
with the problem is criticized, and it is suggested that the court system
be revised and that child battering teams be instituted at centrally
located hospitals, these teams to consist of a pediatrician, psychiatrist,
social worker, and psychologist.

247 Wichlacz, Casimer R.; Randall, Dolores; Nelson, James H.; et al.
     "The characteristics and management of child abuse in the U.S.
     Army -- Europe." Clin Pediatr 14(6): 545-48, June, 1975. (5
     References).

Reports an epidemiologic study of child abuse and neglect among United
States military families stationed in Germany over a twelve month period.
A rate of 147.4 children per 100,000 were reported to be abused or neglected, and five children died as a result of abuse. These rates are
considered conservative since there are no mandatory child abuse reporting laws in Germany. The rates are significantly higher for this military
population than those reported in two United States civilian cities during 1972. Crowded living conditions, cultural shock, and extended family
separations are cited as possible causes of the high abuse rate among
this military population. Management of child abuse cases among military
families in Germany is hampered by a lack of civilian child welfare resources. Treatment modes consist of punitive military measures taken
against the abusive parents and the development of a foster family care
program through the cooperation of local United States military and
German authorities.

II

Prediction, Detection, and Prevention

A. PREDICTION

248 Asch, Stuart S., and Rubin, Lowell J. "Postpartum reactions: some
unrecognized variations." Am J Psychiatry 131(8): 870-74, August,
1974. (21 References).
Four frequently unnoticed postpartum syndromes and four illustrative case
studies are presented. Child battering is felt to be a postpartum reaction which specifically derives from a reawakening of the mother's childhood conflicts following delivery. Childbirth revives the new mother's
ambivalent conflict with her mother, which she acts out with the new
infant. The depressed reaction of a grandmother to the birth of her first
grandchild is considered. The grandmother reaction is typically manifested by a woman who herself has a history of postpartum depression.
The post adoption reaction of a woman who became psychotically depressed
after adopting an infant was attributed to the new mother's identification
with a mothering figure, as she assumed her new role. The vicissitudes of
the early relationship with the mother's mother is of equal importance to
the adoptive and to the natural mother. The father reaction, seen in a
case in which a man exhibited a radical personality change after the
birth of his first son, was also discussed. Awareness that postpartum
reaction need not involve the parturient, and that similar reactions occur
in successive generations of mothers, should aid in the anticipation of
postpartum psychopathology.

249 Barnett, Barnard. "Battered babies: letter to editor." Lancet
2(7672): 567-68, September 12, 1970. (0 References).
Stresses the point that a service which anticipates a family in crisis
should not be hospital based. The family physician providing antenatal
care is in the best position to predict problems and detect child abuse
in its early stages.

250 ————. "Violent parents: letter to editor." Lancet 2: 1208-9,
April 8, 1972. (6 References).
Cites an incident in which child neglect could have been prevented.
Evidence existed to show that neglect would probably occur, but nothing
was done to avert it. The physician of the family involved was not con-
sulted by the social service agency.

251 Bishop, F. I. "Children at risk." Med J Aust 1(12): 623-28,
March 20, 1971. (11 References).
Outlines a new protocol for preventing, detecting, and handling child
abuse. The distinguishing element is the increase in emphasis on the
psychological status of the parents, particularly for the purpose of

counteracting factors predisposing them to abusive behavior. The most
common features of at risk cases are listed. The protocol had succeeded
to some extent; of the seventy cases of child abuse handled in the new
way, only nine resulted in the issuance of Care and Protection orders.

252   Brody, Howard, and Gaiss, Betty. "Ethical issues in screening for
       unusual child-rearing practices." Pediatr Ann 15(3): 106-12,
       March, 1976. (3 References).
Considers ethical issues arising from Ray Helfer's proposed program for
the screening of parents with childrearing practices or attitudes that
correlate highly with the occurrence of child abuse and for an intervention program for those parents determined to be at high risk by the
screening test. Whether or not such a program should be mandatory or
voluntary is the major issue covered. Arguments in support of a mandatory
screening program emphasize the child's right to be free from physical
and psychologic harm, make analogies between this proposal and other
routine screening programs, such as mandatory venereal disease tests for
hospital employees, and point out that those parents in the most need of
help are the least likely to volunteer for assistance. Arguments in support of voluntary screening and intervention state that a mandatory program would be a serious infringement on the rights of parents and would
increase the chances of receiving false-positive predictions, leading to
public distrust of the health professions. In addition, parents pressured
into a parenting-skills education program may not be motivated to learn
the material anyway, and law enforcement agencies may seek to subpoena
the results of screening tests as a form of evidence in abuse cases. Any
program, whether mandatory or voluntary, should seek a balance between
the rights of all parties involved, minimize the emotional effects of
labeling, and inform participants that screening for a problem does not
definitely diagnose it.

253   Chamberlain, Nancy. "The nurse and the abusive parent." Nursing '74
       4(10): 72-73, 75-76, October, 1974. (0 References).
Examines the role of the nurse in identifying potentially abusive parents
and in working directly with child abusers. The nurse may be able to
pick up clues concerning parents' attitudes toward children if she works
in a prenatal, pediatric, public health, school, or in an emergency room
setting. She should be alert to unusual types of injuries and suspicious
histories. In dealing with abusive parents, the nurse should be non-
judgmental and honest and should attempt to seek relevant information
without alienating the parents. The importance of reporting child abuse
is stressed.

254   De Francis, Vincent; Zaphiris, Alexander G.; Philbrick, Elizabeth;
       et al. Selected reading materials: training workshop on child
       protective services. Denver, Colorado: The American Humane
       Association, Children's Division, 1968. 67p. (Bibliography).
Includes excerpts from various papers presented at a training workshop
for child protective services workers. Data gathered from a study of the
availability, scope, and effectiveness of child protective services in
the fifty states is cited. The preventive role of protective services in
assessing cases of neglect and the coadjutant, non-punitive role of the
juvenile court in recommending remedial treatment for the family as substitutes for punishment are discussed. An examination of the pathology
of neglecting parents uncovered an adult who was immature, impulsive,

unable to make decisions, and weighted down with a sense of failure. A dual approach for the prevention of neglect and abuse is recommended. The primary focus for prevention should be the promotion of an environment conducive to the positive mental health of all persons. The availability of medical, educational, and financial resources for the population at large would begin to meet this criterion. Secondary foci for prevention include the treatment of specific parental problems and improved techniques for predicting potentially abusive parents. Additional articles discuss the statutory and popular definitions of neglect, the different levels of evidence and testimony in court, and the problems involved in the disposition of a case.

255 Friedman, Stanford B., and Morse, Carol W. "Child abuse: a five-year follow-up of early case finding in the emergency department." Pediatrics 54(4): 404-10, October, 1974. (18 References).
Continues a 1968 study by Holter and Friedman. From an original group of 156 children treated for injuries at the University of Rochester Medical Center, fifty-four were selected for a follow-up investigation. The original injuries sustained had been judged a result of abuse, neglect, or accident by Holter and Friedman. The present authors wished to test the reliability of those diagnoses as predictive of subsequent risk to the child and his siblings. They found that children from the suspected abused and neglected groups incurred more high risk injuries such as head injuries, fractures and burns, whereas children from the accident group sustained less serious lacerations and ingestions. In addition, only 50 percent of the siblings from the accident group, as compared with 72 and 80 percent of the siblings from the abused and neglected groups, suffered injuries during the five-year interval. The statistical evidence, however, is not definitive enough to allow the generalization of the findings.

256 Gordon, R. R. "Predicting child abuse: letter to editor." Br Med J 1(6064): 841, March 26, 1977. (0 References).
Presents a method for the detection of potential child abusers by identifying six perinatal characteristics of the mother. It is suggested that the social causes of infant abuse and cot deaths may be different.

257 Helfer, Ray E.; Schneider, Carol; Hoffmeister, James K.; et al. Manual for use of the Michigan Screening Profile of Parenting (MSPP). East Lansing, Michigan: Michigan State University, 1977. 17p. (Bibliography).
Describes the administration of and uses for the MSPP as a tool in measuring parental attitudes. The questionnaire is formulated on the assumptions that most parents want to react positively toward their children, and a parent's performance is, to a great extent, determined by his childhood experiences with his own parents. The questionnaire has a seven-point agree-disagree format and measures five clusters of variables: Relationship with Parents; Emotional Needs Met; Dealing with Others; Expectations of Children; and Coping. The MSPP is a screening, not a diagnostic, instrument. Its use in research is stressed.

258 Hurd, Jeanne M. "Assessing maternal attachment: first step toward the prevention of child abuse." JOGN Nurs 4(4): 25-30, July-August, 1975. (0 References).
The obstetric nurse is viewed as being in an ideal position to detect the early signs of child abuse, before the actual violence has begun. She

can observe and assess maternal attachment as expressed through contact,
feeding behavior, and the attitudes the mother verbalizes toward the
responsibilities of child care. An effective referral system is necessary
in each hospital, so that nurses who strongly suspect a disturbed parent-
child relationship may ensure that further investigation and follow-up
procedures are instituted. It is emphasized that a nurse's observation
and assessment of maternal responsiveness and further evaluation (if
necessary) become as important in postnatal procedure as routine physical
examination.

259   Lynch, Margaret A., and Roberts, Jacqueline. "Predicting child abuse:
        signs of bonding failure in the maternity hospital." Br Med J
        1(6061): 624-26, March 5, 1977. (18 References).
In a study conducted at a maternity hospital, fifty abused or high risk
children were compared to fifty controls. Five factors were frequently
found in the abused group: (1) admission to a special baby care unit;
(2) indications of emotional disturbance; (3) mother's age being twenty
or less; (4) referral to a social worker; and (5) some degree of concern
(recorded) about the child's welfare. There were more unemployed fathers
and unsupported mothers in the abused group, more complications in pregnancies for this group, and many more pre-term babies born in the high
risk group. These findings indicate a need for measures to predict the
probability of child abuse.

260   McKenzie, Michael W.; Stewart, Ronald B.; Roth, Sally S. "Child
        abuse -- what the pharmacist should know." J Am Pharm Assoc
        15(4): 213-17, April, 1975. (20 References).
Broadly considers the phenomenon of the abused child. The pattern of
child abuse is highlighted, along with criteria depicting potential child
abusers and precipitating events.

261   Mitchell, Ross G. "The incidence and nature of child abuse." Dev
        Med Child Neurol 17(5): 641-44, October, 1975. (2 References).
Investigates the incidence, manifestations, and probable causes of child
abuse in our society. It is recommended that highest priority be placed
on recognizing abuse at its earliest stages and on recording the pattern
and nature of reported injuries. Eventually, with the help of such
information, an early warning system for abuse could be developed and
measures for preventing further abuse initiated.

262   Mogielnicki, R. Peter; Mogielnicki, Nancy; Chandler, James E.; et al.
        "Impending child abuse: psychosomatic symptoms in adults as a
        clue." JAMA 237(11): 1109-11, March 14, 1977. (7 References).
Demonstrates through three case histories that adults who are potential
or actual child abusers may develop functional symptoms (such as paralysis, headaches, or dizziness) that result in their seeking emergency
medical help. In psychiatric counseling, it is revealed that these
patients have a fear of losing control and acting out violently when
dealing with their children. By recognizing the association between
adults with functional symptoms and the potential for child abuse, social
services can provide intervention before serious child injury occurs.

263   Olson, Robert J. "Index of suspicion: screening for child abusers."
        Am J Nurs 76(1): 108-10, January, 1976. (0 References).
Presents a means for the early detection of problem parents by evaluating
family structures and classifying them in terms of four behavioral pat-

terns known to breed maltreatment of children. This screening index can be instrumental as a warning to initiate preventive action and is especially effective in a hospital maternity unit, where families whose children are at risk can be identified more easily. Four case studies of child abuse resulting from each of the four types of failures are cited.

264 "Parents about to abuse." Emerg Med 9(9): 213-14, 216, September, 1977. (2 References).
Several case histories illustrate that psychogenic weakness and paralysis can identify an abusive parent or one with tendencies to abuse. Physicians should question such patients about their present family situations and their childhood backgrounds. Some methods of interviewing the patient are included.

265 Paulson, Morris J.; Afifi, Abdelmonem A.; Chaleff, A.; et al. "An MMPI scale for identifying 'at risk' abusive parents." J Clin Child Psychol 4(1): 22-24, Spring, 1975. (13 References).
Evaluates the use of a Minnesota Multiphasic Personality Inventory (MMPI) in the diagnosis of thirty-three abuse prone parents. The raw scores were turned into T scores so that the MMPI profile sheet could serve as a measure of pathology. The technique is seen as yielding great potential in identifying the predisposition to abuse.

266 Paulson, Morris J.; Afifi, Abdelmonem A.; Schwemer, Gregory T.; et al. "Parent Attitude Research Instrument (PARI): clinical vs. statistical inferences in understanding abusive mothers." J Clin Psychol 33(3): 848-54, July, 1977. (0 References).
Describes and gives the statistical results of a test given to measure the parental attitudes of abusive and non-abusive mothers. Since many studies have shown that abusive parents have pathological childrearing attitudes, it was thought that perhaps this test, the Parent Attitude Research Instrument (PARI), could be helpful in identifying potentially abusive parents. PARI was given to forty-four abusive mothers referred to the UCLA Child Trauma Intervention Project. It was given also to a control group, seventy mothers from the UCLA Pediatric Well-Baby Clinic. Both groups were primarily of the same socioeconomic standing (lower). Results showed that the test could correctly classify abusive and non-abusive mothers only 65 percent of the time and, hence, was not a reliable instrument to use alone in trying to identify potentially abusive parents. The study also cautions against overinterpretation of clinical data.

267 Polansky, Norman A., and Pollane, Leonard. "Measuring adequacy of child caring: further developments." Child Welfare 54(5): 354-59, May, 1975. (5 References).
Deals with the problem of defining, measuring, and identifying neglect. In order to measure the adequacy of child caring, the Childhood Level of Living Scale was developed. It was oirginally administered to sixty-three Appalachian poverty level families, and later to ninety-three families on AFDC, to test the scale's reliability and to determine how readily it could be administered by other staff members. Reliability coefficients were used to determine internal consistency of the tool. Findings indicated that although thirty-one of the seventy-seven sample items could be eliminated, the remainder proved to be highly reliable.

268 Wild, D. "Baby battering and its prevention." Midwives Chron Nurs Notes 84(1002): 242-44, July, 1971. (5 References).

Describes a surveillance system for the prevention and early detection
of child abuse. Various factors predisposing parents to abusive behavior
are listed, and the formal process for reporting suspected cases of child
battering is outlined. Courses of action available to county medical
officers receiving such reports are suggested.

B. DETECTION

269   Adelson, Lester. "Homicide by starvation." JAMA 186(5): 458-60,
      November 2, 1963. (2 References).
Decries the plight of the nutritionally "battered child" and suggests ways
to prevent such abuse. Five cases of starvation and the problems inherent
in those cases are described. The children were all under nine months of
age, and three of the five were born out of wedlock. The starved children
had had no medical observation or attention until they were brought dead
or dying to the hospital. The challenge is one of prevention. It is
necessary to attend closely to the "poor eater" or the failure to thrive
infant. Comparisons between the physically battered child and the nutritionally battered child are drawn. For example, in both cases, there is
often a discrepancy between the facts related by the parents and the
medical evidence.

270   Boardman, Helen E.; Barbero, Guilio J.; Morris, Marian G.; et al.
      The neglected battered-child syndrome. New York: Child Welfare
      League of America, 1974. 46p. (Bibliography).
Contains three articles on different aspects of child abuse. The first,
"Who Insures the Child's Right to Health?" discusses identification of
and legislation for abused children and calls for criteria to distinguish
between parents who can be helped to be responsible and those who cannot.
The second, "Malidentification of Mother-Baby-Father Relationships
Expressed in Infant Failure to Thrive," uses case studies to show that
babies admitted to the Children's Hospital of Philadelphia with a diagnosis of failure to thrive were often reflecting the depression or negative self-image of the mothers. The babies began to thrive when the
mothers could identify their infants with some good trait in themselves
rather than with some weakness. The third, "Role Reversal: A Concept
in Dealing with the Neglected/Battered-Child Syndrome," postulates that
reversal of the dependency role (in which parents turn to their children
for protection and nurturing) is a constant factor in child neglect and
abuse cases and can be used to diagnose the battered child syndrome.

271   Camps, F. E. "When infant death occurs." Nurs Mirror 133(20):
      14-15, November 12, 1971. (0 References).
Considers the various causes of infant death, focusing chiefly upon the
phenomenon of sudden unexpected death. Unsympathetic neighbors are urged
to be fair to bereaved parents, even those suspected of fatally beating
or neglecting their children. Current research into the mysterious sudden deaths of young infants is set forth, along with the two leading
theories concerning the phenomenon (one suggests a viral infection, the
other an allergic reaction). Both are given credence.

272   Fontana, Vincent J. "Battered child syndrome and brain dysfunction:
      letter to editor." JAMA 223(12): 1390-91, March 19, 1973. (3
      References).

Physicians must be reminded that child battering is the last phase of a range of symptoms comprising the maltreatment syndrome. Many of the less overt symptoms--such as emotional deprivation and nutritional neglect-- precede and help to predict abusive behavior.

273 Gurry, Desmond L. "Temper tantrums." Med J Aust 2(17): 948-51, October 21, 1972. (3 References).
Discusses the appropriate use of punishment in the curbing of temper tantrums. Physicians are advised to observe the behavior of the child having the tantrum and the response of the child's parents to the tantrum, since either could present cause for alarm.

274 Harris, M. J. "Discussion on 'the battered child syndrome.'" Aust J Forensic Sci 3(2): 77-78, December, 1970. (0 References).
Stresses the high probability of child abuse as the actual source of so- called "accidental" injury in young children, along with the frightening rate of recurrence of the battered child syndrome (30 percent). The identification of abusive and potentially abusive parents might be aided by improved communication among hospitals and among representatives of the medical, legal, and social professions, and the police. Other recommenda- tions include attention to the detection of abusive tendencies among pregnant women, the earlier diagnosis of abuse by physicians, and the wider availability of welfare agency services.

275 Helfer, Ray E. "What to do when the evidence hardens." Med Times 101(10): 127-28, October, 1973. (2 References).
All children suspected of being abused must be hospitalized for a thorough examination before a final diagnosis is made. Parents should be inter- viewed to determine their potential for abuse. Once information on both the parents and the child is assembled, the professionals who gathered it should confer with each other to reach a diagnosis. Combined team efforts for treating child abuse should be developed in all communities where more than twenty-five abuse cases are reported annually.

276 Hudson, Phoebe. "The doctor's handy guide to chronic child abuse." J Med Soc NJ 70(11): 851-52, November, 1973. (0 References).
Lists guidelines for the early detection of child abuse. These guide- lines are intended for use by physicians. Clues for observing both the mother and her child, as well as suggestions for interviewing the mother, are provided.

277 Koel, Bertram S. "Failure to thrive and fatal injury as a continuum." Am J Dis Child 118(4): 565-67, October, 1969. (13 References).
Points out that infants who are hospitalized for failure to thrive and later discharged to the home may be at risk of serious injury or death. Three case histories are presented in which the child was treated for failure to thrive, discharged, and subsequently readmitted in a critical condition due to physical abuse. Two of these infants died. Nutritional and developmental improvement of infants in the hospital is not sufficient treatment for the underlying problem--a defective parent-child relation- ship. Comprehensive follow-up treatment and support of the entire family is indicated if subsequent abuse is to be prevented.

278 O'Toole, Thomas J. "The speech clinician and child abuse." Lang Speech Hear Serv Sch 5(2): 103-6, April, 1974. (7 References).

Indicates that the speech clinician could play a role in the fight against child abuse, since such professionals come into close contact with a wide variety of children. Speech clinicians are urged to learn the signs of child abuse, to study the current laws on the problem, and to work to strengthen them.

279 Ounsted, Christopher. "Battered baby syndrome: tape review." Dev
     Med Child Neurol 10(1): 133-34, February, 1968. (0 References).
Supports the contention of Keith Simpson on his tape that medical professionals must be alert to the possibility of child battering in all cases of injured children. The reviewer disagrees with Simpson's belief that most batterers are of low intelligence and social class, maintaining that his contact with such parents is not restricted to members of any one stratum of society.

280 Parry, Wilfred H., and Seymour, Margaret W. "Battered-baby syndrome:
     letter to editor." Br Med J 3(5774): 584, September 4, 1971.
     (1 Reference).
Suggests that when one case of child abuse is detected in a family, the other children be examined for signs of battering as well.

281 Reinhart, John B., and Elmer, Elizabeth. "Love of children -- a
     myth?" Clin Pediatr 7(12): 703-5, December, 1968. (8 References).
Pediatricians fail to recognize child abuse because they believe that all parents love their children. This myth can be rebuked if the fact that children are often an emotional and financial burden to their parents is accepted. Incidences of maternal deprivation and neglect are presented. Several successful programs for the rehabilitation of abusive and neglectful mothers are presented. Physicians are urged to stop denying the existence of child abuse and to work instead toward recognition and treatment of the problem.

282 "'Team' held best hope in child-abuse intervention." Pediatr News
     9(3): 76, March, 1975. (0 References).
Assesses the utility of hospital-based child abuse teams, with particular reference to the one organized at the DeWitt Army Hospital. Team members at DeWitt include a psychiatrist, psychologist, pediatrician, emergency room physician, social services representative, hospital registrar, and community health nurse. The team is seen as increasing the chance for identifying cases, and providing continuous service to both child and parents; there is also the strong possibility that the team approach reduces mortality rates from child abuse.

283 Toby, Jackson. "An evaluation of early identification and intensive
     treatment programs for predelinquents." In: Raab, Earl. Major
     social problems. 3rd ed. New York: Harper & Row, 1973. 342-50.
     (4 References).
Challenges the assumptions and basis of early identification and treatment programs for predelinquents. The examination of two major studies, the Cambridge-Somerville Youth Study and the New York City Youth Board Prediction Study, shows that since the basis for determining predelinquency is unclear, the treatment plan must also be unclear. It is uncertain in both studies whether early identification is based on the inherent personality traits of the youngster or on the delinquent family and social milieu which surround him. Parental rejection or neglect could reinforce delinquent tendencies either by damaging the child's personality develop-

ment or by driving the child to seek acceptance from his peer group (possibly delinquent) in the neighborhood. Both studies were concluded to be inadequate because they could not resolve satisfactorily the following problems: (1) failure to establish firm criteria for identifying predelinquents; (2) inability to achieve accuracy in predictions; (3) confusion about what kind of intensive treatment would be effective; (4) confusion about how early such treatment should start; (5) how to avoid self-fulfilling prophecies in predicting delinquents; and (6) no clear understanding of the causes of delinquency.

C. INVESTIGATING AND REPORTING

1. GENERAL INVESTIGATIONS

284 Colclough, I. R. "Victorian government's report on child abuse: a reinvestigation." Med J Aust 2(27): 1491-97, December 30, 1972. (8 References).
Analyzes a study on child abuse conducted by the Victorian Government Committee. Oral and written evidence, obtained from various sources and medical superintendents from twelve hospitals, attempted to locate cases of maltreatment. Although very few cases were reported, the following reasons suggest that the study's findings failed to reflect the true incidence of abuse: (1) one hospital did not reveal information; (2) there was lack of enthusiasm on the part of several medical superintendents; and (3) the classification systems used by the hospitals were variable and very general. There was a significant discrepancy between the results of the Committee's survey and those of a similar survey conducted by a medical student. The latter found twenty-six cases of maltreatment occurring over a fourteen year period. Sixteen hospitals were visited, including seven of the hospitals contacted by the Government Committee. It is felt that the Committee's methods of investigation were quite inadequate for their purpose, and that the present system of voluntary reporting of abuse is ineffective. It is concluded that the community lacks adequate means for the protection of the abused child.

285 Geddis, D. C., and Thomas, P. S. "Identification of possible non-accidental injury in a casualty department." J Ir Med Assoc 70(3): 80-82, March 19, 1977. (15 References).
Investigated 386 casualties of children under four years of age to ascertain whether some of the deaths could be due to non-accidental injury. Criteria were developed to indicate which cases warranted further investigation. These included a delay of more than twenty-four hours between accident and attendance, history of previous fracture, inadequate history recorded on casualty chart, associated appearance of neglect, and others. If a child met one or more of these criteria, the patient's general practitioner and health visitor were asked if the injury could have been caused by physical abuse. It was concluded that non-accidental injury was a possible cause of death in nine cases.

286 Michael, Marianne K. "Follow-up study of abused children reported from university hospitals." J Iowa Med Soc 62(5): 235-37, May, 1972. (1 Reference).
Details a follow-up study of twenty-eight abused children reported from Iowa's University Hospital between 1965 and 1969. Questionnaires were

mailed to the local county where the referral had been made to investigate the social situation of the child at the time of the abusive incident and at present. Results indicate that at the time of the abuse, 85 percent of the children were two years old or younger. Twelve of the twenty-eight cases were the first and only child. In 57 percent of the sample families, both the natural father and mother were present in the home. Seven fathers and seven mothers had known medical or psychiatric problems prior to the incident of abuse. At the time of writing, twenty-six of the twenty-eight children were living with their natural mothers, and two were with adoptive mothers. Several plans for the management and prevention of child abuse, including family planning clinics, additional research in the area, a central registry for reporting abuse, and family life education classes, are recommended.

287 U.S. Congress. Senate. Committee on Labor and Public Welfare. Sub-
      committee on Children and Youth. Rights of children, 1972, Part I:
      Examination of the sudden infant death syndrome: Hearings. 92nd
      Congress, 2nd session, January 25, 1972. Washington, D.C.: U.S.
      Government Printing Office, 1972. 230p. (Bibliography).
A record of the Senate hearings conducted under the leadership of Senator Walter F. Mondale, chairman of the Subcommittee on Children and Youth of the Committee on Labor and Public Welfare, to examine what little is known about the sudden infant death syndrome, the greatest cause of death in infants under one year of age, and to encourage further research into its causes and its prevention.

288 U.S. Office of Child Development. Research and Evaluation Division.
      Research, demonstration, and evaluation studies, fiscal year 1972.
      Washington, D.C.: U.S. Government Printing Office, 1972. 61p.
      (DHEW Publication no. (OCD) 73-30).
Studies sponsored by the Department of Health, Education, and Welfare through the Office of Child Development in fiscal year 1972 are enumerated by subject area. Information presented includes amount and duration of each grant, along with a description of the project's goals and names and addresses of project directors.

2. THE ROLE OF PROFESSIONALS

289 American Humane Association, Children's Division. Guidelines for
      schools to help protect neglected and abused children. Denver,
      Colorado: The American Humane Association, Children's Division,
      1971. 6p.
Reviews the responsibility of educators in the problem of child abuse. Teachers can be instrumental in early detection and are encouraged to report. A list of indicators of abuse and neglect is included.

290 Anderson, John P.; Fraser, F. Murray; Burns, Kevin. "Attitudes of
      Nova Scotia physcans to child abuse." NS Med Bull 52(5): 185-89,
      220, October, 1973. (5 References).
Presents the results of a survey of the knowledge and attitudes of 144 Nova Scotia physicians and 703 other professionals about child abuse. The findings of the survey showed that 33.3 percent of the physicians and 36.0 percent of the other professionals had contact with between one and five cases of suspected child abuse within three years prior to being questioned. These figures confirm the fact that many suspected cases go un-

reported. Indeed, fewer than 50 percent of the physicians were aware of their legal obligation to report. An increasing professional acceptance of the abusive parent's need for treatment rather than punishment was indicated by the high percentage of respondents (69.4 percent--physicians; 74.0 percent--others) who believed that almost anyone could, at some time, injure a child in his care. Many respondents felt that they themselves had the capacity to injure a child (41 percent--physicians; 35.8 percent-- others). An analysis of the response suggested a number of recommenda- tions, including the establishment of a central registry to identify cases of abuse, comprehensive preventive services, and an interdiscipli- nary team approach to treatment.

291 Broadhurst, Diane D. "Project protection: a school program to de- tect and prevent child abuse and neglect." Child Today 4(3): 22-25, May-June, 1975. (1 Reference).
Describes a school program for the management of child abuse and neglect cases in Montgomery, Maryland called Project Protection. The project consisted of three phases. The policy revision phase included a state- ment of the obligations of all school personnel to report suspected cases of abuse and neglect and provided explicit definitions of these conditions. The second phase was composed of interdisciplinary conferences and staff educational programs geared toward the early identification and effective reporting of suspected cases. The third phase involved curriculum develop- ment to help school personnel and other interested community members to understand the causes of child abuse and to explore possible preventive measures. Academic courses investigated the relationship between violence, stress, and child abuse, studied the patterns of growth and development of the maltreated child, and reviewed the role of child protective services in the treatment of child abuse cases.

292 Browne, Kenneth M. "Wilful abuse of children." Nebr Med J 50(1): 598-99, December, 1965. (0 References).
Outlines the role of the physician in the diagnosis and reporting of suspected cases of child abuse and his potential value to the police in their investigations. Two illustrative case examples are briefly pre- sented.

293 Chang, Albert; Oglesby, Allan C.; Wallace, Helen M.; et al. "Child abuse and neglect: physicians' knowledge, attitudes and experi- ences." Am J Public Health 66(12): 1199-1201, December, 1976. (10 References).
Questionnaires were mailed to a sample of 3,000 pediatricians, radiolo- gists, and other physicians to investigate their knowledge, attitudes, and experiences in the field of child abuse and neglect. The results indicated that most respondents believed that physicians should report cases of child abuse, while fewer believed that physicians usually report them. A minority believed that the existing services were adequate, although a majority felt that awareness of the problem was increasing. It is concluded that education on the procedures for reporting abuse, development of reliable systems for detection of abuse, and clarification of the roles of community agencies are needed.

294 Colucci, N. D., Jr. "The schools and the problem of child abuse and neglect." Contemp Educ 48(2): 98-100, Winter, 1977. (7 References).

Discusses the contributions that schools can make toward detecting and reporting abused and neglected children. Measures to facilitate action by schools include special detection training programs for teachers. Educators should be informed of their responsibility to report suspected cases of abuse, and they should be given specific instructions regarding reporting procedures. Improved communication between schools and protective service agencies, as well as a campaign to educate the public about abuse, are essential.

295 Crown, Barry; Redlener, Irwin; Benson, Irene. "Attitudes to children's accidents: letter to editor." Lancet 1(7959): 590, March 13, 1976. (0 References).
Refutes the idea that parents should be given the benefit of the doubt when there is even the slightest indication that child abuse could have occurred. Observations of the parents' behavior can often lead to suspicion of abuse on the part of the physician. These suspicions must be followed through if the rights of the child are to be protected.

296 Dennis, James L. "Child abuse and the physician's responsibility: editorial." Postgrad Med 35(4): 446, April, 1964. (0 References).
Cites statistics of a 1962 survey indicating the incidence of reported child abuse in the United States. Increased physician protection through effective laws and examination of causal factors are presented as a means of coping with the problem of prevention.

297 Duke, R. F. N. "Attitudes to children's accidents: letter to editor." Lancet 1(7953): 257, January 31, 1976. (0 References).
Suggests that investigating a child's injuries for suspected abuse can be damaging to the parents if it is later determined that the injuries were, in fact, accidental. Parents should be given the benefit of the doubt when the physician is merely suspicious that abuse may have occurred.

298 Education Professions Development Consortium. Lift a finger: the teacher's role in combating child abuse. Houston, Texas: Education Professions Development Consortium C, 1975.

299 Fontana, Vincent J. "Recognition of maltreatment and prevention of the battered child syndrome: letter to editor." Pediatrics 38(6, Part I): 1078, December, 1966. (0 References).
Urges physicians to educate themselves about early signs of maltreatment in order to prevent severe child abuse. Despite some pediatricians' reluctance to report such cases, it is their moral responsibility and the only means of protecting these children from further harm.

300 Griggs, Shirley A., and Gale, Patricia. "Abused child: focus for counselors." Elem Sch Guid Couns 11(3): 186-94, February, 1977. (13 References).
Illustrates the role of the educator and school counselor in the detection of child abuse and neglect through two exemplary stories. Abused children often rely on repression, withdrawal, and self-deception as a means of coping with a hostile family environment. Upon suspecting a case of child abuse, the counselor must be ready to fulfill the requirements of the child abuse reporting law in his state.

301 Harriman, Robert L. "Child abuse and the school." For a summary
     see: Diss Abstr Int 36A(9): 5689, March, 1976.

302 Kibby, Robert W.; Sanders, Lola; Creaghan, Sidney; et al. "The
     abused child -- the need for collaboration." Thrust Educ Leadersh
     4(5): 11-13, May, 1975. (5 References).
Summarizes the motivation, content, and results of a symposium and workshops on child abuse in a California school district. Educators learned
that only a fraction of child abuse cases are reported, and that abusive
parents are found in all socioeconomic groups. Teachers must begin to
assume responsibility for detecting child abuse, contacting parent and
social worker, and familiarizing themselves with techniques of family
intervention. The symposium and workshops emphasized that cooperation
among teachers, social workers, sheriff's office, and other agencies is
necessary to successfully prevent child abuse.

303 "Lesson not yet learned: editorial." Br Med J 1(5956): 477-78,
     March 1, 1975. (3 References).
Refers to an abuse incident in which a three-year-old boy suffered permanent injury. It was felt that the injury could have been prevented by
more vigorous action on the part of the physician and the social worker
involved. Although alert professionals must be ready to act in such
cases, the long-term solution of the problem of child abuse depends upon
the alleviation of debilitating social and economic conditions.

304 Mindlin, Rowland L. "Child abuse and neglect: the role of the
     pediatrician and the Academy." Pediatrics 54(4): 393-95, October,
     1974. (10 References).
Pediatricians are called upon to further educate both themselves and the
community in the recognition and management of child abuse. Freedom
from legal liability should encourage more physicians to report suspected
cases, while group decision-making in formulating individual treatments
will better assure the child's welfare.

305 Morse, Thomas S. "Child abuse, a neglected form of trauma:
     editorial." J Trauma 15(7): 620-21, July, 1975. (4 References).
Reviews the surgeon's role in the management of child abuse. Surgeons
are encouraged to increase their participation in reporting and recording suspected cases of abuse. A lack of participation can lead to tragic
results for the child involved.

306 Pickett, Lawrence K. "Role of the surgeon in the detection of child
     abuse." Conn Med 36(9): 513-14, September, 1972. (5 References).
The role of the surgeon in the detection and reporting of suspected abuse
is outlined. In Yale-New Haven Hospital, attending physicians report
such cases to the DART (Detection, Appraisal, Referral, and Treatment)
multidisciplinary committee for the management of child abuse. A central
registry on all families where abuse has been suspected or proven is
maintained by the Welfare Department of the State of Connecticut for use
by the committee of physicians.

307 "Protecting children from abuse and neglect: phase II." Curr
     Public Health 7(10): 1-4, November-December, 1967. (21 Refer-
     ences).
Reviews the problem of child abuse, with particular focus on the responsibility of physicians to report suspected cases, and the provision of

protective services by the community. Prevention is discussed in terms
of breaking the chain of abuse which binds families from generation to
generation.

308 "Reporting of child abuse by school personnel: editorial." Public
     Health Rep 84(1): 219-20, January, 1969. (0 References).
In Syracuse, the schools serve as the largest source of reports regarding
child abuse, particularly in the case of older children whose injuries
might not require medical attention. But despite the fact that staff
members in the schools are required to report suspected abuse, many are
unaccountably afraid to perform this duty.

309 Ryan, James H. "The battered child deserves a better deal." Prism
     1(5): 39-43, August, 1973. (0 References).
Examines two instances in which the failure of the physician to adequately
investigate a case of child abuse led to unfortunate results--in one case,
the death of a child and in the other, the child's permanent removal from
his home.

310 Santhanakrishnan, B. R.; Shetty, M. Vasanthakumar; Raju, V.
     Balagopala. "PITS syndrome." Indian Pediatr 10(2): 97-100,
     February, 1973. (5 References).
Describes three cases of battered children in detail, illustrating that
in each instance a distraught mother was responsible for the injuries.
In order to prevent further abuse, the emotional, social, and economic
stress suffered by childrearing mothers in Indian society must be lifted.
Physicians need to play a more active role in reporting suspected cases
of battering. Successful treatment depends on consistent detection as
early as possible.

311 Schmitt, Barton D. "What teachers need to know about child abuse
     and neglect." Educ Dig 41(7): 19-21, March, 1976. (0 Refer-
     ences).
Because the teacher is in a strategic position to identify and report
child abuse and neglect, guidelines for detection and intervention are
presented. If a child often comes to school with many bruises, wears
long clothing on a hot day, or is very aggressive, abuse should be
suspected. If the child brings meager lunches to school, or consumes
huge quantities of the school lunch, then nutritional deprivation is a
possibility. A child is being neglected medically if he is not provided
with needed eyeglasses, immunizations, or general health care. When
physical abuse is suspected, the teacher should contact the child protective agency immediately. In the case of nutritional and medical neglect,
the teacher should notify the parents first in order to call attention
to the child's needs. If the parents' care of the child does not improve, the case should then be reported to the child protective agency.

312 Sgroi, Suzanne M. "The abused child -- physicians' obligations:
     editorial." Conn Med 39(7): 418, July, 1975. (0 References).
The mandatory child abuse reporting law and the services designed to
facilitate the reporting process in Connecticut are outlined. Private
physicians tend to report suspected abuse cases far less frequently than
hospital emergency rooms; their obligation to report is stressed.

313 Simons, Betty, and Downs, Elinor F. "Medical reporting of child
     abuse: patterns, problems, and accomplishments." NY State J Med
     68(17): 2324-30, September 1, 1968. (6 References).

Analyzes the patterns of medical reporting of child abuse between 1964
and 1967 in New York City. Most reporting was done by hospitals, while
physicians in private practice and school personnel reported significantly
fewer cases. It was discovered that whenever an amendment to the child
abuse law or a particular case of abuse received a great deal of attention in the media, the amount of reporting would increase dramatically
for the following month. Thus, reporting patterns appeared to reflect
reporter sensitivity to the problem rather than actual changes in the
incidence of abuse. Reasons for failure to report abuse and suggestions
for improving recognition and reporting are given.

314   Smith, Selwyn M. "Child injury intensive monitoring system: letter
      to editor." Br Med J 3(5880): 593-94, September 15, 1973. (0
      References).
Asserts the view that improvements in already adequate monitoring systems
will not alter physician reluctance to provide essential information nor
insure effective management of the battered baby syndrome.

315   Trouern-Trend, John B. G., and Leonard, Martha. "Prevention of child
      abuse: current progress in Connecticut -- I: 'The problem.'"
      Conn Med 36(3): 135-37, March, 1972. (5 References).
Severe physical injury is only at the extreme end of a wide spectrum of
child abuse. The causes of physician underreporting, such as failure or
reluctance to recognize the problem, fear of punitive action to oneself,
the child or his family, and ignorance of reporting legislation are discussed. Several factors that can lead to the suspicion of child abuse
are outlined, including the type of injury, the presence of a stressful
family situation, and a time delay in seeking treatment for an injury to
a child.

316   Wolff, Howard. "Are doctors too soft on child beaters?" Med Econ
      43(21): 84-87, October 3, 1966. (0 References).
Discusses the frequent failure of physicians to report cases of child
abuse. The major reasons for this failure are enumerated with examples.
A number of physicians simply have not gained experience in diagnosing
child abuse, and so they fail to recognize its symptoms. Others, despite
the immunity granted them by the reporting laws, and despite the injunction to report all suspected cases, are reluctant to damage their relationships with their patients, and fear that they may accuse innocent
parties and do permanent harm. This is especially true of private
practitioners; often if the parents are well-dressed and well-spoken,
the physician finds the charge of abuse incongruous. Such physicians are
advised of the grave consequences of their failure to act.

3. HOSPITALS, AGENCIES, AND CENTRAL REGISTERS

317   Berlow, Leonard. "Recognition and rescue of the 'battered child.'"
      Hospitals 41(2): 58-61, January 16, 1967. (8 References).
Describes the battered child syndrome in general terms ranging from
definitions, causes, and physical manifestations to legislation designed
to facilitate reporting and treatment. Lists of the typical behavior
patterns of battered children and battering parents are included as guidelines for recognizing them in hospital situations. Once cases are
recognized, the problem is ensuring that they are reported. All too often
physicians are reluctant to do so. Here hospitals can play a major role

by thoroughly investigating a child's injuries and by taking responsibility for reporting them to the proper authorities.

318   Besharov, Douglas J. "An appraisal of current use and abuse of central registries." In: National Symposium on Child Abuse, 5th, Boston, 1974. Collected papers. Denver, Colorado: The American Humane Association, Children's Division, 1976. 110-14. (0 References).

Discusses the ineffective use of central registries. Agencies are not using registries in prevention or treatment nor is the information contained in the registries up-to-date or specific. All reports need a follow up which indicates whether the report was valid or not, a procedure not being practiced. In order to protect their rights, registry families should have access to their files in case they wish to petition for the emendation of erroneous information.

319   "Child abuse registry aids in prevention." Pediatr News 9(4): 58, April, 1975. (0 References).

Reports on the success of a central registry in Dade County, Florida. The registry has provided new insight into the identification, treatment, and prevention of child abuse.

320   Cullinan, T. R. "Children at risk." Lancet 2(7575): 966-67, November 2, 1968. (3 References).

Stresses the need for at risk registers to be used by general practitioners for the purpose of monitoring the growth and progress of children who might not otherwise, for health or environmental reasons, develop normally. Children included in the register would remain under the observation of a pediatrician and a health visitor.

321   Danckwerth, Edward T. "Techniques of child abuse investigations." Police Chief 43(3): 62-64, March, 1976. (0 References).

The police officer investigating suspected child abuse must be mindful of the priorities of this responsibility. First, he must protect the child, taking the child into immediate protective custody if abuse is suspected. Then he must gather evidence for possible prosecution. Most evidence in child abuse cases consists of physical evidence, as well as information gained in interviews and investigations of medical records. Common signals to which the officer investigating abuse should be alerted are listed. Immediate arrest of suspected parents is not as necessary as immediate protection of the child, because arrest makes prosecution unavoidable, and child abuse is best treated by a multidisciplinary approach.

322   Diggle, Geoffrey, and Jackson, Graham. "Child injury intensive monitoring system." Br Med J 3(5875): 334-36, August 11, 1973. (10 References).

Analyzes a computer-based system of recording and processing critical information about child abuse. Implementation of the system is designed to progress in three stages from acquiring lesser to more comprehensive information on an ever-increasingly broader geographical basis. Although the problem of maintaining medical confidentiality is an immediate concern when processing information in systems of this magnitude, the organizers feel that the system protects the rights of parents and children while helping communities accurately assess the incidence of abuse.

323   Fraser, Brian. "Towards a more practical central registry (child
      abuse cases)." Denver Law J 51(4): 509-28, 1974. (50 Refer-
      ences).
Examines the concept, necessity, and problems associated with a central
registry. The purpose of such a registry is to compile research
about the identification process, assist the physicians and courts in
diagnosis, and aid social service agencies in follow-up. Information
compiled by the central registry is offered only to those people permitted by the law, such as physicians, agencies, and others. To solve the
problem of transience between states, a federal central registry is
suggested which would be based on a standard definition of abuse. An
appendix stating the statutory provisions for central registries, locations, accessibility, and safety factors of each state is included.

324   Goldacre, Patricia, and Hoffman, Mary. "From baby farms to yo-yo
      children." Times Educ Suppl 3134: 20-21, July 4, 1975. (0
      References).
Argues against the feasibility of a national registry which would list
the names of all injured children for purposes of investigating child
abuse. Such a register could: (1) cause unfair suspicion and punishment
of parents in cases of a child's accidental or self-inflicted injuries;
(2) destroy confidentiality for psychiatrists and other professionals
and, hence, scare off people who might otherwise seek help; (3) cause
abusive families to move around even more to avoid attention, creating
more of the kind of isolation that often leads to abusiveness in the
first place; and (4) further damage the emotional state of the abused
child or increase the abusive parent's hostility of the child.

325   Hessel, Samuel J., and Rowe, Daniel S. "Rights of parents and chil-
      dren: letters to editor." N Engl J Med 283(3): 156-57, July
      16, 1970. (2 References).
Responds to a previous article outlining a program for hospital detection
and registration of abuse families. The legal rights of registry families
are of concern as the justification of keeping files on families whose
cases are never reported to state agencies is questionable, and the
terminology used to label abuse patients remains unclearly defined. The
author of the criticized article responds that concern for parents'
rights is valid, but that the primary consideration is the protection of
the child and not prosecution of the parents.

326   Hudson, Phoebe. "How to set up a no-budget battered child program."
      J Med Soc NJ 70(6): 441-42, June, 1973. (2 References).
Describes an effective no-budget system for reporting suspected cases of
battered children in Bergen County, New Jersey, and stresses that this
system could be initiated by other counties with little effort. Prior to
these procedures, the problems of reporting and obtaining professional
and legal counsel had become so acute that a small group of professionals
took action and outlined how their county could quickly remedy the situation. They first aroused community concern through the media and distributed pamphlets to medical professionals outlining reporting procedures.
They also obtained legal representation for the child from the prosecutor's office.

327   Ireland, William H. "The mission and functions of central regis-
      tries." In: National Symposium on Child Abuse, 5th, Boston, 1974.
      Collected papers. Denver, Colorado: The American Humane Associa-
      tion, Children's Division, 1976. 106-9. (0 References).

The purpose of central registries should be to identify and record information about potential or previous abusers. Agencies should be able to use information collected by registries to predict abuse, to develop programs for its control, and to evaluate the effectiveness of existing procedures and laws.

328 ————. "A registry on child abuse." Children 13(3): 113-15, May-June, 1966. (0 References).
Reports on the effectiveness and operation of the Illinois state central registry of abuse cases. Central registries generally provide for: (1) a definition of the problem; (2) a program of control; (3) the recording and analysis of information; and (4) the evaluation of programs. The administration of each state registry is based on the state's reporting laws. The Illinois system files only those cases reported by hospitals or persons required by law to report. The family is investigated, a report is made, and necessary aid offered. Welfare departments throughout the state may obtain information previously gathered on a family through the registry and can avoid duplicated efforts. The registry has been helpful in alerting the public about the incidence of abuse.

329 Lovens, Herbert D., and Rako, Jules. "A community approach to the prevention of child abuse." Child Welfare 54(2): 83-87, February, 1975. (4 References).
Relates the efforts of one community to establish a cross-indexed register to identify children living in potentially abusive or neglectful homes. The goals of the multidisciplinary Vulnerable Child Committee include: (1) early identification of vulnerable children; (2) preventive intervention which will enable parents to solve their problems before they resort to abusive behavior; and (3) education of the general public and professionals in the manifestation of child abuse and neglect.

330 Nyden, Paul V. "The use of authority." Public Welfare 24(3): 239-45, 252, July, 1966. (4 References).
Defines and discusses child abuse--its history, legal ramifications, diagnosis, and treatment. The need for cooperation between physicians, the court system, and law enforcement agencies is stressed, as is the role of the community, schools, and hospitals in preventing or identifying child abuse.

331 Reinitz, Freda G. "Special registration project on the abused child: letter to editor." Child Welfare 44(2): 103-5, February, 1965. (2 References).
Examines an experiment in registering abused children by the Philadelphia-Camden Social Service Exchange. Children registered with the Exchange who were believed to be severely endangered by abuse or neglect received special notation in the registry, which later facilitated referrals to courts, hospitals, and other agencies, and enabled the Exchange to provide some kind of survey of the severity of child abuse in the area. Similar action by all agencies and hospitals receiving children is recommended.

332 Rowe, Daniel S.; Leonard, Martha F.; Seashore, Margretta R.; et al. "A hospital program for the detection and registration of abused and neglected children." N Engl J Med 282(17): 950-52, April 23, 1970. (9 References).

A hospital program, established for the detection and registry of child abuse and neglect cases, is described. A committee was established at Yale University Medical Center for policy development, staff consultation, and review of suspected cases. Once abuse seems indicated by the committee, the staff member is urged to report the case to the state health or welfare department, and the patient's name is filed in the center's registry. Results of the program indicate a discrepancy between the number of abuse cases reported to the center and those reported to the state agencies. Physicians are more at ease reporting suspicions within the center where they work; evidence accumulated by the registry often supports their findings. Other strengths of the program include twenty-four hour access to the registry files, the listing of high risk and neglected children, and the staff's heightened awareness of the possibility of abuse.

333 Sheridan, Mary D. "Children at risk: letter to editor." Lancet
    2(7577): 1077-78, November 16, 1968. (1 Reference).
Argues that the at risk register should do more than just identify at risk children, but it must see to it that all such infants and their families receive health, social, and educational services regularly as the child develops.

334 Wathey, Richard, and Densen-Gerber, Judianne. Preliminary report on
    the sociological autopsy in child abuse deaths. Presented at the
    American Academy of Forensic Sciences Twenty-seventh Annual Meeting.
    Chicago: Odyssey Institute, 1976. 22p.
Illustrates the method of sociological autopsy of the events and background leading to child abuse resulting in the death of the child. Joanie's background led to the abuse of her own child. A lack of interagency cooperation caused confusion and indecisive planning for Joanie's welfare. Adoption or permanent foster home placement early in her life, in retrospect, seemed a necessity. Yet she was passed from one foster home to another, repeating her mother's own cycle of drug addiction and prostitution. After authorities allowed her to have a child and marry a drug addict at age fifteen, signs of the baby's abuse, though noted, were not reported to a protective agency. This omission was critical in light of the infant's subsequent death. Consistent treatment, decisiveness, and interagency cooperation appear to be the crucial preventive steps in similar instances.

335 Whiting, Leila. "The central registry for child abuse cases: re-
    thinking basic assumptions." Child Welfare 56(1): 761-67,
    January, 1977. (2 References).
Evaluates the function of central registries. The question of whether central registries can function without names is raised. The purposes of the registry are to receive reports on a twenty-four-hour basis, analyze the procedures of various local departments, keep records of families of suspected or confirmed abuse, and analyze statistics of child abuse incidence. It is a misconception that registries can be used to "track" abusive families, as statistics show that these families do not leave their communities once they are reported. Because information on the registry is not always accurate and up-to-date, it is suggested that codes replace names on the registry in order to protect rights of privacy. If central registries are to be useful in evaluating current programs, accurate information must be reported immediately. The trend to computerize central registries is criticized, as machines have been known to print

out confidential information by mistake. The best method of protecting children is by immediate investigation of reports and not by computer-operated registries.

D. PREVENTIVE MEASURES

1. PROTECTIVE PROGRAMS AND CENTERS

336   Allen, Anne, and Morton, Arthur. This is your child: the story of the National Society for the Prevention of Cruelty to Children. London: Routledge and Kegan Paul, 1961. 198p.

337   Allison, Patricia K. "Exploration of a program of preventive inter- vention in the early parent-infant interaction." For a summary see: Diss Abstr Int 35A(7): 4689-90, January, 1975.

338   Alvy, Kerby T. "Preventing child abuse." Am Psychol 30(9): 921- 28, September, 1975. (43 References).
Two approaches to understanding the problem of child abuse, namely, the comprehensive approach and the narrow approach, are presented. The first approach defines abuse in a broad sense. It stresses children's rights in society and distinguishes three types of abuse: collective, institu- tional, and individual. Furthermore, it accuses all of society of either intentionally or unintentionally contributing to abuse by not adequately guaranteeing the protection of children's rights and health. The narrow approach avoids defining broad based values about children. Instead, it focuses on the individual perpetrators and victims of abusive acts. Cur- rent legislation represents this second approach. A discussion of the causative factors related to abuse, as well as abuse prevention tactics, is included. The stress is on the cultural toleration of violence and physical force in American caretaker-child interactions. Programs with prevention potential, as well as an assessment of the effectiveness of current abuse prevention efforts, are outlined.

339   American Academy of Pediatrics. Committee on Infant and Preschool Child. "Maltreatment of children: the battered child syndrome." Pediatrics 50(1): 160-62, July, 1972. (10 References).
A published statement on child abuse from the 1966 AAP Committee on Infant and Preschool Child is reviewed six years later. Several of the original recommendations for the reporting of child abuse and for the protection of the abused child are again supported. Additional recom- mendations for comprehensive prevention programs are added, however, since the earlier suggestions, even where implemented, have not been effective in reducing child abuse.

340   Anderson, C. Wilson. "Making family life safe for children." Public Welfare 23(2): 87-93, April, 1965. (9 References).
Discusses the changes which have occurred in available child welfare ser- vices over the last several decades. One major shift has been toward the preservation of the family, toward the treatment of the child within the family, and the improvement of the family environment, rather than the removal of the child. The most significant shift has occurred in the expansion of the concept of child welfare from being an optional service to becoming a policy priority. In that direction, much progress still needs to be made if the welfare of children is to be truly advanced.

341 Ayoub, Catherine, and Pfeifer, Donald R. "An approach to primary
     prevention: the 'At-Risk' program." <u>Child Today</u> 6(3): 14-17,
     May-June, 1977. (0 References).
Describes an interdisciplinary hospital-based child protection team organized by Hillcrest Community Hospital in Tulsa, Oklahoma, with special
emphasis on the At-Risk prevention program. The At-Risk program is
designed to detect potential abusers and to promote healthy parent-child
relationships. It consists of three basic functions: (1) in-patient
screening of infants and children; (2) in-patient protocol and teaching
programs in child and family health; and (3) a pediatric At-Risk Out-
patient Clinic. The program's outstanding success rate indicates that
family-oriented abuse prevention is possible.

342 Bard, M., and Zacker, J. "The prevention of family violence:
     dilemmas of community intervention." J[.]Marriage Fam 33(4): 677-
     82, 1974. (15 References).
Analyzes the problems involved in community prevention of intrafamilial
violence and describes a training program for police officers directed
at meeting these difficulties. The prevention of intrafamilial violence
has been hindered, first, by the traditional reluctance of poorer families (the group most plagued by intrafamilial violence) to approach a
social agency for help before violence has actually broken out, and
second, by the limitation in the ability of police officers to respond
effectively to requests for help in forestalling these outbreaks. The
program outlined met these problems by offering eighteen inner-city
police officers special training in mediating family disputes at a university psychological center. These officers intervened, during a
twenty-two month period, in 1,388 incidents involving 962 families. No
homicides occurred in the families concerned, none of the specially
trained intervening officers was assaulted (an impressive record given
the high probability of injury), and the special unit seemed well
received by the community.

343 Bilainkin, George. "Children in peril." <u>Contemp Rev</u> 201: 67-71,
     February, 1962. (0 References).
A rhetorical plea for greater protection for the abused and neglected
children of the United Kingdom. The National Society for the Prevention
of Cruelty to Children is criticized for its stance of keeping families
intact even when a child's life and welfare are threatened.

344 Broadhurst, Diane D. "Policy-making: first step for schools in
     the fight against child abuse and neglect." <u>Elem Sch Guid Couns</u>
     10(3): 222-26, March, 1976. (1 Reference).
Describes Project PROTECTION, a model program designed to identify and
prevent child abuse and neglect. The motivation, actual statement, and
implementation of the policy are discussed.

345 Burn, J. L. "The problem of the child neglected in his own home."
     <u>J R Sanit Inst</u> 72(4): 326-36, July, 1952. (0 References).
Reports on the problems, diagnosis, and treatment of child neglect. The
common feature in problem families is spiritual poverty and lack of purpose or vision for the future. Typical ills which may be blamed for
neglect, such as bad housing, poor health, or poverty, are often used as
rationales for neglect by the parents, but their remedy would not necessarily alter the child's plight. Team diagnosis is required to sort
through and understand complexities such as these. Preventive measures,

such as the strengthening of family and community life and legislative changes, are the primary steps toward remedying the situation. Case conferences among fieldworkers are also highly recommended as a means of sharing expertise and organizing case action.

346 Burne, Brien H. "Experts and child abuse: letter to editor." Br
     Med J 4(5939): 290-91, November 2, 1974. (0 References).
Discusses points of a previously published paper on the battered child by Selwyn M. Smith and Ruth Hanson. Burne affirms their multidisciplinary approach to the study of the battered child. A new community pediatric service consolidating the expertise and professional concern of general practitioners, psychologists, and clinical medical officers, should be available to all children and their parents as a preventative measure.

347 Carrington, William. "First aid in counseling: the deserted wife,
     husband, or children." Expository Times 78(11): 327-31, August,
     1967. (0 References).
Emphasizes the importance of the initial interview with the deserted husband or wife. The specific needs and immediate counseling of the deserted child are presented.

348 Cary, Ara C., and Reveal, Mary T. "Prevention and detection of
     emotional disturbances in preschool children." Am J Orthopsychiatry
     37(4): 719-24, July, 1967. (5 References).
Reviews a service conducted for mothers and preschool children by the Grand Rapids Child Guidance Clinic. The service is available to any family in the community, is voluntary, and consists of ten weekly meetings of twelve mothers with a psychiatric social worker while their children attend nursery school. Through lectures and discussion, the program is intended to give mothers a general assessment of their children's emotional growth. The nursery school provides the child with experiences conducive to healthy ego development and identifies those children who need some special therapeutic intervention. About 120 families participate in the clinic each year. It has been found that sensitive mothers who are generally tolerant of themselves and others respond particularly well.

349 Challenor, B., and Onyeani, L. "Health and legal services in a
     disadvantaged community." Am J Public Health 63(9): 810-15,
     September, 1973. (44 References).
Discusses the provision of a coordinated program of legal, medical, and social services to poor communities, with particular reference to the demands made by child abuse cases in these services. Improvements in the current coordination of services provided to the disadvantaged are enumerated; the establishment of a legal advocacy program is especially urged.

350 "Children in danger: editorial." Lancet 1(7866): 1090-91, June
     1, 1974. (4 References).
The British Paediatric Association's 1966 report and other early efforts to direct public attention to the problem of child abuse are cited. It notes the areas in which further work must be done, now that the problem has been generally recognized. Interdisciplinary problem solving—involving the cooperation of the police, social workers, and physicians—is recommended to institute and oversee training and to insure the follow-up of battering families. Further studies of the etiology of child abuse

are needed. Preventive measures must be taken to protect new babies
born into abusive families, which are likely to require the mobilization
of lay organizations and the clergy, as well as professionals.

351 Christy, Duane W. "Marshalling community resources for prevention
     of child neglect and abuse." In: National Symposium on Child
     Abuse, 4th, Charleston, S.C., 1973. Collected papers. Denver,
     Colorado: The American Humane Association, Children's Division,
     1975. 39-48.
Suggests causes and solutions for child abuse and neglect. Most abusive
parents are young and, because they were abused as children, often expect
their children to satisfy their needs. Reasons for child abuse and
neglect include family stress, handicaps of the child, alcoholism, drug
abuse, and parental immaturity. Treatment must include a variety of
twenty-four-hour community services provided by several disciplines.
Abusive and neglectful mothers need therapy and guidance in order to
facilitate the development of positive maternal behavior.

352 Court, Joan. "The battered child syndrome -- I: The need for a
     multidisciplinary approach." Nurs Times 67(22): 659-61, June
     3, 1971. (12 References).
Addresses the causes of battering and the importance of caring for the
parents as well as the children. Potentially dangerous parental behavior
must be detected early. In order to do so, medical and social professionals have to develop a higher index of suspicion and learn to recognize
symptoms of battering parents. Intervention measures must be initiated
while the situation is still urgent and while those involved recognize
the immediate need for help. Unnecessary delays can mean that treatment
procedures will never materialize. Although many agencies need to be
involved in intervention and treatment actions, the pressures and anxieties aroused while working with these families often lead to a lack of
cooperation and considerable tension among the agencies.

353 De Francis, Vincent. Accent on prevention. Denver, Colorado: The
     American Humane Association, Children's Division, 1957. 5p.
Funds should be appropriated not only for control and treatment of juvenile delinquency, but also for prevention of delinquency through community
recreation programs, street gang projects, and child protective services.
Neglect is seen as a primary cause of delinquency, and the child protective services are seen as the most effective way of preventing or
correcting neglect.

354 Ebeling, Nancy B. "Implications for protective service practice of
     recent advances in theory and practice." In: National Symposium
     on Child Abuse, 5th, Boston, 1974. Collected papers. Denver,
     Colorado: The American Humane Association, Children's Division,
     1976. 40-46. (5 References).
Presents an overview of current approaches to and attitudes about child
abuse. A deeper commitment by communities leading to improvements in
child protective services has accompanied a greater emphasis on children's
rights. More comprehensive legislation has increased the necessity for
communities to organize their available resources so that these new laws
can be implemented effectively. The multidisciplinary approach is the
most recent and effective model, although supportive services such as
day care or mothers' aids are needed. The dissemination of information
about individual programs is encouraged.

355   Emery, John, and Howells, John G. "Experts and child abuse: letters
      to editor." Br Med J 4(5935): 43-44, October 5, 1974. (3 Refer-
      ences).
Responds to an article describing the failures of protective services
which lead to the death of an abused child. The courts had returned the
child to its natural parents. In the future, greater interagency cooperation, stronger legal representation, identification of potential abuse,
immediate action to protect the child, and a change in society's reluctance to remove children from their natural parents will prevent more
deaths. The investigation of cot deaths as the result of abuse is also
encouraged.

356   Fairburn, Anthony C. "Small children at risk: letter to editor."
      Lancet 1(7796): 199-200, January 27, 1973. (0 References).
Briefly describes an intensive, interdisciplinary monitoring system of
families with preschool children who are thought to be at risk of severe
deprivation or physical abuse.

357   Fenby, T. Pitts. "The work of the National Society for the Preven-
      tion of Cruelty to Children (N.S.P.C.C.)." Int J Offender Ther
      16(3): 201-5, March, 1972. (0 References).
The efforts of the NSPCC to interrupt the cycle of child abuse and juvenile delinquency by working with parents and young children are outlined.

358   Ferro, Frank. "Protecting children: The National Center on Child
      Abuse and Neglect." Child Educ 52(3): 63-66, November-December,
      1975. (1 Reference).
Reports progress made by the National Center on Child Abuse and Neglect
and cites the importance of contributions made by educational personnel
toward protecting children. A list of the demonstration and research
projects and contracts that received federal funds through the National
Center during its first year is provided. One of the projects receiving
appropriations is discussed in detail. It was designed by the Education
Commission of the States to research the role of educational systems in
controlling child abuse and neglect. A description of various members
of the United States Department of Health, Education, and Welfare Intradepartmental Committee on Child Abuse and Neglect, organized by the
Office of Child Development, is also included.

359   Galdston, Richard. "Preventing the abuse of little children: the
      Parents' Center Project for the Study and Prevention of Child
      Abuse." Am J Orthopsychiatry 45(3): 372-81, April, 1975. (11
      References).
Examines the Parents' Center Project for the Study and Prevention of
Child Abuse established in 1969 in Brighton, Massachusetts, under the
support of the Grant Foundation, Inc. The project was designed to investigate intervention measures to protect abused children without removing
them from their families. Forty-six families with seventy-three children
participated in the program's two essential components, namely, the
Center, a therapeutic day care unit for treating the children, and the
Parents' Group, a weekly meeting where parents could ventilate their
personal problems. At the Center, the children showed marked improvement
in physical and psychic growth. Their parents showed less improvement,
however. During treatment, attempts were made to determine the causes
and persistence of the parents' complex and deeply rooted problems. Abuse
was a desperate attempt to avoid the pain of facing personal dissatisfac-

tion with their own lives, especially in terms of their sexuality. In spite of the parents' negligible improvement over the five years studied, treating them was found to be an integral part of treating the children.

360 Gaylin, Jody. "New help for battered children, and their parents." Psychol Today 11(1): 93-94, June, 1977. (0 References).
Reports on measures to prevent child abuse, instituted at the National Center for Prevention and Treatment of Child Abuse and Neglect in Denver. These measures include psychotherapy for parents, residential treatment for entire families, an at-home lay therapy program, a crisis nursery, and a therapeutic play school for abused children. An estimate places the Center's rate of success at more than 50 percent.

361 Green, Frederick C. "Help in preventing lead poisoning and child abuse." Young Child 31(5): 404-5, July, 1976. (2 References).
Two health problems relevant to infants and preschoolers—lead poisoning and child abuse—deserve special attention because of the potential for prevention if comprehensive health services were available to all children. It is emphasized that strong linkages between health programs in child caring facilities and community health facilities be established so that these problems could be alleviated.

362 Helfer, Ray E. "Early identification and prevention of unusual child-rearing practices." Pediatr Ann 5(3): 91-105, March, 1976. (12 References).
Compares programs for the early identification and prevention of unusual childrearing practices with similar models developed for diseases such as cystic fibrosis, polio, and measles. Child abuse is a severe manifestation of unusual childrearing practices and/or problems in parent-child interaction. Early identification programs for these behavior patterns could involve the administration of confidential Child Rearing Surveys to high school students and to pregnant women and observations of mothers with their babies in the delivery room and of both parents at first feedings. Those persons identified to be in the high risk category could be offered an intervention program. Possible objectives of these programs include teaching parenting skills, giving information about child development, developing trust in others, enhancing self-esteem, providing age-appropriate activities for children, and teaching methods of problem solving, crisis intervention, and resolution to parents. The prevention counterpart of Helfer's plan consists of: (1) offering courses in parenting and early child development to school-aged children as well as to persons enrolled in adult education programs; (2) encouraging immediate contact between parents and infant in the delivery room; (3) providing mother-baby aides in the hospital to facilitate maternal bonding; and (4) arranging home visits by volunteers or staff aides for up to six months after delivery.

363 Hepworth, H. P. "Looking at baby battering: its detection and treatment." Can Welfare 49(4): 13-14, July-August, 1973. (0 References).
Emphasizes the necessity for improving child health and welfare services in the fight against child abuse.

364 Housden, Leslie G. The prevention of cruelty to children. London: Cape, 1955. 406p. (Bibliography).

Presents a detailed historical overview of the work of the National Society for the Prevention of Cruelty to Children (NSPCC) in nineteenth century and present day Britain. In the last century, young children suffered both from their parents' acts of passive neglect and active cruelty. Infants were neglected by working mothers; abandoned children were compelled to wander about the streets begging and stealing; and whole families were crowded into squalid one-room living quarters where there was never enough to eat and often no bed or fire for minimal comfort. Children were regarded as their parents' possessions and were accordingly sent to work at a young age to the mines, textile factories, or as chimney sweeps where they were injured, killed in freakish accidents, or simply robbed of all human dignity. Other forms of cruelty to children were more blatant. Many desperate unwed mothers found shelter in lying-in houses. After the infant was born, the mother paid another woman to care for him or adopt him. The caretakers operated "baby farms" where infants were slowly starved, drugged with laudanum to still their crying, or killed outright if the mother had paid a flat fee instead of a weekly subsistence allowance. Moreover, it was the custom for private wet-nurses to get pregnant, find a position, and then abandon their own infants in order to nurse another woman's child for pay. Infant insurance and death clubs were common in Victorian England. For a small fee, newborns could be insured by their parents against burial expenses.

Certain unscrupulous parents saw this insurance as justification for neglecting their child. Infants were suffocated, starved, beaten, and poisoned with alcohol or teething powders. Orphans suffered equal persecutions when boarded out or sent to the workhouses. Living conditions in this century are often as crowded and unsanitary as in the previous. The NSPCC annually investigates hundreds of cases of child neglect and cruelty. Preventive measures which would improve both the social and the physical environments are advocated. Some of the recommendations include specific measures such as premarital counseling and instruction in home management and child care. Young children should be exposed to appropriate mothering models from infancy onward in order to cultivate for society a healthier and more responsible future generation of parents.

365 Kempe, C. Henry, and Silver, Henry K. "The problem of parental criminal neglect and severe physical abuse of children." AMA J Dis Child 98(4): 528, October, 1959. (0 References).
Summaries of a discussion of numerous case studies illustrating the problems of criminal neglect and physical abuse of children. The physician, social welfare agency, and legal system are seen as all too frequently failing in their responsibility to protect children, particularly when the harm done could have been foreseen and prevented.

366 "Maria Colwell and after." Br Med J 1(5903): 300, February 23, 1974. (5 References).
The problems inherent in the prevention of child abuse and other forms of intrafamilial violence, especially in the identification of potentially violent situations, are examined. One important barrier to effective prevention of such violence is the frequent lack of cooperation among physicians, social workers, and police officers in recognizing, reporting, and treating violence within the family. The study calls for follow-up studies evaluating measures designed to improve the utilization of the community's resources for dealing with child abuse and other forms of non-accidental injury in the home.

367 Mayer, J. "Protecting the pre-school child: edited by Paul Gyorgy and Anne Burgess: book review." Pediatrics 38(4, Part 1): 702, October, 1966. (0 References).

A review of Protecting the Pre-School Child, edited by Paul Gyorgy, M.D., and Anne Burgess, M.D. (Philadelphia: J. B. Lippincott Co., 1965), a work which contains the contributions of nutritionists, health educators, agriculturalists, social workers, and community development specialists. The collection is found to be a valuable source in the study of the nutritional needs of preschool children and of the difficulties involved in the fulfillment of these needs.

368 Nagi, Saad Z. "Child abuse and neglect programs: a national overview." Child Today 4(3): 13-17, May-June, 1975. (7 References).

The results of a national survey on child abuse and neglect are presented. Seven types of agencies and groups of respondents were interviewed, including child protective services, juvenile and family courts, police and sheriff departments, school systems, public health departments, hospital medical personnel, and hospital social services departments. The rate of reporting in all counties studied was 7.6 per 1,000. Of all the reports of abuse and neglect made in Florida (the state with the most effective reporting system), about 60 percent were eventually substantiated as entailing abuse and/or neglect. If this rate is projected to the national population, about 555,000 cases of child abuse and/or neglect would be substantiated annually. Police departments were the most consistent source of child abuse reports to child protective agencies, while private physicians were the least consistent. Several survey questions dealt with the temporary placement of abused children. Reports from protective services indicated that the majority of children are placed in foster homes, but some are placed with relatives or in detention homes. About 56 to 75 percent of the population lived in areas where there were no centers on child abuse and neglect, no treatment programs, nor interagency coordinative mechanisms. When respondents were asked to assess the effectiveness of child abuse programs, public health and protective service agencies representing 28 percent of the population rated them as largely ineffectual. When asked what services the programs lacked, counseling, placement facilities, and financial support were frequently indicated.

369 Newberger, Eli H. "Interdisciplinary management of child abuse: problems and progress." In: National Symposium on Child Abuse, 4th, Charleston, S.C., 1973. Collected papers. Denver, Colorado: The American Humane Association, Children's Division, 1975. 16-26.

Examines interdisciplinary management, accepted beliefs about management, and an ideal model for prevention and control of child abuse. Multidisciplinary management often suffers from lack of understanding and communication blocks between disciplines. Accepted beliefs on management stress early identification, prompt intervention, multidisciplinary management, and a helpful rather than punitive attitude. A model system for prevention and control of child abuse should recognize abuse as a family crisis requiring a variety of twenty-four-hour services provided by the community, including legal aid.

370 Paulson, Morris J. "Child trauma intervention: a community response to family violence." J Clin Child Psychol 4(3): 26-29, Fall, 1975.

Surveys the phenomenon of child abuse, and outlines the role of the community in managing the problem.

371 Pfeifer, Donald R., and Ayoub, Catherine. "An approach to the pro-
     phylaxis of child abuse and neglect." <u>J Okla State Med Assoc</u>
     69(5): 162-67, May, 1976. (0 References).
A community hospital SCAN (Suspected Child Abuse and Neglect) team consisting of pediatricians, social workers, and pediatric mental health
nurses was established to identify and treat child abuse. With this program, however, the team could not intervene on behalf of the family until
abuse had already occurred. Therefore, a comprehensive program for the
prevention of child abuse was developed to identify the potentially
abusive or at risk family, to provide in-patient training for parents in
child health care and mothering techniques, and to establish an out-
patient pediatric clinic where at risk families could receive on-going
medical care, support, and continued help with childrearing and environmental problems. Since the program's official beginning in 1975, approximately 270 patients have been seen in the prevention program. No patient
has had to be hospitalized for abuse or neglect over the past nine months
except for the initial evaluation of new patients, demonstrating that the
program has been effective in preventing child abuse.

372 Pringle, Mia Kellmer. "Reducing the costs of raising children in
     inadequate environments: prevention -- impossible dream or essen-
     tial reality?" In: Talbot, Nathan B., ed. <u>Raising children in
     modern America</u>. Boston: Little, Brown, 1974. 212-15. (0 Refer-
     ences).
Stresses that neglect and deprivation prevention measures are meant to
ensure and to promote the emotional and intellectual development of all
children in society. A primary prevention program, aimed at promoting
social education, would handle all matters of family life, including child
development, parental rights, violence, and deprivation. Secondary prevention would involve providing emergency relief for families, supple-
menting the at risk children's home environment with quality care, and
preserving the unity of the family. Tertiary prevention would be
developed on a multidisciplinary basis to provide long-term rehabilitation for child victims.

373 "Program for child abuse prevention begun jointly by two major
     agencies." <u>Community Top</u> 2(7): 1, 1975.

374 Scott, Pena D. "The tragedy of Maria Colwell." <u>Br J Criminol</u>
     15(1): 88-90, January, 1975. (1 Reference).
Extrapolates certain lessons which can be gleaned from the tragic account
of the death by battering of Maria Colwell. Social work personnel must
relay any vital information necessary for the disposition of a custody
case. Neighbors need to inquire into the welfare of the children of
others. Finally, it may be necessary that natural, but abusive, parents
be under the same stringent scrutiny as foster or adoptive parents.

375 Stone, Richard; Lynch, Margaret A.; Roberts, Jacquie. "Predicting
     child abuse: letters to editor." <u>Br Med J</u> 1(6072): 1349-50,
     May 21, 1977. (1 Reference).
An editorial response confirming the suggestion that coordinated efforts
in hospitals and in the community are needed to predict and to prevent
child abuse. More specifically, it recommends that antenatal examinations in the home be conducted, that midwives be used to identify potential abusers in the community and in the hospitals, and that the size of
antenatal clinics be reduced.

376 Toland, Marjorie. "Abuse of children -- whose responsibility."
     Conn Med 28(6): 438-42, June, 1964. (10 References).
Recognizes the child abuse problem in Connecticut and suggests preventative measures. More protective casework services and more cooperation
to develop non-punitive services for family and child are recommended.

377 "Too hurt to cry! Parental abuse of children is a growing national
     evil; its prevention and the protection of its victims are jobs
     for all of us." Ill Soc Serv Outlook 1: 4-6, April, 1966.

378 "Training unit on child abuse prevention opens." Pediatr News
     7(3): 17, March, 1973. (0 References).
Describes the facilities and activities of a National Training Center for
the Prevention and Treatment of Child Abuse, established by the Robert
Wood Johnson Foundation at the University of Colorado. Facilities for
the diagnosis and treatment of child abuse are supplemented by courses
for physicians, lawyers, judges, social workers, and legislators. Therapy
is provided for families in which abuse may occur; included in this is a
day care nursery which gives abuse prone parents the opportunity to
observe role models interacting with their children.

379 "Violence to children." Lancet 1(8026): 1374, June 25, 1977. (0
     References).
Comments on a report made by the British Select Committee on Violence in
the Family. To reduce the grim statistics on battered children in
Britain, the Committee suggests home births and/or more humane hospital
routines to reinforce the very important bonding that occurs between
mother and child immediately after birth and to reduce the stress on new
mothers.

380 White House Conference on Children, Washington, D.C., 1970. Report
     of Forum 23. Washington, D. C.: U.S. Government Printing Office,
     1970. 372-86. (0 References).
Urges the nation to set as one of its highest priorities the helping of
children in trouble. The detection of problem children, and the prevention of abuse and neglect during the early stages of a child's development, namely, from birth to thirteen years of age, would be the most
effective way to control crime. Prevention means insuring that children's
needs are met when they are young, and it requires that adequate funds
be available to design and maintain constructive child-oriented programs.
Children needing such programs include abandoned infants, battered,
neglected, and sexually abused children, as well as emotionally disturbed
and retarded youngsters. Schools and courts are called upon to intensify
their efforts to detect problem children and to prevent delinquency.
Society must stop ignoring children in trouble and wasting human potential.
Among the report's recommendations are the suggestions that federal funding for children reflect their proportion of the population and that
legislation guaranteeing an adequate annual income for all families be
enacted.

381 Wolkenstein, Alan S. "The fear of committing child abuse: a dis-
     cussion of eight families." Child Welfare 56(4): 249-57, April
     1, 1977. (10 References).
Reviews eight families with a neurotic fear of abusing their children,
though none had actually abused a child yet. All the mothers had felt
negative feelings during pregnancy, and all had been laughed at or pres-

sured when they had expressed their fears about harming their child. A
"life-line procedure" (a therapist available at all times for as along as
necessary) revealed a typical pattern of recovery: (1) relief at being
believed at last; (2) rage at family members who had not believed them;
(3) denial of the original problem; and (4) a realization of both their
potential for violence and their access to help in solving their problem.

382   Zalba, Serapio R. "The abused child -- II: A typology for classi-
        fication and treatment." Soc Work 12(1): 70-79, January, 1967.
        (46 References).
Outlines a systematic typology for diagnosing and treating abusive families based on identification of the following criteria: (1) the impending danger to the child; (2) the source of the parent-child dysfunction;
and (3) the immediate reason for the abusive outburst. When the personality of the abusing parent is the source of the family dysfunction, the
abusive behavior is classified as uncontrollable and the child should be
placed in protective custody while the parent receives intensive psychiatric care. The three personality types which fall under this classification are: (1) the psychotic parent; (2) the uncontrollably hostile
and angry parent; and (3) the depressed or passive-aggressive parent who
resents having to tend to his child's needs. The typology also recognizes
three situations in which the abusive behavior can usually be modified
while the child remains at home. The cold, compulsive parent who sternly
disciplines his child and the impulsive parent experiencing marital conflict can be helped through group therapy and marriage counseling.
Parents suffering from an identity crisis caused by environmental stress
can be helped through practical supportive measures such as vocational
training, homemaker services, and others. Agency intervention and treatment strategy, therefore, must address the hidden family dysfunction if
treatment is to benefit both the child and the parent.

2. HEALTH VISITORS

383   Davies, Jean M. "The battered child syndrome -- detection and pre-
        vention." Nurs Mirror 140(22): 56-57, June, 1975. (0 Refer-
        ences).
The British system of detecting and preventing child abuse is briefly
described. The health visitor, who selectively visits families in a
particular population cluster, is the professional best positioned to
detect early signs of stress, neglect, or injury. She becomes known in
her district as a friendly contact, and neighbors are quick to report
concern. Other methods of detection and prevention cited are parent
craft classes given publicly for expectant parents, and neighborhood play-
groups and nurseries designed to relieve mothers from confinement in the
home. When injury is suspected, the child should be examined in the hospital and the social services department informed. A case conference,
composed of the involved professionals, then considers full social and
medical reports, and recommends long-term management as well as immediate
care provisions for the child.

384   Kempe, C. Henry. "Approaches to preventing child abuse: the health
        visitors concept." Am J Dis Child 130(9): 941-47, September,
        1976. (0 References).
Examines two approaches to the prevention of child abuse. The first involves the evaluation of parents and their reaction to their unborn or

newborn children during prenatal, postpartum, and pediatric checkups at
clinics and in physicians' offices. A list of warning signals which
indicate when a family is at risk or in need of extra services is provided.
The second approach involves the development of a universal health care
visitors program. The visitor would ideally be a mother who wanted to
share her experience with other young families. She would contact the
family during pregnancy and continue to provide guidance and support after
the infant's birth. She would inform the parents about immunizations,
nutrition, child development, and periodic examinations by a physician.
She would also be a valuable source of information for the family physician. For such a program to be effective, it would have to be compulsory.

385 Norman, Mari. "A lifeline for battering parents." Nurs Times
      70(39): 1506-7, September 26, 1974. (0 References).
The health visitor is seen as an underrated professional who can play a
vital role in the prevention of child abuse. Health visitors are state
registered nurses with extensive obstetric experience. They routinely
visit all families after the birth of a new baby, and are, therefore, not
perceived to be a threat, like the social worker or the National Society
for the Prevention of Cruelty to Children inspector. They have the
ability to recognize signs of potential child abuse and can continue
visits to a family according to their assessment of need. Two case histories are cited in which a health visitor was able to intervene in the
prevention of abuse. It is strongly recommended that the health visitor's
work be recognized by other professionals. She has no statutory powers
to enable her to take positive action, and social workers or NSPCC inspectors who do not understand the scope of her work, sometimes fail to take
action on her report.

386 Pringle, Mia K. "Identifying deprived children." Proc R Soc Med
      67(10): 1061-62, October, 1974. (15 References).
Stresses the need for early detection of at risk child abuse victims.
Visits by health personnel to families as well as friendly neighborhood
clinics might encourage parents to seek professional help in raising
their children.

387 Smith, Clement A. "The battered child." N Engl J Med 289(6):
      322-23, August 9, 1973. (13 References).
Although detection, diagnosis, and effective treatment initiated swiftly
are all important goals for handling child abuse, the ultimate goal is
its prevention. Intervention measures must be taken as soon as a high
risk family is identified. The program for postnatal home visits by
health visitors in Aberdeen, Scotland is described as a productive means
for identifying children who might be abused and for offering mothers
support services.

3. FAMILY PLANNING

388 Gunn, Alexander D. G. "The neglected child." Nurs Times 66(30):
      946-47, July 23, 1970. (0 References).
Reports on the incidence and symptoms of neglected children in England
and Wales. One in ten children seen by the NSPCC each year is a victim
of maltreatment. Neglect ranges from deliberate cruelty to the absence
of affection, symptoms of which include fractured ribs, lice, malnourishment, and depression. Of major concern is the learned pattern of parent-

ing these neglected children acquire and pass on to successive generations. Suggested preventive measures include birth control education and
available abortions to prevent unwanted children, along with increased
nursery care facilities.

389 Hardin, Garrett. "We need abortions for the children's sake." In:
     California Conference on Abortion, San Francisco, 1969. Abortion
     and the unwanted child. Edited by Carl Reiterman. New York:
     Springer, 1971. 1-6. (3 References).
A plea for the legalization of abortion on demand. The findings of a
Swedish study are presented which indicate that children whose mothers
had been denied abortions tended to exhibit poorer mental and physical
health than children who had been wanted. There was also a higher incidence of child abuse in the unwanted group.

390 Khan, Hamid A. "Population explosion: a pediatric problem." Br
     Med J 2(5528): 1475-77, December 17, 1966. (0 References).
Reprints an address given at the Annual Meeting of the British Medical
Association in conjunction with the Pakistani Medical Association. The
tragic implications of the population explosion in Pakistan are surveyed,
and members of the medical profession are urged to educate people regarding the need for population control.

391 Klerman, Lorraine. "Adolescent pregnancy: the need for new poli-
     cies and new programs." J Sch Health 45(5): 263-67, May, 1975.
     (8 References).
"Inappropriate pregnancies" (a phrase preferred to "unwanted pregnancies")
are related to four societal problems: (1) the absence of a sense of
purpose and commitment to any overriding social goal; (2) the lack of a
meaningful role for people under the age of twenty; (3) the narrow and
constricting definition of the women's role in society; and (4) the gap
between the sexual practices of young people and society's attitude
toward them.

392 Lebensohn, Zigmond M. "Legal abortion as a positive mental health
     measure in family planning." Compr Psychiatry 14(2): 95-98,
     March-April, 1973. (8 References).
Expresses concern over the harmful physical and emotional effects of
abortion. Psychiatrists are called upon to concern themselves more
deeply with the capacity of abortion to do emotional damage. A safer,
more dignified, private and humane means of terminating pregnancy should
be made accessible to all women.

393 Lowry, Thomas P., and Lowry, Anthea. "Abortion as a preventive for
     abused children." Psychiatr Opin 8(3): 15-25, 1970. (0 Refer-
     ences).
Written before the Supreme Court decision against laws limiting legal
abortions, this article discusses several well-known studies of the incidence of child abuse and filicide, and suggests that widening the
availability of legal abortions will help to improve the situation.
Statistics are cited relating legal abortion to the low incidence of child
abuse in Japan. One limitation to the argument is the fact that many
abusive parents had wanted their children and would not have sought
abortions even if they had been available to them.

394 Morgan, Dorothy. "The place of family planning." In: Franklin,
     Alfred White, ed. Concerning child abuse. New York: Churchill
     Livingstone, 1975. 71-72. (0 References).
The initial approach to family planning with the family where battering
has occurred is ideally made through a neighbor, a friend, or a medical
or social worker already acquainted with the parents. Birth control
information should be given to the husband and wife in a joint interview.
There should be adequate time to discuss fears and fantasies about the
use of birth control, and the couple should be allowed to choose which
form they want to use. Family planning can reduce the number of unwanted
children and, therefore, potentially decrease the number of children who
are physically abused or neglected.

395 Oliver, J. E. "Social aspects of the baby battering syndrome in
     relation to family planning: letter to editor." Br J Psychiatry
     126(4): 395-96, April, 1975. (3 References).
Stresses the need for family planning and birth control counseling for
abusive or neglectful parents. Contraceptive advice, if administered
effectively and consistently, could prove to be more effective for preventing battering and neglect in families by discouraging abusive parents,
often young couples, from reproducing before they are capable of rearing
children.

396 Siegel, Earl, and Morris, Naomi M. "Family planning: its health
     rationale." Am J Obstet Gynecol 118(7): 995-1004, April 1, 1974.
     (38 References).
Implies a positive correlation between family size and probability of
child abuse, with discussion of the relation of family size to maternal,
fetal, and newborn mortality rates, prematurity rates, incidence of infec-
tious diseases, and lower intelligence quotients among the children.

397 Ten Have, Ralph. "A preventive approach to the problems of child
     abuse and neglect." Mich Med 64(9): 645-49, September, 1965.
     (15 References).
Contends that primary intervention is necessary to prevent child abuse.
Since studies indicate that many abused children are originally unwanted,
the importance of family planning is emphasized in preventing child abuse.
Unfortunately, physicians and nurses in maternal and child health have
failed to educate people about family planning and the advantages and
disadvantages of various birth control methods. Health departments and
child protective agencies must play a role in family planning and, consequently, a role in the prevention of child abuse.

398 U.S. Congress. Senate. Committee on the Judiciary. Subcommittee
     on Constitutional Amendments. Abortion: Hearings. 93rd Congress,
     2nd session. Washington, D.C.: U.S. Government Printing Office,
     1974-76. 2: 391-439.
Presents both a statement criticizing abortion by Samuel A. Nigro, M.D.,
Assistant Professor of Child Psychiatry at Case Western Reserve University, School of Medicine and University Hospital of Cleveland, and a
statement supporting abortion by James W. Prescott, Ph.D., Health Scien-
tist Administrator and Developmental Neuropsychologist at the National
Institute of Child Health and Human Development. Each statement is
accompanied by a study reinforcing their conclusions. Dr. Nigro's argument against abortion is based on four contentions: (1) unwantedness of
born children is not a detrimental factor in itself, but the fact that

children have no rights to demand that adults meet their needs is most troubling; (2) there is no scientific evidence to prove that unwantedness of a pregnancy results necessarily in unwantedness of the child from that pregnancy; (3) unwantedness is an attitude that can fluctuate; and (4) the idea of abortion and the concept of survival being totally dependent upon wantability are both harmful to a child's emotional well-being. Dr. Nigro warns against mistaking unwantedness as harmful and abortion as its cure. On the other hand, Dr. Prescott stresses the consequences of denied abortions, citing statistics from Scandinavian, Czechoslovakian, and American studies to support his arguments. He emphasizes that unwanted- ness is harmful to the child and to society in the long run. Extensive cross cultural studies on abortion, which compare and contrast societies permitting abortion to those punishing it, and studies which draw paral- lels between societies exhibiting violent behavior and those that offer their children little affection, are presented. To summarize, Dr. Prescott maintains that legalized abortion should help contribute posi- tively to the quality of human life in general.

4. ADULT EDUCATION

399 "The abused child." Todays Educ 63(1): 40-43, January-February, 1974. (11 References).
Teachers and school administrators can play a significant role in report- ing and treating cases of child abuse. Preventive measures offered include the discouragement of corporal punishment in schools so that children will not grow up believing that physical force is an appropriate means of human behavior; education-for-parenthood programs which would instruct teenagers of both sexes in child care; and PTA discussions of positive methods of disciplining children with stress on professionals and community agencies which can assist parents with childrearing.

400 Connecticut Child Welfare Association. Child abuse and neglect: facts you should know. Hartford, Connecticut: The Connecticut Child Welfare Association, n.d. 6p.
Discusses child abuse reporting in Connecticut. The definition of abuse and the personality traits of abusing adults are given. Although a variety of professionals are required to report, all citizens are encour- aged to do so. Reports are made to the Protective Services Division of the Connecticut State Department of Children and Youth Services which has a hot-line for evening hours. All reports are investigated within twenty-four hours; emergencies receive immediate service.

401 Education Commission of the States. Education policies and practices regarding child abuse and neglect and recommendations for policy development: Education Commission of the States Child Abuse and Neglect project report no. 85. Denver, Colorado: Education Com- mission of the States, 1976. 72p.
Presents the findings of a nationwide survey of education policies and practices with regard to child abuse. One section discusses and analyzes the currently limited involvement of the educational community in the efforts to control child abuse, and suggests how that involvement should be broadened. This assessment is followed by specific policy recommenda- tions for the development of educational programs.

402 Eickhoff, Louise F. W. "Inadequate mothers: letter to editor."
Lancet 2(7889): 1152-53, November 9, 1974. (0 References).
Certain women will always be inadequate mothers, but with the constant
help and direction of physicians and nurses, the pattern of loving mothering can be taught.

403 Feshbach, S., and Feshbach, N. D. "Alternatives to corporal punishment; implications for training and controls." J Clin Child Psychol
2(3): 46-49, Fall, 1973. (17 References).
Explores an alternative to corporal punishment which uses behavior modification techniques to achieve the end of constructive behavior. The method
is based on the premise that the origins of misbehavior can be understood
in terms of these determinants: the child has no control over his ego;
he does not understand the rules of conduct or what happens when he fails
to follow them; his actions can be either habitual and heedless instrumental acts, or premeditated instrumental acts.

404 Fruchtl, Gertrude F., and Brodeur, Armand E. "The battered child:
know enough to care -- care enough to know." Cathol World
209(1252): 156-59, July, 1969. (0 References).
The need for education of the public on the subject of child abuse is
emphasized. Silence on the part of physician, parents, and friends has
been a great obstacle to the detection and treatment of abused children
in the past. Battered children are not only physically traumatized by
abuse, but also suffer extensive mental and emotional ramifications. The
role of the physician and social worker are of primary importance in the
treatment of the abused child and his family.

405 Gil, David G. "What schools can do about child abuse." Am Educ
5(4): 2-4, April, 1969. (0 References).
Addresses educators about the problems of child abuse and their role in
its prevention. Teachers need to educate themselves to recognize the
signs of abuse and to work closely with school counselors and community
agencies. Courses on family life which discourage physical discipline
should also be offered to parents and children. The results of a 1965
study by Brandeis University suggest that the acceptance of force in
childrearing is the most basic factor leading to child abuse. Other
factors include: (1) childrearing traditions and practices of various
social classes or ethnic groups; (2) environmental chance circumstances;
(3) environmental stress factors; and (4) deviant behaviors. However,
the study also indicates that the incidence of abuse has been exaggerated,
and that its occurrence can be correlated with poverty. Preventive measures include rendering physical force unacceptable as a means of punishment, eliminating poverty, and establishing a wide range of social
services.

406 Gordon, Thomas. What every parent should know. Chicago: National
Committee for Prevention of Child Abuse, 1975. 32p.
A readable, supportive guide with straightforward principles for the
average parent to make use of in his relationships with children. The
author sets out to alter traditional notions about parenting and replace
the deeply engrained pattern of abusive parenting with constructive and
more effective methods of childrearing. Parents must first recognize
that children do not misbehave; rather their actions are signals to adults
that they have basic needs which must be met. Power and punishment should
not be employed in solving family conflicts. In dealing with older

children it is recommended that a parent talk about his own needs and request the child's cooperation. Suggestions for modifying an infant's displeasing behavior, such as crying or fussing, include: trying to anticipate the infant's immediate need and then fulfilling it, gently substituting another behavior, communicating with non-verbal messages, and changing the environment. A credo summarizes the philosophy of building a happy and healthy parent-child relationship.

407   Lindenthal, Jacob J.; Bennett, Arletha; Johnson, Sylvia. "Public
        knowledge of child abuse." Child Welfare 54(7): 521-23, July,
        1975. (0 References).
To investigate the extent of public knowledge about child abuse, seventy-five adults in Newark, New Jersey were administered structured interviews on the subject. Seven out of ten people interviewed had heard or read about child abuse during the past year. Three out of ten persons had knowledge of a specific incident of abuse. Fewer than one out of four people knew about child protective services in the community. In order to measure the propensity for child abuse, the respondents were asked if there was ever a time when they could hardly refrain from abusing a child. Eighteen percent replied that this had happened to them. No one admitted ever having actually abused a child. Attitudes held toward abusive parents were liberal, with the majority of respondents favoring treatment rather than arrest. Sex, education, and race differences in knowledge are presented.

408   McAfee, Oralie, and Nedler, Shari. Education for parenthood: a
        primary prevention strategy for child abuse and neglect: report
        no. 93 from the ECS child abuse project. Denver, Colorado: Educa-
        tion Commission of the States, 1976. 32p.
Program goals for parent education as a means of combating child abuse are outlined: (1) the importance and complexity of the family unit and the role of the parent should be emphasized; (2) parents should be helped in the formulation of their goals and the understanding of their emotional needs; (3) professionals should be trained in these tasks; and (4) the efforts of organizations should be coordinated so that all existing resources could be utilized in the education of parents.

409   Renvoize, Jean. "Have you stopped beating your baby?" Times Educ
        Suppl 3081: 22, June 14, 1974. (0 References).
A brief overview of the incidence and social diffusion of child battering cases with recommendations for pre- and postnatal parent instruction as one workable preventive measure.

410   Venters, Maurine, and ten Bensel, Robert. "Interdisciplinary educa-
        tion in child abuse and neglect." J Med Educ 52(4): 334-37,
        April, 1977. (11 References).
Describes a course first given in 1975 at the University of Minnesota, School of Public Health, entitled "The Rights of Children and Youth: Neglect and Abuse." Designed for students in the health professions, law, social work, and education, it covered: history of child abuse, developmental needs of children, legal rights of children, and the identification, treatment, and prevention of abuse. The course is expected to help spread information about abuse among numerous professions and, hence, speed interdisciplinary cooperation on abuse problems.

411   Webster, T. "Report from the Education Work Group." <u>Clin Proc</u>
         30(2): 46-48, 1974. (0 References).
Attempts to educate both the general public and individuals most likely
to come into contact with child abuse cases, for example, physicians,
teachers, police officers, and social workers. Efforts to educate the
general public about child abuse should reach both parents who might be
abuse prone and persons who might discover or suspect cases of child
abuse among their friends or families.

5. CHILD CARE

412   "Looking after children." <u>Br Med J</u> 4(5624): 136-37, October 19,
         1968. (0 References).
People and organizations who are paid to look after children in Britain
are required by law to register with the local health authorities. Thus
standards of child care are maintained. Most local authorities demand
that the person in charge of the children be qualified and experienced,
that staff support be adequate, and that provision be made for proper
nutrition and medical care.

413   Nyswander, Dorothy B. "Preventing child casualties on the home
         front." <u>Public Health Nurs</u> 35(9): 493-96, September, 1943. (0
         References).
The great increase in working women during wartime brought with it the
problem of inadequate child care. In 1942, federal funds made possible
the first war nursery and first child care center for working mothers.
The conditions required for funds to establish such services are discussed. This federal program extended the role of the nurse, particularly
the public health nurse.

414   Orriss, Harry D. "Lessons from a tragedy." <u>Nurs Times</u> 70(5):
         140-41, January 31, 1974. (0 References).
Cites the tragic case of Maria Colwell who was returned by social workers
to her stepfather and then beaten to death. Existing child care services
are criticized for failing to coordinate their departments and not put-
ting the child's best interests first.

415   Wagner, Marsden, and Wagner, Mary. <u>The Danish national child-care</u>
         <u>system: a successful system as model for the reconstruction of</u>
         <u>American child care</u>. Boulder, Colorado: Westview Press, 1976.
         183p. (Bibliography).
Describes the highly developed child care system in Denmark and suggests
its use as a model for improving the American system. In Denmark, the
individual child is considered everyone's responsibility. The Child and
Youth Committees (CYC), located in every city and rural hamlet and composed of volunteers, function as neighborhood child advocates. The
goals of the Committee include: (1) the protection of each child; (2)
the promotion of good living conditions for all children; and (3) the
prevention of neglect, abuse, and major health and developmental problems. When cases of neglect or abuse do occur, however, CYC attempts to
solve all problems from within the family. There is no juvenile court
in Denmark. If parents wish to appeal a decision rendered by CYC, they
may take the case to the Supreme Court, but only after having exhausted
all community efforts at a solution.

Each CYC district employs family helpers who guide families through crises by providing practical advice, emotional support, and economic assistance. Day care facilities in Denmark are under CYC supervision. Beginning at age three months, Danish children may attend the all-day kindergartens or after-school recreation centers where they encounter both a comfortable and stimulating learning environment. Mildly handicapped, retarded, and autistic children receive special care and therapy at their own day care centers. Even women who babysit for children in their homes must have a license. Denmark also has a visiting health care program under which public health nurses visit all infants and monitor their developmental progress. Families with at risk children receive additional services and advice. Since the initiation of CYC's intensive child care programs, the infant mortality rate in Denmark has decreased substantially. The successful Danish system has been well received by the public.

6. HOT-LINES

416   Connecticut Child Welfare Association. The Care-Line (Report). Hartford, Connecticut: The Connecticut Child Welfare Association, 1974. 41p.
Reports on the first year of operation of Care-Line. Established in 1973, Care-Line does not give direct service but works statewide, twenty-four-hours a day, seven days a week to give information and referrals about child abuse. A psychologist works during the day, and non-professionals (with professional help available) take calls at night. During the first year, Care-Line took 2,359 calls regarding 3,099 children. Forty-three percent of the callers asked for information; 47 percent needed referrals; and 11 percent requested help in a crisis. Care-Line made 1,012 contacts with outside agencies the first year. The report also gives statistics about the identity of the callers (most frequently relatives or friends of the abusing family); about the ages of the abused children (typically two to eight years old); and about characteristics of the abusing parents (young, frustrated, isolated). Care-Line receives both public and private funding and publicizes its services widely.

417   —————. Child abuse hurts. Hartford, Connecticut: The Connecticut Child Welfare Association, n.d. 6p.
Residents of Connecticut are urged to take advantage of the twenty-four-hour statewide child abuse Care-Line. The staff is qualified to offer referrals, present information about reporting procedures, and to dispatch Emergency Protective Services workers. A brief summary is offered of the dynamics of child abuse and its effects on the community, as well as on the individuals involved.

418   —————. Second annual report of the Care-Line: October 1, 1974–September 30, 1975. Hartford, Connecticut: The Connecticut Child Welfare Association, 1975. 39p.
Summarizes the first two years of operation of the Care-Line, a program of the Connecticut Child Welfare Association. The Care-Line primarily seeks to prevent abuse by providing a phone-in crisis intervention service. During its second year of operation, 2,930 incoming calls were received and a total of 4,267 Care-Line calls were made, including referrals and follow-up calls. Almost half of those calls were received after working hours, and 94.4 percent of all calls originated from lay people. Among professionals, police were the most frequent callers, but there

was a need for increased publicity among all professional groups. Calls primarily requested information, counseling, referrals, or crisis intervention. Frequent calls concerned children who were abused, neglected, or in risky situations. Such children were primarily male, and one-third were under five years of age. The greatest percentage (56.8 percent) of referrals made by Care-Line were made to Protective Services, indicating a need to screen calls more carefully and to draw upon other agencies. Most Care-Line involvement ended when follow-up calls indicated another agency had taken care of the case. This report also describes Care-Line's methods, their staffing, and changing trends from the first to the second year of operation (primarily an increase in activity).

419 ————. <u>Third annual report of the Care-Line:</u> January 1, 1976–<u>December 13, 1976.</u> Hartford, Connecticut: The Connecticut Child Welfare Association, 1976. 50p.
Annual report on the activities of the Care-Line, a service provided by the Connecticut Child Welfare Association to prevent child abuse. During 1976, the Care-Line received 3,846 calls. Fifty-three percent of these calls were received after working hours, an increase from previous years caused by the establishment of a twenty-four-hour protective service system. Calls were categorized into three major types: (1) abuse or neglect reporting calls; (2) prevention of stress calls from parents; and (3) information and referral calls. The greatest number of calls were informational. However, activity was primarily related to reports of abuse or neglect. A 52 percent decrease in the number of calls from unspecified citizens was associated with the attempt to have callers identify themselves. Calls from professional groups had increased overall. The report also gave statistics on the descriptions of various types of child abuse, types of calls handled, and the kinds of services rendered.

420 Hurley, Anitra. "Come and get this kid or I'm going to kill him!" <u>Calif Health</u> 30(1): 12-14, July, 1972. (0 References).
Account of a confidential telephone child abuse hot-line called Child Abuse Listening and Mediation (CALM), Inc. The service is sponsored by community and private funds, and it operates seven days a week, twenty-four-hours a day. About half of the callers are parents afraid of harming their children; in addition, many neighbors, friends, and older children call in. Counseling is not provided; however, the service does supply information concerning professional assistance. The operators at CALM regard their chief role as one of caring and listening.

421 Johnston, C. "Parental Stress Services -- how it all began." J <u>Clin Child Psychol</u> 2(3): 45, Fall, 1973. (0 References).
Parental Stress Service, a community volunteer organization which operates a round-the-clock answering line and referral service for abuse prone parents is described. Its aims include helping parents to learn how to handle stress without becoming violent, referring people who need more intensive help to professional agencies, and educating the public about the problem of child abuse.

422 "My problem and how I solved it: battered child." <u>Good Housekeep-</u><u>ing</u> 178(5): 18ff., May, 1974. (0 References).
A mother suspects that her new neighbor abuses her child. Although the mother has heard the child sobbing, seen the neighbor viciously hit him, and confronted the neighbor on one occasion, she deliberates over her

function as an outsider in child abuse cases. A physician informs her of a hot-line which accepts calls of suspected child abuse and insures the caller's anonymity. The mother uses the hot-line and a social worker immediately visits the family, and as a result, subtle improvements are noticed in the abused child's family.

423 Pike, E. L. "C.A.L.M. -- a timely experiment in the prevention of child abuse." J Clin Child Psychol 2(3): 43-45, Fall, 1973.
     (0 References).
Description of CALM (Child Abuse Listening and Mediating), Inc., a community service in Santa Barbara, California. The organization offers a child abuse hot-line to parents who can call at any time and talk their anger out instead of abusing their children. Once CALM has been called, a volunteer visits the family and tries to establish a friendly, trusting relationship with its members. This contact should encourage the parents to discuss their problems, and perhaps become less preoccupied with them. When the client is more secure and self-assured, the volunteer's work is over.

424 Streshinsky, Shirley. "Help me before I hurt my child." Redbook
     143(6): 85, 151-57, June, 1974. (0 References).
The volunteer-staffed Child Abuse Listening Mediation (CALM) in Santa Barbara, California operates a twenty-four-hour phone counseling service, a visiting volunteer-friend service, and a professional referral system for parents who fear that they may hurt their children.

425 Tapp, Jack T.; Ryken, Virginia; Kaltwasser, Cari. "Counseling the abusing parent by telephone." Crisis Intervention 5(3): 27-37,
     1974.
Description of the operation of a twenty-four-hour child abuse crisis center. Therapeutic approaches are suggested for those handling the calls of abuse prone parents.

III

Causative Factors

A. SOCIOLOGICAL/CULTURAL FACTORS

1. URBAN LIFE AND ENVIRONMENTAL STRESS

426 Bakan, David. Slaughter of the innocents: a study of the battered
child phenomenon. San Francisco: Jossey-Bass, 1971. 128p.
(Bibliography).
Develops the thesis that child abuse and infanticide are primitive evolutionary mechanisms for keeping population levels in balance with the
availability of necessary resources. No distinction is made between
child abuse and infanticide because: (1) child abuse can eventually be
a cause of death; (2) child abuse can lead to sexual dysfunction in the
abused child which inhibits his subsequent reproduction; and (3) even if
the abused child does mature and reproduce, he is likely to abuse his
children which again presents the possibility of death. It is acknowledged that while the instinct for reproduction and survival of the
species would tend to inhibit infanticide, this instinctual mechanism
could work in the opposite direction as well. When overpopulation
threatens the survival of the group as a whole, or overburdens the individual parent, infanticide may naturally occur.

Throughout history the practices of infanticide and child abuse have not
been uncommon, although formal documentation of their occurrence is not
plentiful. A review of the Bible, secular writing, and children's
stories throughout the ages demonstrates that the abuse and murder of
children is a frequent theme in literature, supporting the idea that it
has probably occurred since the beginning of mankind. Still, the practices have only come to the attention of an outraged society in modern
times. The author explains that in modern times technology has provided:
(1) objective tools to document cases of child abuse (the x-ray, for
example); (2) an expansion of resources thereby lessening the burden of
an increased population; and (3) acceptable and humane means of population control through the development of contraceptives. These advances
have uncovered the inherently repugnant nature of infanticide as a means
of population control. That infanticide and child abuse can be demonstrated to have evolutionary origins does not justify their occurrences
in modern technological society. On the contrary, the history of
civilization is a record of man's ability to improve upon his natural
and primitive nature.

427 "Battered babies: editorial." Br Med J 3(5672): 667-68,
September 20, 1969. (5 References).

In seventy-eight cases of child abuse handled by the N.P.C.C., records indicate that there was a thirteen to one chance that parents who had abused the first-born child would subsequently injure a second child. The risk to the younger child had previously been underestimated. The parents involved tended to be young (between twenty and thirty); many of the fathers were unemployed; the families were small; and the victims were very young. The records also noted several instances in which physicians failed to identify the battered child syndrome.

428 Birrell, R. G., and Birrell, J. H. W. "The maltreatment syndrome in children: a hospital survey." Med J Aust 2(23): 1023-29, December 7, 1968. (4 References).
A review of forty-two cases of child abuse located over thirty-one months at Royal Children's Hospital in Melbourne, Australia. A summary of each case is presented in table form. The features characterizing many of the parents include mental ill health or subnormality, alcoholism, severe financial difficulties, out-of-wedlock pregnancies, and single parent status. In 25 percent of the cases, the children were found to have congenital anomalies. A compilation of clinical findings provides diagnostic guidelines for the physician. Radiological examination is particularly stressed as an important diagnostic tool, and physician reluctance to diagnose and report suspected instances of abuse is discussed. The social worker's contribution to case management consists of social assessment of the family, which can aid both in diagnosis and in the formulation of treatment recommendations. Suggestions for combating the problem are based on the assumption that psychiatric help rather than punitive action is needed. Recommendations include: (1) the establishment of a central agency designated to receive reports of suspected abuse and equipped to investigate such reports; (2) mandatory reporting laws which grant immunity from liability to the reporter; (3) professional, interdisciplinary teams to deal with case problems and empowered to remove the child from the home where necessary; and (4) education of health care and hospital workers to the signs and symptoms of abuse.

429 Bosanquet, Nicholas. "Who is really to blame?: editorial." Nurs Times 72(4): 126-27, January 29, 1976. (0 References).
Criticizes a report by a review committee on the murder of a young boy by his mother in King's Lynn, England. The review committee had placed the blame for the child's death on the mother, social worker, and health care visitor. Other causative factors, including a lack of community support services, day nurseries, and foster care facilities, should be blamed for the tragedy.

430 Browder, J. Albert. "Factors in child neglect -- working Indian mothers: letter to editor." Pediatrics 52(6): 888-89, December, 1973. (6 References).
Comments on a study (Oakland and Kane, 1973) which failed to find a correlation between employment of Navajo mothers and child neglect. The misconception of working mothers as frequent child abusers is noted. Characteristics of high risk parents are discussed, and it is suggested that the closeness of the Navajo family may, in fact, prevent the crime.

431 Bush, Sherida. "Child killers: the murderer is often the mother." Psychol Today 10(6): 28-29, November, 1976. (0 References).
Reports on a study by David Kaplun and Robert Reich which examined the records of the Chief Medical Examiner of New York City and found 140

cases of apparent homicide of children under fifteen years of age.
Poverty, alcoholism, drug abuse, criminal activity, and assault were
found to be corollaries of child abuse. Mothers were singled out as the
most frequent perpetrators. Due to insufficient evidence, there were
rarely any murder convictions. Surviving siblings were reported to remain in the custody of forty-six of these parents. In 32 percent of the
families, child abuse was reported again.

432 Bwibo, N. O. "Battered child syndrome." East Afr Med J 48(2):
     56-61, February, 1971. (14 References).
Presents a case report which calls attention to the existence of child
abuse in East Africa. Increasing numbers of unmarried mothers, young
parents living in towns with few or no friends, decreasing extended
family influence, and the delegation of childrearing to friends or relatives are the circumstances cited as favorable to the occurrence of
child abuse.

433 Caffey, John. "The parent-infant traumatic stress syndrome:
     (Caffey-Kempe syndrome), (Battered Baby syndrome)." Am J Roentgenol
     Radium Ther Nucl Med 114: 218-29, February, 1972. (19 References).
Reviews the history of the radiographic discovery of the battered baby
syndrome, to which the designation "parent-infant traumatic stress
syndrome," or PITS syndrome, is applied. Mothers are identified as the
perpetrators of 90 percent of the incidents involving child abuse, and
no special sociological or psychological features differentiate abusers
from non-abusers, according to the author. Stress is the principal cause
of the syndrome, and the prevention is seen to entail whatever social
reform is necessary to provide support for a productive life for abusive
parents and their children.

434 Ceresnie, Steven Joel. "Child abuse: a controlled study of social
     and family factors." For a summary see: Diss Abstr Int 37B(11):
     5826, May, 1977.

435 Chesser, Eustace. Cruelty to children. New York: The Philosophical
     Library, 1951. 159p. (Bibliography).
An analysis of the roots of cruelty to children and its incidence in
modern society. Proposes that cruelty is innate to human nature in its
aggressive striving for power, and that cruelty to children is peculiar
to urban as opposed to primitive societies. When family stability is
threatened by such additional factors as adverse economic and environmental circumstances, lack of education, immaturity and irresponsibility
on the part of the parents, and a deficiency in the maternal instinct,
children become the likely targets of this aggression. Cruelty to
children can be present in three forms: (1) consistent and deliberate
cruelty, the uncontrollable actions of a pathologically sick parent;
(2) episodic active cruelty, the momentarily violent response of a
frustrated or overburdened parent; and (3) passive cruelty or neglect,
the uneducated or unloving parent's continual failure to provide for his
child's basic needs of love, shelter, food, clothing, and medical care.
Though physical neglect is often an unavoidable consequence of poverty,
deliberate emotional neglect is more often found in middle and upper
class homes.

During the calendar year 1949-1950, the National Society for the Prevention of Cruelty to Children investigated 24,102 cases of neglect and

4,286 cases of cruelty to children in England alone. From these statistics it was estimated that in a population of 100 children, six or seven
of these children would be neglected or maltreated sometime during their
childhood. Moreover, 38 percent of neglected and abused children were
unwanted children, and an additional 18 percent came from broken homes.
Social reforms advocated included educating women in matters of contraception and child care and improving urban living conditions. Brief
punishment, paired with long and adequate rehabilitative treatment for
the parent, are seen as most effective in dealing with instances of
cruelty to children.

436   Elmer, Elizabeth. "A social worker's assessment of medico-social
        stress in child abuse cases." In: National Symposium on Child
        Abuse, 4th, Charleston, S.C., 1973. Collected papers.
        Denver, Colorado: The American Humane Association, Children's
        Division, 1975. 86-91.
Presents two studies on the significance of medical and social stress in
child abuse cases. The families of fifty injured patients who had been
admitted to the Pittsburgh Child Guidance Center acted as subjects. A
session with a pediatrician determined the number of medical stress items
operating in the mother-child relationship. An interview with a social
worker produced a score based on the mother's number of social difficulties. In both studies, a comparison of the scores of the abusive mothers
with those of non-abusive mothers showed that abusive mothers showed more
medical and social stress than did non-abusive mothers. The results
imply that management should focus on support designed to alleviate
stresses.

437   Fleck, Stephen. "Child abuse." Conn Med   36(6):   337, June, 1972.
        (0 References).
Contrary to what is generally believed, our society is neither child-
oriented nor future-oriented. The former is evidenced in the number of
school bond issues that are voted down and the vetoing of bills regarding
day care centers. The latter is evidenced by the fact that adequate
dissemination of birth control information is not provided. Unfortunately, the result is unwanted and abused children.

438   Fontana, Vincent J. "Battered children: letter to editor." N Engl
        J Med 289(19): 1044, November 8, 1973. (3 References).
Emphasizes that physicians need to be reminded of the battered child
syndrome, so that they will maintain a high degree of concern for the
future of abused children. Personal, as well as social factors linked
with abuse, are mentioned. Society is called upon to take extensive
measures to stop the cycle of violence.

439   ————. "Child abuse in megalopolis." NY State J Med   76(11):
        1799-1802, October, 1976. (4 References).
Reports on the problems and approaches to child abuse in New York City
as a representative megalopolis. The isolation, poverty, unemployment,
and fragmented family life prevalent in a large city promote conditions
for child abuse, primarily affecting minority groups. Adequate community
services and health care facilities are essential to counteract these
factors, but they are the first to lose funding when cutbacks occur. A
program developed at the New York Foundling Hospital Center is cited for
its successful approach. Initial objectives centered around keeping the
family together, promoting self-help, and preventing further abuse. The

six components of the program are: (1) a multidisciplinary team approach; (2) surrogate mothers; (3) a hotline; (4) an in-resident facility for mother and child; (5) a halfway house; and (6) an out-patient program. Varied approaches are needed, including methods for identifying families in need of help.

440 Gelles, Richard J. "Child abuse as psychopathology: a sociological critique and reformulation." Am J Orthopsychiatry 43(4): 611-21, July, 1973. (29 References).
Criticizes the psychopathological model for explaining and treating child abuse. The study stresses that child abuse is not caused solely by psychopathic parents and, as a result, treatment designed to eliminate psychopathy is of little value. Instead, child abuse rises in the context of society from many sociocultural influences. Factors such as socioeconomic status, employment, sex, and the previous history of violence of the parents can all have some bearing on the incidence of abuse. Important variables such as unwanted pregnancies, the legal entanglements involved in abortions, and unhealthy childrearing practices have also been found to be significant contributing factors. Rather than continue with misdirected treatments after the abuse has already occurred, it is necessary to develop effective detection procedures and preventive measures.

441 Gil, David G. "A sociocultural perspective on physical child abuse." Child Welfare 50(7): 389-95, July, 1971. (18 References).
A nationwide study on physical child abuse citing the sociocultural factors that precipitate child abuse and discussing the contention that the sanctioning of the use of force with children is endemic in our society. In order to begin to prevent child abuse, a combination of efforts must be made on many levels. Assistance needs to come through education, legislative action, efforts to eliminate poverty, and the active participation of social services aiming at reducing family stress and carrying out intervention measures.

442 Gottlieb, David H., ed. Children's liberation. Englewood Cliffs, New Jersey: Prentice-Hall, 1973. 181p.
A series of articles dealing with children's rights and social factors which are detrimental to children. Exploration of the reasons for the current approach and view of childhood, along with suggestions as to how the situation could be improved, are included.

443 Hudson, Bob. "Whose responsibility? 'battered' children (Great Britain)." Munic Public Serv J 83: 999-1001, August 1, 1975; 83: 1021ff., August 8, 1975.

444 "In a nation of boredom: editorial." Med Sci Law 16(1): 1, January, 1976. (0 References).
The disruption of the family unit, the reliance on television as a major form of entertainment for children, and the indifference of parents (including working mothers) to the lives of their children, are cited as recent societal trends contributing to child abuse. In races and religions where a strong family unit is considered to be important, as in the Jewish culture, non-accidental injury, physical deformity, and speech defects are rarely seen in children.

445 Justice, Blair. Violence in the city. Fort Worth, Texas: Leo Potishman Fund, 1969. 289p.

446   Justice, Blair, and Duncan, David F. "Life crisis as a precursor
        to child abuse." Public Health Rep 91(2): 110-15, March-April,
        1976. (25 References).
Investigates the relationship between the number and intensity of life
change events experienced by a parent and the occurrence of child abuse.
Thirty-five abusing parents and thirty-five non-abusing matched controls
were administered the Social Readjustment Rating Scale which consists of
forty-three items dealing with life change events such as the death of
a spouse, marriage, personal injury, change to a different line of work,
change in residence, pregnancy, vacation, and others. A comparison of
the two groups revealed that the abusing parents had experienced a
greater number and intensity of life changes in the twelve months prior
to the abuse of their children than the non-abusing parents had experienced during the same time period. The authors explain that an excessive
amount of either pleasant or unpleasant life change events creates a
magnitude of stress which can exceed the parent's ability to cope with
his/her child. It was also discovered that abusing parents are in
constant search of a symbiotic relationship with another person and will
subject themselves to excessive life changes and crises in order to
elicit a caring response from other people. Several suggestions for the
prevention of child abuse include: (1) the development of services to
assist people in adjusting to life changes and crises; (2) the use of
the Social Readjustment Rating Scale to detect which parents have experienced a great deal of change, so that they can be given counseling and
guidance; and (3) the transformation of society in order to eliminate at
least selected life crises caused by unemployment, lack of opportunity,
and poor health care delivery systems.

447   Kittrell, Ed. "In defense of children." Child Today 6(1): 28-29,
        January-February, 1977. (0 References).
A statement deploring society's negligent attitude toward children.
Children in our society have become a low priority and subject to adult
indifference. Having children is no longer unavoidable and often regarded
as a financial and personal threat to anyone seeking the good life.
Society encourages us to avoid emotional confrontations and to worship
the illusion of youth. Children are a direct and powerful challenge to
both and will continue to be neglected as long as our present value system
remains intact.

448   Maurer, Adah. "Institutional assault on children." Clin Psychol
        29(2): 23-25, Winter, 1976.
American society and its institutions are characterized as fostering
violence toward children. Further, psychologists today continue this
assault through their attempts to condition the suppression of undesirable behavior.

449   Moore, Pamela. "A look at the disintegrating world of childhood:
        editorial." Psychol Today 9(1): 32ff., June, 1975. (0 Refer-
        ences).
Reports the work of psychologist Urie Bronfenbrenner on the American
family. Using statistics on marriage, divorce, birth, mortality, income,
jobs, education, and household composition, Bronfenbrenner found that
the environment for children in the country is progressively worsening.
The family is disintegrating, mothers are spending less time with their
children, the job market is restricted, and working patterns are too
inflexible to accommodate the needs of the family.

450 Newberger, Eli H. "Report from the Research Work Group." Clin
       Proc Child Hosp 30(2): 49-51, 1974. (0 References).
The report indicates that extensive research into the causes and prevention of child abuse continues to be a pressing need, and that such
research should be multidisciplinary and unbiased, should involve the
community, and should pay more attention to the long-term effects of
child abuse.

451 Sattin, Dana B., and Miller, John K. "The ecology of child abuse
       within a military community." Am J Orthopsychiatry 41(4): 675-
       78, July, 1971. (11 References).
A study conducted within a military population to determine whether abusive parents live in poor, socially disorganized neighborhoods with
highly transient populations, while non-abusive parents live in different
residential areas. The addresses of thirty-nine families with proven
abuse and fifty-seven families with non-abuse were plotted on a map of El
Paso. It was discovered that twenty-nine out of thirty-nine abusive
families lived in the "Dyer St." area of El Paso, which is a run-down
area with small rented houses and a busy commercial district. Only
twenty-six of the fifty-seven non-abusive families lived in this area.
It was concluded that child abuse was significantly more likely to occur
in the Dyer St. area than in other areas of the city. The relationship
between abuse and residence is explained by referring to personality and
economic factors which may lead certain families with a potential for
child abuse to choose the Dyer St. area as their home, and/or to environmental and financial stresses resulting from life in the Dyer St. area
which may contribute to subsequent abuse.

452 Scott, Winifred J. "Attachment and child abuse: a study of social
       history indicators among mothers of abused children." For a
       summary see: Diss Abstr Int 35B(12): 6113, June, 1975.

453 Sendi, Ismail B., and Blomgren, Paul G. "A comparative study of
       predictive criteria in the predisposition of homicidal adolescents."
       Am J Psychiatry 132(4): 423-27, April, 1975. (13 References).
Investigates the degree to which homicidal behavior can be predicted.
The psychodynamics of thirty adolescents--ten of whom had committed
homicide, ten of whom had threatened or attempted it, and ten random
youths hospitalized for psychiatric problems--are examined. The presence or absence of various criteria predicting homicidal behavior was
noted in each subject. It was concluded that the presence of a well-
defined predisposition toward homicide could not be supported, and that
environmental factors were crucial in reinforcing homicidal behavior.

454 Shaheen, Eleanor; Alexander, Doris; Truskowsky, Marie; et al.
       "Failure to thrive -- a retrospective profile." Clin Pediatr
       7(5): 255-61, May, 1968. (14 References).
Study of forty-four patients in the Children's Hospital of Philadelphia
whose growth failure could not be traced to organic etiology. Environmental and clinical investigation revealed that: (1) in fourteen of
the cases, there had been some kind of disruption in caretaking of the
patient and his siblings; (2) strong suspicion of battering or abandonment was noted in twelve cases; and (3) marital instability was reported
in fifteen of the forty-four cases. Other clinical and social variables
are studied and the need for further investigation and possible intervention by the physician in failure to thrive cases is suggested.

455 Sills, J. A.; Thomas, L. J.; Rosenbloom, L. "Non-accidental injury:
        a two-year study in central Liverpool." Dev Med Child Neurol
        19(1): 26-33, February, 1977. (12 References).
Between 1973 and 1974, seventy-six children were admitted to Royal
Liverpool Children's Hospital in England for injuries resulting from
suspected physical maltreatment. In every case, the child was immediately admitted to the hospital, the Social Services Department was
informed, and a case conference was held at the hospital within a week.
Taking part in the case conference were the social workers, health
visitors, police superintendent, and physicians involved with each family.
The conferences decided what should be done to ensure the safety and
proper development of all children in the family, and what treatment plan
should be followed. An analysis of the case conference records revealed
that twice as many boys as girls were the victims of child abuse. Fourteen of the seventy-six children had been low birth weight infants (a
higher percentage than in the population at large), and fifty-five had a
history of previous injury. Thirty-three of the mothers had become
pregnant at an early age (before twenty-four years) and twenty-nine of
the children were illegitimate. Environmental stress caused by poor
housing, psychiatric illness, marital instability, and unemployment was
prevalent among these families. It is concluded that factors such as
male sex, illegitimacy, low birth weight, previous injuries, early
pregnancy, and environmental stress may predispose some families to non-
accidential injury.

456 Taylor, Craig. "The 'battered child': individual victim of family
        brutality." In: Bryant, Clifton D., and Wells, J. Gipson, eds.
        Deviancy and the family. Philadelphia: F. A. Davis, 1973. 209-15.
        (4 References).
Focuses on two causative factors of child abuse: (1) the type of child,
and (2) the change in family structures. Babies suffering from digestive
disorders, diaper rash, or hunger are apt to be victims of abuse because
their incessant crying can exacerbate a postpartum depression and further
fray new parents' nerves. Sedating crying babies is recommended for
mother and child. However, low income or uneducated families often do
not have such remedies available to them. Illegitimacy or doubt of
paternity also tends to increase a child's chances of being abused. The
fragmentation of the extended family by urbanization and industrializa-
tion is another cited cause for increased abuse. Mothers lack the
examples and help of other female members of their family, and their
ignorance increases their self-doubt and feelings of inadequacy in their
new mothering role. Mothers who have chosen to have children in place
of a career doubly resent a demanding baby and feel their failure afresh.
Marriages and families begun at an early age place additional hardships
on young people still establishing their identities as well as their
relationship with one another. Child abuse, once condoned as part of
childrearing or religious practices, has now moved outside the normal
societal context and is considered irrational and deviant behavior.

457 Tizard, Jack. "Three dysfunctional environmental influences in
        development: malnutrition, non-accidental injury, and child-
        minding." Postgrad Med J 51(2): 19-27, 1975. (32 References).
Suggests that three environmental conditions, namely, malnutrition, non-
accidental injury, and child-minding, be considered as the primary causes
of developmental disruptions in children. Home stimulation and good
nutrition are essential for a child's intellectual, personality, and

growth. Although malnutrition is still a contemporary problem, it is a diminishing one. In today's society the primary factors prohibiting the health and development of children have to do with a breakdown in child-rearing practices. A further cause of child abuse can be attributed to environmental stress leading to psychological tension in families. The increasing proportion of working mothers creates home child care problems and raises the need for public day care centers. Research to develop effective measures for relieving environmental stress and providing adequate child care services is needed.

458 U. S. National Institute of Mental Health, Office of Program Planning and Evaluation. "Studies of urban life and mental health." In: National Institute of Mental Health. Mental health of urban America. Washington, D. C.: U. S. Government Printing Office, 1969. 140p. (Bibliography).
Description of the research programs of the National Institute of Mental Health which focus on the impact of the urban environment upon mental health. The dynamics of child battering among the poor are highlighted, along with the effects upon mental health of crowding, cultural deprivation, migration, family disintegration, and other concomitants of urban life.

459 Woods, Merilyn B. "The unsupervised child of the working mother." For a summary see: Diss Abstr 29A(11): 4110, May, 1969.

460 Zalba, Serapio R. "The battered child." Sci Dig 70(6): 8-13, 63, December, 1971. (0 References).
Points out the salient characteristics of abusive parents. Most of the parents suffer both internal personal stress, as well as external social or economic stress. As a rule, abusive parents are highly impulsive, socially isolated, experience marriage problems, and even struggle for survival. The problem of battering parents is not restricted to any social class, which aggravates attempts to assess the incidence of abuse in society. It is certain, however, that communities need to invest substantially in social services that provide counseling for parents and protection for children.

2. POVERTY AND SOCIAL DEPRIVATION

461 Arnold, Mildred. "Children in limbo." Public Welfare 25(3): 221-28, July, 1967. (1 Reference).
Originally presented at the National Conference on Social Welfare, this description of the plight of certain children identifies those groups of children whose environments are least conducive to their healthy development. These groups include the children of migrant workers, children who drift from one foster home to another, institutionalized children, neglected and abused children, and children of working mothers who are unable to provide adequate substitute care.

462 Bwibo, N. O. "Battered child syndrome." East Afr Med J 49(11): 934-38, November, 1972. (13 References).
Presents eight case studies of battered children in East Africa. The following circumstances are believed to precipitate abuse: broken homes, environmental strains and stress, poverty, and social deprivation. Other causative factors include disciplinary measures which become extreme and

premeditated murderous attacks. The clinical features for detecting child abuse and the procedure for management of the problem in East Africa are briefly outlined.

463 "Children who die through social disadvantage." Br Med J 2(6042): 962-63, October 23, 1976. (14 References).
In an analysis comparing number of deaths among children to social class, it is shown that death rates for the lowest social class is twice those of the highest class. Explanations consider the variance of diseases and effectiveness of treatment between the different classes. Recommendations aim at finding the causative factors for various diseases and reevaluation of curative and preventative services for all children.

464 Coll, Blanche D. "Deprivation in childhood: its relation to the cycle of poverty." Welfare Rev 3(3): 1-10, March, 1965. (34 References).
Evidence is presented to support the existence of a relationship between economic, cultural, and emotional deprivation in childhood on the one hand and educational achievement and measured intelligence, on the other.

465 Cottle, Thomas J. "A child is being beaten by Naomi Feigelson Chase: book review." New Repub 173(21): 28-30, November 22, 1975. (0 References).
A review of A Child is Being Beaten describes the book as a monumental study of child abuse with significant historical value. Family life has suffered under the effects of the capitalistic system. Society's mistreatment of children, especially poor and disadvantaged children, is undeniable and seems to be a result of multiple social ills such as poverty, lack of health care, and unemployment. In order to combat the lack of day care centers, inadequate schooling, the ineffectiveness of over-extended social work case loads, as well as congested judiciary proceedings involving abuse cases, society must revolutionize its attitudes toward children, childrearing, and family life.

466 Elmer, Elizabeth. "A follow-up study of traumatized children." Pediatrics 59(2): 273-79, February, 1977. (17 References).
Presents a follow-up study of seventeen abused children matched with seventeen children who were accident victims. All the children were from the same geographic area, members of the lower class, and patients in the same hospital. Physical and social evaluations showed little difference between the two groups. The families of both groups engaged in similar amounts of violent behavior and were equally disorganized and drug dependent. Many of the children in both groups related fears about actual persons who might harm them. One hypothesis emerging from the study is that conditions of lower class living may be as powerful an influence on the course of a child's development as abuse itself.

467 Francis, H. W. S. "Child health: points of concern." Public Health 81(1): 245-51, November, 1966. (11 References).
Discusses areas of particular concern in the prevention of child abuse. Poverty generates an atmosphere of stress which is conducive to child abuse; physicians should be sensitive to the signs of abuse and neglect, and caseworkers should recognize the relationship between abuse/deprivation and emotional disturbances.

468 Garbarino, James. "A preliminary study of some ecological corre-
      lates of child abuse: the impact of socioeconomic stress on
      mothers." Child Dev 47(1): 178–85, March, 1976. (12 References).
In an attempt to correlate child abuse and the degree to which mothers
are given support for the parent function, data on the rates of child
abuse/maltreatment for counties in New York State are examined according
to socioeconomic and demographic indices. The data suggests that the
degree to which mothers in a particular county are subjected to socioeconomic stress without adequate support systems accounts for a 36 percent variance in child abuse/maltreatment rates across the counties,
while economic conditions which affect the family more generally account
for a 16 percent variance. These results point to suggested treatment
modalities of income supports, child care services, and educational
development opportunities to relieve pressure on the isolated, poor
mother.

469 Garber, Clark M. "Eskimo infanticide." Sci Mon 64(2): 98–102,
      February, 1947. (6 References).
Describes the process and causes of Eskimo infanticide through a review
of the literature. The economic hardships of Eskimo life forced women to
kill their female or deformed babies without regard to the resulting
lack of marriageable females. Male babies were rarely killed as they
became providers. Intentional abortion was rare.

470 Gil, David G. "Physical abuse of children." Pediatrics 45(3):
      510–11, March, 1970. (0 References).
David Gil responds to Vincent Fontana's criticism of his article entitled
"Physical Abuse of Children." Dr. Gil states that while battering of
individual children is a problem, the greater abuse is to the millions
of American children who live in poverty and without proper care or
education.

471 ————. "Unraveling child abuse." Am J Orthopsychiatry 45(3):
      346–56, April, 1975. (6 References).
Introduces a unique set of criteria for explaining the dynamics of child
abuse. Included is a value-based definition of child abuse, characterized by two related yet contrasting approaches for understanding the
nature of abuse, namely, "level of manifestation" and "levels of causa-
tion." Abuse is manifest on the home level, the institutional level,
and the societal level. The causal dimensions are complex and diverse.
They range, in part, from society's dominant value premises, including
its concept of humans in relation to the nature of its major institutions and society's degree of commitment to the self-actualization of
all children. Further causal dimensions include society's implicit
sanction of the use of force in adult-child relations. Social forces
such as poverty, and certain alienating circumstances inherent in many
jobs and professions, can trigger stress and frustration. In some
individuals this can cause a loss of self-control that ends in violence
against children. Preventing abuse means eliminating its causes.
Political involvement is essential if primary prevention is to be
achieved.

472 Giovannoni, Jeanne M., and Billingsley, Andrew. "Child neglect
      among the poor: a study of parental adequacy in families of three
      ethnic groups." Child Welfare 49(4): 196–204, April, 1970.
      (7 References).

Compares 186 Black, Caucasian, and Spanish-speaking abusing and non-abusing mothers from poverty backgrounds. Abusing mothers tended to be under greater stress in their current situation than those in the control group, the stress being a more significant factor in the abuse than the abusing mothers' early childhood experiences. They had more marital difficulties, less money, weaker family ties, and knew little about community resources, and as homemakers, they were unable to respond to the needs of small children. The results suggest that child abuse should not be treated as an individual problem, but as a community responsibility. Relieving stresses exacerbated by poverty is a suggested approach to prevention.

473 "Hard times for kids too: child abuse as a consequence of economic
     strain." Time 105(11): 88, March 17, 1975. (0 References).
Cases and statistics are reviewed which indicate that economic strain is an increasingly important factor in child abuse.

474 Lewis, Hylan. Child rearing among low-income families. Washington,
     D. C.: Washington Center for Metropolitan Studies, 1961. 17p.
Examines the childrearing practices of low income families in the District of Columbia. Families from different community situations were compared in terms of how they direct the development of their children. Attention is also focused on the practicality and availability of voluntary community programs to assist low income families. A total of sixty-six families were observed and classified as either "subclinical," or "preclinical," or "clinical" dependents. The poor were not a completely homogenous group. An important distinction between the hardcore "undeserving" poor and the hard luck "deserving" poor was emphasized. The willingness of families, regardless of category, to participate voluntarily in community projects was related to their own expectations of making a personal contribution to the improvement of childrearing.

475 Newberger, Eli H. "Child abuse and neglect: toward a firmer
     foundation for practice and policy." Am J Orthopsychiatry 47(3):
     374-75, July, 1977. (0 References).
Research in the field of child abuse and neglect has too long been derived almost exclusively from social agencies that handle children from poor and socially marginal families. For a variety of reasons, these families are the most accessible to study. However, efforts to address the social universality of the problem, as well as attempts to handle sexual misuse of children and institutional abuse, are urgently needed.

476 Oakland, Lynne, and Kane, Robert L. "The working mother and child
     neglect on the Navajo reservation." Pediatrics 51(5): 849-53,
     May, 1973. (10 References).
The histories of thirty-three neglected Navajo children were compared to those of forty-nine controls in an attempt to isolate causes of child neglect, defined as poor family environment, malnutrition, failure to thrive, maternal deprivation, battering, or rejection. No significant difference was found between the negligent mothers and the control mothers in age, education, or employment. There was a higher incidence of neglect among unmarried mothers and those with smaller families, however. The assumption that working mothers would be more likely to neglect their children proved unfounded, but it was emphasized that Navajo working mothers leave their children with the extended family.

477 Pasamanick, Benjamin. "A child is being beaten." Am J Orthopsy-
     chiatry 41(4): 540-56, July, 1971. (0 References).
Discusses the detrimental effects of hunger and malnutrition on children.
The problems of hunger and poverty are deep-seated social ills with vast
and crippling repercussions. Government cannot allow hunger to become a
political or economic issue. Adequate nutrition is a humanitarian issue
that should take precedence over all other social, political, and
economic concerns. Proposals for a system of child advocacy are detailed
and a call for immediate action to improve the plight of neglected
children is made.

478 Polansky, Norman A.; Borgman, Robert D.; DeSaix, Christine; et al.
     The faces of poverty for Appalachian children. Athens, Georgia:
     Georgia University, School of Social Work, 1971. 14p. (Bibliog-
     raphy).
Summary of the results of a series of interviews by the Georgia University School of Social Work with two groups of poor families living in
Appalachia--the one group comprising sixty-five self-supporting families,
and the other ninety-one families receiving Aid to Families with
Dependent Children. The project represented an attempt to elaborate the
impact of poverty on the Childhood Level of Living Scale. It was found,
in general, that the self-supporting families provided higher levels of
emotional support and stability than did the AFDC families, although both
groups offered roughly the same levels of survival necessities. A lower
Childhood Level of Living frequently corresponded to the appearance of
schizoid tendencies and lower intelligence in the children.

479 Polansky, Norman A.; Borgman, Robert D.; DeSaix, Christine. Roots
     of futility. San Francisco: Jossey-Bass, 1972. 272p. (Bibliog-
     raphy).
Probes the complex interrelationships among poverty, child neglect, and
maternal behavior in rural southern Appalachia. In a countryside that
has undergone few progressive changes during several hundred years of
settlement, the cycles of deprivation and futility have repeated themselves uninterruptedly. A pilot study aimed at discerning the effects
of maternal personality on childrearing in an impoverished environment
uncovered the roots of this futility cycle and raised suggestions for
further research and grass-roots curative action.

Ten mothers with youngsters of four or five years of age were involved
in the pilot study. All of the mothers had failed to provide adequate
care for their children; legally, however, they were not guilty of
neglect since they shared the child's bleak environment and the dearth
of nutritious food, clothing, and other basic comforts. After several
interviews at home with a rural social worker, each mother was evaluated
on the Childhood Level of Living Scale to determine the relative levels
of physical and emotional/cognitive care which she provided for her
child. Following psychological testing, the mothers were next rated on
a Maternal Characteristics Scale. The following personality traits were
generic of the mothers: (1) an infantile personality; (2) a close and
clinging symbiotic attachment to their children; and (3) verbal inaccessibility. Two distinct maternal models were identified. The majority
of the mothers displayed an apathetic-futile outlook. These women saw
no hope for their situations, were unresponsive, detached both from
family members and outside contacts, and projected a demeanor of emotional
numbness. Their children were frequently lethargic, withdrawn, and less
capable of performing visual and motor skills. The second group of

mothers displayed signs of an impulse ridden character. Their behavior
was infantile, and in relationships with all other persons, they were
the dependent party. Hostility and defiance were marked in their children.

A second field study in similar rural surroundings attempted to describe
which children experienced the greatest risk of neglect. Sixty-five
mothers of poor but self-supporting families were questioned about their
own social histories and their childrearing practices. An examination
of the data revealed that women of marginal intelligence and from families
whose parents were retarded or deviant, who had not held a job for at
least a year, and who had dated sparsely but married young, were more apt
to neglect their children.

Intervention into the homes of these inadequate mothers and their children must be sensitive and directed toward long-range as well as immediate betterment. Counseling, day care centers, homemaker services, and
family planning education will help to transform the mothers' isolated
and dreary environment into more pleasant and manageable surroundings.
Most importantly, the neglected children of Appalachia will begin to
receive the physical and emotional attention that they need to break out
of the cycle of futility.

480   Polansky, Norman A.; DeSaix, Christine; Sharlin, Shlomo. "Child
      neglect in Appalachia." In: National Conference on Social Welfare,
      98th, Columbus, Ohio. Proceedings: Social Work Practice. New
      York: Columbia University Press, 1971. 33-50. (Bibliography).
Report on a project investigating the impact of welfare upon the Childhood Level of Living Scale. Two groups of poor Appalachian families
were compared, the one group being self-supporting and the other group
receiving Aid to Families with Dependent Children. In terms of the
physical necessities of food, housing, and medical care, no significant
differences were found between the AFDC families and the self-supporting
group. However, the child from the self-supporting family tended to
receive more in the way of clothing, mature discipline, and intellectual
stimulation than his AFDC counterpart. Recommendations are made to
improve the handling of child neglect in Appalachia by social workers.

481   Schlieper, Anne. "Mother-child interaction observed at home." Am
      J Orthopsychiatry 45(3): 468-72, April, 1975. (16 References).
An account of a nursery school evaluation project in which the interaction
of seven middle class mother-child pairs was observed at home and compared to that of sixteen mother-child pairs from a lower socioeconomic
group. In contrast to other studies which have reported that lower class
mothers interact less with their children, this study revealed few inter-
actional differences between the two socioeconomic groups. The fact that
the families were observed in the home seems to account for the disagreement with prior studies, most of which were performed in laboratories and
classrooms. The lower socioeconomic status mothers tended to direct
their children more than the middle class mothers, and also tended to
interact slightly more with their children.

482   Singh, Rev. J. A. L., and Zingg, Robert M. Wolf-children and feral
      man. New York: Harper and Row, 1942. 379p. (Bibliography).
Explores the question of whether idiocy is natural or acquired in cases
of feral men and of children isolated by guardians. One author, Rauber,
argues in favor of acquired idiocy or dementia ex separatione. In such

isolation, either the mind remains intact and can continue to develop, or it cannot. Since the most intensive learning occurs during the first two years of life, it seems reasonable to assume that early learning deprivation can lead to a kind of brain atrophy. However, another researcher, Francis N. Maxfield, considers that a wild child's recovery would indicate that isolation in early childhood has little or no permanent effect on the mental and personal development of any child born normally intelligent; cases in which little improvement occurs even when excellent after-care has been given, would indicate an innate mental deficiency. Detailed case histories of the wild-boys of Kronstadt and Aveyron and of two isolated girls are included.

483 Stover, William H., Jr. "Assumptions on battering questioned: letter to editor." Pediatrics 55(5): 748, May, 1975. (3 References).
Questions the assumptions underlying a statement made in a recent journal article (Lauer, B.; Broeck, E. T.; Grossman, M. "Battered child syndrome: review of 130 patients with controls." Pediatrics 54: 67, 1974), that minority and non-white children are less likely to be abused than are white children.

484 Tulkin, Steven R. "An analysis of the concept of cultural deprivation." Dev Psychol 6(2): 326-39, 1972. (58 References).
Many social scientists seem to be unaware of the degree to which the concept of "cultural deprivation" is ethnocentric. Many social programs designed to compensate for this deprivation are ineffective because of their ethnocentric failure to see cultural differences objectively, to understand the effects of specific experiences, and to appreciate the degree to which the majority culture both is deprived in its own way and has deprived minorities of the political and social amenities taken for granted by the majority. The literature regarding cultural relativism is reviewed, and numerous examples of differing cultural values are cited. Emphasis is placed on the need for guidelines for social research which take cultural differences into account objectively and which make the research more relevant to community needs.

485 Yelaja, S. A. "The abused child -- a reminder of despair." Can Welfare 49(2): 8, 10-11, March-April, 1973. (0 References).
Suggests that the focus upon individual pathology in the problem of child abuse and neglect has clouded the fact that these tragedies are symptoms of social pathology. This societal neglect will probably continue to sustain the causes of poverty and continue its effects.

B. PSYCHOLOGICAL CAUSES

1. PSYCHOLOGICAL STUDIES OF ABUSIVE PARENTS

486 Adelson, Lester. "Slaughter of the innocents: a study of forty-six homicides in which the victims were children." N Engl J Med 264(26): 1345-49, June 29, 1961. (0 References).
A study of forty-six homicides of infants and pre-adolescents provides a breakdown of the victims by age, race and sex, and considers the relationships between assailants and victims, the circumstances of death, the fates of the assailants and the cause of death. Thirty-six children

were slain by a parent or close relative. Seventeen of the assailants
were mentally ill or psychotic; nine fathers, however, killed their children in fits of anger following the child's prolonged crying or other
frustrating behavior. Methods and motives in these cases tended to be
wholly dissimilar from those in instances of adult homicide. Three
infants were starved to death and asphyxiation was found to be the cause
of sixteen children's deaths. Three children died in a parent's unsuccessful attempt at suicide. Owing to the absence of witnesses and lack
of external evidence of trauma in most cases, a thorough autopsy alone
uncovered evidence of non-accidental internal injury. In the disposition of these cases, all but one assailant was taken into custody, tried,
and sentenced to a prison term or to a mental hospital.

487   Bach-y-Rita, George, and Veno, Arthur. "Habitual violence: a
        profile of 62 men." Am J Psychiatry 131(9): 1015-17, September,
        1974. (13 References).
Presents results of a study of sixty-two men in prison, the aim of which
was to establish personality and environmental characteristics related to
habitually violent behavior. The most striking finding was the high
rate of self-mutilation among the prisoners--five to six times greater
than the rate expected among a prison population. Many had had unstable
family lives. A high frequency of seizures, concussions, and hallucinations among the subjects (especially during childhood) might be an
indication of hemological impairment. Four sub-groups were defined in
the population: (1) self-destructive, anxious demanding men who suffered
from anxiety, restlessness, and depression; (2) men who were quiet and
withdrawn, possessing delusional systems; (3) a group similar to the
first group, but not as self-destructive; (4) prisoners who were not
self-destructive and did not suffer from delusions. It is suggested
that careful analysis of the psychopathology and past history of prisoners
be conducted as a means of assuring effective treatment. The effect of
environmental deprivation in childhood is pointed out as a possible
catalyst for stimulus-seeking through violent behavior in later life.

488   "Battered child." Newsweek 71(23): 68-69, June 3, 1968. (0
        References).
Briefly describes the injuries common to abused children and highlights
one case study of a battered child to illustrate that with help, these
children can survive and prosper. Frequently, children need to be
separated from their parents in order to recover and lead healthy lives.
Several suggestions as to why parents abuse their children are provided.
Abusing parents come from all professions and social backgrounds and
were often abused or neglected themselves as children.

489   Bennie, Ernest H. "No not non-accidental injury!: letter to
        editor." Lancet 2(7991): 913, October 23, 1976. (2 References).
There may be a connection between the self-destructive or suicidal
behaviors of a parent and his/her physical maltreatment or murder of the
children. The author finds that a high proportion of abusing parents
have various forms of schizophrenia.

490   Bennie, Ernest H., and Sclare, A. B. "The battered child syndrome."
        Am J Psychiatry 125(7): 975-79, January, 1969. (4 References).
A review of ten cases of the battered child syndrome focusing upon the
psychological profile of the assailant. Of the ten parents who assaulted
their children, all were found to be plagued by feelings of inadequacy

and impulsive behavior. The attack on the child usually represented a displacement of aggression against a disturbed domestic situation. The battered child syndrome includes the following features: (1) the assailant, who is the child's parent or parent surrogate, has been involved in a prior emotional crisis with another child; (2) there is a history of repeated assault; (3) the child injured is usually the youngest in the family; (4) there is marital friction; (5) the other children are well cared for; (6) the assailant's explanation of the trauma does not match the injuries.

491 Berkowitz, Leonard. "The expression and reduction of hostility." _Psychol Bull_ 55(5): 266-68, September, 1958. (22 References). Formulates two hypotheses concerning the relationship between an individual's overt aggression and his aggressive drive. The first hypothesis states an individual will act on his aggressive tendencies more often when parents have allowed aggressive behavior. The second hypothesis indicates that the repeated punishment of aggression increases the instigation to aggression. Numerous studies are cited in support of these two hypotheses.

492 Block, Myrna. "Child abuse: what can we do to stop it?" _Forecast Home Econ_ 19(3): F-24-F-28, March, 1974. (2 References). Examines why certain parents abuse their children. Maltreatment by their own parents, young marriages, and an inability to cope with a normal amount of stress complicate the parent's role of a disciplinarian. Legal provisions to protect children and prosecute abusers are listed. Alternatives to removing the child from the home are described, including programs which instruct women in mothering, Parents Anonymous, and outpatient family help sessions.

493 Blumberg, Marvin L. "Psychopathology of the abusing parent." _Am J Psychother_ 28(1): 21-29, January, 1974. (9 References). Considers personality traits of abusing parents and treatment approaches which attempt to maintain the structural integrity of the family. There has been general reluctance to recognize the problem of child abuse until recently, when attention to the problem has become widespread. Parent concealment of abuse and physician reluctance to report makes it impossible to estimate the true incidence of child battering. Popular misconceptions hinder efforts to find solutions to the problem. These include the idea that a universal mothering instinct insures the infant's well-being and the concomitant notion that an abusive mother suffers from psychosis. No specific psychiatric diagnosis can be applied to all child abusers, and numerous factors underlying the problem must be considered. Parents who can afford to escape parenting for some period of time during the day do better than parents who must nurture their children twenty-four hours a day, which perhaps accounts for the fact that mothers are the most frequent abusers. There are, however, some common denominators in the psychopathology of child abusers. Parents typically were abused or neglected themselves, and failed to develop the ability to love. They are narcissistic, immature, have poor ego control and low self-esteem. Role-reversal is a frequent dynamic, in which the mother wants the child to comfort and love her, and interprets the child's crying as rejection and, therefore, as a justification for punishment.

Different treatment approaches have been advocated, including individual psychoanalytically oriented psychotherapy, and direct psychotherapy with ancillary support for the child. Treatment difficulties arise from the patient's distrust of authority figures, making positive transference difficult to achieve, and from the therapist's negative counter-transference. Therapy must be aimed at improving the patient's self-image and ego strength. It must be combined with a rehabilitation program for both the parent and the child, in which an appropriate mothering figure can satisfy the patient's needs for nurturance while teaching her suitable childrearing techniques. Group therapy is also considered, and is felt to have a good probability of success for some. Self-help groups remove the threat of an untrusted authority figure, diminish guilt because of the presence of other offenders, and their anonymity suits the temperament of the person with a poor self-image. Up to half of all cases may be untreatable and removal of the child from his parents becomes the only alternative.

494   Boisvert, Maurice J. "The battered child syndrome." Soc Casework
        53(8): 475-80, October, 1972. (5 References).
Twenty cases of battered children and their families were carefully studied in order to develop a typology of the abusing parent that would systematically identify where the basic problem lies, what causes and maintains the problem, and what can be done to eliminate it. Two major typologies emerged: uncontrollable and controllable battering. The uncontrollable battering typology was divided into four classifications of personality types--psychotic, inadequate, passive-aggressive, and sadistic. For parents falling into this typology, battering was a result of a long-standing personality problem and was, therefore, considered uncontrollable. The controllable battering typology was divided into classifications--displacement of aggression and cold-compulsive discipline. Among parents of this typology, battering resulted either from a situational crisis or from a misconception about the use of physical punishment as discipline. Differential treatment strategies, prognoses for rehabilitation, and probabilities of recurrence of abuse are provided for each of the typologies.

495   Brown, John A., and Daniels, Robert. "Some observations on abusive
        parents." Child Welfare 47(2): 89-94, February, 1968. (1
        Reference).
From the perspective of social casework, an investigation of the psychological dynamics which lead to and result from child abuse. The emotional and behavioral patterns characteristic of the abusive parents are traced for the benefit of social workers who may be called upon to help treat families in which abuse has occurred. The parent is frequently limited intellectually, crippled emotionally, and preoccupied with his own needs. The worker is advised not to petition for the child's removal from the parents except as a last resort, since the removal will only aggravate the existing damage and will often punish the non-abusive as well as the abusive parent.

496   Calef, Victor. "The hostility of parents to children: some notes
        on infertility, child abuse, and abortion." Int J Psychoanal
        Psychother 1(1): 76-96, February, 1972. (4 References).
Discusses the various causes and manifestations of parental hostility. Four case studies are presented.

497   Chandra, R. K. "The battered child." Indian J Pediatr 35(246):
        365, July, 1968. (0 References).

A plea for greater awareness of the psychological circumstances which usually accompany the physical abuse of children. The cases of suspected child abuse, the emotional problems of both the parents and the abused child are frequently subordinated to the physical symptoms of abuse, although awareness of these psychological aspects of child abuse by the examining physician could lead to its detection and prevention. Both parents and children should be met with understanding.

498 Cohen, Michael I.; Raphling, David L.; Green, Phillip E. "Psycho-
       logic aspects of the maltreatment syndrome of childhood." J
       Pediatr 69(2): 279-84, August, 1966. (6 References).
Study of the psychologic motivations of abusing parents made by the Pediatric and Psychiatric Services, United States Air Force Hospital, Forbes Air Force Base, Kansas. Twelve children diagnosed as abused were followed for a two year period. Psychiatric data collected on four of the parents indicated that they tended to be young, immature, and unable to defer their needs for those of their families. These unmet dependency needs, combined with stressful events, commonly precipitated abuse. Two of the parents had themselves been abused as children; aggression felt toward their parents and/or spouse was often thus misplaced. None of them were diagnosed as having a neurotic or psychotic illness. Military life was not viewed as an influence in three instances, and one situation was exacerbated by the husband's absence overseas.

499 Collins, Gary G. "The psycho-social characteristics of child
       abusers." For a summary see: Diss Abstr Int 36A(5): 2520,
       November, 1975.

500 Court, J. "Battering parents." Soc Work 26(1): 20-24, January,
       1969. (22 References).
Focuses on the problems of determining the dynamics of child abuse, i.e., what types of parents are prone to abuse and what does the child do, if anything, to provoke the abuse. Therapy should be directed toward enabling the parent to recognize his own feelings and to thereby gain some control over them.

501 Criswell, Howard D., Jr. "Why do they beat their child?: commen-
       tary." Hum Needs 1(9): 5-7, March, 1973. (0 References).
Discussion of the identification and treatment of abuse-prone parents. The inclination to child abuse is seen in all social strata, and is usually associated with the parent's own traumatic or deprived childhood, coupled with present feelings of inferiority. It is estimated that 80 percent of these parents could be sufficiently rehabilitated to receive permanent custody of their children. The efforts of the Denver Center for the Study of the Abused and Neglected Child to treat parents predisposed to abuse are described. It is suggested that obstetricians could help prevent abuse through the prenatal identification of the inclination to abuse.

502 Dailey, Timothy B. "The labeled deviant as victim or culprit: the
       case of child neglecters. A study of the factors that influence
       the imputation of deviance." For a summary see: Diss Abstr Int
       36A(2): 1105, August, 1975.

503 David, Lester. "The shocking price of parental anger." Read Dig
       85(509): 181-86, September, 1964. (0 References).

Indicates that cases of the battered child syndrome are not limited to
low socioeconomic groups. Typically, parents that abuse children are
self-centered, weak and dependent, and possess feelings of hatred. Cited
are two developments--x-ray evidence and the drafting of a model child
protection law--which will increase protection and prevention.

504 Disbrow, Mildred A. "Parents who abuse their children." Wash State
       J Nurs 42-45(13): 5-9, Summer, 1972. (17 References).
Examines factors which hamper accurate and complete reporting, including
a reluctance of professionals to believe that parents would injure their
own children, a fear of legal complications, and a concern about disturbing the therapeutic relationship. Characteristics of abusing parents,
such as having unrealistic expectations of the child, a tendency to
isolate themselves from others, and a personal insecurity and lack of
identity, are reviewed. The nurse can play a significant role in the
detection and treatment of child abuse and neglect.

505 Flynn, William R. "Frontier justice: a contribution to the theory
       of child battery." Am J Psychiatry 127(3): 375-79, September,
       1970. (6 References).
Two case studies indicate that the abusing parent is not necessarily
psychotic or the victim of his own parents' abuse; rather, a malfunction-
ing of the ego defense system occurs, leading to an inappropriate expression of anger. Excessive denial and repression prevent the patients'
linking one angry episode with another or recognizing this misplaced
anger toward their spouses. In both cases, genetic determinants act as
factors in their choice of which child to abuse. The theory of weakened
ego control supports psychotherapy as a form of treatment for such
patients.

506 Fontana, Vincent J. "Further reflections on maltreatment of chil-
       dren: letter to editor." NY State J Med 68(16): 2214-15,
       August 15, 1968. (10 References).
Describes the psychological reasons for parental abuse of children.
Societal violence is also implicated as a possible sociological explanation for abusive behavior. Further emphasized is the urgent need for
legislative action, educating society to the problems and extent of maltreatment behavior, effective reporting of abuse cases by physicians,
and new treatment alternatives for both the children and the parents.

507 Frank, George H. "The role of the family in the development of
       psychopathology." Psychol Bull 64(3): 191-205, September, 1965.
       (148 References).
A review of the literature of the past forty years concerning the connection between childhood events--especially in relation to the mother--and
the subsequent development of schizophrenia, neurosis, and other psychological problems. The conclusion was drawn that the families of people
with such disorders do not substantially differ from the families of so-
called "normal" people.

508 Gluckman, L. K. "Cruelty to children." NZ Med J 67(426): 155-59,
       January, 1968. (15 References).
Origins and subtle manifestations of cruelty to children throughout
history are discussed from a clinical psychiatrist's point of view. A
child may be maltreated because he is unwanted or because physical punishment is culturally or religiously sanctioned. It is difficult for the

physician to talk directly with a child about maltreatment because an adult guardian is usually present during any examination or visit. Organic brain disease, personality structure disorder, sadism, and attitudinal pathosis are listed as possible causes for parental abuse of children. Psychiatric disorders of the child can also form the basis of differential diagnosis and treatment of the child. Although cruelty is inherent in mankind, the role of preventive medicine is to ensure that individuals are reasonably protected from uncontrollable, destructive drives.

509   Hanson, Ruth, and Smith, Selwyn. "I.Q. of parents of battered babies: letter to editor." Br Med J 1(5905): 455, March 9, 1974. (7 References).
Dr. Clare A. Hyman's criticism (December 22, p. 739) of the authors' paper (November 17, p. 388), which investigates the intellectual functioning of battering parents, is refuted. The authors defend their use of a short form of the Wechsler Adult Intelligence Scale, with comprehension, vocabulary, block design, and picture arrangement subtests, as best reflecting the inability of parents to foresee the consequences of their actions. Results show a fifteen point I.Q. difference between index and control groups. It is argued that Dr. Hyman's conclusion that the low verbal abilities of battering parents can be attributed to withdrawal, depression and non-communicativeness is unjustified.

510   Harrington, J. A. "Violence: a clinical viewpoint." Br Med J 1(5794): 228-31, January 22, 1972. (11 References).
Various theories of the cause of violence are described, including the frustration/violence theory, various psychodynamic and personality theories, imitation, group factors, biological theories of aggression, and neurophysiology of violence.

511   Horn, Pat. "The child-battering parent: sick but slick." Psychol Today 8(7): 32-33, December, 1974. (0 References).
A concise summary of the psychological characteristics typically associated with battering parents, modified by the findings of psychologist Logan Wright, is offered. Personality and I.Q. tests performed on two groups of parents, battering and non-battering, revealed that the former group has a high ability to appear normal. Abusive parents showed high scores on the MMPI L scale, which measures aggression and lack of control, and the MMPI K scale, which indicates that the respondent is falsifying his answers. There is a marked attempt to disguise violent impulses.

512   Hughes, A. F. "The battered baby syndrome -- a multidisciplinary problem." Case Conf 14(8): 304-8, 1967. (13 References).
Briefly surveys the problems of child abuse in Britain from both medical and psychological perspectives. The characteristics of victims, incidents, and perpetrators of child abuse are described, with special attention to the profile of the kinds of parents involved. Opposition to the instigation of criminal proceedings against the parents on the grounds that such actions further damage the fragile home situation is implied.

513   Hyman, Clare A. "I.Q. of parents of battered babies." Br Med J 4(5894): 739, December 22, 1973.
A critique of Dr. Selwyn M. Smith's study on child abuse which revealed that nearly half of the abusing mothers tested had a subnormal or lower

I.Q. A counter investigation pointed out that significant differences between normal and battering parents showed up only in their respective abilities to use verbal concepts, the latter being decidedly lower.

514 Isaacs, Susanna. "Neglect, cruelty, and battering." Br Med J
     3(5820): 224-26, July 22, 1972. (7 References).
Discusses the personality characteristics of abusing parents and how these parents can be helped to recover their ability and desire to care for their children. A non-judgmental and understanding approach is recommended, as opposed to a retributive and punishing one.

515 Komisaruk, Richard. "Clinical evaluation of child abuse-scarred
     families: a preliminary report." Juv Court Judges J 17(2): 66-
     70, Summer, 1966. (0 References).
A report of a study performed by the Clinic for Child Study on some sixty-five families in which child abuse had occurred. The report chiefly concerns the parents who perpetrated the abuse: mental retardation was fairly common among them, they were relatively young and narcissistic, and showed signs of passive dependency. A number of them had lost a significant parental figure early in life. It is suggested that the ego of an abusive parent is usually too weak to control his aggressive impulses. Recommendations are made for the rehabilitation of disturbed families.

516 Lascari, Andre D. "The abused child." J Iowa Med Soc 62(5):
     229-32, May, 1972. (6 References).
The causes, diagnosis, and management of child abuse are discussed. Procedures for reporting child abuse in accordance with the Iowa State law are outlined. An understanding approach to the abusive parents is recommended, and criminal prosecution is strongly discouraged.

517 Lukianowicz, Narcyz. "Battered children." Psychiatr Clin 4(5-6):
     257-80, 1971. (44 References).
Eighteen cases of child battering in Northern Ireland were studied so that the psychodynamics of the syndrome could be traced. The drafting of child abuse legislation on the American model is urged, with particular stress upon mandatory reporting and protection for reporting agencies.

518 Lund, Susan J. N. "Personality and personal history factors of
     child abusing parents." For a summary see: Diss Abstr Int
     36A(6): 3053, December, 1975.

519 Novick, Jack, and Novick, Kerry K. "Beating fantasies in children."
     Int J Psychoanal 53(2): 237-42, 1972. (17 References).
In investigating conscious beating fantasies in children, it is found that the fantasies started in disturbed boys at puberty and were the permanent focus in the boys' psychosexual life. This problem is connected to "an early sadomasochistic relationship to the mother." In girls, at a much younger age, these fantasies were considered a normal stage.

520 Odlum, Doris M. "Neglected children." R Soc Health J 79(6):
     737-43, November-December, 1959. (1 Reference).
Child abuse is a far-reaching problem which has been insufficiently recognized by society. Some common manifestations of cruelty and neglect, which are felt to be inseparable entities and elusive of defini-

tion, are described. The underlying causes of this syndrome are multiple.
Categories of parents likely to abuse their children are suggested: (1)
the physically ill parent; (2) the mentally defective or subnormal parent;
(3) the psychopathic parent; (4) the psychotic parent; and (5) the neurotic parent. The effects of neglect are variable and dependent upon the
temperament of the child. Children respond primarily in two ways: they
may become isolated and introverted or aggressive and anti-social. Social
factors, such as poor housing conditions or the necessity of the mother
working full-time, may also contribute to the potential for abuse.
Neglect or abuse does not necessarily occur at the hands of the primary
parent. The institutionalized child may be deprived of the affection and
attention necessary for his adequate development. A host of social
agencies exist which can deal with the problem of abuse. Their services
must be coordinated to allow for early detection and intervention, and
treatment efforts should be directed to the family as a whole instead of
the present tendency to deal with the situation piecemeal.

521 O'Hearn, Thomas P. "A comparison of fathers in abusive situations
     with fathers in non-abusive situations." For a summary see: Diss
     Abstr Int 35B(7): 3591, January, 1975.

522 Paulson, Morris J.; Afifi, Abdelmonem A.; Chaleff, Anne; et al. "A
     discriminant function procedure for identifying abusing parents."
     Suicide 5(2): 104-13, Summer, 1975. (12 References).
Thirty-three abusive parents and 100 matched controls were administered
the Minnesota Multiphasic Personality Inventory (MMPI). Discriminant
function analyses were performed and separate scales were derived for
males, females, and both sexes combined. Male abusers were characterized
as more hedonistic, self-centered, suspicious, and in conflict with
parental and societal demands. Female abusers demonstrated counter-
culture behaviors, suspicion, distrust, and concern over the motives of
their peer group. In this study, 100 percent of the males and 93 percent
of the females were correctly classified as abusing or non-abusing, which
demonstrates the effectiveness of this psychometric procedure in identifying abusive parents. A cross-validation study with a large, crosscultural sample is required to positively demonstrate the effectiveness
of the procedure in identifying the potential abuser.

523 Paulson, Morris J.; Afifi, Abdelmonem A.; Thomason, Mary L.; et al.
     "The MMPI: a descriptive measure of psychopathology in abusive
     parents." J Clin Psychol 30(3): 387-90, July, 1974. (12
     References).
Uses the MMPI to compare the psychopathology of sixty abusing parents
with a non-abusing control group of similar lower-middle class background and a history of psychiatric care. The subjects were divided into
three categories--abusers, passive abusers, and absolute non-abusers--
and separated by sex. The female passive abusers measured highest on
scales of interpersonal isolation and depression, while the abusing
females measured higher in aggression and authority conflict. For males,
the abusing fathers show marked psychotic symptoms. It is concluded that
abusive fathers and mothers are psychologically different and predict
that the MMPI will facilitate early identification of abusing parents in
the future.

524 Paulson, Morris J.; Schwemer, Gregory T.; Bendel, Robert B.
     "Clinical application of the Pd, Ma and (OH) experimental MMPI

scales to further understanding of abusive parents." J Clin Psychol 32(3): 558-64, July, 1976. (26 References).

Fifty-three adults who were positively identified as responsible for injuring or severely neglecting a child and 113 matched controls were administered the following scales of the MMPI (Minnesota Multi-phasic Personality Inventory): (1) the Pd scale which identifies the amoral, asocial, and emotionally immature personality; (2) the Ma scale which reflects the potential for overactivity, emotional excitement, flight of ideas, and impulsive behavior; and (3) the OH (overcontrolled hostility) scale which tests for the rigid inhibition of aggressive behavior. A 2 X 2 Analysis of Variance procedure was performed to test for the independent effects of experimental group (abusing or non-abusing) and sex of subject, and for any interaction effects between group and sex. It was found that the abusing group showed significantly higher mean scores on the Pd and Ma scales than the control group, which indicates a greater degree of psychosocial pathology, impulse predisposition, and driveness potential on the part of abusers. On several of the Pd subscales, females (from both experimental groups) showed a significantly higher mean score than males, signifying a greater degree of counter-culture conflict, family discord, and authority problems on the part of women. Only one of the seventeen scales showed an interaction effect, and the OH scale did not differentiate between groups, sexes, or interaction. By acquiring an understanding of the personality characteristics of abusing parents, the early identification and effective treatment of potential abusers becomes possible through personality assessment.

525 Reiner, Beatrice S., and Kaufman, Irving. Character disorders in parents of delinquents. New York: Family Service Association of America, 1959. 179p. (Bibliography).

Describes the character disorders of neglectful parents and the treatment plan. The impulse-ridden disorder is discussed according to pregenital levels of development and requires objective treatment by social workers knowledgeable in behavioral theories. The oral character disorder is characterized by low self-esteem and ineffective parenting for both young and older children. These parents are often a financial burden to their communities. Parents with an anal stage disorder have a wide range of behavioral characteristics, including aggression, sado-masochism, and rebellion which require the social worker to adapt treatment methods to individual cases. Those suffering from a phallic-ureathral conflict show kleptomania, competitiveness, and a tendency to act out conflicts.

Treatment of any disorder involves four stages. The first stage focuses on the establishment of a relationship between the caseworker and the client. During the second stage, the client strengthens his self-image by identifying with his model, the caseworker. The third stage aims at establishing the client's individual identity so that in the fourth stage, the client can acquire self-understanding and relinquish treatment in favor of a more mature relationship with the caseworker. It is suggested that fathers be included in the treatment of disturbed mothers, that psychotics not be treated according to the methods described, that, in the client's best interests, cases be transferred as little as possible, and that caseworkers be emotionally strong and receive support from their agencies. The need for coordinating community services is stressed.

526 Rodenburg, Martin. "Child murder by depressed parents." Can Psychiatr Assoc J 16(1): 41-47, February, 1971. (15 References).

Discussion of child murder in terms of incidence and predictability. It is argued that a depressed person, who is likely to turn his aggression onto himself and commit suicide might, if he is a parent, be inclined to filicide as well. Over a tenth of the homicides in Canada in 1968 were child murders, most of the victims being between one and five years of age. An etiology is offered for this phenomenon: the major factors seem to be a disturbed personality in the parent, particularly an inability to handle aggression, and a non-nurturing relationship with the child. When these factors are combined with a depressive illness, the risk of child murder becomes high.

527 Satten, Joseph; Menninger, Karl; Rosen, Irwin; et al. "Murder with-
out apparent motive: a study in personality disorganization." Am
J Psychiatry 117(1): 48-53, July, 1960. (13 References).
The personality structures of four murderers who killed without apparent motive show several common characteristics: (1) lifelong lack of control over aggressive impulses; (2) blurring of boundaries between fantasy and reality with periods of altered consciousness; (3) shallow emotional reactions; and (4) a violent and primitive fantasy life. These character-istics seem to have sprung from a history of parental violence, often sexual, severe emotional deprivation, and ego weakness. Also, all the men had childhood speech difficulties, a finding which confirms the con-nection between their lack of impulse control and their inability to discharge energy into verbal rather than motor outlets. Their victims often had little reality for them as persons, representing, instead, themselves or a key figure from a past traumatic experience. Future research needs to: (1) distinguish these murderers from other murderers and from others with the same problem but who do not kill; (2) determine significance of each factor described; and (3) learn to identify and control these individuals before they kill.

528 Schwartz, E. K. "Child murder today." Hum Context 4(2): 360-61,
1972. (0 References).
Describes a seminar conducted for psychologists and playwrights conceived with the theme of filicide. The principal topic was the parents' denial of their own hostility toward their children.

529 Scott, Pena D. "Fatal battered baby cases." Med Sci Law 13(3):
197-206, July, 1973. (18 References).
A case study of twenty-nine fathers, each charged with killing his child, compared with two non-fatal child abuse studies. Certain demographic characteristics emerge as criteria for differentiating the fatal from the non-fatal group, such as differences in marital status, previous history of violent crimes, biological paternity, and location of the injuries on the victims. Sentencing of the fathers, who were charged with murder, appeared to be arbitrary and ranged from probation to life imprisonment with twenty-one of them receiving substantial prison sen-tences. Since so many do have to serve time, prison treatment facilities, where men can receive help to overcome their personality disorders, are essential. Receiving follow-up care after leaving prison, such as family counseling through a psychiatric clinic, could also be helpful.

530 Segal, Rose S. "A comparison of some characteristics of abusing
and neglecting, non-abusing parents." For a summary see: Diss
Abstr Int 32A(6): 3434, December, 1971.

531   Sheriff, Hilla.   "The abused child." J SC Med Assoc 60(6): 191-
         93, June, 1964. (3 References).
Presents general characteristics and numerical dimensions of the problem
of the abused child, and includes a brief list of the personality traits
of the abusing parent. The clinical picture and the use of x-ray for
diagnosis are described. Brief attention is given to solutions involving
therapeutic counseling and legal protection.

532   Silver, Larry B.   "The psychological aspects of the battered child
         and his parents." Clin Proc Child Hosp 24(11): 355-64,
         December, 1968. (1 Reference).
Discusses psychological characteristics of the battering parent and the
resulting psychological effects on the battered child. The purpose of
the study is to formulate behavior patterns that could be used to detect
abusers so that preventive measures can be taken. In order to accentuate
the characteristics of battering parents and children, the report con-
trasts the behavior patterns of parents whose children were accidentally
injured with the behavior of battering parents, as well as the behavior
of accidentally injured children with battered children. A discussion
session with the author responding to specific questions related to
abuse concludes the articles.

533   Smith, Selwyn, M.; Hanson, Ruth; Noble, Sheila. "Parents of bat-
         tered babies: a controlled study." Br Med J 4(5889): 388-91,
         November, 1973. (24 References).
A study designed to formulate a psychological profile of abusing parents.
Results indicate that child abusers are generally young people, who have
experienced parenthood prematurely, and are more likely to be from a
lower social class. The study included 214 parents of battered babies.
Each of the parents was examined for personality or psychopathic disorders. Findings reveal that 76 percent of the mothers and 64 percent
of the fathers had abnormal personalities. Slightly less than half of
the mothers were neurotic and more than half of the fathers with abnormal
personalities were psychopaths. Criminal records and the results of
intelligence tests for all parents were recorded. Because many of the
children who are returned home are battered again, protecting the child
must be the most important concern. When there is little hope of rehabilitating the parents, the child should be removed from the home.

534   ————. "Parents of battered children: a controlled study."
         In: Franklin, Alfred White, ed. Concerning child abuse. New
         York: Churchill Livingstone, 1975. 41-48. (0 References).
The parents of 134 children with inflicted injuries were compared with
the parents of fifty-three children with accidental injuries in order
to study the characteristics of the abusive parent. Both groups of
parents were administered the Wechsler Adult Intelligence Scale, the
Eysenck Personality Inventory, and the General Health Questionnaire. It
was found that abusive parents were of significantly lower social class
than the controls. Seventy-six percent of the mothers and 64 percent
of the fathers in the abusive group had an abnormal personality. Psychotic reactions were observed in four mothers and one father in the
abusive group. Significantly fewer of the non-abusive parents had
abnormal personalities, and none were found to be psychotic. Approximately 29 percent of the fathers and 11 percent of the mothers in the
abusive group had a criminal record. Of the control group, none of the
mothers and only two of the fathers had a criminal record. It was found

that nearly half of the abusive mothers were of borderline or subnormal intelligence. The average age of the abusive mothers at the birth of their first infant was 19.7 years, while the average age of the national sample at the birth of the first child was 23.3 years. It may be concluded that battering is associated with youthful parenthood, lower social class, parental criminality, intellectual subnormality of the mother, and personality abnormality in both parents.

535 Smith, Selwyn M.; Honigsberger, Leo; Smith, Carol A. "EEG and personality factors in baby batterers." Br Med J 3(5870): 20-22, July 7, 1973. (13 References).
Investigates EEG findings and accompanying personality disturbances among child abusers. Eight out of thirty-five subjects were found to have abnormal EEG's and to be persistent batterers, and six out of these eight were classed as aggressive psychopaths. These findings tentatively suggest that a sub-group among child abusers resembles those who commit other acts of violence and may not respond to the supportive tactics pervasively employed in treatment programs for abusive parents.

536 ————. "EEG and personality factors in child batterers." In: Franklin, Alfred White, ed. Concerning child abuse. New York: Churchill Livingstone, 1975. 49-55. (0 References).
Thirty-five battering parents and sixteen of their spouses were subjected to EEG examination. The parents were divided into two groups—those with normal and those with abnormal EEG's. Of the thirty-five battering parents, eight (23 percent) had demonstrably abnormal EEG's. These eight parents were found to be of low intelligence, though no lower on the average than were those subjects in whom no EEG abnormality could be shown. All eight subjects with abnormal EEG's could be classified as having a personality disorder. The presence of an abnormal EEG in almost one-quarter of the cases suggests that in at least a sub-group of battering parents, there may be an organic basis for the violent, antisocial behavior against their children. It may, therefore, be dangerous to assume that all parents who batter their children do so because they received inadequate mothering as children.

537 Spinetta, John J., and Rigler, David. "The child-abusing parent: a psychological review." Psychol Bull 77(4): 296-304, April, 1972. (88 References).
Reviews the literature of the previous decade to obtain generalizations on the psychological characteristics of the abusing parent. Results indicate that economic and social stresses alone are not responsible for abuse, although they may add to the causative factors within the parent's personality. Many abusing parents were themselves abused and deprived as children. In addition, their knowledge of childrearing may be limited and include expectations that the child meet their needs. While the literature has come to agree that these parents rarely show severe psychotic tendencies, there is evidence of character disturbance and unchecked aggressive impulses. Merrill's three clusters of parental personality characteristics are listed, along with a brief criticism of a national survey citing poverty as a major factor in child abuse cases.

538 Thatcher, Aileen A. "Personality correlates of abuse and neglect in children." For a summary see: Diss Abstr Int 37B(9): 4658-59, March, 1977.

539 Van Stolk, Mary. <u>The battered child in Canada.</u> Toronto, Canada:
       McClelland and Stewart, 1973. 127p. (Bibliography).
Explores the various dimensions of the child abuse syndrome, with particular attention given to the state of the problem in Canada. A sketch of
the battering parent suggests that gross misperceptions of the child's
capabilities, the sincere belief that terrible things will happen to the
child if he does not learn to obey authority, and punitive responses to
the child's failure to meet the parent's needs are typical. The battering parent does not identify with the child as a human being and cannot
feel his predicament. A hypothetical situation in which a child's feeding, toilet-training, and crying behavior leads to abuse illustrates some
of the stress factors in a parent-child relationship which can cause a
pattern of abuse to emerge. Although child batterers are found in all
walks of life, there is no evidence to indicate that all people are
potential child abusers. Specific intrapsychic mechanisms interact with
environmental and cultural factors to produce a child abuser. The
acceptance of the act of battering by the non-battering parent, however,
does reveal a tolerance for violence which is cultural as well as individual.

Gross forms of child battering are only one aspect of a larger problem
of violence in society. Corporal punishment of children is commonly
accepted and the authority of the parent is felt to be inviolable. "Soft
core" abuse of children is a widespread and socially accepted phenomenon.
This cultural pattern and the pervasiveness of media violence provides
a model of behavior for both children and adults. Violence breeds
violence, as it is sanctioned as an appropriate response to stress. In
order to challenge those cultural attitudes which are destructive to
healthy childrearing practices, new models for parenthood need to be
taught, with the media as a key component in an extensive educational
effort.

Although cultural reform is stressed as a necessary part of any long-
term solution, the role of the physician in dealing with existing cases
of abuse is also discussed. It is felt that the social worker attempting
to intervene in problem families is often hampered by the physician's
unwillingness to document abuse and by the court's lack of understanding
of the battered child syndrome. Extensive legal and social reform is
necessary in Canada in order to insure that the rights of the child are
given precedence over parents' rights, that abuse is consistently
detected and reported, and that adequate services for its treatment,
such as good child-care institutions, foster homes, and follow-up of
abused children, are established.

540 Wasserman, Sidney. "The abused parent of the abused child."
       <u>Children</u> 14(5): 175-79, September-October, 1967. (6 References).
Points out the potential for violence within all of us and calls for a
sensitive look at the needs of the abusive parent. Abusing parents of
all social classes have common psychological characteristics: they were
denied security, safety, and love as children. Therapy for the parents
is a long process and necessitates steady, firm authority from one
nurturing person in order to develop a close, dependable, secure, and
trusting relationship. The community must also develop a positive
working attitude toward the family so that they do not feel excluded and
rejected.

541 Wolff, Wirt M., and Morris, Larry A. "Intellectual and personality
     characteristics of parents of autistic children." <u>J Abnorm Psychol</u>
     77(2): 155-61, April, 1971. (26 References).
Presents the results of a study of the demographic, intellectual, and
personality characteristics of five sets of parents with autistic children. The parents were found to be moderately well-educated and socio-
economically above-average. They were slightly above average intellectually, but the findings did not support the widespread assumption that
the parents of autistic children are usually well above average in mental
capacity. And, contrary to another assumption, these parents were not
cold or remote, but were normally demonstrative. The mothers' personality
patterns resembled those of mothers of disturbed children. These findings
suggest that the preconceptions of the scientific community regarding the
environments of autistic children need revision, and that the psychogenic
etiology of autism may not be valid.

542 Wright, Logan. "The 'sick but slick' syndrome as a personality
     component of parents of battered children." <u>J Clin Psychol</u> 32(1):
     41-45, January, 1976. (13 References).
Thirteen parents convicted in court of battering their children and thirteen matched controls were given a battery of personality tests, including
Rorschach, Minnesota Multiphasic Personality Inventory, and Rosenzweig
Picture Frustration Study. On those scales where the social desirability
of the items were more obvious, the battering parents appeared healthier
than the control group. That is, they demonstrated low bizarre content,
high intro-punitiveness, and high conformity. However, on those scales
where the socially desirable response was more ambiguous, the battering
parents appeared significantly more disturbed. These findings indicated
that the battering parents did have psychological problems but that they
presented themselves as healthy and unlikely to abuse their children
whenever possible. This combination of personality traits was labeled
the "sick but slick" syndrome.

543 Young, Leontine R. "The behavior syndromes of parents who neglect
     and abuse their children." For a summary see: <u>Diss Abstr</u> 24(8):
     3456, February, 1964.

2. PSYCHOLOGICAL PROFILES OF THE ABUSIVE MOTHER

544 Anthony, E. James, and Kreitman, Norman. "Murderous obsessions in
     mothers toward their own children." In: Anthony, E. James, and
     Benedek, Therese, eds. <u>Parenthood: its psychology and psycho-</u>
     <u>pathology</u>. Boston: Little, Brown, 1970. 479-98. (19 References).
Presents a study of forty women who experienced murderous impulses toward
their children. These impulses were accompanied by overwhelming feelings
of remorse, shame, and tenderness. Approximately half of these women
were diagnosed as obsessional and half as depressives. The murderous
wish remained a fantasy in nearly all instances and rarely led to episodes
of severe abuse or neglect. In fact, these women often expressed reactive
overconcern about their children's health. Half of the patients reported
an intensification of their aggressive impulses toward the child before
and during their menstrual period. In addition to impulses centered on
the child, the women often had fears about attacking strangers, committing
suicide, or making inappropriate sexual advances. Most of the patients
had been depressed at some stage of their illness.

The following factors emerged in the psychotherapy of these women: (1) general sense of being unloved in childhood; (2) the absence of maternal models for identification; (3) a profound ambivalence toward their own parents; (4) exposure to interparental aggression; and (5) an inadequate system of ego defenses. In families of at least two children, the hostile feelings of the mother were usually directed toward one particular child (nineteen out of twenty-one cases). In seventeen cases, the only child was the object of aggressive impulses. Selection of the disliked child was frequently related to the identification of that child with the parent's own mother, father, or sibling. It is suggested that these findings may elucidate the nature of postpartum psychoses as well as the psychodynamics of infanticide, filicide, and homicide.

545 Bardon, D.; Glaser, Y. I. M.; Prothero, D.; et al. "Mother and baby
       unit: psychiatric survey of 115 cases." Br Med J 2(5607): 755-
       58, June 22, 1968. (22 References).
A group of 115 mothers who had become mentally ill during or shortly after pregnancy were permitted to bring their infants with them while they were treated at a psychiatric hospital. The results were not conclusive: two mothers committed suicide in the follow-up period, one died of pulmonary embolism in the hospital, 89 percent were deemed able to care for their infants after treatment, but there had been no prior evidence that the mental illness had interfered with maternal care. Nevertheless, the unit was described as moderately successful.

546 Bishop, Frank. "Perception, memory, and pathological identification
       as precipitating factors in parental attacks on children." Med J
       Aust 2(7): 243-45, August 16, 1975. (4 References).
Three case histories of abusing mothers and psychological explanations for the abuse are presented. Each mother failed to perceive her infant or child as a unique individual. Certain personality or behavioral traits of the child reminded the mother of other people or past situations in her life that were very disturbing or intolerable to her. During times of stress, the mother would project these distressing memories onto her child. (For example, the child might become identified with the mother's parent or estranged husband.) Then, the mother would lash out against the child as if he were this other hated person. An understanding of why an incident of child abuse occurs can only be acquired if the meaning of the child's behavior to the parent at the moment of maltreatment is explained.

547 Brody, Sylvia. "A mother is being beaten: an instinctual deriva-
       tive and infant care." In: Anthony, E. James, and Benedek,
       Therese, eds. Parenthood: its psychology and psychopathology.
       Boston: Little, Brown, 1970. 427-47. (18 References).
Examines the beating fantasy and its relationship to maternal behavior. The study is based on the hypothesis that a mother has the unconscious wish to be beaten by her father. Defenses against this wish range from complete sublimation to repression and identification with the aggressor. One hundred twenty-two mother-infant pairs were observed during feeding acts. Mothers were classified into one of seven types according to their behavior during feeding, each type representing the use of a different defense. The greater ability of the mother to sublimate the fantasy, the healthier was her relationship with her child. Abuse was likely to occur when mothers interpreted an internalized image of the beating father as badness on the part of the child or when they identified

with the aggressor and disguised the beating as physical discipline for
moral reasons.

548 Dalton, K. "Paramenstrual baby battering: letter to editor." <u>Br
     Med J</u> 2(5965): 279, May 3, 1975. (1 Reference).
Suggests that many otherwise model mothers may impulsively injure their
children in a moment of premenstrual irritability. The author's clinical
experience confirms this hypothesis, but further research is needed to
determine the true incidence of menstrually-related child abuse. Pro-
gesterone therapy is an effective means of alleviating the condition,
which can be rapidly resolved if recognized.

549 Evans, Alan Lee. "Personality characteristics of child-abusing
     mothers." For a summary see: <u>Diss Abstr Int</u> 37B(12): 6322,
     June, 1977.

550 Evans, S. L.; Reinhart, J. B.; Succop, R. A. "Failure to thrive:
     a study of 45 children and their families." <u>Am Acad Psychiatry J</u>
     2: 440-57, 1972. (16 References).
Forty families with children who were failing to thrive were distributed
into three profile groups, which were generally determined by the characteristics of the mother. The attributes singled out as indicative
included the mother's psychological make-up, her perceptions of her children, and her management of her family. As a result of this retrospective study, it was concluded that the failure to thrive syndrome can be
corrected only through aggressive intervention.

551 Farley, F. H. "Birth order and a two-dimensional assessment of
     personality." <u>J Pers Assess</u> 39(2): 151-53, 1975. (8 References).
Investigation of the possible correlation between birth order and degree
of extraversion/introversion and neuroticism in personality. One hundred
forty-one women were given the Eysenck Personality Inventory, on which
extraversion and neuroticism register as high scores. No correlation
was found.

552 Floyd, Linda M. "Personality characteristics of abusing and neglect-
     ing mothers." For a summary see: <u>Diss Abstr Int</u> 36B(7): 3600,
     January, 1976.

553 Forrest, Tess. "The family dynamics of maternal violence. <u>J Am
     Acad Psychoanal</u> 2(3): 215-30, 1974.
Discusses the psychodynamics of the maternal filicidal impulse, which is
regarded as a universal phenomenon. Four case studies are presented to
demonstrate the long-term, inter-generational effects of literal and
symbolic maternal violence. An approach to therapy is described.

554 Gibbens, T. C. N. "Female offenders." <u>Br J Hosp Med</u> 6(3): 279-
     86, September, 1971. (44 References).
Female criminals are shown to be more disturbed emotionally than male
criminals, according to an analysis of the typical characteristics and
typical crimes of female offenders. Women who murder or abuse their
children seem to suffer from depression or physical/mental exhaustion.

555 Katz, Morton L. "A comparison of ego functioning in filicidal and
     physically child-abusing mothers." For a summary see: <u>Diss Abstr
     Int</u> 36B(11): 5798, May, 1976.

556   Kenel, Mary E. "A study of the cognitive dimension of impulsivity-reflectivity and aggression in female child abusers." For a summary see: <u>Diss Abstr Int</u> 37B(3): 1438, September, 1976.

557   Melnick, Barry, and Hurley, John R. "Distinctive personality attributes of child-abusing mothers." <u>J Consult Clin Psychol</u> 33(6): 746-49, December, 1969. (31 References).
Ten abusive mothers and ten matched controls were given five subscales of the California Test of Personality (CTP), the Family Concept Inventory (FCI), the Manifest Rejection (MR) scale, and a set of twelve TAT cards. Analysis of the tests revealed that abusive mothers had lower self-esteem, less family satisfaction, a greater degree of pathogenicity, less need to provide nurturance, higher frustration of dependency needs, and a less openly rejecting attitude toward children than the non-abusive controls. The abusive mothers' low need to provide nurturance suggests that these women have a deficient capacity to empathize with their children's needs. Their frustrated need for dependence reflects feelings of being unable to cope with the responsibilities of life. The unexpected finding that abusive mothers are less rejecting of their children on the MR scale than non-abusive mothers can be explained by their increased defensiveness about having injured their child. These findings are inconsistent with the view that abusive mothers have "normal" personalities.

558   Myers, Steven A. "Maternal filicide." <u>Am J Dis Child</u> 120(12): 534-36, December, 1970. (6 References).
A brief description of the most common characteristics of maternal filicide, based on a study of thirty-five cases occurring in Detroit between 1940 and 1965. Most of the mothers who killed their children were found to be psychotic at the time of the act, most frequently suffering from a psychotic depression, and a large group appeared to be schizophrenic. Symptoms of the mother's disturbed state included anorexia, insomnia, fatigue, agitation, guilt, and a resentment of interference. A number of the women were suicidal, although their depression was not associated with the common postpartum depression, which is more often linked with neonaticide.

559   Polansky, Norman A.; DeSaix, Christine; Sharlin, Shlomo A. <u>Child neglect: understanding and reaching the parent</u>. New York: Child Welfare League of America, Inc., 1976. 94p. (Bibliography).
Child neglect and abuse are not identical conditions: the personalities of the parents and the long-term effects on the children may be quite different. A child is neglected when he is malnourished, without proper shelter, without supervision, lacking essential medical care, denied normal experiences that produce feelings of being loved and wanted, exploited, emotionally disturbed due to problems in the home, or exposed to unwholesome and demoralizing circumstances. It is often difficult to distinguish neglect from a generalized poor standard of living. The Childhood Level of Living Scale (presented in Appendix A) can be used to measure the quality of physical and emotional/cognitive care of the child. In order to treat child neglect, a psychodiagnosis of the neglectful mother must be made. The Maternal Characteristics Scale (presented in Appendix B) and an assessment of the parent's verbal accessibility (or readiness to express feelings and attitudes) are tools that can help in this diagnosis.

There are five types of neglectful mothers: the apathetic-futile mother, the impulse-ridden mother, the mentally retarded mother, the mother in reactive depression, and the psychotic mother. The apathetic-futile mother is characterized by an emotional numbness, low competence in most areas, verbal inaccessibility, and a pervasive attitude that nothing is really worth doing. Children of these mothers are often withdrawn, lethargic, and intellectually retarded. The impulse-ridden mother is restless and unable to tolerate stress or frustration. She craves excitement and is manipulative of other people. As a result, the children of impulsive neglectful mothers show hostile-defiant behavior. The mentally retarded mother is often childlike and unable to make appropriate adult judgments. Her intellectual deficit may lead to child neglect because she is not likely to notice early symptoms of illness or to follow through on medical directions when her child is ill. Because the mother is unable to provide cognitive stimulation for the child, the cycle of school failure, social ineptness, and eventual retardation is likely to be repeated. The mother in reactive depression is incapacitated by grief. She is unable to care for the physical and emotional needs of her children, and they are likely to show evidence of emotional disturbances. Finally, the psychotic mother is characterized by social withdrawal, inappropriateness of mood, bizarre behaviors, delusional thinking, hallucinations, and/or severe anxiety. A child's personality can obviously be damaged by identification with a psychotic parent. Differential treatment approaches for each type of neglectful mother and their children are presented.

560 Sheridan, Mary D. "Intelligence of 100 neglectful mothers." Br
    Med J 1(4958): 91-93, January 14, 1956. (4 References).
Intelligence tests were administered to 100 women who had been convicted of willful neglect. They were to receive training at Mayflower, a Salvation Army home in Plymouth, England. The results indicated that the intelligence curve for these women followed a similar pattern compared to the normal curve. However, it was skewed to the lower end of the scale with the average I.Q. being 79.8. Also, there was a small percentage of I.Q.s which fell at the high end of the scale. These findings suggested that there were a significant number of subnormal women represented in the study. Follow-up studies (still in progress at the time of writing) indicated that seventy-six mothers had derived benefits from the residential training in child care, cooking, housework, laundry, and shopping.

561 Smith, Selwyn M., and Hanson, Ruth. "Failure to thrive and anorexia
    nervosa." Postgrad Med J 48(560): 382-84, June, 1972. (14
    References).
A woman with a history of anorexia nervosa battered her oldest son and starved her second child to death. The case is described, including the results of psychological tests given to both parents. A possible link between the mother's anorexia nervosa and her abusive behavior is highlighted.

562 Wisner, Joan Jones. "Mothers who neglect: differentiating factors
    of their daily lives." For a summary see: Diss Abstr Int 38A(2):
    1028, August, 1977.

C. DYNAMICS OF PREGNANCY AND THE NEONATAL PERIOD

1. PRENATAL INDICATORS OF ABUSE

563 Brosseau, B. E. "Battered child and unwanted pregnancy: letter to
     editor." Can Med Assoc J 112(9): 1038, May 3, 1975. (2
     References).
This letter refutes the claim of a previous article that unwanted infants
comprise the majority of battered children.

564 Corry, Peter C. "Children at risk: letter to editor." Br Med J
     1(6068): 1084, April 23, 1977. (0 References).
A response to a study which found that a significant number of a group
of abused children come from families with perinatal risk factors.
Results show that 10 percent of the non-abused group also had these risk
factors.

565 Court, Joan. "Nurture and nature: the nurturing problem." In:
     Franklin, Alfred W., ed. Concerning child abuse. New York:
     Churchill Livingstone, 1975. 106-12. (0 References).
Discusses the causes and treatment for improper child care. Abusive and
neglectful parents often experience the same treatment as children and
are ill-prepared to care for their own offspring. A history of the
parents during the prenatal period can aid in the prediction of potential
abuse. Family stresses involving finances, marriage, or too many offspring can lead to abuse. Traditionally, treatment has focused on the
medical needs of the child, but attention to the psychosocial needs of
both parents and child is desired.

566 Court, Joan, and Robinson, W. "The battered child syndrome."
     Midwives Chron Nurs Notes 83(990): 212-16, July, 1970. (13
     References).
Several of the psychosocial traits which characterize abusive parents
are enumerated for the benefit of midwives taking care of pregnant women
and young mothers. The expectation is that the midwives will recognize
the potential for abusive behavior among their patients and will be able
to help these mothers counteract these tendencies in themselves and
develop loving relationships with their children.

567 Fanaroff, Avroy; Kennell, John H.; Klaus, Marshall H. "Follow-up
     of low birth weight infants -- the predictive value of maternal
     visiting patterns." Pediatrics 49(2): 287-90, February, 1972.
     (8 References).
The surviving child of a high-risk pregnancy is a likely victim of battering and failure to thrive. A retrospective study (1969) of premature
babies placed in an intensive care nursery for longer than two weeks
included observations of maternal visiting patterns and their relation
to the incidence of battered babies. The frequency of visits and telephone calls to the nursery were recorded. It was found that disorders
of mothering occurred in high proportions among infrequent visitors.
These findings suggest a need to identify mothers at risk. Recommendations include recording the frequency of visits and phone calls made by
parents and actively encouraging parents to visit the intensive care
nursery.

568 Fomufod, Antoine K. "Low birth weight and early neonatal separation
     as factors in child abuse." <u>J Natl Med Assoc</u> 68(2): 106-9, March,
     1976. (16 References).
A review of studies demonstrating that low birth weight of an infant and/
or hospitalization in the immediate newborn period may lead to subsequent
child abuse. Early separation of the mother from the child impairs the
establishment of a warm, mother-infant relationship. This situation,
along with other factors, can contribute to the child abuse syndrome.
Definite steps should be taken through the efforts of obstetrics and
pediatrics to permit mothers to interact with their babies while they are
hospitalized so that a strong maternal-infant bond can be formed. The
family situation and parental visiting behavior should be carefully
reviewed so that potential child abusers can be identified and helped
through the coordinated efforts of an interdisciplinary child abuse treatment team.

569 Fomufod, Antoine K.; Sinkford, Stanley M.; Louy, Vicki E. "Mother-
     child separation at birth: a contributing factor in child abuse:
     letter to editor." <u>Lancet</u> 2(7934): 549-50, September 20, 1975.
     (5 References).
Describes a retrospective study of child abuse cases over a one-year
period with particular emphasis placed on the birth weight and gesta-
tional age of the infant, neonatal problems, and duration of the infant's
hospital stay immediately after birth. The results indicate that low
birth weight and infant separation at birth due to neonatal hospitalization are possible factors in the etiology of child abuse.

570 Guttmacher, Alan F. "Unwanted pregnancy: a challenge to mental
     health." <u>Ment Hyg</u> 51: 512-16, 1967. (5 References).
Discussion of the emotional and behavioral disturbances (among them,
child battering) which frequently result from unwanted pregnancies.
Examples of such problems are cited and their social implications are
drawn. Members of the mental health community are urged to help prevent
the mental illnesses associated with unwanted children by increasing
their support for Planned Parenthood.

571 Hedges, Wallace H. V. "The American dream and the unwanted child."
     For a summary see: <u>Diss Abstr Int</u> 38A(2): 869, August, 1977.

572 Holman, R. R., and Kanwar, S. "Early life of the 'battered
     child.'" <u>Arch Dis Child</u> 50(1): 78-80, January, 1975. (7
     References).
Studies the obstetric histories and early lives of twenty-eight abused
children designed to locate factors that could be used as indicators for
predicting abuse. Several significant factors emerged, namely, prematurity, low birth weight, and poor antenatal care. Further environmental stresses such as prolonged separation of mother and child after
birth, illness, an undesirable home environment, and parental psychological problems appear to contribute to abusive behavior in susceptible
individuals.

573 Klein, Michael, and Stern, Leo. "Low birth weight and the battered
     child syndrome." <u>Am J Dis Child</u> 122(1): 15-18, July, 1971.
     (11 References).
An investigation to determine the correlation between low birth weight
and risk to battering. The study, which reviewed fifty-one cases of

abused babies over nine years, revealed that 23.5 percent were low birth weight babies. Although several factors were difficult to control over the nine year period (such as changes in diagnostic criteria), the 23.5 percent figure was excessive when compared to the low birth weight of 9 to 10 percent in the general population of Montreal. It is suggested that mothers of premature babies be encouraged to have contact with their children while they are still very sick, in order to strengthen the bond between them and avoid an extended separation. This would also give the staff a chance to watch the mother's attitude toward her baby, helping her gain insights into her ability to care for the child. In this way, high risk relationships could be detected early and intervention measures initiated.

574 Lynch, Margaret A. "Ill-health and child abuse." Lancet 2(7928):
       317-19, August 16, 1975. (14 References).
Compares the early lives of a group of abused children with their non-abused siblings in order to examine the assertion commonly made by abusive parents that one particular child, the abused child, is much more difficult to raise. Results of the investigation indicated that six factors significantly differentiated the early lives of the abused children from the non-abused children: (1) abnormal pregnancy; (2) problem labor or delivery; (3) neonatal separation; (4) other separation during the first six months; (5) illnesses in the child during the first year; (6) illnesses in the mother during the first year. This suggests that child abuse can be the result of a difficult pregnancy. The treatment of parents during and immediately following pregnancy would help prevent abuse.

575 Maginnis, Elizabeth; Pivchik, Elizabeth; Smith, Nancy. "A social
       worker looks at failure to thrive." Child Welfare 46(1): 335-
       58, January, 1967. (5 References).
An examination of the non-organic growth failure syndrome from the perspective of the social worker. The families of some 151 children (average age: 12.5 months) admitted to a hospital for failure to thrive were studied and interviewed by welfare workers. The interviews revealed that the birth of the child had been accompanied by stress in most of the families, and that a significant proportion of the mothers had either wanted a child of the opposite sex, or not wanted a child at all. The families came from a number of socioeconomic groups, were not particularly mobile, and almost half of the parents questioned had come from intact families, features which differed from the expected background information. Most of the parents seeking medical help did not seek caseworker intervention, which suggests that hospital social workers should prolong the exploratory phase of the treatment in order to help parents see their own involvement in the problem.

576 Pasamanick, Benjamin. "Ill-health and child abuse: letter to
       editor." Lancet 2(7934): 550, September 20, 1975. (2 Refer-
       ences).
Describes the results of a longitudinal study of the sequelae of prematurity. A significant linear relationship was found between the degree of maternal tension and signs of brain dysfunction in the infant. In addition, it was discovered that the neurologically abnormal child had a tense mother. These defects in the infants could elevate parental stress and ultimately precipitate child abuse.

577 Sauer, L. W. "Pediatric problems of teen-age parents: editorial."
     <u>J Int Coll Surg</u> 43(5): 556-59, May, 1965. (0 References).
Pediatric problems such as prematurity, birth defects, infection, and
child abuse occur more frequently in the children of teen-age parents
than in other children. Some reasons for their occurrence and means of
prevention are offered.

578 Severo, Richard. "The tragedy of Joanne." <u>Senior Scholastic</u>
     109(14): 23-26, March 24, 1977. (0 References).
Recounts the background of a mother, Joanne, accused of criminal neglect.
Neighbors from Joanne's past described her as withdrawn and "not belonging." Most of her high school life was spent with children or animals.
She left home as a means of self-discovery and eventually ended up in a
tenement apartment in New York, where she purchased a pet dog. Becoming
pregnant, as a result of rape, Joanne never asked for anyone's assistance
during pregnancy. While in the hospital at the time of her baby's birth,
no one detected her need for psychological and social work help. Joanne
and her baby were released on September 5, the day before Labor Day.
Since her money had been locked in the hospital's property room and, due
to administrative procedure, could not be returned to her until the day
after Labor Day, she left the hospital with no money to feed herself,
her baby, or her dog. On Labor Day, Joanne returned to the hospital for
her money. During her absence, the hungry dog killed the infant. In
light of this history, charges against Joanne were dropped and she
received immediate monetary assistance and counseling.

579 Sloan, R. E. G.; Horrobin, R.; Wiffin, E. M. "Antenatal battering:
     letter to editor." <u>Br Med J</u> 4(5945): 655, December 14, 1974.
     (0 References).
Reports on one case of threatened antenatal battering by a mother-to-be.
A close watch of women during the prenatal period might point out those
mothers who run a high risk of becoming child abusers.

580 Smith, Selwyn M., and Hanson, Ruth. "134 battered children: a
     medical and psychological study." <u>Br Med J</u> 3(5932): 666-70,
     September 14, 1974. (61 References).
Low birth weight babies and all children under two years of age suffer
a particular risk of being abused. The child is not always the single
scapegoat of the family, but in many instances a sibling has also been
battered or has even died. In addition to fractures and bruises, many
children suffer scalds and burns, injuries often reported as accidental
by parents. After measuring the children's locomotor development, hearing, speech, personal-social behavior on the Griffiths' Mental Development Scales, the authors conclude that battering often results in
permanent neurological impairment and may lead to developmental retardation.

581 Stern, Leo. "Prematurity as a factor in child abuse." <u>Hosp Pract</u>
     8(5): 117-23, May, 1973. (9 References).
Discussion of the often-noticed coincidence of intensive care and prematurity with child abuse. A causal relationship is suggested: the
premature infant usually stays in the hospital away from his parents
for a longer period of time than full-term infants, and this prolonged
separation may inhibit parent-child bonding at a crucial stage, thus
fostering neglect and perhaps abuse of the child later on. This theory
has been borne out by a number of case histories. The experience of the

Montreal Children's Hospital in encouraging parents of hospitalized newborns to stay with and care for their infants resulted in more positive
parent-child attitudes than are usually observed in cases of neonatal
hospitalization.

582 Tompkins, Kevin J. "The unwanted pregnancy: letter to editor."
     Can Med Assoc J 112(3): 279-80, February 8, 1975. (0 References).
Reproves S. H. Stone and K. E. Scott, authors of "The Unwanted Pregnancy"
(1974), for their irresponsible and unproven suggestion that unwanted
children become beaten and neglected children.

2. PARENT-TO-INFANT BONDING FAILURE

583 Besdine, Matthew. "Nurturing and ego development." Psychoanal Rev
     60(1): 19-43, Spring, 1973. (147 References).
Discusses the relationship between mothering and the intellectual development of the child. The quality, quantity, and intensity of mothering are
regarded as the variables most significantly affecting the child's intellectual and emotional growth. It has been found that problems like
retardation in the mother ultimately develop in the child, not because
of brain damage, but because the child's responses have been geared to
the mother's limited intelligence, and, therefore, only those neural
patterns producing simple, dull behavior have developed. Five kinds of
mothering are identified: negligent (or abusive) mothering (most prevalent among the poor and disadvantaged), reluctant mothering, average
mothering, dedicated (or "Jewish") mothering, and Jocasta mothering. The
"best" type is the dedicated mother, while the Jocasta mother is most
likely to produce a gifted, but often troubled, individual.

584 Bylinsky, Gene. "New clues to the causes of violence." Fortune
     87(1): 134-42, 146, January, 1973. (0 References).
Discussion of the status of current research into the causes of violent
behavior. Both physiological and environmental causes are treated, with
considerable discussion of neurological research on animals. Support is
cited for the concept that maternal deprivation--particularly in the
areas of touching and handling--is ultimately connected to the development of violent behavior patterns. According to the theory, maternal
deprivation actually produces brain damage of a sort, in that normal
neurological circuits are not established.

585 "Child abuse: family social disease: editorial." Can Ment Health
     21(6): 16-17, November-December, 1973. (0 References).
Traces the cause of child abuse and child neglect to a mothering deficiency in either parent. The negligent or abusive parent, instead of
functioning as a competent adult responsible for the welfare of a helpless child, imposes his own emotional needs on the child and demands
gratification. The process is often repeated in the next generation.

586 Clark, Karen N. "Knowledge of child development and behavior inter-
     action patterns of mothers who abuse their children." For a
     summary see: Diss Abstr Int 36B(11): 5784, May, 1976.

587 Court, Joan, and Kerr, Anna. "The battered child syndrome -- II: A
     preventable disease?" Nurs Times 67(23): 695-97, June, 1971.
     (16 References).

Regards the battered child syndrome as an advanced symptom of parental pathology and focuses attention on the needs of the battering parents. Not all parents are capable of mothering. Potential for nurturing could be detected early if nurses and physicians were aware of the symptoms in mothers that indicate anxiety and frustration leading to violence. For example, the mother who reappears frequently in a medical or welfare clinic with unfounded concerns for her child's health may actually be indirectly seeking guidance for her own feelings. Others who do not make their needs known are difficult to detect. Common to most battering parents is a history of deprivation. Consequently, treatment should include an extended period of mothering and caring for the parents themselves. The treatment should be carried out by a multidisciplinary team with one central mother figure, whose model behavior would serve as an example for the parents.

588 Fischhoff, Joseph; Whitten, Charles F.; Pettit, Marvin G. "A psychiatric study of mothers of infants with growth failure secondary to maternal deprivation." J Pediatr 79(2): 209-15, August, 1971. (8 References).
A study of twelve mothers whose infants failed to thrive because of maternal deprivation suggests that this deprivation is frequently linked to character disorders in the mother. The mothers studied tended to be disorganized, rigid, and unable to adapt to new circumstances, did not plan ahead or think actions through. These character disorders cannot be treated in normal psychotherapy; rather, intervention measures are necessary which give the mother direction and help to bring about behavioral changes. In the meantime, the infant, in order to be protected from neglect, should probably be placed in a foster home.

589 Fraser, William. "Maternal deprivation reassessed by Michael Rutter: book review." Dev Med Child Neurol 14(5): 687, October, 1972. (0 References).
Commends Michael Rutter's book, Maternal Deprivation Reassessed, as a valuable sourcebook for all pediatricians, child psychiatrists, and others who work with emotionally disturbed or delinquent children. It is pointed out that although maternal bonds are important, the child can also develop bonds with other persons and can, theoretically, be deprived of the love of any of these important persons.

590 Freedman, David A., and Brown, Stuart L. "On the role of coenesthetic stimulation in the development of psychic structure." Psychoanal Q 37(3): 418-38, July, 1968. (30 References).
Presents detailed case descriptions of two children of a psychotic mother who suffered extreme isolation and a near total lack of maternal care from birth. Their subsequent development, followed closely through periods of foster and adoptive care, showed intellectual progress but no improvement in the ability to differentiate self from others and to form attachments to external objects. It is speculated that the capacity to cathect objects has its basis in early coenesthetic stimulation, with which these children had minimal experience. An account of two children raised by wolves substantiates this hypothesis. They received rich, albeit highly distorted stimulation, and were thus able to form strong libidinal attachments. Significantly, their well-defined ego structures interfered with their intellectual achievements, as the distortions in their learning had to be unlearned before progress in the normal human sphere could be accomplished. Other cases, although of an anecdotal

nature, support the hypothesis that nutriment in the coenesthetic mode is a prerequisite for the development of a unifying concept of the self and for interpersonal attachments.

591 Freud, Anna. "The concept of the rejection mother (1955 [1954])."
     In: Freud, Anna. The writings of Anna Freud, Volume IV: Indica-
     tions for child analysis and other papers, 1945-1956. New York:
     International Universities Press, 1968. 586-602. (2 References).
Delineates the ways in which a mother may reject her child. The mother
who has a baby unwillingly is likely to be a rejecting mother. Rejection
can occur from external causes such as marital or financial difficulties
or from internal conflict over accepting the role of motherhood. The
mother who vacillates between acceptance and rejection often produces the
most harmful effects on the child. Rejection may also occur as the
result of the mother's abnormal or psychotic personality. Even where
positive attachment is found, a sudden separation of mother and child is
nonetheless experienced by the child as a rejection. Fluctuations in
affection or the birth of a sibling also signal a kind of desertion to
the child. A mother's feelings commonly vary with the developmental
stages of her infant's growth. Also, the closer the relationship of
mother to child, the more closely the child identifies her with both his
pleasures and his pain. Thus, even the devoted mother may in this way
be rejecting to the child.

592 Grygier, T.; Chesley, Joan; Tuters, Elizabeth W. "Parental depriva-
     tion: a study of delinquent children." Br J Criminol 9(3): 209-
     53, July, 1969. (49 References).
Studies the correlation between parental deprivation (for example, the
death, separation, or faulty image of a parent) and juvenile delinquency.
It was found that paternal and maternal deprivation could not be separated from each other. No control group was used, so that no causal
factors could be established.

593 Horenstein, David. "The dynamics and treatment of child abuse: can
     primate research provide the answers?" J Clin Psychol 33(2):
     563-65, April, 1977. (9 References).
Relates a 1964 study by comparative psychologists (Seay, Alexander, and
Harlow) regarding the transfer of mothering skills from one generation
of monkeys to the next and suggests that its findings could provide
insight into the problems of the abusive parent. Infant monkeys deprived
of intimate contact with their mother and provided only the bare
mechanics of mothering, such as cleansing and feeding, were studied. It
was found that infants raised without intimate maternal contact did not
develop intimate maternal behavior. In fact, many became abusive
mothers. Although it would be faulty to assume that direct parallels
between human and monkey behavior can be drawn, these findings do
indicate the following in terms of treatment for human child abusers:
(1) experience in mothering encourages the development of normal maternal
behavior; and (2) the detrimental effects of poor or abusive mothering
can be offset or eliminated, if the infants or normal mothers are raised
together with those of motherless mothers. This suggests that mothering
can be taught in a supervised therapeutic nursery setting, where peer
interaction would benefit both the children and the mothers.

594 Jenkins, R. L., and Boyer, A. "Effects of inadequate mothering and
     inadequate fathering." Int J Soc Psychiatry 16(1): 72-78, Winter,
     1969-1970. (5 References).

The relationship of adequate mothering and fathering to behavioral stability in children is discussed. The evaluation of 1,500 child clinic
cases in terms of criteria for mothering and fathering indicated that
inadequate mothering was most likely to coincide with abnormal behavior
in children. Inadequate fathering was also associated with behavior
problems, but the correlation was weaker than it had been with inadequate
mothering.

595 Kennell, John H., and Klaus, Marshall H. "Care of the mother of
     the high-risk infant." <u>Clin Obstet Gynecol</u> 14(3): 926-54, 1971.
     (25 References).
Discussion of the desirability of increasing contact between mother and
infant in the neonatal period. The practice of rooming the infant with
the mother is recommended over the standard isolation of the child in
the nursery; the indication is that the bonding between mother and child
is strengthened by neonatal contact. Four case studies are presented
describing abnormal birth situations in which the physician needed to
prepare the parents.

596 Klaus, Marshall H., and Kennell, John H. "Mothers separated from
     their newborn infants." <u>Pediatr Clin North Am</u> 17(4): 1015-37,
     November, 1970. (71 References).
Discussion of the possible differences in maternal behavior arising from
differing amounts of early contact with newborns. Mothers allowed to
spend more time with their children in the neonatal period were more
inclined to fondle, talk to, and gain eye contact with their infants.
It was suggested that the entire range of mothering disorders from minor
insecurities to child battering may be at least partly related to the
early separation of the child from the mother. The incidence of child
battering and failure to thrive appeared to be higher among children who
were premature or whose stay in the hospital after birth was otherwise
prolonged.

597 Leaverton, David R. "The pediatrician's role in maternal depriva-
     tion: illustrative cases and an approach to early recognition."
     <u>Clin Pediatr</u> 7(6): 340-43, June, 1968. (29 References).
Presents three case studies of the effects of maternal deprivation on
children seen at an Air Force Base hospital. Pediatricians are advised
to take the possibility of maternal deprivation seriously, and the cases
described suggest several features characteristic of maternal deprivation: (1) a history of emotional disturbance in the mother's family or
of marital difficulties between the patient's parents; (2) frequent
visits to medical personnel; (3) one mother's indifference to the child;
and (4) underdiagnoses of mental illness in either the patient or his
mother. It is argued that maternal deprivation produces emotional as
well as physical effects, and that the syndrome must be viewed from both
a medical and psychosocial perspective. It is a problem to which
transient military families are particularly vulnerable because of the
absence of long-term emotional support for the parents and the frequent
lack of community facilities on military bases.

598 Ounsted, Christopher; Lynch, Margaret; Roberts, Jacqueline. "No
     not non-accidental injury!: letter to editor." <u>Lancet</u> 2(7991):
     913, October 23, 1976. (0 References).
Child abuse is presented as a symptom of an underlying bonding failure.
There is no connection between the severity of physical damage perpetrated

on a child and the prospects of recovery for the whole family in treatment. Once child abuse is recognized and the processes that lead to it
identified, its recurrence can be prevented.

599 Prescott, James W., and McKay, Cathy. "Child abuse and child care:
      some cross-cultural and anthropological perspectives." In: U. S.
      National Institute of Child Health and Human Development. National
      Conference on Child Abuse. Washington, D. C.: U.S. Government
      Printing Office, 1973. 53p. (73 References).
A statistical study of a 400 culture sample indicates that a significant
causal relationship exists between somatosensory deprivation in infancy
and childhood on the one hand and adult physical violence (including
child abuse) on the other. It was found that societies that are characterized by high physical affection (fondling, caressing, playing with
infant) and permissive premarital sexual behavior (another form of somatosensory stimulation) are extremely unlikely to be physically violent.
Underlying neurobiological mechanisms are suggested to explain this
connection. Social and physical characteristics of the environment--
poverty, mother-child households, small extended families, complexity of
society and others--are seen as mediating variables which contribute to
violence (and child abuse) indirectly by making it difficult for adults
to provide infants with physical affection and by repressing or punishing
premarital and/or extramarital sexual behaviors.

600 Ribble, Margaret A. "The right to a mother." In: Ribble, Margaret
      A. The rights of infants: early psychological needs and their
      satisfaction. New York: Columbia University Press, 1947. 3-14.
      (0 References).
Describes the importance of mother love for the healthy mental and
physical growth of an infant. Babies whose physical needs are adequately
met but who are deprived of mothering fail to thrive. This disease,
known as marasmus, was quite commom prior to the use of substitute mothers
in hospitals and institutions. Because the baby upon birth is incomplete
and relies on the mother entirely, the loving nurturance provided by the
mother is a necessary extension of the prenatal state. Separation in
early infancy causes the child to regress in breathing and eating habits
and can cause severe psychological damage.

601 Rosenthal, David; Wender, Paul H.; Kety, Seymour, S.; et al.
      "Parent-child relationships and psychopathological disorder in the
      child." Arch Gen Psychiatry 32(4): 466-76, April, 1975. (22
      References).
Discusses a retrospective study of the relative contributions of genetic
and environmental factors to schizophrenic disorders. Chosen for the
study were 258 adult subjects, representing four categories of parent/
child relationships: (1) adoptees with a schizophrenic biological
parent; (2) adoptees with no family history of mental illness; (3)
adoptees whose biological parent(s) exhibited schizophrenic or manic-
depressive disorders; and (4) non-adoptees with a disturbed parent.
After being interviewed about their relationships with their parents and
given a psychiatric examination, the subjects were ranked into twenty
categories on the basis of the quality (from good to bad) of the parental
relationships. It was found that contrary to the assumptions that
environment is everything and that genes play a negligible role in the
formation of personality, the children of mentally disturbed biological
parents tended to exhibit signs of mental illness at a rate which seemed

only slightly susceptible to the influence of environment. On the other hand, environmental factors did prove to be significant in the case of individuals without a family history of mental illness. Longitudinal studies are recommended to test and refine the implications of this study.

602 Stone, Frederick H. "Psychological aspects of early mother-infant relationships." Br Med J 4(5781): 224-26, October 23, 1971. (0 References).
A psychological exploration of early mother-infant relationships. A wide variety of methods can be successful in caring for the individual needs of infants. Mothers need only be aware of and respond to their own babies' individual and unique demands to promote a healthy mother-infant relationship. However, disorders in the relationship do occur and can be caused either by variations in infant activity levels to which a normal mother may react inappropriately, or by serious psychological problems in the mother that disrupt her behavior toward her baby. In addition, certain social situations, such as family attitudes toward the new baby, can be cause for distress and depression in the mother and can disturb the delicate balance between herself and the baby. Ways to prevent these disorders are suggested.

603 ten Bensel, Robert W., and Paxson, Charles L., Jr. "Child abuse following early postpartum separation: letter to editor." J Pediatr 90(3): 490-91, March, 1977. (6 References).
Describes a study which suggests that the postpartum separation of mother and child is a causative factor of child abuse.

604 Tulkin, Steven R., and Kagan, Jerome. "Mother-child interaction in the first year of life." Child Dev 43(1): 31-41, March, 1972. (11 References).
Description of a project in which thirty middle-class and twenty-six working class mothers were observed interacting with their first-born female infants. The quality of the mothers' responses to their daughters' behavior was recorded at five-second intervals in their own homes, and the mothers were interviewed informally after the observation period. As expected, it was found that the middle-class mothers engaged in more verbal interaction with their daughters and tended to provide a greater variety and amount of stimuli to them. The working class mothers frequently explained their conduct in terms which indicated that they discounted the effect of environment on infants and generally assumed that the child's inherent nature could not be influenced by their maternal behavior. The middle-class mothers assumed a more active role and seemed to act upon much more definite childcaring goals than did the working class mothers. This data suggests that people need to be made more aware of the impact of the environment upon children.

3. INFANTICIDE

605 Arboleda-Florez, Julio. "Infanticide -- some medicolegal considerations." Can Psychiatr Assoc J 20(1): 55-60, February, 1975. (24 References).
Discussion of the Canadian law relating to infanticide. Medical aspects, including the possibility of postpartum mental illness as a common cause of child-murder, are explained. A distinction is drawn between neonaticides and infanticides. While infanticides are often committed for

"altruistic" reasons (sparing the child from an unhappy life), neonaticide is simply a means of relieving oneself of an unwanted child. The legal considerations involved in handling a case of infanticide are discussed.

606 Asch, Stuart S. "Crib deaths: their possible relationship to postpartum depression and infanticide." J Mount Sinai Hosp 35: 214-20, 1968. (18 References).

Discusses the possibility that a large proportion of so-called "crib deaths" are actually infanticides resulting from postpartum depression. The psychological features which often--or even usually--accompany pregnancy include the mother's fantasized identification with her own mother and with her unborn child. In some cases, a pregnant woman projects her unacknowledged hatred of her own mother onto herself and her child. Most women experience depression at the loss of the fantasized self and baby, but quickly readjust to the new real person in their lives. However, disturbed women cannot make this adjustment and their postpartum depression deepens, often aggravated by the psychosis brought on by the pregnancy. In this depressed state, they kill their infants. The infanticidal impulse must be recognized as a common feature of human experience.

607 Bloch, Dorothy. "Some dynamics of suffering: effect of the wish for infanticide in a case of schizophrenia." Psychoanal Rev 53(4): 531-54, Winter, 1966-1967. (35 References).

Freud identified the Oedipus Complex as the nucleus of neurosis, but neglected to analyze the psychological implications of the first half of the Oedipus narrative--the attempted killing of Oedipus as an infant by his parents. The pervasiveness of the wish for infanticide can only be suspected; however, the assumption of a widespread infanticidal impulse provides the most logical explanation for the schizophrenic and self-destructive behavior of many adults who as children repressed their recognition of parental hostility. Several manifestations of this psychiatric syndrome are discussed, and case histories and courses of treatment of several psychiatric patients are given.

608 Browne, William J., and Palmer, Anthony J. "A preliminary study of schizophrenic women who murdered their children." Hosp Community Psychiatry 26(2): 71, 75, February, 1975. (3 References).

The characteristics of nine schizophrenic women who murdered at least one of their children are reported. All of the women had had frequent thoughts of suicide and several had, at one time, tried to kill themselves. Seven of the women came from broken homes. All of the women had been guilty of child neglect before the murder. The crimes are seen as projections of the women's own self-destructive tendencies and an attempt to save the child from an unhappy life. Although the crimes were committed in psychotic states, the mothers expressed a great deal of guilt and some attempted symbolic "restoration" of the child. The schizophrenic reaction to the child murderer is often signaled by postpartum depression or early rejection of an infant.

609 Brozovsky, Morris, and Falit, Harvey. "Neonaticide: clinical and psychodynamic considerations." J Am Acad Child Psychiatry 10(4): 673-83, October, 1971. (10 References).

Presentation of two case histories involving neonaticide, with an analysis of their common features and the implications of these for the

psychiatric consideration of neonaticide. Both mothers were poor and
unmarried adolescents, and both had been threatened with abandonment by
their mothers in the event that they became pregnant. Likewise, both
refused to recognize the fact that they were pregnant and were surprised
at the appearance of a baby. Both young women threw their infants out
the bathroom window and one briefly became amnesiac. Being forced to
acknowledge their pregnancies threw the young and dependent mothers into
a psychologically disorganized state in which they identified with their
aggressor mothers and destroyed their children.

610 Button, J. H., and Reivich, Ronald S. "Obsession of infanticide:
    a review of 42 cases." Arch Gen Psychiatry 27: 235-40, August,
    1972. (37 References).
A review of forty-two psychiatric patients at a university medical center
who were reported to have infanticidal fantasies. Many of these patients
had been first-born, adopted, or only children, and a number of them had
gone through traumas or behavioral problems in childhood. While the
psychotic patients described overt infanticidal impulses, a number of the
others feared that they might want to harm their children. Treatment
consisted of supportive psychotherapy and chemo or convulsant therapy.

611 Calef, Victor. "The unconscious fantasy of infanticide manifested
    in resistance." J Am Psychoanal Assoc 16: 697-710, 1968. (7
    References).
Proposes the existence of a psychological syndrome among women in which
infanticide fantasies serve as the expression of a defense against a
repressed Oedipal Conflict. In the case study presented, a female
patient of a male psychiatrist also unconsciously rejected both the pur-
chase of her new house and the insights of her psychoanalytic sessions
as forbidden Oedipal offspring.

612 Cameron, J. Malcolm. "Infanticide." Nurs Times 67(44): 1371-72,
    November 4, 1971. (3 References).
A description of various attitudes toward infanticide among primitive
societies is followed by a brief review of the legal status of infanticide
in the British Islands, along with a discussion of the problems in
detecting and prosecuting cases of infanticide. Injuries symptomatic of
infanticide are described, with a caveat concerning the difficulty of
ascertaining these injuries.

613 Evans, Philip. "Infanticide." Proc R Soc Med 61: 36-38, December,
    1968. (19 References).
Discusses the phenomenon of infanticide around the world. Various reasons
for infanticide are enumerated, including religion, the disposal of extra
or undesirable children, financial gain, anger, and maternal psychoses.

614 Harder, Thøger. "The psychopathology of infanticide." Acta Psychiatr
    Scand 43: 196-245, 1967. (48 References).
A compendium of case histories of nineteen persons (fourteen women and
five men) in Denmark who killed or attempted to kill their children. The
three women who killed their newborn infants are grouped separately from
the remaining eleven women, who were, in turn, grouped into three diagnostic categories: five cases were manic depressive, five indicated
psychogenic psychoses, and one was classified as neurotic. Two of the
five men were psychotic. Psychological profiles and histories are provided for all the subjects.

615 Knight, Bernard. "Forensic problems in practice -- IX: Infant
       deaths." Practitioner 217(1299):   444-48, September, 1976. (0
       References).

Infant deaths present a number of medical and legal difficulties. Still-
birth is defined as a child born after the twenty-eighth week of pregnancy
which did not at any time show signs of life after being completely
expelled from the mother. It is pointed out that if a child was destroyed
while even a foot remained inside the mother, that this could not be
considered homicide until the Infant Preservation Act was passed in 1929.
Infanticide is the killing of a live-born child by a willful act of
omission or commission. It is extremely difficult to distinguish between
the newborn infant that is smothered to death and the stillborn infant.
The battered child syndrome can be a cause of infant death, and the
medicolegal problem is distinguishing between accidental and non-accidental injury. Evidence of repetitive injuries, implausible explanations
for the causes of injuries and the nature of the injuries can lead to
confirmation of the battered child syndrome. Cot deaths occur in one out
of 500 infants, usually between two weeks and two years of age. Frequently, a child is put to bed with mild symptoms or no signs of illness
and is found dead the next morning. The cause of cot deaths is not
known.

616 Lukianowicz, Narcyz. "Attempted infanticide." Psychiatr Clin
       (Basel) 5(1): 1-16, 1972. (15 References).

An analysis of the records of the Northern Irish women who attempted to
kill their children, six having also attempted suicide and five having
tried to kill their spouses. It was found that religion, social class,
housing, and the sex of the children did not seem to influence the infanticidal impulse, but most of the women had had unhappy childhoods and
ambivalent feelings toward pregnancy. Personality and psychiatric disorders appeared in a number of the women. The attempts at infanticide
took four forms: (1) actual physical violence against the child; (2)
unclear forms of physical threats against the child's life; (3) fears
that one might threaten a child's life; and (4) verbal threats to kill
children.

617 ————. "Infanticide." Psychiatr Clin (Basel) 4(3): 145-58,
       1971. (31 References).

Presents eighteen case histories illustrating the psychodynamics of child
abuse from the parent's point of view. Most of the abusing parents
studied were young mothers of one or two children who had not wanted
their children and felt hostile toward their husbands. The typical
abused child was either the youngest or the only child in the family.
The abusing mothers exhibited various personality disorders, ranging
from psychopathy to hysteria, were immature, needed ego-bolstering, and
had had relatively unhappy (though not especially eventful) childhoods
themselves. Official apathy toward the problem is condemned.

618 Rascovsky, Arnaldo, and Rascovsky, Matilde. "The prohibition of
       incest, filicide, and the sociocultural process." Int J Psychoanal
       53(2): 271-76, 1972. (26 References).

Presentation of the argument that filicidal impulses on the part of the
parent--a universal pattern in human psychology--began in the ancient
supression by the parent of the child's incestuous drives. This suppression was accomplished early by means of murder, and later by increasingly
ritualized killings (child sacrifice) which ultimately became almost

entirely symbolic (circumcision) and covert (discipline, scolding). However, in unstable parents under stress, the filicidal impulse reasserts
itself more overtly and results in child abuse or even murder.

619   Resnick, Phillip J. "Child murder by parents: a psychiatric review
        of filicide." Am J Psychiatry 126(3): 73-82, September, 1969.
        (64 References).
A review of world literature on the murder of children over twenty-four
hours old by a parent (filicide) from 1751 to 1967 revealed 131 cases.
The filicides can be classified on the basis of apparent motive. The
altruistic murder is carried out to relieve a child of his suffering or
to avoid abandonment after a parent's suicide. Filicide can take place
while a parent is acutely psychotic or experiencing an epilepsy attack
or hallucinations. An unwanted child due to illegitimacy or financial
pressures is another reason why a parent may murder his child. In a
violent outburst a parent may "accidentally" murder a child when this
was not his conscious intention. Finally, a parent may murder a child
in order to obtain revenge against a spouse. The psychodynamics of the
filicidal impulse are explored. To prevent filicide, psychiatrists
should be alert to the potential of their suicidal and depressed adult
patients to murder their children. Parents who express fear about harming their children should be hospitalized, and social agencies should be
available to assume the care of unwanted children.

620   ————. "Murder of the newborn: a psychiatric review of neonati-
        cide." Am J Psychiatry 126(10): 1414-20, April, 1970. (51
        References).
It is proposed that the killing of newborn infants differs radically in
nature from the killing of older infants and children, so much so that
the use of a special term--neonaticide--is recommended. After a study
of some thirty-seven cases in which parents--principally mothers--killed
their newborn children, it was found that neonaticide differs from
filicide in the following ways: the perpetrator is almost always the
mother, she is younger than the parents who commit filicide, more likely
to be unmarried, less likely to be psychotic, and she usually kills the
infant because she does not want it, the most usual reason for this
rejection being the child's illegitimacy. The present legal status of
neonaticide is reviewed.

621   Scott, Pena D. "Parents who kill their children." Med Sci Law
        13(2): 120-26, April, 1973. (26 References).
Attempts to classify motivations for filicide, based on case histories
from England and Wales. To increase objectivity, motivation is deliberately limited here to the source of the impulse to kill, as determined
by clinical observation of the parent's personality and circumstances.
Five sources of homicidal impulse include the elimination of an unwanted
child, mercy killing, mental pathology, arousal by the victim, and displacement onto the victim of anger at something else. In the cases
discussed, 44 percent of the fathers killed when their children stimulated the attack, while the filicidal mothers tended to be mentally ill.

622   ————. "Victims of violence." Nurs Times 70(27): 1036-37,
        July 4, 1974. (0 References).
The motives of the parent who murders his child are outlined. In one-
third of the cases, the parents were diagnosed as mentally ill, while in
another third, the parents suffered from severe stress and found them-

selves unable to meet the demands of childrearing. In another one-sixth of the cases, the murder was based on a deliberate parental decision to rid himself of the child, and in the final sixth of this population, the motive of revenge or aggression stimulated the crime, although the child was not even the source of hostility in some instances. It is suggested that the nurse become aware of the dynamics of child-murder, as it may help her to accurately spot and report potentially dangerous parent-child situations.

623 Winnik, H., and Horovitz, M. "The problem of infanticide." Br J
      Criminol 2: 40-52, July, 1961. (6 References).
Studies the incidence and etiology of infanticide in Israel. It was found that infanticide was most often committed by young women and usually within twenty-four hours after birth. The infants were most often strangled, and their corpses disposed of haphazardly. Prior to the act the mothers had attempted to deny or conceal their pregnancy and many had been rejected by their families. After delivery the mothers experienced acute anxiety. The act of infanticide was more an expression of the mother's suicidal wish than an act of deliberate homicide. The twelve women brought to the attention of the study were treated compassionately by the court. Seven of the twelve were soon married and quickly bore other children whom they loved and nurtured.

D. FAMILY DYSFUNCTION

1. GENERAL FACTORS

624 Askwith, Gordon K. "A follow-up study of neglectful parents."
      For a summary see: Diss Abstr 24(4): 1732, October, 1963.

625 Bennett, A. N. "Children under stress." J R Nav Med Serv 60(1-2):
      83-87, Spring-Summer, 1974. (10 References).
A brief description of the causes of child abuse, the characteristics of the battering parent, the symptoms which should alert the physician to the diagnosis, and suggestions for treatment.

626 Bossard, James H. S. "Parents with problem attitudes." In:
      Bossard, James H. S. The sociology of child development. New
      York: Harper, 1948. 331-49. (10 References).
Describes problem family situations designed to classify characteristics common to families with specific behavior irregularities. Preliminary examinations led to the current approach for studying families, in which the family is viewed as a group of interacting persons, whose inter- actions and reactions to their environment are influenced by special sets of circumstances. This approach made it possible to identify several groups of parents with problem attitudes: (1) parents who reject their children; (2) parents who magnify and distort their responsibili- ties; and (3) parents who disregard the personalities of their children. Each of these types is described, documented with case histories, and discussed in detail.

627 Bryant, Clifton D. "Problems of institutional ineffectiveness."
      In: Bryant, Clifton D. Social problems today: dilemmas and
      dissensus. Philadelphia: Lippincott, 1971. 167-340. (0 Refer-
      ences).

A collection of fifteen previously published articles, divided into three groups. The first is concerned with marriage and the family, the second discusses the family and includes material on child abuse, and the third group deals with education.

628 Burland, J. Alexis; Andrews, Roberta G.; Headsten, Sally J. "Child abuse: one tree in the forest." Child Welfare 52(9): 585-92, November, 1973. (0 References).
An in-depth study of the records of twenty-eight abused children, illustrating that attention must be given to the needs of the parents and children involved, not to the fact that abuse has occurred. The physical evidence of abuse is only one fraction of the total problem. The family's problems that led to the abuse must be investigated in order to bring about effective treatment. Various cases are presented to illustrate casework considerations, the parents dependency needs, and the advantages of bringing the family together as opposed to placing the children in long-term foster care.

629 Byassee, J. E., and Murrell, S. A. "Interaction patterns in families of autistic, disturbed, and normal children." Am J Orthopsychiatry 45(3): 473-78, April, 1975. (20 References).
The results of an experiment comparing the interaction in six normal families with the interaction in six families with disturbed and autistic children challenge assumptions regarding the psychogenic nature of autism. The Ferreira and Winter Unrevealed Differences Task was used in the experiment; the parents of disturbed children disagreed more than parents in the other families, but there was no difference between the families with normal children and those with autistic children. The implication is that no correlation exists between the severity of deviant behavior on the part of the children and the severity of family abnormality.

630 Colbach, Edward M. "Psychiatric criteria for compassionate reassignment in the Army." Am J Psychiatry 127(4): 508-10, October, 1970. (4 References).
Discusses the task of evaluating requests for the compassionate reassignment of military personnel because of psychological problems within the family. Neglect of children by a disturbed wife is one standard mentioned in Army regulations and a case in point is very briefly described.

631 Cordell, Chris. "The abused child." Imprint 21(2): 34, 47-48, April, 1974. (0 References).
Brief explanation of the history and reasons behind child abuse. Battering parents are viewed as insecure, frightened parents, and ambivalent toward the demands of their role in childrearing. The nurse is seen as a major resource in the early detection of child abuse cases. Several characteristics of battered children are described: they rarely cry, do not often seek out parental reassurance, approach situations suspiciously, and are often unresponsive to the outside world. A team approach involving the nurse and the social service agency is recommended as an effective means of dealing with suspected abuse cases.

632 Elmer, Elizabeth. "Child abuse: a symptom of family crisis." In: Pavenstedt, E., and Bernard, V. W., eds. Crisis of family disorganization: programs to soften their impact on children. New York: Behavioral Publications, 1971.

633 ————. Children in jeopardy: a study of abused minors and their
     families. Pittsburgh: University of Pittsburgh Press, 1967.
     125p. (Bibliography).
Results of a research study of thirty-one children who had been admitted
to Children's Hospital of Pittsburgh at varying times during a thirteen
year period for multiple bone injuries. The retrospective study consisted of interviews with the natural or foster mother at home and in the
hospital where each study child was given a complete pediatric, psychological, and psychiatric examination. The purpose of the study was to
ascertain whether the original hospitalization had been the result of
abuse or not; and, if so, to characterize the abusive families both at
the time of, and following, the abusive incident. After weighing all
data, eleven families were classified as abusive, twelve as non-abusive,
and eight remained unclassified.

Mothers were questioned concerning current methods of discipline used in
the home, their estimation of the child's physical and social development,
and their own roles in the family and community. At the time of the
interviews, the abusive families exhibited a greater degree of family
dysfunction than the non-abusive families. Indicators of this dysfunction included: marital difficulties, a disorganized household, inconsistent discipline, and a negative attitude toward the study child.
Research into each family's childbearing history uncovered the significant
statistic that injury to the study child frequently occurred during or
immediately after pregnancy. Stress caused by a premature birth or by
bearing several children at close intervals have precipitated the abusive
incident.

Fifty-six percent of the study children had been under ten months of age
when first brought to the hospital. Subsequent to hospitalization,
eleven of the abused children had changed living situations. In an
improved environment the majority of these children had developed normally,
although many were hampered by physical scars, low intelligence, and
personality problems. Owing to the serious nature of the injuries
inflicted and the young ages of the children, it is not surprising that
over half of the abused children were diagnosed as retarded.

634 Fontana, Vincent J. "Which parents abuse children?" Med Insight
     3(10): 16-21, October, 1971. (8 References).
Reviews recent medical findings useful in diagnosing the battered child
syndrome. The sociological, psychological, and physical characteristics
of at risk families are summarized. Stress is placed on the role of the
physician in recognizing, treating, and preventing child abuse.

635 Gardiner, Muriel. The deadly innocents: portraits of children who
     kill. New York: Basic Books, 1976. 190p.
Presents character portraits of ten youthful murderers. Although the
author is a practicing psychoanalyst, clinical case histories are not
attempted. Rather, the story of each young person is presented as he
thought, felt and experienced it. Neither clear recommendations for
methods of rehabilitation nor firm conclusions about the reasons for
violent crime emerge from these histories; their intent is to further
the reader's understanding of why a particular youth committed a crime.
The homicides discussed tended to be motivated either by passion, in
which case the crime was committed alone and was not premeditated, or by
the desire for material gain, in which case the crime was likely com-
mited by two or three young people with some degree of planning. In all

instances, the normal adolescent drive toward aggression and self-asser-
tion and the need for adventure became distorted and was inadequately
controlled. In every case, the home life of the offender was extremely
bleak, and the young person had no one whom he could love or with whom
he could identify. Each case review stresses the debilitating consequences of prison life to the young person, as it exacerbates his isolation and his feelings of worthlessness, which can only serve to deepen
his hatred of the world and to promote a future of criminality upon his
release from prison.

636 Gershenson, Charles P. "Child maltreatment, family stress, and
        ecological insult: editorial." Am J Public Health 67(7): 602-3,
        July, 1977. (7 References).
Argues that child abuse and other pediatric social illnesses, such as
neglect and the failure to thrive syndrome, are symptomatic of family
dysfunction. The pediatrician's concern for the child's physical
recovery and the social worker's effort to modify the surrounding environment do little to heal the stress, violence, and confusion experienced by
other family members. A comprehensive public health approach designed to
help the family through all stages of childrearing would best treat both
the physical and psychological traumas of the family.

637 Helfer, Ray E. "The etiology of child abuse." Pediatrics 51(4,
        Part II): 777-79, April, 1973. (0 References).
Suggests three possible causes of child abuse that could be used to
recognize the potential for abuse in parents and families and to prevent
it before it happens. The first area discussed is the parent's potential
for abuse. Four considerations emerge as indicative of a potential for
violence: (1) history of poor mothering in the parents' childhood; (2)
degree of isolation from others who are concerned about them and who
could offer help; (3) problems within their marriage; and (4) attitudes
toward and expectations of their children. Secondly, it is suggested
that an unusual child can, to a degree, provoke his parents to abuse him.
Finally, family crises can also upset the stability of inter-familial
relationships and cause a potential abuser to lose control. Such crises
need to be identified early so that intervention can occur quickly to
avert disaster.

638 Holter, Joan C., and Friedman, Stanford B. "Etiology and manage-
        ment of severely burned children." Am J Dis Child 118(5): 680-
        86, November, 1969. (8 References).
Suggests that the management of burns in children should take into consideration the circumstances in which the burns occurred. In a review
of thirteen cases of burns in pre-adolescent children, only three of the
burns are assessed to be true accidents resulting from momentary lapses
in supervision. The other ten cases all suggested that the burns were
reflections or products of a disturbed family situation, three of the
cases involving actual child abuse, in which the children were scalded
with hot water. The deliberately injured children tended to be younger
than the other burn victims. It is recommended that, given the low
incidence of purely accidental burns, physicians keep in mind the possibility that the family of the burn victim may have to be carefully
approached, and may benefit from therapy of some kind.

639 Howells, John G. "Ill-health and child abuse: letter to editor."
        Lancet 2(7932): 454, September 6, 1975. (0 References).

Suggests that ill-health may be a secondary cause of child abuse. The
primary underlying cause precipitating the illness could actually be
family emotional stress. Resolving the stressful situation would then
be more effective treatment for preventing further abuse than merely
attending to the illness itself.

640   Johnson, Adelaide M., and Szurek, S. A. "The genesis of antisocial
        acting out in children and adults." Psychoanal Q 21(3):   323-43,
        July, 1952. (18 References).
Psychoanalytic treatment of parent and child has revealed that the origin
of a child's antisocial behavior lies with one or both parents' unconscious permission and encouragement of the child's actions. The parent's
own unconscious desires are thus gratified by the actions of the child.
In making a scapegoat of the child, the parent also satisfies his hostile
impulses toward him. Although a major theory indicates guilt as the
cause for acting out, parental influence, combined with the self-protective
need for detection in order to prevent further destructiveness, is
emphasized. The mechanisms of various acting out behaviors are described.

641   Justice, Blair, and Justice, Rita. The abusing family. New York:
        Human Sciences Press, 1976. 288p. (Bibliography).
Presents a model of the abusive family which focuses upon pathologic
symbiosis in the family and stressful change as precursors of child abuse.
Thirty-five abusing and thirty-five non-abusing parents of similar age,
income, and educational background were interviewed. It was found that
abusive parents had experienced excessive change in their lives--such as
the death of a relative, a divorce, sexual difficulties, or loss of
employment--during the twelve month period prior to the onset of their
abusive behavior. All the changes were serious and required rational
decision-making, something the parents were not able to effect smoothly.

Abusive families also exhibited unhealthy symbiosis. To promote its
physical and emotional health, an infant needs to experience a symbiotic
attachment with its mother; however, should this attachment continue
beyond the time when the child ought to begin forming a separate identity,
the results can be destructive. The authors found this exact behavior
within their survey population. Each spouse sought care and nurturing
from his child. If the child failed to respond adequately, the parent
struck out at him.

In group therapy work with abusive parents, each spouse was encouraged
to develop a sense of differentiation and separateness. To accomplish
this, the therapists utilized transactional analysis, behavioral modification therapy, and group dynamics. Through transactional analysis a
spouse perceived how he continually obstructed his mate's space for action
and decision-making by inflexibly adhering to the role of parent, adult,
or child and forcing the mate to play a complementary, but equally
restrictive, role. In behavioral modification therapy each group member
was asked to set specific goals for himself in the following problem
areas: symbiosis, isolation, talking and sharing with mate, impatience/
temper, knowledge of child development, and employment. The therapists
suggested that each parent ask his spouse, another group member, or any
mature adult to fulfill his needs, rather than demand such age inappropriate behavior from his child. As therapy continued and each member made
significant changes in the six problem areas, he experienced fewer crises
and was better equipped to cope with these crises. When the therapist,
the parent in question, and the rest of the group acknowledged the

parent's overall progress, it was determined safe for the child to return home.

642   Nurse, Shirley N.   "Familial patterns of parents who abuse their children."   Smith Coll Stud Social Work   35(1):   11-25, October, 1964.   (13 References).
Twenty case records involving parental abuse were studied in order to test the validity of several hypotheses regarding the battered child syndrome.   These hypotheses included the beliefs that only one child is usually victimized in a family, that the parents protect each other, that the child does not provoke the attack, and that abusive parents are not remorseful, and may be mentally ill or retarded.   The findings bore out most of the hypotheses.

643   Sarsfield, James K., and Dowell, A. C.   "Parents of battered babies: letter to editor."   Br Med J   1(5908):   637, March 30, 1974.   (0 References).
Attempts to qualify the conclusion of S. M. Smith and his colleagues (November 17, 1973, p. 388) that psychiatric assessment of battering parents is useful in the management of this problem.   It was found that a large minority (47 percent) of the battered children they surveyed were not living with their natural parents at the time of battering.   It is concluded that irregularities among the family groups of battered children must have a bearing on the circumstances leading to child abuse.

644   Smith, Selwyn M.   "Parents of battered babies: letter to editor."   Br Med J   2(5916):   443, May 25, 1974.   (4 References).
The assertion of J. K. Sarsfield and A. C. Dowell (March 30, 1974, p. 637) that anomalies of family status have a bearing on child abuse, is supported.   It is noted that lack of family cohesiveness is an important precursor of baby battering, and that the similarities between baby battering and other forms of deviant behavior are striking.   Prevention, rather than treatment alone, must be vigorously pursued.

645   Terr, Lenore C.   "A family study of child abuse."   Am J Psychiatry   127(5):   665-71, November, 1970.   (15 References).
Reports on a six year study of the relationships within ten families of abused children.   The abusing parent's fantasies about the maltreated child, though highly individual, commonly involved fear or disappointment in the child.   Another strikingly important element among the families was the passive-dominant relationship between the parents and the expression of anger with one another displaced onto the offspring.   The child's physical traits, the nature of his birth as well as his own retaliatory behaviors also contributed to his abuse.   These findings support similar studies and indicate the importance of treatment for the entire family.

646   Woodworth, Robert M.   "The physician and the battered child syndrome in the United States and in Oklahoma."   J Okla State Med Assoc   67(11):   463-75, November, 1974.   (53 References).
An all-inclusive account of the terminology, history, incidence, etiology, diagnosis and legal aspects of the battered child syndrome.   Three categorical causes are investigated: (1) the parents must have potential to abuse;   (2) children of a certain physical or emotional makeup share a higher risk of suffering abuse; and (3) a series of crises, often unrelated to the child himself, precede the abusive act.   Factors pointing to possible child abuse, such as poor general health, failure to thrive,

and a history of similar incidents in the family, are listed. The study
investigates the ramifications of mandatory reporting of cases of suspected child abuse and subsequent legal protection for the reporting
physician. Specific child abuse laws passed in Oklahoma and other preventive action are cited.

2. MARITAL STRESS

647 Braen, B. B., and Forbush, J. B. "School-age parenthood: a national
     overview." J Sch Health 45(5): 256-62, May, 1975. (55 Refer-
     ences).
Discussion of various aspects of the problem of school-age parenthood,
focused principally on attempts in the last decade to understand and
alleviate the problem and help those most affected by it. The Children's
Bureau is commended for initiating the first in a chain of demonstration
schools providing comprehensive community-based services. The National
Alliance Concerned with School-Age Parents have advocated the protection
of the rights of school-age parents, and have effected the passage of
legislation prohibiting discrimination by educational institutions
against school-age mothers.

648 Gayford, J. J. "Wife battering: a preliminary survey of 100 cases."
     Br Med J 1(5951): 194-97, January 25, 1975. (9 References).
One hundred battered wives, most of them from the Cheswick Women's Aid
Hostel, were interviewed by means of an open questionnaire. Topics
investigated included their injuries, medical histories, patterns of
abuse, parental and marital histories. All the marriages appeared to be
disastrous, and the children involved in them, endangered. Both husbands
and wives frequently came from families with histories of violence,
despite the variety of socioeconomic backgrounds reflected in the whole
group. Recommendations are made concerning sanctuaries and therapy for
such women and their children.

649 Hellsten, Penetti, and Katila, Olavi. "Murder and other homicides,
     by children under 15 in Finland." Psychiatr Q 38(1): 54-74,
     1965. (9 References).
Presents detailed case histories of five adolescent boys who committed
homicide (in four cases against a parent) in Finland. The features
common to the histories are enumerated. Disturbed marital relations
characterized all the families. The weak and withdrawing fathers generally could not offer admirable and affectionate role models to their
sons, while the mothers tended to be cold, superficial, egotistical, and
aggressive, especially toward their husbands. According to results of
follow-up studies, all of the boys had displayed character deviations
of some sort, but none of them was psychotic nor had any of them become
a criminal.

650 Kirkpatrick, Francine K. "Patterns of role dominance-submission
     and conflict in parents of abused children." For a summary see:
     Diss Abstr Int 36B(11): 5800, May, 1976.

651 Martin, Helen L. "Antecedents of burns and scalds in children."
     Br J Med Psychol 43(1): 39-47, March, 1970. (15 References).
Studies the family psychodynamics surrounding burn injuries of fifty
children. Although these injuries were claimed by parents to be acci-

dental, the coincidental circumstances, such as the presence of other
people and the preoccupation of the mother with other family problems,
suggests the accidents were not entirely fortuitous. Marital stress and
a lack of closeness with the parents' own families often left these persons in an isolated position with few internal or external supports.
Conflicts among family members also indirectly played a part in the
child's injury. However, the pattern displayed by these parents differed
from those of other battering parents in that accurate explanations were
readily offered, guilt was evident, and accidents were not repeated.

652 Moore, Jean G. "Yo-yo children." Nurs Times 70(49): 1888-89,
     December 5, 1974. (1 Reference).
Home situations in which the parents continually argue and even use violence against each other can produce emotionally battered children.
These children are often parcelled between parents or moved from relative
to relative as their parents' marriage undergoes constant upheaval.

653 ————. "Yo-yo children -- victims of matrimonial violence."
     Child Welfare 54(8): 557-66, September-October, 1975. (7 Refer-
     ences).
The significant features of the "yo-yo" syndrome as revealed in a study
of twenty-three cases of violent married couples and their children are
presented. The syndrome is characterized by alternating marital violence
(resulting in severe bruising, broken jaws, and knife wounds) and restlessness (evidenced by frequent marital separations, reunions, and family
moves). Eighty percent of the children of these marriages were adversely
affected. Scapegoating, in which a child was favored by one parent and
rejected by the other, was common. Sometimes a child would be used as
a pawn by his parents. For example, one parent might threaten to harm
the child in order to force his partner to give in to his demands. School
problems were frequent among the "yo-yo" children and often resulted from
a lack of sleep or from the constant moves of the family from one school
district to another. Finally, the children of these marriages often
turned the familial aggression inward, resulting in physical and
emotional problems of their own. In thirteen of the twenty-three cases,
the grandparents encouraged or exacerbated the marital problems. The
parents themselves were inadequate individuals with poor self-esteem who
often unconsciously created the violence about which they complained.
When treating these couples, the social worker must play the role of the
caring, but firm, parent. When dealing with the children, the social
worker must convey that somebody cares and interpret what is happening
in the family. Further research in this area is desperately needed.

654 Sauer, Louis W. "Problems of teen-age parents." PTA Mag 59(2):
     27-28, October, 1964. (0 References).
The problems of teen-age parents are discussed in a question-answer
forum. The battered-baby syndrome, which often appears in teen-age
marriages, is briefly described.

655 Smith, Selwyn M.; Hanson, Ruth; Noble, Sheila. "Social aspects of
     the battered baby syndrome." Br J Psychiatry 125(589): 568-82,
     December, 1974. (73 References).
Evaluates the social and familial characteristics of 214 abusive parents.
Seventy-one percent of the mothers conceived premaritally and 36 percent
of the battered children were illegitimate. A high percentage of parents
acknowledged marital discord and lack of family cohesiveness. Fifty-

four percent of the mothers described themselves as lonely with little
activity outside of the home. It is concluded that improved material
surroundings will not reduce child battering, but more social contacts
and activities could alleviate the anxieties which perpetuate child battering from generation to generation.

656   Sussman, Sidney J. "The battered child syndrome." Calif Med
        108(6): 437-39, June, 1968. (18 References).
A study of twenty-three incidents of child abuse in California investigates the socio-medical aspects of the battered child syndrome. A
general review of family characteristics noted a tendency toward small,
intact family units with young parents and children in which functioning
was hampered by multiple problems and stresses. Clinical findings are
also reviewed and physician participation in the later phases of case
management is encouraged.

3. INADEQUATE PARENTING PRACTICES

657   Anderson, George M. "Child abuse." America 136(21): 478-82, May
        28, 1977. (0 References).
Ascribes the widespread incidence of child abuse in the United States,
England, and Germany to traditional beliefs of parental supremacy and
filial obedience. Episodes of abuse occur in all levels of society; the
environmental stress of poverty, however, is a major contributing factor
to such abusive outbursts. It is argued that foster placement provides
an incomplete and negative solution to the problem of abuse. Several
effective treatment programs (most sponsored by volunteer groups) are
described.

658   Bendix, S. "Drug modification of behavior: a form of chemical vio-
        lence against children?" J Clin Child Psychol 2(3): 17-19, Fall,
        1973. (30 References).
Questions the efficacy of using amphetemines to treat hyperkinetic children, on a number of grounds. It is often difficult to separate truly
dysfunctioning hyperkinetic children from creative or non-conforming
children. Amphetemines have not been shown to improve a child's capacity
to learn and to handle his problems; they simply mask his problems. And
dependence on amphetemines often develops when a child is regularly
treated with such drugs.

659   Binion, Rudolph; Fine, Rubin; Langer, William; et al. "The evolu-
        tion of childhood: commentaries." Hist Child Q 1(4): 576-603,
        Spring, 1974. (8 References).   ·
Responses to Lloyd deMause's psychogenic theory of history ("The evolution
of childhood," Hist Child Q 1(4): 503-75, Spring, 1974), in which it is
proposed that the developments in human history grew out of changes in
the relationships between parents and children. Both positive and negative commentary is included. The favorable remarks praise deMause for
granting the existence of hostile impulses within the family and for
adding validity to Freud's conclusions. The negative responses faulted
deMause for being simplistic and "monocausal," and for giving short
shrift to the lower classes and "primitive" societies in his study.

660   Borgman, Robert D. "Intelligence and maternal inadequacy." Child
        Welfare 48(1): 301-4, January, 1969. (4 References).

An exploration of the relationship between limited intelligence and failure to provide adequate care, conducted via a comparison between a group of inadequate mothers and a control group from similar socio-economic circumstances. It was found that limited intelligence was related to inadequate mothering only below an I.Q. level of sixty. No other difference appeared to exist between the negligent and the non-negligent mothers in terms of age, number of children, or literacy level.

661 Buglass, Robert. "Parents with emotional problems." Nurs Times 67(32): 1000-1001, August 12, 1971. (0 References).
The battered baby problem involves parents, as well as children, who need help. Young English mothers, under twenty-five, who are generally immature, with unstable personalities, and poorly prepared and equipped motherhood, are discussed. Most of them are isolated with their children in new high-rise flats, unrelieved by other adult company and without support. These mothers might benefit most from a team approach in which psychiatric treatment is first aimed at treating acute symptoms, then at establishing a long-term support program with psychiatric treatment casework, and measures aimed at altering the environment as far as this is possible, to provide greater stability and more social contact.

662 "Cruelty to children." Br Med J 1(1956): 1286-87, June 2, 1956. (1 Reference).
Discusses the highlights of the report of a Joint Committee of the British Medical Association and the Magistrates Association. According to this report, neglect and cruelty to children are largely due to ignorance and thoughtlessness rather than deliberate action. Another section of the report is devoted to the medical factors involved in cruelty and neglect such as the mental and emotional stability of the parents. Recommendations include coordination between various services and the need for additional consultation before making any major decision involving the child's future.

663 Dine, Mark S., and Stark, Stanley N. "Slaughter of the innocents: letters to editor." JAMA 223(1): 81-82, January 1, 1973. (3 References).
Emphasizes that parents are responsible for the safety of their children. Several cases are reported where proper supervision by a parent or guardian was missing. Neglectful behavior can be as detrimental as overtly abusive behavior.

664 Jayaratne, Srinika. "Child abusers as parents and children: a review." Soc Work 22(1): 5-9, January, 1977. (33 References).
States that there is little empirical evidence to prove the frequently repeated statements that abusive parents are inadequate in parenting ability, and are themselves the products of an abusive upbringing. Such statements might be true but are not valid without any comparison studies of non-abusing parents; no adequate comparison studies have been made. The author also asks "reparenting" programs (for example, programs to teach abusing parents better methods of childrearing) first to examine: (1) the difference in practice between abusers and non-abusers; (2) the cultural and class differences in parenting practices; and (3) the program's own cultural assumptions about childrearing.

665 Johnson, Charles F. "Why children fail." Med Times 104(12): 81-83, December, 1976. (0 References).

Describes ways in which poor parenting deprives children of their basic rights and aggravates feelings of failure. Children deserve to be planned for, to be wanted, and to develop in ways that will build their self-esteem. Parental expectations which the child cannot meet cause him to feel like a failure. These feelings, in turn, lead to behavior problems, anxiety, and loss of confidence. Areas in which children can succeed need to be emphasized. Knowledgeable parenting can prevent these problems. Access to genetic counseling, as well as mandatory junior high school courses in child care and the family, are suggested.

666   Kogelschatz, J. L.; Adams, P. L.; Tucker, D. M. "Family styles of fatherless households." J Am Acad Child Psychiatry 11(1-4): 365-83, 1972. (7 References).
Investigates the effect of paternal absence in children. A group of fifty-two fatherless children were compared to fifty-three children from homes which were intact. A number of differences between the two groups were found, but none substantial enough to make fatherlessness a factor which has any more influence than economic class does upon a child's problems. The fatherless children did tend to exhibit a slightly greater number of behavioral problems and neuroses, and among children whose fathers had been absent for two years or longer, psychoses and mental retardation were more prevalent.

667   Landsmann, Leanna. "Child abuse is no myth: interview with Ellen M. Thomson." Instructor 83(5): 84-85, January, 1974. (1 Reference).
Tension, immaturity, and ignorance of the stages of child development can precipitate child battering. Programs such as Parents Anonymous and the Foster Grandparent program can help parents with the rearing of their children and in coping with anxiety.

668   Lewis, Hilda. "Unsatisfactory parents and psychological disorders in their children." Eugen Rev 60(2): 129-39, June, 1968.
Summary of the results of an investigation into the relation between parental inadequacy and psychological problems in children, based on observation of some 500 children. There is an attempt to correlate the type of behavior problem with the nature of disturbance in the child's behavior. The hypothesis that maternal deprivation yielded detrimental effects on young children was not substantiated by the data.

669   Newberger, Carolyn M., and Newberger, Eli H. "Inadequate mothers: letter to editor." Lancet 1(7897): 42-43, January 4, 1975. (4 References).
The cause of child abuse is too complex to simply attribute it to inadequate mothering.

670   Oliver, J. E. "Parents of battered children: letter to editor." Br J Psychiatry 128(5): 509, May, 1976. (0 References).
Two differences between childrearing behavior of abusive parents and of controls are pointed out: (1) battering parents attenuate accounts of typical rearing practices and incidents of battering; and (2) battering parents have a poor or inaccurate conception of normality.

671   Pinkerton, P. "Pediatric psychiatry: the pathology of parent/child interaction." Nurs Mirror 142(1): 56-58, January 15, 1976. (0 References).

Discusses the two major patterns of parental attitude and behavior leading to emotional disturbance in the child--overprotection and rejection.
A parent may become overprotective when the child has a physical or
emotional handicap, or when the death of another child, previous miscar-
riages, or generalized stress has aroused anxiety and fear in the parent.
The child responds to this protective behavior by becoming either over-
dependent or defiant. A parent may become rejecting if the child is seen
as a burden or has a congenital defect, or if the mother never learned
how to be a nurturant adult. The consequences of this pattern of parent/
child interaction is often non-accidental injury to the child and emotional stunting. It is important for the nurse to recognize these
damaging patterns of parenting and to work constructively with the parent
in order to improve them.

672 Polansky, Norman A.; Borgman, Robert D.; DeSaix, Christine; et al.
     Mental organization and maternal adequacy in rural Appalachia.
     Athens, Georgia: Georgia University, School of Social Work, 1969.
     15p. (Bibliography).
Reports on a study made in Appalachia of sixty-seven mother-child pairs
to discover the relationship between maternal personality and the child's
level of care. Although it was found that mothers with strong egos
tended to deliver a higher level of care, the findings imply that the
family's socioeconomic level may be the most influential factor since
it seemed to exhibit a strong positive correlation with both variables.
These findings are interpreted to suggest that the problem of inadequate
maternal care is not to be solved through "social thinking."

673 ————. "Two modes of maternal immaturity and their consequences."
     Child Welfare 49(6): 312-23, June, 1970. (27 References).
Presents the results of a study to determine the effect of the mother's
immaturity on her children. Chosen for the study were sixty-four mother-
child pairs from low-income, rural Appalachian families. Children were
four to five years of age. Based on observations of the family and
interviews with family members, mothers were rated on an Apathy-Futility
continuum, characterized by dependency and rash responses to tension.
Children were rated on a scale based on their physical and emotional
environment. The greater the mother's immaturity on both scales, the
more unhealthy was the child's environment. Children of mothers rated
high on the Apathy-Futility scale exhibited withdrawal, lethargy, and
dependency, while children of mothers rated high on the Childishly
Impulsive scale showed hostility and definance. Though treatment is
difficult because these personality traits are so deeply-rooted, it
must begin with concrete assistance in the form of economic aid and
casework service.

674 Polansky, Norman A.; DeSaix, Christine; Wing, Mary Lou; et al.
     "Child neglect in a rural community." Soc Casework 49(8): 467-
     74, October, 1968. (19 References).
The personality of the inadequate mother is profiled on the basis of
interviews and psychological tests administered to ten mothers from
rural southern Appalachia. The results suggest a typology involving
early arrest and fixation of personality development.

675 Smith, Selwyn M., and Hanson, Ruth. "Interpersonal relationships
     and child-rearing practices in 214 parents of battered children."
     Br J Psychiatry 127(6): 513-25, December, 1975. (41 References).

A study of childrearing practices of 214 parents of battered babies indicating a pattern of prematurely high performance expectations with no apparent conception of their young child's limited abilities. However, results also indicated that the demanding behavior of the battering parents was generally not excessive in comparison with others of the lower social classes except in three instances: maternal emotional over-involvement, demands for obedience, and use of physical force for punishment. Difficulties with interpersonal relationships, including marital problems, appeared to contribute to the unhappiness that provoked violence in susceptible parents.

676 Smith, Sona, and Deasy, Patrick. "Child abuse in Ireland--Part II: Why does it occur?" J Ir Med Assoc 70(3): 70-74, March 19, 1977. (10 References).

Part II of a comprehensive study on child abuse which analyzes the medical and social work hospital records of 126 families in order to investigate the causes of child abuse. Geographical location of the family (urban or rural), social class, and family size were not found to be related to child abuse. Neither were other socioeconomic factors such as poverty, financial difficulties, or stressful living arrangements associated with its occurrence. A higher incidence of child abuse was related to inadequacy of parents (as determined by their immaturity, irresponsibility, and inability to cope), limited maternal intelligence, parental personality disturbance or psychiatric illness, alcoholism, and marital problems. A history of violence in the home correlated highly with the presence of alcoholism and marital problems. It was also strongly related to active physical abuse of a child as opposed to passive neglect.

677 Stultz, Sylvia L. "Childrearing attitudes of abusive mothers: a controlled study." For a summary see: Diss Abstr Int 37B(3): 1419, September, 1976.

4. DISCIPLINE AND FAMILIAL VIOLENCE

678 Bandura, Albert, and Walters, Richard. "Method" and "Techniques of discipline: results from parent interviews." In: Bandura, Albert, and Walters, Richard. Adolescent aggression. New York: Ronald Press, 1959. 6-9, and 217-46. (0 References).

Studies fifty-two adolescent boys and their parents correlating aggression and parental discipline. Twenty-six boys had histories of aggressive behavior, and twenty-six were used as a control group. The relationship of the boys to their mothers was a central ingredient in the development of antisocial behavior. The mothers of the aggressive boys tended to discipline less frequently, less effectively, and less consistently. When discipline was imposed, it was resisted more strongly by the aggressive boys, reflecting hostility and anxiety over the parents' control. The degree of affection and warmth associated with discipline was greater in the control group. It was found that these parents used reasoning more often, whereas the parents of the aggressive group tended toward more coercive, punitive measures. The fathers of the aggressive boys were particularly viewed by the sons as harsh, and it was suggested that this more aggressive manner of discipline in conjunction with the mother's lack of demands complimented the development of aggressive tendencies.

679 Becker, Wesley C. "Consequences of different kinds of parental
     discipline." In: Hoffman, Martin L, and Hoffman, Lois, eds.
     Review of child development research, Vol. I. New York: Russell
     Sage Foundation, 1964. 169-208. (87 References).
A study of the consequences of different methods of parental discipline
using several sets of variables: love vs. hostility and restrictiveness
vs. permissiveness. Hostile parents generally used power-assertive
methods of discipline (beating, shouting, threatening), while warm
parents generally used love-oriented discipline (praising, reasoning,
showing disappointment, withdrawing love). Power-assertive discipline
seemed to promote in the child aggression, resistance to authority, and
externalized reactions to wrongdoing (fear of punishment, projected
hostility). Love-oriented discipline seemed to foster acceptance of
responsibility, guilt, and other internalized responses to wrongdoing.
Restrictive discipline promoted good social behavior but also tended to
make the child fearful, dependent, inhibited, or dull. Permissive discipline made a child more outgoing and assertive, but seemed to foster
increased aggression and decreased persistence. Interactions between
restrictive vs. permissive and hostile vs. warm discipline are also
examined, as are the consequences of inconsistent discipline. A consistent, warm, permissive discipline seems to produce the best results
in children.

680 Brandon, Sydney. "Physical violence in the family: an overview."
     In: Borland, Marie, ed. Violence in the family. Atlantic
     Highlands, New Jersey: Humanities Press, 1976. 1-25. (25 Refer-
     ences).
Describes patterns of physical violence occurring between family members.
Results of various studies on non-accidental injury to children are
cited. Extreme violence is likely to be inflicted by the father or
father substitute. Many of these fathers have prior criminal records.
The mothers tend to come from deprived backgrounds and to possess
limited nurturing capacities. A common treatment difficulty occurs when
the worker is drawn into the parents pattern of denial. Management
procedures stress carefully planned teamwork to maintain the integrity
of the family while protecting the child. Suggested preventive measures
include parent education and improved means of detecting stress. Other
aspects of family violence discussed are incest and wife battering.
Gambling, drug abuse, jealousy, and victim provocation are cited as
related causes of family violence. Society should provide the means for
family members, particularly wives, to establish independent lives when
they can no longer cope with a violent family structure.

681 Button, A. "Some antecedents of felonious and delinquent behavior."
     J Clin Child Psychol 2(3): 35-37, Fall, 1973. (0 References).
The theory that violence leads to violence is asserted by means of a
study of the influence of punishment on the behavior of young people.
One hundred and eighty delinquent and non-delinquent boys were compared
according to their family backgrounds. It was generally found that
severe physical and psychological abuse served as punishment for many of
the delinquents, while few of the non-delinquents were ever punished
harshly.

682 Cutts, Norma E., and Moseley, Nicholas. "Observations on methods
     of discipline." In: Cutts, Norma E., and Moseley, Nicholas.
     Better home discipline. New York: Appleton-Century-Crofts, 1952.
     213-26. (0 References).

A collection of observations on various methods of discipline and suggestions for guiding children's behavior effectively and constructively.
The methods of discipline discussed include the use and abuse of punishment, deprivation, isolation, and spanking. It is stressed that misbehavior, if persistent despite punishment, may only be aggravated by
further punishment. Also, punishment should never be misconstrued as a
substitute for proper supervision. The fundamental guiding principle
for good discipline is "to make right" what has gone wrong. When a child
misbehaves, he should have to face the consequences and accept the
responsibility of correcting the situation.

683 Dolder, Suzy J. "Differential attitudes towards punishment and
       child abuse." For a summary see: Diss Abstr Int 36B(7): 3598,
       January, 1976.

684 Erlanger, Howard S. "Social class and corporal punishment in child-
       rearing: a reassessment." Am Sociol Rev 39(1): 68-85, February,
       1974. (37 References).
Reviews Bronfenbrenner's paper entitled "Socialization and Social Class
Through Time and Space" (1958) and other studies which attempt to establish a correlation between corporal punishment and social class, parents'
level of education, family income, race, and religion. Data was self-
reported and parents were asked the frequency with which they had been
spanked as children and whether they would spank their own children in
certain hypothetical situations. The demographic results were not consistent with the conventional notion that working class parents usually
employ physical punishment, whereas middle class parents resort to psychological techniques of punishment. Instead, data from all social classes,
races, and age groups overlapped. These findings lead us to reevaluate
certain stereotypic behaviors which we associate with the lower class,
such as working class authoritarianism, tendency toward physical violence,
relationship to child abuse, and the subculture of violence.

685 Feshback, N. D. "The effects of violence in childhood." J Clin
       Child Psychol 2(3): 28-31, Fall, 1973. (25 References).
Critical assessment of the effectiveness of corporal punishment. Such
discipline is seen as aggravating a child's anxiety and hostility, rather
than making him more cooperative. The child is actually made less able
to control his impulses by corporal punishment. A more effective approach
has been to focus on reinforcing cooperative behavior and ignoring aggressive behavior.

686 Fischhoff, J. "The role of the parents' unconscious in children's
       antisocial behavior." J Clin Child Psychol 2(3): 31-33, Fall,
       1973. (8 References).
A discussion of the pattern wherein a parent unable to handle his own
frustrations unconsciously encourages the child to act out his own
negative impulses in an antisocial way. The parent's subsequent punishment of the child is frequently brutal and represents an attempt to deny
the original impulse. Such inconsistent behavior confuses the child and
leads to more severe behavioral and psychological problems.

687 Fontana, Vincent J. Somewhere a child is crying: maltreatment --
       causes and prevention. New York: Macmillan, 1973. 268p.
A descriptive, often emotional account of battered and neglected children
in New York City's Foundling Hospital. As a pediatrician and medical

director of the hospital, Fontana not only treated the young victims but was responsible for working with child protection agencies, social workers, district attorneys, and others involved in the management of child abuse.

But the story belongs to the children; and sadly, the story often ends in failure and death. Frequently Fontana lists the instances of death by abuse in newspaper fashion, citing only the final and horrible details. But other times he traces the child's history from pregnancy through death and any follow-up legal action. The book honestly points out the mistakes and oversights of social workers, police, and others, including Fontana himself, overburdened with investigative and custody cases.

Fontana struggles with the question of how to break the cycle of violence, neglect, and sexual abuse which is passed from parent to child, and decides that the accepted pattern of childrearing in our culture is much at fault. Most abusing parents do not recognize that they are indulging themselves, instead of disciplining their child, when they continually beat or torment that child. Parental attitudes must be altered to a level of wholesome affection toward and acceptance of the child in every family. To implement this change, a return to the concept of the extended family is in order.

As a society we need to change our attitudes about children's rights and initiate legislative action to guarantee these rights. The prevalent attitude is that children have no rights after being born, except, perhaps, to be clothed and fed. But the child's right of life and happiness can only be asserted by others--by concerned neighbors, teachers, physicians, or children's advocates. Fontana urges personal involvement on the community level by being parent-aides or simply by being helpful and neighborly. In urban areas he recommends the establishment of central clinics for the diagnosis and treatment of child abuse. Finally, he favors federal legislation which would be specific and enforceable, covering all aspects of minors' rights. Solutions advocated by others, such as abortion on demand, he sees only as treating the symptoms of the disease and not any possible cause.

The author reiterates the findings of Mayor Lindsay's task force on abuse, along with the following recommendations: (1) only experienced social workers should handle abuse cases; (2) one judge should follow through on a specific case of abuse; and (3) the judge's decision to return the child to his parents' custody should only be made after personal consultation with the physician and social worker involved in the case. The chapter entitled "A child's day in court" is the account of an assistant district attorney's success in bringing a child abuser to justice: a belated, but nonetheless sincere, effort at asserting a child's rights.

688 Goldstein, Jeffrey H.; Davis, Roger W.; Herman, Dennis. "Escalation of aggression: experimental studies." J Pers Soc Psychol 31(1): 162-70, 1975. (39 References).
Describes an experiment which investigates the dynamics of escalating aggression. Subjects could offer any of ten levels of increasingly positive reinforcement for correct responses or any of ten levels of negative reinforcement. It was found that, regardless of whether the first reinforcement was strong or weak, the subjects always raised the level of the reinforcement--that is, it either became strongly positive or strongly negative. These findings support the disinhibition theory of either hostile or friendly behavior. These results have application to the study of the battered child syndrome which also involves the escalation of aggression in this case against a child.

689 Goode, William J. "Force and violence in the family." J Marriage
      Fam 33(4): 624-36, November, 1971. (17 References).
Evaluates the appropriate and harmful uses of force within the family
structure. Generally, the threat of force has its constructive and
inevitable presence in any social unit, so long as the application is
just and understandable. When a member of the family feels that physical
or psychological force is applied unfairly to him, the results could
include the disruption of the family. Physical force is found to be used
more commonly in lower class families, while middle class families apply
psychological pressure. Child abuse is discussed as a perversion of the
normal use of force in the family.

690 Harrison-Ross, Phyllis, and Wyden, Barbara. The black child -- a
      parent's guide. New York: Peter H. Wyden, 1973. 360p.
Discusses the special discipline-sex related problems in black families.
The report focuses on mother-son relationships and suggests that black
mothers who are too strict with their young sons cause their sons to
grow up fearing women. At the same time, black women have traditionally
been forced into situations that cause them to fear men and sexual contacts. This fear is then carried over into their relationships with
their sons in the form of severe punishment. Steps must be taken to
encourage fathers to become involved with their children and to assume
more of the responsibility for disciplining them.

691 Havens, Leston L. "Youth, violence, and the nature of family life."
      Psychiatr Ann 2(2): 18-29, February, 1972.
Discusses the currently emerging image of family life as harboring much
potential for physical and psychical violence. This shift from the post-
war idealization of family harmony is compared to the revision of attitudes toward the family which resulted from the publication of Freud's
studies. Intra-familial violence is explored in its various manifestations, which include patricide, matricide, filicide, infanticide, child
battering, and spouse murder. Genetic, psychological, and environmental
influences in the dynamics of family violence are investigated, along
with the role of the family in mental illness, particularly in its violent manifestations.

692 Justice, Blair; Justice, Rita; Kraft, Irvin A. "Early warning signs
      of violence: is a triad enough?" Am J Psychiatry 131(4): 457-
      59, April, 1974. (9 References).
Suggests that fighting, temper tantrums, getting along with others, and
truancy behavior in children may predict violence in adulthood, especially if these symptoms occur together or excessively.

693 Lourie, Reginald S. "The roots of violence: an essay on its nature
      and early developmental determinants." Early Child Dev Care 2:
      1-12, January, 1973.

694 Loveland, Robert John. "Distinctive personality and discipline
      characteristics of child-neglecting mothers." For a summary see:
      Diss Abstr Int 38B(1): 368, July, 1977.

695 Lystad, Mary H. "Violence at home: a review of the literature."
      Am J Orthopsychiatry 45(3): 328-45, April, 1975. (162 Refer-
      ences).

Reviews recent studies on violence in families. The studies cited examine violence in terms of psychological, social, or cultural factors. They raise theoretical questions concerning the causes of violence and discuss the implications of each for reducing violence. Incidence estimates and reports on violence in married couples are also reviewed. Numerous studies have attempted to reach an understanding of abuse toward children by parents or caretakers, as well as an understanding of acts of extreme violence by children. Any study that would develop a comprehensive theory of family violence has to encompass psychosocial as well as cultural considerations. Most importantly, individual acts of violence at home need to be examined within the boundaries of social and cultural norms. Services to families must focus on basic individual needs that are not being met at home and provide community support as needed. Areas for further research into family violence are suggested.

696 Mintz, A. A. "Battered child syndrome." Tex Med 60(2):   107-8,
      February, 1964. (0 References).
Presents the idea that the battered child is only a symptom of a family disease, which must be treated as such. The battered child is described as a scapegoat, providing for the release of aggression which insures the rest of the family's survival. The battering parent has characteristically held the same position within his own family. Legal action is difficult due to insufficient evidence or conflicting attitudes of physicians regarding treatment of the parents. Family treatment is recommended.

697 Sayles, Mary Buell. "Unwanted." In: Sayles, Mary Buell. The
      problem child at home: a study in parent-child relationships.
      New York: The Commonwealth Fund Division of Publications, 1928.
      209-26. (1 Reference).
A case report illustrating the effects of using negative reinforcement, to the exclusion of positive reinforcement, in order to direct a child's behavior. Repeated attempts on the part of the subject to find satisfaction in relations with his parents were blocked and frustrated by punishment. Consequently, the subject became gradually more and more antagonistic and delinquent. A direct relationship was drawn between parental rejection, along with unreasonable, inconsistent punishment, and delinquency in children.

698 Sourkes, Barbara M. "Parental neglect and lashing out: maladaptive
      styles of coping." For a summary see: Diss Abstr Int   37B(8):
      4170, February, 1977.

699 Steele, Brandt F. "Violence in our society." Pharos Alpha Omega
      Alpha 33(2): 42-48, April, 1970. (0 References).
Traces a cause and effect relationship between beatings a parent received as a form of discipline, and beatings he administers to his own child. Such beatings are usually perceived as normal by the parent, severe as they may be; their severity seems justified to the parent by the severe treatment he received as a child. Because the parent believes that the batterings are necessary in maintaining discipline, he cannot recognize their brutality even after he has been imprisoned for child abuse. Typical cases are described.

700 Steinmetz, Suzanne K. "The use of force for resolving family con-
      flict: the training ground for abuse." Fam Coord 26(1): 19-25,
      January, 1977. (0 References).

Conclusions based on a questionnaire, completed by seventy-eight people between eighteen and thirty years old, concerning methods of resolving conflicts within their families. All families have conflict and, hence, have the potential to be abusive to children; and violence seems to be a learned method of problem solving. Our society sanctions a certain amount of forceful control of behavior, and it is easy for people to go beyond force to violence in dealing with a spouse or child. Data showed that virtually all families used verbal aggression, and many used physical aggression also in resolving conflicts. Four types of patterns emerged, all combinations of high or low verbal and high or low physical aggression: screaming sluggers, silent attackers, threateners, and pacificists. Since children pattern their own subsequent behavior on the models given them, "normal" families are seen as potential training grounds for abuse.

701 Steinmetz, Suzanne K., and Straus, Murray A., eds. <u>Violence in the</u>
     <u>family</u>. New York: Harper and Row, 1974. 337p. (Bibliography).
A comprehensive selection of articles which explore the origins and effects of intra-family violence and its relationship to societal violence. The conceptual framework provided by the authors to organize the various and often controversial arguments contained in the articles hinges on the following points: (1) violence is a fundamental part of family life and is not present only in pathological instances of wife beating or child abuse; (2) the family is a system within a larger social system and intra-family violence is only one element in a complex societal pattern of normals and values; and (3) the psychopathological view of violent behavior which derives from psychoanalytic theory is an insufficient explanation of the problem unless placed in a sociocultural context.

This approach to violence challenges the idea that it is primarily a lower class phenomenon, that it is biologically linked to sex and, therefore, a pre-determined aspect of human behavior, and that modified expressions of aggression have the cathartic effect of reducing tension and so preventing severe future episodes of violence. The catharsis theory derives from the psychoanalytic idea that aggression is necessary and must find some channeled means of release; the sociocultural approach would view such release as providing a model for achieving short-term satisfaction and, therefore, as reinforcing future aggressive outbursts.

Part One offers an analysis of the function of force and violence in the family. Violence is seen as a resource which can be used to achieve desired ends and which is relied upon when other resources such as money, status or respect are lacking. If the flow of transactions within a family system is imbalanced and family members perceive themselves as giving more than they are getting, then feelings of rage will naturally ensue if members are unable to get what they need through other means.

Part Two examines violence between spouses and kin. It is emphasized that the problem of violence tends to be ignored except when it escalates to the point of murder or child abuse. Little is known about the frequency and intensity of fights and slapping between spouses. This unexplored area of human relationships needs to be understood if the fundamental causes of violence are to be uncovered and if those features of society which promote violence are to be altered. The articles in this section offer various theories of violence, including the idea that violence provides the American male with a means of compensating for feelings of masculine inadequacy, that violence stems from frustration due to the inability of family members to fulfill culturally prescribed roles, that violence plays a role in family dynamics in that some families require the acting out of violent behavior in order to maintain family equilibrium, and that violence derives from environmental stress factors such as poverty and the lack of upward mobility. Articles with a clinical orientation suggest that one means of controlling violence is to have the family therapist teach methods of fair and constructive fighting. The ethological approach is also represented by an article comparing human and animal behavior.

Part Three focuses on the problem of child abuse. It is granted that pathological child abusers exist, but the larger problem has its roots in accepted patterns of social behavior. Physical punishment is still an almost universal mode of child discipline which can be replaced by alternative approaches to childrearing. Several articles consider the etiology of child abuse and theorists of both the psychopathological and the socio-cultural schools are represented. Also included in this section are clinical approaches to the treatment of existing instances of child abuse, with an emphasis upon the necessity for long-term, supportive relationships between the abusing parent and the worker.

Part Four looks at the family as a training ground for societal violence. A significant controversy exists between the biological, deterministic view of violence and the view which maintains that violence is socially learned behavior. Analyses of student revolutionaries and pro-war students suggest some factors which contribute to social and individual approval of violence as a means of problem-solving or control. Some family factors are identified which tend to produce the violence-prone child, such as the placing of high value on toughness, the use of physical punishment as a means of discipline, and the lack of value consensus among family members. Means of learning non-violence in a family context might include a return to an extended family system, but far more needs to be learned about this aspect of human behavior.

702 Wittels, Fritz. "Sadistic tendencies in parents." In: Calverton
    V. F., and Schmalhausen, Samuel D. The new generation. New York:
    Macaulay, 1930. 41-54. (1 Reference).
A commentary on the long-standing attitude on the part of parents that children are property to be punished and manipulated at will. Children, the recipients of sadistic parental behavior, are at the same time taught to love their parents. Imagining revenge when in reality faced with impotence, a child is tortured by guilt feelings. Sadistic practices toward children in many societies are not only reflected and passed on in families, but also in cultural traditions, including fairy tales and religious writings such as the Old and New Testaments. Sadism itself develops and persists unconsciously. In order to eliminate it, parents must be made to realize the harm they are inflicting upon their children and future generations.

5. THE GENERATIONAL CYCLE OF ABUSE

703 "The battering parent." Time 94(19): 77-78, November 7, 1969.
    (0 References).
Reviews several studies of child abuse which focus treatment on the battering parent. A study of sixty families by Brandt F. Steele and Carl B. Pollock indicated that parents who abuse their children were themselves abused, neglected, or deprived as children. These parents expect

their children to fulfill their needs, and abuse results when this does not happen. Legal action or temporary intervention for the sake of the child only may exacerbate the parent's feelings of rejection. C. Henry Kempe's study suggests, however, that the parent sees abuse as rightful punishment, a view reinforced by the social sanction of physical punishment. Kempe advocates treatment which provides the parent with the kind of attentive parenting he has never had. There have been no repeaters in 400 families receiving this treatment.

704 deMause, Lloyd. "Psychohistory and psychotherapy." Hist Child Q
      2(3): 408-14, Winter, 1975. (0 References).
Advocates an expansion of psychohistorical research on the grounds that most modes regarded as psychopathic today have their origins in attitudes which were universally accepted at some earlier point in human history. Various examples of such attitudes and their historical manifestations are discussed. Child abuse and child murder are included among the horrible phenomena which were at one time culturally sanctioned.

705 Fontana, Vincent J. "Child abuse and neglect -- a social disease."
      J NY State Sch Nurse Teach Assoc 5(4): 18-21, June, 1974. (0
      References).
A rousing and succinct overview of the problem of child abuse in the United States. Child abuse is viewed as a social disease in which violence begets violence in generation after generation and through which will result the eventual disintegration of our society if present trends are not curbed. The best approach to cure is in the establishment of a multidisciplinary network of protection in each community. This would involve coordination of efforts of physicians, courts, and social service agencies to facilitate enlightenment of the masses, adequate treatment programs, and efficient implementation of procedures and laws pertaining to child abuse. Finally, government funding will be necessary to finance the entire network.

706 Freedman, David A. "The battering parent and his child: a study in
      early object relations." Int Rev Psychoanal 2(2): 189-98, 1975.
      (30 References).
General survey of the literature studying battered children, defining the syndrome of child abuse and describing the "typical" attack. It is argued that the predisposition to abuse is transmitted from generation to generation through the mother's treatment of her child in the earlier months of life. The syndrome has been traced as far back as four successive generations in a single family.

707 Green, Arthur H.; Gaines, Richard W.; Sandgrund, Alice. "Child
      abuse: pathological syndrome of family interaction." Am J
      Psychiatry 131(8): 882-86, August, 1974. (16 References).
Rejects the presupposition of an abusive personality and argues, instead, that child abuse is a dysfunction of parenting. Adults who are unable to adjust responsibly to the role of parenting may themselves have been childhood victims of abuse. As parents, they now reenact their childhood traumas in their own children. A child with any physical or psychological abnormality has an increased chance of being abused, because he is seen as a copy of the parent's own defective self-image. Finally, environmental factors such as illness, estrangement, or death in the family increase the stress on the parent and can cause him to mete out his distress or anger on the most readily accessible victim.

708 Hanks, Susan E., and Rosenbaum, C. Peter. "Battered women: a study
     of women who live with violent alcohol-abusing men." Am J Ortho-
     psychiatry 47(2): 291-306, April, 1977. (0 References).
A study of twenty-two women and their violence-prone, alcohol-abusing
male partners to determine not only why women stay in such relationships,
but also how they might be contributing to the perpetuation of violence.
Attempts are made to link the subjects' history in intra-familial strife
to their choice of mates and to their continued use of violence in interpersonal relationships.

709 Kastel, Jean. "Sally P., a case record: the deprived child of a
     deprived mother." In: Kastel, Jean. Casework in child care.
     London: Routledge and Kegan Paul, 1962. 264-77.
Outlines the case history of a neglected child whose mother was also
ignored and abandoned as a child. The mother's apparent cold uncaring
attitude toward her child was the result of her own neglected upbringing
(repeated desertions by the mother left the child severely disturbed).
The anger of the caseworker toward the mother and his protective attitude
toward the child prevented a helpful therapeutic intervention.

710 Morris, Marian G., and Gould, Robert W. "Role reversal: a necessary
     concept in dealing with the 'battered child syndrome.'" Am J Ortho-
     psychiatry 33(2): 298-99, March, 1963. (0 References).
Summarizes the findings of a study of twenty abusive parents. Role reversal was found to be a key operant principle in the thought patterns
and behavior of parents who batter their children. Such parents perceive
that their infants possess an adult capacity to willfully displease or
judge them. In their natural dependency, the children are linked to their
grandparents who could not be pleased and who did not meet the needs of
the current parents. Brutality perpetuates itself through the generations
as each new set of parents considers it their natural prerogative to beat
their offspring for seemingly aggressive dependency. Parents studied in
the twenty cases typically did not feel guilty for their brutality, but
did fear punishment from the outside world, which the baby in his role-
reversal position represented. In addition, such parents were frequently
isolated and did not seek help from agencies.

711 Morris, Marian G.; Gould, Robert W.; Matthews, Patricia J. "Toward
     prevention of child abuse." Children 11(2): 55-60, March-April,
     1964. (12 References).
Presents observations resulting from two studies of neglected and battered children. The studies indicated that abuse is passed down through
families for generations. Abusing parents tend to fall in three group-
ings: (1) responsive to treatment by the hospital team; (2) responsive
to combined services of the hospital and community agencies; and (3)
unresponsive parents. Interviewing which clarifies the parents' attitude
toward the child, themselves, and their own parents helps establish a
treatment plan. Differences between nurturing and abusing parents are
listed in detail, centering primarily around the parents' immediate
expressions of concern for the child. These characteristics are illustrated by case histories. The reactions of the well-cared-for child and
the neglected child are also contrasted by the former's reliance on his
parents and the latter's fear and withdrawal. It is indicated that these
findings are a tremendous aid to diagnosis and prevention. Establishing
accountability and coordination among agencies, along with proper legislation, are suggested to be crucial.

712   Neill, Alexander S.   "Cruelty."   In: Neill, Alexander S.   The
       problem family.   New York: Hermitage Press, 1949.   123-33.   (0
       References).
Examines the unconscious sexual motivations of cruelty and their effects
on the development of children.   Society condones cruelty by the expectation of its use in enforcing discipline and laws.   Yet cruelty practiced
on children, even when the conscious motive is to benefit the child,
results in the child also learning to be cruel.   The repression of a
child's natural impulses by his parents only serves to bury the material
in the unconscious to re-erupt as anger or hate.   Abolish that middle
unconscious of guilt, and one's desires can be expressed in a free and
open manner devoid of cruelty.   Sexual expression, when repressed and
denied, seeks its outlet in cruelty and sadism, and the maltreatment of
children often has this repression as its cause.

713   Oliver, J. E., and Cox, Jane.   "A family kindred with ill-used
       children: the burden on the community."   Br J Psychiatry   123(572):
       81-90, July, 1973.   (12 References).
A family pedigree is presented in which representatives from at least
three generations were subjected to abuse or severe neglect as children.
Many family members received extensive social and medical help from
various professionals, which failed to prevent the tendency toward child
abuse in subsequent generations.   This family is representative of other
such families under study by the authors.   The prevalent emphasis upon
maintaining children within their own family units at all costs is called
into question.   Skilled family planning advice must be incorporated into
the helping services offered to such families.

714   Oliver, J. E., and Dewhurst, K. E.   "Six generations of ill-used
       children in a Huntington's pedigree."   Postgrad Med J   45(530):
       757-60, December, 1969.   (8 References).
Discusses Huntington's pedigree of six generations and the detrimental
effect upon children reared in such families.   The interaction of genetic
and environmental factors is illustrated.   Attention is directed to
legislation on family planning and therapeutic abortion in such cases.

715   Oliver, J. E., and Taylor, Audrey.   "Five generations of ill-treated
       children in one family pedigree."   Br J Psychiatry   119(552):
       473-80, November, 1971.   (15 References).
A detailed description of five generations of abused children.   This
family pedigree is representative of a number of others, also under study,
which make disproportionate demands upon community services without
significant benefit.   Numerous family members suffer from mental illness,
profound personality disturbances, and degrees of subnormal intelligence.
The prevention of abuse requires a more thorough understanding of the
parents' psycho-social histories and of emotional disorders which are
untreatable by social support alone.   The identification and surveillance
of disturbed family systems should be accompanied by adequate birth control services.   Problems relating to effective family planning are discussed.   Removal of the child must sometimes be considered as the only
humane course of action.

716   Ostow, M.   "Parents' hostility to their children."   Isr Ann Psy-
       chiatry   8(1):   3-21, April, 1970.   (15 References).
Suggests a connection between a parent's hostility toward his child and
his childhood hostility toward his parents or siblings.   Various types

of infantile impulses in parents are categorized in terms of the parent's childhood repression and adult redirection of them toward his children. The histories of parents characteristically vulnerable to this process are grouped into patterns as are the family situations which typically elicit the parents' buried impulses.

717 Parker, Barbara, and Schumacher, Dale N. "The battered wife syndrome and violence in the nuclear family of origin: a controlled pilot study." Am J Public Health 67(8): 760-61, August, 1977. (0 References).

Compares the characteristics of battered and non-battered wives. No significant difference existed between battered and non-battered women in age, race, number of children, educational background, years of marriage, and the atmosphere of their childhood families. Of the fifty women interviewed, twenty reported battering. Those who came from homes where their mothers were battered were more likely to be abused by their husbands. Abusive husbands had less education than non-abusive husbands. There was no correlation between a woman's abuse as a child and her subsequent abuse as a wife. A discussion stresses the responsibility of medical and legal professionals in dealing with this problem.

718 Peterson, Karen. "There's a link between animal abuse and child abuse." PTA Mag 68(10): 14-16, June, 1974. (0 References).

Childhood cruelty to animals is both a response to possible child abuse at home and a precursor of the criminally violent adult. Children should be taught that all life is important and should not be allowed to torture or kill an animal with impunity.

719 Silver, Larry B.; Dublin, Christina C.; Lourie, Reginald S. "Does violence breed violence?: contributions from a study of the child abuse syndrome." Am J Psychiatry 126(3): 404-7, September, 1969. (11 References).

The family records of abused children who came into contact with the District of Columbia child protective services between June and December of 1963 were reviewed in 1967. These records not only provided information on the contacts of these families with social agencies since 1963, but also yielded historical data from up to twenty years before the reported incident of abuse. In more than half of the thirty-four cases studied, abuse on the part of one or both parents toward each other or siblings was discovered. In four of the instances, the abusive parent had himself been abused as a child. Seven abused children had already come to the attention of the courts for delinquent or assaultive behavior. Longitudinal reviews of families over three generations show that some abused children become the abusive parents of tomorrow and that violence does appear to breed violence. Other patterns of defensive adaptation to child abuse are also discussed with nine case reports presented in detail.

720 Van Stolk, Mary. "Beaten women, battered children." Child Today 5(2): 8-12, March-April, 1976. (15 References).

The problem of battered wives is compared with the problem of battered children. Like older children who have been abused, many women do not seek help because of shame about how they are being treated. As in child abuse, wife beating cuts across all socioeconomic classes. Alcohol may play a significant role in wife as well as child battering. Many women are pregnant when they are assaulted, increasing the probability that unborn children are battered in the womb. As in the case of child abuse, society does not want to get involved in the private affairs of the family. In Canada, wife beating is not recorded statistically by any agency. More reliable statistics are needed to make a clear assessment of the nature and extent of the problem.

721 —————. "Who owns the child?" Child Educ 50(5): 258-65, March, 1974. (31 References).
Analyzes the anthropological and historical framework which allows child abuse to perpetuate itself in North American society. Western society has always affirmed the parent's right to demand absolute obedience of a child and has looked upon the child as property. When a child is exposed to harsh discipline and abuse instead of nurturing, he grows up believing that force is an effective childrearing methodology. The need to end punitive and archaic childrearing practices and recognize the individual child's basic human rights is emphasized.

722 Zilboorg, Gregory. "Sidelights on parent-child antagonism." Am J Orthopsychiatry 2(1): 35-43, January, 1932. (0 References).
Suggests the necessity of examining unconscious parental attitudes in the treatment of the child. Antagonism between parent and child may be caused by unresolved conflicts from the parent's own childhood which are projected onto his own child. For instance, the father who has never resolved his competitive feelings toward his brother may unconsciously repeat that competition with his son. Often these parents appear to be well-adjusted concerned parents who strongly desired children. In some parents, the baby at first represents a relaxation of their superego through which they revive the id impulses of their childhood. Later, they punish this relaxation by imposing their harsh superego onto their child. Recognizing these factors in the parent-child relationship is an important factor in the treatment of maladjustment in children.

6. THE CHILD'S ROLE IN PROVOKING ABUSE

723 Berg, Pamela I. "Parental expectations and attitudes in child-abusing families." For a summary see: Diss Abstr Int 37B(4): 1889, October, 1976.

724 Friedrich, William N., and Boriskin, Jerry A. "Ill health and child abuse: letter to editor." Lancet 1(7960): 649-50, March 20, 1976. (5 References).
Describes the analysis of 424 cases of physical child abuse. Correlations were run between children with certain disorders--physical disease, learning problems, emotional disturbances--and the incidence of abuse. Results showed a greater severity of abuse involving children under six years of age and those having childhood disorders.

725 —————. "The role of the child in abuse: a review of the literature." Am J Orthopsychiatry 46(4): 580-90, October, 1976. (46 References).
A review of the literature on the role of the child in abuse. Certain characteristics of a particular child may make him vulnerable, unattractive, or difficult to care for, producing parental stress reactions and precipitating abuse. The premature baby is more likely to be restless and irritable. A child born with mental or physical deficiencies may be

more vulnerable to scapegoating. There appears to be genetic predispositions for some children to be difficult, unable to adapt, or unresponsive to physical contact. Certain children are perceived as being "different" by their parents for understandable or unexplainable reasons. Studies have demonstrated that these "special" children make up a greater proportion of the abused and neglected than do "normal" children. Although this child may be at greater risk of abuse, he is not the sole contributor to the abusive situation. Abuse is probably the product of a special child, a special parent, an immediate or long-term crisis, and a cultural tolerance for corporal punishment. More research in the area of child abuse is needed before its complete etiology can be determined.

726 Laury, Gabriel V. "The battered child syndrome: parental motiva-
        tion, clinical aspects." Bull NY Acad Med 46(9): 676-85,
        September, 1970. (17 References).
Explores the battering parent's motivation for abuse. The parent abuses the child to discipline him "for his own good" or to quell what is considered to be unacceptable or annoying behavior. The mother may blame the child for her lost youth, or the father may suspect that the child is not his own. Both parents may feel the child does not live up to their expectations. Psychopathic parents may use the child for sexual gratification or allow the child to become a part of their delusional system. In some cases, the abuse is impulsive and without apparent reason. Unconsciously, parents may ventilate their own hostility and frustrations or satisfy their own needs through child abuse.

727 Milowe, Irvin D., and Lourie, Reginald S. "The child's role in the
        battered child syndrome." J Pediatr 65(6): 1079-81, December,
        1964. (0 References).
Through the presentation and discussion of cases of child abuse, four categories are delineated. Discussion revolves around the first: defects in the child as a precipitating factor. It is noted that occasionally these children are again beaten in foster homes, due to particularly irritating behavior on the part of the child.

728 Nichamin, Samuel J., and Fontana, Vincent J. "Battered child syn-
        drome and brain dysfunction: letters to editor." JAMA 223(12):
        1390-91, March 19, 1973. (4 References).
It is suggested that babies with minimal brain dysfunction may provoke unstable parents to attack them. The behavior of these babies is often radically atypical in infancy and becomes increasingly more difficult to handle at the toddler and preschool age. Although there has been little or no research in this area, it is suspected that minimal brain dysfunction is a genetic trait passed from parent to child. Information about emotional disturbances in teens and their relationship to perceptual deficits needs to be gathered, so that these young adults can be identified and possibly treated with psychostimulant medication. A second letter points to the importance of preventing child abuse by developing techniques for predicting potential abusers and detecting cases of abuse early.

729 Rubin, Jean. "The need for intervention." Public Welfare 24(3):
        230-35, July, 1966. (0 References).
In a discussion of the incidence of child abuse it is pointed out that children under age three are most susceptible to abuse. Abusive parents frequently expect age-inappropriate behavior from their children. Owing

to a basically unstable and unrewarding marital relationship, the non-
abusive spouse frequently encourages the abusive behavior or becomes a
passive witness. When parents fail, it is society's responsibility to
intervene and protect abused children. Well-publicized reporting laws
and a central registry can aid in identifying at risk children.

730   Soeffing, Marylane. "Abused children are exceptional children."
      Except Child 42(3): 126-33, November, 1975. (28 References).
Reviews data and literature concerning the relationship between child
abuse and handicapped children. Numerous studies reveal the susceptibility of the handicapped to abuse. Others describe severe handicaps
resulting from abuse such as mental retardation, emotional disturbance,
physical defects, and growth failure. The responsibility of educators
to identify and report suspected cases of abuse and neglect is emphasized,
since schools can play an important role in controlling the number of
abused and handicapped children. An outline of current programs for
managing child abuse and suggestions for futher research projects are
included.

731   Steele, Brandt F. "Parental abuse of infants and small children."
      In: Anthony, E. James, and Benedek, Therese, eds. Parenthood:
      its psychology and psychopathology. Boston: Little, Brown, 1970.
      449-77. (24 References).
Describes the psychological characteristics of abusive parents based on
a study of sixty families in which child abuse occurred. Abusive parents
are often depressed, immature, and dependent. They tend to be isolated,
unable to ask for help, and suspicious and distrustful of others. Many
of these parents were themselves abused as children. Their early childhood experiences result in a lack of motherliness, a narcissistic concern
for self, and a tendency toward moral masochism or self-deprecation.

The pattern of childrearing in abusive families is characterized by:
(1) the parents' conviction that the child exists in order to satisfy
their needs; (2) the parents' misperception of the infant as bad, dis-
obedient, inconsiderate, unloving, or bothersome; and (3) the parents'
belief that the child should be punished if he cannot meet their expectations and satisfy their needs. These parental attitudes, in conjunction
with the cultural acceptance of the use of physical punishment as a form
of discipline and the parents' own upbringing, create a family dynamic
in which child abuse is likely to occur. Other factors which affect the
likelihood of child abuse are the nature of the child and the behavior of
the non-abusive spouse. Premature or sickly infants and children with
congenital defects require more care than normal children and are less
able to respond to parental needs. They are, therefore, more likely to
stimulate parental attack. The non-abusive spouse often encourages, or
at least condones, the abusive parent's behavior.

To successfully treat the abusive parent, the psychiatrist must examine
his own feelings about child abuse, establish a supportive relationship
with the patient, help the abusive parent to overcome his/her reluctance
to seek and accept help from others, and bring about change in parental
attitudes which lead to child abuse.

732   Symonds, Percival M. "Parental rejection: a denial of love and an
      expression of hate toward child," and "Parental ambivalence: over-
      protection or overindulgence as a reaction formation against
      hostility." In: Symonds, Percival M. The dynamics of parent-

child relationships. New York: Columbia University Press, 1949.
11-50, and 89-93. (14 References).

Two chapters discuss parental rejection and ambivalence toward children.
Rejection of a child manifests itself in a number of ways, primarily
through neglect, separation, denial, and humiliation. An obvious expression of rejection is through punishment or maltreatment. Threats, even
when not acted upon, still register as an expression of hostility. The
earlier it occurs, the more serious rejection is in its effect on the
child. A child's responses to rejection are just as numerous. Attempts
to gain affection, attention-getting behavior, hyperactivity, and helplessness are common reactions. Psychopathic, unstable tendencies or
counterhostility may also develop. Some children repress their counterhostility by becoming perfectionists, by withdrawing, or by regressing.
Parental neglect can cause retardation. Mild neglect, however, can
produce some positive traits, such as increased independence in the
child. Dynamic factors motivating a parent's hostility may be the
economic burden of a child, his interference with a career or marital
relationship, or his failure to meet expectations. Unconscious factors
may include a revival of Oedipal conflicts, self-hatred, or projections
of negative feelings for one's spouse. Ambivalence in a parent may mask
hostility and is often revealed by an inconsistent alteration between
hostility and overprotection or overindulgence. Ambivalence seems to
cause more antisocial characteristics in the child than any other factor.

733 White, G. de L.; Househam, K. C.; Ngomane, D. "Child abuse among
     rural blacks: letter to editor." S Afr Med J 50(39): 1499,
     September, 1976. (0 References).

Presents two case histories of rural black children who suffered non-
accidental injuries and malnutrition while in the care of relatives.
Both children had florid kwashiorkor, a disease caused by poverty and
ignorance. It is suggested that the irritability and apathy of a child
with kwashiorkor may have annoyed the guardians and percipitated the
abuse.

7. DRUG-ADDICTED MOTHERS

734 Carr, J. N. Maternal drug dependence incidence, drug use patterns,
     and impact on children. New York: Odyssey House, 1975. 18p.
     (Bibliography).

Mothers who are drug dependent jeopardize their children's well-being.
Exposure to drugs during pregnancy, along with interference in the develop-
ment of mother-infant attachment, yield severe impairments in children.
Provision for services are recommended.

735 Coppolillo, H. P. "Drug impediments to mothering behavior." Addict
     Dis 2(1): 201-8, 1975. (14 References).

Describes the physiological and behavioral obstacles which prevent female
addicts from assuming a mothering role with their infants. The addict's
orientation is basically materialistic. A developing mother-child
symbiotic relationship, however, requires that the mother meet her
child's needs before she herself can be gratified. A course of action for
assisting the infant through the withdrawal syndrome is explained.
Similarities between addicted and abusive mothers are noted.

736   Densen-Gerber, Judianne, and Rohrs, C. C.   Drug-addicted parents
        and child abuse. New York: Odyssey House, 1975. 16p. (Bibliog-
        raphy).
A sharp criticism of the current negligent attitude of the public and,
particularly of health professionals, toward the children of drug addicts.
It is presently assumed that the parents are fit to raise their children
as long as they are receiving therapy. It has been found that drug
addicts are irresponsible parents, and that they usually fail to accommodate their lives to new children. The children of those drug addicts
who cannot make the necessary adaptations required by parenthood should
be removed from the destructive environments into which they were born.

737   "Drug addiction -- spot it early: consultation." Med World News
        13(44): 25ff., November 24, 1972. (0 References).
Report of a forum on drug addiction which included some discussion of the
effect upon the infant of addiction during pregnancy. The forum was
chiefly concerned with the phenomenon of addiction in young people.

738   Lynch, Margaret; Lindsay, Janey; Ounsted, Christopher. "Tranquil-
        izers causing aggression: letters to editor." Br Med J 1(5952):
        266, February 1, 1975. (1 Reference).
Two letters endorse a recent article which noted the interaction between
drug effects and social stimulation. The first indicates that drugs are
frequently prescribed in response to complaints of anxiety and depression.
These are not isolated symptoms, and their causes may continue despite
drug therapy. Recent research has shown that a high proportion of parents
taking certain drugs become hostile to their children. Tranquilizers and
antidepressants should be dispensed with extreme caution, particularly to
mothers of young children. A second letter suggests that the dangers of
impulsive self-poisoning also exists with these tranquilizers. A study
undertaken at Walton Hospital, Liverpool, verifies this finding. Drug
prescription in place of psychotherapy is faulted.

739   Neuberg, R.; Fraser, A.; Weir, J. G.; et al. "Drug addiction in
        pregnancy." Proc R Soc Med 65(10): 867-70, October, 1972. (11
        References).
Discussion, with several case histories, of drug addiction in infants.
Such addiction can be cured easily, but the risk of recurrence is high
if the infant returns to the mother who initiated his addiction during
pregnancy. Early adoption of the child is recommended.

740   Nichtern, S. "The children of drug users." Ann Prog Child Psy-
        chiatry Child Dev 10: 545-51, 1974. (0 References).
Calls attention to the plight of the children of heroin addicts. Most
are withdrawn, neglected, and malnourished, and a number are physically
abused.

741   Weir, J. G. "The pregnant narcotic addict: a psychiatrist's impres-
        sion." Proc R Soc Med 65(10): 869-70, October, 1972. (0 Refer-
        ences).
Describes a British drug-dependency center. Although drug addicts are
not likely to concern themselves with prenatal care, many are changed by
pregnancy and childbirth in such a way that they are willing to undertake
the proper care of their children.

IV

Manifestations

A. DIAGNOSTIC TECHNIQUES

742 Allen, Hugh D.; ten Bensel, Robert W.; Raile, Richard B. "The
      battered child syndrome: Part I: Medical aspects." Minn Med
      51(12): 1793-99, December, 1968. (12 References).
Discusses the physiological symptoms of abuse as an aid to the physician
diagnosing the battered child syndrome. Eighteen case histories are
detailed in table form.

743 Bamford, Frank N. "Medical diagnosis in non-accidental injury of
      children." In: Borland, Marie, ed. Violence in the family.
      Atlantic Highlands, New Jersey: Humanities Press, 1976. 50-60.
      (7 References).
Outlines the physician's responsibilities in diagnosing cases of suspected child abuse. A history of the patient must be taken with special
attention paid to the parents' attitudes and to their manner of giving
information. A child's previous injuries and treatment are often concealed, and thus their possibility must be carefully investigated. The
article describes the characteristic symptoms of five types of non-
accidental injury: (1) head injuries; (2) bone injuries; (3) soft tissue
injuries; (4) burns; and (5) injuries of the chest and abdomen. Some
abuse injuries can be discovered by x-ray examinations, but because certain conditions (such as subdural hematomas) can result from conditions
other than abuse, the physician must consider alternative diagnoses.
Since a diagnosis of abuse often rests on opinion rather than fact, the
medical examiner must entertain all possibilities.

744 Baron, Michael A.; Bejar, Rafael L.; Sheaff, Peter J. "Neurologic
      manifestations of the battered child syndrome." Pediatrics 45(6):
      1003-7, June, 1970. (13 References).
Presents a case study which illustrates that symptoms of the battered
child syndrome can be mistaken for primary disease of the nervous system.
Apathy, stereotyped movement, and abnormal posture combined with slow
development, stretch reflex changes, and increased startle reaction
appear to be the symptoms of organic brain disease. However, the dis-
appearance of these symptoms after brief hospitalization, along with the
presence of bruises and bone fractures at various stages of healing,
indicate maltreatment. The danger of misdiagnosis is stressed; undetected
abuse commonly leads to further batterings.

745 "The battered baby: editorial." Br Med J 1(5487): 601-3, March
      5, 1966. (0 References).

A memorandum by the Special Standing Committee on Accidents in Childhood of the British Pediatric Association. The most common symptom of child abuse is severe physical/emotional neglect, including the failure to thrive syndrome. The principal concern of the memo is with recommendations regarding the official management of discovered cases. Included are extracts from current British legislation relating to child abuse.

746   "Battered children and abusive parents." Roche Med Image 10(4):
       28-32, August, 1968. (0 References).
A photographic essay describes in lay terms the methods employed by the Los Angeles Children's Hospital in the diagnosis of child abuse. The physician's responsibilities include detecting the problem, reporting it to the proper authorities, and testifying in court to insure the child's future safety. A discussion of the characteristics of abusing parents suggests that they often project unacceptable feelings about themselves onto their children. Resources for the treatment of these parents are inadequate, necessitating the child's removal from the home in many cases.

747   Baxter, S. J., and Rees, B. "The immunological identification of
       foetal haemoglobin in bloodstains in infanticide and associated
       crimes." Med Sci Law 14(3): 163-67, July, 1974. (6 References).
Evaluates an anti-human fetal hemoglobin reagent used for the purpose of distinguishing between adult blood and that of infants under six months of age. The substance may be used in cases of infanticide or illegal abortion to prove the presence of fetal blood. The results obtained using anti-HBF are believed to be fairly accurate, and it is suggested that this method be employed over other techniques.

748   Birrell, J. H. W. "The 'maltreatment syndrome' in children." Med
       J Aust 2(24): 1134-38, December 10, 1966. (9 References).
Defines and outlines the history of the maltreatment syndrome, whose range of characteristics is illustrated by a discussion of six cases. The syndrome is not widely recognized due to general disbelief that such atrocities occur. Hospital staff also tend to be oriented toward treatment rather than prevention, and the symptoms are so diverse they are difficult to classify. Clinical features include: (1) a child under three years of age; (2) parents whose story is contradicted by the child's appearance; and (3) bruising around the head and appendages. Radiographic findings frequently show many fractures at various stages of healing. The family's background is disturbed, with one child serving as the focus of its discontent. There is a high incidence of repeated abuse which makes early recognition of symptoms and responsive legislation critical to prevention.

749   Blount, June G. "Radiologic seminar CXXXVIII: the battered child."
       J Miss State Med Assoc 15(4): 136-38, April, 1974. (5 Refer-
       ences).
Radiologic recognition of the characteristic signs of skeletal injury is a helpful guide to establishing the diagnosis of physical abuse. Common physical manifestations of the battered child syndrome are described in order to assist diagnosis. These include multiple fractures in different stages of healing, exaggerated periosteal reactions, frequent metaphyseal fragmentation with epiphyseal separation, soft tissue injuries, head injuries, and evidence of prior injury unexplained by history.

750   Bolz, W. Scott. "The battered child syndrome." Del Med J 39(7):
       176-80, July, 1967. (13 References).

A case history of a battered child illustrating that physicians must recognize and report instances of abuse. The child involved had repeatedly been brought into the hospital for injuries and ailments, but because the family's socioeconomic status was not that expected of child abusers, the physicians did not indicate a high index of suspicion in their diagnoses. The cause of the child's death first became evident during the autopsy. A detailed description of the clinical findings is presented. When gross discrepancies between physical findings and the parent's claims arise, physicians must recognize the possibility of inflicted injury, regardless of socioeconomic status.

751 Bowen, D. A. L. "The role of radiology and the identification of foreign bodies at post mortem examination." J Forensic Sci Soc 6(1): 28-32, January, 1966. (13 References).
Describes several uses of radiology, including its value in the diagnosis of battered children. X-rays provide excellent court evidence.

752 Brodeur, Armand E. "Child abuse." Emerg Med Serv 6(2): 49-60, March-April, 1977. (11 References).
Three categories of child abuse are outlined: physical trauma, neglect and deprivation, and psychological maltreatment. The article provides both absolute and suggestive criteria for diagnosing child abuse and outlines the legal and medical steps to be taken for management of child abuse cases.

753 Bussey, Kenneth L., and Rapp, George F. "The battered child syndrome." J Indiana State Med Assoc 67(6): 383-85, June, 1974. (6 References).
Attempts to stimulate awareness of the problem of child abuse in the medical community. The article offers a brief history of the literature describing cases of abuse, the first presented in 1888 and the last in 1962, and a summary of a 1973 review of 110 cases of battered children. Roentgenograms are thought to be the best diagnostic tool for discovering the battered child syndrome. The physical findings most commonly associated with child abuse are described, as are means of distinguishing this syndrome from scurvy, syphilis, osteogenesis imperfecta, osteomyelitis, and tuberculosis. The medicolegal aspect of the problem, which in Indiana includes mandatory reporting and immunity from prosecution for the reporter, are reviewed.

754 Caffey, John. "Significance of the history in the diagnosis of traumatic injury to children." J Pediatr 67(5, Part 2): 1008-14, November, 1965. (13 References).
Suggests methods of obtaining diagnostic information in cases of trauma in children. The incidence of deliberate child abuse is downplayed, even in cases in which the parents are not forthcoming with the necessary information. Many parents of accidentally injured children are ashamed to acknowledge the accident; in some cases they may be unaware of it altogether. The disciplinary beating of a child often inadvertently and innocently produces severe injuries for which the parents should not be held responsible.

755 Cameron, J. Malcolm. "The battered baby." Nurs Mirror 134(23): 32-38, June 9, 1972. (22 References).
The battered child syndrome is discussed, with particular emphasis on the reluctance of the physician to make the diagnosis of battering. The

physician tends to accept the parent's explanation of the injury, and
frequently diagnoses a case of child abuse as something else (such as
scurvy or syphilis). The most characteristic signs of child abuse are
given; these include both external and internal injuries. Physicians
are urged to take child abuse into consideration when presented with such
symptoms, the parents' explanation, appearance, and behavior notwith-
standing.

756 ————. "Battered child syndrome." Leg Med Annu 0(0): 123-34,
     1974. (32 References).
Emphasizes the importance of the physician's role in recognizing the
battered child syndrome. Characteristic signs of trauma which the physician should look for in his examination of the injured child or in an
autopsy include: (1) distribution of surface marks (bruises, burns and
abrasions); (2) finger-tip bruises on elbows and knees caused by grip-
ping the child; (3) ocular injuries; (4) skeletal fractures; and (5)
injury to the mucosa of the upper lip. Subdural hemorrhage and ruptured
viscera (particularly the liver) are the two internal injuries which most
often prove fatal.

757 ————. "The battered baby syndrome." Practitioner 209(1251):
     302-10, September, 1972. (12 References).
Discusses the ramifications of diagnosing the battered child syndrome.
The syndrome is defined and subdivided into four classifications.
Characteristic injuries such as bruises, lacerations, and lesions to the
eyes, bones and viscera are covered. Other diagnostic features include
a marked discrepancy between the clinical findings and the history of
the injury supplied by the parents, a delay in seeking treatment for the
injured child, and the presence of long-standing emotional, marital, or
financial problems in the family. The physician has a moral obligation
to the child and to his parents to carefully consider the diagnosis of
abuse and to report all suspected cases.

758 Cameron, J. Malcolm; Johnson, H. R. M.; Camps, F. E. "The battered
     child syndrome." Med Sci Law 6(1): 2-21, January, 1966. (12
     References).
This study, conducted by the Department of Forensic Medicine of The
London Hospital Medical College, examines the battered child syndrome,
its frequency, and the reasons for the relative lack of public knowledge
in this area. Arriving at a commonly used definition is difficult,
especially when distinguishing between "willful" and "accidental" causes.
Physicians who are unable to accept the fact that parents can batter
their children look for alternative diagnoses. However, knowledge of
common symptoms, a low threshold of suspicion, and radiological examination should abate such errors. In general, the children are under three
years of age with a mean age of 14.3 months. The sex incidence is equal,
although more patients abuse children of their own sex. Perhaps the
most important diagnostic sign is the discrepancy between the parents'
story and the child's appearance or the radiological findings. Multiple
fractures, bruises around the head, face, neck and appendages, all in
various stages of healing, are common. Ninety percent of those that die
have had previous injuries. Internal injuries are most often in the
skull, with subdural hemorrhages in two-thirds of the cases. Abused
children are generally not wanted and are born into families where discord is present. The parents, often of low intelligence and with personality disorders, fall into four categories: (1) parents who deliberately

kill the child; (2) parents who inflict persistent spontaneous violence; (3) parents subject to violent outbursts; and (4) foster parents. Denial of guilt was common among the parents, who often admitted their actions after conviction. A knowledge of these characteristics and legal protection for physicians are recommended for prevention.

759 Cameron, J. Malcolm, and Rae, L. J. Atlas of the battered child syndrome. New York: Longman, 1975. 90p. (Bibliography).
A comprehensive guide to the diagnosis of the battered child syndrome. Parental behaviors that should raise suspicions of physical abuse include: (1) a delay in seeking treatment for a child's injury; (2) a vague or implausible explanation for the child's injury; and (3) inappropriate agitation or rejection of the child by the parents. Skin surface findings which can lead to the diagnosis of abuse are bruises, lacerations, and burns of different colors and ages, which have a distribution suggestive of inflicted injury. These include finger tip bruises and bite marks. Fractures in various stages of reparative change are diagnostic of the battered child syndrome if they can be differentiated from bone lesions caused by childhood diseases such as osteogenesis imperfecta, scurvy, congenital syphilis, osteomyelitis, and others. Radiographs of head, metaphysial, rib, and long bone injuries resulting from physical abuse and radiographs of bone lesions resulting from disease are presented, along with detailed clinical observations to distinguish the two.

Visceral injuries from blunt trauma should be suspected in any child with abdominal complaints even if no skeletal fractures, head injury, or external bruising are present. Rupture of the liver and abdominal viscera with tearing of the mesentery can occur from a diffuse blow to the child's relaxed abdomen without any external bruising of the abdominal wall appearing. Ocular damage or disease which can result from physical abuse include bruising around the eyes of the child, conjunctival hemorrhages, anterior segment injuries, retinal detachment, intraocular hemorrhage, optic atrophy, and squinting. Drawings of eyes damaged by physical abuse and methods of distinguishing inflicted ocular damage from hereditary or accidental trauma are presented.

As soon as non-accidental injury is suspected, the child should be admitted to the hospital for observation and safety. The family physician, health visitor, and social and law enforcement agencies should be notified immediately. Close cooperation between professionals from many disciplines is essential if the battered child syndrome is to be managed effectively.

760 "Child abuse often goes undetected." Med World News 8(6): 10, 1967.
The widespread ignorance of medical personnel regarding the symptoms of child abuse and procedures for reporting suspected cases is revealed in a survey conducted at the Children's Hospital in Washington, D.C.

761 "Child abusers: signaling for help." Sci News 111(14): 214-15, April 2, 1977. (0 References).
Cites examples in which such physical symptoms as weakness, paralysis, and vomiting--where no physiological cause could be detected--were indications of psychological trauma in abusive or potentially abusive parents. Medical personnel are advised to be alert to such symptoms in distressed parents, and to respond with assistance to both the parent and the child.

762   Cochrane, W. A.   "The battered child syndrome."   Can J Public Health
        56(5):   193-96, May, 1965.   (11 References).
A physician's introduction to the battered child syndrome, which is felt
to be insufficiently recognized in Canada.   Typical physical findings
associated with child abuse, the usefulness of roentgenologic exams in
diagnosis, and some common characteristics of abusive families are discussed.   After further investigations into the nature and size of the
problem, legislative reform, which would institute mandatory reporting
and protection from liability for the reporter, is needed.

763   Connell, John R.   "The devil's battered children: the increasing
        incidence of willful injuries to children."   J Kans Med Soc   64(9):
        385-91, September, 1963.   (7 References).
Three representative case studies are used to underline the difficulties
existing in establishing a diagnosis of child abuse.   Physicians are
beginning to establish an identifiable portrait of the battered child.
An acrostic abstract of the typical symptoms of child abuse is offered.

764   Cremin, B. J.   "Battered baby syndrome: letter to editor."   S Afr
        Med J   44(36):   1044, September 12, 1970.   (5 References).
Notes the prominent role of the radiologist in detecting child abuse.

765   Donnan, S. P. B., and Duckworth, P. M.   "Suspected child abuse:
        experience in Guy's Hospital Accident and Emergency Department."
        Guys Hosp Rep   121(4):   295-98, 1972.   (5 References).
Describes a study of children up to four years of age with physical injuries or fractures admitted to the Accident and Emergency Department of
Guy's Hospital, London, England.   Injuries were classified as suspicious
according to the following criteria: (1) delay in treatment; (2) unusual
time of hospital admission; (3) unusual cause of injury; (4) unusual
injury; and (5) failure to appear at a follow-up appointment.   The Medical
Social Work Department's suspected child abuse cases were then checked
to see if any had been referred as questionable by the Accident Department.   The study indicated that many allegedly abused children were not
originally referred.   However, suspected cases did seem to follow predictions made by other studies of parental characteristics such as
youth, low social class, financial difficulties, and repeated abuse.
Future plans include keeping a register of all children under four years
old with physical injuries or signs of neglect.

766   Elmer, Elizabeth.   "Child abuse: the family's cry for help."   J
        Psychiatr Nurs   5(4):   332-41, July-August, 1967.   (6 References).
Presents a case history of an infant whose injuries and general family
situation exhibited some of the features of the battered child syndrome.
The admitting physician diagnosed the child's injuries as resulting from
child abuse and contacted the police.   Some of the hospital personnel,
on reading the physician's diagnosis, treated the infant as a battered
child and interpreted its behavior as that of a battered child.   The
case is cited as a warning against the dangers of prematurely diagnosing
child abuse and of developing a punitive attitude toward the parents
involved.   In this case, it was unclear whether abuse had actually
occurred, and the hasty action of the professionals involved only served
to exacerbate the family's disturbance.   Medical personnel are urged to
show more understanding of the parents in such situations.

767 ————. "Identification of abused children." <u>Children</u> 10(5):
180-84, September-October, 1963. (10 References).
Examines a follow-up study of fifty children with multiple bone injuries.
The purpose of the study was to aid in the establishment of objective
criteria on child abuse. Bone injuries in infants and young children have
been documented as related to child abuse. The x-ray examination is
cited as a starting point for the exploration of social factors. The
study was designed to learn the present status of former patients and to
learn the kinds of families in which abuse occurs. Of the children in
the study group, all had repeated injuries, signs of which were discovered
during a single hospitalization. The group of patients studied decreased
in size as age increased. The incidence of death or serious defect was
high. A second study will be concerned with newly admitted patients and
their families.

768 Elmer, Elizabeth; Gregg, Grace S.; Wright, Byron; <u>et al</u>. "Studies
of child abuse and infant accidents." <u>Ment Health Program Rep</u>
(5): 58-89, December, 1971. (13 References).
Discusses two major studies of child abuse involving fifty families over
thirteen years at the Children's Hospital of Pittsburgh. The first
investigation was a follow-up study of these children designed to trace
their developmental patterns over time. Significant observations were
made of attitudes and behaviors typical of battering parents, of the correlation between low birth weight and increased abuse, and of the long-
term effects of abuse on children. The second study was conducted to
establish guidelines for distinguishing injuries caused by abuse from
those that are accidental. Careful attention was given to the modes of
discipline used by mothers of very young infants, and it was found that
in most instances, they were physically punishing their babies by the
time infants were twenty-four months old. In fact, 41 percent began this
practice with babies under six months of age. In order to diagnose abuse
correctly, physicians must be familiar with the normal injuries of children. Suggestions for preventing abuse and improving child abuse laws
are included.

769 Fatteh, A. V., and Mann, G. T. "The role of radiology in forensic
pathology." <u>Med Sci Law</u> 9(1): 27-30, January, 1969. (14 References).
Explores the wide utility of post-mortem radiation in the determination
of a number of medical questions. Observation of long-bone fractures of
varying ages and presence of subdural hematoma can aid in the identification of the battered child syndrome.

770 Follis, Peggy. "Recognizing non-accidental injury in children."
<u>Nurs Times</u> 71(51): 2034-35, December 18, 1975. (0 References).
Describes an interdisciplinary team approach to the management of child
abuse in Preston, Lancashire, England. The nurse is cited as the most
important link in the referral chain of child abuse cases from physicians
in all departments of the hospital to the non-accidental injury specialist, who examines all children suspected of being physically abused.
Implausible explanations for injuries to children should alert the nurse
or physician to the possibility of maltreatment. When abuse is suspected,
a complete physical examination, along with a full skeletal x-ray should
be carried out. Medical evidence is of utmost importance if the case is
eventually taken to court.

771 Fontana, Vincent J. "When to suspect child abuse." <u>Med Times</u>
       101(10): 116-22, October, 1973. (4 References).
Lists the signs and symptoms of three categories of child abuse that
should be included in a physician's index of suspicion: (1) history;
(2) physical examination; and (3) radiologic manifestations. It is
important that a complete x-ray examination is done in order to conclu-
sively diagnose the battered child syndrome. Suspected cases of battering must then be reported to the proper authorities.

772 Fontana, Vincent J.; Donovan, Denis; Wong, Raymond J. "The 'mal-
       treatment syndrome' in children." <u>N Engl J Med</u> 269(26): 1389-94,
       December 26, 1963. (10 References).
Describes and defines the clinical and social manifestations, along with
the preventive measures of the maltreatment syndrome in children.
Typical case histories are utilized to underline the range of diagnostic
and social problems encountered. Preventive measures outlined include
increasing physician awareness of the symptoms. Cooperative, integrated
efforts of all social and legal agencies are also emphasized.

773 Gans, Bruno. "Battered babies -- how many do we miss?: letter to
       editor." <u>Lancet</u> 1(7659): 1286-87, June 13, 1970. (0 References).
Presents a typical case history of abuse which illustrates the unwillingness of professionals to entertain the possibility of maltreatment. The
child had been in the hospital six times in four months before abuse was
suspected and subsequent court action taken. The court dismissed the
case. Dr. C. Henry Kempe's insistence that this case was a classical
illustration of the battered child initiated a reopening of proceedings
which led to the removal of the child from his home.

774 ————. "Unnecessary x-rays?: letters to editor." <u>Br Med J</u>
       1(5695): 564, February 28, 1970. (0 References).
The appropriate use of x-rays is discussed. Reducing the availability
of radiographic treatment is medically irresponsible, increases the pain
of the patient, and creates legal difficulties. When the injured patient
is a child under two years of age, complete skeletal x-rays are necessary
to detect possible battering. However, x-rays should not be ordered if
the result will not change the treatment of the case.

775 Green, Karl. "Diagnosing the battered child syndrome." <u>Md State
       Med J</u> 14(9): 83-84, September, 1965. (4 References).
An overview of the physical findings which should alert the physician
to suspect child abuse. Radiologic examination and discrepancies
between clinical observations and history are key factors in the diagnosis of child battering. The physician's responsibility to make the
correct diagnosis and to take the appropriate steps to protect the
child's future welfare is emphasized.

776 Greengard, Joseph. "The battered child syndrome." <u>Am J Nurs</u>
       64(6): 98-100, June, 1964. (3 References).
Urges physicians and nurses to familiarize themselves with the symptoms
of the battered child syndrome. Clinical and radiologic indications of
abuse are described. X-rays have proven very helpful in diagnosing child
abuse in cases of long bone fractures and fractures at different stages
of healing. Aspects of treatment and prevention are presented, along
with a typical case history.

777 Gregg, Grace S. "Infant trauma." <u>Am Fam Physician</u> 3(5): 101-5,
     May, 1971. (0 References).
Accents the responsibility of the physician to analyze the causes of
infant trauma. Often the child's injuries are accidental. However,
accidents themselves are frequently the result of parental carelessness.
Caring properly for children requires parents to provide an adequately
safe environment in which a minimum of active and passive accidents take
place. Because it is often difficult to determine if an infant's injuries
have been caused by abuse or by accidents, the physician has to depend on
other external signals from the parents and the general condition of the
baby. When the physician does suspect abuse, he must report it to the
proper authorities in order to guarantee the child's safety and procure
professional help for the parents.

778 Gregg, Grace S., and Elmer, Elizabeth. "Infant injuries: accident
     or abuse?" <u>Pediatrics</u> 44(3):   434-39, September, 1969. (9 Ref-
     erences).
An analysis of the injuries of 113 infants treated at Children's Hospital
of Pittsburgh revealed that eighty-three were accidental and thirty
resulted from physical abuse. Injuries sustained by the abused group
tended to be more severe. Developmental lags and failure to thrive were
also more common among the abused group. Abused infants were more often
the first or second-born child. Economic and personal stress among the
parents was observed for both the accidental and abusive injury group,
demonstrating that stress can sometimes distract parents from safety concerns or precipitate an aggressive attack. Most of the accidental injuries could have been avoided if proper safety precautions had been
observed. Therefore, the physician is warned that both accidental and
abusive injuries reflect a lapse in adequate child care.

779 Grosfeld, Jay L., and Ballantine, Thomas V. N. "Surgical aspects of
     child abuse [trauma-x]." <u>Pediatr Ann</u> 5(10):   106-20, October,
     1976. (10 References).
Following the presentation of six case studies illustrating the various
manifestations of child abuse found at the James Whitcomb Riley Hospital
for Children at Indiana University, the salient points in the diagnosis
of such cases are discussed. Suspicious injuries include an unexplained
injury, evidence of repeated skin or soft tissue injuries, or repeated
fractures, evidence of sexual abuse, characteristic x-ray changes, suspicious or contradictory parental histories, unexplained subdural hematoma, visceral abdominal injuries with a suspicious history, and overall
poor care or malnutrition. The importance of the anatomic location of
the injury in relation to the motor development of the child, as well as
the possibility of the injury being inflicted by an older sibling, is
cited.

780 Hall, Malcolm H. "A view from the emergency and accident depart-
     ment." In: Franklin, Alfred White, ed. <u>Concerning child abuse</u>.
     New York: Churchill Livingstone, 1975. 7-20. (0 References).
Increasing experience in the recognition of non-accidental injury often
enables the emergency department personnel to discover the physically
abused child while the injuries are still minimal. Child abuse should
not be viewed as a homogeneous syndrome. On the contrary, it can be
classified into five types: active abuse--leading to ordinary violence,
bizarre violence, or death; and passive abuse--leading to physical neglect
or failure to thrive. The final diagnosis in the case of non-accidental

injury depends upon a combination of factors: (1) the physical signs
obtained in the examination of the child; (2) the history of the cause of
injuries provided by the parents; and (3) the results of the initial investigation into the social background of the family. X-rays should be
considered in conjunction with the clinical record. Bruises are the
most valuable clinical finding in a minor case of non-accidental injury.
They often take the shape of the instrument of physical abuse, such as
the hand, belt, or piece of wood. It is important to remember that the
shape of the object in a bruise can only be seen when the limb or trunk
is examined in the position that it was when the injury was inflicted.
Cigarette burns and bite marks are also diagnostic. The successful management of non-accidental injury requires the cooperation of the medical
profession, the social services, the voluntary societies, and the police
forces.

781 Hazlewood, Arthur I. "Child abuse: the dentist's role." NY State
      Dent J 36(5): 289-91, May, 1970. (7 References).
Provides dentists with background information on child abuse and a description of their medical and legal responsibilities in such cases.
Since dentists do not typically hospitalize children, thorough history
taking and immediate reporting of suspected cases are recommended alternatives.

782 Holter, Joan C., and Friedman, Stanford B. "Child abuse: early
      case finding in the emergency department." Pediatrics 42(1):
      128-38, July, 1968. (11 References).
Studies the incidence and management of maltreated children seen in the
emergency room of the University of Rochester Medical Center in New York.
Two independent surveys were conducted, during which time all accidents
involving children under six years of age were systematically examined.
Approximately 10 percent of these accidents were judged to represent
suspected abuse, and in another 10 percent, the accidents were believed
to be related to gross neglect on the part of the parent. The nature of
the injury appeared to be empirically related to a diagnosis of suspected
abuse. If the child had sustained head injuries, fractures, limb injuries,
burns, contusions or bruises, he was more likely to be diagnosed as
abused (high risk) than if he was seen for lacerations and ingestions
(low risk). The families of both high and low risk children had experienced many recent stressful situations, but the low risk families were
better able to cope with their problems than the high risk group. The
importance of early identification of child abuse in the emergency room
of hospitals is stressed. A multidisciplinary professional staff should
be a part of every emergency facility so that such cases can be efficiently and adequately managed.

783 Hussey, Hugh H. "The battered child syndrome: unusual manifesta-
      tions." JAMA 234(8): 856, November 24, 1975. (1 Reference).
Reviews unusual manifestations of the battered child syndrome that have
been reported in the literature. They include retinal hemorrhages, subgaleal hematomas, handprint bruises, bite marks, genital injuries, a
tear in the floor of the mouth due to forced feeding, traumatic cysts of
the pancreas and liver, repeated poisonings, and others. Physicians
should be alerted to the extraordinary range of non-accidental injuries
in children.

784 Hwang, Woon T.; Chin, Carmel; Leng, Lam K. "Battered child syndrome
     in a Malaysian hospital." Med J Malaysia 28(4): 239-43, June,
     1974. (19 References).
A detailed statistical analysis of seven cases of the battered child syndrome aimed toward stimulating interest in the diagnosis and management
of the problem. Three tables diagram the injuries sustained by the
victims, the characteristics of the abuser, and the follow-up treatment
of the children.

785 Isaacson, E. K. "The emotionally battered child: letter to editor."
     Pediatrics 38(3): 523, September, 1966. (0 References).
Advises pediatricians to become more cognizant of the role they can play
in the prevention of child abuse among the families of their patients.
The pediatrician is called upon to regularly devote a segment of every
examination to inquiries concerning the home life of the child.

786 Jackson, Graham. "Child abuse syndrome: the cases we miss." Br
     Med J 2(5816): 756-57, June 24, 1972. (10 References).
Draws attention to the findings of a study reviewing 100 cases of child
injuries for evidence of battering. The results indicate that eighteen
of these were misdiagnosed. All of the patients were under two years of
age. The group consisted of seven boys and eleven girls; five children
were black. There was ample evidence at the time to confirm a diagnosis
of abuse, particularly for the major diagnostic feature--discrepancy
between parents' explanation of the injury and the clinical findings.
The conclusion drawn is that the present system of diagnosis is incomplete. Extra steps should, therefore, be taken to review diagnosis of
injuries to children under four years of age.

787 James, Hector E., and Schut, Luis. "The neurosurgeon and the bat-
     tered child." Surg Neurol 2(6): 415-18, November, 1974. (10
     References).
A breakdown of the neurological findings in forty-five cases of child
abuse at Children's Hospital of Philadelphia is reported. The statistics
indicate that most victims suffer multiple injuries--injuries that cannot always be determined only from radiological tests. Imperative is
the immediate intervention of a neurosurgeon to detect and correct the
complications of abuse.

788 Kempe, C. Henry; Silverman, Frederic N.; Steele, Brandt F.; et al.
     "The battered-child syndrome." JAMA 181(1): 17-24, July 7, 1962.
     (18 References).
Introduces the term, the battered child syndrome, to describe children
who have received serious physical abuse. A nation-wide survey of hospitals provides data on the incidence of the problem. The clinical
manifestations vary widely, but the radiologic features of the syndrome
should alert the informed physician to the presence of abuse. Psychiatric
knowledge pertaining to the problem is meager, and multiple factors may
motivate the abusing parent. Methods which can aid the physician in
identifying and obtaining information from such a parent and the typical
sociopsychological causes of abuse are considered. Two condensed case
histories depict some of the problems encountered in dealing with the
battered child syndrome. Radiologic examination of the battered child
is discussed both as a diagnostic tool and as a useful guide in case
management. The physician's concern should be to make the correct diagnosis so that he can institute proper therapy and protect the child from

future trauma. He should report abuse to the appropriate agency in his
community.

789 Krige, H. N. "The abused child complex and its characteristic x-
     ray findings." S Afr Med J 40(21): 490-93, June 11, 1966. (8
     References).
Outlines the diagnostic signs of child abuse, particularly those related
to skeletal trauma. The general practitioner, often the first professional aware of maltreatment, needs to recognize presenting characteristics of abuse, including physical, emotional, and social patterns. Early
diagnosis is crucial, as 50 percent of abuse cases suffer repeated injuries or death. Physicians are warned against eagerly ascribing
symptoms to a new disease or to an established disease with similar
symptoms. Various types of bone injuries commonly found are presented
to illustrate this point. Radiological findings are extremely helpful
in establishing etiology early.

790 Laskin, Daniel M. "The battered-child syndrome: editorial." J
     Oral Surg 31(12): 903, December, 1973. (0 References).
Attempts to educate the oral surgeon to the problem of child abuse.
Common fallacies about the battered child syndrome are dispelled, and the
role of the oral surgeon in reducing its incidence is discussed. The
syndrome should be brought to the attention of dental students and
residents, suspected cases reported, and the various signs and symptoms
learned.

791 Leikin, Sanford L., and Guin, Grace H. "Clinical pathological con-
     ference: the battered child syndrome." Clin Proc Child Hosp
     19(11): 301-6, November, 1963. (2 References).
Presents a medically detailed description of a four-and-one-half-year-
old battered child. A physical examination and the laboratory findings
ruled out all possible diagnoses until only the battered child syndrome
remained as a probable cause. Precautions which physicians should take
in verifying such a diagnosis are included.

792 Levine, Milton I. "Child abuse: a pediatrician's view." Pediatr
     Ann 5(3): 6-9, March, 1976. (0 References).
An introduction to a symposium on child abuse and neglect. The physician
has a responsibility to diagnose child abuse which has many social,
medical, and legal ramifications.

793 ————. "Traumatic injuries in children -- modern concepts: a
     pediatrician's view." Pediatr Ann 5(10): 4-7, October, 1976.
     (0 References).
An introduction to an issue devoted to traumatic injury in children.
Articles included address the topics of splenectomy, emergency management of the injured child, acute traumatic injuries to the abdomen,
thorax and head, and surgical aspects of child abuse.

794 "The maltreated child." Med J Aust 2(24): 1155-56, 1966. (6
     References).
Presents an early overview of the phenomenon of the battered child syndrome. The extensive use of radiation in detection is urged, and the
separation of the child from his parents is recommended.

795 "MD has [a] role in child abuse cases: editorial." Pa Med 73(9):
    192, September, 1970. (0 References).
Physicians are called upon to be alert to symptoms of child abuse in
routine examinations and to report them to the local welfare authorities.
Statistics on child abuse in Pennsylvania are cited, and abusive parents
are described as being outwardly normal, but actually suffering from
insecurity, insensitivity, and tendencies toward impulsiveness, psychopathic deficiency, and schizophrenia.

796 Meadow, Roy. "Munchausen syndrome by proxy: the hinterland of child
    abuse." Lancet 2(8033): 343-45, August 13, 1977. (4 References).
Describes two cases in which mothers gave physicians false information
about their children's symptoms and, thus, subjected their children to
much unneeded or harmful medical treatment. In one case, the mother
tampered with the child's urine samples, causing the girl to endure countless examinations and treatments with drugs, which themselves caused
unpleasant side effects. In the other case, the mother gave her son
frequent, toxic doses of salt, which eventually killed the boy. She, too,
lied to physicians about the boy's symptoms. Both mothers had hysterical,
depressed personalities, and had a history of falsifying their own medical
records.

797 Mowat, Alex P. "The battered baby syndrome." Dist Nurs 14(2):
    26-27, May, 1971. (0 References).
Overviews the problem of child battering in Britain and the usual procedures for detecting and alleviating it. Clinical features of child
abuse fall into three main categories: (1) the battered child subjected
to repeated physical injury (bruises, fractures, and others); (2) the
child subjected to deliberate sadistic cruelty over a period of time
(beatings, scaldings, and others); and (3) the neglected, undernourished
child. Other factors commonly associated with the syndrome are: (1)
parents who expect children to meet their emotional needs; (2) social
deprivation such as poor housing, unemployment; and (3) the lack of supportive extended family members. Cases are typically managed by a team
of involved professionals who review the entire situation and attempt to
strike a balance in decision making between the rights of the parents and
the best interests of the child.

798 Newberger, Eli H., and McAnulty, Elizabeth H. "Family intervention
    in the pediatric clinic: a necessary approach to the vulnerable
    child." Clin Pediatr 15(12): 1155-61, December, 1976. (28
    References).
Reviews the records of seventy-five pediatric patients from fifty families who were seen at the out-patient Family Development Clinic at
Children's Hospital Medical Center in Boston. All of the families referred to the clinic had children with various physical and behavioral
problems symptomatic of family crisis in the home. The clinic provided
primary health care for the children and diagnostic and referral services
for the family. The most common diagnosis was parent-child crises with
behavioral problems (26 percent), followed in decreasing frequency by
child abuse and neglect (23 percent), failure to thrive (9 percent),
multiple accidents (9 percent), and well child care (8 percent). Seventy-
nine percent of the children seen at the clinic had chronic health
problems such as growth lags, seizure disorders, psychomotor retardation,
and others. Ten percent of the families had environmental problems such
as inadequate or overcrowded housing. At the end of the study period,

fourteen of the nineteen children with growth problems showed a significant improvement in weight. Referrals for evaluation and treatment from
the clinic were as follows: 26 percent for psychologic evaluations, 19
percent for community health or social services and day care, 4 percent
for better housing, 11 percent for speech evaluation and treatment, and
8 percent for dental treatment. Further study is needed before the
associations between different childhood physical and behavioral symptoms
on the one hand, and various familial crises on the other, can be understood.

799 O'Neill, James A., Jr.; Meacham, William F.; Griffin, Paul P.; et al.
     "Patterns of injury in the battered child syndrome." J Trauma
     13(14): 332-39, April, 1973. (10 References).
A clinical analysis of typical, recurring injuries in battered children.
Of the 110 battered children seen over a five-year period, most were
under two years of age. These children had suffered many types of injuries, the most common being soft tissue trauma. However, fractures
and head injuries appeared with regularity, as well as combined or
repeated injuries in various stages of healing. The study illustrates
that physicians need to familiarize themselves with the evidence of the
battered child syndrome, so that they can recognize it, diagnose it, and
initiate treatment at once.

800 Parry, Wilfrid, H.; Seymour, Margaret W.; Smith, Selwyn, M. "Child
     abuse syndrome: letters to editor." Br Med J 3(5818): 113-14,
     July 8, 1972. (1 Reference).
Responses regarding Graham Jackson's article (Br Med J, June 24, 1972)
on the misdiagnosis of child abuse. The first letter contends that the
regular re-examination of hospital records proposed by Jackson must be
supplemented by a community-based scheme of detection and that Jackson's
article did not constitute a significant contribution to the literature.
The second letter commends Jackson's recognition of the existence of
many undiagnosed cases of abuse. The author briefly summarizes some of
his own findings which are in agreement with Jackson's and concludes with
the reminder that an accurate diagnosis is not enough. Hospital and community management of the problem is still inadequate.

801 Pashayan, H., and Cochrane, W. A. "Maltreatment syndrome of chil-
     dren." NS Med Bull 44(1): 139-42, June, 1965. (6 References).
Reports on a study of seven maltreated children carried out at the
Children's Hospital in Halifax. The authors gear their observations
toward a clarification of the maltreatment syndrome. A brief description
of physical findings, diagnostic procedures, and psychosocial characteristics of abusive parents provides guidelines for the physician who
is responsible for detecting abuse cases. The seven case examples are
presented.

802 "Physicians [are] told how to deal with child abuse." JAMA 211(1):
     35, January 5, 1970. (0 References).
Report of Ray E. Helfer's speech at a symposium urging that emergency
room physicians consider child abuse diagnoses in all cases of traumatic
injury to small children. A pediatrician should be consulted, but
parents should not be accused in the emergency room.

803 Potts, William E., and Forbis, Oriel L. "Willful injury in child-
     hood -- a distinct syndrome." J Arkansas Med Soc 59: 266-70,
     December, 1962. (8 References).

A general overview of the battered child syndrome, focusing on physiological signs of abuse. A brief discussion of radiologic indices of battering is included, as is an outline of some of the personality characteristics of the abusing parent. The need for increased awareness of the child abuse problem and the adaptation of laws to secure the rights of children are stressed.

804   Riley, H. D. "The battered child syndrome: general and medical
       aspects." South Med Bull 58(3): 9-13, June, 1970. (16 Refer-
       ences).
Reviews the history of child abuse and the responsibilities of physicians in its detection and prevention. A checklist of suspicious injuries and other symptoms of child abuse is provided for use in examining, taking medical histories, and making observations.

805   Sarsfield, James K. "Battering -- dangers of a backlash: letter
       to editor." Br Med J 2(5909): 57-58, April, 1974. (0 Refer-
       ences).
J. W. Woodward's concern (March 9, p. 452) about the possible harmful effects of precipitant action in the investigation of suspected cases of baby battering is seconded. A case is cited in which a skin lesion suspected of being a deliberatly inflicted burn was later diagnosed as toxic epidermal necrolysis. Consultation with the family physician prevented an investigation of the parents.

806   Schmitt, Barton D. "What teachers need to know about child abuse
       and neglect." Child Educ 52(3): 58-62, November, 1975. (8
       References).
The signs and symptoms of physical abuse, nutritional deprivation, drug abuse, medical care neglect, sexual abuse, emotional abuse, severe hygiene neglect, and educational neglect are presented so that teachers can detect them in the school setting. Guidelines for appropriate teacher responses to suspected abuse are provided.

807   Schmitt, Barton D., and Kempe, C. Henry. "The pediatrician's role
       in child abuse and neglect." Curr Probl Pediatr 5(5): 3-47,
       March, 1975. (54 References).
Presents a comprehensive discussion of the manifestations, diagnosis, treatment, and prevention of child abuse and neglect. Particular attention is given to the subjects of physical abuse and nutritional neglect. Physical abuse should be considered in any child with skin bruises, soft tissue swellings, burns, fractures, and head, eye, visceral, and central nervous system injuries that could have resulted from inflicted trauma. Vague explanations or discrepant histories of the injuries, a delay in seeking medical care, blame on a third party (such as the babysitter) for the injuries, alleged self-injury in a small infant, or repeated suspicious injuries are diagnostic of the battered child syndrome. Psychosocial risk factors which are suggestive of physical abuse indicate past records of mental illness or criminal conduct of the parents, serious marital discord, social isolation, inappropriate standards for the child's behavior, and others. A lack of parental concern for the hospitalized child can also be a clue to the diagnosis. Nutritional neglect is diagnosed by a paucity of subcutaneous tissue, underweight, and malnourishment in the child. Most mothers involved in maternal deprivation feel deprived and unloved themselves. If an infant is found to be severely undernourished, he should be hospitalized immediately and placed

on a nutritional rehabilitation program. A rapid weight gain documents
the diagnosis of caloric deprivation.

Detailed guidelines for the initial management of child abuse or neglect
by the physician include: (1) hospitalizing and treating the child; (2)
attaining necessary laboratory tests; (3) informing the parents of the
diagnosis; (4) reporting the case to the child protective agency; (5)
examining all siblings of the abused child within twelve hours; (6)
obtaining hospital social service consultation within forty-eight hours;
(7) attending a multidisciplinary dispositional conference on the case;
(8) providing expert medical testimony for cases going to court; and
(9) making sure that the child protective agency is providing psychosocial
follow-up and treatment for the child and his family. Prevention of
child abuse and neglect entails identifying potential abusers or high
risk parents in prenatal clinics, delivery rooms, hospital nurseries, and
pediatricians' offices, and offering them special follow-up care, support,
child care education, discipline counseling, family planning, and other
services.

808 Shaw, Anthony. "Would you have missed this battered baby?" Hosp
      Physician 9(3): 59, 62-63, March, 1973. (6 References).
Demonstrates, through a case history, the process which leads to a diagnosis of battered child syndrome. An intern, a resident, and an attending physician are shown discussing a case of apparently routine infantile
subdural hemotoma in which child abuse had not been considered. The
child's thinness and unexplained minor bruises arouse the suspicions of
the resident and attending physician, and a more thorough examination
and history reveal that the suspicions are warranted. Clues which should
alert the physician's suspicions of child battering are listed.

809 Silverman, Frederic N. "Unrecognized trauma in infants, the bat-
      tered child syndrome, and the Syndrome of Ambroise Tardieu."
      Radiology 104(2): 337-53, August, 1972. (96 References).
Describes the clinical and radiographic manifestations of child abuse.
Clinically observable symptoms include mucosal, cutaneous, and ocular
lesions, malnutrition, and unusual timidity. X-rays frequently reveal
new and healing fractures and variations in bone density, lung contusions,
duodenal, mesenteric and jejunal changes, and retroperitoneal hematoma.
Ambroise Tardieu, a nineteenth century Professor of Legal Medicine in
Paris, is given credit for first noting the conjunction of symptoms now
called the battered child syndrome.

810 Smith, E. Ide. "Trauma in children." J Okla State Med Assoc
      62(11): 511-17, November, 1969. (13 References).
Discusses the etiology, diagnosis, and treatment of trauma in children.
The difficulty of identifying symptoms of child abuse is acknowledged
and greater care in the examination of trauma patients is therefore
suggested. Five tables are included.

811 Starbuck, George W. "The recognition and early management of child
      abuse." Pediatr Ann 5(3): 27-41, March, 1976. (13 References).
The recognition of child abuse depends, in part, upon the willingness of
the examining physician to consider the possibility of its occurrence.
Characteristic signs of abuse are presented, along with thirty-one
plates of photographs and x-rays of children with inflicted injuries.
Early management of child abuse by the physician includes: (1) immediate
hospitalization of the abused child during the acute crisis phase; (2)

reporting of the case to the proper authorities; (3) gaining the cooperation of the parents; (4) documenting abuse with photographs, x-rays, and
laboratory tests; and (5) working with an interdisciplinary child protection team to arrange for the treatment of the child and family.

812 Storey, Bruce. "The battered child." Med J Aust 2(20): 789-91,
       November 14, 1964. (10 References).
Cites a number of case histories selected to alert Australian physicians
to the problem of the battered child. A brief review of important
studies follows. The clinical findings are presented, along with diseases
whose symptoms may complicate diagnosis.

813 Teuscher, G. W. "The battered child -- a social enigma: editorial."
       J Dent Child 41(5): 336-36, September-October, 1974. (0 Refer-
       ences).
Encourages dentists who daily treat children with mouth and teeth injuries to be aware of the child abuse syndrome and to join other professionals in treating the far-reaching problem.

814 Weller, Carolyn M. R. "Assessing the non-accidental injury." J
       Emerg Nurs 3: 17-26, March-April, 1977. (25 References).
Outlines a procedure for the emergency room staff to follow in examining
a victim of suspected child abuse. The emergency room nurse should first
obtain a medical history from the child's parents, including their version of how the injury was sustained. Secondly, the behavior of both
the child and his parents must be observed. Abusive parents frequently
do not touch or otherwise comfort their injured child. The actual
physical examination should cover the following six areas: (1) the state
of the child's clothing (feces caked, or otherwise indicative of neglect);
(2) the overall condition of the skin with attention to soft tissue
injury and the distribution of bruises, burns, and skin lesions; (3)
evidence of intra-abdominal injuries, such as bleeding or visceral bruising; (4) a radiologic skeletal examination which will date all bone
injuries and point out any metaphyseal injuries; (5) evidence of head
injuries, usually the most severe injury likely to be suffered, examples
of which include subdural hematoma and retinal hemorrhage; and (6) signs
of the whiplash syndrome in infants. If the medical diagnosis indicates
non-accidental injury, the child should be admitted to the hospital and
the appropriate child protective agency notified.

815 "Willful injuries to children." Whats New (228): 3-5, Summer,
       1962. (10 References).
Although the history of childrearing practices shows that modern society
is more humanitarian than societies of the past, individual cases of
child abuse will occur frequently. Battering parents tend to develop
strategies to conceal willful injuries to their children, making detection difficult. Roentgenographic examination is most valuable in the
diagnosis of the battered child syndrome. Complete autopsies on all
children who die under unknown circumstances are advocated.

816 Woods, Walter. "Expanding our responsibility: editorial." J Dent
       Child 42(2): 86, March-April, 1975. (0 References).
Urges dentists to watch for signs of child abuse--including malnutrition,
facial and oral lesions, lip lacerations, and fractured teeth--in their
young patients.

B. ABUSE: PHYSICAL SIGNS

1. SUBDURAL HEMATOMAS AND OTHER HEAD INJURIES

817   Adelson, Lester. "The battering child." JAMA 222(2): 159-61,
      October 9, 1972. (7 References).
Cites five case studies of infants less than one year of age who were
killed by children age eight years or younger. All five infants died
from craniocerebral trauma resulting from blunt violence to the head.
None of the infants showed evidence of previous neglect or abuse. Two
of the child assailants were mentally retarded, but the other three were
apparently normal. These studies emphasize the vulnerability of infants
to the anger and jealousy of slightly older children.

818   Ameli, N. O., and Alimohammadi, A. "Attempted infanticide by inser-
      tion of sewing needles through fontanels: report of two cases."
      J Neurosurg 33: 721-23, December, 1970. (5 References).
Describes two instances of an ancient and still practiced method of killing an unwanted baby through the insertion of a sewing needle through
the fontanel. In both cases, the victims survived and were in their
thirties when diagnosed. One had been suffering from epilepsy and the
other from headaches and hemiparesis, but these symptoms did not appear
until the patients were in their twenties.

819   Benstead, J. G. "Infantile subdural haematoma: letter to editor."
      Br Med J 3(5766): 114-15, July 10, 1971. (0 References).
A letter referring to A. N. Guthkelch's paper on infantile subdural hematoma (May 22, 1971) upholds its significance for pathologists who deal
with these cases. Infant fatalities resulting from this injury may be
divided into three categories, according to the obvious degree of injury
to the head and to other parts of the body.

820   Berenberg, W. "Toward the prevention of neuromotor dysfunction."
      Dev Med Child Neurol 11(1): 137-41, February, 1969. (0 Refer-
      ences).
Outlines the efforts which are needed in order to prevent brain damage
in children, with particular reference to cerebral palsy. The reduction
of the incidence of child abuse is listed as one angle of attack on the
problem.

821   Bysshe, Janette. "A battered baby." Nurs Times 72(25): 986-87,
      June 24, 1976. (0 References).
Cites a case study of an eleven-month-old girl with a head injury who
was brought to a hospital in Hackney, England, by her mother. The
article discusses how and why the diagnosis of non-accidental injury was
made and reviews the past medical and social histories of the mother and
child. Because the risk of repeated battering was high, the child was
placed in the home of a relative.

822   Caffey, John. "On the theory and practice of shaking infants: its
      potential residual effects of permanent brain damage and mental
      retardation." Am J Dis Child 124(2): 161-69, August, 1972.
      (24 References).
Alerts physicians to the pathogenic effects of shaking and whiplashing
infants and small children. Shaking children is possibly the root cause

of mental retardation, subdural hematomas, retinal lesions, and other cerebrovascular injuries. Many parents shake their children as a form of mild reproof, or toss them in play. Yet the effects of such motion, possibly undetected for months or years, can be greater than a direct blow on the head or face. The heavy head, weak neck muscles, and the softness of the skull and brain make the young child particularly vulnerable to injury of this sort. Even noise and other vibrating stimuli can inflict damage. Brief histories of twenty-seven children reflect these findings.

823 ————. "The whiplash shaken infant syndrome: manual shaking by the extremities with whiplash-induced intracranial and intraocular bleedings, linked with residual permanent brain damage and mental retardation." Pediatrics 54(4): 396-403, October, 1974. (32 References).
Manual shaking of infants can seriously injure or even kill a child while leaving no external evidence of trauma. However, the unsupported head of the infant when whiplashed is vulnerable to intracranial and intraocular hemorrhaging. Additional physical indications of shaking include fever, hyperactive reflexes, bulging fontanel, and enlarged head. Even habitual casual shaking of infants can lead to mild mental retardation and mild cerebral palsy. A nationwide educational campaign advising parents of the kinds of injuries which can arise from even playful shaking of infants is needed.

824 Collins, Camilla. "On the dangers of shaking young children." Child Welfare 53(3): 143-46, March, 1974. (1 Reference).
Whiplash shaking as a punishment for misbehavior or playfully dangling a young child by his limbs can cause blood clots, bone and joint damage, and in extreme cases, permanent brain damage or even death. Owing to his heavy head and weak neck muscles, the infant is especially vulnerable to whiplash injury. The toddler may injure himself while playing on a slide or seesaw or in certain acrobatic games such as "crack the whip."

825 Craft, A. W.; Shaw, D. A.; Cartlidge, N. E. "Head injuries in children." Br Med J 4: 200-203, October 28, 1972. (12 References).
Reports a study of 200 cases of head injuries in New Castle, United Kingdom. Physicians made neurological examinations and extracted histories from parents. Most victims were under age three. Injuries usually occurred during the day as a result of bicycling accidents and falls from windows, chairs, and stairs. The six children who had been injured between the hours of twelve midnight and four in the morning were victims of parental abuse. Of the two children who died, one had been abused.

826 Eckert, William G. "Slaughter of the innocents." J Fla Med Assoc 54(13): 256, March, 1967. (0 References).
Documents a case study of a thirteen-month-old child who died from injuries to the head. When an autopsy was performed to investigate the physician's suspicions that violence had caused the child's death, many further signs of abuse, such as multiple fractures in various stages of healing, were discovered. These signs, along with the additional injuries that had originally aroused the examiner's suspicions, were evidence that the child had repeatedly been abused before the fatal injury took place. The child's father was found guilty of manslaughter and then given a suspended sentence.

827   Groff, Robert A., and Grant, Francis C. "Chronic subdural hematoma:
         collective review." Surg Gynecol Obstet 74(1): 9-20, January-
         June, 1942. (82 References).
Summarizes the current literature on subdural hematoma, including matters
of etiology, pathology, symptomatology, and treatment. A distinction is
made between acute and chronic subdural hematoma. It is suggested that
the former be termed "subdural hemorrhage" due to its rapid development.
The etiology of subdural hematomas remains uncertain. However, they can
be divided into infammatory and hemorrhagic types of either traumatic or
non-traumatic, called "spontaneous" in origin. Various probable causes
are outlined and described in detail. Although the location of subdural
hematomas is relatively similar in most cases, their sizes vary radically,
averaging from fifty to 200 ccs. They appear in solid or fluid form, or
even a combination of both. Subdural hematomas occur in infants as well
as in the aged. When the injury is trauma-induced, its symptoms may not
surface until days, months, or years following the incident. Guidelines
for diagnosing it are provided. Surgical removal is recommended as the
most effective treatment. However, various treatment procedures are
described as appropriate, depending on the condition of the patient.

828   Guarnaschelli, John; Lee, John; Pitts, Frederick W. "Fallen fon-
         tanelle (Caida de Mollera): a variant of the battered child
         syndrome." JAMA 222(12): 1545-46, December 18, 1972. (12
         References).
Presents a case history of an infant with subdural hematoma resulting
from the attempts by the folk healer to cure the infant of "fallen fon-
tanelle." Physicians dealing with patients of Latin-American background
should familiarize themselves with the folk remedies for childhood disorders so that variants of the battered child syndrome can be recognized.

829   Guthkelch, A. N. "Infantile subdural haematoma and its relation-
         ship to whiplash injuries." Br Med J 2(5759): 430-31, May 22,
         1971. (11 References).
Points out that the subdural hematoma in a battered child may not only
be the result of a direct blow to the head, but also of violently shaking the child. When whiplash to the head causes an injury, the subdural
hematoma is very often bilateral and accompanied by no external signs
of abuse. Therefore, it is imperative that medical examiners recognize
the possibility of assault even when there may be no evidence of injury
such as bruises or other external marks. Indeed, whiplash injuries to
the head can be even more serious than a sudden direct blow.

830   Haas, L. "Injured baby: letter to editor." Br Med J 20(5): 645,
         September 11, 1965. (0 References).
Subdural hematoma in an infant, in association with multiple epiphysial
injuries, points to a diagnosis of deliberate abuse rather than to birth
trauma. A case history in which epiphysial injury was at first unsuspected is presented.

831   Hawkes, C. D. "Craniocerebral trauma in infancy and childhood."
         Clin Neurosurg 11(7): 66-75, 1964. (8 References).
Presents extensive descriptions of head injuries which may appear in
child abuse cases. Physicians are urged to exercise extreme caution when
a head injury in an infant or child is discovered. The degree of severity is not always immediately obvious in that the immature nervous system
responds differently to trauma than does that of an adult. Since many

of these types of injuries are accompanied by vomiting and drowsiness, it is especially important that these symptoms be carefully observed. Possible indications of the battered child syndrome should be noted when head injuries are present.

832 Heiskanen, O., and Kaste, M. "Late prognosis of severe brain injury in children." Dev Med Child Neurol 16(1): 11-14, February, 1974. (9 References).

Thirty-six children who had suffered brain injury and unconsciousness were the subjects of this follow-up study. The academic performance of these children was noted between four and ten years after the injury. About half of the children suffered a decline in school performance. (Eight of these subjects had to attend schools for the mentally handicapped). Children who had been unconscious for two or more weeks usually suffered a severe decline in academic abilities. Most of the children had been injured in traffic accidents. While prognosis for recovery is better for children than for adults who receive brain injuries, lasting impairment is still quite common.

833 Henderson, J. G. "Subdural hematoma and 'battered baby': letter to editor." Br Med J 3(5619): 678, September 14, 1968. (11 References).

Emphasizes the need for more research into the significance of subdural hematomas in relation to child abuse.

834 Ingraham, Franc D., and Matson, Donald D. "Subdural hematoma in infancy." J Pediatr 24(1): 1-37, January, 1944. (13 References).

Presents a report, complete with statistics, from ninety-eight case records collected over six years, on the occurrence and management of subdural hematoma in infants during the first two years of life. Early detection of subdural hematomas is the responsibility of pediatricians and general practitioners, whereas treatment is best carried out by an experienced neurosurgeon. The single most prominent cause of subdural hematoma in infancy is trauma to the head. A detailed analysis of the symptoms, including failure to gain weight, fever, vomiting, irritability, coma, convulsions, and paralysis, is presented. Enlarged heads do not frequently accompany subdural hematoma. Diagnosing it is in many ways problematic. History, physical examination, and x-ray findings often provide insufficient evidence to reach an accurate diagnosis. In fact, in many instances puncture of the subdural space is the only procedure that can indicate the presence of a subdural hematoma. It is, therefore, extremely important that the lesion be suspected, even when there is little external evidence to warrant a subdural puncture. A detailed summary of the pathologic findings, as well as graphic representation of the pathology of subdural hematoma, is included.

Treatment procedures vary according to the age of the patient and the development of his brain, for the pathologic physiology of the disease varies greatly once the brain is fully grown. In infancy, subdural hematomas must be removed. The method applied has to be designed to affect a gradual release of pressure prior to ultimate radical removal. Procedures for performing subdural taps, bilateral Burr holes, and bone flaps are presented, as well as additional guidelines for the care of the patient involved. The number of infants found to be suffering from subdural hematoma is directly proportional to the ability of physicians to identify it.

835 Jennett, Bryan. "Head innuries in children." <u>Dev Med Child Neurol</u>
       14(2): 137-47, April, 1972. (10 References).
Head injuries, which account for nearly one-sixth of the general surgical
admissions at children's hospitals, result from three causes: car accidents, falling, and battering. The management of such injuries is discussed, and an illustrative account is given of effective management of
a typical case from diagnosis to convalescence.

836 Lis, Edward F., and Frauenberger, George S. "Multiple fractures
       associated with subdural hematoma in infancy." <u>Pediatrics</u> 6(6):
       890-92, December, 1950. (1 Reference).
Documents a medical history of a ten-week-old male infant with subdural
hematoma and multiple fractures of the flat bones. A comparison of
Caffey's report, noting the association of subdural hematoma and multiple
bone fractures, is drawn. The etiology of the injuries remains unestab-
lished.

837 Lorber, John, and Bhat, Usha S. "Posthaemorrhagic hydrocephalus:
       diagnosis, differential diagnosis, treatment, and long-term
       results." <u>Arch Dis Child</u> 49(10): 751-62, October, 1974. (8
       References).
Cites case reports on forty-seven infants treated for intracranial hemorrhaging. This condition may be a result of accidental injury, child
abuse or, occasionally, blood disease. Four of the forty-seven cases
were confirmed or suspected child abuse. Treatment procedures are
described. Of the thirty-two survivors, many suffered brain damage or
physical handicap as a result of the hemorrhage.

838 MacKeith, Ronald. "Speculations of non-accidental injury as a cause
       of chronic brain disorder." <u>Dev Med Child Neurol</u> 16(2): 216-18,
       April, 1974. (16 References).
For every child who has died with subdural hematoma due to battering,
there are at least four children who are mentally or physically incapacitated. The annual death rate and annual rate of cases of incapacitation
in the United Kingdom and the United States are approximated. It is
suggested that children who present with cerebral palsy or a severe mental
handicap, with no apparent causative factor, may be previously abused
children, brought for assessment when the parents have matured and abuse
has ceased. The possibility of earlier abuse should be considered.

839 ─────. "Speculations on some possible long-term effects." In:
       Franklin, Alfred White, ed. <u>Concerning child abuse</u>. New York:
       Churchill Livingstone, 1975. 63-68. (0 References).
Head injuries are frequent manifestations of the battered child syndrome.
Some of these injuries result in death, some in complete recovery, but
others lead to lasting deficits in cerebral functioning. In a study of
749 cases of battered children, Kempe (1962) reported that 10.4 percent
of the battered children died, and that 15 percent were left with
permanent brain damage. There is also evidence to show that 20 percent
of those infants who suffer non-accidental injury will be educationally
handicapped later in life. They may also develop emotional maladjust-
ments and become child batterers themselves as adults. It is possible
that a person with brain injury is more vulnerable to environmental
stresses and is, thus, less equipped to cope effectively with the demands
of small children. In one-half of the children with cerebral palsy and
half of the mentally deficient children, no adequate cause of their dis-

ability can be identified. It is hypothesized that non-accidental injury
and the associated deprivation may account for ninety new cases of
cerebral palsy and 150 new cases of severe mental handicap in the United
Kingdom every year.

840   Meacham, W. F. "The neurosurgical aspects of the battered child."
        South Med Bull 58(3): 33-36, June, 1970. (0 References).
The head injuries characteristic of child abuse are enumerated and described, and their treatment is outlined. Particular attention is focused
on the diagnosis of battering-induced subdural hematoma, which is distinguished from non-traumatic hematoma. Subdural taps are recommended
for treatment. It is suggested that physicians who note some of the head
injuries symptomatic of abuse examine the child for several other characteristic trauma and report the matter to the appropriate body.

841   Moyes, Peter D. "Subdural effusions in infants." Can Med Assoc J
        100(5): 231-34, February 1, 1969. (13 References).
The symptoms, etiology, diagnosis, and treatment of subdural hematomas
are discussed with particular reference to sixty cases diagnosed and
treated over a ten year period. Most of the patients were under a year
in age; four cases involved child abuse.

842   O'Doherty, N. J. "Subdural haematoma in battered babies." Dev Med
        Child Neurol 6(2): 192-93, April, 1964. (3 References).
Describes the clinical signs of a subdural hematoma in child abuse cases.
Subdural hematoma is cited as a cause of death or retarded development in
battered children and, therefore, warrents careful diagnosis. Important
clinical signs include vomiting or convulsions, preretinal hemorrhages,
and excessive fluid derived from a subdural puncture.

843   Oliver, J. E. "Microcephaly following baby battering and shaking."
        Br Med J 2(5965): 262-64, May 3, 1975. (8 References).
Child battering has not been sufficiently recognized as a causal factor
in certain types of microcephaly and mental retardation. Three case
studies illustrate that violent or frequent shaking of babies or bruising
to the heads of young children often leads to brain damage.

844   Payne, E. E. "Unusual fatal brain injury due to knitting needle."
        Br Med J 2(5517): 807-8, October, 1966. (3 References).
Reports an incident in which a thirteen-month-old boy died after a knitting needle punctured his neck and penetrated eight centimeters into
his brain. His mother had been present during the injury. The death
was ruled accidental.

845   Russell, Patricia A. "Subdural haematoma in infancy." Br Med J
        2(5459): 446-48, August 21, 1965. (19 References).
Discusses the diagnosis and treatment of twenty-five cases of subdural
hematoma in children under the age of two years. In three of the cases,
child abuse was suspected as a cause of injury; in fourteen cases, there
was no history of trauma. The symptoms of the condition in most instances
were convulsions, vomiting, and drowsiness. Early diagnosis is regarded
essential in the prevention of permanent brain damage.

846   Salmon, James H. "Subdural hematoma in infancy: suggestions for
        diagnosis and management." Clin Pediatr 10: 597-99, October,
        1971. (5 References).

Subdural hematoma may be difficult to diagnose in infants. The subdural
tap technique is highly recommended with the reminder that physicians
take care to avoid contamination. The technique is described and its
application demonstrated with several case histories.

847 Sarsfield, James K. "The neurological sequelae of non-accidental
       injury." Dev Med Child Neurol 16(6): 826-27, December, 1974.
       (9 References).
A compendium of long-term studies concerned with the neurological consequences of baby battering. The incidence of cerebral palsy and mental
retardation among such children is considerable and may possibly indicate
existence of the handicap prior to the battering incident.

848 Schulman, K. "Late complications of head injuries in children."
       In: Congress of Neurological Surgeons, Miami, Florida, 1971.
       Proceedings: Clinical neurosurgery. Baltimore: Williams and
       Wilkins, 1972. 371-80. (16 References).
Reviews treatment prescribed for the late complications arising from head
injuries in children, including those resulting from abuse. Chronic subdural hematomas and repeated severe closed head injuries are pointed to
as possible symptoms of battering.

849 Silber, David L., and Bell, William E. "The neurologist and the
       physically abused child." Neurology (Minneap) 21(10): 991-99,
       October, 1971. (14 References).
Presents six detailed case reports of physically abused children with
five of the six showing cerebral trauma. Because of the high incidence
of this type of injury, neurologists play a key role in diagnosing and
reporting suspected cases of abuse.

850 Smith, Marcus J. "Subdural hematoma with multiple fractures." Am
       J Roentgenol Radium Ther Nucl Med 63(3): 342-44, March, 1950.
       (2 References).
Sets forth a case report of an infant presenting with subdural hematoma,
skull fractures, and multiple long bone fractures. No history of trauma
was indicated, and no conclusions as to the origin of the injuries were
reached.

851 Till, Kenneth. "A neurosurgeon's viewpoint." In: Franklin, Alfred
       White, ed. Concerning child abuse. New York: Churchill Living-
       stone, 1975. 56-62. (0 References).
This neurosurgeon usually treats only those victims of child abuse suffering from an intracranial lesion requiring neurosurgical care. The
children are referred from a number of hospitals spread over a large
geographical area. Upon admission, the infants are characteristically
pale and inactive. Vomiting, seizures, weakness of limbs, and shallow
slow breathing may be present when injury to the brain has been sustained.
A common complication of head injury is subdural hematoma, a collection
of fluid over the surface of the brain. Half of the babies who have
subdural hematoma also have retinal hemorrhages which result from a rapid
rise in pressure within the head. Between 5 and 10 percent of these
infants will be uneducable as a result of the head injuries; another 10
percent will later prove to be educationally subnormal, leaving 80 percent with normal intelligence. Epilepsy appears to develop in between
1 and 5 percent of children with head injury. A small percentage have
a loss of vision due to retinal hemorrhage.

852 "Whiplash injury in infancy." <u>Med J Aust</u> 2(9): 456, August 28, 1971. (1 Reference).
Although subdural hematoma in infants is frequently a result of direct injuries to the head, it can also be caused by shaking the infant violently. Such whiplash injuries are not always the result of parental violence. However, the possibility of willfully inflicted trauma must be considered in all instances of subdural hematoma, even in situations where there is no previous history of parental abuse.

2. SKELETAL INJURY

853 Adams, Patricia C.; Strand, Roy D.; Bresnan, Michael J.; <u>et al</u>. "Kinky hair syndrome: serial study of radiological findings with emphasis on the similarity to the battered child syndrome." <u>Radiology</u> 112(2): 401-7, August, 1974. (16 References).
Depicts the serial roentgenographic changes of the long bones in two patients with Menkes' syndrome and documents the vascular and central nervous system changes of the condition. One case in particular demonstrates the radiographic similarity of Menkes' syndrome (probably caused by copper deficiency) to the infant abuse syndrome.

854 Akbarnia, Behrooz A., and Akbarnia, Nasrin Owsia. "The role of [the] orthopedist in child abuse and neglect." <u>Orthop Clin North Am</u> 7(3): 733-42, July, 1976. (20 References).
After a brief discussion of the incidence and manifestations of the abused child and abusing parent, the orthopedic physical findings of child abuse are presented. Findings are broken down into three categories--metaphyseal fractures, diaphyseal fractures, and miscellaneous lesions, including those of the skull, rib, and thoracolumbar. Diagnostic x-ray films are presented as examples. The orthopedist is prevailed upon to report these findings and to become more involved in the team approach for management of abuse, particularly by means of the skeletal work-up.

855 Akbarnia, Behrooz; Torg, Joseph S.; Kirkpatrick, John; <u>et al</u>. "Manifestations of the battered-child syndrome." <u>J Bone Joint Surg (Am)</u> 56A(6): 1159-66, September, 1974. (13 References).
A compilation of the orthopedic injuries resulting from child battering as observed in 231 children admitted to St. Christopher's Hospital for Children in Philadelphia between 1965 and 1972. Thirty-six percent of the children had orthopedic injuries, the most common being multiple long bone and rib fractures, impactions, deformity of joints, and widened sutures of the skull. Periosteal new bone formation was singled out by the authors as a pathognomonic symptom of child battering. Numerous fractures in multiple stages of healing provide further evidence of child battering.

856 Altman, Donald H., and Smith, Richard L. "Unrecognized trauma in infants and children." <u>J Bone Joint Surg (Am)</u> 42A(3): 407-13, April, 1960. (10 References).
Presents cases of bone lesions due to traumatic injury. It is suggested that attempts be made to recognize adult or sibling-induced trauma, thus potentially saving the child's life.

857 Astley, Roy. "Multiple metaphyseal fractures in small children (metaphyseal fragility of bone)." <u>Br J Radiol</u> 26(311): 577-83, November, 1953. (4 References).

Reviews six medical histories of infants with multiple metaphyseal frac-
ture-like defects. It is suggested that these clinical and radiologic
findings are symptoms of a generalized bone disease in small children.
All six cases were characterized by an absence of history to account for
the widespread lesions and an apparent lack of pain. Although the possibility that parents could have been responsible for inflicting the
injuries is recognized, no history of trauma in these cases was elicited.
Instead, the syndrome was believed to be associated with some structural
abnormality of non-mineral constitution of the growing skeleton and was
labeled metaphyseal fragility of bone.

858 Baker, David H., and Berdon, Walter E. "Special trauma problems in
     children." Radiol Clin North Am 4(2): 289-305, August, 1966.
     (21 References).
Describes skeletal trauma in children and its relation to the battered
child syndrome. Radiologic evidence of metaphyseal avulsion, of new and
old injuries, or of slipped epiphysis are indicators of abuse. Head
injuries resulting in subdural hematomas also signal maltreatment and
call for complex body x-rays. Bone growth which stimulates trauma,
diseases which increase the susceptibility of fracture, as well as abdominal, skull, and cervical spine bone trauma, are described.

859 Bakwin, Harry. "Multiple skeletal lesions in young children due to
     trauma." J Pediatr 49(1): 7-15, July, 1956. (8 References).
Examines three case histories of infants with multiple bone lesions suggesting that such injuries as subperiosteal ossification, metaphyseal
fractures, avulsions, impacted fractures, and epiphyseal displacement
are common in infants and young children. The etiology of this syndrome
remains unclear. However, clinical evidence and radiologic findings
indicate that the probable cause of skeletal changes is trauma, despite
the absence of a history of trauma.

860 ————. "Roentgenologic changes in the bones following trauma
     in infants." J Newark Beth Israel Hosp 3(1): 17-25, January,
     1952. (0 References).
Sets forth six case reports of infants with traumatic lesions of the
bones. Such lesions are often misdiagnosed and believed to be complications due to scurvy, syphilis, or general bone disease such as fragilitas
ossium. Skeletal lesions tend to be multiple and show developments that
are unique to infants. Such roentgenological changes are difficult to
detect and are only visible when fractures are present. Inflicted trauma
is not suspected as the cause of these complications. Instead, they are
considered to be the result of repeated accidents.

861 Barmeyer, George H.; Anderson, Lee R.; Cox, Walter B. "Traumatic
     periostitis in young children." J Pediatr 38(2): 184-90,
     February, 1951. (16 References).
The limping leg of young children is often caused by periosteal separation. The child usually recovers on his own.

862 Barness, Lewis A. "What's wrong with the hip?" Clin Pediatr
     9(8): 467, August, 1970. (0 References).
Documents a case history of a ten-week-old boy brought to an emergency ward
with a sudden swelling of the left leg. After a number of tentative diagnoses were considered, an x-ray revealed a fractured femur. An intern,
however, had, by taking a comprehensive history, already made the diag-

nosis of battered child. It is suggested that better initial histories would speed correct diagnoses.

863 Bhattacharya, A. K. "Multiple fractures." Bull Calcutta Sch Trop Med 14(3): 111-12, July, 1966. (0 References).
Two siblings, victims of the battered child syndrome, were subjects for a case study. Multiple fractures, the simultaneous illness of the brother and sister, the improvement of both when hospitalized, and a lack of pathological cause following extensive examination indicate abuse. The report is believed to be the first of its kind from India.

864 Blockney, N. J. "Observations on infantile coxa vara." J Bone Joint Surg (Br) 51B: 106-11, February, 1969. (11 References).
Observations on the occurrence of the "infantile" variation of the condition coxa vara (as opposed to "congenital" coxa vara). The association of infantile coxa vara with the battered child syndrome in a number of cases observed leads to the conclusion that infantile coxa vara should not be considered congenital or developmental.

865 Caffey, John. "Infantile cortical hyperostosis." J Pediatr 29(5): 541-59, November, 1946. (4 References).
Infantile cortical hyperostosis is of undetermined cause and is considered a new syndrome in infants. It is characterized by deep swelling of soft tissues and cortical hypertoses in the neighboring bones. It usually occurs between three weeks and twenty months of life.

866 ————. "Multiple fractures in the long bones of infants suffering from chronic subdural hematoma." Am J Roentgenol Radium Ther Nucl Med 56(2): 163-73, August, 1946. (10 References).
Reviews six case studies of infants with chronic subdural hematoma as well as multiple fractures in the long bones. No history of injury that could account for these complications and no general or localized disease predisposing the bones to fractures were determined. It is merely suggested that the presence of unexplained fractures in the long bones should signal physicians to conduct an examination for possible subdural hematoma. Conversely, evidence of a subdural hematoma should signal the need for a complete roentgen examination. The ultimate cause of both difficulties remains undetermined. It can only be stated that the bone changes do not seem to be the result of one single traumatic episode.

867 ————. "Some traumatic lesions in growing bones other than fractures and dislocations: clinical and radiological features." Br J Radiol 30(353): 225-38, May, 1957. (16 References).
Describes various cases of traumatic lesions in growing bones of children other than fractures and dislocations. These are not necessarily of abusive origin, but pediatricians are cautioned to be alert to that possibility. The overall concern is that physicians be aware that in young patients there exists a high prevalence of traumatic injuries—accidental or non-accidental—particularly in cases presenting painful swollen lesions in the extremities. Such symptoms should be examined immediately for traumatic origin versus more sophisticated causal agents as vitamin deficiencies, infections, metabolic imbalances, and others.

868 ————. "Syphilis of the skeleton in early infancy: the non-specificity of many of the roentgenographic changes." Am J Roentgenol Radium Ther Nucl Med 42(5): 637-55, November, 1939. (35 References).

Surveys fifteen medical cases involving skeletal difficulties of questionable origin in non-syphilitic infants. Syphilitic infants have long been known to have skeletal problems, while non-syphilitic infants with skeletal problems have been largely ignored. This report analyzes the syphilitic-like skeletal changes found in non-syphilitic infants and relates the findings that roentgenographic skeletal lesions--such as osteochondritis, osteoperiostitis, and osteomyelitis--cannot be interpreted as sole indicators of syphilis in infants. These lesions appear under many varied conditions. No conclusive explanation for the origin of such lesions is offered however.

869 ————. "Traumatic cupping of the metaphyses of growing bones." Am J Roentgenol Radium Ther Nucl Med 108(3): 451-60, March, 1970. (13 References).
Describes residual traumatic cupping of the metaphyses, and metaphyseal cupping which results from prolonged immobilization. Such immobilization has produced metaphyseal cupping in victims of tuberculosis and polio as well as in victims of child abuse. The bones at the knee are the most commonly affected. Photographs of x-rays of the condition in both abused children and those immobilized because of illness are included.

870 Cozen, Lewis. "Office treatment of childhood hip conditions: Part I." Med Times 99(11): 150-52ff., November, 1971. (0 References).
The incidence and treatment of childhood hip conditions, including those resulting from suspected abuse, are detailed.

871 Cullen, John C. "Spinal lesions in battered babies." J Bone Joint Surg (Br) 57B(3): 364-66, August, 1975. (5 References).
Presents five case histories of young children with spinal injuries resulting from suspected physical maltreatment by either a parent or guardian. Radiographs of the damaged spines are reproduced. On the basis of spinal injury alone, it is difficult to diagnosis non-accidental injury. In each of the children presented, there were associated injuries to the limbs or skull, which made the diagnosis more certain. The importance of having a full radiological survey of children suspected of being maltreated is emphasized.

872 Fairburn, Anthony C., and Hunt, A. C. "Caffey's 'third syndrome' -- a critical evaluation ('the battered baby')." Med Sci Law 4(2): 23-26, April, 1964. (3 References).
Examines seven cases of multiple fractures in children resulting from abuse by parents. The article discusses the syndrome of "metaphysical fragility" as an alternate explanation to abuse. However, repeated fractures strongly suggest a battered child and require thorough investigation.

873 Fiser, Robert H.; Kaplan, Joseph; Holder, John C. "Congenital syphilis mimicking the battered child syndrome: how does one tell them apart?" Clin Pediatr 11(5): 305-7, May, 1972. (7 References).
A case history of congenital syphilis which mimicked the battered child syndrome is presented. Congenital syphilis causes bone lesions in the infant which resemble those resulting from physical abuse. Radiographs of such lesions are reproduced in the article. To distinguish between the two diseases, it is recommended that repeated serologic testing of the mother for venereal disease be administered throughout the entire

pregnancy. Treatment provided for syphilis even in the last month of gestation can reduce the degree of fetal infection significantly.

874 Fisher, Samuel H. "Skeletal manifestations of parent-induced trauma in infants and children." South Med J 51(8): 956-60, August, 1958. (11 References).
Cites six cases of parent-induced skeletal trauma in infants and children. In order to prevent further abuse, physicians must maintain a high index of suspicion in diagnosing such cases. One of the six children studied showed unique and unusual roentgen changes, illustrating a relatively new and undocumented bone development behavior of recurrent parental abuse.

875 Frauenberger, George S., and Lis, Edward F. "Multiple fractures associated with subdural hematoma in infancy." Pediatrics 6(6): 890-92, December, 1950. (1 Reference).
Case history of a ten-week-old male infant, brought to the hospital suffering from what was believed to be osteogenesis imperfecta. Further study over a ten week period revealed multiple fractures of the ribs and leg and subdural hematoma. No etiology could be established in this particular case, and the need for further study of the linkage between subdural hematoma and multiple fractures in infants is stressed.

876 Friedman, Morris S. "Traumatic periostitis in infants and children." JAMA 166(15): 1840-45, April 12, 1958. (4 References).
Describes the clinical and radiographic manifestations of traumatic periostitis. The disease involves the stripping of the periosteum, subperiosteal hemorrhaging, and in some cases, periosteal calcification. Although clinical symptoms may resemble pseudoparalysis or scurvy, roentgenograms can reveal traumatic periostitis and can be helpful in differentiating it from other, more serious skeletal lesions. Case studies including x-rays illustrate these findings.

877 Griffiths, Alan L. "Fatigue fracture of the fibula in childhood." Arch Dis Child 27(136): 552-57, December, 1952. (14 References).
Reviews eight case histories of children, aged two-years-two-months to eight years, with fatigue fracture of the fibula. Comparison of these eight cases to other cases recorded in the literature on fatigue fractures are drawn. Trauma is discounted as a probable cause for such fractures. Instead, they are attributed to the excessive stress caused by jumping and skipping on strongly curved fibulae, a defect that may predispose to the evolution of fatigue fractures, especially in combination with badly worn shoes.

878 Griffiths, D. L., and Moynihan, F. J. "Multiple epiphysial injuries in babies: 'battered baby' syndrome." Br Med J 2(5372): 1558-61, December 21, 1963. (15 References).
Describes epiphysial injuries to babies suffering from the battered child syndrome. Five children are described whose symptoms are characteristic: (1) unexplained swelling at the ends of the long bones; (2) x-ray changes; (3) elevated temperature; and (4) leucocytosis. The importance of a skeletal x-ray for discovering other possible lesions is emphasized. The radiological signs of this syndrome are unmistakable, although they resemble other conditions such as scurvy. The 10 percent rate makes the cooperation of physicians imperative despite their disblief and unwillingness to get involved.

879 Gwinn, John L., and Barnes, George R., Jr. "Radiological case of
     the month." Am J Dis Child 109(5): 457-58, May, 1965. (5
     References).
Documents a case history of an abused five-week-old female revealing
multiple rib fractures at various stages of healing and metaphyseal fracture of the left femur. These findings, along with the misleading history
related by the parents, led to a clinical diagnosis of battered child
syndrome.

880 Gwinn, John L.; Lewin, Kenneth W.; Peterson, Herbert G., Jr. "Roent-
     genographic manifestations of unsuspected trauma in infancy."
     JAMA 176(11): 926-29, June 17, 1961. (13 References).
Presents the child abuse problem with emphasis on roentgenographic manifestations in repetitive trauma cases.

881 Hayden, John W. "Pathologic fractures in children." Wis Med J
     68(11): 313-18, November, 1969. (12 References).
Describes the various types of pathologic and stress fractures in children's bones, including the insufficiency fracture (associated with
scurvy). This fracture is often confused with the battered child syndrome, since a number of the symptoms are similar.

882 Hiller, H. G. "Battered or not -- a reappraisal of metaphyseal
     fragility." Am J Roentgenol Radium Ther Nucl Med 114(2): 241-46,
     February, 1972. (3 References).
A reconsideration of epiphyseal plate fractures in the diagnosis of battering. A retrospective two year study of fracture cases of children
under three years of age was conducted at the Royal Children's Hospital.
It was found that not one out of the 145 cases reviewed was of the
epiphyseal plate type, despite the range and severity of the injuries
considered. It was inferred that epiphyseal plate fractures occur rarely
in the normal infant, and that their presence is a stronger indicator of
an underlying bone defect than of abuse.

883 Jones, Henry H., and Davis, Joseph H. "Multiple traumatic lesions
     of the infant skeleton." Stanford Med Bull 15(3): 259-73,
     August, 1957. (14 References).
Reviews the literature on multiple skeletal lesions in infants and includes a summary of five case reports of undiagnosed trauma. Forty-two
cases of multiple skeletal lesions were chosen from the literature to be
studied. Evidence drawn from these cases indicate that they were all the
result of inflicted trauma, instead of an underlying susceptibility to
fractures. Early diagnosis of the lesions is strongly encouraged and
in certain cases removal of the child from the home is recommended so
that the patient can have an opportunity to fully recover. Because subdural hematoma is often discovered in infants with multiple fractures,
physicians should routinely examine the patient for evidence of its
presence. The converse is also true. When subdural hematoma is discovered initially, physicians should conduct a skeletal survey to detect
fractures.

884 Kogutt, M. S.; Swischuk, Leonard E.; Fagan, C. J. "Patterns of
     injury and significance of uncommon fractures in the battered
     child syndrome." Am J Roentgenol Radium Ther Nucl Med 121(1):
     143-49, May, 1974. (15 References).

Examines the patterns of injury identified in ninety-five physically abused children through case history and x-ray. It was found that fractures of the long bones and other bone changes tended to accompany child abuse.

885   Lentle, B. C.   "Pycnodysostosis: a case report."   J Can Assoc Radiol
       22(3):   210-14, September, 1971.   (13 References).
Documents a case history of a child suffering from pycnodysostosis, a rare bone disease. A number of its symptoms are also characteristic of the battered child syndrome, including multiple bone fractures.

886   Lloyd-Roberts, G.   "The diagnosis of injury of bones and joints in
       young babies."   Proc R Soc Med   61(12):   1299-1300, December 12,
       1968.   (1 Reference).
Some injuries to the bones and joints of infants are characteristic of child abuse. X-rays and schematic drawings illustrate healing patterns unique to infants who have incurred injuries as a result of assault. Multiple skeletal lesions varying in maturity and unexplained subdural hematoma constitute evidence that often support a diagnosis of abuse.

887   McHenry, Thomas; Girdany, Bertram R.; Elmer, Elizabeth.   "Unsus-
       pected trauma with multiple skeletal injuries during infancy and
       childhood."   Pediatrics   31(6):   903-8, June, 1963.   (14 Refer-
       ences).
A study of experiences at the Children's Hospital of Pittsburgh concerning fifty abused children with multiple injuries to the skeleton. The article discusses the various presenting complaints, the ages of the patients, and family backgrounds. The most frequent injuries found were disabled extremities, skin lesions, convulsions, and general failure to do well. The children ranged in age from one month to eight years old, and 60 percent of them were under nine months old. Information about the families was not always available but tended to show that the parents: (1) were impulsive in their behavior; (2) showed little guilt or concern about the injured child; (3) had marital problems; and (4) had themselves had a deprived childhood.

888   Mackler, S. F., and Brooks, A. L.   "Diagnosis and treatment of skele-
       tal injuries in the battered child syndrome."   South Med Bull
       58(3):   27-32, June, 1970.   (16 References).
Discusses the utility of radiography in identifying and confirming the battered child syndrome. The most frequent radiological evidence of abuse includes the predilection of the epiphyses and adjacent metaphyses, exaggerated periosteal reaction, multiple lesions in different bones, lesions in various stages of healing, and skull fractures. The basis for a diagnosis of child abuse is differentiated from other diseases with similar symptoms.

889   Miller, Donald S.   "Fractures among children: I.   Parental assault
       as causative agent."   Minn Med   42(9):   1209-13, September, 1959.
       (7 References).
Describes bone fractures caused by parental assault. Physicians can identify fractures caused by abuse by the presence of multiple injuries, by radiological examination which will often reveal older, healing injuries, and by ruling out rare diseases which may resemble these bone injuries. Subdural hematoma or accompanying signs of neglect and malnutrition also suggest abuse. A thorough and probing history must be taken from the parents to confirm abuse as the cause of injury.

890 Quigley, Thomas B.; Banks, Henry H.; Leach, Robert E.; <u>et al</u>.
     "Advances in the management of fractures and dislocations in the
     past decade." <u>Orthop Clin North Am</u> 3(3): 793-825, November,
     1972. (220 References).
A lengthy survey of developments with respect to the treatment of skeletal
injuries in both children and adults. The discussion of children's injuries is brief and includes some mention of the incidence of skeletal
injuries as the result of child abuse.

891 Roaf, Robert. "Trauma in childhood." <u>Br Med J</u> 1(5449): 1541-43,
     June 12, 1965. (3 References).
Summarizes the nature of physical injuries commonly undergone by young
children. The distinguishing characteristics of various accidental
fractures, such as greenstick fractures and pulled elbows, are presented.
Bone damage inflicted on battered children can be distinguished by a
subperiosteal formation on the long bones.

892 Rose, Cassie B. "Unusual periostitis in children." <u>Radiology</u>
     27(2): 131-37, August, 1936. (0 References).
Gives examples of five case histories with similar radiologic findings,
but with varying diagnoses. These cases illustrate the need to collect
and to coordinate histories and clinical findings, so that x-rays can be
interpreted consistently in the future. The case reports involve children with unusual bone developments from age six months to four-and-one-
half years. Four cases showed multiple lesions. X-ray findings alone
are not sufficient evidence upon which to base a diagnosis. Furthermore, unusual bone developments found in one area should warn a physician
to make a complete skeletal survey to determine if more changes are
present. Suggested causes for the radiologic findings include trauma,
scurvy, osteomyelitis, syphilitic or rachitic periostitis, tumors, and
tuberculosis.

893 Silverman, Frederic N. "The battered child." <u>Manitoba Med Rev</u>
     45(8): 473-77, October, 1965. (10 References).
Documents radiologic indicators of skeletal injuries commonly seen in
battered children. Three groups of children who are often victims of
abuse are listed as: (1) children injured as a result of parental
attempts to protect them from another injury such as a fall; (2) children
whose injuries are due to a lack of protection; and (3) children who are
victims of intentional abuse. Three cases representing each group are
provided. Possible psychological factors precipitating abuse in parents
are still sketchy at best, but abnormal emotional and violent reactions
to frustration appear to be typical. Legal and social channels for
reporting and investigating suspected cases need to be established in
order to support the physician in his diagnosis and thereby encourage
him to acknowledge abuse.

894 ————. "The roentgen manifestations of unrecognized skeletal
     trauma in infants." <u>Am J Roentgenol Radium Ther Nucl Med</u> 69(3):
     413-27, March, 1953. (9 References).
Cites three case studies of infants with fractures that were initially
unsuspected. Two of the three infants had metaphysial lesions. In each
case, before the roentgen examinations revealed the fractures, no effort
was made by the attending physicians to obtain an accurate history of
the child's injuries. Emphasis is placed on considering the possibility
of caretaker-inflicted injury when the clinical manifestations show

bizarre skeletal lesions in different stages of development and when no
adequate history to explain them is given.

895   Silverman, Frederic N., and Gilden, Jerome J. "Congenital insensi-
        tivity to pain: a neurologic syndrome with bizarre skeletal
        lesions." Radiology 72(2): 176-90, February, 1959. (29 Refer-
        ences).
Examines the case histories of two sisters presenting unusual skeletal
lesions and an overwhelming indifference or insensitivity to pain. When
first admitted for medical attention, neither trauma nor congenital insensitivity to pain were considered in the diagnosis. Both young girls
had a history of recurrent skeletal injuries, yet neither of them suffered
significant pain considering the seriousness of their injuries. Some
years later, after the syndrome of congenital insensitivity to pain was
established, one of the sisters was reevaluated. It was then discovered
that her skeletal lesions were the result of repeated trauma to her
bones. Congenital insensitivity to pain occurs in varying degrees and
is perhaps a hereditary condition.

896   Snedecor, Spencer T.; Knapp, Richard E.; Wilson, Harrison B. "Trau-
        matic ossifying periostitis of newborn." Surg Gynecol Obstet
        61(3): 385-87, September, 1935. (0 References).
Describes injuries to muscles and bone areas of babies as a result of
too much traction on arms or legs during breech births.

897   Snedecor, Spencer T., and Wilson, Harrison B. "Some obstetrical
        injuries to long bones." J Bone Joint Surg (Am) 31A(2): 378-84,
        April, 1949. (11 References).
In breech deliveries of the first born, injuries to the long bones often
occur. These can be decreased if less force is used and more care taken
in turning lower extremities.

898   Stone, J. S. "Acute epiphyseal and periosteal infections in infants
        and children." Boston Med Surg J 156(26): 842-48, June 27, 1907.
        (0 References).
Discusses bone and joint lesions found in children. These lesions differ
from those found in adults and, as a result, often go undetected. The
importance of physicians' knowing human anatomy typical of each stage of
development is stressed. Includes case histories.

899   Swischuk, Leonard E. "The battered child syndrome: radiologic
        aspects." South Med Bull 58(3): 24-26, June, 1970. (6 Refer-
        ences).
Describes the identification of battering-induced skeletal injury by
means of radiation. The injuries discussed include epiphyseal-metaphyseal
traumas (resulting from twisting) and their healing patterns; spiral
fractures (due to rotary stress); and other injuries to the skull, clav-
icle, ribs, and spine.

900   ————. "The beaked, notched, or hooked vertebra: its signifi-
        cance in infants and young children." Radiology 95(3): 661-64,
        June, 1970. (9 References).
Explains the occurrence of beaked, notched, or hooked vertebra in children. Although its occurrence is common in a number of seemingly unrelated conditions, its placement is almost always at the thoracolumbar
junction, accompanied by thoracolumbar kyphosis. If an infant is forced

to sit up too soon, kyphosis increases as does the stress on interverte-
bral discs. Muscular hypotonia may account for the vertebral notching
which occurs in cases of child abuse.

901 ————. "Spine and spinal cord trauma in the battered child syn-
     drome." Radiology 92(3): 733-38, March, 1969. (8 References).
A description of spinal injuries resulting from child abuse, complete
with detailed case histories and roentgenograms of damaged spines. Possible mechanisms for the various injuries are discussed. The presence
of spinal injury in itself does not establish the diagnosis of the battered child syndrome. It should be assessed in conjunction with other
roentgenographic and clinical findings. Because patients with uncompli-
cated spinal fractures are often asymptomatic, initial detection of the
injury often rests with the radiologist.

902 Teng, Ching Tseng; Singleton, Edward B.; Daeschner, C. W., Jr.
     "Skeletal injuries of the battered child." Am J Orthop 6(10:
     202-7, October, 1964. (15 References).
Presents five case reports and summarizes the physiological indicators
of child abuse. These clues include: (1) metaphyseal infractions or
fragmentations, subperiosteal hemorrhages and epiphyseal-metaphyseal
separations; (2) multiplicity of injury; and (3) fresh and healing lesions
in the same bone. Physicians are urged to be suspicious of all such
cases and, if child abuse is indicated, the physician should report the
family to law enforcement and/or social agencies.

903 Weston, W. J. "Metaphysial fractures in infancy." J Bone Joint
     Surg (Br) 39B(4): 694-700, November, 1957. (8 References).
Documents three case histories of infants with metaphyseal fractures.
In two of the cases the fractures probably resulted from obstetrical
trauma, but in the third case, repeated direct injury to the left shoulder
was inflicted and admitted by the parents. Previously, fractures involving bone destruction and periosteal new bone development were misdiagnosed
as syphilis, tuberculosis, scurvy or osteomyelitis. In all three cases
the fractures were responsive to treatment and healed rapidly.

904 Woolley, Paul V., and Evans, William A., Jr. "Significance of
     skeletal lesions in infants resembling those of traumatic origin."
     JAMA 158(7): 539-43, June 18, 1955. (7 References).
Summarizes the questions raised in the recent literature concerning the
diagnosis of obscure, unrecognized skeletal complications in infants.
The study investigates the origin of multiple skeletal lesions accrued
over an extended period of time in twelve infants in order to determine
if they were trauma-inflicted. No history adequately explaining the
lesions was given. Up to now such lesions have been categorized as syndromes of unknown etiology. The most common manifestations are subdural
hematoma and metaphysial fragility. An investigation into the patients'
surroundings at home revealed that the twelve infants under study reportedly came from unstable families. When the infants were removed from
their homes they recovered rapidly and no new signs of skeletal irregularities developed. Evidence supports the unpleasant conclusion that
skeletal lesions in infants are often a result of the repeated use of
force against them.

905 Wurfel, Lois J., and McCoy, W. T. "Radiographic features of the
     battered child syndrome." J Coll Radiol Aust 9(3): 220-23,
     October, 1965. (6 References).

A description of the radiologic features of twenty-six cases of child abuse. Gross fractures, metaphyseal fractures, epiphyseal displacements and periosteal reactions were noted. Difficulties occurring when a radiographic exam is attempted on an infant are discussed. Radiologic findings remain central in the diagnosis of child abuse, and often there is no other evidence for the syndrome.

3. INTERNAL TRAUMA

906   Bongiovi, Joseph J., and Logosso, Ronald D. "Pancreatic pseudocyst occurring in the battered child syndrome." J Pediatr Surg 4(2): 220-26, April, 1969. (11 References).
A detailed account of the first documented case of pancreatic pseudocyst resulting from physical abuse. The five-year-old child was treated successfully with external drainage. Pseudocyst of the pancreas should be considered in a child with fever, vomiting, abdominal pain, and an abdominal mass. The possibility of intraabdominal injury in the battered child should not be overlooked by the examining physician.

907   Bratu, Marcel; Dower, John C.; Siegel, Bernard; et al. "Jejunal hematoma, child abuse, and Felson's sign." Conn Med 34(4): 261-64, April, 1970. (15 References).
Describes intramural hematoma of the jejunum and its relation to child abuse. One child, his injuries, and their repair are described in depth. The rarity of such injuries often leads to missed diagnosis. However, cases reported in the literature indicate that many cases are of boys of school age who are prone to heavy activity. Vomiting and constipation are common symptoms, and x-rays often reveal an intramural mass. Treatment includes draining of the hematoma and possible surgery if the intestinal block remains.

908   Dargan, E. L. "Pancreatic pseudocysts in childhood." J Natl Med Assoc 58(3): 179-81, May, 1966. (13 References).
Suggests that pancreatic pseudocysts be checked for in the differential diagnosis of abdominal masses in abused children.

909   Eisenstein, Elliot M.; Delta, Basil G.; Clifford, John H. "Jejunal hematoma: an unusual manifestation of the battered-child syndrome." Clin Pediatr 4(8): 436-40, August, 1965. (30 References).
Documents a case of a thirty-eight-month-old male with intramural hematoma of the jejunum secondary to abuse. This is believed to be the only reported case with these features.

910   Gornall, P.; Ahmed, S.; Jolleys, A.; et al. "Intra-abdominal injuries in the battered baby syndrome." Arch Dis Child 47(252): 211-14, April, 1972. (13 References).
Compares the intraabdominal injuries of six children resulting from physical abuse with the intraabdominal injuries of sixty-nine other children resulting from accidents. Liver and intestinal injuries, usually accompanied by external bruising, are most common among battered children. Kidney and spleen injuries, often found in conjunction with other visceral lesions, are most common among children involved in accidents. The case histories of the six battered children are presented in detail, along with x-rays and photographs. Two of the battered children died because their parents delayed obtaining treatment for them.

911 Hamlin, Hannibal. "Subgaleal hematoma caused by hair-pull: letter
      to editor." JAMA 204(4): 339, April 22, 1968. (4 References).
The most frequent cause of subgaleal hematoma is abusive hair-pulling,
according to this author.

912 Keeney, Ronald E. "Enlarging on the child abuse injury spectrum."
      Am J Dis Child 130(8): 902, August, 1976. (4 References).
A three-and-one-half-year-old girl was admitted to a hospital semicon-
scious with a severely bruised face, pancreatitis, and lytic bone lesions.
Her father alleged that the injuries were caused by a supposed car
accident in which she hit her head on the dashboard. Blatant discrepancies between the explanation for the child's injuries and the actual
findings was an indication that the child had been abused.

913 Kim, Taek, and Jenkins, Melvin E. "Pseudocyst of the pancreas as
      a manifestation of the battered-child syndrome: report of a case."
      Med Ann DC 36(11): 664-66, November, 1967. (12 References).
Describes a case history of a three-year-old boy who suffered pseudocyst
of the pancreas after blunt trauma to the abdomen. This condition often
follows abdominal trauma and needs to be recognized by physicians as
evidence of the battered child syndrome. The boy's mother was suspected
of inflicting the injury.

914 Kunstadter, Ralph H.; Singer, Myron H.; Steinberg, Rose. "The
      'battered child' and the celiac syndrome." Ill Med J 132(3):
      267-72, September, 1967. (11 References).
A detailed three-year medical and social case history of a boy with celiac
disease who was three years, nine months old when first admitted to the
hospital is described. The child was eventually removed from his family
and made rapid improvement. It is concluded that the cause of celiac
disease includes physical abuse or neglect.

915 McCort, James, and Vaudagna, James. "Visceral injuries in battered
      children." Radiology 82(3): 424-28, March, 1964. (10 Refer-
      ences).
Studies ten children, ranging in age from five to thirty months, with
initially unexplained visceral trauma. Medically detailed descriptions
of the injuries are provided. Malnutrition was noted in one child, poor
development in three, and severe anemia in two, suggesting that a positive correlation exists between neglect and abuse. The role of the
physician in detecting and reporting incidents of abuse is emphasized.
The avoidance of further injury to the child requires that the potential
for abuse be recognized and that the child be protected or removed from
his environment.

916 Morris, T. M. O., and Reay, H. A. J. "A battered child with pharyn-
      geal atresia." J Laryngol Otol 85(7): 729-31, July, 1971. (4
      References).
Physical manifestations and associated problems involving a possible congenital pharyngeal defect are presented for a seven-month-old female,
two of whose siblings were seriously abused by their parents. It was
thought likely that her condition placed her at increased risk of battering, given the associated difficulty with feeding. The case illustrates the necessity for careful follow-up of abused children and their
siblings.

917 Orton, Clive I. "Loss of columella and septum from an unusual form
     of child abuse." Plast Reconstr Surg 56(3): 345-46, September,
     1975. (6 References).
Presents a case report of two children, ages six and eight, who suffered
injuries of the nasal columella and septum because their mother had been
obsessively scouring the nasal secretions from their noses since infancy.
After the mother was separated from her children, the younger child was
provided a reconstruction of the columellar loss.

918 Owens, Mark P.; Wolfman, Earl F., Jr.; Chung, George K. "The manage-
     ment of liver trauma." Arch Surg 103: 211-15, August, 1971.
     (18 References).
Studies the treatment and mortality rate of liver trauma. The surgical
and post surgical procedures are described. Statistics show that mortality rates for both penetrating and blunt liver trauma have decreased
drastically between 1955 and 1969 due to medical advancement. Death is
more likely to occur where more than one organ is injured in addition to
liver damage. Various causes of injury with resulting mortality rates
are charted and discussed. Three cases involved battered children, one
who died.

919 Pena, Sergio D. J., and Medovy, Harry. "Child abuse and traumatic
     pseudocyst of the pancreas." J Pediatr 83(6): 1026-28, December,
     1973. (4 References).
Cites three case studies of children under three years of age with traumatic pseudocysts of the pancreas. Although abdominal trauma is quite
common in schoolage children and is usually an accident, abuse should be
strongly suspected if the child is under three and no appropriate explanation for the injury is given.

920 Rees, Alan; Symons, John; Joseph, Michael; et al. "Ventricular
     septal defect in a battered child." Br Med J 1(5948): 20-21,
     January 4, 1975. (13 References).
Summarizes the case history of a five-year-old girl with a ventricular
septal heart defect (V.S.D.) caused by a beating by her stepfather.
Photographs taken during surgery to correct the defect are reproduced.
The appearance of cardiac failure two weeks after the child was beaten,
the position of the defect, and the presence of an overlying aneurysm
confirmed the diagnosis of traumatic V.S.D.

921 Schechner, Stephen A., and Ehrlich, Frank E. "Case reports: gastric
     perforation and child abuse." J Trauma 14(8): 723-25, August,
     1974. (20 References).
Gastrointestinal lesions, reported to be the most common lesions suffered
by battered children, are produced by crushing, decelerating, or compres-
sing traumatic forces upon the visceral region. Accounts of two such
cases resulting from abdominal blows to a child who had just eaten are
given.

922 Slovis, Thomas L.; Berdon, Walter E.; Haller, Jack O.; et al.
     "Pancreatitis and the battered child syndrome: report of 2 cases
     with skeletal involvement." Am J Roentgenol Radium Ther Nucl Med
     125(1): 456-61, October, 1975. (14 References).
Two detailed cases of pancreatitis in children resulting from physical
abuse are presented, along with gastrointestinal and skeletal illustrations. Pancreatitis is unusual in children under age five and should

alert the physician to the possibility of abuse. Abdominal trauma is the
most common cause of the disorder in children. The roentgenographic
signs of pancreatitis are coarsened duodenal mucosa, obstruction of the
duodenum, or widening of the duodenal loop. Bone lesions are often seen
following pancreatitis. Enzymes released from the pancreas during acute
inflammation may reach the blood stream and react with the fat in the
bone morrow, causing hydrolysis and subsequent necrosis.

923   Stone, Richard K.; Harawitz, Alan; San Filippo, J. Anthony; et al.
      "Needle perforation of the liver in an abused infant." Clin
      Pediatr 15(10): 958-59, October, 1976. (6 References).
Relates a case of abdominal trauma in an abused child. The injury had
resulted from a needle pierced into the infant's liver. The diagnosis
of non-accidental injury was confirmed when records indicated that the
infant's sibling had been admitted to the hospital for abuse. The re-
examination of the sibling revealed new signs of trauma. Both children
were placed in a foster home. A group such as the Battered Child Committee can be utilized in the detection, diagnosis, and treatment of
battered infants.

924   Suson, Eduardo M.; Klotz, Donald, Jr.; Kottmeier, Peter K. "Liver
      trauma in children." J Pediatr Surg 10(3): 411-17, June, 1975.
      (15 References).
Among urban children studied who had experienced blunt abdominal trauma,
approximately one-third sustained liver injury, though more apparent
injuries were often treated first. More awareness on the part of physicians of liver injury is suggested. The most frequent causes of this
injury were: falls, vehicles striking pedestrians, and violent child
abuse.

925   Talbert, J. L., and Felman, A. H. "Identification and treatment of
      thoracoabdominal injuries in 'battered children.'" South Med Bull
      58(3): 37-43, June, 1970. (16 References).
Surveys the methods for assessing the extent of abdominal and genitouri-
nary injuries, and their utility in identifying cases of child abuse.

926   Thomas, Meirion, and Cameron, Alan. "Rarity of non-accidental
      penetrating injury in child abuse: letter to editor." Br Med J
      1(6057): 375, February 5, 1977. (0 References).
Although penetrating injury is not commonly associated with the battered
child syndrome, the possibility of non-accidental injury should always
be considered. A case study of the thirteen-month-old child with a penetrating injury is presented.

927   Tomasi, Lawrence G., and Rosman, N. Paul. "Purtscher retinopathy
      in the battered child syndrome." Am J Dis Child 129(11): 1335-
      37, November, 1975. (16 References).
Purtscher retinopathy--a hemorrhagic angiopathy resulting from sudden
compression of the thorax--should be added to the differential diagnosis
of hemorrhagic retinopathy in infancy and to the list of physical findings
associated with child abuse. Two case studies illustrate the importance
of a complete ophthalmological examination in infants for whom battering
is a possible diagnosis.

928   Touloukian, Robert J. "Abdominal visceral injuries in battered
      children." Pediatrics 42(4): 642-46, October, 1968. (15 Refer-
      ences).

Retrospective study of five cases of fatal abdominal visceral injuries caused by abuse. Pathological findings were commonly found in the duodenum, proximal jejunum, pancreas, and mesentery. A blow or punch to the mid-abdomen was the probable cause of the injuries which were usually accompanied by multiple ecchymoses and fresh bruises. Among childhood deaths due to battering in Rhode Island, visceral injuries comprised 25 percent. The need to suspect visceral injury in any abused child who has abdominal complaints is stressed.

929 ————. "Battered children with abdominal trauma." GP 40(6): 106-9, December, 1969. (0 References).
A description of abdominal trauma in children due to non-accidental injury is presented, along with illustrations, x-rays, and photographs. Visceral injury should be suspected in any child with abdominal complaints who has multiple ecchymoses and fresh bruises covering his body. The organs most likely affected in abdominal injury due to battering are the pancreas, duodenum, mesentery, and proximal jejunum. The most important diagnostic test for abdominal injury due to physical abuse is a careful physical examination. Other methods of differentiating accidental from non-accidental trauma are also discussed.

930 ————. "Visceral injury caused by trauma in children: abstract." Mod Med 37(22): 117, November 3, 1969. (0 References).
Kidney and spleen injuries are most common in blunt abdominal trauma, and these may go undiagnosed in abused children in spite of their battered appearance. Prompt diagnosis of these injuries is suggested.

4. VISUAL PROBLEMS

931 "Child with congenital glaucoma may be [the] victim of parental abuse." US Med 11(14): 6, July 15, 1975. (0 References).
Describes a case history of a nine-week-old battered child presenting congenital glaucoma. Symptoms included hazy corneas with unusually high interocular pressures and a mass lesion in the iris, with further examination showing a separation of the iris from its attachment. Treatment included a trabeculectomy in both eyes. The presence of other facial and chest injuries suggested abuse. Physicians were urged not to overlook the possibilities of abuse in child injuries and to report these suspicions.

932 Coyle, J. Terrence, and Smith, Ronald E. "Alkali retinopathy: letters to editor." Arch Ophthalmol 94(9): 1629, September, 1976. (2 References).
Symptoms of child abuse which were overlooked in a recent article are cited. Lye burns of the eye do not entirely account for all of the child's retinal damage. The response to this letter explains the particular child's situation further, while generally agreeing that abuse must be considered in cases of ocular trauma.

933 Friendly, David S. "Ocular manifestations of physical child abuse." Trans Am Acad Ophthalmol Otolaryngol 75(2): 318-32, March-April, 1971. (16 References).
Deals with the eye injuries which are often symptomatic of child abuse. Examining physicians need to keep in mind the possibility of abuse in diagnosing such injuries. Five case histories are presented which link

eye injuries with abuse. Mention is made of a study of a group of abused children which describes ocular injuries in one-fourth of the cases.

934 Harcourt, Brian, and Hopkins, David. "Ophthalmic manifestations of the battered-baby syndrome." Br Med J 3(5771): 398-401, August 14, 1971. (18 References).
Eight out of eleven cases of battered babies with ocular manifestations of their abuse suffered permanent impairment of the visual function. It is emphasized that a significant number of abused children suffer from severe visual handicap. The presence of severe intraocular hemorrhages should raise the suspicion of abuse and lead to careful assessment of the chances for recovery of full visual function.

935 ————. "Permanent chorio-retinal lesions in childhood of sus-pected traumatic origin." Trans Ophthalmol Soc UK 93: 199-205, 1973. (7 References).
Details the etiology of retinal hemorrhages, complete with photographs of damaged eyes. Because retinal hemorrhages occur as a result of a rise in intracranial blood pressure--such as being swung by the feet or trunk compression--abuse should be suspected as a possible cause. Diagnostic features to distinguish retinal lesions due to physical abuse from those due to other causes are carefully outlined.

936 Kiffney, G. T., Jr. "The eye of the battered child." Arch Ophthalmol 72: 231-33, August, 1964. (3 References).
Describes a case study of a seven-month-old victim of the battered child syndrome. Clinical findings reveal bilateral retinoblastoma or bilateral organized vitreous hemorrhage secondary to trauma. Traumatic retinal detachment is therefore considered a possibility in the differential diagnosis of retinoblastoma.

937 Morgan, Gwyn, and Mushin, Alan S. "Ocular injury in the battered baby syndrome: report of two cases." Br J Ophthalmol 55(5): 343-47, May, 1971. (11 References).
Details the clinical and pathological features of eyes removed from two battered children. In the first case, the original diagnosis was Coat's disease. Six months later, the child lost his eye, clearly because of post concussional injury. Clinicians, particularly ocular pathologists, must consider the possibility of battering in diagnosing childhood ocular conditions such as pseudoglioma, Coat's disease, lens dislocation, and intraocular haemorrhages of any kind.

938 Mushin, Alan S. "Ocular damage in the battered-baby syndrome." Br Med J 3(5771): 402-4, August 14, 1971. (10 References).
Documents twelve cases of the battered child syndrome in which vision was permanently impaired. Such impairment in one or both eyes occurred in twelve out of twelve battered babies with ocular damage. The frequency of permanent damage is not widely recognized; all infants suspected of being battered should be referred to an opthalmologist for ocular examina-tion both at the time of injury and at follow-up.

939 Mushin, Alan S., and Morgan, Gwyn. "Ocular injury in the battered baby syndrome: report of two cases." Br J Ophthalmol 55: 343-47, (11 References).
Two case histories illustrate some of the more common eye injuries which can result from child battering. Ocular pathologists are advised not to

mistake eye injuries which are traumatic for pseudogioma, Coat's disease, lens dislocation, or intraocular hemorrhage.

940   Tseng, Stanley S., and Keys, Marshall P. "Battered child syndrome simulating congenital glaucoma." Arch Ophthalmol 94(5): 839-40, May, 1976. (7 References).

A child previously diagnosed with congenital glaucoma was later discovered to be suffering from maltreatment. In addition to glaucoma, probably induced by trauma, the child showed gross signs of neglect. A review of research on ocular injuries related to abuse cases is given, with the warning that maltreatment should be considered when allegedly congenital glaucoma is present.

941   Weidenthal, Daniel T., and Levin, Daniel B. "Retinal detachment in a battered infant." Am J Ophthalmol 81(6): 725-27, June, 1976. (7 References).

Presents a detailed case report of a twelve-week-old battered infant with bilateral retinal detachments. Surgery was performed on the right eye to reattach the retina, and limited vision was restored. Retinal damage due to physical abuse can be differentiated from damage resulting from congenital anomalies by a complete medical and social history, other evidence of abuse, the location of the retinal pathology, and absence of a lens coloboma.

942   Zadik, Donna. "Social and medical aspects of the battered child with vision impairment." New Outlook Blind 67(6): 241-50, June, 1973. (22 References).

Cases of abuse among children with visual defects are studied. Demographic data regarding socioeconomic level, age, sex of the child, and perpetrators were found to be similar to the general population.

5. POISONING

943   Brings, E. G. "Sudden and unexpected death: letter to editor." Pediatrics 39(5): 792-93, May, 1967. (2 References).

A report of two cases in which alcohol consumption led to the asphyxiation of children with nasal congestion. It is suggested that the use of nasal decongestants in small children may also result in sudden unexpected death.

944   Dershewitz, Robert; Vestal, Bonita; MacLaren, Noel K.; et al. "Transient hepatomegaly and hypoglycemia: a consequence of malicious insulin administration." Am J Dis Child 130(9): 998-99, September, 1976. (22 References).

Reports the case of a three-and-one-half-year-old black girl admitted to a hospital on two separate occasions with severe hypoglycemia. Although hypoglycemic episodes occurred frequently in childhood, it was determined that this girl's problem was due to malicious insulin administration. Distinguishing signs of deliberate insulin poisoning are excessive amounts of the substance in the plasma at the time of the episode associated with transient hepatomegaly. These medical findings in conjunction with a family history and evaluation of the incident should lead to the suspicion of inflicted insulin overdose.

945 Dine, Mark S. "Tranquilizer poisoning: an example of child abuse."
      Pediatrics 36(5): 782-85, November, 1965. (17 References).
Relates a case report of a parent deliberately poisoning her child with
tranquilizers. Parallels between this type of abuse and other forms of
maltreatment are drawn. Abusing parents typically deny any responsibility
for the injury. In this instance, the mother's repeated denials significantly delayed a proper diagnosis. Physicians need to be alert to the
symptoms of drug ingestion as a form of child abuse and to exercise
routine tests to detect intoxication. The study urges physicians to report
a high index of suspicion in their final diagnoses in order to facilitate
the detection of abuse in general.

946 Fleisher, David, and Ament, Marvin E. "Diarrhea, red diapers, and
      child abuse." Clin Pediatr 17(9): 820-24, September, 1977. (19
      References).
Offers three case studies of babies given laxatives containing phenolphthalein by their mothers. The children all had to be hospitalized for
intense diarrhea, and all showed pin-red stools or urine. All three
mothers, though apparently good parents, were found to be psychologically
disturbed. Physicians are warned to consider phenolphthalein poisoning
as a form of child abuse when a patient's intractable diarrhea cannot be
traced to usual causes.

947 Jones, M. Douglas, Jr., and Helfer, Ray E. "A teething lotion
      resulting in the misdiagnosis of diphenylhydantoin administration."
      Am J Dis Child 122(3): 259-60, September, 1971. (3 References).
A four-month-old boy, in his third hospital admission, was being examined
for failure to thrive symptoms and possible child abuse. It was discovered by the method of Svensmark and Kristensen that serum diphenylhydantoin levels were faultily recorded in the child. It was suspected
that parents had administered diphenylhydantoin to the boy as a sedative.
The parents claimed, however, to have given him only a multivitamin preparation and Dr. Hand's teething lotion. Further investigation revealed
constituents in the commercial teething preparation acted as agents and
led to fallacious results in the determination of diphenylhydantoin
concentration in serum.

948 Lansky, Lester L. "An unusual case of childhood chloral hydrate
      poisoning." Am J Dis Child 127(2): 275-76, February, 1974.
      (10 References).
A three-year-old comatose patient was found to have been repeatedly
poisoned by her mother. Those indicators of coma related to toxic-
metabolic encephalopathy are listed, along with several additional case
reports of chloral hydrate intoxication.

949 Malee, Thomas J. "Drug abuse in a small community." Rocky Mt Med J
      69(5): 66-67, May, 1972. (0 References).
Relates a case study of a five-year-old girl who ingested an overdose of
Placidyl from her mother's medicine cabinet. The mother was a known
drug user, and this knowledge facilitated the diagnosis of the child's
comatose condition.

950 Pickering, Douglas. "Neonatal hypoglycemia due to salicylate poison-
      ing." Proc R Soc Med 61: 40, December, 1968. (5 References).
Cites a case of aspirin poisoning in a nineteen-day-old girl. It could
not be determined whether the poisoning had been accidental or intentional
since the child's parents contradicted each other.

951 ————. Salicylate poisoning as a manifestation of the battered
      child syndrome." Am J Dis Child 130(6): 675-76, June, 1976.
      (1 Reference).
Details a non-accidental salicylate poisoning of an infant (from aspirin)
as the first episode of child abuse. Due to the difficulty in distinguishing deliberate from accidental poisoning, the infant was discharged
from the hospital to her mother. Later she was readmitted for treatment
of injuries resulting from a severe beating. It is recommended that
blood and urine samples from battered infants be analyzed upon admission
to the hospital.

952 Pickering, Douglas; Moncrieff, Martin W.; Etches, P. C. "Non-
      accidental poisoning and child abuse: letter to editor." Br Med J
      1(6019): 1210-11, May 15, 1976. (4 References).
Presents two case histories of non-accidental poisonings and stresses the
need for suspicion of poisoning in high risk families having children
hospitalized for inexplicable illnesses.

953 Rogers, David; Tripp, John; Bentovim, Arnon; et al. "Non-accidental
      poisoning: an extended syndrome of child abuse." Br Med J 1(6013):
      793-96, April 3, 1976. (7 References).
Six case studies of children who were deliberately poisoned by their
parents are presented. Features which may lead to the detection of non-
accidental poisoning include: (1) bizarre symptoms with no apparent
pathological explanation; (2) knowledge that the drug is available to the
parent; (3) history of parental overdose or abuse; (4) psychosocial stress
in the family; (5) episodic illness in the child; and (6) detection of
the drug in the child's urine, blood, or gastric contents. A plan for
the management of cases of non-accidental poisoning is outlined, and the
underlying causes of this form of abuse are briefly examined.

6. OTHER PHYSICAL SIGNS

954 Adelson, Lester. "Homicide by pepper." J Forensic Sci 9(3): 391-
      95, July, 1964. (3 References).
Describes an unusual case of child abuse. A child died of asphyxia when
her mother poured black pepper into her mouth, resulting in a blockage
of the air passageways. The large difference in physical size and
strength between adults and children makes the employment of such bizarre
homicidal techniques relatively easy.

955 Anderson, William R., and Hudson, R. Page. "Self-inflicted bite
      marks in battered child syndrome." Forensic Sci 7(1): 71-74,
      January-February, 1976. (5 References).
Bite marks on a child abuse victim can be a clue to the identification
of the abuser. A dental examination of all individuals having contact
with the victim should be carried out if bite marks are present. Dental
photographs and impressions can then be compared to the pattern of bite
marks on the victim's body. The possibility that the bites were self-
inflicted should not be dismissed without investigation. In the autopsy
of a three-year-old girl, it was determined that the bite marks on her
arms were self-inflicted. It was believed that the child had bitten
herself in an effort to stiffle crying or to cope with intense pain.

956   Barta, Rudolph A., and Smith, Nathan J. "Willful trauma to young
      children, a challenge to the physician." Clin Pediatr 2(10): 545-
      54, October 19, 1963. (0 References).
Several case studies illustrate the deliberate infliction of injury upon
very young children--six of them only a few months old. Perhaps because
most of the children came from middle-class families, the diagnosis of
battered child syndrome was resisted by the attending physician until
damage had been compounded in some cases. Photographs of x-rays are
included.

957   Berant, Moshe, and Jacobs, J. "A 'pseudo' battered child." Clin
      Pediatr 5(4): 230-37, April, 1966. (8 References).
Presents the case history of a two-year, eight-month-old boy whose condition resembled the battered child syndrome but was later diagnosed as
scurvy. The child's poor health, painful swellings of the legs, shoulder
and arm, a possible fracture, and the confused history presented by a
pregnant, unhappy mother indicated possible abuse. Further examination
of the child, coupled with the behavior of the parents during the child's
hospitalization, discounted the possibility of maltreatment. A presentation of family history and differential diagnoses are included.

958   Bhattacharya, A. K., and Mandal, J. N. "Battered child syndrome:
      a review with a report of two siblings." Indian Pediatr 4(4):
      186-94, April, 1967. (9 References).
A comprehensive review of American and British literature is given for
the purpose of increasing knowledge of child abuse in India. The clinical
findings of two cases of battered children, reportedly the first to be
recorded in India, are described in detail. A call for a complete investigation of the prevalence of the battered child syndrome in India is
made.

959   Boysen, Bette E. "Chylous ascites: manifestation of the battered
      child syndrome." Am J Dis Child 129(11): 1338-39, November,
      1975. (8 References).
A twenty-month-old boy was admitted to the hospital with burn scars,
healing fractures, and a grossly distended abdomen. The diagnosis of
chylous ascites was made and confirmed, with the origin presumed to be
traumatic. No previously reported cases of chylous ascites secondary to
abuse were found in a review of the literature.

960   Butler, Karen O. "Accidental injury?" J Emerg Nurs 3: 43-45,
      March-April, 1977. (4 References).
Describes an emergency medical team's correct diagnosis of child abuse
in the case of a thirteen-month-old girl. Although an initial medical
examination uncovered no suspicious abnormalities, a skeletal x-ray
revealed multiple fractures. A complete pediatric physical uncovered
ecchomyotic marks on the face and arm, indications that the child was
forcibly grabbed by an adult. The child's passive behavior during the
examination first alerted the attendant staff to the possibility of non-
accidental injury.

961   Debenham, Arthur E. "Cruelty and neglect." In: Debenham, Arthur
      E. The innocent victims: a warning to parents, a textbook of
      crimes committed by and against children. Sydney, Australia:
      Edwards and Shaw, 1969. 99-123.
Details case histories of severely abused or neglected children in Australia. Accounts of the disposition of their cases are outlined.

962   Galdston, Richard. "The burning and the healing of children."
      Psychiatry 35(1): 57-66, February, 1972. (8 References).
A clinical study of 100 burned children ranging in age from ten months to
sixteen-and-one-half years. Fourteen children were burned by adults, five
as the result of deliberate abuse, ten by other children and seventy-six
by themselves. Direct interviews, sustained observations of parents and
children, and staff reports presented during hospitalization provided
the basis for the author's conclusions. Three causal factors were identified in every incident: a burning agent, the presence of a child, and
the absence of adult attention or supervision. These factors are discussed individually, with particular consideration given to the subtleties
of parent-child interaction and the factors which may cause a child to
perceive the loss of parental control, allowing his own impulses to erupt.
The lack of adult supervision ranged from chronic and severe neglect to
temporary lapses in ordinarily high-attention situations. Marital discord
was found in association with self-inflicted, accidental burns in older
boys. Considerable discussion is devoted to the psychological effects
of the burning and healing process and to the extended role of the nurse.

963   Gillespie, Robert W. "The battered child syndrome: thermal and
      caustic manifestations." J Trauma 5(4): 523-34, July, 1965.
      (18 References).
Nineteen children (ranging in age from one day to ten years), who had
received willfully inflicted thermal injuries, were the subject for this
Nebraska-based study. The study's purpose was to determine the incidence
of thermal injuries in the battered child syndrome and to identify injury
characteristics which would point to a diagnosis of abuse. Reports from
practicing physicians, city and county officials in Lincoln, the office
of the coroner in Omaha, and a review of hospital records constituted the
basis of the study. All children showed evidence of repeated abuse and
many suffered multiple burns inflicted at different time intervals.
Injury was attributed to parent psychosis in four instances and to parent
alcoholism in three. Eight cases were triggered by the child's minor
misbehavior or enuresis and in four instances the child was unwanted by
the parents. Clinical findings at variance with the history and the
location of burns on parts of the body which would rule out self-inflicted
injury are cited as signs pointing to willful abuse. Attention should be
directed to associated injuries and to the presence of malnutrition. The
repetitious nature of these injuries is an indictment of society's failure
to intervene to protect the child. The true frequency of thermal injury
cannot be determined until adequate reporting systems are instituted but
its occurrence is clearly enough established to warrant measures insuring
the child's protection.

964   Joos, Thad H. "Child abuse: a different point of view: letter to
      editor." Pediatrics 45(3, Part I): 510-11, March, 1970. (4
      References).
Discusses a subtle form of child abuse--a refusal to remove a pet from
the home when it causes allergic disease in the child.

965   Keen, J. H.; Lendrum, J.; Wolman, B. "Inflicted burns and scalds
      in children." Br Med J 4(5991): 268-69, November 1, 1975. (8
      References).
A survey of children presenting with burns or scaldings over a three
year period in a British hospital revealed that sixteen children had been
the probable victims of child abuse. Several indications of non-acci-

dental burns or scaldings are enumerated. They include contradictory or vague explanations of how the injury occurred, burns to the buttock or perineum, dip scaldings with a clear margin on the hands and feet in children old enough to have pulled away, cigarette or repeated burns, and burns found in conjunction with other injuries such as fractures or subdural hematomas. Skeletal x-rays, case conferences, and intervention by social services are suggested procedures for the management of suspected cases of non-accidental burns.

966 Kempe, C. Henry. "Uncommon manifestations of the battered child syndrome." Am J Dis Child 129(11): 1265, November, 1975. (2 References).
Delineates eleven rare manifestations of physical abuse.

967 Koch, Charles; Minuchin, Salvator; Donovan, Woodrow M. "A case of somatic expression of family and environmental stress." Clin Pediatr 13(10): 815-18, October, 1974. (0 References).
A case history of an eighteen-year-old girl who suffered from a variety of physical and psychological problems at different stages of her life is used to illustrate the impact of various social forces on a child's well-being. Physicians tended to view the girl's symptoms independent of her environment and history. It was revealed that upsets in her family life (including placement in several different foster homes, abuse, and lack of emotional support) may, in fact, have been responsible for the patient's physical and emotional instability.

968 Laing, S. A., and Buchan, A. R. "Bilateral injuries in childhood: an alerting sign?: letter to editor." Br Med J 2(6041): 940-41, October, 1976. (0 References).
Reports a study of 481 nursery school children having 1,543 accidental injuries over a two month period. None of the injuries were found to be bilateral, which suggests that a child having bilateral trauma should alert the examining physician to the possibility of child abuse. In order to provide assistance in distinguishing accidental from non-accidental injury cases, a small number of senior physicians with expertise in the area of child abuse are available to give advice to general practitioners in Leicestershire, England.

969 Levine, Lowell J. "The solution of a battered-child homicide by dental evidence: report of case." J Am Dent Assoc 87(6): 1234-36, November, 1973. (0 References).
Illustrates the use of dental evidence in solving a battered child homicide case. Bite marks found on a dead baby were used by a dentist to identify the assailant, a four-and-one-half-year-old child. Details of the investigative procedures involved in linking human bite marks with individuals are given.

970 Lung, Richard J.; Miller, Stephen H.; Davis, Thomas S.; et al. "Recognizing burn injuries as child abuse." Am Fam Physician 15(4): 134-35, April, 1977. (0 References).
Presents five case histories and photographs of children with burns due to child abuse. When burns are distributed in an unusual way on the body and are claimed to be caused by accidental scalding, child abuse should be suspected.

971 Miles, A. E. "Forensic aspects of odontology: a museum exhibit."
     Proc R Soc Med 64(2): 112, February, 1971. (3 References).
Describes a new exhibit, "Forensic Aspects of Odontology," on display in
the Royal College of Surgeons Odontological Museum. One aspect of the
exhibit covers bite marks, a potential feature in the battered baby syndrome.

972 Nelson, Gerald D., and Paletta, F. X. "Burns in children." Surg
     Gynecol Obstet 128(3): 518-22, March, 1969. (14 References).
Discusses methods of treating burns in children, with reference to the
treatment of 460 patients who were given acclusive dressings without
topical agents. The ages of the children and causes and types of burns
are enumerated, along with the effects of the treatment. Child abuse was
ascertained in only one case but was suspected in others.

973 Nixon, James, and Pearn, John. "Non-accidental immersion in bath-
     water: another aspect of child abuse." Br Med J 1(6056): 271-
     72, January 29, 1977. (5 References).
Summarizes a study of near-drownings and bathtub deaths of young children.
Infants were most often the victims of accidental immersion, whereas
toddlers were frequently deliberately immersed by their parents. Most
parents were overcome by remorse upon seeing their child lose consciousness and sought emergency medical attention. Pneumonia and other respira-
tory ailments are possible consequences of deliberate immersion.

974 Nong the Anh. "Pseudo-battered child syndrome: letter to editor."
     JAMA 236(20): 2288, November, 1976. (2 References).
Points out that a Vietnamese child with ecchymoses and bilateral bruises
on his/her chest and back may be misdiagnosed as physically abused. It
may be that the child was given "Cao Gio," a home treatment which consists of using a boiled egg or coin to scratch the balsamed skin of the
sick person to help rid the body of "bad winds."

975 Palmer, C. H., and Weston, J. T. "Several unusual cases of child
     abuse." J Forensic Sci 21(4): 851-55, October, 1976. (8 Refer-
     ences).
Among all childhood deaths in New Mexico during 1974 and 1975, nine
resulted from child abuse or neglect. Included in this toll were children of Indian, Spanish-American, Anglo and Negro descent, ranging in
age from three months to five years. In this article, four of these
cases are presented in detail. One death was due to complications resulting from gross medical neglect, while the others resulted from
physical abuse inflicted by parents or close relatives. The cases presented are considered to be unusual because of the distribution of
pathologic findings or because of problems encountered in court presentation of the case.

976 Pickel, Stuart; Anderson, Charles; Holliday, Malcolm A. "Thirsting
     and hypernatremic dehydration -- a form of child abuse." Pediatrics
     45(1, Part I): 54-59, January, 1970. (13 References).
Presents three cases of hypernatremic dehydration in children whose
mothers deprived them of fluids. Treatment of the physical condition
indicated that these children did not have the sodium deficits normally
associated with dehydration. The severity of the dehydration, evidence
of bruising, and reports from outside observers indicated all three children suffered from periodic water deprivation, a form of child abuse not
commonly recognized.

977   Polomeque, F. E., and Harrston, M. A., Jr. "'Battered child' syn-
         drome: unusual dermatological manifestation." <u>Arch Dermatol</u> 90:
         326-27, September, 1964.
Describes the dermatological nature of a battered child who is abused by
his parents and four siblings. The pediatrics division of a New Orleans
hospital found human bites imprinted on the child's body. The child also
suffered from malnutrition and growth retardation.

978   Priestley, B. L. "Drug addiction and the newborn." <u>Proc R Soc Med</u>
         65(10): 26, October, 1972. (6 References).
Describes the symptoms and treatment of drug addiction in newborn infants,
with the warning that the long-term effects of the dependence and the
withdrawal from it might be irreversible. Separation of the infant from
his parents is recommended.

979   Robertson, I., and Hodge, P. R. "Histopathology of healing abra-
         sions." <u>Forensic Sci</u> 1(1): 17-25, April, 1972. (3 References).
Accounts of a histological analysis of skin abrasions from the bodies of
accident victims. The intent was to determine criteria for assessing
the amount of time between injury and death.

980   Seville, R. H. "Elastic band injuries: letter to editor." <u>Br Med J</u>
         1(5592): 643, March 9, 1968. (0 References).
Relates a case in which a rubber band wrapped around a child's neck resulted in injury. The case serves as an example of the possibility that
subconscious motivations may operate in injuries which are patently accidental.

981   Sims, B. G., and Cameron, J. Malcolm. "Bite-marks in the 'battered
         child syndrome'." <u>Med Sci Law</u> 13(3): 207-10, July, 1973. (8
         References).
Bite marks have become an increasingly frequent manifestation of the
battered baby syndrome. Three case reports of children under three years
of age, one who had been severely abused, and two who had been fatally
injured, are discussed. Procedures for determining the assailant are
often effective, and the clinical findings can be used as evidence in
court.

982   Stone, Nelson H.; Rinaldo, Lucille; Humphrey, Charles R.; <u>et al</u>.
         "Child abuse by burning." <u>Surg Clin North Am</u> 50(6): 1419-24,
         December, 1970. (0 References).
Describes the incidence, symptoms, and management of child abuse by burning. Of all burned patients admitted to the Children's Division of Cook
County Hospital over a four year period, 4.2 percent were deliberately
abused. The patients averaged three years of age, with boys being the
most frequently maltreated. When a physician suspects abuse, the child
is hospitalized and the parents are referred to a medical social worker.
The Committee on Child Abuse evaluates the family, and if the abuse
diagnosis is confirmed, it is reported to the Department of Children and
Family Services which determines future action.

983   Sussman, Sidney J. "Skin manifestations of the battered-child
         syndrome." <u>J Pediatr</u> 72(1): 99-101, January, 1968. (5 Refer-
         ences).
Skin lesions are a more common finding in abuse than are intracranial
trauma and bone changes. The characteristics which distinguish abuse-

associated skin lesions from other conditions are listed. Most importantly, lesions that are not the result of deliberate injury tend to have
non-specific shapes, to be of similar age, and to be located on the
extremities. Eleven case histories are documented.

984   Swanson, David W.; Bratrude, Amos P.; Brown, Edward M. "Alcohol
      abuse in a population of Indian children." Dis Nerv Syst 32:
      835-42, 1971. (22 References).
Studies the effect of excessive consumption of alcohol upon the Calville
Indians, particularly its impact among a group of forty-two young people
ranging from two to sixteen years in age. Many of these children had
become alcoholics, and many of them had parents who were alcoholics.
Drunkenness was conventionally accepted; in the young people it led to
promiscuity, pregnancy, delinquency, and various forms of violence,
including suicide.

985   Tate, R. J. "Facial injuries associated with the battered child
      syndrome." Br J Oral Surg 9(1): 41-45, July, 1971. (7 Refer-
      ences).
The incidence of facial trauma in battered children has increased in the
past few years and now occurs more often than trauma to other parts of
the body. Facial injury may result from a blow intended to silence a
crying or screaming child. A correct diagnosis is paramount to insure
the future safety of the battered child. Several case studies are presented.

986   Wei, Stephen H. "Prevention of injuries to anterior teeth." Int
      Dent J 24(1): 30-49, March, 1974. (114 References).
Discusses the reasons for the increase of traumatic injuries to anterior
teeth and their treatment. Depending on the age of the child, there are
different reasons for the injury. Accidents most likely occur when a
child is very hungry, tired, or hyperactive. Play activity and bicycle
and automobile accidents also cause dental injury. Dentists must be
especially alert for symptoms of the battered child syndrome when treating oral injuries. If he recognizes bruises, abrasions, bite marks,
hematomas, or other symptoms, the dentist must help prevent further abuse
to the child.

987   West, S. "Acute periosteal swellings in several young infants of
      the same family, probably rickety in nature." Br Med J 1(1425):
      856-57. April 21, 1888. (0 References).
Several children of the same family with acute periosteal swellings
attributed to rickets are described. A relationship between the quality
of milk in the diet and the resulting rickets or scurvy is suggested.
Syphilis is also considered among the various physicians' opinions
listed.

988   Wickes, Ian G., and Zaidi, Zafar H. "Battered or pigmented?:
      letter to editor." Br Med J 2(5810): 404, May 13, 1972. (0
      References).
Suggests the possibility that the presence of Mongolian spots—grey-blue
areas of pigmentation on various parts of the body—may lead to a diagnosis of battering. Although this pigmentation is rarely of clinical
significance, the possibility of battering should not be precluded. Two
very brief case studies are presented.

989 Yeatman, Gentry W.; Shaw, Constance; Barlow, Matthew J.; et al.
      "Pseudo-battering in Vietnamese children." Pediatrics 58(4):
      616-18, October, 1976. (2 References).
Describes the lay practice of "Cao Gio" for the treatment of fever,
chills, and headaches in Vietnamese children. The practice consists of
applying oil to the back and chest, massaging the skin until warm, and
scraping the skin with the edge of a coin until petechiae and purpura
appear. Physicians should be aware of this pseudo-battering when dealing with Vietnamese families.

C. ABUSE: PSYCHOLOGICAL EFFECTS

990 Babow, Irving, and Babow, Robin. "The world of the abused child:
      a phenomenological report." Life-Threatening Behav 4(1): 32-42,
      Spring, 1974. (11 References).
An account of an interview with a twenty-one-year-old woman who had been
abused as a child by her mother and who later attempted suicide. Such
a phenomenological report may be of use in discovering the relationship
between child abuse and self-destructive behavior.

991 Bender, Barbara. "Self-chosen victims: scapegoating behavior
      sequential to battering." Child Welfare 55(6): 417-22, June,
      1976. (4 References).
Presents case histories of two battered children with a compulsive need
to provoke punishment from everyone with whom they came into contact.
Their scapegoating behavior is attributed to a sense of guilt resulting
from feelings of anger and aggression toward the abusive parent, an inability to deal with aggression, a confused sexual identity, and a sense
of inferiority. Gradual improvement resulted from treatment utilizing
symbolic play therapy.

992 Bloch, Dorothy. "Fantasy and the fear of infanticide." Psychoanal
      Rev 61(1): 5-31, Spring, 1974. (10 References).
Discusses children's fears of being killed by their parents; fears which
may stem from the witnessing of the parents' violent behavior and childhood feelings of guilt. In some cases, a child will construct a defensive fantasy, using the concept of an imaginary creature to represent the
parent. The child displaces his terror and is able to still look upon
his parents favorably. Often, a child will convince himself he is bad
and, therefore, deserving of parental hostility. A case study of a five-
year-old girl who felt her parents wanted to kill her is included, as are
some recommendations for treatment.

993 Bloom, Lawrence A. "Communication skills of abused children." For
      a summary see: Diss Abstr Int 36A(12): 7728, June, 1976.

994 Buist, Neil R. M. "Deliberate injury of children: letter to editor."
      Br Med J 4(5894): 739, December 22, 1973. (0 References).
Draws needed attention to the psychological abuse of children, which is
difficult to detect and can have lasting repercussions long after the
abuse is terminated. Concentrated efforts to define all aspects of psychological abuse are necessary in order to equip the social, medical, and
legal authorities with enough information to detect, treat, and hopefully
prevent emotional disturbance.

995 Christiansen, James L. "Educational and psychological problems of abused children." For a summary see: Diss Abstr Int 36A(9): 5988, March 1976.

996 Clyne, Max B. Absent: school refusal as an expression of disturbed family relationships. London: Tavistock, 1966. 269p. (Bibliography).
Absence from school may be related to deeper disturbances in the child's life. Attendance at school is the first contact where a child extends his relationships on a large scale; problems experienced in regular attendance may be an early sign of difficulties. Symptoms, treatment, etiology, and prevention of absenteeism from school are discussed in detail.

997 Elmer, Elizabeth. "Hazards in determining child abuse." Child Welfare 45(1): 28-33, January, 1966. (7 References).
Delineates conclusions relative to diagnosing child abuse reached as the result of a follow-up study of thirty-three allegedly abused children formerly suffering from multiple bone injuries. The study's original goal was the evaluation of these children's current status physically, intellectually, and socially. The secondary aim of the study was to determine common characteristics among their families. Problems included defining the limits of abuse, and determining the cause of multiple bone injuries. The study indicated that hasty and false accusations of caretakers damage parents and children psychologically, especially when added to the stress factors found to be present in non-abusive and abusive families at the time of injury.

998 Elmer, Elizabeth, and Gregg, Grace S. "Developmental characteristics of abused children." Pediatrics 40(4, Part I): 596-602, October, 1967. (12 References).
A follow-up study of the developmental characteristics of twenty children hospitalized for multiple bone injuries as a result of assault or gross neglect. These children were originally part of a group of fifty children who were admitted to Children's Hospital of Pittsburgh from 1949 to 1962, but who, for various reasons, including death, could not all be included in the final results. In 1963 the reevaluation began and consisted of the following methods: (1) interviews with the mothers emphasizing family history and child care; (2) questionnaires assessing parental attitudes of the mothers; (3) medical examinations of the children consisting of pediatric, psychiatric, audiometric, psychological, and skeletal evaluations; and (4) a review of school records to help estimate each child's intellectual functioning. In light of the information gathered, an assessment of the children's current condition was made. Results showed that many of the children exhibited signs of mental retardation, varying degrees of emotional disturbance, speech problems, and other physical defects related to previous injuries. In fact, only two were normal in all areas. Abuse was the sole cause of physical defects in one-third of the children. The other problems could have been due to prematurity, maternal deprivation, and child care practices stemming from different social environments. Some observations are made concerning the variations in child care practices from one racial group to another. Evidence indicated that prolonged neglect is more common among whites than blacks, that premature babies may cause more stress for whites than for blacks, and that black mothers perhaps have more family support while raising their children. The two normal children were black. Be-

cause the sequelae of abuse and neglect are extensive and, except for
growth failure, virtually irreversible, it is imperative that abuse be
detected early.

999   Endler, N. S.   "The case for person-situation interactions."   Can
       Psychol Rev   16(1):   12-21, January, 1975.   (78 References).
Examines the controversy between personologists and social psychologists
regarding the relation of personality to behavioral change, the former
holding that the change derives from some element in the individual's
personality, and the latter arguing that events, not personality, bring
about shifts in behavior.   Because neither exclusionist view has proven
conclusive, it is suggested that the interaction of events and personalities be studied.

1000   Galdston, Richard.   "Observations on children who have been phys-
        ically   abused and their parents."   Am J Psychiatry   122(4):   440-
        43, October, 1965.   (0 References).
Summarizes observations about physically abused children which have been
gathered over five years at Children's Hospital Medical Center, Boston.
Close human contact while hospitalized is strongly recommended for these
anxious or completely passive children to repair arrested and atrophying
ego skills.   Such contact often stimulates a return of appetite.   Parents
require psychotherapy to divert the focus of their pathology from their
children to its true source in their past.   They are described as ambivalent toward their children, perceiving in them the qualities of adults
who have once caused them pain.   Sensing their own hostility toward their
children, the abusing parents will often arrange for an alternate caretaker.   The breakdown of this arrangement frequently precipitates a confrontation with the child.   A reversal of traditional family roles is
also cited as a source of abuse.

1001   Gambino, Vincent.   "Psychological abuse related to interruptions
        in the psychosocial and cognitive development of disturbed chil-
        dren."   For a summary see: Diss Abstr Int   37A(8):   4983, February,
        1977.

1002   Gay, James R.   "A comparison of abused, neglected, and normal chil-
        dren utilizing the Children's Behavioral Classification Project."
        For a summary see: Diss Abstr Int   37B(6):   3073, December, 1976.

1003   Green, Arthur H.   "Self-destructive behavior in physically abused
        schizophrenic children."   Arch Gen Psychiatry   19(2):   171-79,
        August, 1968.   (23 References).
A study designed to test the hypothesis that the occurrence of self-
mutilation bears a significant relationship to a prior history of physical abuse.   Seventy school age schizophrenic children were divided into
two groups according to the presence or absence of previous physical
abuse.   Self-mutilatory behavior was shown to be significantly related
to abuse.   Infantile headbanging was also noted to be a precursor to
self-mutilation but was separate and distinct from abuse.   Detailed
examination of case histories, several of which are presented, reveal
that physical abuse occurs in a context of severe rejection.   Abusive
mothers experienced severe deprivation and excessive physical punishment
as children and endowed their children with their own feelings of worthlessness.   Parental abuse of the child is alternated with parental withdrawal from the child, so that the child may tend to repeat the painful

experience in order to establish fundamentally needed contact with the parent. It is speculated that pain is associated with contact, and that the child learns to hurt himself in order to re-experience the pleasurable elements of parental attacks. If this theory is correct, then self-mutilation will persist until the basic needs for tactile stimulation and body contact are supplied in a more appropriate manner. It is suggested that the connection between physical abuse and self-destructive behavior be studied in non-schizophrenic children.

1004   Gross, Seymour Z. "Critique: children who break down in foster homes; a psychological study of patterns of personality growth in grossly deprived children." J Child Psychol Psychiatry 4(1): 61-66, April, 1963. (10 References).
Disagrees with the methods and interpretation of conclusions reported in an article with the same title by J. M. Williams. It is determined that Williams has not found the means to predict breakdowns by using psychological tests.

1005   Hagebak, R. W. "Disciplinary practices in Dallas contrasted with school systems with rules against violence against children." J Clin Child Psychol 2(3): 14-16, Fall, 1973. (0 References).
Suggests a connection between corporal punishment and behavior problems in the Texas school systems. Schools practicing corporal punishment seemed to have more discipline problems than schools not using corporal punishment. The implication is that corporal punishment tends to frustrate children and make them hostile or apathetic.

1006   Jenkins, R. L., and Hewitt, Lester. "Types of personality structure encountered in child guidance clinics." Am J Orthopsychiatry 14(1): 84-94, January, 1944. (1 Reference).
Discusses the effects of poor parenting on boys and presents three schemes that capsulize the boys' various personality types according to probable family backgrounds and common behavioral characteristics. The three types are depicted as follows: (1) excessive inhibitions, internal conflict, and neurosis; (2) inadequate inhibitions, external conflict, and unsocialized; and (3) inhibition toward in-group only, group conflict, and pseudosocial. Attention is focused on psychotherapy for treating male children presenting such symptoms.

1007   Katz, Julian. "Depression in children." Med J Aust 1(16): 592-94, April 16, 1977. (3 References).
Summarizes symptoms and treatment of depression in children. Until recently, both professionals and parents have overlooked depression in children. As a possible manifestation of mental abuse, depression needs definition and treatment. An infant expresses depression through physical signs, such as sleep or feeding disturbances, while the older child exhibits antisocial behavior, withdrawal, and habit disorders. Because depression of one or both parents is often found as a corollary, family-oriented treatment is suggested.

1008   Kline, Donald, and Christiansen, James L. Educational and psychological problems of abused children: final report. Logan, Utah: Utah State University, Department of Special Education, 1975. 175p.   ERIC Document ED 121 014.
Presents a study of the educational and psychological problems of 138 school age abused children. Data was derived from juvenile court records.

The frequency of special education placement, speech therapy, psychological counseling, institutional placement, academic achievement, and other behaviors was determined. Results showed that abused children were more likely to be placed in classes for the educably retarded and emotionally disturbed, to be in psychiatric institutions, to have psychological problems, and to achieve lower academic scores.

1009   Laury, Gabriel V., and Meerloo, Joost A. M. "Mental cruelty and child abuse." Psychiatr Q (Suppl.) 41(2): 203-54, 1967. (58 References).

A lengthy discussion of an invisible but very damaging form of child abuse--mental cruelty. Mental cruelty encompasses a whole range of parental activities and attitudes, from attempts to discipline and perfect the child, to unconscious or covert encouragement of behavior problems. Mental cruelty can accompany physical abuse, but more commonly, it represents a substitute for it. In all its aspects, mental cruelty is a form of aggression not channeled into constructive outlets. The pattern of mental cruelty can be altered and new, less aggressive behavior can be learned.

1010   ————. "Subtle types of mental cruelty to children." Child Fam 6(2): 28-34, Spring, 1967. (0 References).

Describes many forms of mental cruelty directed at children. Mental health agencies should become centers for prevention as well as for treatment. Treatment itself needs to be directed toward the family as a unit as opposed to care of the child in isolation. Early detection, coupled with an efficient system of social care, is necessary to curb the incidence of mental abuse to children.

1011   Lester, David. "Self-mutilating behavior." Psychol Bull 78(2): 119-28, August, 1972. (60 References).

A review of the literature concerned with self-mutilation, principally in terms of the various forms such behavior can assume, their etiology, the possible connections between self-mutilation and suicidal impulses and behavior. It has generally been found that children and animals neglected by their parents are prone to self-mutilation, both as a needed physical stimulus and as a means of attracting the attention of their parents.

1012   Loomis, W. G. "Management of children's emotional reactions to severe body damage." Clin Pediatr 9(6): 362-67, June, 1970. (14 References).

Examines the patterns of emotional trauma exhibited by severely burned children, as well as the various methods for managing the trauma. In a study involving sixteen badly burned children admitted to Colorado General Hospital over a two-year period, it was found that the child tended to view his pain as punishment for the misdeed that produced the burn, and that, in many cases, the burned child also seemed to mistrust the mother (herself guilty over the accident) for failing to protect him. This mistrust was in several cases extended to the hospital staff. As people often do in suffering pain, the children regressed to more infantile behavior and some withdrew into silence altogether. The staff, while permitting the early regressive behavior, pushed the children to abandon their withdrawal tactics when they improved physically. Foster grandparents proved quite effective in this endeavor. Several case studies are presented, including one in which the child had been scalded. The child had also been neglected and battered and was completely withdrawn. He failed to respond to the efforts made by the staff to reach him and died in the hospital.

1013 Martin, Harold P., and Beezley, Patricia. "Behavioral observations of abused children." Dev Med Child Neurol 19(3): 373-87, June, 1977. (27 References).
Reports on a study designed to trace the physical status, the neurological function, and the subsequent intellectual abilities of fifty abused children approximately four-and-one-half years after they were first identified as abused. The study also made further investigations into the psychological impact of physical abuse on these children. Results yielded no common psychological profile for the group; however, many showed signs of low self-esteem and of certain types of symptomatic behavior that encouraged others to reject them. One salient feature common to most was a minimal ability to enjoy themselves. Social interaction with peers was also often inappropriate for their respective ages. The severity of the physical attacks against the children was secondary to other environmental factors, such as unstable family structure, punitiveness, impermanence of home life, and rejection by parents, in influencing the psychological development of the children.

1014 ————. "Prevention and the consequences of child abuse." J Oper Psychiatry 6(1): 68-77, Fall-Winter, 1974. (38 References).
Examines four potential long-term effects of maltreatment on abused children. These effects can result from the abuse itself, from the circumstances which give rise to it, or even from therapeutic measures intended to correct the situation. The types of damage include: (1) physical damage to the central nervous system as a result of injury or poor nutrition; (2) emotional damage resulting from the psychological climate of the child's family; (3) psychological trauma generated by the therapeutic removal of the child from an abusive environment; and (4) variations in the child's inherent psychic equipment as a result of abuse.

1015 O'Keefe, Edward J. "Comparison of high- and low-impulse groups on two tests of motor inhibition." Percept Mot Skills 37(2): 435-41, October, 1973. (14 References).
Details an investigation of the possible correlation between motor inhibitions and impulsivity. Eighty high-impulse and low-impulse boys who had been either delinquents or abused and abandoned children were given tests to measure their motor inhibition. Delinquents were not differentiated from non-delinquents. The tests found no consistent correlation between motor inhibition and impulsivity.

1016 Reidy, Thomas J. "The social, emotional and cognitive functioning of physically abused and neglected children." For a summary see: Diss Abstr Int 37B(1): 476, July, 1976.

1017 Shengold, Leonard. "The effects of overstimulation: rat people." Int J Psychoanal 48(Part 3): 403-15, 1967. (24 References).
Examines the psychoanalytic aspects of the behavior patterns of people who were sexually abused as children. These people are the victims of overstimulation and carry its effects with them for the rest of their lives. A few characteristic effects of overstimulation--illustrated by four case histories--could be listed as rage, paranoia, a craving for some kind of explosive action to end the overstimulation, a build-up of

"massive" defenses, regression of the ego, a confusing battle between feelings of love and hate, and an overpowering need to re-experience the overstimulation. Parallels between these behaviors and those of Oedipus, characters in Shakespeare's King Lear and Orwell's 1984, are drawn. Frequent references are also made to Freud's well known case of the Rat Man.

1018 Steele, Brandt F. "Child abuse: its impact on society." J Indiana
      State Med Assoc 68(3): 191-94, March, 1975. (0 References).
Reprints an address delivered to the Colorado State Medical Association on the social repercussions of child abuse. The high incidence of mental retardation as a result of brain damage or skull fracture places a hardship on school systems which are unlikely to provide the special attention the abused child needs. Juvenile delinquents interviewed in several studies recall a high incidence of childhood abuse, as do several political assassins whose personal histories are briefly noted. The tendency to abuse is passed from generation to generation. The necessity of re-educating parents of young children and expectant parents about child-rearing practices must be coupled with an alertness to the high risk parent.

1019 Stephenson, P. Susan, and Lo, Nerissa. "When shall we tell Kevin?:
      a battered child revisited." Child Welfare 53(9): 576-81,
      November, 1974. (8 References).
A case study is presented of a fourteen-year-old boy who was placed in foster care at age nineteen months due to severe abuse which left him permanently handicapped. The study follows the boy's development, noting his problematic behavior both with his foster parents and at school. His difficulties escalated when he reached puberty, and were marked by a growing hostility toward his foster parents and increased aggressive activity outside of the home. It was postulated that his behavior was due, in part, to a displacement of feelings about his rejection by his own parents, and it was therefore decided to inform him of his mother's abuse of him. Gradual improvement was noted as this distressing information was assimilated. Foster children typically idealize their absent parents, take out their feelings on their foster parents, and blame themselves for their parents' desertion of them. Many children are unable to perceive and accept the reality of the deficits of their own parents until they have acquired the ability to think abstractly which comes with adolescence. The decision to inform foster children of the reasons for placement should be seriously considered, as it may help to further acceptance of self and the foster family.

1020 Tooley, Kay M. "The young child as victim of sibling attack."
      Soc Casework 58(1): 25-28, January, 1977. (3 References).
Focuses on the child who is the victim of serious, life-endangering sibling attack. Little attention has been given to the psychological effects on victims of sibling attack. It has commonly been difficult to secure permission from parents to study them. One case illustrating the psychological impact of repeated sibling attacks on a six-year-old younger brother is described in detail. Therapy for the child was slow at first. However, he later became remarkably responsive to treatment and showed no sign of psychotic behavior at the end of his stay in the hospital. In this case, as in many others like it, the physician was unprepared to take action to remove the child from danger. Child abuse caused by sibling attack must be reported, for although the parent was not the aggressor, he failed to protect the child from the assaults of the sibling.

1021   Wick, Emil C., Jr.   "A study of the development of self-concept in physically abused children."   For a summary see: <u>Diss Abstr Int</u> 37B(9): 4715, March, 1977.

D. NEGLECT

1. PHYSICAL EFFECTS

1022   Barbero, Giulio J., and Shaheen, Eleanor.   "Environmental failure to thrive: a clinical view."   <u>J Pediatr</u>   71(5): 639-44, November, 1967. (10 References).
Surveys four types of children who fail to thrive: (1) children with systemic symptoms; (2) children without systemic symptoms; (3) those with signs of recently inflicted injury; and (4) those with primary systemic disease.   The discussion includes a case history for each category.

1023   Bullard, Dexter M.; Glaser, Helen H.; Heagarty, Margaret, C.; et al. "Failure to thrive in the 'neglected' child."   <u>Am J Orthopsychiatry</u> 37(4): 680-90, July, 1967. (13 References).
In one-third of the 151 children admitted to the Boston Children's Hospital Medical Center between 1958 and 1965 for failing to thrive, no organic illness could be found.   The growth of forty-one of these children after hospitalization was followed over varying lengths of time; the family environment was observed, among other variables.   Although the continued retardation of physical, mental, or emotional growth is commonly associated with parental neglect, the follow-up study revealed no consistent connection between neglect and failure to thrive.   A number of the children who did not make normal progress did come from families with problems, but the kinds of emotional impediments or disturbances noted were too varied and often too subtle or complex to be subsumed under the term "neglect."   The development of a more flexible and specific language for assessing mother-child interaction is particularly recommended.

1024   ————.   "Failure to thrive in the 'neglected child'."   In: Chess, Stella, and Thomas, Alexander, eds.   <u>Annual progress in child psychiatry and child development, 1968</u>.   New York: Brunner/ Mazel, 1968.   540-54.
Discusses four case reports of children admitted to the hospital for failure to thrive.   The study investigates the possible causal relationship between maternal neglect or deprivation and the failure to thrive syndrome, a serious growth disorder.   Determining specifically what constitutes maternal deprivation and its effects should be thoroughly investigated.   Observing mother-child interaction in the home is suggested in order to carefully study the relationship between physical and emotional nutrients in infancy.

1025   Coleman, Rose W., and Provence, Sally.   "Environmental retardation (hospitalism) in infants living in families."   <u>Pediatrics</u>   19(2): 285-92, February, 1957. (10 References).
Evaluates the case reports of two infants found to be suffering from retarded physical development.   Both children were raised at home, but suffered from maternal deprivation.   While both mothers were present, they failed to give their infants needed attention and affection.   Additional physical, emotional, and social stimulation is viewed as good

therapy in these cases. The failure to thrive syndrome is differentiated from: (1) disorders affecting the central nervous system; (2) retardation secondary to insufficiencies in other organ systems; and (3) development hindered by infantile psychosis.

1026 "Events in puberty." Br Med J 4(5626): 317-18, November 2, 1968. (0 References).
Reports a number of cases of a new syndrome attributable to maternal deprivation. The manifestations include dwarfism, low body weight, abdominal distension, and perversion of appetite followed by ravenous eating. These symptoms were often accompanied by circulatory disturbances with coldness of the extremities, blotchiness, and discoloration. In ten of the cases reported, the children had been rejected by their mothers, and in three cases, the mothers were depressed.

1027 Glaser, Helen H.; Heagarty, Margaret C.; Bullard, Dexter M., Jr.; et al. "Physical and psychological development of children with early failure to thrive." J Pediatr 73(5): 690-98, November, 1968. (27 References).
Discusses the syndrome of non-organic growth failure as it was manifested in the cases of fifty children. The hospital records of the children were reviewed, and evaluations of the child and his family were conducted by pediatricians, psychiatrists, psychologists, and social service workers. Despite the evidence in the literature linking failure to thrive with deprivation, no such connection was discovered in the cases studied here. Most of the parents were emotionally stable, although over one-third of the families studied had experienced a disruption. Six of the children were removed from bad environments. No consistent pattern of sequelae was found, and most of the children, while still failing to thrive, exhibited normal psychological and mental development. Several, however, were mentally retarded.

1028 Goldson, Edward; Cadol, Roger V.; Fitch, Michael J.; et al. "Nonaccidental trauma and failure to thrive: a sociomedical profile in Denver." Am J Dis Child 130(5): 490-92, May, 1976. (16 References).
The medical charts of 140 children discharged from Denver General Hospital (DGH) in 1971 through 1972 with diagnoses of non-accidental trauma or failure to thrive were reviewed. It was found that most children were under three years of age at the time of the incident. The birth weights of the abused children were lower than those of non-abused children born at DGH during 1971. This finding suggests that the mother-infant separation that often occurs among low birth weight infants in the hospital may disrupt the bonding process and predispose the child to abuse. White children were more often abused than non-whites, which could reflect a lack of support systems for the white population. Bruising was the most prevalent injury, followed in decreasing frequency by fractures, failure to thrive, abandonment, burns, and death. The abuser was the biologic parent of the child in 70 percent of the cases. Both married and single individuals abused their children, which indicates that the problem affects all forms of family structure. More hospitalizations for child abuse occurred during the Spring and Fall months, suggesting that there is a greater need for preventive services during those periods.

1029 Green, Orville C. "Sizing up the small child." Postgrad Med 50(4): 103-9, October, 1971. (4 References).

Reviews several cases of undersized children, including some instances
in which placement in a more nurturing environment produced a remarkable
improvement in size and health. Most undersized children actually grow
at normal rates, but have delayed bone age; their problems are genetic
and, therefore, untreatable. Cases in which the problem is hypothyroidism
can be treated medically. But in a third category of undersized children,
growth failure is actually secondary to physical or emotional depriva-
tion--and sometimes physical abuse. Children may be diagnosed for pituitary insufficiency who are actually suffering from parental neglect.
Physicians treating such children are advised to watch for symptoms of
neglect or battering.

1030 Hepner, R., and Maiden, N. C. "Growth rate, nutrient intake and
      'mothering' as determinants of malnutrition in disadvantaged chil-
      dren." Nutr Rev 29(10): 219-23, October, 1971. (12 References).
Two groups of disadvantaged children--one set exhibiting vitamin A deficiencies characteristic of malnutrition, the other set with normal vitamin
A levels--were pair-matched for age, sex, race, neighborhood, and school
of attendance. The experiment found no correlation between malnutrition
and per capita income, expenditures on food, or Polansky's Childhood
Level of Living Scale, which attempted to measure both material and emotional support in the family. However, there did seem to be a strong
connection between the quality of mothering, one factor in the scale,
and malnutrition, the suggestion being that inadequate mothering may
exacerbate a predisposition to malnutrition in the child.

1031 Hock, Yeoh O., and Hwang, Woon T. "A battered child." Med J
      Malaysia 30(1): 43-47, September, 1975. (7 References).
The case history of a six-year-old girl who was battered by her mother
is detailed. Physical examination of the child revealed that she was
below the third percentile in height and weight. Psychological tests
indicated that the girl was handicapped in all major areas of functioning with an overall Intelligence Quotient of 67. Analysis of the family
dynamics demonstrated that the mother was not receiving adequate attention and assurance from her husband and, therefore, made excessive
demands upon her daughter. When the child was unable to satisfy her
mother's needs, she was physically abused. The child was eventually
separated from the family and placed in her grandmother's home where she
could attend a nearby school for the mentally retarded.

1032 Ironside, Wallace. "The infant development distress (IDD) syndrome:
      a predictor of impaired development?" Aust NZ J Psychiatry 9(3):
      153-58, September, 1975. (6 References).
Compares the progress of eight infants exhibiting the Infant Development
Distress syndrome with that of eight normal infants over a six year
period. It was found that most of the IDD children had been abused by
their parents. It is concluded that the so-called IDD syndrome actually
signifies a disturbed mother-child interaction whose symptoms first
appear in the early months of life.

1033 Kirchner, Sandra G., and Lee Ying T. "X-ray of the month." J Tenn
      Med Assoc 66(11): 1053-54, 1056, November, 1973. (7 References).
Radiological findings for a twenty-two-month-old white male admitted to
the hospital at the request of his local health department for failure
to thrive are presented and discussed. Differential diagnoses include
congenital indifference to pain, Vitamin A intoxication, osteogenesis

imperfecta, scurvy, syphilis, lesions of neuroblastoma, and leukemia.
These possibilities are eventually eliminated and the final diagnosis of
child abuse is made.

1034   Krieger, Ingeborg. "Food restriction as a form of child abuse in
       ten cases of psychosocial deprivation dwarfism." Clin Pediatr
       13(2): 127-33, February, 1974. (16 References).
An investigation of the eating habits of ten malnourished children brought
to Children's Hospital of Michigan revealed prolonged food deprivation and
neglect by their mothers. By withholding food, a mother typically believed that she could punish her child for his garbage eating habits or
even for his resemblance to an unkind father or husband. Seven children
showed signs of intestinal malabsorption, but this was proven to be a
result, not a cause, of malnutrition. Physical abuse was suspected in
six children. Feeding experiments were designed to encourage weight gain
in the children, and consenting mothers underwent psychotherapy.

1035   Lampard, F. Gillian, and Reid, Dorothy A. "Nanook of Eskimo Point."
       Nurs Times 65(46): 1472-73, November, 1969. (0 References).
Documents a case study of a twenty-month-old Eskimo boy who was found
almost dead and frozen at Eskimo Point in Canada. The child was taken
to a nearby nursing station where he was revived. The child was eventually placed with another family who could better care for his needs.
Apparently, the boy had a history of surgery and repeated illness, and
his natural mother was incapable of coping with his medical problems.

1036   MacCarthy, Dermod. "Physical effects and symptoms of the cycle
       of rejection." Proc R Soc Med 67(10): 1057-61, October, 1974.
       (12 References).
Dwarfism in deprived children, commonly attributed to severe emotional
neglect, is seen to result from the inadequate nutrition which frequently
accompanies maternal rejection. The diagnosis of dwarfism and malnutrition may be missed because mothers often give histories of the child
eating well and because dwarfism may occur without overt appearance of
malnutrition. It is regretted that children are not routinely measured
as well as weighed, as leg length is the best immediate indicator of the
deprivation syndrome. The pediatrician's remedial role in the cycle of
deprivation is emphasized. Insufficient protein and calorie intake during the first three years of life can result in permanent impairment.

1037   Money, John. "The syndrome of abuse dwarfism (psychosocial dwarf-
       ism or reversible hyposomatotropism): behavioral data and case
       report." Am J Dis Child 131(5): 508-13, May, 1977. (12 Refer-
       ences).
Illustrates, by a specific case, the characteristics of abuse dwarfism
and reversible hyposomatotropism. Confined most of his life to a closet,
beaten, deprived of sufficient food and sleep, the boy at age sixteen
had the height and weight of an eight-year-old. The pituitary dysfunction corrected itself when he was removed from his parents' home, and
by age twenty-one, he had achieved the height of a fourteen-year-old and
the weight of a twelve-year-old. His I.Q. increased twenty-nine points
in seven years, and his speech, originally unintelligible, improved
enormously. As pain agnosia or stoicism during pain is common in these
cases, the boy was at first hesitant to discuss his abuse. His social
adjustment was difficult, and as he tested his new environment, he
actually invited the continuation of abuse. While he did have an aware-

ness of sex and showed signs of secondary sexual characteristics, he was primarily interested in finding a foster family rather than a mate. Foster care was denied by the agencies responsible for him, and he remained under institutional care.

1038   Money, John, and Wolff, Georg. "Late puberty, retarded growth and reversible hyposomatotropinism (psychosocial dwarfism)." <u>Adolescence</u> 9(33): 121-34, Spring, 1974. (12 References).
Documents a case study of extreme childhood neglect and isolation which retarded statural growth and delayed the onset of puberty in twelve adolescents. Growth retarding variables in the environment included poor food intake, chronically disturbed sleep, lack of fresh air and exercise, and physical abuse by other family members. When the children were transferred to a facilitative environment, intellectual growth increased substantially, and statural growth, along with signs of puberty, advanced to levels more commensurate with the child's age.

1039   Money, John; Wolff, George; Annecillo, C. "Pain agnosia and self-injury in the syndrome of reversible somatotropin deficiency (psychological dwarfism)." <u>J Autism Child Schizo</u> 2(2): 127-39, April-June, 1972. (27 References).
Examines a study of thirty-two children who exhibited both physical and behavioral symptoms of the failure to thrive syndrome. These include both growth retardation and self-inflicted injury. A number of these children had been abused by their parents. After the children had been removed from their homes to more therapeutic environments, their symptoms were reversed.

1040   "Mother confines three [children] to house for ten years." <u>Life</u> 49(9): 29-30, August 29, 1960. (0 References).
A photographic account of three dwarfed children confined to their home for ten years, including details of their confinement and release. It is speculated that their dwarfed condition is due to a pituitary deficiency which may be congenital or the result of early malnutrition.

1041   Oates, R. K. "The child who fails to thrive." <u>Med J Aust</u> 1(9): 300-302, February 26, 1977.
Failure to thrive may be defined as failure to maintain a previous growth pattern. To claim the existence of such a condition requires objective observation and recording. Failure to thrive may be organic (metabolic disorders, defective absorption) or non-organic (emotional deprivation, inadequate nutrition) in origin. When organicity is excluded, an approach which offers guidance for the mother can be effective.

1042   Patton, Robert G., and Gardner, Lytt I. <u>Growth failure in maternal deprivation</u>. Springfield, Illinois: Charles C. Thomas, 1963. 94p. (Bibliography).
Six infants brought to the hospital for the failure to thrive syndrome were diagnosed as maternally deprived. Although the infants had received adequate nourishment at home, they had not been touched or talked to by their mothers. At least one parent in each family was emotionally disturbed. Upon admission to the hospital, the infants were lethargic, avoided contact with other persons, and showed limited motor activity. All exhibited retarded skeletal growth; in fact, the average ratio between height and chronological age was 42 percent. During the recovery period the infants displayed a "radar gaze" or fixed stare. Growth

charts and photographs document the infants' accelerated growth following
intense mothering both in the hospital and in subsequent foster home
settings. The relationship between deprivation and later intelligence
and personality development is examined. Additional clinical studies and
experiments with animals focusing on the problems of maternal deprivation
and institutional care are also reviewd.

1043 ————. "Influence of family environment on growth: the syndrome
      of 'maternal deprivation.'" Pediatrics 30(6): 957-62, December,
      1962. (27 References).
Reviews case studies of six children suffering from failure to thrive,
believed to be a result of unsatisfactory emotional and social environments. A review of several studies of deprivation is included.

1044 Pollitt, Ernesto; Eichler, Aviva W.; Chan, Chee-Khoon. "Psycho-
      social development and behavior of mothers of failure-to-thrive
      children." Am J Orthopsychiatry 45(4): 525-37, July, 1975. (22
      References).
A study designed to determine if mothers of failure to thrive children
show signs of psychopathology that would adversely affect their children's
physical and psychological growth. Data comparing the index group to a
group of matched controls were collected in the following areas: (1)
early childhood environment of mothers; (2) marital history; (3) mental
health; (4) marital adaptation; and (5) emotional and social relationship
with the child. Findings indicate that the mothers of failure to thrive
children did not show signs of severe psychopathological behavior. In
fact, significant differences between the two groups emerge only in terms
of physical affection and verbal interaction. In both instances the index
group showed a lesser degree of participation with their children.

1045 Powell, G. F.; Brasel, J. A.; Blizzard, R. M. "Emotional depriva-
      tion and growth retardation simulating idiopathic hypopituitarism."
      N Engl J Med 276(23): 1271-78, June 8, 1967. (28 References).
Details the histories and physical symptoms of thirteen children whose
failure to grow was initially diagnosed as idiopathic hypopituitarism,
but which actually was the result of emotional deprivation. The family
and personal histories of the children were often elicited with difficulty,
but they provided information crucial to the ultimate diagnosis of deprivation and the successful treatment of it. In most cases, a disturbed
family history was accompanied by bizarre behavior on the part of the
child (withdrawal, eating garbage, drinking from the toilet bowl). Treatment usually required the removal of the child--at least temporarily--
from the family environment. Physicians are advised to consider the
possibility of non-organic growth failure due to deprivation in all cases
of undersized children.

1046 Richmond, Julius B.; Eddy, Evelyn; Green, Morris. "Rumination: a
      psychosomatic syndrome of infancy." Pediatrics 22(1): 49-54,
      July, 1958. (3 References).
Studies four ruminating infants and their mothers. Rumination appears to
be a baby's way of compensating from within for the nurturing that the
mother is unable to provide. Onset typically occurs at three to four
months of age. Missed diagnosis can result in death.

1047 Riley, R. L.; Landwirth, J.; Collipp, P. J.; et al. "Failure to
      thrive: an analysis of 83 cases." Calif Med 108(1): 32-38,
      January, 1968. (13 References).

Of the eighty-three cases of failure to thrive, twenty-six yielded evidence linking maternal deprivation to the child's condition. The deprived children had no organic malady, and most of them grew rapidly after admission to the hospital. The specific deficiencies in the child's home environment could not always be ascertained, but clear evidence was found for improper feeding, malnutrition, and parental neglect. Child abuse had occurred in several cases. It is recommended that physicians be alert to the possibility of maternal deprivation and the necessity to save the child from a destructive environment.

1048   Robertson, Isobel. "Follow-up of five severely deprived and malnourished siblings, after their placement in foster care." S Afr Med J 50(21): 799-800, May 15, 1976. (3 References).
Describes the results of a study of five neglected and malnourished siblings who were removed from their home and placed in foster care. The weights and heights of each child were recorded at the time of placement and at intervals over the following six years. Each child showed a rapid gain in weight in the first two years of foster care, but the increases in height were not as marked. The dwarfing effect of malnutrition was most pronounced among the older children. All of the siblings were slow at school, but this could not be attributed solely to early malnutrition because other factors—such as the shock of a changed environment, physical illness, and a late start in attending school—may have contributed to the intellectual retardation as well.

1049   Rutter, Michael. "Maternal deprivation reconsidered." J Psychosom Res 16: 241-50, 1972. (28 References).
Attempts to define so-called "maternal deprivation" more precisely by treating different manifestations of it (or problems believed to be manifestations of it) separately. The term "maternal deprivation" has been used too broadly to retain much meaning, and its implications of failure on the part of the mother is not necessarily accurate. Problems associated with maternal deprivation should be linked to more specific causes: acute distress is most likely the result of a break in the bonding process which would probably occur if the infant were to be separated from any human being with whom bonds had begun to form; physical and intellectual impairment are both seen as a result of experiential privation, and dwarfism, of nutritional privation; delinquency is related to discord in the family unit; and affectionless psychopathy may result from the child's failure—for whatever reason—to develop bonds early in life.

1050   Schutt-Aine, Joseph C.; Drash, Allan L.; Kenny, Frederic M. "Possible relationship between spontaneous hypoglycemia and the 'maternal deprivation syndrome': case reports." J Pediatr 82(5): 809-13, May, 1973. (9 References).
Presents a study in which hypoglycemia and temporary decrease in adrenocorticotrophic hormone (ACTH) in children seemed to be definitely linked to the maternal deprivation of these children. Three case studies are presented; the information includes the symptoms, treatment, and medical and family history of each child. The findings indicate an association between a poor family environment and reversible abnormal pituitary-adrenal axis; growth improved after the child's environment was changed. It is suggested that attending physicians consider the possibility of deprivation in treating hypoglycemic children.

1051   Silver, Henry K., and Finkelstein, Marcia. "Deprivation dwarfism."
       J Pediatr 70(3):   317-24, March, 1967. (27 References).
Reports on the new syndrome of "deprivation dwarfism." The term is used
to describe a set of physical conditions--extreme short stature, voracious
appetite, and a marked delay in skeletal maturation--which can be associated with emotional deprivation. The report is based on a study of nine
children, four to sixteen years in age, who displayed the physical symptoms
of the syndrome. Interviews with five of the parents yielded the conclusions that the families involved were significantly disturbed, and the
children, emotionally deprived. The parents were depressed and withdrawn
or aggressive and rejecting, and three of the five mothers had experienced
similar treatment by their parents. In three of the five cases, the
emotional deprivation of the children was accompanied by signs of physical
neglect and/or abuse. The children placed in foster care reversed their
symptoms and grew normally. The children who could not be placed in foster
homes exhibited no change in their symptoms.

1052   Talukder, M. Q., and Dawson, K. P. "Nutritional marasmus in an
       affluent society." Practitioner 212(1269):   359-62, March, 1974.
       (6 References).
Summarizes the case history of a child with severe marasmus due to under-
feeding. This child neglect was the result of a withdrawn mother in a low
income family.

1053   "Their prison was home." Newsweek 56(6):   43, August 8, 1960.
       (0 References).
Cites the case of three dwarfed children who had been confined to their
home for ten years. The mother, who has three other children, said that
she hid them at first in order to be able to find housing, and later
because they were different from other children. The story of their
escape and their previous home life is told. Physicians were unable to
account for their small statures, as they are neither anemic or undernourished.

1054   Togut, Myra R.; Allen, John E.; Lelchuck, Louis. "A psychological
       exploration of the nonorganic failure-to-thrive syndrome." Dev Med
       Child Neurol 11(5):   601-7, October, 1969. (13 References).
Examines nine cases of the failure to thrive syndrome. All of the children studied were the youngest members of their families. The mothers
exhibited normal intelligence but showed signs of high levels of anxiety,
insecurity and guilt, were unable to deal with aggressive and sexual
impulses, and seemed overwhelmed by their family responsibilities. The
children improved in the hospital, but their progress slowed when they
were returned home.

1055   Trube-Becker, Elisabeth. "The death of children following negli-
       gence: social aspects." Forensic Sci 9(2):   111-15, March-April,
       1977. (10 References).
Discusses the symptoms and outcomes of severe neglect. The incidence of
neglect is difficult to ascertain, for it rarely receives exposure unless
signs of physical maltreatment emerge at the same time. Symptoms of
neglect include intense emaciation, dry puckered, scaly skin, lack of
subcutaneous fatty tissue, and an aged face. The characteristics of fifty-
four infant neglect cases that ended in death are cited. In every case
the family was in extremely poor financial and social condition, and in
most instances, the mothers were too young and had no preparation for

mothering. Whenever positive parental influence is lacking, the community should provide a substitute.

1056 Watt, J. M. "Ill-thrift." NZ Med J 75(480): 285-87, May, 1972. (11 References).
The failure to thrive syndrome results from emotional deprivation and is characterized by such signs as retarded physical and mental development and apathetic behavior. Recommendations are made regarding diagnosis, and an attack on the syndrome is urged.

1057 Whitten, Charles F.; Pettit, Marvin G.; Fischhoff, Joseph. "Evidence that growth failure from maternal deprivation is secondary to under-eating." JAMA 209(11): 1675-82, September 15, 1969. (18 References).
A report of an investigation of the premise that infants often fail to thrive because they receive inadequate mothering. Thirteen underweight and maternally deprived children between the ages of three and twenty-four months were removed to a hospital environment and were fed amounts of food which approximated their reputed intake at home, but were otherwise left alone. Eleven of these children showed an accelerated weight gain even when the hospital atmosphere simulated the maternal deprivation of their homes. It was concluded that psychological maternal deprivation does not necessarily result in failure to thrive, and that the mothers of the subjects had simply not been offering the amount of food to their children which they had reported.

2. PSYCHOLOGICAL EFFECTS

1058 Bakwin, Harry. "Psychologic aspects of pediatrics: emotional deprivation in infants." J Pediatr 35(4): 512-21, October, 1949. (27 References).
The severe mortality rate of institutional infants results from emotional deprivation. Loss of appetite, listlessness, and unresponsiveness are common symptoms of hospitalism. Yet the lack of its occurrence in pre-mature, newborn, or cerebrally damaged babies indicates that conscious cerebral functioning is necessary before this condition arises. A lack of sensory stimulation is indicated as the cause of illness; babies who are given the most attention on the ward or who are removed to responsive homes recover rapidly, providing the deprivation has not lasted beyond three or four months. Hospitals encourage staff to handle and play with babies and may arrange accommodations for mother and child during a hospital stay.

1059 Bowley, Agatha H. The psychology of the unwanted child. Edinburgh: E. & S. Livingstone, 1947. 112p.
Investigates the psychology of the unwanted or uprooted child. In order for a child to develop normally in both a physical and a psychological sense, his needs for affection, security, recognition, and a sense of belonging to a group must be met. However, when a child is emotionally rejected by his parents, he experiences feelings of unworthiness and inferiority. Moreover, the parent's desertion, death, divorce, or re-marriage can create serious repercussions in the child. Problems with tantrums, bedwetting, destructiveness, and stealing may develop. Various programs aimed at helping the unwanted child readjust to the living situation at home or a new environment are evaluated. The following

factors must be taken into consideration before a treatment plan can be prescribed: (1) the environment where the child will be living; (2) the child's emotional, physical, and intellectual endowment; and (3) the child's personality and his ability to relate to other people and cope with trying circumstances. The advantages and disadvantages of placement in a foster home, residential nursery, school for maladjusted children, and state institution are discussed. Narrative reports and statistical analyses of the readjustment processes as seen in different children are presented.

1060   Caldwell, Bettye M. "The effects of psychological deprivation on human development in infancy." Merrill-Palmer Q 16(3): 260-77, July, 1970. (59 References).
An assessment of current research priorities in the study of the relationship between psychosexual deprivation and development in infancy. Most investigations of this topic are categorized as "enrichment type" approaches and are found to be inconclusive. Emphasis is placed upon the need for improving techniques for evaluating the psychosexual environment and development of a child, along with his susceptibility to deprivation.

1061   "Child bereavement: editorial." Br Med J 1(5538): 445-46, February 25, 1967. (27 References).
Discusses the difficulty in ascertaining a relationship between childhood bereavement and eventual psychological disorders. Several studies have established a connection while others have failed to find any reliable pattern. It is equally difficult to determine how the age and sex of the bereaved child influence his vulnerability to mental illness after his loss. It is suggested that the resilience and strength of the family as a whole have a great influence over the child's ability to recover.

1062   Erikson, Erik H. "Early ego failure: Jean." In: Erikson, Erik H. Childhood and society. 2d ed. New York: W. W. Norton, 1963. 445p.
The characteristics, problems, and progress of a six-year-old schizophrenic child are detailed. Her symptoms included withdrawal from human contact, lack of speech, and fascination with objects, especially instruments or machines. It is suggested that the child's possible failure to respond to the mother as an infant may have caused a withdrawal of the parent. An early four-month separation and an interruption of breast feeding forced by illness in the mother seem unlikely to account for the child's condition, although they undoubtedly exacerbated it. The resulting ego weakness manifested itself in her inability to separate self from other and in her conviction that her hands were hurtful, destructive instruments. She became fascinated with parts of people that she could touch. She blamed herself for the early separations and was extremely self-punitive. Gradually, with understanding help from her mother, she engaged in finger play, improving her relationship with her hands. Discovering a surprising gift for piano playing helped her view her hands as a source of pleasure rather than destruction.

1063   Freud, Anna. "Special experiences of young children: particularly in times of social disturbance." In: Soddy, Kenneth, ed. World Federation and Infant Development, Proceedings: Mental health and infant development. New York: Basic Books, 1956. 141-60.
Observations about young children raised under wartime conditions. These special circumstances create a means of studying factors impossible to

recreate through experimentation, such as the sudden loss of parents. The younger child displays the loss through physical disorders such as feeding or sleep disturbances. The toddlers regress in their behavior and are unable to resume close relationships immediately. Interactions among peers include more aggressiveness and group identification. Memory recall is less available, and a child often remembers his real parents as ideal and views his substitute parents as bad. These findings raise numerous issues which are briefly discussed. These include the question of the good versus the bad set of parents, separation patterns and day care, transference of parental anxiety to the child, resolution of the Oedipal Complex where the father is missing, repression of fearful experiences versus mastery, and conditions of adoption.

1064 Goldfarb, William. "Psychological privation in infancy and subsequent adjustment." Am J Orthopsychiatry 15(2): 247-55, April, 1945. (5 References).
Studies infant deprivation in institutional children compared with infants who were cared for in foster homes. Four groups of equated pairs at various mean ages, namely, at the ages of three years, six years, eight years, and twelve years, were studied. Findings indicate that severe institutional infant deprivation is characterized by an extreme meagerness of stimulation. It results in a predictable basic defect of total personality, characterized by a problem in concept formation and by an attitude of passivity and emotional apathy. This often later turns into hyperactivity and disorganization. Related aggressive behavior lacks goal-orientation. The study also distinguishes between a deprivation experience and a rejection experience, the latter being more amenable to treatment.

1065 Haka-Ikse, Katerina. "Child development as an index of maternal mental illness." Pediatrics 55(3): 310-12, March, 1975. (5 References).
Depression in the mother often inhibits the development of the child, but pediatricians, by focusing on the child's problem, may fail to connect it to the mother's mental illness. Such mothers should be treated for their illnesses; maternal supplements or even substitutes may be necessary for the child's well-being.

1066 Hirksyj, Peter. "Nursing care study: Naomi a case of neglect." Nurs Mirror 139(20): 83-84, November 14, 1974. (0 References).
Summarizes a case study of a two-year-old child, admitted to University College Hospital in London. She was obese, non-verbal, and was suffering from a severe cough and from diarrhea and vomiting, attributed to gastroenteritis. An acute absence of maternal care and stimulation in the home situation was discovered. After a week in the hospital, the child's condition had improved and she returned home. Home help was directed to assist the family. The parents were also encouraged to contact the hospital if further problems arose.

1067 Hood, Catriona. "Children abandoned in long-stay hospitals." Child Care Health Dev 2(4): 239-50, July-August, 1976. (18 References).
Sixty-eight children residing in eight long-stay hospitals for handicapped, retarded, and emotionally ill pediatric patients were examined to investigate the problem of child abandonment in long-stay hospitals in England. A child was defined as abandoned if he or she was under

eighteen years of age and had not been visited by his parents, nor gone home in the six months preceding the study. It was found that almost one-fifth of the children studied met this definition of abandonment and that a child could be at risk of abandonment regardless of the nature of his handicap. Over half of the abandoned children had been admitted to a residental setting before the age of five, and the early admission in itself appeared to be a factor in the abandonment of a fairly high pro-portion of children. Marital instability and other environmental stresses were common among the parents of abandoned children and contributed to their decision to abandon their child. Medical attitudes of rejection toward the child's handicap and a lack of effort on the part of the insti-tution to foster family contacts were also considered to be causative factors in the abandonment of children in long-stay hospitals.

1068 Howells, John G. "Visiting children: letter to editor." Br Med J
      2(5488): 676-77, March 12, 1966. (6 References).
The traditional assumption that children separated from their mothers automatically run the risk of emotional damage is refuted. Studies are cited which indicate that separation from the mother does not, in and of itself, result in emotional problems, and that the type of care which the child is given has a greater effect over his ultimate mental health.

1069 Jacobson, Shirley; Fasman, Jean; DiMascio, Alberto. "Deprivation
      in the childhood of depressed women." J Nerv Ment Dis 160(1):
      5-14, January, 1975. (26 References).
Investigates the hypothesis of a connection between adult depression and childhood deprivation, defined as the "loss or absence of an emotionally sustaining relationship." The subjects against whom the hypothesis was tested were 347 depressed female in-patients and 114 female out-patients, with a control group of 198 normal women. No association could be found between actual childhood loss (such as the death of a parent) and adult depression, but there was evidence of a connection between adult depres-sion and less overt forms of childhood deprivation such as the mental illness of a parent.

1070 King-Meese, Ruth E. "A descriptive study of self-concept and be-
      havior of indigent/neglected children in the Tennessee Home
      Community Program." For a summary see: Diss Abstr Int 35A(9):
      5926, March, 1975.

1071 "Koluchova's twins: editorial." Br Med J 2(6041): 897-98,
      October 16, 1976. (34 References).
This response to Koluchova's study of severely deprived twins emphasizes the importance of developmental reversals caused by excellent alternative child care, as well as the preventive qualities of the early mother-child bonding relationship. Studies by Clarke and Clarke are cited in support of the first assertion; findings by Bowlby and research described by a Ciba symposium support the latter claim.

1072 Michell, Guy. "Maternal deprivation." Dev Med Child Neurol 5(1):
      42-44, 1963. (9 References).
Reviews some of the literature on the effects of deprivation of maternal care on the young child. Distinctions among the definitions of separa-tion, deprivation, and multiple mothering figures are made. Maternal deprivation in institutional situations is said to produce: (1) a delay in infants' vocal and smiling behavior; (2) failure to respond to human

contact; (3) retarded motor performance, language, and social development; and (4) an early lack of interest in toys, although after the first year, the child prefers objects to people. Two studies of the effect of increased maternal attention on the social and vocal responses of institutionalized infants are cited.

1073   Moss, Sidney Z., and Moss, Miriam S. "Surrogate mother-child relationships." Am J Orthopsychiatry 45(3): 382-90, April, 1975. (25 References).
Analyzes the sensitive process in which a relationship develops between a child and a surrogate mother. Particular attention is paid to the difficulties of establishing a new bond and the potential damage which can be done by the loss of the original parent. The new bond will in a variety of ways be influenced by the old one.

1074   Mulford, Robert M. Emotional neglect of children. Denver, Colorado: The American Humane Association, Children's Division, 1958. 11p. (Bibliography).
Examines the problems of recognizing and treating the emotional neglect of children. A brief history traces the growing awareness of emotional neglect and its effects. It is defined as deprivation resulting from the parents' failure to provide the love and security necessary for normal emotional development. Attitudes toward neglect as a physical rather than an emotional phenomenon need changing, particularly in the courts where the recognition of the harm of emotional neglect is not being used constructively. Treatment should attempt to change the parents' attitude toward their children and develop effective parental care.

1075   Nye, Ivan F. "Child adjustment in broken and in unhappy unbroken homes." Marriage Fam Living 19(4): 356-61, November, 1957. (6 References).
Discusses the question of whether children in broken homes are better off psychologically than children whose unhappy families have remained intact. Findings of a study of 780 adolescents suggested that the children from broken homes fare somewhat better than children from intact, unhappy homes on several counts. They seemed better adjusted and less inclined to delinquency and psychosomatic illness.

1076   Prescott, James W. "Early somatosensory deprivation as an ontogenic process in the abnormal development of the brain and behavior." In: Conference on Experimental Medicine and Surgery in Primates, 2nd, New York, 1969. Medical primatology, 1970. New York, Basel: Karger, 1971. 356-75. (92 References).
Suggests that certain behavioral abnormalities thought to be the result of maternal-social deprivation are also symptomatic of impaired neurophysiological functioning. The study investigates the neurobiological effects of early somatosensory deprivation. Literature on mammalian maternal-social deprivation supports the contention that serious emotional-behavioral disorders are linked to developmental somatosensory deafferentation that is caused by early deprivation of the somatosensory system. This presupposes the concept that sensory systems need sensory input in order to grow normally. The somatosensory system itself, comprising a motor sensory feedback system, consists of sets of non-movement and movement senses. When early motor movements within the system are constricted, sensory deprivation takes place. Isolation-reared mammals deprived of motor feedback commonly exhibit chronic self-stimulation be-

havior and hyperexcitability, both stimulus-seeking behaviors. Cannon's
Law of Denervation Supersensitivity is used to suggest that insufficient
somatosensory stimulation during early development does, indeed, cause
supersensitivity and hyperexcitability in cerebellar functioning. Moreover, the cerebellum integrates and regulates sensory-emotional and motor
functions, specifically the reticular and limbic systems, which are
independent "activation" systems. Consequently, emotional-behavioral
pathologies such as violent-aggressive and autistic-withdrawn behavior
may be related to disorders in the cerebellum "inhibitory" regulatory
system. Numerous neurochemical and electrophysiological studies point
out the differences in the near-receptor and distance-receptor functioning and their combined influence on early psychobiological and psychosocial development. Guidelines for research, stressing the importance of
identifying pathologic violent personalities, are included.

1077   Prugh, Dane G., and Harlow, Robert G. "'Masked deprivation' in
       infants and young children." In: World Health Organization.
       Deprivation of maternal care: a reassessment of its effects.
       Geneva: World Health Organization, 1962. 9-29. (81 References).
Reports a study of the type of maternal deprivation which is concealed,
because it is emotional in nature. Nevertheless, it can result in emotional damage equivalent to that arising from the more obvious forms of
maternal deprivation such as death or separation of the mother.

1078   Roberts, Albert R., ed. Childhood deprivation. Springfield,
       Illinois: Charles C. Thomas, 1974. 209p. (Bibliography).
Several forms of childhood deprivation, particularly physical, emotional,
familial, and social deprivation, are prevalent in American society. The
impact upon the developing child of extreme poverty, physical abuse, lack
of mothering in infancy, and separation from a parent due to divorce or
death is examined.

Children raised in poverty stricken areas lack the home stability, medical
treatment, and educational facilities necessary to improve their situation.
Nevertheless, programs such as Head Start, Home Start in rural areas, day
care centers, and child welfare services can help the disadvantaged to
overcome social deprivation at an early age. Infants deprived of human
contact encounter difficulties later in their emotional and social development. Antisocial behavior, stunted growth, and a delay in language skill
acquisition are consequences of a lack of social contact, most importantly
with a mother. The preschooler who is separated from his natural parents
and placed in a foster home will usually experience grief, guilt, anger,
and a preoccupation with the lost parent. Unless the foster parents are
sympathetic and encourage the child to act out his grief, the child's
personality may be permanently impaired by this loss. Children living
with one parent after a divorce have often already endured at least two
years of pre-divorce tension and turbulence. Forcing a child to choose
which parent to live with involves not only a rejection of the other
parent, but of part of his own developing self. In addition, a child's
attitude toward marriage begins to form between the ages of three and
six, so that a child who lives through one marriage failure has a greater
chance of duplicating that failure in his own subsequent marriage.

The abused child is usually multiply deprived. Adequate food, shelter,
love, and communication with others are denied him while he is simultaneously physically assaulted. It is important to treat the parents
and the complex motivations for abuse, rather than approaching all cases

punitively, if the cycle of abuse is to be halted. Child abuse, along with all manifestations of either familial or social deprivation, is a transcultural problem awaiting an educated and sensitive solution.

1079 Rohner, Ronald P. They love me, they love me not: a worldwide study of the effects of parental acceptance and rejection. New Haven, Connecticut: HRAF Press, 1975. 300p. (Bibliography). Discusses the deleterious effects of rejection on the personalities and developmental processes of children. A "universalist" view of human nature is taken; the biological bases of behavior are acknowledged, as are certain crosscultural similarities in needs and developmental tendencies. The importance of learning is also noted. Despite the fact that many uniformities in the human species exist, people are unique in that their environmental experiences and patterns of behavioral conditioning vary. The need for positive responses or acceptance is seen to be an innate one, common throughout all cultures. Since it is such a basic need, its absence in childhood can produce permanent and obvious damage. Rejection may lead to: hostility, aggression, dependency, poor self-esteem, phychological instability, and difficulties in relating to others. Crosscultural studies of parental acceptance/rejection are cited and discussed. Questions are raised concerning: (1) the best means of testing the universalist theory with respect to parental treatment; (2) the personality characteristics which distinguish accepting from rejecting parents; (3) the effects of environmental factors on parental attitudes; (4) the relationship between social and psychological variables and their combined effects on acceptance/rejection; and (5) the effects of the sex of both the child and the parent on style of parenting. Recommendations for further study of the universal implications of parental love or lack of love are outlined.

1080 Salk, Lee. "On the prevention of schizophrenia." Dis Nerv Syst 29(1): 11-15, January, 1968. (27 References). Numerous theories concerning the causes and prevention of infantile schizophrenia or autism are outlined. It is suggested that autism has an intermediate physiological cause--that structured mechanisms in the sensorium have failed to develop. But this failure is itself most likely the result of sensory deprivation in the early days of life. Human and animal studies in support of this etiology are discussed. It is concluded that infants who are handled often by their mothers have stabler dispositions, interact better with others, and develop a greater range of response than infants who are left to "cry it out" at other than feeding or changing times. It is recommended that hospitals allow much more contact between mother and infant in the neonatal state.

1081 Schermerhorn, Wanda S. "The neglected child's perception of the public school experience." For a summary see: Diss Abstr Int 31A(12): 6352-53, June, 1971.

1082 Senn, Milton J. E. "A relook at the effects of maternal deprivation." Children 9(6): 237-39, November-December, 1962. (2 References). Reviews John Bowlby's 1951 monograph on the effects of maternal deprivation on the mental health of children. Bowlby's intent was to demonstrate to child care workers that the psychological milieu in which infants are reared influences decisively their personality development. Important changes in British child care services were made in response to his report: institutions were critically evaluated, hospital staffs encouraged more frequent visiting by parents, and foster homes were generally considered to be more suitable than institutions. Further investigations into the problem of child care have produced some qualifications of the Bowlby view. Most significantly, researchers are now more hopeful about opportunities for restoration to normal development after deprivation. Evidence still remains of severe impairment of long standing as a result of deprivation, and there continues to be a need for caution in considering the placement of children.

1083 Spitz, Rene A. "Hospitalism: an inquiry into the genesis of psychiatric conditions in early childhood." Psychoanal Study Child 1: 53-74, 1945. (29 References).
Examines the effects of institutionalization on children under one year of age. Two groups of 164 institutionalized children were compared; two other groups totaling thirty-four children served as controls. The presence of a mother or mother substitute was found to be the most important factor in assuring normal development. Children in the nursery group, although more severely handicapped by background than those in the foundling home group, rose markedly on the developmental curve, surpassing the descending curve of the foundling group at four months. This is the age at which the foundling babies were weaned, and their lives thereafter had little human contact. The nursery babies were born of delinquent mothers who inundated their babies with care. Differences in toys, visual stimulation, locomotion, and personnel are discussed.

1084 Vaughan, Mark. "Hungry children scavenge in Portsmouth dustbins." Times Educ Suppl 2911: 3, March 5, 1971. (0 References).
Parental neglect, reported by school leaders in Portsmouth, England, has driven a number of school children to scavenging for food. The children are generally in need of medical attention and display defensive aggressive behavior in their play. Blame is placed on the lack of liaison between schools and the city's children's department and between the welfare agencies themselves. An effective welfare program is greatly needed.

1085 Wald, Max. Protective services and emotional neglect. Denver, Colorado: The American Humane Association, Children's Division, 1961. 20p. (Bibliography).
The symptoms and causes of emotional neglect are multiple and complex. Such habit disorders as nail biting, enuresis, and head banging or such conduct disorders as tantrums, lying, and destructiveness are manifestations in a child of emotional neglect. Supportive casework for neglectful families involves practical assistance in addition to counseling. Attributes of the casework staff include a firm, yet warm, approach, patience, and dedication. The nature of casework treatment demands small caseloads, interagency cooperation, and further research.

1086 Werkman, Sidney L. "Hazards of rearing children in foreign countries." Am J Psychiatry 128(8): 992-97, February, 1972. (14 References).
Various clinical psychiatric problems appear in children whose parents (usually businessmen, missionaries, military personnel, and members of the United States Foreign Service) have raised them overseas. While fathers in the United States may not play a large role in childrearing, a foreign career often necessitates an even greater commitment to one's career. Mothers often have servants abroad and neglect their children.

Several case histories, illustrating the sexual and emotional problems which can result when a child is left to be cared for by a servant are noted. Other problems suffered by children raised in foreign countries include feelings of alienation which arise from a lack of parental commitment to a homeland and separation upon returning to the United States from abroad.

1087   Werner, Emmy; Simonian, Kenneth; Bierman, Jessie M.; <u>et al</u>. "Cumulative effect of perinatal complications and deprived environment on physical, intellectual, and social development of preschool children." <u>Pediatrics</u> 39(4): 490-505, April, 1967. (21 References).
Analyzes the relationships among perinatal complications, quality of early childhood environment, and physical/intellectual/social development. Six hundred and seventy children born in 1955 in Kauai, Hawaii, were scaled according to type and severity of perinatal complications. Ethnic origins, mother's age and intelligence, socioeconomic status, and family stability had no discernible effect on the incidence of perinatal complications. The quality of each family's environment (socioeconomic status, family stability, maternal intelligence) was also noted, most of the families proving to be average or slightly above. When the study group children reached age two, they were given physical and psychological examinations. Among those children with severe perinatal stress, there was an increasing probability of a lag in physical/intellectual/social development. The effect of the family environment on the child's development seemed to increase with the severity of the perinatal complications.

1088   Young, H. Boutourline. "Deprivation of maternal care." <u>Dev Med Child Neurol</u> 5(5): 520-31, 1963. (13 References).
Selectively reviews the literature on the role of maternal deprivation in causing psychological disorders. The need for more thorough, longitudinal studies of the problem of deprivation is emphasized. Criticisms of: (1) animal experiments; (2) the view of maternal deprivation as only one facet of a collection of adverse factors; and (3) studies of the effects of the quality of mothering and time of separation on mental health of the child, are included.

3. MENTAL RETARDATION AND LEARNING PROBLEMS

1089   Brandwein, Harold. "The battered child: a definite and significant factor in mental retardation." <u>Ment Retard</u> 11(5): 50-51, October, 1973. (4 References).
Because of the high incidence of head trauma and resulting brain injury in the child abuse statistics, it is deduced that child abuse has materially contributed to mental retardation, although it is impossible at this point to determine the statistical incidence of mental retardation as a result of child abuse.

1090   Clarke, A. D. B. "Commentary on Koluchova's 'severe deprivation in twins: a case study.'" <u>J Child Psychol Psychiatry</u> 13(2): 103-6, June, 1972. (8 References).
The rapid cognitive development of several severely deprived children upon rescue confirms the findings of the Koluchova study of severely deprived twins. Theories stressing the importance of early learning require reassessment; reinforcement of early learning may be the critical factor.

1091 D'Ambrosio, Richard. "No language but a cry." Good Housekeeping
      171(8): 64-67ff., August, 1970. (0 References).
A physician's account of the dramatic, heart-rending recovery of an abused
child from mute withdrawal and physical deformity. As an infant, the
child had been burned and beaten by her alcoholic and mentally ill parents.
She was removed from the home and eventually placed in an institution for
girls run by Catholic nuns. At age twelve, the girl suffered severe
curvature of the spine, crossed eyes, and pronounced varicose veins of
the legs. She would not talk to anyone or play with the other children.
Therapy began with the physician spending long hours talking to the child
and engaging in play activities, but the child did not respond until two
years had passed. Once an initial breakthrough had been made, recovery
was fairly rapid. The child gained the ability to communicate with
others, had several operations to correct physical deformities, and completed a course in child care at a nearby school so that she could work
in a nursery. She left the institution at age eighteen.

1092 Erickson, Marilyn T. "Effects of social deprivation and satiation
      of verbal conditioning in children." J Comp Physiol Psychol 55(6):
      953-57, December, 1962. (11 References).
Studies the effects of social deprivation and satiation on the verbal
task performance of elementary school children under two types of reinforcement. Forty sixth grade children were randomly assigned to four
experimental groups. Forty-eight pairs of nouns were presented succes-
sively to each subject, the correct response being the choice of the
animate noun from each pair. The subjects were requested to choose the
work they liked better. During the pretask session, half of the subjects
were socially deprived and half were socially satiated. During the
verbal conditioning session, half were presented with the social rein-
forcer "good" following each correct response, and half were presented
with a marble. The results demonstrated the possibility of verbal conditioning in sixth grade children. A short period of social deprivation
was found to increase the efficiency of social reinforcement relative to
a comparable period of social satiation.

1093 Koluchova, Jarmila. "The further development of twins after severe
      and prolonged deprivation: a second report." J Child Psychol
      Psychiatry 17(3): 181-88, July, 1976. (3 References).
A follow-up report on the development of twins who were severely deprived
and mistreated by their stepmother from age eighteen months to seven
years. During these years, their intelligence quotient was subnormal,
speech development was retarded, and they had rickets. The predictions
of speech pathologists and pediatricians for the recovery of the twins
were pessimistic. But at age fourteen, the I.Q. scores, speech development, and social adjustment of the boys was normal. No psychopathological features were identified. Their successful recovery was attributed
to the loving care that they had received from their foster family, to
their understanding but challenging teachers, to speech specialists, and
to their on-going relationship with a clinical psychologist. A ten-year-
old girl who was also severely deprived and cruelly treated by a psychopathic mother until age four lived with the same foster family as the
twins. She had made progress in her development as well, although she
still exhibited some severe problems in social adjustment and ability to
concentrate. The twins had each other, however, during their period of
social isolation and cruelty, while this child had been completely alone.
The diagnosis of severe deprivation must be distinguished from that of

mental subnormality. Even gross damage suffered by severely deprived children can be remedied if the proper care is given.

1094 ———————. "Severe deprivation in twins: a case study." J Child
     Psychol Psychiatry 13(2): 107-14, June, 1972. (2 References).
Presents a case study of twins deprived of emotional and social contacts from age eighteen months to seven years. The twins, kept by a psychopathic mother and a passive father, were refrained from contact with their siblings or neighbors. They were often beaten and locked in a basement with no stimuli except a table and two bricks. Upon discovery, they were placed in a hospital, then moved to a children's home, and then to living in a warm, responsive foster home. During this time, they progressed from a mental age of three years to a level average for their present age, and their motor skills also developed rapidly. The excellence of their progress, when compared to other cases of deprivation, is linked to their twinship. This case provides important data for the study of early childhood development and deprivation.

1095 Koski, Marvin A., and Ingram, Eben M. "Child abuse and neglect:
     effects on Bayley Scale scores." J Abnorm Child Psychol 5(1):
     79-91, 1977. (15 References).
Documents a statistical study used to examine the effects of abusive or neglectful family situations on the test-taking behaviors of children. More specifically, the study was designed to investigate relationships between certain observed behaviors and test scores on the Mental Developmental Index (MDI) and the Psychomotor Developmental Index (PDI) for thirty-eight normal control children, thirty-eight failure to thrive (FTT) children, and forty-six victims of non-accidental trauma (NAT). Results indicate that the physical abuse of children significantly depresses mental functioning but is not detrimental to motor functioning. Neglect, however, adversely affects both mental and motor development. Males and females also exhibit distinctly different responses to physical abuse and to neglect in terms of attention span, social relationships, and mental deterioration. These variables indicate that prior to testing, the physically abused males experienced patterns of abuse different from the physically abused females.

1096 Martin, Harold P.; Beezley, Patricia; Conway, Esther F.; et al.
     "The development of abused children: Part I. A review of the
     literature; Part II. Physical, neurological and intellectual
     outcome." Adv Pediatr 21: 25-73, 1974. (144 References).
Reports on a two-part study of the impact of abuse on children. The authors first review the child abuse literature of the past thirteen years and conclude that further study of the effect of the abusive environment upon child development must be initiated. Factors associated with the home environment which may be additionally detrimental to the abused child are examined, including undernutrition, maternal deprivation, sexual abuse, severe psychiatric disturbance in parents, and social and/or economic disadvantage.

The second part of the study is a report of the physical and intellectual functioning of fifty-eight abused children several years after being returned to a home environment. The children's neurologic status, physical growth, head circumference and birth weight were graphed. Intellectual tests such as the Wechsler Intelligence Scale and the Peabody Picture Vocabulary Test were administered. Children with a history of head trauma

scored significantly lower than those children who registered no neurologic impairment. Moreover, children still living in a punitive or unstable home environment generally scored lower than those who enjoyed
improved home relations. In addition, when earlier scores were available,
the latter group generally showed marked improvement over previous results.
It is concluded that professionals should insist that the abused child
be taken to an environment where growth and development will be stimulated rather than impeded.

1097   Morse, Carol W.; Sahler, Olle J. Z.; Friedman, Stanford B. "A
        three-year follow-up study of abused and neglected children." Am
        J Dis Child 120(5): 439-46, November, 1970. (10 References).
Presents the results of a follow-up study of twenty-five children hospitalized between 1963 and 1966 for injuries diagnosed as the sequelae
of abuse or neglect. The goal of the study was to determine which children had prospered since their initial hospitalization and why. Methodology consisted of interviewing mothers about the following three concerns: the child's present state of health and his intellectual and
emotional development, interim changes in the family such as a change in
living situations, and the mother's estimate of the value of any agency
intervention subsequent to the child's hospitalization. Study findings
indicated that 35 percent of the children were subsequently treated for
repeated abuse or neglect. Nine children showed signs of mental retardation, and six were emotionally disturbed. Of the nine mentally retarded
children, eight had been so before the abusive incident; thus it is con-
ceivable that the retardation provoked the parent's abusive reaction.
Six children, however, developed normally. This group of children
appeared to be enjoying a happy mother-child relationship. Moreover,
agency involvement with these six families was generally regarded as
supportive and helpful. These last two factors, therefore, became the
criteria for predicting whether or not an abused child would prosper if
returned to his parents.

1098   Ramanujam, B. K. "Psychiatric problems of children seen in an urban
        center of Western India." Am J Orthopsychiatry 45(3): 490-96,
        April, 1975. (0 References).
Surveys the types of problems encountered in a child guidance clinic in
Western India, based on observations of some 498 children between the
ages of five and twelve. A high proportion of the clientele exhibited
chronic brain syndrome and mental retardation; an injury to the central
nervous system had occurred in 49 percent of the cases. Other problems
included retardation due to malnutrition, cultural deprivation, learning
inhibitions, and neurotic and speech disorders. Many of the children's
emotional problems were regarded as a reflection of the familial and
marital difficulties of young parents caught in the transition of a
developing nation from the extended to the nuclear family group.

1099   Ringler, Norma M.; Kennell, John H.; Jarvella, Robert; et al.
        "Mother-to-child speech at 2 years -- effects of early postnatal
        contact." J Pediatr 86(1): 141-44, January, 1975. (9 Refer-
        ences).
Analyzes effects of extended neonatal contact between mothers and their
first children upon the quality of the mother's later conversation with
her child. Ten young mothers were chosen from two groups, one having
spent the usual amount of time with their infants in the first three days
after delivery, the other group having been given an extra sixteen hours

with their children during this period. The speech patterns of these mothers to their children were compared when the children were one month, one year, and two years old. The mothers who had had extended contact with their newborns tended to use more sophisticated and open-ended constructions with their children at the age of two. They gave fewer commands, asked more questions, and used more adjectives and words per preposition than did the other mothers. These findings lead to the recommendation that hospitals regularly allow mothers to spend more time with their newborns.

1100   Rosen, Shirley R.; Hirschenfang, Samuel; Benton, Joseph G. "Aftermath of severe multiple deprivation in a young child: clinical implications." Percept Mot Skills 24(1): 219-26, February, 1967. (0 References).

A clinical study of a young child who suffered physical and mental retardation as a result of parental neglect and abandonment. Although she was three years old, the child had the vocal development of a four-month-old baby who had never left his crib and was retarded in all areas of development. A month-by-month treatment program aiming for the acquisition of basic motor skills, language, and an awareness of self is outlined in the study. Follow-up evaluations of his progress revealed consistent growth in all developmental areas, but also some evidence that he may have had some form of organic brain damage in addition to mental retardation.

1101   Sandgrund, Alice; Gaines, Richard W.; Green, Arthur H. "Child abuse and mental retardation: a problem of cause and effect." Am J Ment Defic 79(3): 327-30, November, 1974. (11 References).

Cites an experiment designed to uncover the relationship between child abuse and mental retardation. Sixty cases of moderate abuse were compared with two thirty-member control groups of neglected children and non-abused children. Families from all three groups received public assistance. Twenty-five percent of the abused children, 20 percent of the neglected children, and 3 percent of the non-abused children were found to be retarded. Observing the correlations between retardation and abuse and neglect, an additional question is raised: does cognitive impairment precede abuse or result from it?

1102   Schmidt, Wilfred H. O. "The child as animal educandum: social deprivation." In: Schmidt, W. H. O. Child development: the human, cultural, and educational context. New York: Harper and Row, 1973. 30-37. (6 References).

Describes two children in extreme social isolation for the first six years of life. Anna, an illegitimate child, was rejected by her mother, taunted by her brother, and left in a chair in a dark room for six years. Upon discovery, she was placed in an institution for nine months and was later removed to a good foster home. However, her advances in speech and social adjustment remained small, even at the time of her death three years later. Isabelle, another illegitimate child, also remained isolated in a dark room for six years with her deaf-mute mother. However, upon discovery, her advances in speech and social development were so rapid that after two years of expert training, she appeared to be a child of normal intelligence. Isabelle's mother's acceptance and constant presence appears to be the critical difference between these two cases. Although Isabelle and her mother could not communicate verbally, they did communicate through physical gesture. The close relationship with her mother allowed Isabelle to establish contact quickly once in the outside world.

1103   Sharlin, Schlomo A., and Polansky, Norman A.   "The process of in-
        fantilization."   Am J Orthopsychiatry   42(1):   92-102, January,
        1972.   (15 References).
Infantilization, which is defined as the process by which individuals are
encouraged not to develop competence and independence, is explored.
Fifty-two somewhat retarded children and their mothers were observed and
interviewed over a twelve to thirty month period in an attempt to identify
infantilizing behavior and attitudes.   Children were designated infantile
if their I.Q.'s decreased more markedly than normal over the period of
the project.   Other concomitants of infantilism included low gross muscle
coordination and visual clinging to the mother.   It was found that the
infantilized children had been protected overzealously by their mothers,
that the child's handicap had made the mother reluctant to criticize and
punish him.   Forty other variables producing infantile behavior were
identified.

1104   Stott, D. H.   "Abnormal mothering as a cause of mental subnormality:
        a critique of some classic studies of maternal deprivation in the
        light of possible congenital factors."   J Child Psychol Psychiatry
        3(2):   79-91, April-June, 1962.   (31 References).
Hypothesizes that some of the early childhood handicaps such as impaired
motor development, physical malformations, and infantile diseases, often
believed to be caused by maternal deprivation may, in fact, actually be
a result of congenital damage.

E. VIOLENCE AND CRIME

1105   Climent, Carlos E., and Ervin, Frank R.   "Historical data in the
        evaluation of violent subjects: a hypothesis generating study."
        Arch Gen Psychiatry   27(5):   621-24, November, 1972.   (9 References).
Forty violent subjects were compared with forty non-violent subjects in
tests conducted at Boston City Hospital.   The results generated four
hypotheses for further study: (1) that there is positive correlation between brain injury and violence; (2) that a link between neurotic childhood traits and adult violent behavior is not evident; (3) that violent
individuals have more suicidal impulses than non-violent persons; and
(4) that criminality is independent of violent behavior, the former being
related to cultural factors, and the latter to individual factors.   Data
also revealed that violent subjects were more likely to be unemployed
and to be referred to the hospital as violent by someone other than themselves.   This non-referred group generally tended to be more socially
disorganized than self-referrals.   Violent subjects were also beaten more
often as children.

1106   Curtis, George C.   "Violence breeds violence -- perhaps?"   Am J
        Psychiatry   120(4):   386-87, October, 1963.   (5 References).
Suggests that today's battered children become tomorrow's violent criminals and murderers.   Both theory and empirical data are offered to
support this claim.   Theoretically, an abused child must build up great
hostility against his parents, hostility that will vent itself somewhere.
Also, such a child is given a model of destructive venting of hostility
and will likely imitate his parents in that respect.   Clinical studies
of murderously aggressive children frequently showed that they were themselves abused children.

1107   Duncan, Glen M.; Frazier, Shervert H.; Litin, Edward M.; et al.
       "Etiological factors in first-degree murder." JAMA 168(13):
       1755-58, November 29, 1958. (0 References).
Studies the family background of six criminals and its relationship to
their subsequent crimes. The prisoners were from middle class families
and were not suffering from an organic diseases or psychoses. Two of
the prisoners were psychotic at the time of their crimes and were not
brutally abused as children. Four prisoners received abuse from at least
one parent, treatment which they later imitated as solutions to frustration. Consistently, the prisoners' female victims were seductive, then
rejecting, while male victims were threatening. Unconscious homosexual
tendencies reflect the parents' preferential treatment of a sister.
Prevention of such manifestations of abuse rests on the family physician's
awareness of and intervention in brutal family situations.

1108   Duncan, Jane W., and Duncan, Glen M. "Murder in the family: a
       study of some homicidal adolescents." Am J Psychiatry 127(11):
       74-78, May, 1971. (9 References).
Reports on a retrospective study investigating five cases of homicidal
adolescents, in order to illustrate behaviors and family situations that
augment an adolescent's potential for committing homicide. It reveals
that in each case the youth's actions were a response to the progressive
deterioration of his interpersonal relationship with the victim, to events
that had become increasingly unbearable, and often to a deep feeling of
despair and helplessness after non-violent solutions to his problems had
failed. The study also shows that a history of parental violence is
frequently present in cases of adolescent homicide. An outline of specific criteria for evaluating a youth's potential for violent behavior
is provided.

1109   Field, Jack G. "Two types of recidivist and maternal deprivation."
       Br J Criminol 2(4): 377-81, April, 1962. (8 References).
Studies two types of recidivist in an attempt to link delinquent behavior
with maternal deprivation. Of the ninety-three subjects, forty-two were
in Corrective Training Programs in prison, while fifty-one were serving
Preventive Detention sentences. Maternal deprivation was indicated in
approximately 17 percent of each sample group. In addition, these per-
centages did not differ significantly from those found to be true in a
sampling of the general population. The study does not, however, rule
out the possibility of other forms of childhood deprivation or abuse as
contributing to delinquency in later life.

1110   Geha, Richard. "For the love of Medusa: a psychoanalytic glimpse
       into gynecocide." Psychoanal Rev 62(1): 49-77, Spring, 1975.
       (51 References).
A Freudian interpretation of the motives behind the murder of women. Some
of the literature concerning the dynamics of this crime are discussed, and
several brief case histories are included. It is assumed that a desire to
commit matricide is at the root of every gynecocide.

1111   Jenkins, Richard L.; Gants, Robert; Shoji, Takeshi; et al. "Inter-
       rupting the family cycle of violence." J Iowa Med Soc 60(2):
       85-89, February, 1970. (0 References).
Documents a case history of an abused child who, in turn, battered other
children. The child, severely beaten and humiliated by his stepfather,
vacillated between extreme fear and extreme hatred. During therapy, as

his fears lessened, his withdrawn silent self would turn obstreperous and abusive. Continued therapy and positive foster home placements allowed him to balance his expression of these feelings in more socially acceptable ways.

1112 King, Charles H. "The ego and the integration of violence in
      homicidal youth." Am J Orthopsychiatry 45(1): 134-45, January,
      1975. (9 References).
Studies the motivation and treatment of nine homicidal youths. Disruptive homelife, educational deprivation, and inability to cope characterize the backgrounds of these adolescents. Abandoning a traditional approach to treatment, this study employs an ecological perspective. The causes of homicide and the actual behavior are placed in a total environmental framework.

1113 Miller, Derek, and Looney, John. "The prediction of adolescent
      homicide: episodic dyscontrol and dehumanization." Am J Psychoanal
      34(3): 187-98, Fall, 1974. (25 References).
Analyzes the psychological syndrome which predisposes murderous behavior. A number of cases are cited to support the idea that the distinguishing factor in the "predictable" homicide is his ability to dehumanize others. Because of this weakness in ego development, certain stresses precipitate violent behavior. In some persons, the slightest irritant can lead to murder. In a number of cases, the tendency toward dehumanization began in the brutalization and neglect of the murderer by his parents.

1114 Pemberton, David A., and Benady, D. Roger. "Consciously rejected
      children." Br J Psychiatry 123(576): 575-78, November, 1973.
      (6 References).
Defines "consciously rejected children" as children who have been excluded from the family. They exhibit aggression, reject parents, lie, steal, and possess other negative behaviors. Such consciously rejected children tend to be the products of unstable marriages where, particularly, the mother is ambivalent about her role.

1115 Prescott, James W. "Before ethics and morality." Humanist 32(6):
      19-21, November-December, 1972. (0 References).
Human violence is linked to sensory deprivation and parental neglect in childhood. The effects of deprivation in animals and the relationship between sensory stimulation and normal brain development are also discussed.

1116 Richette, Lisa Aversa. The throwaway children. Philadelphia:
      J. B. Lippincott, 1969. 342p.
A stark portrait of "throwaway" children--delinquent, battered, sexually abused, or abandoned--taken from the transcripts of the juvenile court in Philadelphia. Squalid neighborhoods and incidents of psychological deprivation, corruption, and abuse at home are described. The role of the court in deciphering the complex motives which lead these misused children to become thieves, rapists, and murderers in adolescence is discussed. The collapse of the family and the loss of childhood happiness is reenacted in each vignette.

1117 Rolston, Richard H. "The effect of prior physical abuse on the
      expression of overt and fantasy aggressive behavior in children."
      For a summary see: Diss Abstr Int 32B(5): 3016, November, 1971.

1118 Sadoff, Robert L. "Clinical observations on parricide." <u>Psychiatr</u>
      <u>Q</u> 45(1): 65-69, 1971. (3 References).
Presents the histories of two cases of parricide--one the killing of a
mother and the other, of a father--both acts performed by young men. In
both cases, the youth felt himself to be trapped in an unhealthy and
abnormal relationship with the parent: the parent mistreated the child
(in some cases, physically abused him) while the child felt attached in
some way to the parent and, therefore, unable to break free by more conventional means. Both boys felt relieved and liberated after the parri-
cides.

1119 Tanay, Emanuel. "Proceedings: adolescents who kill parents --
      reactive parricide." <u>Aust NZ J Psychiatry</u> 7(4): 263-77, December,
      1973. (17 References).
Explores the crime of reactive parricide--the murder of a parent, which
is prompted by the cruel behavior of the victim. The factors examined in
relation to the crime are: (1) the personality of the parent; (2) the
victim's effect on the family, especially the killer; (3) the personality
of the surviving parent; (4) the relationship between the parents; (5)
the nature of family life both before and after the killing; (6) societal
reaction to the family; and (7) treatment of the perpetrator. The homicide is viewed as an adaptive act. Since an abused child is often not
protected by society from a sadistic parent, murder may simply be the
child's extreme reaction to an intolerable situation. The need for
increased understanding of reactive parricide is stressed as a means of
preventing its occurrence. Two detailed case histories are given.

V

Treatment

A. OVERVIEW

1120 Alberts, M. E. "Child abuse: editorial." <u>J Iowa Med Soc</u> 62(5):
      242, May, 1972. (0 References).
Briefly reviews the history of child abuse and concludes with a summary
of the 1972 statement by The American Academy of Pediatrics. The statement calls for: (1) mandatory reporting by physicians; (2) agencies
equipped to take action when necessary; (3) services to be provided for
problem families; (4) protection of the child; (5) a central registry
for all cases of child abuse; and (6) immunity from lawsuits for physicians reporting such incidents. Future recommendations include prediction of high risk situations, establishment of crisis management centers,
day care centers and diagnostic and/or treatment centers, and the use of
lay assistance in aiding distressed families.

1121 "Battered babies." <u>Can Med Assoc J</u> 101(7): 98, November 1, 1969.
      (0 References).
Emphasizes the need for child protection agencies. The National Society
for the Prevention of Cruelty to Children (NSPCC) holds the opinion that
rather than remove abused children from their homes, the problem families
should receive help.

1122 Bennett, Robert F. "Families in stress, children in peril."
      <u>Compact</u> 10: 13, 16, Summer, 1976. (0 References).
For treatment of child abuse problems, rehabilitation is considered more
effective than punishment. Clear legal definitions of abuse and quick
identification of abused or potentially abused children are important;
and all professions and agencies should cooperate to help abused children
and their families. The laws of most states are widening the categories
of people required to report suspected abuse and are requiring penalties
for those who fail to report. However, society as a whole needs to do
more to prevent abuse. Citizens must know what the problem is, what
agencies exist to handle it, and how individuals can get involved.
Federal aid would help; but in the long run, only cooperation between
government, public and private agencies, and private citizens will avail.

1123 Bishop, Frank. "The maltreatment of children: some unresolved
      problems." <u>Med J Aust</u> 2(7): 245-49, August 16, 1975. (11
      References).
Unresolved problems in the management of child abuse are discussed. An
overemphasis is placed on physical findings with little attention given
to the emotional, social, personality development, and intellectual
manifestations of maltreatment. Professionals are often reluctant to

report suspected abuse, because they feel that protection of the parents from criminal prosecution is more important than protection of the child from serious injury or death. A lack of follow-up research on battered children who are separated from their families, as compared to those who are treated at home, makes it difficult to determine whether or not separation is a viable treatment strategy. Any research in this area would be confounded by the fact that children who are separated from their families were generally subjected to more severe injury or neglect than those allowed to remain at home. Finally, the manner in which child abuse is handled in the courts is inappropriate and counterproductive. Most parents are psychologically disturbed at the moment that maltreatment occurs, but there is no evidence that punishment through the criminal courts can effect any lasting change in this emotional disturbance.

1124 Bishop, Julia A. "Helping neglectful parents." Ann Am Acad Polit
      Soc Sci 355(5): 82-89, September, 1964. (6 References).
Summarizes the goals and functions of child protective services in cases of child neglect. A protective services agency depends upon its links to the community, which provides it with reports of neglected children. Its main goal is to insure the protection of the child, and its chief tenet is that the inadequately functioning, neglectful parent is not necessarily incapable of improved functioning. The protective services worker attempts to provide parents with an opportunity to maximize their capacities and must use non-conventional casework methods to do so. The legal auspices under which the agency functions is an important dimension of the role it can play with parents. It is emphasized that child abuse must be distinguished from neglect in terms of etiology, treatment approach, and prognosis.

1125 Blue, M. T. "The battered child syndrome from a social work view-
      point." Can J Public Health 56(5): 197-98, May, 1965. (0
      References).
Widespread recognition of the problem of child abuse in Canada is a recent phenomenon which has led to some sensational news reporting and calls for legislative reform. Legislation enacted in the United States is seen as motivated by punitive feelings against abusive parents. The article tries to desensationalize child abuse. Trained social workers need to be skilled in the diagnosis and treatment of the personality symptoms of the battering parent. Interdisciplinary professional efforts and the acceptance of responsibility by everyone in society to report cases of abuse is more important than legislative action.

1126 Booz-Allen and Hamilton, Incorporated, Washington, D.C. An assess-
      ment of the needs of and resources for children of alcoholic
      parents. Springfield, Virginia: National Technical Information
      Service. 183p. (Bibliography). For ordering information see:
      Government Reports Announcements and Index 75(14): 32, July 11,
      1975.
Presents findings and recommendations of a study which evaluated the special needs of children of alcoholic parents and the community and national resources available to help them. For a sample study population of fifty teenagers and young adults in the Philadelphia area, the authors estimate that there are twenty-eight million children nationally living in homes with at least one alcoholic adult.

Alcoholic families are beset with numerous problems. Children are deprived of warmth, affection, and a supportive parent figure. The home environment is inconsistent and tense, and children become unwilling witnesses to angry and sometimes violent conflicts between parents. In addition to emotional neglect, some children suffer verbal, physical, or sexual abuse at their parents' hands. Emotionally, a child will be tormented by feelings of resentment, embarrassment, fear, hatred, and loneliness. If a child is continually subject to such an environment, he will exhibit such problems as temper tantrums, problems in school, delinquency, experimenting with alcohol or drugs, and attempts at suicide. Nevertheless, many children devise means of coping with their unhappy family lives. These coping mechanisms include: (1) flight, especially the young child's hiding under a bed or at a relative's; (2) fight, particularly during adolescence; and (3) becoming a perfect child, an overachiever, or one who attempts to solve all the family's problems.

Like all children, the children of alcoholic parents have a basic right to enjoy their childhood. In addition, their primary needs must be met, if not by their parents, then by other persons in the extended family or in the community. These primary needs include protection, compensatory parenting, respect, respite, attention, a positive environment, and the right to seek help and treatment. Present resources, however, do not meet these needs. Child and family care agencies favor clients with certain crisis-oriented problems, such as child abuse or divorce, and they traditionally deal solely with limited populations. Unless a child of an alcoholic parent has behavior problems of his own, he may never come into contact with any supportive community resources. The establishment of integrated treatment programs for the entire alcoholic family are recommended. Special services should be delegated for the child, however, and these should be readily accessible to him. Most importantly, perhaps, legislation granting children the right to seek and receive treatment without parental consent must be passed.

1127 Brieland, Donald. "Protective services and child abuse: implications for public child welfare." Soc Serv Rev 40(4): 369-77, December, 1966. (18 References).
Surveys the development of protective service agencies and expresses concern for the future of such agencies under child abuse legislation. The range of services provided by such agencies throughout the country is depicted, along with the interaction of these agencies with the hospitals and law enforcement system. The difficulties faced by the protective service agencies since the passage of child abuse legislation lie mainly in the increase of the burden placed on the understaffed agency. The increase in reported cases and the growing pressure for rapid investigation of these cases add to the work load.

1128 "Child abuse." Nurs Forum 3(2): 7-9, 1964. (0 References).
Traces a child abuse case from hospital admission through legal prosecution.

1129 Daniel, Jessica H. "Ethical, professional and technical dilemmas of cultural and social class discrepancy between professionals and clients." In: National Symposium on Child Abuse, 5th, Boston, 1974. Collected papers. Denver, Colorado: The American Humane Association, Children's Division, 1976. 53-62. (0 References).
Presents some dilemmas encountered in identifying and treating child abuse. In the absence of sufficient data, it is difficult to identify a family in crises, particularly one above the lower socioeconomic class.

Consequently, most abuse cases involve the low income family. The problem of court intervention involves deciding when and how to use the courts, the conflict of awarding custody, and the role of the professionals as advocate of the child, the parents, or the family unit.

1130   De Francis, Vincent. Child protective services in the United States:
       reporting a nationwide survey. Denver, Colorado: The American
       Humane Association, Children's Division, 1956. 16p. (Bibliography).
Proposes a definition of child protective services based on a 1954
national survey undertaken by the Children's Division of The American
Humane Association. Protective services are primarily distinguished from
private social agencies by their uninvited intervention on behalf of the
child at the bequest of the community. The Children's Bill of Rights
written by the New York State Youth Commission clearly indicates the
responsibility of the community to protect its children. The aim of
protective services, then, is to provide a casework service which guarantees these rights. Because the services' approach is rehabilitative
rather than punitive, changes in the home which are necessary for the
child's welfare and the strengthening of family unity are goals. Though
protective services do not provide child welfare services such as financial aid and foster home placement, it is responsible for contacting
welfare agencies for their services when necessary.

1131   ————. The fundamentals of child protection: a statement of
       basic concepts and principles. Denver, Colorado: The American
       Humane Association, Children's Division, 1955. 71p.
Presents basic philosophy, responsibilities, and operating methods of
child protective services, distilling years of practical experience to
create a manual for new workers. Protective services should actively
reach out to help, to treat, and to prevent problems, since parents of
neglected children rarely seek help voluntarily. An expression of the
community's concern for its children, the child protective service has
the right to use its authority, both legal and moral, to safeguard children. Its responsibilities are greater than most social service agencies,
for it must satisfy the community as well as the client. Its operation
necessarily depends on other available community services, and all
services should cooperate closely. The author suggests a three-step
process for handling each case: fact-finding, diagnosis, and treatment.
He outlines and explains in detail each of the three.

1132   ————. "Parents who abuse children." PTA Mag 58(3): 16-18,
       November, 1963. (0 References).
Argues for an increase in child protective services, outlining the aims,
activities, and achievements of those already in operation. A general
profile of child abuse is given, including a description of the needs of
abusive parents. Help and guidance for these parents are listed as the
key solutions to abuse problems.

1133   ————. Protective services and community expectations. Denver,
       Colorado: The American Humane Association, Children's Division,
       1961. 17p.
Evaluates the role and function of protective services in the community.
The strength of society depends on its most fundamental unit, the family;
and protective services should work both to correct and to prevent problems which weaken the family. Because neglect situations tend to foster
delinquency and to be self-perpetuating, prevention of neglect is stressed

to save the community money otherwise lost to crime and to save families
before the child is seriously damaged. Physical neglect, being invisible,
brings about the majority of referrals to protective services. Emotional
neglect, being less tangible, poses three problems for the child protective workers: (1) Being less visible, an emotional neglect case rarely
gets referred to protective services until it has already become a full-
blown crisis. Protective services should ask for help from other community facilities (schools, for example) in spotting early signs of
emotional neglect; (2) State laws are often outdated and ambiguous on the
subject of emotional abuse and, hence, do not give protective services
the legal support needed; (3) The vagueness of the emotional neglect laws
often renders caseworkers ineffective in court. They should hire legal
consultants. In all ways, a community should cooperate to prevent neglect,
abuse, and delinquency of children.

1134 "Deliberate injury to children." Br Med J 4(5884): 61-62, October
      13, 1973. (6 References).
Provides a brief discussion of the child battering problem, stressing that
families need help, not punishment, for their actions. Injuries resulting
typically from abuse are discussed, as well as the personality of the
battering parent and the parent's social problems. The importance of
maintaining records of abused children in all hospitals for cross-refer-
encing is emphasized.

1135 Drake, Frances M. "The position of the local authority." In:
      Franklin, Alfred White, ed. Concerning child abuse. New York:
      Churchill Livingstone, 1975. 85-94. (0 References).
The local social service authority must carry out the protective functions
of society toward all children in need of care. It has the power to
remove a child from his home and perhaps break up a family. However,
individual workers of the authority are not free agents and must work
within the statutory constraints placed upon them. In recent years, evidence of child battering is often discovered in a hospital setting. But
because medical personnel are reluctant to report such cases to the local
authority, delays in investigation and treatment inevitably occur. It
should be a statutory obligation for medical personnel to report abuse to
the local authority where a central register of all reported cases should
be maintained. The first consideration of the local authority when a
report of suspected child abuse has been made is the well-being and
safety of the child. If there is evidence of physical assault, the child
should be removed from the home while an assessment of the family situation is made. The local authority has the power to establish residential
family treatment centers and day care nurseries, and to provide financial
help to low income groups where environmental stress may precipitate child
abuse. It has an expanding, supportive role which can ensure the proper
development and safety of the child as well as provide help to the parents
and family.

1136 Franklin, Alfred White, ed. Concerning child abuse: papers pre-
      sented by the Tunbridge Wells Study Group on non-accidental injury
      to children. New York: Churchill Livingstone, 1975. 189p.
      (Bibliography).
Presents a selection of brief expository papers and reports of studies
which examine the responsibilities, concerns, and theoretical findings of
those persons involved in the medical, social, and legal management and
treatment of the child abuse syndrome. A pediatrician outlines the

external signs of abuse and neglect and cautions attendant physicians in
emergency rooms to thoroughly investigate even minor injuries in children,
for these often prove to be warning signs of potentially serious or fatal
abuse. Neurological manifestations of brain contusion in infants are
described, and procedures for diagnosing the extent of cerebral damage
are discussed.

Results of a study aimed at discovering a correlation between abnormal
EEG readings and the personality of child abusers indicate the possible
existence of a subgroup of child batterers who more closely conform to
other aggressive and violent criminal types than to the general population.
An in-patient setting for family psychotherapy offering individual nurturing to mother and child illustrates how both a protective and therapeutic
atmosphere can mend the cycle of abuse.

The roles of the social worker, health visitor, police, and the local
authority are examined. It is recommended that social workers receive
legal training in the fundamentals of landlord-tenant relationships, adoption procedures, legal aid, and other areas of concern which often trouble
families. Because of their extensive knowledge of families within a
particular neighborhood, health visitors can refer at risk families to
the appropriate social services for counseling and treatment. Reasons
cited for involving the police in child abuse cases include their efficiency in gathering information and their twenty-four-hour availability.
Local social service authorities serve not only protective, but also
diagnostic functions in preparing a program for the treatment of the whole
family.

Additional essays explain legal problems in reporting child abuse in Great
Britain, along with standard procedures for criminal and juvenile court
hearings there. Appendices include height and weight charts to be used
during the course of a physical examination in assessing the failure to
thrive syndrome in a young child.

1137 Gritz, Francine S. "Administrative problems to program implementation in child protective services." In: National Symposium on
Child Abuse, 5th, Boston, 1974. Collected papers. Denver, Colorado:
The American Humane Association, Children's Division, 1976. 94-96.
(0 References).
Suggests methods of effective administration in protective services.
Agencies need full-time administration, adequate, well paid staff, and
caseload controls. The supervisor must be versatile, responsible, and
able to maintain a high level of morale among staff members. Community
groups must contribute to the educational process.

1138 Harrison, Stanley L. "Child abuse control centers: a project for
the Academy?" Pediatrics 45(5): 894-95, May, 1970. (2 References).
Sets forth a proposal involving the formation of child abuse control
centers, similar to poison control centers. They would be located in
hospitals or public health centers and would: (1) offer twenty-four-hour
services; (2) remove children from dangerous home situations; (3) report
cases requiring further investigation; (4) work with existing agencies to
place children in foster homes; (5) refer parents to psychiatrists if
necessary; (6) serve as court consultants; (7) offer reports to the
state's central registry; and (8) supply the community as well as physicians and social workers with information about the child abuse problem.

1139 Irwin, Theodore. To combat child abuse and neglect. (Public
      Affairs Pamphlet No. 508). New York: Public Affairs Committee,
      1974. 28p.
Summarizes the problem of child abuse, including methods of treatment and
the way various professionals and concerned laymen can help with the
problem.

1140 Kadushin, Alfred. "Protective services." In: Kadushin, Alfred.
      Child welfare services. New York: Macmillan, 1974. 221-91.
      (160 References).
Protective services may take on the responsibility of strengthening an
unstable home, helping parents to care for their children, or removing
the child from an unhealthy environment. A brief history of child welfare services is offered. The situations in which protective services
are required include: (1) physical abuse; (2) inadequate fulfillment of
basic environmental needs; (3) absence of proper medical care; (4) infrequent school attendance; (5) exploitation or overwork; and (6) exposure
to "unwholesome circumstances." Examples are given of each type of abuse.
Protective service intervention is often offered without the client's
request; community groups or individuals seek agency response. The agency
is responsible for protecting the child until he appears to be safe, and
in some cases, the agency may turn to the courts in an effort to maximize
their effectiveness. Neglect is a more common complaint than abuse.
While neglect is described as a response to social stress, abuse is said
to be a product of psychological stress. An evaluation of the existing
protective services system in the United States concludes by noting its
general effectiveness. Problems in the system include the need for
standard definitions of "adequate parental care" and of the "rights of
parents and of children." It is also difficult to hire qualified protective service workers. A discussion of new trends in the provision of
protective services includes: (1) an emphasis on family cooperation,
rather than on strict law enforcement; (2) an increase in public agency
involvement, as opposed to volunteer participation; (3) the institution
of more aggressive case-finding procedures; (4) widespread concern with
child welfare-oriented legislation; (5) community acceptance of protective service agencies; and (6) the employment of sociotherapy, rather
than a purely psychotherapeutic approach to counseling.

1141 Kempe, C. Henry. "Child abuse and neglect." In: Talbot, Nathan
      B., ed. Raising children in America. Boston: Little, Brown,
      1974. 173-88. (0 References).
Discusses the problem of child abuse and neglect, and relates the nature
of the problem to the social, economic, and political system in America.
Formerly, children were regarded as the property of their parents, who
could treat them or dispose of them as they wished. Recently, however,
Americans have begun to regard children as being merely in the care of
their parents and belonging to themselves. This attitude parallels the
philosophy of childrearing which exists in a totalitarian system, where
children belong to the state and, therefore, receive broad and continuing
support for their mental and emotional welfare. Although American law
demands compulsory education from age six, it offers no provisions for
guaranteeing basic safety to children under six and certainly no provisions for developing environmental circumstances for optimal growth.
Mandatory reporting laws are a first step toward providing protection,
but their effectiveness depends on the quality of the follow-up action
of child protective service units.

Treatment can be productive for the 90 percent of abusive parents not suffering from some severe pathological disorder. In cases where treatment is not successful, there should be a socially acceptable alternative --to dissolve families and to absolve parental rights voluntarily or involuntarily so that every child receives minimal support. Society must have access to children from a very early age and must provide regular health supervision for all. A system of health visitors is suggested whereby regular contacts are made with all families with newborns, regardless of social class. Further recommendations to improve the quality of care to all children include: (1) swift and appropriate action by protective services and juvenile courts; (2) a national child abuse registry; (3) interim foster care; (4) innovative treatment modalities such as Families Anonymous; (5) legal training in law school for court judges and lawyers who will face making decisions about child protection; and (6) family life education.

1142 ————. "A practical approach to the protection of the abused child and rehabilitation of the abusing parent." Pediatrics 51(4, Part II): 804-12, April, 1973. (1 Reference).
Points out effective and practical ways to protect abused children and to treat their abusing parents. The successful child advocacy program in Aberdeen, Scotland, where a team of health visitors contacts every household to gather information that could be used to identify potential abusers, is discussed. A combination of protection and treatment programs, such as crisis hot-lines, crisis nurseries, homemakers, and day care centers, should be present in every community. Another innovative program that deserves special attention is the foster grandmother or mother surrogate program. Most importantly, society needs to recognize that many people do not like their children and will never be capable of mothering. In such cases there should be a socially acceptable way to remove the child and place him in foster care. Children need love and mothering. When their own parents cannot provide these essentials, the child should have the chance to find them outside of the home.

1143 Kempe, C. Henry, and Helfer, Ray E., eds. Helping the battered child and his family. Philadelphia: J. B. Lippincott, 1972. 313p. (Bibliography).
Numerous articles, covering many aspects of the treatment of the battered child and his family, are presented. Part I outlines the procedure for evaluating the potential for parents to abuse their children, describes the kind of therapeutic relationship that should be developed with the parents, discusses different types of therapeutic agents that can work successfully with the family (including social workers, foster grandparents or parents aids, visiting nurses, homemaker services, crisis nurseries, and Mothers Anonymous), and lists the goals of therapy when working with battering parents.

Part II provides guidelines for the detection of child abuse through examination of the child, outlines procedures that emergency room physicians and school personnel should use when reporting cases of abuse to the child protective services, discusses the kinds of treatment battered children may need (including individual therapy and/or placement in a foster home), and lists the criteria for determining whether a home is safe enough for a battered child to be allowed to return to the family. Also included in this section is a discussion on the effects of child abuse on a child's subsequent intellectual, motor, and personality development, and his prognosis for recovery with and without intervention.

Part III assesses the current state of protective services throughout the United States and recommends that public policy support a system of state funding and supervision of child protective programs. This section also demonstrates how an interdisciplinary hospital-based team for the management of child abuse cases operates, and discusses the team's relationship with community and child protective services. It is emphasized that a full-time professional person is needed to coordinate the activities of the treatment team, protective services, the police, the courts, the foster parents, and the family to avoid confusion and inefficient handling of child abuse cases.

Part IV analyzes the involvement of the courts, law enforcement officers, attorneys, and judges in child abuse cases. Child abuse cases are treated in two different contexts by the law--in civil and criminal proceedings. Prosecution of an abusing parent under criminal law is considered to be a punitive, non-therapeutic approach which is totally ineffective in the handling of child abuse cases. If child abuse is treated as a civil matter, the judge can bring together the expertise of the lawyer, physician, social worker, police, clergy, and educator to plan a treatment program for the abusive parents and to provide for the safety and welfare of the abused child. The ultimate goal of the civil proceeding is to strengthen the family and reunite its members if possible. Appendices to this book include a preliminary report on a questionnaire that is successful in predicting which parents will abuse their children and a description of The Center for the Study of Abused and Neglected Children in Denver, Colorado.

1144   Lewis, Harold. "Parental and community neglect: twin responsibilities of protective services." Children 16(3): 114-18, May-June, 1969. (14 References).
Community and parental neglect are mutually supporting contributors to the problem of child neglect, as illustrated by the child whose medical needs are overlooked in an area where medical services are seriously deficient. Social agencies widely ignore the problem of community neglect, which is said to exist where there "is evidence of persistent, inadequate, insufficient provision of resources for child care." Comprehensive agency goals should include the promotion of positive community conditions and community leaders must be identified as part of the agency's client group. Innovative types and combinations of services, focused on the child, must be directed against this multidimensional problem.

1145   Makepeace, Dorothy. "The neglected child." Practitioner 174(1042): 483-87, April, 1955. (0 References).
Examines the viable options available to abusing parents and abused children. The nuclear family is by far the most superior situation for child-rearing although at times it may become necessary to remove a child from its parents' home. Better education in childrearing, mobilization of existing services, and prophylactic psychiatry may aid in the prevention of child abuse and neglect.

1146   Mulford, Robert M. "Child abuse: intervention and treatment, edited by Nancy B. Ebeling and Deborah A. Hill: book review." Child Welfare 55(3): 226, 1976. (0 References).
Briefly reviews Child abuse: intervention and treatment by Nancy Ebeling and Deborah Hill. Comments are made as to the content and quality of the work.

1147   Nagi, Saad Z.   Child maltreatment in the United States -- a cry for
help and organizational response: appendix.   Columbus, Ohio: The
Ohio State University, 1976.   295p.
Appendix to a report on the maltreatment of children.   Research tools are
presented, including sample forms for interviewing individuals from child
protective services, school systems, courts, and police departments.

1148   National directory of child abuse services and information.   Chicago,
Illinois: National Committee for Prevention of Child Abuse, 1974.
101p.
Lists nationwide child abuse services as of 1974 for use by individuals
in the community seeking referral help or by agencies seeking to coordinate their services with other service programs.   There are four categories of listings as follows: (1) a listing of child abuse services by
state/city, with brief descriptions of each program and pertinent contact
information; (2) a geographical index of child abuse services by state/
city; (3) an alphabetical index of child abuse services; and (4) an index
of child abuse agencies listed according to the services they provide,
such as consultation, referral, and training.

1149   National Symposium on Child Abuse, 1st, Rochester, N. Y., 1971.
Collected papers.   Denver, Colorado: The American Humane Association, Children's Division, 1972.   72p.   (Bibliography).
The proceedings of a symposium held in Rochester, New York, on October
19, 1971, deals with the problem of child abuse from the points of view
of medical, social work, and legal professionals.   A medical social
worker, a pediatrician, and a psychiatrist examine the topics of identification of abuse among other injuries treated in the emergency room,
protection of the child victim, the need for supportive services to
abusive families, and the medical responsibility to report.   A second
panel discusses the role and function of child protective services in
the treatment and prevention of abuse.   Examples of non-punitive and
supportive interaction between social worker and parent are described.
An explanation of juvenile court proceedings and of important Supreme
Court decisions regarding the juvenile court are provided.

1150   Newberger, Eli H., and Daniel, Jessica H.   "Knowledge and epidemiology of child abuse: a critical review of concepts."   Pediatr
Ann 5(3):   15-25, March, 1976.   (23 References).
Reviews the following problems in the management of child abuse and
neglect: (1) insufficient financial backing to develop services capable
of dealing with the needs of the family and child; (2) a lack of solid
theoretical and practical understanding of the origins of child abuse
and how it should be treated; (3) a deficient system of diagnosis which
often places the physician in the role of "detective;" and (4) an ineffective referral process which often alienates the already frightened,
confused, and isolated family from the sources of assistance.   Our knowledge of the epidemiology of child abuse is limited because reliable data
on its actual recorded incidence are lacking and research in the area is
frequently defective.

1151   Oettinger, Katherine B.   "The abused child."   Child Educ 41(5):
235-37, January, 1965.   (0 References).
The prevalence of child abuse, which is thought to be on the increase,
demands society's active attention to the problem.   Early identification
and reporting of suspected cases by physicians is the first step, and

social agencies responsible for intervening must do whatever is necessary
to protect the child. A greater understanding of abusive parents is
needed. Educators and community leaders should be informed of the problem,
and agencies must be officially sanctioned if their efforts are to be
effective.

1152 "Out of the closet: authorities face up to the child-abuse prob-
      lem." US News World Rep 80(18): 83-84, May 3, 1976. (0 Refer-
      ences).
Surveys various organized efforts around the country to fight child abuse,
including self help groups, interdisciplinary child protection teams,
family group therapy, and new state legislation. A higher incidence of
abuse among families of United States servicemen than in the general
populace is noted.

1153 Parfit, Jessie. "Community child care: letter to editor." Br Med
      J 1(5588): 382, February 10, 1968. (1 Reference).
The necessity for increasing and upgrading the staffs of community child
care programs is emphasized. Information on these programs must be made
available to physicians.

1154 Rosenfeld, Alvin A., and Newberger, Eli H. "Compassion vs control:
      conceptual and practical pitfalls in the broadened definition of
      child abuse." JAMA 237(19): 2086-88, May 9, 1977. (20 Refer-
      ences).
Identifies and discusses the problems and conflicts that arise in child
abuse treatment because of the "lack of a rigorous practical and theoretical framework for law and for clinical practice." On the one hand,
child protection laws have grown rapidly, requiring intervention in child
abuse cases. On the other hand, research has shown that abusive parents
are themselves victims more than criminals and are in need of help and
understanding. Social workers and other helping professionals are thus
left to make a sometimes risky choice between compassion and control in
abuse cases. Threats of force may alienate the parents from the social
worker or make them more abusive to the child; but too much compassion
may seem to condone the parents' actions and leave them free to continue
to abuse (or even kill) the child. Some standards are offered for guiding
the difficult decisions between compassion and control.

1155 Ryan, Jamice, ed. Social services and the family. Durham, North
      Carolina: Learning Institute of North Carolina, 1975. 63p. ERIC
      Document ED 110 175.
A compilation of brief articles and selected materials on child abuse and
neglect, child advocacy, services, family problems, and parent education.

1156 Sampson, Paul. "Medical progress has little effect on an ancient
      childhood syndrome." JAMA 222(13): 1605-12, December 25, 1972.
      (0 References).
Reports a panel discussion focused on the topic of child abuse. The panel
consisted of physicians, lawyers, social workers, and police officers.
The areas covered in the discussion included the incidence and sociology
of child abuse, the child abuse reporting laws, parental therapy and its
place within the sociolegal apparatus for managing child abuse, and the
role of physicians, social workers, and police in the identification and
prevention of child abuse.

1157   Simpson, D. W.   "Non-accidental injury to preschool children in
       New Zealand."   NZ Med J   81(531):   12-15, January 8, 1975.   (13
       References).
Because physical maltreatment and neglect of children is difficult to define and physicians are reluctant to report suspected abuse, many cases
are left undetected.   Effective treatment strategies have been developed,
but the programs only reach a selected sample of cases.   A reexamination
of treatment and preventive facilities in New Zealand is urgently needed.
If a proposed Children and Young Persons Bill becomes law, it will
alleviate some of the shortcomings of existing legislation; but it will
also create an acute shortage of reception centers for abused children
and treatment facilities for abusing parents.   Education of young people
in the areas of parenthood and child care, and training of paramedical,
social work, and school personnel in the recognition of child abuse are
effective strategies for the prevention of child maltreatment and neglect.

1158   Smith, Sona, and Deasy, Patrick.   "Child abuse in Ireland -- Part
       III: Recognition and management."   J Ir Med Assoc   70(3):   75-79,
       March 19, 1977.   (23 References).
Part III of a comprehensive study on child abuse deals with the detection
and treatment of child abuse in Ireland.   Signs of child abuse present in
the abused child (disturbed behavior such as "frozen watchfulness,"
severe malnutrition, rigidness, failure to thrive, and others) and in the
parents of abused children (a mother who avoids normal baby check-ups or
has inappropriate expectations for the child, parents whose reports of
injuries are inadequate, maternal depression, and others) are outlined.
Once the diagnosis of child abuse has been established, an interdisciplinary team should make a decision regarding treatment.   Several alternatives are available: short-term or long-term supervision in the home,
short-term or long-term residential treatment with parents' consent, or
long-term care through court order.   The author points out that it is
difficult to obtain a court order to remove a child from the home in
Ireland and that termination of parental rights is not a legal possibility.   The major requirement for prevention of child abuse is considered
to be education.   Also, physicians treating mothers of small children
for psychiatric illness should be alerted to the possibility of child
abuse.

1159   U.S. Department of Health, Education, and Welfare.   Child abuse
       and neglect programs.   Springfield, Virginia: National Technical
       Information Service, 1976.   296p.   For ordering information see:
       Government Reports Announcements and Index   76(20):   31, October,
       1, 1976.
A comprehensive directory providing brief descriptions of over 1,700
private and publicly funded child abuse and neglect programs in the United
States as of the summer of 1975.   Information given includes the program
name, administering organization, address, director, and an abstract
describing the services, clientele, staffing, funding, and coordination
of the program.   Program director, organization, and subject indices complete the volume.

1160   U.S. National Center for Child Abuse and Neglect.   Child abuse and
       neglect: the problem and its management.   Volume 2:   The roles and
       responsibilities of professionals.   Washington, D.C.:   U.S. Govern-
       ment Printing Office, 1976.   89p.   (Bibliography).   (DHEW Publica-
       tion no. (OHD) 75-30074).

The second booklet in a series of three published by the National Center
on Child Abuse and Neglect. Professionals are urged to emphasize the
therapeutic approach in working with abusive parents. Social workers
should listen to, respect, and nurture troubled parents. Supportive
services and paraprofessional help can alleviate the stress on the worker.
A chapter devoted to the Child Protective Services (CPS) in Hennepin
County, Minnesota, describes the functions and effectiveness of this
highly specialized program. Because CPS subunits work closely with the
family in rehabilitation, a very small percentage of all cases reach the
juvenile court for custody hearings. The role of the physician in diagnosing and reporting abuse, and acting as a medical consultant on the
multidisciplinary team is outlined. The work of the Abused and Battered
Child (ABC) Unit of the Los Angeles Police Department is described. The
specially trained officers of the male/female teams investigate all reports of physical and sexual abuse in addition to coroners' reports of
all unexplained deaths of children under twelve. The teacher's role in
identifying abuse and neglect, her obligation to report, and her subsequent supportive role with the child in the classroom are discussed.

1161 U.S. National Center for Child Advocacy. Child advocacy programs:
      1975. Washington, D.C.: U.S. Department of Health, Education,
      and Welfare, 1975. 118p. ERIC Document ED 130 212. (DHEW
      Publication no. (OHD) 76-30082).
Lists child advocacy programs which offer direct service and/or planning
and coordination. The programs are described as to their purposes and
activities and listed by states and regions. Two indexes list programs
for easy reference.

1162 Wall, Charles M. "Child abuse: a societal problem with educational
      implications." Peabody J Educ 52(3): 222-25, April, 1975. (2
      References).
Defines child abuse and discusses sociological patterns which characterize the abusers and the abused. Hospitals, police, welfare agencies, and
social workers most frequently report child abuse, but many cases still
go unreported. Effects of abuse are listed--broken bones, mental retardation, and speech defects being primary among them. The most effective
treatment is for existing agencies to work together to improve the environmental conditions which lead to abuse. Family planning, placement
for unwanted or abused children, and educational and psychological
services would help. Schools, too, should do more to prevent child abuse
by learning abuse laws, recognizing abuse symptoms, and reporting suspected abuse. Teachers can serve as role models to teach children non-
violent methods of solving problems, and schools can initiate programs
in all aspects of parenting.

1163 Wright, Walter, Jr. "Policies and standards for optimum child
      protection." In: National Symposium on Child Abuse, 5th, Boston,
      1974. Collected papers. Denver, Colorado: The American Humane
      Association, Children's Division, 1976. 102-4. (0 References).
Defines some administrative practices of a model protective service.
Administrators and supervisors must support their practitioners, particularly by relieving the emotional strain. Caseloads should be controlled,
specialists should be used when necessary, and consultation with medical,
psychological, and legal professionals should be provided.

B. COMMUNITY AND HOSPITAL SERVICES

1. MULTIDISCIPLINARY EFFORTS

1164 "Aid to abused and neglected children." Intellect 102(2357): 415,
      April, 1974. (0 References).
Describes the planning of a project to assess the efficacy of a community
program of services for abused children. The project will make available
a wide range of medical, legal, and social services, and will assess the
impact of such resources upon abused children and their parents. Investigators intend to develop risk profiles, which will assist in the early
identification of child abuse, and a treatment model which will be workable in large urban areas.

1165 Avery, Jane C. "The battered child: a shocking problem" Ment
      Hyg 57(2): 40-43, Spring, 1973. (0 References).
Although reporting laws have facilitated the detection of abuse, they are
not intended to curb the incidence of child abuse. Protective intervention, carried out by a multidisciplinary community network of professionals who treat the family as a unit, is needed. Singling out the
parents for punishment does little to improve their parenting practices.
Any program that effectively provides the legal and psychological services
necessary in handling abuse will be expensive.

1166 Barnett, B. "Battered babies: letter." Br Med J 4(5680): 432,
      November 15, 1969. (0 References).
Greater communication between physicians and social workers in treating
and preventing child abuse is emphasized.

1167 Bates, Talcott; Elmer, Elizabeth; Delaney, James J. "Health based
      problems in child abuse and neglect." In: National Symposium on
      Child Abuse, 5th, Boston, 1974. Collected papers. Denver, Colorado:
      The American Humane Association, Children's Division, 1976. 32-37.
      (6 References).
Presents a study of several multidisciplinary health based programs. Most
teams consist of a pediatrician, a social worker, a psychiatrist, and a
psychologist, with no member working with the problem of child abuse full-
time because of the stress involved. All programs have written guidelines
and criteria on how to handle cases. The majority are referred from
emergency rooms, although the various programs show referrals from other
sources, depending on the community and its attitudes. The cost factor
and the availability of community resources for the programs are also
discussed. Problems which programs are trying to resolve involve civil
liberties, such as confidentiality and consent, photography, and registries.

1168 "The battered: editoral." Lancet 1(7918): 1228-29, May 31,
      1975. (0 References).
Widespread attention has been given to the problem of physical child
abuse, and consequently, hospital staffs are now quick to report suspicions of battering. The result is that busy professionals expend a great
deal of time at the multidisciplinary conferences which are called during
the early phases of case management. Although such conferences are
essential, professional overreaction to suspected child abuse is not now
uncommon, and trivial cases absorb valuable resources which should be

directed elsewhere. Non-abusive, troubled families and children are also
in need of rehabilitative services.

1169   Besharov, Douglas J.   "Building a community response to child abuse
       and maltreatment."   Child Today   4(5):   2-4, September-October,
       1975.   (3 References).
The management of child abuse in many communities involves uncoordinated,
fragmented programs which waste manpower, blur responsibility and accountability, and fail to provide follow-up referrals and treatment for
troubled families.   The community response to child abuse is often denial
and hostile rejection of the abusing parents.   Treatment of child abuse
should be a community process, however.   All citizens should become aware
of the prevalence of child abuse and recognize that protection of the
abused child must come through rehabilitation and strengthening of the
entire family.   Public support and funding for a comprehensive, indigen-
ous, and responsive program for the management of child abuse should be
obtained.

1170   Blumberg, Marvin L.   "Treatment of the abused child and the child
       abuser."   Am J Psychother   31(2):   204-15, April, 1977.   (10
       References).
Abusing parents suffer from loneliness, low self-image, and a lack of ego
strength.   Defense mechanisms such as repression, denial, and projection
contribute to the self-defeating behavior that so often leads these
parents to violence against their children.   Psychotherapy for the parents, as well as the physically and emotionally tramatized children, is
often not enough.   Therefore, a multidisciplinary approach that includes
the services of social workers, of the court, and of child placement is
recommended.   Suggestions for preventive methods, such as screening
questionnaires used to identify potential abusers, are included.

1171   Bryant, Harold D.; Billingsley, Andrew; Kelly, George A.; et al.
       "Physical abuse of children in an agency study."   Child Welfare
       42(3):   125-30, March, 1963.   (11 References).
Reveals the results of a study on child abuse in a Massachusetts community.   Referrals of abuse are primarily made by relatives and legal
authorities, such as the police and probation officers, and neighbors.
Physicians and hospitals refer only 9 percent of the cases.   Abusing
parents have similar personalities: aggressive, hostile, compulsive, and
dependent.   Most were abused as children.   The study illustrates the
importance of a coordinated effort among the family, physician, social
worker, and court to effectively combat child abuse.

1172   "Concerning child abuse: editorial."   NZ Med J   85(583):   191-92,
       March 9, 1977.   (27 References).
Reviews the difficulties in identifying and treating child abuse.   Because
the range of symptoms and causes of child abuse extends from physical
abuse to maternal deprivation, the complexity of factors requires a multidisciplinary team approach.   Management must consider not only individual
aspects of a case, but also society's responsibility to the problem of
abused children.

1173   Court, Donald; Lister, James; Franklin, Alfred W.; et al.   "Experts
       and child abuse: letters to editor."   Br Med J   3(5934):   801-2,
       September 28, 1974.   (1 Reference).
Effective cooperation in managing child abuse cases necessitates understanding and respect for the function of each expert by the others.

1174   Cupoli, J. Michael, and Newberger, Eli H.   "Optimism or pessimism
       for the victim of child abuse?"   Pediatrics   59(2):   311-14,
       February, 1977.   (18 References).
Stresses the need for a more optimistic approach in the treatment of child
abuse.   Means of attaining this goal include using interdisciplinary techniques in family health care, fostering an atmosphere of respect for children and families in the pediatrician's office, considering the symptoms
of child abuse as one group of medical manifestations of a family in
distress, and recognizing the importance of prevention as well as treatment of the problem.

1175   Dawe, Kathleen E.   "Child abuse in Nova Scotia."   Aust Paediatr J
       9(4):   294-96, December, 1973.   (0 References).
Summarizes the design, findings, and recommendations of the first Canadian
research project on child abuse.   The project was developed within the
framework of an interdisciplinary approach and consisted of two parts.
Part I involved gathering data about the management of battered and maternally deprived children, the main focus of which was the abused child
himself.   Part II was an attitudinal study which attempted to ascertain
the attitudes of professional groups about child abuse.   Although a
variety of recommendations were suggested by the project's findings,
stress was placed on the necessity for interdisciplinary cooperation in
response to the complex problems involved.

1176   De Francis, Vincent.   "Child protection -- a comprehensive, coor-
       dinated process."   In: National Symposium on Child Abuse, 4th,
       Charleston, S. C., 1973.   Collected papers.   Denver, Colorado: The
       American Humane Association, Children's Division, 1975.   5-14.
Presents an overview of the problem of child abuse, stressing interdisciplinary management.   Prevention through identification of potential abuse
families and education of the young concerning family structure and
management is suggested.   After a review of the Child Protective Service
Act of 1875 and the medical model of the 1960's, the interdisciplinary
approach is favorably critiqued.   Honolulu's program, consisting of caseworkers, a pediatrician, a psychiatrist, and a psychologist, serves as
an example.   Although an interdisciplinary approach provides a balanced
management, other community services are needed, including juvenile
courts, mental health services, homemaker services, day care centers,
public health nursing, and law enforcement.

1177   ————.   Community cooperation for better child protection.
       Denver, Colorado: The American Humane Association, Children's
       Division, 1959.   20p.   (Bibliography).
To protect children from neglect and abuse, child protective agencies
must have the cooperation of other community agencies, such as the juvenile court, the police, the school, the church, and other family and
children's services.   Roles and responsibilities of each agency need to
be understood.   The function of the court is not to administer child
protective services, but to handle the judicial processes once the petition of neglect has been filed.   The court determines parents' right to
custody, decides on separation and placement, reviews evidence, and enters
judicial orders.   The police can help most not by prosecution of neglect
cases but by preventing exploitation of children in hazardous or prohibited employment, by suppressing community activity that may lead to
delinquency, and by protecting children from criminal abuse.   Schools
can help by early identification of problem children and by providing

family-life education. The church can help by instilling spiritual values
and by redirecting families toward higher moral values. Other services
which should be available in the community are shelter care, homemaker
services, and family counseling agencies. These and other agencies can
all enrich the protective agency's potential for helping neglected children and their families.

1178   Ebeling, Nancy B., and Hill, Deborah A., eds.   Child abuse: inter-
       vention and treatment. Acton, Massachusetts: Publishing Sciences
       Group, 1975. 182p.
Consists of a compilation of papers written by various professionals involved in Children's Advocates, Inc., a Boston area interdisciplinary
committee on child abuse and neglect. The organization believes that
abuse and neglect are symptoms of serious family unhappiness or dysfunctioning; therefore, Children's Advocates tries to treat the entire family
unit. The book's twenty-six essays cover a wide range of topics, but
they repeatedly emphasize the need to integrate the abusive family into
an informed and caring community. Abusive parents are often aggressive,
hostile, overly concerned with order and routine, and incapable of expres-
sing warmth. Their view of reality is often distorted and, consequently,
they mistrust others, particularly professionals whom they fear will remove their child. By showing concern for the parents as individuals, the
social worker can construct a trusting relationship with them. As the
parent accepts his dependence upon the social worker and is in a sense
"re-parented," he achieves a sense of self-worth. Treatment progresses
smoothly when the social worker takes into account the parents' abilities
to make changes, the needs of the children, and the resources available.

Community resources, such as those available in the Boston area, lessen
the workload of social workers and public agencies while offering less
threatening means of treatment for already disturbed families. Volunteer
or paraprofessional services such as parent-aides, homemaker services,
and day care facilities provide parents with support in day-to-day tension
situations. Self-help groups such as Parents Anonymous promote regular
socialization for members while insuring them of personal and telephone
contact at crisis times. If individual or group treatment should fail,
placement of the child in a foster home may be necessary. An essay pertinent to this topic offers suggestions for a smooth readjustment process.
Preplacement visits with the social worker, natural parents, and foster
parents will provide a sense of continuity between the two settings for
the child. Subsequent visits by the natural mother to the foster mother's
home will allow her to learn cooking, mothering, child care, and other
valuable home management skills.

An essay on child abuse and the law points out that legislation itself
cannot control abusive behavior; however, a good and well-publicized law
can be preventive in that it prescribes the limits of acceptable conduct.
Arguments for and against the establishment of a central registry for
cases of abuse and neglect are given. Prevention and detection programs
such as mandatory physical/psychological examinations of all preschool
children, increased state funding, and improved education programs as
positive means of checking the problem of child abuse are recommended.

1179   Ellinger, A. J.; Dudding, Burton; Kretchmer, Helen; et al. "Neuro-
       pediatrics conference: battered child syndrome." Minn Med 49(9):
       1429-36, September, 1966. (5 References).

Reports a presentation made at a neuro-pediatric conference by all professionals involved in one child abuse case. The medical examination
and history, at odds with the presenting information given by the parents,
suggested the battered child syndrome. A non-punitive, therapeutic
approach was adopted by the hospital social worker, who regarded the
parents as heavily burdened by financial, educational, and marital pressures. The father, age twenty-one, and the mother, age eighteen, were
forced by this pregnancy to marry. The mother was evaluated by the
psychologist as emotionally detached and immature; the father was viewed
as insecure and anxious. The child was placed in the custody of the
maternal grandparents with the hope that the parents' situation could
improve enough for her to be returned to them. Final recommendations
included legal custody of the child by the county until the family situation could be reevaluated.

1180 "Experts and child abuse: editorial." Br Med J 3(5932): 641-42,
      September 14, 1974. (2 References).
The lack of coordination between different departments of social services
and the fallibility of judgment of many young social workers have led
numerous child abuse cases to become real tragedies. The author supports
more legal protection for children in disputes of custody, along with the
establishment of speciality teams manned by a psychiatrist, a pediatrician, and a senior social worker in every hospital region as a means of
more efficient prevention and treatment.

1181 Fontana, Vincent J. "Factors needed for prevention of child abuse
      and neglect: letter to editor." Pediatrics 46(2): 318-19,
      August, 1970. (0 References).
Suggests improvements in the management of child abuse cases. Recommendations include the establishment of interdisciplinary programs combining
legal, medical, and social expertise and the necessity of adequate funding
to support child abuse and protection laws.

1182 Furst, William D. "A pediatric generalist's experience with child
      abuse and neglect in a small, isolated community." Pediatr Ann
      5(3): 79-87, March, 1976. (0 References).
A physician in a small, isolated community presents the means he employed
to develop an interdisciplinary team to treat child abuse in his community, with three case studies illustrating the actual handling of the
cases. Suggested guidelines enumerated for stimulating community participation include: (1) educating and informing paramedical and ancillary
personnel; (2) discussing with colleagues; (3) encouraging the inclusion
of child abuse in nursing education; (4) speaking at local bar association meetings and inviting lawyers to panel discussions; (5) developing
programs for public education; (6) organizing inservice educational
programs for teachers; and (7) including nursing students in treatment
programs.

1183 Guandolo, Vincent; Silver, Larry B.; Barton, William; et al. "Grand
      rounds: the battered child syndrome." Clin Proc Child Hosp
      23(5): 139-60, May, 1967. (23 References).
Reviews the literature on the battered child syndrome relating to how
physicians came to recognize the physical signs of trauma, as well as
psychiatric literature documenting reactions and attitudes typical of
battering parents and battered children. Criminal prosecution in cases
of abuse is difficult, even impossible, when the evidence is insufficient.

All too often punitive action makes the parents resentful and aggressive, placing the child in even greater danger. To avoid this conflict, communities need a multidisciplinary network of medical and social services aimed at helping the child and the parents as soon as battering is first detected.

1184 Helfer, Ray E., and Pollock, Carl B. "The battered child syndrome." Adv Pediatr 15: 9-27, 1968. (19 References).
Comprehensively reviews all aspects of child abuse, including history, incidence, legal implications for the physician, chief symptoms and their detection, radiologic evidence, psychiatric aspects, and various community sources available to the physician to combat child abuse. A multidisciplinary approach is needed for the management of child abuse. The child protective services could compile all available data, coordinate the activities of involved persons and agencies, and maintain complete records on each family. The police are often involved in the initial investigation following a report of child abuse. School personnel should report an obviously neglected or abused child to the protective services. The social worker should work with the parents to develop a positive helping relationship. The physician has the primary responsibility to detect and treat the medical aspects of the battered child syndrome and to serve in a supervisory role over the child protection team.

1185 Holter, Joan C., and Friedman, Stanford B. "Principles of management in child abuse cases." Am J Orthopsychiatry 38(1): 127-36, January, 1968. (9 References).
Procedures for multidisciplinary team diagnosis and management of child abuse are outlined. The team must plan for the protection of the abused child upon discharge from the hospital. If the parents have been unresponsive to professional help, the child may have to be placed in temporary foster care. The medical social worker must act as coordinator for all agencies and persons involved in a particular case. The homemaker who visits the family routinely can teach the parents principles of childrearing. Child abuse is often a "cry for help" on the part of the parents, and working with these families is a challenging experience.

1186 Jackson, R. H. "Trauma in childhood: letter to editor." Br Med J 2(5456): 299-300, July 31, 1965. (0 References).
The tendency of specialists to treat the problem of child abuse from one angle only is criticized. Child abuse centers, which would bring together specialists from various disciplines to study the problem in a more integrated manner, should be established.

1187 Klibanoff, Elton B. "Child advocacy in action: Massachusetts' Office for Children." Child Educ 52(3): 70-72, November-December, 1975. (0 References).
In spite of the recent gains in understanding abusing families and in developing effective crisis intervention procedures, child protective services remain characterized by a lack of coordination, fragmented organization, and obscured visibility from the community. These factors seriously limit a community's chances for helping families in distress. Two measures that could lead to improved coordination and cooperation among agencies are introduced as follows: (1) one local agency must be designated as the coordinator and monitor of all family services; and (2) the public must be informed as to how to contact the protective service network, so that action can be taken promptly. The Massachusetts'

Office for Children, an agency solely responsible for coordinating and monitoring protective services, has incorporated both suggested measures into its organization.

1188 Leese, Stephanie M. "Children in danger -- the causes and preven-
      tion of baby battering by Jean Renvoize: book review. Br J
      Psychiatry 128(4): 411-12, April, 1976. (0 References).
Jean Renvoize's book on child battering is critically reviewed. Although the contributory circumstances leading to baby battering are fairly well known, the book may exert pressure for the appointment of a coordinator between all professionals involved in child abuse cases. It may also ensure that a report of a committee studying child abuse is not filed and forgotten.

1189 McQuarrie, Howard G.; Gibbs, Charles E.; Meyer, Hermann, B. P.;
      et al. "Statement on child abuse and neglect: letter to editor."
      JAMA 238(5): 427, August 1, 1977. (0 References).
Proposes that the desired goal of early detection and prevention of child abuse can best be realized in the working concept of a professional multi-disciplinary family treatment team.

1190 Morris, Vivian G., and Taneja-Jaisinghani, Vijay. "A call for
      action on the child abuse problem." J Home Econ 68(5): 17-20,
      May, 1976. (11 References).
Incidence statistics, treatment programs, and legislation regarding child abuse are discussed in order to alert the home economist to the problem. The role of the home economist in the management of child abuse includes: (1) providing expert testimony to Congress; (2) becoming politically active in the area of legislation; (3) supporting preventive programs aimed at reducing environmental stress suffered by abusive families; and (4) joining multidisciplinary teams of professionals for the thorough treatment of the problem once it has occurred.

1191 Nixon, H. H. "Non-accidental injury in children: introductory
      comment from B.P.A. and B.A.P.S." Br Med J 4(5893): 656-57,
      December 15, 1973. (3 References).
Stresses the need for local child protection committees composed of social, medical, and law enforcement professionals dedicated to the detection, prevention, and treatment of non-accidental injuries. The proper use of management systems is essential to assure that action is initiated, re-gardless of which professional faction first receives notice of suspected instance of abuse. Suggestions offered by the Department of Health and Social Security for referral systems are presented.

1192 "Non-accidental injury." Lancet 1(8011): 611-12, March 12, 1977.
      (0 References).
In London, case conferences are regarded to be a vital element in dealing with incidents of non-accidental injury. In the past, however, there has been a failure in the coordination of various services, particularly between the police department and social service agencies.

1193 "One problem, two answers." Economist 255: 31, May 3, 1975. (0
      References).
Reiterates the need for cooperation among social work agencies and per-sonnel who work with abusive and neglectful families. Information and decision-making must be shared in order that the child be optimally protected.

1194 Oppe, Thomas E. "Problems of communication and co-ordination."
      In: Franklin, Alfred White, ed. Concerning child abuse. New York:
      Churchill Livingstone, 1975. 155-61. (0 References).
Describes the difficulties of an interagency system as it related to child
abuse. A discussion of the various disciplines--law, social work, health
care, and journalism--identifies their roles in the problem of child abuse
and presents the difficulties encountered in each discipline's approach.
Identification is often mishandled due to failures in diagnosis, interagency communication, and gathering data. Treatment is complex because
it must not only address the needs of the child, but also the needs of
the parents. Skilled workers and interagency cooperation is essential.

1195 Polier, Justine M. "Professional abuse of children: responsibil-
      ity for the delivery of services." Am J Orthopsychiatry 45(3):
      357-62, April, 1975. (0 References).
Examines the responsibilities of medical, social, and legal professionals
for either providing or denying their services to children. The efforts
of all professionals involved in determining the fate of abused children
should be united to work toward the singular goal of delivering whatever
services are needed to halt the abuse of children and to protect those
who suffer from it. A discussion of the changing rights of children, as
reflected in recent federal court decisions, is included.

1196 Rappaport, Mazie F., and Finberg, Laurence. "The neglected child
      -- collaborative approaches to recognition and management." Clin
      Pediatr 2(9): 521-24, September, 1963. (8 References).
Reveals two case studies of parental neglect. The best protection for
the child in both cases results from a cooperative effort of pediatricians, social workers, community agencies, juvenile courts, and the
parents. A Baltimore study of prenatal care is also described. Twenty-
five percent of mothers in the study lacked prenatal care and 15 percent
were insufficiently registered at the advertised community service for
antenatal obstetric records. It is believed that prenatal neglect is an
important type of child neglect in urban areas.

1197 Reeb, Kenneth G.; Melli, Marygold S.; Wald, Max; et al. "A con-
      ference on child abuse." Wis Med J 71(10): 226-29, October, 1972.
      (2 References).
Four professional viewpoints are expressed in a conference on child abuse.
All conferees agreed that society's inability to realize the existence
of the problem was the first barrier to be overcome in its solution. A
pediatrician on the panel discussed the necessity of educating the physician as to the etiology of abuse, so that he can recognize high risk
situations and function as a link between potentially abusive families
and health, social, and legal agencies. The panel's radiologist described
the physical findings which point to a diagnosis of child battering. A
social worker emphasized the importance of both physician and community
awareness of available resources and discussed the social service aspects
of the prevention and treatment of abuse. A lawyer contributed information about the legal snarls which frequently hamper effective action in
abuse cases. The legal process is concerned with affording justice to
the defendent and, therefore, cannot be sufficiently focused on the well-
being of the child. Juvenile rather than criminal court proceedings may
be more appropriate, and the social agency bringing a case to court must
be aware that it carries the burden of proof in establishing evidence of
abuse.

1198   Schmidt, Rebecca.   "What home economists should know about child
       abuse."   J Home Econ   68(5):   13-16, May, 1976.   (8 References).
Describes child abuse as a medical, psychiatric, legal, social, and
familial problem requiring multidisciplinary professional management.
Treatment strategies and services are discussed, including hospital child
protection teams, school reporting systems, parent aides, parents anonymous groups, and crisis nurseries.   The role of the home economist is to
report cases of suspected abuse to the proper authorities, to become
involved in multidisciplinary treatment teams, and to conduct educational
programs on parenting and child development in the community.

1199   Terr, Lenore C., and Watson, Andrew S.   "The battered child re-
       brutalized: ten cases of medical-legal confusion."   Am J Psychiatry
       124(10):   1432-39, April, 1968.   (15 References).
Analyzes the process of handling cases of battered children by examining
the cases of ten children and their families.   Over two years, records
concerning the medical, social, and legal actions taken in each case were
kept.   These records were then utilized to determine the effects of each
process upon the children and families.   Findings indicate that there
was confusion and a general lack of direction in each phase of treatment.
In order to eliminate some of this confusion, several specific courses of
action are encouraged.   Efficient and comprehensive treatment will be
forthcoming only if the process remains a multiagency effort.   Coordination of these agencies is the key to improvement.

1200   "Theory and practice."   Nurs Times   71(18):   678, May 1, 1975.
       (0 References).
Several brief case histories revealing gross inadequacies in the management of child abuse are documented.   Critical failures of communication
between medical and social professionals, along with excessive caseloads
for social workers and insufficient legal powers to remove an abused child
from a dangerous home environment, all contribute to the deficiencies in
the current system for handling child abuse.

1201   U.S. National Center for Child Abuse and Neglect.   Child abuse and
       neglect: the problem and its management.   Volume 3:   The commun-
       ity team: an approach to case management and prevention.
       Washington, D.C.:   U.S. Government Printing Office, 1976.   208p.
       (Bibliography).   (DHEW Publication no. (OHD) 75-30075).
Community team management of child abuse involves identification,
diagnosis, treatment, and education.   Specific tasks pertinent to identification are: reporting, investigation, intervention, assessment, and
disposition.   Resources necessary for this first stage of case management
include a central register and a twenty-four-hour crisis hot-line.
Practical suggestions for setting up a hot-line, in addition to telephone
listening techniques, are presented.

The goal of treatment for parents is to replace the abusive pattern of
behavior with a more responsible and loving method of childrearing.   The
following programs have been effective in rehabilitating abusive parents:
community mental health agencies, psychotherapy, group therapy, parent
aides, homemaker services, visiting nurses, and self-help groups.   Alternatives to foster care placement for abused children are proposed.   While
their parents are undergoing separate treatment, children can receive
positive nurturing in therapeutic day care centers, play groups, and
crisis nurseries.   Planning, administrative, and play/educational activities for operating a therapeutic day care center are given.

The discussion of education includes considerations for public education, professional education, and conducting a multimedia public information campaign. Primary prevention programs are needed which will identify at risk families, provide crisis management and parent training, and stress community support and willingness to help in improving family life.

1202 "Violence at home." Public Health 84(2): 53-56, January, 1970.
      (0 References).
Evaluates a report of seventy-eight abused children by the National Society for the Prevention of Cruelty to Children. Although certain correlations between the family situation and the battering are valid, the report is criticized for not being more specific regarding the emotional background of the battering. In addition to the dissemination of information and an understanding approach to parents as means of prevention and treatment, the report should have recommended the need for a multidisciplinary approach. All interested services should be alerted and consulted concerning the suspicion of child abuse. To follow the report's suggestion that one service handle reporting would thwart effective management.

1203 Weaver, Edward T. "Child protection -- a service concept and
      system." In: National Symposium on Child Abuse, 5th, Boston, 1974.
      Collected papers. Denver, Colorado: The American Humane Associa-
      tion, Children's Division, 1976. 6-14. (0 References).
Advocates the integration of various aspects of societal intervention. Child abuse is a product of many socioeconomic difficulties of the family, such as low income, poor housing, lack of health care, and general family conflict. Treatment is often ignorant of these causal factors. Communities must provide adequate incomes, better housing, counseling services, and should recognize the interrelatedness of all human services. Resources should be used to prevent abuse. A discussion of the Child Abuse Prevention and Treatment Act is included.

1204 Yates, Patricia K. "Community relationships -- problems and frus-
      trations." In: National Symposium on Child Abuse, 5th, Boston,
      1974. Collected papers. Denver, Colorado: The American Humane
      Association, Children's Division, 1976. 97-101. (0 References).
Describes the conditions under which protective services operate. The community is a conglomeration of agencies operating according to federal, state, and local laws. Problems arise when laws and community standards are in conflict. The complications resulting from the child reporting laws that broke out rapidly in the 1950's demonstrate the difficulties that occur when laws are passed without defined administrative procedures for implementation. Procedures must be followed by all agencies in order to avoid confusion about responsibilities.

1205 Zalba, Serapio R. "Battered children." Transaction 8(9/10):
      58-61, July-August, 1971. (0 References).
Presents a sociological view of the battered child syndrome. Traditionally there has been an unwillingness on the part of social agencies to intervene in families where a child may be suffering from abuse. This reluctance has begun to change with the advent of out-reach programs and with the accumulation of experience over the years in the field of social work and psychology. Progress has been made in defining the characteristics of battering parents and estimating the incidence of abuse. Nevertheless, community coordinated treatment programs will not become more

effective without greater financial support and a willingness of the citizenry to report suspected cases of abuse.

2. STATE, CITY, AND COUNTY PROGRAMS

1206 Ball, Margaret. "Issues of violence in family casework." Soc
      Casework 58(1): 3-12, January, 1977. (5 References).
Sketches the efforts of the Family Service of Detroit and Wayne County to work with cases of violence and abuse. Many of the violent clients treated by the Family Service showed histories of violence and abuse in early childhood. Several case histories of clients are included. Casework intervention measures as outlined are geared toward helping the client gain an understanding of the conditions that can potentially contribute to violent behavior and offers ways to control his impulses.

1207 Brieland, Donald. "Emergency protective services in Illinois."
      Child Welfare 44: 281-83, May, 1965. (0 References).
Reports a recently instituted plan for emergency protective service to abused and neglected children in Illinois. Telephoned reports of suspected child abuse or neglect are relayed by a central answering service to the appropriate local agency for investigation. Information disseminated also includes a description of state and local resources for dealing with cases of child abuse and a discussion of the responsibilities of the officials involved.

1208 Burt, Marvin R., and Blair, Louis H. Options for improving the care
      of neglected and dependent children: program analysis applied to
      local government. Washington, D.C.: The Urban Institute, 1971.
      138p.
Presents alternative programs for the care of neglected and dependent children. The aims of the presentation are to improve the care of children in Nashville and Davidson County, Tennessee, and to develop and demonstrate improved methods by which local governments can analyze their programs and policies. The immediate objectives of the existing program in Tennessee are: (1) to reduce the number of neglect and dependency petitions filed with the juvenile court; (2) to keep the child in his home until the case is decided upon; and (3) to keep the child in his home when long-term care is required. Four types of programs for short-term care and two types for long-term care are suggested and described. Short-term programs are twenty-four-hour intake screening, emergency caretaker service, emergency foster homes, and homemaker service. Long-term alternatives are intensive casework supervision and a foster home program. National recommendations are offered for improved child care systems.

1209 Cassidy, Richard K. "Public assistance services to children in
      Columbus, Ohio." Natl Probat Parole Assoc J 6(1): 47-50, January,
      1960. (0 References).
Discusses the problems and development of public assistance services to children in Columbus, Ohio. Limited finances and competition for funds between public social agencies markedly interfered with services. The public felt that the welfare department should provide only for the physical needs of children. In 1959, after a Public Welfare Committee was formed to coordinate programs, services improved considerably. Planning encompassed the community, unified resources, and avoided duplication of

aids. Later, the Welfare Department offered rehabilitative assistance
geared toward strengthening family life, with needed expansion in casework and counseling.

1210   Cherry, Barbara J., and Kuby, Alma M. "Obstacles to the delivery
       of medical care to children of neglecting parents." Am J Public
       Health 61(3): 568-73, March, 1971 (4 References).
The Bowen Center in Chicago, a neighborhood demonstration project, is
designed to provide supportive services for hard-to-reach, severely disturbed families who neglect their children. Services such as health
care, public assistance, employment, counseling, and legal representation
are available. The Center's staff includes professional social workers
and teachers, and untrained child care workers. The Center has worked
with thirty-six families over the past three years. These families are
characterized by marital instability, poverty, physical and mental illness, and antisocial behavior. Strategies to help these families should
not punish their inadequate behavior, but attempt to draw on strengths
that they may bring to the situation. The neighborhood-based family
clinic is an appropriate start for assisting these families in the care
of their children. However, basic attitudinal as well as organizational
changes within the health care delivery system may be necessary if this
population is to be reached effectively.

1211   "A child protection service on a 24-hour, 365-day basis." Child
       Welfare 49(3): 168, March, 1970. (0 References).
Describes a twenty-four-hour child protection service provided by the
Children's Aid Society of Metropolitan Toronto. The dangerous nature of
after-hours work and the lack of opportunity for long-range involvement
have led to the employment of male law students rather than social workers
to staff the service. Training, supervision, and rotation schedules are
explained.

1212   Christy, Duane W., and Paget, Norman W. Innovative approaches in
       child protective services. Denver, Colorado: The American Humane
       Association, Children's Division, 1969. 24p. (Bibliography).
The first article of this pamphlet tells of the community services offered
by the Children's Protective Services of the Ohio Humane Society for the
management of child abuse. The agency's youth referral center and maternal and infant care programs, its effective use of volunteers, and the
responsibilities of the multidisciplinary team are described. The second
article discusses various innovative approaches to child abuse management
used by the Children's Aid Society of Buffalo. In relating to the community, the agency has made successful use of the mass media and has
organized conferences on such topics as neglect and the child abuse and
neglect reporting law. An emergency live-in parent service, homemaker
service, and the agency's twenty-four-hour availability insure prompt
intervention on behalf of the children of the community. The work of
three service teams--applications team, study and diagnostic team, and
emergency casework team--and two treatment teams--multiple problem family
team and child abuse team--is outlined. The success of the family day
camp and parent education programs is reported.

1213 De Francis, Vincent. Children who were helped through protective
      services. Denver, Colorado: The American Humane Association,
      Children's Division, 1960. 14p. (Bibliography).

Narrates four case histories illustrating the successful intervention by
child protective services workers into the homes of troubled families.
All cases were referred to the agency by concerned citizens who recognized
the need for professional and therapeutic help.

1214   Donnison, David V.   The neglected child and the social services;...
       Manchester, England: Manchester University Press, 1954.   152p.
       (Bibliography).
Examines the role of various public and private social service organizations in the management of neglect cases in the English cities of Manchester and Salford as of 1954.   Criteria used by the agencies for measuring neglect included: (1) the necessity for frequent visits by a health
visitor or school welfare officer; (2) the presence of two or more
illegitimate children in the home; (3) the desertion or imprisonment of
the father; and (4) failure of the father to find employment and support
his family.   After intervention by public agencies and voluntary societies,
families received help in finding employment, housing, and keeping a
budget in addition to instruction in housekeeping and child care.   A
Mutual Register established for the two cities provided a readily available index of all assistance given to persons in the area and was useful
in keeping in touch with families and avoiding duplication of services.
An evaluation of the level of cooperation between the various agencies
is provided.

1215   Giles, Rosalind.   "Facilities and services for neglected children
       in Texas."   Natl Probat Parole Assoc J   6(1):   62-65, January, 1960.
       (2 References).
Outlines the services provided for neglected children in Texas.   Protective services attempt to improve family life and to protect the child from
further maltreatment through the help of caseworkers and homemakers.   In
some instances, children are removed from the home until conditions
improve or until they can be placed for adoption.   Because 227 counties
lack protective services and trained personnel, the Department of Public
Welfare needs to develop more programs, to provide inservice training for
personnel, and to coordinate group efforts toward protective services,
foster care, and adoption.

1216   Gretton, John.   "When no one is minding the children."   Times Educ
       Suppl   3056:   4, December 21, 1973.   (0 References).
Cites the problems of a social service system in a London borough which
retards early intervention efforts in child abuse cases.   The uneven distribution of resources, which promotes care for the aged at the expense
of the young or which focuses attention only on the toddler, severely
handicaps youth workers.   The social service's lack of a community base
also hampers work; they must rely on other better known community agencies such as hospitals and schools for information.   This dependency
prevents the needed early warning system.   Poor relations and diminished
trust between professions, along with a lack of professional status
attributed to social workers, are also detracting variables.

1217   Hammell, Charlotte, L.   "Preserving family life for children."
       Child Welfare   48(10):   591-94, December, 1969.   (1 Reference).
The Delaware County (Pennsylvania) Child Care Services offers homemaker
service, therapeutic nursery for preschoolers, emergency shelter, and a
day care center, in addition to expanded psychiatric, psychological, and
legal services.   The emphasis of the agency is on helping parents care

for their children rather than providing substitute parental care. Because it is the disadvantaged segment of the population which produces
the majority of neglected and dependent children, preservation of family
life depends upon the development of programs to insure adequate standards
of living for all families. Such programs could include guaranteed income,
low income housing, job training, medical assistance, and appropriate
education. A truly preventive program would also provide skilled evaluation of the capacity for men and women of childbearing age to be good
parents.

1218   Juvenile Protective Association. Report of the Bowen Center
        Demonstration Project: 1965-1971. Chicago, Illinois: Juvenile
        Protective Association, 1975. 170p.
Reports on the Bowen Center Project, conducted by the Juvenile Protective
Association in Chicago from 1965 to 1971. Recognizing that child abuse
is just one symptom of a staggering constellation of family problems, the
Project sought to provide a wide range of integrated services for severely
dysfunctional families. Their goal was not only to protect the child, but
also to help the family toward a process of growth and stability which
would help them to stop the continuing cycle of neglect and defeat. The
Project Center gathered under one roof facilities for counseling, day
care, homemaker services, temporary shelter, tutoring, foster case,
emergency financial aid, and health service assistance. The report described: (1) the way the program was put together; (2) the kind of families they helped; (3) the kinds of services provided; and (4) an outline
of the cost of services. A follow-up study four years later showed
significant improvements in many of the families.

1219   Lange, Gus B. "Facilities for neglected children in the Portland,
        Oregon, urban area." Natl Probat Parole Assoc J 6(1): 44-47,
        January, 1960. (1 Reference).
Outlines existing services for neglected children in Portland, Oregon.
Receiving its referrals from the juvenile court, the Women's Protective
Division of the Portland Bureau of Police and private citizens, the
Children's Department of the County Public Welfare Commission has had
primary responsibility for protective services, including a specialized
service within the Commission which deals with child neglect. Private
and public agencies handle institutional care and adoptions. Expansion
is needed in the area of casework, preventive counseling, special foster
home placement, homemaker services, and receiving facilities. The school
system and a community program, the Portland Children's Treatment Study
Project, are cited for their innovations.

1220   Massachusetts Society for the Prevention of Cruelty to Children.
        Annual Reports (1-17, 1881-1897). Boston: Wright & Potter, 1882.
These reports discuss the foundation, philosophy, methods, and accomplishments of the Massachusetts Society for the Prevention of Cruelty to
Children. Each report includes: (1) a list of the Board of Government;
(2) President's Address; (3) Treasurer's Report; (4) Report of the Home
Committee on the workings of the temporary haven where abused children
were kept until suitable placement was found; (5) Report of the General
Agent--the bulk of the annual report, discussing their work, problems
faced, criticisms, abuse laws, kinds of abused children helped, and
typical causes of abuse (alcohol, then as now, being a leading factor in
abuse); (6) statistical summary of the year's work; (7) specimen cases of
abuse to keep public aware of the necessity for such a society; and (8)

lists of donors, members, agents, and kindred societies in America and abroad. Overall, these reports reflect the Society's steady devotion to the rights of children, a consistent increase in the number of abuse cases handled, the development of more child abuse laws, and a growth in public awareness concerning the problems of child abuse.

1221 Miller, Mary B. "Community action and child abuse." Nurs Outlook
     17(3): 44-46, March, 1969. (1 Reference).
Public health nursing students systematically investigated the management of child abuse in a community in North Carolina. They convinced powerful members of the health department that a more comprehensive program was necessary to deal with the problem, and enlisted the aid of the community in developing a standardized procedure for reporting child abuse cases to the child welfare department. Preliminary findings revealed that three months after the project had been initiated, the number of child abuse reports had increased.

1222 Nesi, William A. "Facilities and services for dependent and neg-
     lected children in Cleveland." Natl Probat Parole Assoc J 6(1):
     53-55, January, 1960. (0 References).
Outlines the procedures of the Cuyahoga County Welfare Department in Cleveland. Acting on referral, the agency offers care to homeless, dependent, and neglected children either through a foster home program or casework services to families, the goal being the reunion of the family.

1223 New York (State). Board of Social Welfare. Director of child
     caring institutions and agencies. Albany, New York: New York
     State Board of Social Welfare, 1973. 91p.
Lists child caring institutions and agencies in New York State. The directory contains a listing, alphabetically, by county, and by type of service, as well as a directory of the Board of Social Welfare. Each separate listing describes location, history, personnel, program and admission policies, and services provided by the agency or institution.

1224 New York (State). Department of Social Services. 1975 annual
     report for the provision of child protective services in New York
     State. Albany, New York: New York State Department of Social
     Services, 1976. 30p. (Publication no. 1200).
Reprints the 1975 annual report on the operations of state and local child protective services in New York. Also included are recommendations for further legislation concerning child abuse and many tables giving statistical information about incidence, distribution, and variety of child abuse.

1225 New York (State). Legislature. Assembly. Report of the Select
     Committee on Child Abuse. Albany, New York: New York State
     Assembly, 1972. 168p.
Presents findings and recommendations of the New York Assembly's state-wide investigation of child abuse treatment and management programs. New York State has an expensive, but poorly managed, child welfare system. Although 3,244 cases of suspected abuse were reported in 1971 (three-fourths of which originated in New York City), many children never came to the attention of the authorities and of those who did, many were shuffled from agency to agency or simply lost with the paperwork.

Widespread poor management among the different child protective services was uncovered. Fragmentation of agency responsibility caused delays in

crisis intervention. Agencies often duplicated information-taking procedures and failed to communicate with each other. One agency refused to
accept reports from non-mandated sources, such as the police. In court,
many cases were dismissed due to lack of evidence because many social
workers did not know how to conduct a proper investigation. To avoid these
problems, the committee recommended that agency staff be highly trained
and specialized. It was suggested, moreover, that hospital social
workers take over the long-term investigative aspects of cases first seen
in the hospital.

Numerous problems associated with foster care placement were examined.
It was found that foster care was generally inadequate and expensive.
The committee advised that adoption procedures be reexamined and simplified so that the current average twenty-two month period could be
shortened.

In the judicial network, a separate child abuse division of the family
court with periodically rotating judges was advocated as a means to amend
the present overcrowded docket. In this manner the judge would be able
to make a proper evaluation of the home situation before returning the
child to his abusive or neglecting parents or placing him in a foster or
adoptive home. Lastly, the committee advised that existing social, legal,
and judicial services be reorganized with an emphasis upon coordination
of services before any additional expenditures are contemplated.

1226 Newberger, Eli H.; Haas, G.; Mulford, Robert M. "Child abuse in
     Massachusetts." Mass Physician 32(1): 31-38, January, 1973.
     (23 References).
Analyzes the current status of both the problem of child abuse in Massachusetts and the attempt to deal with it. The inadequacies in the data
and in the child protective services in the state are pointed up, and the
recommendations of the Governor's Advisory Committee on Child Abuse,
which focused on the treatment of cases after they are discovered, are
included.

1227 North Dakota. Social Service Board. Protective services for chil-
     dren. Bismark, North Dakota: North Dakota Social Service Board,
     1974. 12p.
Excerpts, from the administrative manual of the North Dakota Social
Services Board, gives information concerning referral practices, protective services available (including those for children on Indian reserva-
tions), and procedures for reporting neglected or abused children.

1228 "One child dies daily from abuse; parent probably was abused."
     Pediatr News 9(4): 3, 59, April, 1975. (0 References).
Describes the work of the National Center for the Prevention and Treatment of Child Abuse at the University of Colorado. The Center is sponsored by the Office of Child Development in conjunction with private
foundations, and the service provided is free of charge. At present,
five pilot programs have been started: (1) group psychiatric sessions
for abuse prone parents; (2) lay therapy for the isolated parent; (3) a
crisis nursery which takes care of children in emergencies; (4) a school
and nursery school providing therapy for abused children; and (5) Circle
House, a residential center which houses and treats troubled families.

1229 Paget, Norman W. "Emergency parent -- a protective service to chil-
     dren in crisis." Child Welfare 46(7): 403-7, July, 1967. (0
     References).

The operation of an Emergency Casework After-Hours Service by the Children's Aid Society and the Society for the Prevention of Cruelty to Children in Buffalo, New York is discussed. Instead of removing children left alone at night from their homes--a traumatic experience--the emergency service dispatches an adult volunteer to stay with the children through the night. Emergency parents are drawn from the general populace; each stays on call for one week at a time. The program has proven to be successful and inexpensive.

1230 Paneth, J. "Deflation in an inflationary period: some current social health need provisions." Am J Public Health 62(1): 60-63, January, 1972. (5 References).
Reports the inadequacies of the welfare system in New York City with particular criticism of the scanty aid provided for pregnancy and post-natal care. Many children of welfare families are malnourished, receive no medical care, and live in poor housing. A Mt. Sinai Hospital program is described which attempts to help families on welfare make the most of public services, and which provides emergency aid for acute medical needs.

1231 Penner, G. Lewis. "Multidisciplinary cooperation for protecting children." In: National Symposium on Child Abuse, 4th, Charleston, S. C., 1973. Collected papers. Denver, Colorado: The American Humane Association, Children's Division, 1975. 27-31.
Examines the function of the Bowen Center in Chicago as a family service. The Center's goal is to work toward the maintenance of the family unit. Neglected children receive meals, education, and health care. Because abusive and neglectful parents often have infantile personalities, the Center provides them with social functions and home managing instruction as therapeutic and developmental activities.

1232 Pickett, John. "The management of non-accidental injury to children in the city of Manchester." In: Borland, Marie, ed. Violence in the family. Atlantic Highlands, New Jersey: Humanities Press, 1976. 61-87. (15 References).
Describes a special unit set up in Manchester, England designed to protect children from repeated non-accidental injury. The unit's main functions are to provide services for the family of the abused child, to arrange consultations among professionals, and to maintain a case register. The unit must also coordinate services within Manchester, undertake research, and provide information. The unit team, consisting of a leader, five members, and a coordinator, is on call twenty-four hours a day. They focus on preserving the life and health of the child, preferably within his own home, and on providing supportive therapy to the abusing parents. A monitoring service ensures that cases are handled correctly and that the various agencies are in proper communication.

1233 Pizzo, P. D.; Cochintu, A.; Bean, S. "Child abuse and day care." Voice Child 7(1): 1-6, January, 1974. (5 References).
Reviews the problem of child abuse, with focus on the role played by day care agencies in the discovery and treatment of child abuse. Several features common to cases of child abuse are listed (abusive parents were abused by their parents and are ambivalent toward their children), along with the avenues for action most frequently taken by day care centers discovering cases of child abuse. The agencies are warned to avoid common pitfalls in dealing with child abuse.

1234   Scherer, Lorena.   "Facilities and services for neglected children
       in Missouri."   Natl Probat Parole Assoc J   6(1):   66-68, January,
       1960. (0 References).
The referral procedures and aims of Missouri Child Welfare Services are
summarized.   Improving care for the child in his own home has been found
to benefit parents and children in 66 percent of the cases seen during a
twelve month period and has proved more economical for the county than
placement.   After referrals are received from juvenile court or from the
county welfare staff, a child welfare worker initiates contact with the
family and arranges for a treatment plan.   Termination occurs when the
family can adequately care for the child or when a placement has been
arranged for the child.

1235   Schmidt, Dolores M., and Johnson, Betty.   "Facilities and services
       for neglected children: protective service for neglected children
       in Denver."   Natl Probat Parole Assoc J   6(1):   40-43, January,
       1960. (1 Reference).
Describes the functions of child protection services in Denver.   As the
liaison between the police department and the Child Welfare Division, the
Juvenile Bureau investigates police reports of abuse and neglect, referring some cases to the Child Welfare Division for social work, and removing children from situations of immediate danger.   The Child Welfare
Division receives referrals from other community agencies and private
citizens.   Once it is established through consultation with the Juvenile
Bureau that a referral is not an emergency, the child welfare worker contacts the family, sets up weekly meetings, and arranges for the special
services they might need.   A study indicated that three out of four families improved their situation under the care of protective services.

1236   Solomon, Theo; Berger, Deborah; Pessirilo, Gloria.   Final report:
       the Mayor's Task Force on Child Abuse and Neglect.   New York: Human
       Resources Administration, Special Services for Children, December
       15, 1970.   99p.
Presents the findings and recommendations of the Mayor's Task Force on
Child Abuse and Neglect in New York City.   After interviewing persons of
all levels of responsibility in hospitals, social service agencies,
schools, and law enforcement agencies, specific recommendations in the
areas of investigation, disposition, rehabilitation, and education were
offered.

The report advises that the operation of the central registry be expanded
to a twenty-four-hour basis and that the system be computerized to deal
more efficiently with new reports and with requests for information by
a physician suspecting prior non-accidental injury to a child he is currently treating.   To insure immediate protective care to the greater
number of abused and neglected children, the committee urges that only
one agency receive reports and that one social worker be responsible for
all aspects of a single case.

Disposition of abuse and neglect cases often poses monetary problems to
the city and emotional problems to the family.   As alternatives to placement, expanded homemaker services and day care facilities can be employed.
Extending a child's stay at a supposedly short-term facility for several
months or retaining children in the hospital after completion of medical
treatment are discouraged.   Rather, short-term placement should be designed either to return the child to his home after a safe interim or to
find appropriate foster or adoptive parents.   The study advocates increased

foster home care rates for hard to place children and the establishment
of less restrictive criteria for foster parents.

Observing the paucity of psychiatric programs available to help abusive
parents, the Task Force advises the creation of alternative mental health
programs designed exclusively for abusive and neglecting parents. These
programs would include: group therapy, lay therapy, residential family
treatment, homemaker services for neglecting parents, Parents Anonymous,
and visiting public health or psychiatric services. In the field of
education, the report urges the establishment of a center for the study
of child abuse and neglect in New York City. The center would provide
additional training for physicians, pediatricians, social workers, police
officers, lawyers, and judges involved in the treatment and management of
child abuse. In addition, the center would carry on its own research and
dispense information regarding reporting laws, placement alternatives,
and court procedures.

1237 Tocchio, Octavio J. "Procedural problems inhibiting effective
        county and community-wide resolution of battered child problems."
        Police 14(5): 16-21, May-June, 1970. (3 References).
Considers the problems physicians and local officials in Fresno County
face with respect to the handling of maltreated children. One major difficulty lies in the lack of continuity and resulting lack of experience
among the juvenile court judges who must decide the disposition of the
children brought before them. Other problems include the provision of
therapy for emotionally and physically damaged children and their parents,
the need to expand the capacities of welfare agencies, and the clarification of existing child welfare legislation.

1238 Varon, Edith. "The client of a protective agency in the context of
        the community: a field study of the Massachusetts Society for the
        Prevention of Cruelty to Children." For a summary see: Diss Abstr
        22(12): 4429, June, 1962.

1239 Ward, David M. "Citizen responsibility in the development of pro-
        tective services." Natl Probat Parole Assoc J 6(1): 50-53,
        January, 1960. (0 References).
Offers an overview of the development of protective services within the
Division of Child Welfare of the Cuyahoga County Welfare Department in
Cleveland from 1875 to 1959. In 1956, the concern that no protective
services existed for neglected children prompted an investigation by a
lay citizen's committee. It was concluded that the community needed
specialized protective services and that the Division of Child Welfare of
Cuyahoga County should be responsible for such services.

1240 Winston, Ellen. "The responsibility of the state public welfare
        agency for the neglected child." Natl Probat Parole Assoc J 6(1):
        59-62, January, 1960. (0 References).
The responsibilities of state public welfare agencies serving neglected
children are outlined. Primary responsibilities are to aid the family
so that the child may remain in the home and to provide the same standard
of care to children in all areas.

3. PRIVATE PROGRAMS

1241 Berkeley Planning Associates. First site visit report -- Part II:
      Community system: evaluation, demonstration program in child abuse
      and neglect. Berkeley, California: Berkeley Planning Associates,
      October, 1974. 80p.
Evaluates eleven child abuse and neglect demonstration programs at the
following sites: Adams County, Colorado; Arlington, Virginia; Bayamon,
Puerto Rico; East Baton Rouge Parish, Louisiana; a three county area in
rural Arkansas; portions of Los Angeles County; Neah Bay Indian Reservation in Washington; St. Louis, Missouri; St. Petersburg, Florida; Tacoma,
Washington; and Union County, New Jersey. Information is presented in
tabular format concerning the characteristics of the community served by
the projects; the incidence of abuse; the scope, penalties, waivers, and
other special features of each state's reporting laws; the functions of
all community agencies which receive and handle cases of suspected abuse;
and the degree of coordination among the different community agencies.

1242 Cassert, Hilda P. "Homemaker service as a component of casework."
      Soc Casework 51(9): 533-43, November, 1970. (9 References).
Assesses the contribution of a homemaker service to a caseworker agency.
The homemakers are sent by the agency to help out overburdened families
who have appealed to the agency for assistance. The homemakers, generally
older women trained by the agency for this specific role, stay all day
with the family for as long as it is necessary. They are expected to
offer non-intrusive childrearing models to the mothers they stay with and
to help with decisions regarding household management. They need to be
tactful and sensitive to the needs and impulses of their case families.
The service has proven quite successful in the preservation of troubled
families.

1243 Cohn, Anne; Clemons, Donald; DeGraaf, Beverly J.; et al. Second
      site visit report: evaluation, demonstration program in child
      abuse and neglect. Berkeley, California: Berkeley Planning
      Associates, December, 1974. 78p.
Highlights of a second series of evaluative visits to ten child abuse and
neglect demonstration projects. The purpose of the visits was to appraise
the level of progress made in implementing the individual diagnostic and
treatment programs, and to identify any further problems in internal program operation or with other community agencies. Examples of program
activities observed include: (1) preparation of a curriculum for foster
parents in Adams County, Colorado; (2) a special group therapy session
for adolescents at Pro-Child in Arlington, Virginia; (3) a community
crisis home network in St. Louis, Missouri; (4) plans for a maternity
ward based prediction and prevention program in St. Petersburg, Florida;
and (5) basic training in the fundamentals of child development for pregnant women in Bayamon, Puerto Rico.

1244 Doris, John L. "Child abuse and neglect: an introduction to the
      Family Life Development Center." Hum Ecol Forum 5(2): 4-7,
      Autumn, 1974. (0 References).
Gives a brief description of the history of child abuse laws and names
of organizations involved with child abuse. A list of eight activites
of the Family Life Development Center (Cornell University, Ithaca, New
York) is outlined.

1245 "Final child abuse project workshop is held." Natl Assoc Soc
      Workers News 22(8): 8, September, 1977. (0 References).
Reports a series of workshops held at the end of the twelve month operation of the Child Abuse and Neglect Training Project. Over 800 social
workers, lawyers, nurses, psychologists, and other professionals attended
the NASW-sponsored workshops on the training project held throughout the
year. Materials presented at the workshops are listed and include techniques for identifying abused and neglected children, an investigation of
the psychosocial dynamics of families, audovisual illustrations, and
instruction in the management of abuse and neglect by the community.

1246 Galdston, Richard. "Violence begins at home." J Am Acad Child
      Psychiatry 10(2): 336-50, April, 1971. (7 References).
Despite gains made in the recognition and diagnosis of child abuse, efforts
to prevent and treat it have not kept pace. The Parents' Center Project
was founded in order to escalate the use of preventive measures and
organized treatment procedures. The Center objectives include protecting
the child while treating the parent, studying causal forces of violence
in families, and serving as a training center for personnel dealing with
family violence. The Project Center consists of the child care facility
staffed by child case workers, and a parent group which meets once a week
under the leadership of several social workers. The need for centers
designed to help parents of preschool children and to assist the community
in curtailing the spread of violence is stressed.

1247 Garber, Michael. "Neighborhood-based child welfare." Child Welfare
      54(2): 73-81, February, 1975. (0 References).
Discusses the importance of keeping troubled children in the familiar surroundings of their own neighborhoods, even when the parents cannot handle
the custody of the child. A neighborhood group home for boys in the
Washington Heights area of New York is described. The home had three
functions: it served as a long-term facility, an emergency residence for
children in times of family crisis, and a halfway house for boys recently
leaving institutional placement for their homes. The group home was able
to utilize neighborhood resources in identifying and aiding troubled
families.

1248 Helfer, Ray E. A self-instructional program on child abuse and
      neglect. Evanston, Illinois: American Academy of Pediatrics,
      Committee on Infant and Preschool Child, 1974.

1249 Helfer, Ray E., and Wheeler, John S., eds. "Child abuse and the
      private pediatrician." Feelings Their Med Significance 14(3):
      May-June, 1972. (3 References).
Reports the establishment of a community SCAN program (Suspected Child
Abuse and Neglect) in Allentown, Pennsylvania. Emphasis is given to
responsibilities of private physicians in dealing with child abuse cases.

1250 Hinton, Cornelia, and Sterling, Joanne W. "Volunteers serve as an
      adjunct to treatment for child-abusing families." Hosp Community
      Psychiatry 26(3): 136-37, March, 1975. (0 References).
Evaluates the success of a child abuse management program staffed by
volunteers as a result of insufficient funds. Hiring and training procedures for the volunteers are presented. These volunteers are primarily
responsible for offering neglectful or abusive parents support services
and friendship in order to encourage them to develop social outlets.

Volunteers are also trained in mothering techniques so they can demonstrate acceptable childrearing practices for the parents to follow in the
home.

1251 Lobsenz, Norman. "One woman's war against child abuse." Good
      Housekeeping 181(1): 81-82, 118-19, July, 1975. (0 References).
Documents the story of one woman's successful effort to establish a SCAN
(Suspected Child Abuse and Neglect) team in Little Rock, Arkansas, with
particular emphasis on the reparenting and support given by volunteer
workers to abusive parents. A list of agencies which parents can contact
for help is provided.

1252 Mukundarao, Kathirisetti. "Perceptions of community need and its
      resolution: a case study of a community effort to protect its
      neglected children." For a summary see: Diss Abstr 24(4): 1735,
      October, 1963.

1253 "Non-accidental injury to children." Br Med J 4(5884): 96-97,
      October 13, 1973. (0 References).
Summarizes the resolutions of the Tunbridge Wells Study Group on non-
accidental injuries to children. Various professional groups were represented; their primary concern was the provision of maximum support to the
family.

1254 Richette, Lisa Aversa. "Who catches the throwaway child?" Trans
      Stud Coll Physicians Phila 40(4): 219-25, April, 1973. (0 Refer-
      ences).
Records a lecture given by the author of The Throwaway Children. Community intervention for the prevention of child abuse, legal representation
for the victims, and therapeutic treatment, rather than punishment, for
the offenders are advocated. Projects such as CALM (Child Abuse Listening
and Mediation) are described. The lecture ends with a plea to women in
the audience to "permeate a male-created world of violence" with their
empathy and energy.

1255 "Shelter." New Yorker 45(20): 21-22, July 5, 1969. (0 Refer-
      ences).
Offers a distressing account of the overcrowding conditions of The Children's Center, a New York facility for the temporary shelter of abused,
delinquent, or neglected children, staffed by fifteen nurses and 220
child care workers.

1256 Stringer, Elizabeth A. "Homemaker service in neglect and abuse.
      Part II: A tool for case evaluation." Children 12(1): 26-29,
      January-February, 1965. (5 References).
Emphasizes the role of homemaker services in the treatment of child
neglect and abuse. Case studies illustrate the homemaker's contributions
in case finding and evaluation. Her direct observations of the facts
allow her to assess family strengths and weaknesses and to assist other
professionals in a comprehensive approach to the problem of abuse.

1257 Suarez, Mary L., and Ricketson, Mary A. "Facilitating casework
      with protective service clients through use of volunteers." Child
      Welfare 53(5): 313-22, May, 1974. (16 References).
Analyzes a program whereby volunteers assist in direct protective services. Once the roles of social worker and volunteer are clearly dif-

ferentiated, the volunteers prove helpful to the clients, social workers, and entire agency.

1258   Willner, Milton; Willner, Florence; Mooney, Eileen. "The forgotten children: an agency does double duty." Child Welfare 55(6): 423-30, June, 1976. (2 References).
Describes the Service to Children in Their Own Homes Program, operating out of the Porter-Leath Children's Center in Memphis, Tennessee. The Center is situated in the black ghetto, where living conditions are poor, and recreational, educational, and health services are minimal. The program consists of small groupwork sessions in which disadvantaged children (age six to eighteen) can discuss their feelings of anger and self-disparagement, establish realistic goals for self-improvement, and learn to relate more effectively with their peers and adults. Leaders of the small groups consult regularly with the children's teachers to see that they are receiving maximum assistance from the school system. In addition, the group leaders maintain contact with the children's families and give practical assistance such as providing transportation of parents and children to health clinics and interceding on their behalf with landlords, utility companies, and bill collectors. Other services include job finding and training programs for young adults and their parents, and field trips to libraries, parks, and museums. Program assessment demonstrated that the children's school achievement and behavior improved with several mothers reporting that they had found the services to be helpful.

4. COMMUNITY-BASED TEAMS

1259   Arthur, L. J. H.; Moncrieff, Martin W.; Milburn, W.; et al. "Nonaccidental injury in children: what we do in Derby." Br Med J 1(6022): 1363-66, June 5, 1976. (14 References).
Relates one community's program for dealing with child abuse. A team of physicians, policemen, and social workers cooperatively handle each case. When abuse is suspected by a pediatrician, the parents are informed that it will be reported. The police investigate every report of abuse and obtain, preserve, and present evidence when required by law. A special forensic physician testifies in court when necessary. A team social worker usually retains a twenty-eight-day "place of safety" order for the child and begins casework with the family immediately. Criminal prosecutions for assault occur in only a few cases. Two case histories are presented as illustrations of how the team operates.

1260   Bean, Shirley L. "The Parents' Center Project: a multiservice approach to the prevention of child abuse." Child Welfare 50(5): 277-82, May, 1971. (0 References).
Examines the efforts of a social agency to develop an interdisciplinary approach to the treatment of abused children and their parents. A Parents' Center was created, in which the agency's medical director supervised the medical care of the children. Parents were involved in group therapy and were encouraged to participate in the Center's extensive day care services. The Center's research aims include the development of new techniques for the treatment of families with patterns of child abuse, the training of personnel, and the study of the origin and effects of violence within families.

1261 Beswick, Keith; Lynch, Margaret A.; Roberts, Jacqueline. "Child
      abuse and general practice." Br Med J 2(6039): 800–802, October
      2, 1976. (15 References).
Studies a child abuse prevention program used by a primary health team in
Oxfordshire, England. The team consisted of four family physicians,
nurses, health visitors, and midwives. The team meets regularly with the
local social service office. The population consisted of 9,250 patients
from the physicians' general practice. Of this population, thirty families were determined to be at risk. Criteria used for identification of
at risk families are outlined. Management of these families involved:
(1) a diagnostic interview; (2) a twenty-four-hour crisis telephone service; (3) the establishment of a therapeutic relationship between a primary
physician and the parents; (4) regular health care care for the child;
(5) practical help in easing the stresses of daily living; and (6) referrals to other agencies. Program evaluation reveals that no serious
incidences of abuse have occurred among the at risk families.

1262 Brem, Jacob. "Child abuse control centers -- a project for the
      academy?: letter to editor." Pediatrics 45(5): 894–95, May,
      1970. (2 References).
Child abuse cases are often mismanaged because physicians are unfamiliar
with child abuse laws and fearful of making reports on parents. Child
abuse control centers with a team approach are recommended.

1263 Burt, Marvin R., and Balyeat, Ralph. "A new system for improving
      the care of neglected and abused children." Child Welfare 53(3):
      167–79, March, 1974. (5 References).
Documents a three year study in Metropolitan Nashville and Davidson County
to coordinate various child neglect and emergency welfare services into a
single efficient program. With funding from the United States Children's
Bureau, Emergency Services (EMS) was developed to provide caretaker and
homemaker services for children left without parental supervision and to
find temporary foster homes for abused children. The goal of the program
to keep the child at home whenever possible was met, as evidenced by the
significant reduction of institutional placements from 190 in 1971–1972,
to only two in 1972–1973.

1264 Cameron, James S. "Role of the child protective organization."
      Pediatrics 51(4, Part II): 793–95, April, 1973. (0 References).
Examines the role and responsibilities of the New York Child Protective
Service Agency. Its functions often overlap with the functions of other
agencies and professional services. Nevertheless, the Child Protective
Service Agency is the sole authority legally responsible for organizing
community action on behalf of any endangered child. It not only investigates the question of treatment and custody of the child, but also the
type of treatment needed to stabilize the family as a whole. Its effectiveness, however, depends on the cooperation of those responsible for
reporting suspected cases of abuse such as physicians and school officials.

1265 Coffey, Carol. "The protective social worker's view of interdis-
      ciplinary action -- problems and assets." In: National Symposium
      on Child Abuse, 5th, Boston, 1974. Collected papers. Denver,
      Colorado: The American Humane Association, Children's Division,
      1976. 22–25. (0 References).
Discusses the coordination of disciplines as demonstrated by the Hennepin
County Welfare Department, Minnesota. The intake process receives com-

plaints from all members and groups in the community and determines their
validity. Assessment and intervention involves making contact with the
parents and determining the problems. The family, social workers, and
medical, psychiatric, and educational professionals work together to provide solutions.

1266 Cooper, Elizabeth. "Pilot study of protective services in Los
      Angeles." Natl Probat Parole Assoc J 6(1): 56-58, January, 1960.
      (0 References).
Assesses the effectiveness of protective services in Los Angeles County.
A small population from an average, rather than deprived, community was
served by caseworkers with graduate degrees in social work. They acted
on referrals limited to families with children under ten years of age.
The staff discovered that the protective services alone could not handle
all aspects of the cases, proposing the need for auxiliary services and
coordination of existing services.

1267 D'Agostino, Paul A. "Dysfunctioning families and child abuse: the
      need for an interagency effort." Public Welfare 30(4): 14-17,
      Fall, 1972. (0 References).
Examines two programs in Boston which aim at coordinating the efforts of
various agencies to identify, treat, and prevent child abuse. The
Department of Public Welfare has instituted a Division of Family and Child
Services to marshall local resources to aid families lacking parental
skills. It has made possible a third alternative to the old choice between removing the child from his home and leaving him in an unrecon-
structed family environment. The other program, Children's Advocates,
Inc., is a corporation made up of various public and private agencies
whose activities are standardized, coordinated by Children's Advocates,
Inc. The corporation also gathers data, cross references cases of child
abuse and keeps a registry for them, trains volunteers, and distributes
educational materials.

1268 Everett, M. G.; Lewis, I. C.; Mair, Catherine H.; et al. "The
      battered baby syndrome: the Tasmanian approach." Med J Aust
      2(15): 735-37, October 13, 1973. (4 References).
Presents a systematic approach to dealing with the legal, social, and
treatment aspects of the battered child syndrome. A committee is established to coordinate the activities of police, pediatricians, social
workers, and families so that cases of suspected child abuse can be efficiently investigated and managed. One of the primary tasks of this
committee is to inform and educate all members of the medical and related
professions about the procedures for reporting suspected cases of child
abuse, and about available community services for treatment.

1269 Fontana, Vincent J., and Robison, Esther. "A multidisciplinary
      approach to the treatment of child abuse." Pediatrics 57(5):
      760-64, May, 1976. (10 References).
During 1973 and 1974, sixty-two families in New York City participated
in a program for the treatment and prevention of child abuse. The program's two major components are: a three to four month in-patient treatment for the mother and the abused child, and a one year out-patient
follow-up treatment for the entire family. The therapeutic approach
during both treatment phases involves a multidisciplinary team of professionals and paraprofessionals who provide medical, psychiatric, and
social services. During the residential treatment, each mother is

assigned a social worker assistant and a group mother. These paraprofessionals demonstrate appropriate mothering techniques, become supportive friends, and negotiate outside agencies on the mothers' behalf to secure housing, job training, education, and day care for the family. A psychiatrist provides individual and group therapy for the mothers. A behavior modification technique is also employed in which the mother is videotaped while feeding or playing with her child and later reviews the tape with her psychiatrist. In this way, the mother can receive feedback about the quality of her interaction with her child. Program evaluation indicates that the intervention was successful in preventing separation of the mother and child in 65 percent of the cases. A majority of the mothers showed a decrease in stress, improved relationships with family members, and improved emotional stability. All of the children in the program demonstrated improvements in many areas of their development.

1270   Herman, Bernice J. "A cucumber from Roberta." <u>MH</u> 60(2): 19-21,
        Summer, 1976. (0 References).
Describes a treatment program for child abusing parents and their children established by the Child and Family Advocates of Evanston (CFAE). The program utilizes volunteers who visit the family and serve as friends and parent models. Volunteers include school teachers, mothers doing graduate work, church workers, and mothers skilled at mothering. The volunteers receive training in how to understand and interact with the abusing parent. Other groups involved in the program are the schools, police, hospitals, health departments, several counseling services, day care services, universities, and the local mental health association. The CFAE acts as interagency coordinator and as supervisor for the volunteers.

1271   Hill, Deborah. "Communication and collaboration in developing
        approaches to child abuse prevention and treatment." In: National
        Symposium on Child Abuse, 5th, Boston, 1974. <u>Collected papers.</u>
        Denver, Colorado: The American Humane Association, Children's
        Division, 1976. 63-67. (0 References).
The Children's Advocates, Inc. in Boston, Massachusetts is composed of twenty-three agencies, including the Public Welfare Department, Children's Protective Services, hospitals, social agencies, legal agencies, and volunteer groups. The group promotes interagency communication, defines guidelines for the protection of abused and neglected children, disseminates educational information, and develops protective programs.

1272   Jaffe, Peggy E. "Family crisis intervention: demonstration and
        evaluation of a program utilizing mental health paraprofessionals
        and law enforcement officers." For a summary see: <u>Diss Abstr Int</u>
        35B(8): 4178, February, 1975.

1273   Moorehead, Caroline. "Seven-man team helps parents of battered
        babies." <u>Times Educ Suppl</u> 2897: 12, November 27, 1970. (0
        References).
Describes the establishment and procedures of the Battered Child's Research Department set up by the National Society for the Prevention of Cruelty to Children. When a hospital refers an abused child, the seven person team comprising the Battered Child Unit tries first to elicit some response from the parents and to seek temporary custody for the child in the hospital. Evasive at first, the parents become dependent on the team, and once they can begin to request and accept help, improvement in their relationship with their child is possible. These parents, often neglected

as children, tend to be immature, young, and to already have several children who appear well cared for. Increasing available aids for battering parents and improving education for parenthood are two suggested means of prevention.

1274   Nordstrom, Jerry L.   "Child abuse: a school district's response to its responsibility."   Child Welfare   53(4):   257-60, April, 1974. (0 References).
The formation of a child abuse and neglect team in the Adams County (Colorado) School District I is described.   Through inservice presentations, the interdisciplinary team alerted other educators of their responsibilities to abused children, while processing promptly all reported cases through an efficient centralized system.

1275   Sayre, James W.; Foley, Frank W.; Zingarella, Leonor S.; et al. "Community committee on child abuse: a step toward better understanding and cooperation."   NY State J Med   73(16):   2071-75, August 15, 1973.   (9 References).
Relates the development of the Monroe County Committee on Child Abuse, an intra-agency referral and management unit.   Its membership is represented by professionals from social, legal, and medical services.   The committee meets monthly and coordinates the community's efforts to identify and report abuse as well as to provide protective and legal action.   After working together, each of the various professional groups gained a more thorough understanding of their respective roles in handling abuse.   Additional accomplishments, suggested changes, and future undertakings, such as community education programs, Parents Anonymous, and day care centers, are discussed.

1276   Silver, Larry B.; Dublin, Christina C.; Lourie, Reginald S.   "Agency action and interaction in cases of child abuse."   Soc Casework 52(3):   164-71, March, 1971.   (13 References).
Summarizes a five year study of thirty-four child abuse cases.   Data was gathered from hospital and community agency records.   All thirty-four cases were at some time referred to the Women's Bureau by the Children's Hospital of the District of Columbia.   The Women's Bureau then referred 62 percent of the cases to protective services for casework.   No clear statistical correlation between referring cases to protective services and improvements in the families could be drawn.   Nevertheless, continuous and conscientious casework proved to be successful in increasing the parents' ability to care for their children.   Therefore, families should be referred for protective services early, even before the abused child's medical care is terminated.   Although removal of the child appeared to be the primary deterrent for further abuse, it is not the desirable solution.   Cooperative community efforts to treat the family as a unit are suggested.

1277   "Social salvage: editorial."   Br Med J   1(5480):   121, January 15, 1966.   (2 References).
Reviews the functioning of Family Service Units (FSUs) in Britain.   FSUs are groups of health visitors, social workers, and other professionals organized to help families which, for one reason or another, have high potential for child neglect.   Often the "salvage" involves reeducating the parents; FSUs try to help improve living conditions among the families, who are usually poor, and establish friendly relationships with family members.

1278   Surdock, Pete W., Jr. A community's team approach to abuse and
       neglect. Helena, Montana: Montana State Department of Social
       and Rehabilitative Services, 1974. 8p.
Defines and describes a Montana community's team approach to child abuse
and neglect. Two key concepts need to be clear: the role of the team
as a whole and the role of the individual members of the team. The goals
of the team are to share expert knowledge from a variety of professions
and to use that knowledge to improve the delivery of services to abused
children and their families. For this team consultation to be effective,
members must share and accept expertise without "professional chauvinism"
or individual bias. Because child abuse or neglect is a complex problem,
the team composition needs to be both comprehensive and well coordinated.
Essential members of the team include: team coordinator, physician,
county welfare social worker, county attorney, public health nurse, mental
health clinic or psychiatrist, and hospital representative. Montana's
eight community child abuse teams are working well after going through
several typical stages: (1) orientation phase to clarify roles and assign
ultimate responsibility for the abused or neglected family; (2) second
stage to develop trust, confidence, and team morale; and (3) third phase
to plan for continued effectiveness. The child abuse team is regarded
as an exciting, flexible, and effective system for helping the defenseless
child.

1279   Thomson, Ellen M.; Paget, Norman W.; Bates, Doris W.; et al. Child
       abuse: a community challenge. Buffalo, New York: Henry Stewart,
       1971. 169p. (Bibliography).
An in-depth account of the philosophy, background, and operation of an
interdisciplinary child protection agency in Buffalo, New York for the
management of child abuse cases. A total of 376 children from 334 families that were reported as abused from November, 1966 through October,
1969 form the basis for this report. The philosophy of the agency emphasizes the right of society to intervene in the affairs of the family on
behalf of a neglected or abused child, the importance of strengthening
family life and keeping the child at home if possible, the responsibility
of the agency to provide community services for the family and temporary
or permanent placement outside the home for the abused child if necessary,
and the involvement of the agency in the education of professionals and
the public about the problem of child abuse. The major lesson to be
learned from the background of this project is that legislation on child
abuse alone is not enough to encourage the reporting of child abuse cases
to the appropriate agencies. New laws and procedures must be interpreted
to hospitals, private physicians, nurses, and school personnel in order
to significantly increase the number of children reported to them.

All cases of suspected child abuse are brought to the attention of the
coordinating social worker at the child protection agency. His job is to
set the process of investigation and intervention of child abuse cases in
motion. The role of the social worker assigned to a particular case is to
coordinate the activities of physicians, teachers, and other involved
parties, to develop a trusting, supportive relationship with the family,
to assess the psychosocial make-up of the family and its problems, and
to make a decision regarding the treatment of the family or placement of
the child outside the home. The role of the physician is to diagnose and
report cases of suspected child abuse to the protection agency. He orders
laboratory tests, x-rays, and takes photographs of the abused child. The
physician also has the responsibility to testify in court about medical
findings if necessary. The agency attorney must work closely with the

social worker, the physician, the court, the opposing counsel, and the parents in order to obtain a judgment in the best interests and welfare of the child. If a judgment is made to separate the child from the home, the foster care social worker must work sensitively with the child, his parents, and the foster family to provide a corrective experience and bring about change. During the separation, the parents are encouraged to visit the child, provide financial support, and actively participate in follow-up counseling or treatment. The foster care social worker ultimately decides whether the parents have the capacity to resume the care of their child.

Statistical tables are provided which give information about the abused children, the parents, those persons reporting suspected abuse, the circumstances leading up to abuse, and the outcome of abuse cases. It is concluded that: (1) reported cases of child abuse represent a small percentage of the actual number; (2) the assessment and diagnosis of child abuse should be shared by an interdisciplinary team; (3) cases of abuse need special handling and services; and (4) inadequate preparation for parenthood can be seen as a primary cause of child abuse.

1280 Whiting, Leila. "A community multidisciplinary child protection team." Child Today 6(1): 10-12, January-February, 1977. (3 References).

The Montgomery County, Maryland, Child Protection Team's main function is to coordinate prompt agency action in response to reports of child abuse and to offer advice to protective service workers faced with deciding the futures of abused children and their families. The team consists of individuals representing the community's medical, social, and legal professions. Its consultation services are also involved in cases of neglect, including emotional neglect.

1281 Wolkenstein, Alan S. "Evolution of a program for the management of child abuse." Soc Casework 57(5): 309-16, May, 1976. (25 References).

Investigates a program begun in 1967 which manages cases of child abuse in Milwaukee. The Advisory Committee on Child Welfare is no longer concerned exclusively with child abuse, since its purview includes all aspects of child welfare, but abuse and negligence are the most pressing problems it faces. The Committee, made up of physicians, psychiatrists, and a social worker, acts as a referral service for physicians at Children's Hospital, and it also performs diagnostic evaluations and offers therapy programming. The Committee approaches cases with a rehabilitative and non-punitive attitude. No attempt is made to identify the abuser, and an effort is made to keep the child in the home. Recommendations are included for the management of child abuse in other communities.

5. HOSPITAL-BASED TEAMS

1282 American Academy of Pediatrics. A descriptive study of nine health-based programs in child abuse and neglect. Springfield, Virginia: National Technical Information Service, 1974. 115p. (Bibliography). For ordering information see: Government Reports Announcements and Index 75(3): 35, February 7, 1975.

Describes and compares nine nationwide multidisciplinary child abuse and neglect treatment programs. At the time of the survey, Cook County Children's Hospital in Chicago treated severe child abuse cases in its

crises oriented facilities. The hospital had a parent education program
for parents of premature infants, but few additional supportive services
were available in the community. The University of Colorado Medical
Center was found to utilize a Child Protection Team of professionals and
lay therapists who evaluated each child's medical, psychiatric, and family
history. Numerous treatment programs designed for abusive families were
provided. The Infant and Child Protection Committee of the William
Beaumont Army Medical Center in El Paso, Texas, cared for fifty abused
children of military personnel each year. Neglect cases were especially
prominent on the army base. The center reported almost 100 percent parent
cooperation in its treatment program. Kauikeolani Children's Hospital
in Honolulu provided diagnostic and short-term crisis treatment to abused
children. Low income white agricultural families from all parts of the
state were found to be served by the University of Iowa Hospitals in
Iowa City. A surprising 98 percent of all referrals came from private
physicians. Ninety percent of all children diagnosed as non-accidental
injury victims admitted to Children's Hospital of Los Angeles were temporarily removed from their homes. Families did not often receive adequate therapeutic treatment due to poor coordination of community resources. A residential mother and child treatment program was found to
be offered by the New York Foundling Hospital. Patients were all referred from other hospitals. Extensive group and individual therapy was
directed at altering deep-seated and destructive behavior in the mothers.
Children's Hospital of Pittsburgh was found to be successfully incorpor-
ating the SCAN program (Suspected Child Abuse/Neglect) into its pediatric
unit, while a total community program was found at the St. Paul-Ramsey
County Mental Health Center. The child abuse reporting rate by physicians
in that Minnesota county was one of the highest in the nation.

1283   Barnes, Geoffrey B.; Chabon, Robert S.; Hertzberg, Leonard J.
       "Team treatment for abusive families." Soc Casework 55(10):
       600-611, December, 1974. (0 References).
Describes and evaluates the work of a special child abuse team based at
the Sinai Hospital in Baltimore. The team included a full-time social
worker, two full-time paraprofessional community aides, a half-time nurse,
a consulting pediatrician, a consulting psychiatrist, and a secretary.
The social worker coordinated team efforts and provided the major therapy
to the family, as well as being the liaison to other social agencies.
The community aides listened to the families' problems and offered role
models to abusive parents. The pediatrician was responsible for medical
care while the psychiatrist was consulted by the social worker regarding
the psychological needs of each family. The team seemed to perform
successfully, its principal problem being that of financial shortage.

1284   Boardman, Helen E. "A project to rescue children from inflicted
       injuries." Soc Work 7(1): 43-51, January, 1962. (5 References).
Reports a project in the Children's Hospital of Los Angeles which protects the victims of child abuse. The hospital staff emphasizes that
cooperation among physicians, social workers, and the courts is necessary to protect the child.

1285   Brewster, Thomas, and Postel, Kenneth L. "Managing child abuse:
       a multidisciplinary approach for naval hospitals." US Navy Med
       67(10): 8-10, October, 1976. (6 References).
In 1974, at the Naval Regional Medical Center (NRMC), Camp Lejeune, North
Carolina, the NRMC Child Abuse/Neglect Committee was established. The

team includes a pediatrician, psychiatrist, administrator, attorney,
social caseworkers, counselors from the Onslow County Medical Health
Clinic and Red Cross, and nurses from the Navy Relief Society, each with
defined roles. The Committee meets once a week to discuss and follow up
cases. Although it is too early to draw conclusive results, three cases
are presented to demonstrate the team's handling of child abuse.

1286   Chabon, Robert S.; Barnes, Geoffrey, B.; Hertzberg, Leonard J.
       "The problem of child abuse: a community hospital approach." Md
       State Med J 22(10): 50-55, October, 1973. (13 References).
Reviews a multidisciplinary team formed at Sinai Hospital of Baltimore
to deal with child abuse. It consists of medical and social professionals,
as well as a paraprofessional community aide, who provide much of the
direct family service. The Child Abuse Project considers child abuse to
be a social problem and evaluates both psychological and social factors
in the family environment that could be cause for abuse. It has successfully reduced the potential for further abuse in the families under its
care.

1287   Gray, Jane. "Hospital-based battered child team." Hospitals
       47(4): 50-52, February 16, 1973. (1 Reference).
Recommends that hospitals organize multidisciplinary teams of professionals to handle case-finding, documentation, physical examinations,
medical treatment, and follow-up care for battered children and their
families. A physician who strongly suspects that a child has been battered should make certain that the child is admitted to a hospital, where
the child will be safe and extensive physical examinations can be conducted. During the child's hospitalization, the combined efforts of the
physicians, child protective workers, public health nurses, welfare
department, and the appropriate legal authorities should be initiated
and a diagnosis reached. Follow-up care after the child's discharge
should be handled by the hospital team when no appropriate community
agency is available. Learning to recognize the characteristics typical
of battering parents is the key to the prevention of child abuse.

1288   Hildebrandt, H. M., and Bowden, M. L. "The SCAN team: a specialty
       team for suspected child abuse and neglect." Pediatrician 5(3):
       141-55, 1976. (33 References).
Describes a special team (SCAN) for the management of child abuse at Mott
Children's Hospital, University of Michigan Medical Center, Ann Arbor,
Michigan. The team is composed of a staff pediatrician, six house
officers, a social worker, a psychiatrist, and a secretary-coordinator.
The SCAN team developed an effective protocol for the diagnosis and
reporting of suspected cases of child abuse. It also outlined medicolegal procedures for emergency foster placement or hospital retention of
abused children who cannot be safely returned home after treatment. The
SCAN team provides medical examinations for children referred to them by
protective services, school personnel, or law enforcement agencies because of suspected child abuse or neglect. The team also acts as an
information source on the subject of child abuse for interested community
and university organizations. The article reviews two administrative
problems encountered by the team--the reluctance of physicians to identify
and report abuse and time limitations on team members. Problems involving
the management of unusual cases are also discussed. Since the establishment of SCAN in 1971, the number of reported cases of child abuse and
neglect have increased. Sixty-three percent involved children age five
years and under.

1289 Irwin, Clare. "The establishment of a child abuse unit in a children's hospital." S Afr Med J 49(28): 1142-46, July 5, 1975.
      (11 References).
Reports on the establishment of a child abuse center in a children's hospital in South Africa. A study assessing the effectiveness of the unit was conducted. Although a shortage of trained staff influenced the outcome of the study, significant progress was made toward integrating the agencies responsible for handling the problem. The cooperation of the medical profession is sought in setting up further programs.

1290 Joyner, Edmund N., III. "Child abuse: the role of the physician and the hospital." Pediatrics 51(4, Part II): 799-803, April, 1973. (0 References).
Outlines five responsibilities that hospitals should assume in dealing with child abuse: (1) consistent identification of symptoms that appear non-accidental; (2) protection of the child by placing him in the hospital; (3) medical treatment of physical and emotional injuries; (4) reporting of cases to the authorities; and (5) parental rehabilitation. The formation of a child abuse committee or team of medical and social professionals to carry out these responsibilities is recommended. The Child Abuse and Neglect Committee of Roosevelt Hospital in New York serves as a model for successful management.

1291 Kempe, C. Henry. "The battered child and the hospital." Hosp Pract 4: 44-47, October, 1969. (0 References).
Studies the effective deployment of a coordinated approach to intervention in cases of child abuse. The coordination should begin immediately, in the emergency room, drawing on medical, legal, and social work personnel to treat both child and parents. Effective intervention must focus on the rehabilitation of the family. For this reason, civil, rather than criminal, procedures are recommended to the courts.

1292 Kristal, Helen F., and Tucker, Ford. "Managing child abuse cases."
      Soc Work 20(5): 392-95, September, 1975. (31 References).
Describes a child abuse management program established by the Social Work Division at the University of Rochester Medical Center. The coordination of several disciplines in handling child abuse cases is emphasized, as is the transmission of knowledge and experience regarding child abuse to new staff members. The establishment of some set procedure is imperative in managing child abuse cases; at Rochester, the efforts of senior staff members are coordinated by a psychiatric social worker experienced in the problems of children and families. The coordinator follows each case through the hospital, the courts, and agencies. A case study exemplifying the approach is included.

1293 Leivesley, S. "The maltreated child -- a cause for concern." Med J Aust 1(18): 935-36, April 29, 1972. (3 References).
Summarizes the syndrome of child abuse, including incidence, clinical features of the maltreated child, characteristics of the abusing parent, and a team approach to the treatment of the child and his family while the child is hospitalized.

1294 Lister, John. "By the London Post: the price of oil -- death of a baby -- no sex, please -- we're British." N Engl J Med 294(13): 710-12, March 25, 1976. (2 References).

Comments on a report of an infant's death by starvation. The lack of
communication between the family physician, visiting nurse, and social
worker was cited as a contributing factor to the tragedy. The exclusion
of social workers on primary health care teams and the lack of skepticism
on the part of the young social workers are criticized.

1295 Lynch, Margaret; Steinberg, Derek; Ounsted, Christopher. "Family
      unit in a children's psychiatric hospital." Br Med J 2(5963):
      127-29, April 19, 1975. (1 Reference).
Analyzes a program in Park Hospital, a facility designed to treat family
problems. Both mothers and children are admitted to the hospital, which
provides medical care, counseling, and training in techniques of child
care. The unit is thought to be generally successful, especially in its
function of diagnosis and assessment. However, there is a need for
further assessment of live-in treatment facilities, employing a team
approach.

1296 Meyers, Alan; Cooper, Carol; Dolins, David. "Child abuse: hospital
      combats neglected health crisis." Hospitals 48(17): 46-49,
      September 1, 1974. (5 References).
A report on DART, the new Yale-New Haven Hospital's program for the detection, appraisal, reporting, and treatment of abused children or those in
danger of being abused. DART conducts prevention and follow-up visits to
abuse prone families in addition to providing immediate attention to child
victims at the hospital. Self-help groups for parents and educational
programs at local colleges and PTA's have been initiated as DART's outreach has extended to the larger community.

1297 Newberger, Eli H.; Hagenbuch, John J.; Ebeling, Nancy B.; et al.
      "Reducing the literal and human cost of child abuse: impact of a
      new hospital management system." Pediatrics 51(5): 840-48, May,
      1973. (11 References).
Research findings reveal the effectiveness of a new hospital-based interdisciplinary consultation unit in reducing the cost of child abuse in
terms of the financial burden to families and in terms of the risk of
subsequent injury to the abused. The management group, founded in
September, 1970, is called the Trauma X Group. Its functions include:
(1) recording information about each new case of abuse or neglect; (2)
planning continued care for the child; (3) periodically reviewing the
quality of care given; (4) preparing legal juvenile court proposals with
the department of public welfare; (5) educating the medical staff to
detect and control abuse; and (6) improving communications among agencies
handling abuse and neglect. Furthermore, it is responsible for continuing
research aimed at advancing studies in etiology and intervention methods.

1298 Shaw, Anthony, and Carr, Corinne H. "A team approach to child
      abuse." Va Med Mon 101(5): 366-72, May, 1974. (9 References).
Reports on a multidisciplinary team approach to the management of child
abuse at the University of Virginia Medical Center. The team consists
of physicians, social workers, nurses, and a psychiatrist. Consultants
to the team include a juvenile court judge, three professors of law, a
professor of surgery, and others. Steps in the team's management of
abuse--receiving reports, reporting suspected cases to the authorities,
assisting the court in determining abuse or neglect, and filing petitions
for the placement of the child outside the home if necessary--are outlined. The community, educational, and research activities of the team

are also mentioned. Results indicate that of sixty-four children referred by the team for suspected abuse, only eight were subsequently believed to have been accidentally injured. A list of the number of cases and kind of injuries sustained in each age group is provided, along with several detailed case histories.

1299   Wolkenstein, Alan S. "Hospital acts on child abuse." Hospitals
       49(6): 103-6, March 16, 1975. (11 References).
Evaluates the success of a hospital-based multidisciplinary team of professionals organized for treating the victims of child abuse and their families in Milwaukee, Wisconsin. A primary contribution to the success of the Child Health Clinic is the quality of its follow-up treatment services.

6. MEDICAL CARE

1300   Bain, Katherine. "The physically abused child." Pediatrics   31(6):
       895-98, June, 1963. (7 References).
Notes increasing professional recognition of the physically abused child. It is pointed out that due to inadequate record keeping or unreported cases, however, no valid incidence figures on abuse are available. Inaction on the part of physicians is blamed on missed diagnoses, a lack of social conscience, fear, or ignorance. The development of the Model State Law by the Children's Bureau, requiring the reporting of suspected child abuse cases, is discussed.

1301   Bain, Katherine; Milowe, Irvin D.; Wenger, Don S.; et al. "Child
       abuse and injury." Milit Med 130(8): 747-62, August, 1965. (8
       References).
Reprints statements presented before the 1964 Forensic Sciences Symposium at the Armed Forces Institute of Pathology on the subject of child abuse. Discussion ensuing from formal statements followed a question-and-answer format. The presentation served as a general introduction to the problem and spanned a variety of issues. Several physician-participants, including one psychiatrist, shared their personal clinical experience with the problem of abuse. Some issues considered were: (1) mandatory reporting for physicians and hospitals; (2) the function of central registries in case-finding; (3) the questionable accessibility of battering parents to treatment and the need for criteria to guide the removal of children from the home; (4) the characteristics of abusing parents and families and of the abused child; and (5) the role of the obstetrician and pediatrician in the early detection of abuse and the prevention of future occurrences.

1302   Barnett, Bernard. "Violent parents: letter to editor." Lancet
       2(7735): 1208-9, November 27, 1971. (5 References).
Concern is expressed regarding the role of the family physician and the hospital in cases of child abuse. He speaks of the issue of "case conferences," contending that they require time which might more wisely be spent on the problems of management and administration. Recommendations include better education in childrearing and a psychiatric crisis theory which is not so psychodynamically bound.

1303   "The battered child syndrome: editorial." J La State Med Soc
       115(9): 322-24, September, 1963. (4 References).

Reviews an article by Kempe and others reiterating the medical description of the battered child syndrome and much of the numerical data. Physicians are encouraged to report suspicions of abuse, supported by photographs and x-rays, without comment on the person who committed the abuse.

1304   Breslow, Lester. "Proposals for achieving more adequate health care
       for children and youth." Am J Public Health 60(4, Supplement):
       106-22, April, 1970. (11 References).
Discusses the problems in child health care and possible solutions. Major medical problems are created by malnutrition, inadequate dental care, and battering parents. In his address at the Conference on Health Services for Children and Youth, Breslow advocates neighborhood health centers, specific programs for the poor, and increasing federal expenditures. The objectives and services offered by a National Program for Child Health are stated. Training personnel to assume many of the pediatrician's jobs is recommended. Although all the participants agreed on the urgency of the problem, they disagreed on the proper approach and methods of payment.

1305   Callaghan, K. A., and Fotheringham, B. J. "Practical management
       of the battered baby syndrome." Med J Aust 1(26): 1282-84, June
       27, 1970. (3 References).
Presents a plan for the management of child abuse cases at the Adelaide Children's Hospital in Melbourne, Australia. Once the child is admitted to the hospital, he is referred to a clinic which handles abusing families. The registrar arranges for an interview with the parents, a physical examination, a clinical photograph, initiates a routine investigation, arranges for the child to stay in the hospital, and notifies the social welfare department. Individual and cojoint interviews with the parents determine marital history, financial standing, family background, and current stresses. Plans can then be made to deal with the problem. Learning to recognize and manage families in crisis is a crucial element of prevention.

1306   Chadwick, David L. "Child abuse." JAMA 235(18): 2017-18, May
       3, 1976. (2 References).
The role of the family physician in the management of child abuse is examined. The physician should know the signs and symptoms of abuse so that it can be readily identified. In every state, reporting of suspected non-accidental injury is required by law, and the physician should become familiar with the specific procedures for reporting in his locality. On-going medical care must be provided for the child, and steps must be taken to protect him from further injury. The physician should adopt a supportive attitude toward the family, inform the parents that they will be contacted by a social worker from the child protective agency, and make necessary referrals. Finally, the physician has the responsibility of participating in community efforts to establish programs for the prevention and treatment of child abuse.

1307   Coles, Robert. "Terror-struck children." New Repub 150(22):
       11-13, May 30, 1964. (0 References).
Urges public and legal support of physicians in their fight against child abuse. It is pointed out that physicians currently bear the brunt of the responsibility in child abuse cases; they must be well informed about the problems and its causes and must concern themselves with preventive care.

1308   Cooper, Christine. "The doctor's dilemma -- a pediatrician's view."
       In: Franklin, Alfred White, ed. Concerning child abuse. New York:
       Churchill Livingstone, 1975.   21-29. (0 References).
The pediatrician must improve his general understanding of child abuse
and develop expertise in its diagnosis. Whenever a child is injured, the
pediatrician should ask this question: "Is it accident, carelessness,
neglect, or inflicted injury?" He should remember the high mortality and
morbidity rates of inflicted injury. Even minor non-accidental injuries
should be viewed as early warning signs, and the child and his family
should be referred to the hospital for diagnosis, protection from further
injury to the child, and treatment. If the home is not considered to be
safe enough for the child to return, it may be necessary to obtain a
place of safety, care orders, or a supervision order. Specially trained
police should be involved in the multidisciplinary management of child
abuse. However, police interrogation or investigation at an early stage
generally disturbs the developing confidence of the parents and any beginning therapeutic relationships.

1309   Curphey, Theodore J.; Kade, Harold; Noguchi, Thomas T.; et al.   "The
       battered child syndrome: responsibilities of the pathologist."
       Calif Med   102(2): 102-4, February, 1965. (2 References).
Highlights the role of the pathologist in fatal cases of child abuse. His
responsibilities differ from those of the reporting physician, who initiates the investigative process, in that his findings will constitute an
opinion about the guilt or innocence of the suspect. The pathologist's
procedures should include: (1) a consideration of all available information from the attending physician and from hospital records; (2) complete
x-ray studies of the skeleton; (3) documentation of external evidences of
injury supplemented by photographs; and (4) microscopic studies of all
injured areas. Four case studies are illustrative of the points discussed.

1310   Eisen, Peter. "The 'maltreatment syndrome' in children."   Med J
       Aust 1(9): 466-67, March 4, 1967. (0 References).
Advocates the active participation of the medical profession in the fight
against child abuse and neglect. Physicians are called upon to replace
their apathy with a sense of responsibility and stimulate new legislation
for the protection of children.

1311   Erwin, Donald T. "The battered child syndrome."   Med Leg Bull
       130: 1-7, February, 1964. (5 References).
Describes the characteristics and treatment of the battered child syndrome. Incidence is difficult to determine because of unrecognized or
unreported cases. Physicians' reluctance to report stems from disbelief,
fear, and/or ignorance of procedures involved. The parents of these
children, generally unable to control aggressive impulses, were often
victims of abuse as children. The clinical signs range from mild to
severe, but abuse is often repeated and reveals itself through radiographic examination. Obtaining a history of abuse from parents is important for the child's protection and for possible legal prosecution.
Sympathetic questioning by the physician involved is recommended. An
example of procedures to follow in the management of abuse cases is given,
including information about possible legal proceedings against the parents
and the protection of physicians against defamation suits.

1312 Finch, A. T. "Child welfare: what is being done in the field of child conservation." Va Med Mon 57(1): 23-25, April, 1930. (0 References).
Calls for semi-annual medical examination of children between the ages of six months and six years so that defects can be corrected before the child enters school. According to the West Law of Virginia, appropriations are to be made for health examinations of children. A uniform system of examination is necessary, and medical students should receive appropriate training for such purposes. One particular examination plan is discussed. The cooperation of local physicians is necessary for the success of the program.

1313 Fontana, Vincent J. "Battered babies: what the textbooks don't tell you." Med Dimens 19-21, January, 1975. (0 References).
Briefly discusses the maltreatment syndrome. Profiles of abusing families, causative factors, physical manifestations, and treatment are included. The physician's responsibility for detection, reporting, and follow-up are emphasized.

1314 ————. "The diagnosis of the maltreatment syndrome in children." Pediatrics 51(4, Part II): 780-82, April, 1973. (0 References).
Emphasizes the legal responsibility of the physician to report all suspected cases of battered children. A precise list, which clearly defines the signs and symptoms of maltreatment that should be part of any physician's index of suspicion, is included. These signs and symptoms are grouped into the following four categories for immediate reference: (1) history; (2) physical examination; (3) differential diagnosis; and (4) radiologic manifestations. Additional signs manifest themselves in distinctive behavioral patterns typical of abusers and the abused. Often a child's general appearance and state of cleanliness are enough to arouse a physician's suspicions.

1315 ————. "An insidious and disturbing medical entity." Public Welfare 24(3): 235-39, July, 1966. (1 Reference).
Proposes that the term "maltreatment syndrome of children" replace the original expression "the battered child syndrome" because, in addition to physical abuse, children are abandoned, neglected, and emotionally abused. When confronted with unexplained injuries in a child, the physician can reasonably suspect parental maltreatment. Because of the difficulty in obtaining a medical history, the physician needs to employ x-rays and other diagnostic tests in his examination of the child. The paucity of reporting by private physicians is attributed to a lack of awareness of the maltreatment syndrome and the reporting law, in addition to the physician's disliking of legal entanglements. The responsibility of protecting children must be shared by the medical, legal, and social work professions.

1316 Furst, William D. "The medical profession and child abuse in Texas." Tex Med 71(7): 87-89, July, 1975. (6 References).
Outlines a program designed to increase the involvement of the physician in the management of child abuse. Specific guidelines for identifying, diagnosing, and treating the physical and psychological damage to a battered child are provided. Parental support and rehabilitation measures should be taken early inasmuch as the eventual goal of treatment should be to reunite the family. Physicians must regard themselves as integral members of a larger community team of professionals working together to manage abuse.

1317 Green, Frederick C. "Child abuse and neglect: a priority problem
       for the private physician." Pediatr Clin North Am 22(2): 329-39,
       May, 1975. (14 References).
Emphasizes the role of primary care physicians, including private physicians, pediatricians, and surgeons, in recognizing and treating abused
children. Pertinent information regarding the definition of abuse, its
clinical manifestations, and goals in managing abuse cases is translated
into guidelines for physicians responsible for identifying and treating
abuse, as well as for offering family rehabilitation care. Although
state laws now require that physicians report all suspected cases of abuse,
many still hesitate to respond for a variety of reasons, including fear
of having to devote an excess of personal time to the adjudication process.
A failure to report, however, can and has led to criminal action against
the physician.

1318 Gregg, Grace S. "Physician, child-abuse reporting laws, and injured
       child." Clin Pediatr 7(12): 720-25, December, 1968. (13 Refer-
       ences).
Outlines the physician's role in the management of child abuse. In most
states the physician is required by law to report suspected abuse to the
proper authority. To diagnose suspected abuse, the physician should obtain a pertinent history of the injury or presenting problem, give the
child a complete physical examination, assess the dynamics of the family
by observing the parent-child relationship, and be alert for any signs of
economic, marital, or psychological stress which could adversely affect
the parents' ability to care for their child. After a report of suspected
abuse has been made, the physician must decide whether to hospitalize the
child or allow him to return home.

1319 Haller, J. Alex, Jr. "Trauma workshop report: trauma in children."
       J Trauma 10(11): 1052-54, November, 1970. (0 References).
Examines the particular problem of treating trauma in children. Since
children differ from adults in their responses to trauma, physically and
emotionally, treatment facilities and personnel need to plan for these
differences. Common causes of trauma, including parental abuse, are
cited.

1320 Halpern, S. R. "The battered child: letter to editor." Pediatrics
       40(1): 143-44, July, 1967. (0 References).
Sets forth the pediatrician's responsibility to prevent child abuse as an
obligation to his professional ethics.

1321 Hansen, Christian M., Jr. "Physician responsibility in child abuse:
       editorial." J Med Soc NJ 72(7): 559, July, 1975. (0 References).
Comments on the fact that all fifty states have passed child abuse reporting laws but that no increase in the number of cases referred to child
protective services by private physicians has been observed. The author
urges more responsible reporting by physicians and encourages the development of comprehensive treatment programs. Public awareness of the problem should be improved, and physicians should utilize the extensive literature on child abuse in their daily practice.

1322 ————. "A program to introduce medical students to the problem
       of child abuse and neglect." J Med Educ 52(6): 522-24, June,
       1977. (0 References).

Describes and evaluates a summer project developed at the College of
Medicine and Dentistry of New Jersey-Rutgers Medical School, in cooperation with the Protective Services Resource Institute. Designed to overcome physicians' traditional inability or reluctance to recognize abuse
problems, the project assigns students with at least one year of medical
school training to professional social workers from the New Jersey Division of Youth and Family Services for eight weeks. By working with families with abuse problems (real or potential), the students have a chance
to see the social aspects of abuse problems they might have to treat
medically in the future. Students and supervisors alike agreed that the
project offered valuable experience.

1323 Helfer, Ray E. Diagnostic process and treatment programs. Wash-
      ington, D.C.: U.S. Children's Bureau, 1975. 48p. (DHEW Publica-
      tion (OHD) 75-69).
Designed to assist physicians and nurses in the diagnosis and treatment
of child abuse, this booklet contains a wide range of information. Four
phases of treatment are described: (1) the emergency room or office
phase; (2) the diagnostic assessment phase; (3) the acute treatment phase;
and (4) the long-term treatment phase.

1324 —————. "7 guidelines in child abuse cases." Resid Staff
      Physician 19(8): 57-58, August, 1973. (2 References).
Suggests that physicians use a systematic approach in diagnosing child
abuse: (1) child abuse should be suspected in all cases of inexplicable
injury; (2) the child suspected of being abused should always be sent to
a hospital for diagnosis; (3) the parents should be approached firmly but
tactfully, without reference to the suspicion of abuse; (4) they should
be interviewed several times; (5) the child should be thoroughly examined
and laboratory studies should be made; (6) all individuals with information should provide input to the diagnosis; and (7) hospitals handling
twenty-five or more cases of child abuse per year should develop a child
abuse consultation team.

1325 —————. "Why most physicians don't get involved in child abuse
      cases and what to do about it." Child Today 4(3): 28-32, May-
      June, 1975. (1 Reference).
Eight reasons why physicians are reluctant to get involved in child abuse
cases are outlined. They include: (1) insufficient medical training in
the area of child abuse; (2) lack of interpersonal skills; (3) difficulties in working with members of other disciplines as peers; (4) extensive
drainage of time, finances, and emotions in child abuse cases; (5) fear
of testifying in court; (6) minimal personal rewards; (7) inadequate community services; and (8) an inability of physicians to see themselves as
agents for change. To increase their involvement, all medical students
should be given general training in child abuse and neglect. Pediatric
specialists in these areas should be trained, subsidized, and affiliated
with a community or hospital-based multidisciplinary child protection
team. These changes in medical school curriculums and residency training
programs will take some time, but physicians in the areas of abuse and
neglect are needed now. To involve established physicians in child abuse
programs, one or two physicians in the community should be singled out,
asked to be consultants in a couple of abuse cases, invited to a conference about the family, and subtly encouraged to increase their participation in the program. At some point, community financial support for this
physician's activities would be required.

1326 Hick, John F., and Steinschneider, Alfred. "Sudden infant death
      syndrome and child abuse: letters to editor." Pediatrics 52(1):
      147-48, July, 1973. (1 Reference).
Critique and defense of a case report involving two siblings who were
found to be victims of the sudden infant death syndrome. The critique
maintains that the possibility of child abuse was overlooked. The
defense, on the other hand, emphasizes that physicians must proceed with
extreme caution when diagnosing abuse.

1327 Ingraham, Franc D., and Heyl, Henry L. "Subdural hematoma in in-
      fancy and childhood." JAMA 112(3): 198-204, January 21, 1939.
      (7 References).
Offers suggestions for managing infant patients admitted to a medical
facility with subdural hematoma. Treatment procedures for the removal of
clots and membranes are outlined as follows: (1) lumbar puncture and
withdrawal of not more than 10 cc. of fluid; (2) bilateral subdural taps
through the coronal suture; (3) bilateral burr holes; and (4) elevation
of a bone flap. Included are eleven case histories demonstrating the
success of these treatment methods.

1328 Jeffress, J. Elizabeth. "Psychological aspects of pediatric prac-
      tice." J Am Med Wom Assoc 22(9): 630-33, September, 1967. (0
      References).
Cites the vast array of psychological problems with which pediatricians
must deal in treating the illnesses of children. The psychological
aspects of certain childhood illnesses, malformations, and injuries are
emphasized.

1329 Justice, Blair, and Duncan, David F. "Physical abuse of children
      as a public health problem." Public Health Rev 4: 183-200, 1975.

1330 Kalisch, Beatrice J. "What are hospitals doing about child abuse?
      Report of a nationwide survey." Hosp Top 52(6): 21-24, June,
      1974. (6 References).
Reports the results of a 1973 survey of hospital child abuse treatment
programs. Of the 120 hospitals sent questionnaires, eighty-eight responded
and of those, forty-one reported having a child abuse team or program
designed to deal with the problem. Seven types of programs emerged from
the data, ranging from a single person in a hospital acting in a coordinating capacity, to interagency, community-wide programs. The nurses'
role was delineated as were future plans regarding child abuse programs.
The need for federal funding is underlined.

1331 Kempe, C. Henry. "Paediatric implications of the battered baby
      syndrome." Arch Dis Child 46(245): 28-37, February, 1971. (2
      References).
An overview of the battered baby syndrome includes discussions of: (1)
the range of physical findings associated with the problem; (2) the incidence of the problem; (3) the characteristics of battering parents and
some of the common dynamics of the disturbed parent-child relationship;
and (4) the difficulties in diagnosing those cases in which there has
been no blatant physical assault, such as in cases of failure to thrive
babies. Suggestions are offered for the early and late management of
abused children and for the treatment of battering parents. It is emphasized that effective parenting is not guaranteed by a universal mothering
instinct and that society must take responsibility for providing adequate

foster care. Pediatricians must concentrate their attention on early childhood, particularly on the physical and emotional development of the young child. The pediatrician can play a vital role in the prediction, detection, and correction of disturbances in mothering.

1332 Kushnick, Theodore; Pietrucha, Dorothy M.; Kushnick, Judith B.
      "Syndrome of the abandoned small child." Clin Pediatr 9(6):
      356-61, June, 1970. (15 References).
Examines the manner in which the Newark City Hospital handled some thirty-nine abandoned children. A number of these children had been left in the care of others by parents who did not return; the rate of abandonment seemed to increase more noticeably in December. Most of these children were undersized and about half exhibited physical abnormalities. Poverty, crime, and mental illness were pervasive elements in their family backgrounds; most of the children came from Newark's ghetto. One point is emphasized in particular: in many of these cases, the histories and physical examinations were clearly inadequate, and much needed information was missing. It was concluded that the abandoned child represents a low medical care priority, particularly in seasons during which the wards are filled with "really" sick children. Hospitals are advised to look into this problem and to evaluate their handling of other patients from the ghetto population.

1333 Laupus, William E. "Child abuse and the physician." Va Med Mon
      93(1): 1-2, January, 1966. (0 References).
Enumerates the physician's responsibilities in child abuse, highlighting early recognition of maltreatment, treatment, and protection of the child.

1334 Layton, J. J. "The watchdog of medicine." Community Health 4(2):
      58-63, September-October, 1972. (2 References).
The role of the forensic pathologist in detecting child abuse is discussed. The correct diagnosis of child abuse depends not so much upon the pathologist's ability to notice the symptoms, as upon his ability to interpret them accurately, especially in the face of contradictory testimony by the parent.

1335 MacKeith, Ronald. "Notes on education: the doctors." In:
      Franklin, Alfred White, ed. Concerning child abuse. New York:
      Churchill Livingstone, 1975. 149-50. (0 References).
Outlines procedure for physicians in detection and prevention of child abuse. A list of danger signals for detection stresses scrutiny of the parent's account of the injury, characteristic injuries, and suspicious situations. Diagnosis and treatment must include photographs, x-rays, blood counts, and height, weight, and head measurements. Approaches to prevention are primary, secondary, and tertiary which involve, respectively, education in the schools about family life, early evaluation and detection of injuries or problem situations, and interdisciplinary management.

1336 "Medical management of child abuse." J Med Soc NJ 69(6): 551-53,
      June, 1972. (0 References).
Reviews the salient information regarding the battered child syndrome for the benefit of the medical community. Typical victims and perpetrators are described, but the phenomenon is not associated with a particular socioeconomic class. Characteristic injuries are enumerated, and the psychological dynamics of child abuse are traced from the parents' own

histories through their present anxieties and impulses. The importance
of a non-punitive rehabilitative approach to the parents is emphasized.
Requirements and procedures for reporting are set forth.

1337 New York (City). Department of Health. Health Services Administra-
      tion. What physicians must do about child abuse and neglect. New
      York: Department of Health, Health Services Administration, n.d.
      6p.
A guideline for physicians to use in determining whether a child has been
abused or neglected. A list of indicators of child abuse with respect to
the medical history of the injury, the physical examination, and the
radiologic examination are provided. Procedures for reporting a case of
suspected abuse and for retaining custody of the child in the hospital
are explained.

1338 Newberger, Eli H. "Medical management of child abuse." In:
      National Symposium on Child Abuse, 4th, Charleston, S.C., 1973.
      Collected papers. Denver, Colorado: The American Humane Associa-
      tion, Children's Division, 1975. 76-85.
Argues for family-oriented diagnosis and treatment of child abuse. Child
abuse is the result of personal and family turmoil. Therefore, a physician's interrogation should focus more on why the child was injured rather
than how. Several case histories show what often looks like abuse is
actually the product of a reparable situation. A presentation of data on
child abuse accompanies suggestions on how to lower the cost of treating
child abuse and how to coordinate various disciplines.

1339 "No not non-accidental injury!" Lancet 2(7989): 775-76, October
      9, 1976. (10 References).
Briefly reviews the physician's role in the management of child abuse.
The signs and symptoms of the abused and abuser, antecedents to the
incident, interdisciplinary treatment, and systematic family therapy for
the prevention of abuse are discussed. A highly successful preventive
treatment may lead to increased demands on the service, and people may
use the threat of abuse to obtain more counseling. Several parallels
between self-poisoning behavior and child abuse are enumerated.

1340 Patterson, Peter H., and Char, Donald. "Child abuse in Hawaii."
      Hawaii Med J 25(5): 395-97, May-June, 1966. (4 References).
Reports the results of a questionnaire on child abuse developed under the
auspices of the Hawaii State Commission on Children and Youth. The
questionnaire, completed by 393 physicians, basically sought to discover
who treated abused children, how many had been seen, and how they were
handled. Results showed that the majority of cases were identified by
general practitioners and pediatricians, with police receiving one-half
of the reports made. Only 50 percent of abused children were reported.
Due to a lack of severity or proof, unreported cases were handled most
often by counseling the parents. Mandatory reporting with protection
from liability for physicians was the most frequent suggestion for dealing with abuse. Limitations of the study include a lack of a precise
definition for abuse and possible duplication of reports. The responses
indicated considerable concern on the part of Hawaii physicians.

1341 Rosenblum, Herman. "Child abuse: a constant problem: editorial."
      Del Med J 49(4): 238-39, April, 1977. (4 References).

The medical profession's responsibility to recognize and report suspected cases of child abuse is briefly reiterated. Common indicators of abuse are listed.

1342 Sanders, R. Wyman. "Resistance to dealing with parents of battered children." Pediatrics 50(6): 853-57, December, 1972. (15 References).
Discusses the psychological and cultural origins of the individual's resistance to dealing with battered children and their parents. Several examples which illustrate communication difficulties between parents of battered children and the authorities are provided. Some suggestions about how battering parents could be dealt with more effectively are offered.

1343 Shaw, Anthony. "The surgeon and the battered child: editorial." Surg Gynecol Obstet 119(2): 355, August, 1964. (0 References).
Indicates the need for physicians to be alert to the symptoms of the battered child syndrome. It suggests careful assessment, including roentgenologic survey, and presents a suggested course of action for the physician.

1344 Shydro, Joanne; Noyes, Mona K.; Wheeler, John S. "Child abuse." Nursing '72 2(12): 37-41, December, 1972. (0 References).
The child abuse management programs in two hospitals in Pennsylvania are described. Both programs emphasize the importance of dealing with the parents in an understanding way and the necessity of protecting the abused child from any further injury.

1345 Snedeker, Lendon. "Traumatization of children: letter to editor." N Engl J Med 267(11): 572, September 13, 1962. (0 References).
Increased reporting of traumatization of children throughout the country is noted. While the staff at the Children's Hospital Medical Center was, at one time, hesitant to report suspected abuse cases, out of fear of action against the accuser, a set of procedures has since been instituted for reporting. Social service and psychiatric help is available to problem families. The danger of hasty referral to the court is noted, however, as many families profit from the assistance by a social agency and do not require legal constraints.

1346 Sumpter, E. E. "Battered baby syndrome: letter to editor." Br Med J 1(5490): 800-801, March 26, 1966. (0 References).
The hospital must assume the primary responsibility for the welfare of battered children and for the investigation of incidents of suspected child beating. The battered baby syndrome is more serious than the other forms of child neglect, and special handling is required to safeguard the child's physical and mental health.

1347 Till, Kenneth. "Subdural haematoma and effusion in infancy: letter to editor." Br Med J 3(5621): 804, September 28, 1968. (0 References).
Defends a previous paper by the author on the subject of the neurosurgical treatment of battered children. Surgery is only one component of a treatment approach, but there is not sufficient data to provide clear guidelines for the long-term and problematic management of abusing families. Only a small percentage of the author's patients suffered repeated injury. The need to protect the child should be balanced carefully

against the problems involved in removing him unnecessarily from the
parents.

1348   Wolman, Irving J., and Freedman, Alan R.   "The abused or sexually-
       molested child: clinical management." Clin Pediatr 8(5): 16B-
       16C, May, 1969. (0 References).
Summarizes G. S. Gregg's "Physician, child-abuse reporting laws, and injured child; psychosocial anatomy of childhood trauma," Clin Pediatr 7:
720, 1968, and enumerates the specific duties of the physician in protecting the battered child. The physician must learn the history of the
child and evaluate the validity of the parent's report. A detailed list
of abnormal physical manifestations of the skin tissues, bones, eyes,
and abdomen aids the physician in the detection of child abuse.

1349   Woolley, Paul V., Jr. "The pediatrician and the young child sub-
       jected to repeated physical abuse: letter to editor." J Pediatr
       62(4): 628-30, April, 1963. (7 References).
Cites progress made in the prevention of child abuse, particularly the
contributions made by social workers and persons in the legal profession.
Legal action protecting the child, without necessarily convicting the
parent, is favored. Physicians are urged to be aware of the symptoms of
child abuse. Community organization plus further study of the problem
are suggested.

1350   Young, Marjorie. "A comparison of physician responses to child
       abuse, Tulsa County, Oklahoma; 1969 and 1974." J Okla State Med
       Assoc 69(4): 125-27, April, 1976. (0 References).
The responses of ninety-three physicians to a child abuse survey in 1969
were compared to those of seventy-one physicians in 1974. No significant
differences in physician attitudes and reported behaviors were found between the two time periods. In both surveys, the mass media was the
major source of information about child abuse during the year. About 50
percent of the physicians believed that a child should be removed from
his home as a last resort. Approximately 75 percent preferred supervision
and treatment of abusive parents to punishment. Eighty percent reported
that they would actively intervene to protect a child if they thought
abuse was occurring. In the 1969 survey, physicians were questioned about
the need for a central repository for the reporting of child abuse cases.
As a consequence of their affirmative response, a child abuse registry
was established.

1351   Ziering, William. "The battered baby syndrome: letter to editor."
       J Pediatr 65(2): 321-22, August, 1964. (7 References).
Complains of the lack of activity in the prevention of child abuse and
cites the need for interagency cooperation to combat the problem. Physicians, as the first contact with most abuse cases, are urged to extend
their sphere of responsibility beyond the strictly medical one and to
report all suspected cases.

1352   Zuckerman, Kenneth; Ambuel, J. Philip; Bandman, Rosalyn. "Child
       neglect and abuse: a study of cases evaluated at Columbus
       Children's Hospital in 1968-1969." Ohio State Med J 68(7): 629-
       32, July, 1972. (1 Reference).
Reports data collected from a study of sixty children at Columbus Children's Hospital in 1968 through 1969. The results of the study emphasize
the poor quality of the follow-up and treatment program. In most of the

cases, the parents were allowed to determine follow-up treatment. Among those abusers who were prosecuted, few were convicted, and the emphasis was on punishment of the parent rather than protection of the child. Other findings indicated that many children had been abused before and that a majority were five years of age. Poverty was a factor among many of the families, but this trait generally reflected the population served by the hospital. Diminished interagency communication and the reluctance of physicians to report cases are two major problems in the prevention of abuse. Moreover, the lack of criminal convictions frustrate what efforts are made. Suggestions are given about the management of the psychologically abused child.

7. NURSING CARE

1353   Barnard, Martha U., and Wolf, Lorraine. "Psychosocial failure to thrive: nursing assessment and intervention." Nurs Clin North Am 8(3): 557-65, September, 1973. (10 References).
Emphasizes the role of the nurse in the early assessment of the failure to thrive syndrome in infants or children. Procedures a nurse should follow for prevention, detection, and intervention are established. In addition to collecting information about the child's health history, the nurse should be alert to hints of social or emotional dysfunction in the patient and in the family. Areas of investigation should include: family social history, eating patterns, elimination patterns, sleep patterns, growth, and motor, language, and social development. An outline of specific symptoms and modes of intervention is included. Part of the nurse's role is to work with the family to reach an understanding of the problem and to discuss treatment.

1354   Bassett, Louise B. "How to help abused children -- and their parents." RN 37(10): 44-60, October, 1974. (0 References).
Discusses the nurse's role in the detection and treatment of child abuse and focuses upon the behavior patterns characteristic of abusive parents and abused children. Several prenatal symptoms of the predisposition to abuse among women, and various methods for eliciting information and sources for twenty-four-hour support services are presented. The information is directed at enabling nurses to recognize, treat, and prevent incidents of child abuse and to understand the needs of the children and the parents involved.

1355   "The battered child: what the nurse can do." RN 31(12): 43-45, 66-68, December, 1968. (10 References).
Highlights the important role of the nurse in detecting and reporting child abuse. Recognizing injuries caused by abuse, identifying behavior typical of abusing parents, and carefully observing the children themselves are skills the nurse can develop and apply. However, the role of the nurse extends beyond these capabilities. Nurses must first give medical attention to the child and, secondly, try to offer support and guidance to abusing parents. In helping the entire family, nurses can contribute to the prevention of future incidences of child abuse.

1356   Bird, Harmony. "Battered babies: a social and medical problem" Nurs Times 69(47): 1552-54, November 22, 1973. (0 References).
Presents a personal account of student nurse's encounter with a three-and-one-half-year-old battered child and his family. A detailed description

of the baby's physical condition and of the medical treatment administered
to him during his hospitalization is given. In this case the father,
responsible for the child's injury, had a history of an unhappy childhood
himself, and did not have an open relationship with his wife. She, however, developed a close relationship with their social worker, to whom she
reported the history of her husband's violent tendencies. Non-judgmental
attitudes toward parents and cooperation among health workers are essential
ingredients of effective treatment programs.

1357   Carter, Bryan D.; Reed, Ruth; Reh, Ceil G. "Mental health nursing
       intervention with child abusing and neglecting mothers." J Psychiatr
       Nurs 13(5): 11-15, September-October, 1975. (8 References).
Reports a study of mental health nursing intervention with abusing and
neglectful mothers. Mothers were divided among three treatment groups:
a long-term intervention group averaging 5.44 months, a short-term intervention group averaging 1.55 months, and a control group. A visit observation sheet was constructed in order to evaluate areas of concern such
as management and child care skills at the beginning and the end of treatment. Results indicated that communication between mother and child
improved with treatment over six months, whereas the short-term treatment
group did not significantly increase those skills. Although other skills
did improve in both long- and short-term groups, the long-term rather
than the short-term intervention proved more effective for most variables.
Ninety percent of the control group's children were rehospitalized during
the study, indicating the general value of intervention programs.

1358   Davies, Jean M. "A health visitor's viewpoint." In: Franklin
       Alfred White, ed. Concerning child abuse. New York: Churchill
       Livingstone, 1975. 78-81. (0 References).
Because the health visitor visits the home of all children under five
years of age, she is in a unique position to detect early signs of inflicted injury and to recognize the conditions that could lead to it. In
each area there are local multidisciplinary committees for the management
of child abuse consisting of a social worker, health visitor, NSPCC
officer, women police officer from the local force, child guidance worker,
and hospital representative. Whenever child abuse is suspected, the
health visitor should contact the area committee, and the child should be
placed in a hospital or nursery while an investigation is being made.
Several recommendations for the future management and prevention of child
abuse are made. The number of health visitors should be increased to a
ratio of one per 3,000 population. Detailed antenatal and postnatal care
needs to be provided. Better preparation for parenthood, more nursery
or playgroup places, and family planning facilities are needed.

1359   Elmore, Joyce; Alexander, Betty; Lyman, Laura; et al. "The nurse's
       role in the care of the battered child: panel discussion." Clin
       Proc Child Hosp 24(11): 364-74, December, 1968. (1 Reference).
Delineates the responsibilities of the nurse who ministers directly to
abused children and their families. The roles of nurses working in hospital emergency rooms, in prenatal clinics, and in the community as public
health nurses are discussed in detail. Numerous case histories illustrate
guidelines for identifying battered children, for gaining their confidence, and also for recognizing a parent who is a potential abuser. One
study conducted by a public health nurse reviewed maternal punishment
practices and attitudes toward disciplining infants. The study consisted
of a series of simple questions in the form of an interview and was given

to 100 mothers in three clinics. Results indicated that this type of questioning could be useful in clinics for identifying mothers in need of guidance.

1360 "A family affair: editorial." Nurs Mirror Midwives J 133(21):
      26-29, November 19, 1971. (0 References).
A mother and daughter studying nursing describe their experience in re-storing a three-year-old boy who had been removed from the care of a negligent grandmother to health and emotional stability.

1361 Friedman, Allison L.; Juntti, M. Jeanette; Scoblic, Mary A. "Nurs-
      ing responsibility in child abuse." Nurs Forum 15(1): 95-112,
      1976. (25 References).
The nurse's responsibility in each phase of the management of child abuse is examined in detail. First of all, the nurse is in a strategic posi-tion to identify suspected abuse. She is required by Michigan law to report suspected cases to the local protective service worker in the Department of Social Services. She cooperates with other professionals in order to arrive at a definitive diagnosis of abuse, and is involved either directly or indirectly in the treatment process. Direct treatment consists of establishing an on-going supportive, therapeutic relationship with the family, while indirect service involves serving as a member of a multidisciplinary child abuse team. The public health nurse has the responsibility of participating in efforts to prevent child abuse.

1362 Fulk, Delores L. "The battered child." Nurs Forum 3(2): 10-26,
      1964. (17 References).
Addresses the nursing population about the general characteristics of the battered child. Features discussed include: (1) the psychological make-up of the parents and ways they can be approached; (2) symptoms which should arouse suspicion; (3) various legal procedures and current legisla-tion; (4) hospital responsibilities; (5) the necessity for public educa-tion; and (6) the role of the nurse.

1363 Golub, Sharon. "The battered child: what the nurse can do." RN
      31(12): 42-45, 66-68, December, 1968. (10 References).
Discusses the role of the nurse in the detection, management, and preven-tion of child abuse. A wide range of physical manifestations of abuse are outlined. Guidelines for distinguishing physical abuse from acci-dental injuries are also provided. It is emphasized that the nurse has a legal and moral obligation to report suspected abuse to the proper authorities. The nurse should gradually establish a relationship with the abused child who is hospitalized. This relationship enables the child to grow emotionally. The nurse's attitude toward the abusive parent should not be punitive. Obstetrical and visiting nurses can frequently play a role in preventing abuse if they can recognize the signs of a potentially abusive situation and constructively intervene.

1364 Gower, M. D. "Non-accidental injury and the health visitor." Nurs
      Times 72(40): 1563-64, October 7, 1976. (0 References).
Health visitors examine the baby from the tenth day and retain records until the child is five years old. They are, therefore, in an excellent position for detecting non-accidental injury and neglect in children. If the health visitor suspects that a family has a problem, she notifies a senior physician, social worker, or nurse who calls a case conference. If there is reason to suspect abuse, the team must report the case to the

proper authorities and devise a treatment plan for the family. Clear
records of each case should be maintained and made available to all agencies and professionals involved with the family. Emphasis should be
placed on routine health visiting in order to spot early warning signs of
family stress and child maltreatment. Serious incidences of abuse can be
prevented in this way.

1365 Hiller, R. B. "The battered child -- a health visitor's point of
      view." Nurs Times 65(40): 1265-66, October 2, 1969. (0
      References).
A health visitor discusses her point of view on child abuse, emphasizing
the need for team work among professionals. A consideration of the health
visitor's role includes three examples of family situations with high
potential for abuse.

1366 Hopkins, Joan. "The nurse and the abused child." Nurs Clin North
      Am 5(4): 589-98, December, 1970. (1 Reference).
Explores the role of the nurse in dealing with families of abused children. Recognizing the symptoms which indicate abuse is an important
observation skill for the nurse to acquire. Abusing parents tend to
expect their children to behave as adults and are often fulfilling the
expectations their own parents set. These parents commonly lead isolated
lives and need caring, reassurance, and guidance rather than censure and
criticism. Although professionals are often reluctant to become involved,
the nurse is in a non-threatening position to help. Teaching child care
and mothering skills is another important function the nurse can serve.

1367 Johnson, Mildred. "Symposium: the nursing responsibilities in the
      care of the battered child." Clin Proc Child Hosp 24(11): 352-
      53, December, 1968. (0 References).
As part of an introduction to a symposium on child abuse, the various
aspects of the role of nursing in the treatment of child abuse are outlined.

1368 Josten, Lavohn. "The treatment of an abused family." Matern Child
      Nurs J 4(1): 23-24, Spring, 1975. (14 References).
Outlines a public health nurse's approach to treatment of a family suffering from various symptoms of dysfunction, including child abuse. The
characteristics ascribed to abusive parents are: a history of having been
abused by their own parents, feelings of inadequacy, unrealistic childrearing expectations, various personal crises, and difficulty in request-
ing help. The nurse, through modeling behavior, assuming a motherly
(although not overly authoritative) role, offering help only when requested by the family, encouraging empathy for the child, and promoting
a closer relationship between the child's mother and father, was able to
effect notable improvement in family relations. By emphasizing and reinforcing the parents' feelings of self-worth, the nurse gave the parents
confidence in their ability to successfully raise their son. The practice of tailoring family treatment to the individuals' and groups' unique
needs is stressed.

1369 Kalisch, Beatrice J. "Child abuse: What is it? What can be done
      about it?" Nurs Care 7(6): 23-25, June, 1974. (7 References).
Delineates a definition of abuse, examples of battering, and characteristics of abusing parents and abused children. The nurse's role in alleviation of abuse includes detection, reporting, charting, psychological

support to parent and child, and preventive measures. The newest approaches to treatment are described.

1370 ————. Nursing actions in behalf of the battered child." Nurs
      Forum 12(4): 365-77, 1973. (19 References).
Offers nurses a comprehensive guide for handling cases of child abuse.
Nurses can become involved in four basic areas to help combat the problem
of child battering: (1) detection; (2) nurse-parent therapy; (3) alternative community programs; and (4) public reeducation concerning child
development and child care practices. Subtle behavior patterns that can
signal an abusing parent or abused child are outlined as guidelines for
case-finding. Nurse-parent therapy is aimed at establishing a relationship of trust that will help the parents to acquire a healthier self-
image and to break out of their isolation. To accomplish this, nurses
must learn to accept parents without judging them. Nurses can greatly
encourage the development of local crisis centers, homemaker services,
parent aides programs, and also massive education programs to teach people
about child development and socially acceptable childrearing practices.

1371 Kempe, C. Henry, and Hopkins, Joan. "The public health nurse's role
      in the prevention of child abuse and neglect." Public Health Curr
      15(2): 1-4, May, 1975. (9 References).
The role of the public health nurse (PHN) in the prevention of child abuse
and neglect is discussed. First of all, the PHN can become aware of the
signs of potential child abuse, evaluate each family according to these
criteria, and determine whether a family is a high or low risk. If the
family is a high risk or suspected abuse has already occurred, the PHN
may report this to the child protective services. If the family is a low
risk, the PHN may intervene in a constructive way by supporting and educating the family. The qualities of a good therapist are outlined. The
PHN may suggest that the parents utilize other community programs such
as groups for abusive parents in conjunction with their contact with the
PHN.

1372 Learoyd, Sandra, and Williamson, Ann. "The battered child syndrome
      -- nursing care." Nurs Mirror 140(22): 54-55, June 12, 1975.
      (3 References).
Points out the particular problems of nursing abused, but not severely
injured, children in the hospital setting. Often these children are not
among the seriously ill but are in great need of care, handling, and
attention. They need an atmosphere for growth--secure, quiet, unhurried--
not the noisy, bustling ward to which they are often exposed. In treating
these children, the nurse must deal with her environmental and time limitations. She must also adjust to the fact of abuse and learn to communicate with and care for seemingly uncaring parents.

1373 Mundie, Gene E., and Fontana, Vincent J. "Child abuse -- our
      responsibility." J Pract Nurs 24(12): 14-17, December, 1974.
      (1 Reference).
Notes the large number of cases of child maltreatment in the United States
and indicates that available figures do not include the many unreported
instances of child abuse occurring each year. Although the initial reaction of a nurse toward abusing parents may be one of repulsion or anger,
an attempt at empathy is suggested, encouraging deeper understanding of
the perhaps frustrating history and unpleasant financial, social, or
psychological status of the individual. Child abuse requires treatment

rather than punishment. The importance of the social welfare organization
is discussed and a model is offered for the ideal treatment of an abuse
case, utilizing all available resources. A detailed table of characteristics of abusing parents and battered children is included.

1374 Savino, Anne B., and Sanders, R. Wyman. "Working with abusive
      parents: group therapy and home visits." Am J Nurs 73(3): 482-
      84, March, 1973. (8 References).
Describes an out-patient therapy group for abusing parents and a program
for home visits at the request of group members. The group leaders focus
on encouraging the parents to talk freely about the problems that led them
to abuse their children and teaching them to become better parents. Home
visits are made by public health nurses. The nurse's role is to observe
and establish a positive relationship with the parents, so that ideally
her mothering behavior will serve as a model for the parents to imitate.
She must, therefore, refrain from passing judgments or issuing excessive
instructions. Such treatment only makes the parents feel rejected. During the home visits, the nurse can also recommend specific techniques for
handling problems in the children.

1375 Shade, Dolores A. "Limits to service in child abuse." Am J Nurs
      69(8): 1710-12, August, 1969. (3 References).
Defines the public health nurse's role in the management of child abuse
as a preventive one. The nurse should be able to recognize high risk
families and provide information on parenting and child development to
troubled parents. But the nurse should also accept her limitations. The
nurse's major limitation is her lack of preparation as a therapist for
abusive parents. When actual abuse is suspected or family problems are
severe, other social agencies or professionals should be contacted. The
nurse is a health worker, not a policeman, and, therefore, she should not
be required to monitor conditions in the home for evidence of abuse or
neglect. A public health nurse may be subpoenaed, in which case she must
testify in court about her knowledge of the family.

1376 Slack, Patricia. "Planning training for coping with non-accidental
      injury." Nurs Times 72(40): 1561-63, October 7, 1976. (9
      References).
Training programs for nurses on child abuse should cover the areas of prevention, identification, positive action, and follow-up. Seminars should
be held on the deployment of staff resources, communication among members
of interdisciplinary teams, and procedures for reporting and handling
legal problems. Appropriate training may be single or multidisciplinary.

1377 Stainton, M. Colleen. "Non-accidental trauma in children." Can
      Nurse 71(10): 26-29, October, 1975. (7 References).
Defines various degrees of non-accidental trauma inflicted upon children
ranging from child battering to child neglect and, most importantly,
points out how the nurse can effectively participate in detecting, preventing, and treating abuse. A case history illustrating role-model
techniques for the demonstration of proper mothering practices to abusive
mothers is provided.

1378 Tagg, Peggy I. "Nursing intervention for the abused child and his
      family." Pediatr Nurs 2(5): 36-39, September-October, 1976. (9
      References).

The role of the nurse in the identification and treatment of child abuse is emphasized. Characteristics of high risk children and parents are outlined. The hospital staff nurse is the professional having the most contact with a family when a child is brought to the hospital and, therefore, has the best opportunity to recognize these characteristics and offer help. The nurse should cooperate with the hospital child abuse management team by informing its members of her observations, suspicions, and opinions of the family. If child abuse is suspected, the nurse has a responsibility to report the case to the appropriate authorities. When a battered child is hospitalized, the pediatric nurse should encourage the development of a warm relationship between herself and the child. The public health nurse is in a position to provide the best on-going treatment, education, and intervention in the family where child abuse has occurred or is a potential. During visits to the family, the nurse should focus on the parent, give factual information about child development, allow the parent to ventilate angry and frustrated feelings, and include other psychiatric and social work professionals in the treatment if necessary.

8. SOCIAL SERVICES

1379 Ackley, Dana C. "A brief overview of child abuse." Soc Casework
      58(1): 21-24, January, 1977. (3 References).
Offers information about child abuse that can be applied in training non-professionals to work with abusers. Characteristics typical of abusing parents and of abused children are provided in order to sketch the emotional factors involved in the battering syndrome. In many cases, parents can be helped. They need understanding and support, not condemnation.

1380 Bandoli, Larry R. "Leaderless support groups in child protective
      services." Soc Work 22(1): 150, March, 1977. (7 References).
Advocates support groups for social workers in child protection. Because the strain of abuse and neglect cases often leads to turnover in personnel or low staff morale, support groups are needed. A brief history of such groups explains how and why they came into existence. A description of the group in Kern County Welfare Department, California is included.

1381 Beer, Sally. "A medical social worker's view." In: Franklin,
      Alfred White, ed. Concerning child abuse. New York: Churchill
      Livingstone, 1975. 73-77. (0 References).
At University College Hospital, London, any child suspected of having non-accidental injuries is admitted to the pediatric ward. A case conference is convened by the medical social worker and all other professionals involved with the family are invited to attend. At the conference, decisions are made as to whether the child should be temporarily removed from the home for his own safety, and who the primary social worker with the family will be. If a decision is made to remove the child from the home, the police or local social services must be contacted so that a care order can be secured. The most important goal of the primary social worker is to establish a relationship of trust with the parents. Work with these families is often emotionally draining, but can be rewarding as well.

1382 Bezzeg, E. D.; Fratianne, R. B.; Karnasiewicz, S. Q.; et al. "The
      role of the child care worker in the treatment of severely burned
      children." Pediatrics 50: 617-24, October, 1972. (6 References).

Examines a new program of treatment for burned children. The burn victims
were moved from adult wards into the general pediatric ward and caseworkers were provided to reassure and comfort the child and to help him
keep his hospital experience in perspective so that he can reenter the
outside world more easily. The caseworker can also, in cases of non-
accidental burns, arrange for therapy to resolve the family and personal
conflicts which led to the injury.

1383   Billingsley, Andrew. "The role of the social worker in a child
       protective agency: a comparative analysis." For a summary see:
       Diss Abstr 25(9): 5438, March, 1965.

1384   Bourke, William A. "Developing an appropriate focus in casework
       with families in which children are neglected." For a summary see:
       Diss Abstr Int 31A(4): 1891, October, 1970.

1385   Bradford, Kirk A. "Critical factors that affect the judgments of
       protective services workers in child abuse situations." For a
       summary see: Diss Abstr Int 37A(3): 1798, September, 1976.

1386   Butler, Raymond V. "Lend the client an ear." Public Welfare 23(2):
       105-10, April, 1965. (2 References).
Discusses the work of the Bureau of Indian Affairs in family casework on
an Indian reservation. A sample neglect case involving a fifteen-year-
old girl, an alcoholic father, and a neglectful mother illustrates the
author's philosophy in working with neglectful families. These three
basic precepts are: (1) the caseworker must be a sympathetic listener;
(2) he must follow up treatment with the family in order to alleviate any
new hostilities; and (3) he must respect his client's social value system.

1387   "Child abuse project trains care-group." Natl Assoc Soc Workers
       News 22(2): 10, February, 1977. (0 References).
Describes a workshop given by the National Association of Social Workers
to explain a training project for social workers who deal with cases of
child abuse. The project is being funded by the National Center on Child
Abuse and Neglect and the Office of Child Development (HEW).

1388   Davies, Joann. "When the agency must intervene." Public Welfare
       23(2): 102-5, April, 1965. (5 References).
The obligation of the social worker to intervene in cases of neglect is
discussed. The fact that the worker must be concerned with the welfare
of both parent and child is acknowledged, as is the worker's need for
sensitivity, tact, and patience in handling negligent parents. The progress of a neglect complaint is traced (after the "complaint" takes the
form of hints from the negligent parent). Verification of neglect is
briefly discussed.

1389   Davies, Joann F., and Jorgensen, James D. "Battered, but not de-
       feated: the story of an abused child and positive casework."
       Child Welfare 49(2): 101-4, February, 1970. (3 References).
Uses a case study to illustrate an approach to casework which emphasizes
the potential for treatment of the abused child rather than the pathology
that results. Presenting Martin, a maltreated child, with adult role
models whom he could trust facilitated his healthy adjustment to adoption.
Statewide communication between child welfare agencies, immediate consultation, and well-organized staff are essential for adequate, prompt
evaluation and treatment.

1390   Davoren, Elizabeth. "Working with abusive parents: a social
       worker's view." Child Today 4(3): 2, 38-43, May-June, 1975.
       (1 Reference).
Parents are abusive because they have learned destructive parenting patterns from their own parents as children. The role of the social worker
in child abuse is to develop a therapeutic relationship with the parents
that fulfills their needs to feel good about themselves, to be dependent,
to find pleasure in life, and to understand their children and care for
them without feeling inadequate. The successful social worker must be
extremely sensitive to other people, be able to accept rejection without
being devastated by it, and be capable of making life-and-death decisions
about the safety of the children, based on their evaluation of the parent's ability to care for them. Supportive services such as homemakers,
public health nurses, emergency shelter care, parent groups, and emergency
loans can take part of the burden off the social worker's shoulders and
provide for some of the immediate, practical needs of the abusive parents.

1391   De Francis, Vincent. Let's get technical: the "why and what" of
       child protective services. Denver, Colorado: The American Humane
       Association, Children's Division, 1957. 10p. (Bibliography).
A children's bill of rights with the corresponding parental responsibilities is discussed. The role of child protective services is simply to
step into a home, assess the problem, and offer assistance whenever a
parent fails his children. The agency's casework service is non-punitive
and directed toward improving family relationships. Both the parent and
child are treated as clients, but on different levels. A broad definition
of neglect encompassing both the statutory and layman's use of the term
is given.

1392   —————. Special skills in child protective services. Denver,
       Colorado: The American Humane Association, Children's Division,
       1958. 16p.
Special skills necessary for practitioners in child protection include:
(1) an acceptance and support of the authority and responsibility of his
agency; (2) an ability to handle resistance and hostility; (3) an ability
to interpret to the parents the community's concern for both parent and
child; (4) skill in diagnosing and evaluating danger to children; (5)
sensitivity; and (6) a knowledge of the legal process. Aside from special
skills, a worker should also have understanding about the specifics of
actual practice. The article discusses problems inherent in the evaluation of the complaint, in the first interview with the parents, in the
home visit, and in the discussion of the complaint with the parents. A
case history illustrates these difficulties.

1393   Francis, Jo, and Sutton, Andrew. "The battered child and his
       parents: can we help?" Soc Work Today 8(13): 16-18, January 4,
       1977. (16 References).
States that the present concern about non-accidental injury to children
concentrates on identification and possible prediction of the battered
child syndrome rather than on the possibility of actual observation and
treatment within the family. Correlations between the incidence of abuse
and the social conditions of the abusive parents are inconclusive because
other parents in the same situations are non-abusive. More helpful would
be an understanding of the interactions within the abusing family and
intervention measures which deal with those problems in family relationships. Caseworkers with the parents could concentrate on such areas as:

(1) reducing parents' anxiety about child raising; (2) building up the
parents self-confidence and abilities; (3) offering marital help so parents can support each other better; (4) teaching practical childrearing
techniques; (5) giving models of coping behavior; and (6) encouraging
parents to see the rewards of their relationships with their children.
The community also should have a full range of cooperating support services to help abusive families, and parents must know that such help is
available.

1394 Gilman, Merritt C., and Little, Ruby. "Treatment of the rejected
      child." Natl Probat Parole Assoc J 6(1): 24-32, January, 1960.
      (4 References).
Emphasizes the role of the probation officer in the treatment of the
abusing parent or rejected child. The officer must recognize the defensive position of the parent and avoid diagnosis and action on that basis
only, keeping in mind that rejection of the child often repeats what the
parent underwent himself as a child. Casework treatment should emphasize
the experience of the individual in the present situation and avoid
dangers of transference and counter-transference.

1395 Gjenvick, Benjamin A. "Some considerations on the use of profes-
      sional social case work by the physician in problems involving the
      welfare of children." SD J Med Pharm 4(1): 138-41, 143, June,
      1951. (1 Reference).
Presents the role of the social worker in child welfare case work. The
social worker has a key role in the adoption of children, where she explores the situation through office interviews and home visits. The
requisite educational preparation for a social worker is discussed in
detail.

1396 Goldberg, Gale. "Breaking the communication barrier: the initial
      interview with an abusing parent." Child Welfare 54(4): 274-82,
      April, 1975. (17 References).
During the initial interview with a social worker, the abusive parent may
be fearful of the legal or psychiatric consequences of child abuse, guilt-
ridden about having injured his child, ashamed about having lost control
of himself, and suspicious of any "normal" person who claims he wants to
help. The social worker must acquire a set of intervention behaviors
that he can use to engage the abusive parent in open communication with
him. First of all, the social worker should position himself in ways
that are likely to increase the parent's comfort and to convey positive
feelings. When the parent does not express emotion, the social worker
should "reach for feelings" by verbalizing the parent's non-verbal behavior. For example, he might say to the parent, "You look like you are
about to cry." When a parent does express his feelings, it is important
for the social worker to "get with" those feelings, or to show the parent
that he understands. When asking for information, open-ended questions
such as "What happened?" or "What made you angry?" yield more information and sound less like an interrogation than close-ended questions such
as "Did you call Mary?" or "Did you hit your child?" The social worker
can help reduce the parent's uncertainty and anxiety by giving information to the parent about available treatment alternatives and the physical
condition of the injured child.

1397   Gordon, Henrietta L. "Protective service: intake problems," and
       "Services to neglectful parents." In: Gordon, Henrietta L. <u>Case-
       work services for children: practices and principles</u>. Boston:
       Houghton Mifflin, 1956. 371-425. (4 References).
Outlines the various tasks facing the caseworker in child protective services. Protective services is an agency authorized by the community to
intervene in a family for the protection of a neglected child. Its referrals come from other agencies, individuals, and even family members.
In order to protect the rights and privacy of the family, each referral
should be evaluated by an investigation of the complaintee's motives,
his relationship to the family, and the contents of the complaint, specifically the conditions which are harming the children. Once the complaint
is verified, the caseworker must initiate contact with the family, antici-
pating the alarm, anxiety, and defensive behavior this may provoke. The
caseworker's task is to examine the nature of the neglect, to lead the
family to a realization of the problem, and to formulate a rehabilitative
plan with the parents. Their ability to acknowledge their problems, to
define a treatment plan and to follow it will determine their ability to
work toward a satisfactory family relationship and home for their child.
Where this approach fails, the caseworker must contact authorities who
can begin to arrange for the placement of the child.

1398   Higgins, Edward. "Notes on education: the social workers." In:
       Franklin, Alfred White, ed. <u>Concerning child abuse</u>. New York:
       Churchill Livingstone, 1975. 150-51. (0 References).
Focuses on the necessary education for social workers as it relates to
their role in the management team. In addition to their basic training,
social workers must understand their role within their agency, the
authority of the agency itself, and the function of the agency within the
management team. A knowledge of court procedures is essential. Although
an understanding and supportive attitude toward the abusive parents is
necessary, the social worker's primary consideration must focus on the
child.

1399   Holmes, Sally A.; Barnhart, Carol; Cantoni, Lucile; et al. "Work-
       ing with the parent in child-abuse cases." <u>Soc Casework</u> 56(1):
       3-12, January, 1975. (8 References).
Analyzes the attitudes and problems a caseworker can expect to meet when
working with abuse prone parents. Various examples are cited which
demonstrate the behavior patterns of these parents as well as their
expectations of the caseworker. The parent wants both approval and discipline. Many caseworkers make the mistake of sympathetically minimizing
or trying to ignore the parent's problem with abusive behavior, thus
offering approval but no discipline. It is suggested that effective
casework with such clients must manage to engage the client in a constructive, facilitative child-parent relationship without infantilizing the
client.

1400   Hornbein, Ruth. "Social worker's orientations to the use of
       authority in initiating and maintaining a social casework relation-
       ship with parents who abuse and parents who neglect their children."
       For a summary see: <u>Diss Abstr Int</u> 33A(6): 3031-32, December,
       1972.

1401   Horner, Gerald. "Support your social workers (the problem of
       'battered children' in Britain)." <u>Munic Public Serv J</u> 82: 862ff.,
       July 19, 1974.

1402 Howells, John G. "Whose responsibility? -- parent, foster parent, or local authority? (a) separation or death." R Soc Health J 95(5): 257-61, October, 1975. (7 References).
Refutes three misconceptions about the parent-child relationship: (1) that there is always a special bond between parent and child; (2) that the parent-child bond is unique; and (3) that separation of the child from his home is the worst possible outcome for the child. The social worker, in collaboration with other professionals, has the responsibility for the immediate care of the child. Some of the elements of her work are discussed, along with issues about expertise, assessment, the rights of children, and state monopolized child care services.

1403 Hyde, James N., Jr. "Uses and abuses of information in protective services contexts." In: National Symposium on Child Abuse, 5th, Boston, 1974. Collected papers. Denver, Colorado: The American Humane Association, Children's Division, 1976. 56-62. (0 References).
Discusses the use of information as a prelude to treatment. Ideally, a caseworker needs a large data-base from which to evaluate and make decisions. Hearsay evidence is often essential, but the rights of both the parents and the child should be carefully considered. The caseworker frequently must act on the available information whether it is adequate or not. Therefore, decisions should always have short-term consequences. When drastic action is necessary, the caseworker should make the decision in consultation with another professional. The need to explore family strengths is argued.

1404 Jacobucci, Louis. "Casework treatment of the neglectful mother." Soc Casework 46(4): 221-26, April, 1965. (5 References).
Describes a caseworker's approach to negligent mothers which has resulted in effective treatment in a number of cases. The approach is predicated on the assumption that the negligent mother is often a child herself emotionally, has had a poor relationship with her own mother, has developed a negative self-image, feels neglected, isolated, trapped, and unloved, and craves the affirmation of authority figures. The caseworker is advised to assume the temporary role of a substitute mother, concentrating her attention on the client's need for support and demonstrations of affection. At some point, the caseworker may introduce advice very subtly into the relationship, but the approach must always be reinforcing and non-judgmental.

1405 McGowan, Brenda G. "Case advocacy: a study of the interventive process in child advocacy." For a summary see: Diss Abstr Int 35A(10): 6809, April, 1975.

1406 Mitchell, Betsy. "Working with abusive parents: a caseworker's view." Am J Nurs 73(3): 480-83, March, 1973. (0 References).
Presents a caseworker's perspective on the treatment of abusing parents while looking after the best interests of their children. A more effective solution for the treatment of families could perhaps be accomplished by the combined efforts of both nurses and social workers. If, in some instances, health professionals were to go one step beyond referring suspected cases to actually issuing a warning to abusive parents that court action might be taken if they refused to improve, perhaps more children would get the immediate attention at home that they need.

1407 Mitchiner, Myra J. "Providing preventive and protective services
      to children in a public welfare agency." Child Welfare 45(4):
      224-27, April, 1966. (2 References).
Discusses the responsibilities in the public welfare agency of the individual caseworker in providing services for children in need of financial,
psychological, or social assistance. The caseworker should have a working
knowledge of both family dynamics and of agency resources and organization
and public assistance policies. Communication and coordination among the
family receiving help, the caseworker, and the public assistance agency
is stressed. Small caseloads for each worker are recommended as a means
of maximizing effective treatment of the problem.

1408 Mulford, Robert M.; Wylegala, Victor B.; Melson, Elwood F. Case-
      worker and judge in neglect cases. New York: Child Welfare League
      of America, 1956. 31p.
Presents a collection of three articles distinguishing the separate roles
of the caseworkers and the courts in providing protective services to
neglected children and their families. Cooperation between the two is
stressed. Caseworkers often find themselves in need of court action to
carry out their own services or to take over cases when their services
fail to produce results. Consequently, they need to have a clear understanding of the possibilities and limitations of court action, as well as
the rules of providing competent evidence. Guidelines for preparing and
planning court cases are introduced. Statements supporting the caseworker's efforts to convince the courts that children must be protected
from both physical and emotional neglect are also included.

1409 Overton, Alice. "Aggressive casework." Soc Work J 33(3): 149-51,
      July, 1952. (0 References).
Describes a project of protective casework operated by the New York City
Youth Board and Department of Welfare. This type of casework was designed
for a population which requires help but which ordinarily cannot or will
not seek it themselves. Through the Board of Education referral units,
the project learns of families where children are in danger. On receiving
these referrals, the worker writes the family, indicating a visitation
date and the reasons for coming. Home visits are considered an invaluable method of observing family relationships. The aims are to establish
better relations within the family and to help the family become more
comfortable with available community resources. The greatest change
noted in the families has been their increased social effectiveness.

1410 Polansky, Norman A.; Borgman, Robert D.; DeSaix, Christine, et al.
      "Verbal accessibility in the treatment of child neglect." Child
      Welfare 50(6): 349-56, June, 1971. (9 References).
Examines a method for interviewing neglectful mothers in rural areas that
can be used by social workers attempting to improve the mothers' child
care practices. The key to successful interviewing is encouraging the
client to express her important attitudes and feelings, which is called
increasing her verbal accessibility. Verbal accessibility is a useful
diagnostic tool for the social worker, for it is relatively simple to
assess. When a mother is decidedly inaccessible, it can mean that she
is intellectually dull, very immature, neurotically inhibited, or seriously disturbed. A higher degree of verbal accessibility is a sign that
she will be receptive and responsive to treatment. In fact, increasing
a client's willingness and ability to express herself can in itself be
regarded as curative. Several techniques that rural caseworkers apply

in interviews to facilitate verbal accessibility in their clients are
suggested.

1411 Popplestone, Ruth. "Moving the balance from administration to
      practice." Soc Work Today 8(13): 14-15, January 4, 1977. (3
      References).
Warns against the present trend to put too much emphasis on the administrative procedures in dealing with child abuse cases. Although the
administrative systems are designed to protect children, they sometimes
have the opposite effect for the following reasons: (1) they take up
social workers' time with often unnecessary procedures, time which would
be better spent on the personal needs of the abusing family; and (2) the
administrative authorities' anxiety to protect their reputations leads
everyone to overreactions such as indiscriminate visiting of families,
who, in turn, may react to the increased anxiety level by actually becoming more abusive. Social workers need to be able to work without heavy
caseloads or heavy administrative duties and with sound professional support available. Suggestions to improve the present situation are offered.

1412 Rall, Mary E. "The casework process in work with the child and the
      family in the child's own home." In: National Conference of Social
      Work. Casework papers, 1954. New York: Family Service Association
      of America, 1955. 31-43. (0 References).
Stresses the assessment of each family member's need when undertaking
casework services in the home. The caseworker must seek the motives behind the parents' appeal for help. If the needs of parent and child can
be reconciled toward the goal of strengthening the family, home service
can be offered. However, when these needs conflict, placement of the
child must be considered. Illustrations of applied casework principles
are given as well as examples of cases which cannot profit from casework
treatment.

1413 Roberts, Robert W. "A comparative study of social caseworkers'
      judgments of child abuse cases." For a summary see: Diss Abstr
      Int 31A(9): 4894, March, 1971.

1414 Schmidt, Dolores M. "The challenge of helping the 'untreatables.'"
      Public Welfare 23(2): 98-102, April, 1965. (2 References).
Argues that there may really be no such thing as an "untreatable" case
to the able and experienced caseworker, or at least, that the number of
cases designated "untreatable" would drop if enough capable caseworkers
were around to take on the difficult clients. The argument is presented
by means of an example which demonstrates that the even apparently hopeless cases can make progress so long as the caseworker is patient and
sensitive enough. Agencies must make an all out effort to attract such
workers and to help them to exercise their potential.

1415 Stroud, John. "The social worker's role." In: Franklin, Alfred
      White, ed. Concerning child abuse. New York: Churchill Living-
      stone, 1975. 95-105. (0 References).
A history of attitudes and approaches to child protection reveals the
range of variables that services are now considering. Given these, the
social worker needs a system of evaluation which helps his/her role in
each case. In cases of overt physical abuse, procedures must be carried
out quickly. When abuse is suspected but not clearly evident, a thorough
data base must be compiled which includes a medical history of the child,

a history of the parents and the family, and observations about the home situation, particularly the parents' attitude toward the child. Families at risk need periodic review as an on-going diagnosis of the problems and assessment of the child's welfare. The possibility of requiring this procedure through legislation is explored. Although court intervention is sometimes necessary, maintaining the family unit with the assistance of a supervising officer is stressed. An added remark discusses the demands a community makes upon its social workers.

1416 Wasserman, Harry. "Early careers of professional social workers in a public child welfare agency." Soc Work 15(3): 93-101, July, 1970. (11 References).
Assesses the job satisfaction levels of twelve professional child welfare workers whose experiences in a large welfare agency were analyzed over a two year period. The workers had all recently completed their training at the beginning of the period covered by the analysis; most found that they were not allowed to call on the professional skills which they had developed in school, but rather were too overworked and too burdened with procedural regulations to apply what they had learned to the demanding situations they met in their casework. By the end of the two year period, eight of the twelve workers had left the agency.

9. RESPONSIBILITY OF THE SCHOOLS

1417 Batinich, M. E. Mancina. "How school can aid the abused child: principal's role central in protecting children." Chic Sch J 46(3): 57-62, November, 1964. (4 References).
States the need for the school to detect and protect children from abuse, emphasizing the role of the principal. The school may be the first social agency to become aware of the child's maltreatment, and the principal, as spokesperson for the school, must initiate protective legal and social measures. The principal's responsibilities include record keeping, contact with public service agencies and the family, and attending related court hearings. A weakened family structure is cited as the predominant source of abuse. Various methods of treatment are discussed, including a description of child welfare agencies and court proceedings.

1418 Bechtold, M. L. "That battered child could be dead tomorrow." Instructor 77(8): 20, April, 1968. (0 References).
Characteristics of child abuse and methods for handling cases are presented to elementary school teachers. The history of one child illustrates successful counseling and placement.

1419 Broadhurst, Diane D. "Project PROTECTION in Maryland: a school program to combat child abuse." Educ Dig 41(2): 20-23, October, 1975. (0 References).
Examines Montgomery County's school-based plan for combating child abuse and neglect in the state of Maryland, condensed from another article by the author which appeared in Childhood Education in November, 1975. The federally funded plan, called Project PROTECTION, is designed to train educational personnel to recognize the indicators of abuse and neglect, to inform the staff of their legal responsibility to report suspected cases of abuse and neglect, and to teach them the procedures for making reports. Furthermore, the project is developing innovative preventive measures such as school courses dealing with many aspects of the child

maltreatment syndrome. These courses are designed to prepare youngsters for parenthood.

1420 Broadhurst, Diane D., and Howard, Maxwell C. "More about Project PROTECTION." Child Educ 52(3): 67-69, November, 1975. (0 References).

Reports a school system's successful response to the problem of child abuse and neglect. In 1974, Montgomery County, Maryland, initiated a federally funded school-based program called Project PROTECTION: A Multi-disciplinary Approach to Educational Problems Associated with Child Abuse and Neglect. A massive effort to educate school personnel in identifying neglected and abused children was undertaken. Further instructions in-formed the staff of their legal responsibility to report suspected abuse and neglect cases and proper referral procedures. Three case histories illustrate the effectiveness of the program's protective services. Most importantly, Project PROTECTION is engaged in strengthening its preventive capabilities. Forthcoming plans include a high school course on the child maltreatment syndrome which would concentrate on early child develop-ment, the achievement of emotional maturity, and various ways people can learn to cope with stress.

1421 "Child abuse." J Sch Health 45(10): 567, December, 1975. (0 References).

The main thrust of several presentations at the American School Health Association (ASHA) convention are given in this brief report. Legisla-tion, the school's role, incidence, and a school referral program are included.

1422 "Child abuse curriculum." Child Today 6(3): 29, May-June, 1977. (0 References).

Introduces the six-unit curriculum on child abuse and neglect prepared in conjunction with Project PROTECTION, a federally funded program de-signed by the Montgomery County, Maryland Public Schools. The collection of resource materials for training teachers focuses primarily on preven-tion. A contact for obtaining copies of the curriculum is listed.

1423 "Children: the hard case." Newsweek 82(3): 32, July 16, 1973. (0 References).

Government committees are investigating a private school for youths with discipline problems. The director of the school allegedly participated in the physical abuse of his pupils. He was arrested and released on bond, and his school was closed pending decision on the case.

1424 Forrer, Stephen E. "Battered children and counselor responsibil-ity." Sch Couns 22(3): 161-65, January, 1975. (3 References).

Outlines the role of the school counselor in managing the physical and psychological abuse of children and adolescents. Counselors can make significant contributions to the treatment and prevention of child abuse by working directly with abusive parents and abused children and by en-couraging troubled families to take advantage of the lay professional community services available to them. Counselors should also promote curriculum innovations that would include family studies, effective parenting practices, and techniques for coping with stress.

1425 Gittins, John. "Children in trouble." Spec Educ 57(3): 7-9, September, 1968. (0 References).

Reaction to the White Paper, "Children in Trouble," 1968.

1426 Henke, Lorraine J. "A health educator's role in the problems of
      child abuse." Health Educ 6(3): 15-18, May-June, 1975. (3
      References).
Points out the teacher's advantageous position in combating child abuse.
Because teachers see children on a daily basis, they can be an important
source in identifying the abused child, obtaining help for the child and
his parents, and following up on treatment. Symptoms such as aggressive
behavior, truancy, physical scars, and physical neglect may reveal a
child's need for protection. The teacher must handle the situation with
extreme care and must not shirk his responsibility to help the abused
child. Courses in family life and human development are suggested so
that schools produce future loving parents.

1427 Hill, Dorothy Murdock. "Breaking the vicious circle of child
      abuse." Chic Theol Semin Regist 67(2): 66-75, Spring, 1977.
      (0 References).
Presents a personal account by a teacher in Boulder, Colorado, who participated in a federally funded elementary education program called Follow
Through. It was designed as a multidisciplinary approach to reducing
poverty area educational problems. The account itself focuses on the
teacher's successful efforts to break the cycle of child abuse in one
family involved in the program.

1428 Hyman, Irwin, and Schreiber, Karen. "Selected concepts and prac-
      tices of child advocacy in school psychology." Psychol Sch 12(1):
      50-58, January, 1975. (43 References).
Argues that the school psychologist's main responsibility is to insist on
the rights of children, even if that means confronting the educational
bureaucracy. Specific guidelines for three areas in which a school psychologist can work for children's rights are given: (1) identifying,
reporting, and preventing child abuse; (2) eliminating corporal punishment from the schools; and (3) guarding the confidentiality of a child's
record against unwarranted disclosure while granting parents the right to
know the school authorities' findings about their children.

1429 Jordan, June B. "CEC convenes two invisible colleges -- child
      abuse and neglect; learning and behavior problems at the secondary
      level." Educ Train Ment Retarded 12(1): 83-89, February, 1977.
      (0 References).
Summarizes the content of two symposiums sponsored by the Council for
Exceptional Children. In discussing the problem of child abuse and
neglect, such issues as adolescent abuse, the role of the teacher, and
reporting legislation were covered. The second symposium focused on the
problems encountered by handicapped students in secondary schools.

1430 Joyce, Walter C.; Haynes, Edythe; Gardner, Thomas G. "Child [is]
      molested at home." Instructor 79(9): 35, May, 1970. (0
      References).
Discussion of a school principal's alternatives when faced with a case
of possible child molestation occurring in the home of a student. The
child revealed to other classmates, but to no adult, that he was being
molested at home. The principal is advised to seek the aid of the guidance counselor who can interview the child, and of former and current
teachers who can observe behavior which might verify the child's story.
On the basis of this observation and information gathering, the principal
may conclude that these stories are fantasies on the child's part and

suggest professional help. However, if the story appears to be verified, a social agency should be notified. School authorities and school attorneys need to be aware of the investigation.

1431 Leavitt, Jerome E. "The battered child." Instructor 75(7): 50-
      51, 142, 150, March, 1966. (0 References).
Presents educators with the stigma and problems associated with battered children and identifies methods for handling the abused child in the classroom. Due to the disbelief and taboo which have surrounded the topic, parents, educators, and physicians have been slow to recognize the problem of maltreatment. Yet, the high incidence of abuse requires that educators learn all they can about the legal, medical, and social aspects of child abuse.

1432 Leuchter, H. J. "Are schools to be or not to be community health
      centers? letter to editor." Am J Psychiatry 125(4): 575-76,
      October, 1968. (8 References).
Expresses favor of the school's assumption of the role of community mental health centers. Psychiatrists are urged to aid educators having direct contact with disturbed children in the creation of programs which can check the spread of mental illness from generation to generation.

1433 McAnarney, Elizabeth. "The older abused child: letter to editor."
      Pediatrics 55(2): 298-99, February, 1975. (3 References).
Cites two case histories illustrating a need for further research into the abuse of teenagers. Fear of their parents frequently makes teenagers reluctant to report abuse. Because they tend to express their concerns to school authorities, rather than medical or social services, abused teenagers should be identified and studied within schools or other youth center environments.

1434 Rochester, D. E.; Ellis, Mary A.; Sciortino, Sam C. "What can
      schools do about child abuse?" Todays Educ 57(6): 59-60,
      September, 1968. (0 References).
Reports the results of a questionnaire sent to school personnel in order to assess their knowledge of child abuse and their respective roles in handling known cases. Because school officials have such close contact with children, the conclusion is drawn that the schools need to take an active part in detecting and treating abused children.

1435 Sanders, Lola; Kibby, Robert W.; Creaghan, Sidney; et al. "Child
      abuse: detection and prevention." Young Child 30(5): 332-38,
      July, 1975. (9 References).
Two case histories are presented to illustrate how one school handled child abuse before and after the initiation of a joint management program with the county child protective services. The steps taken to educate the school personnel about child abuse and to establish a treatment approach are outlined. It is emphasized that reporting abuse is the first step toward helping the child and his family.

1436 Shanas, Bert. "Child abuse: a killer teachers can help control."
      Phi Delta Kappan 56(7): 479-82, March, 1975. (0 References).
Since children are required by law to go to school, teachers can be the "first line of defense" against child abuse; but too few teachers report suspected abuse through reluctance to get involved or through fear of retaliation from the parents. The article lists symptoms which teachers

should recognize as possible indications of abuse and discusses some
typical causes of abuse. Teachers also should know what kinds of social
agencies can help and what treatment methods for parents are available.
By doing nothing or by using corporal punishment in the classrooms,
teachers worsen the problem of abuse and prolong the repeating cycle
of abuse from one generation to the next. Special educational classes
to help abused children and special classes to train teachers in the
problems of abuse are recommended.

1437 Slack, Georgia. "Child Find." Am Educ 12(10): 29-33, December,
      1976. (0 References).
Studies the Child Find program of the Dade County, Florida school system.
The purpose of the program is to seek out children who are not receiving
an education in any form and to provide them with educational programs
that are suited to their needs. Most of these children are hidden at
home by their families. Child Find specialists are responsible for finding, identifying, and placing them. The details of six case reports,
including one instance of sexual abuse, are included.

1438 Suchara, Helen T. "The child's right to humane treatment." Child
      Educ 53(6): 290-96, April-May, 1977. (22 References).
Expresses the belief of the Association for Childhood Education International that educators must both treat children humanely and help teach
them to be humane themselves. The article discusses in detail: (1) ways
of implementing humane treatment (making sure their needs for physical
growth are filled and fostering a good self-image in them); and (2) ways
of nurturing humaneness in children (creating caring relationships with
them and teaching them to value cultural, ethnic, or religious diversity
among others). Other suggestions to help adults foster humaneness among
children are also listed.

C. SEPARATION AND PLACEMENT

1. DISCUSSION OF PROCEDURES

1439 "Children in care: editorial." Br Med J 3(5564): 512, August
      26, 1967. (0 References).
Cites statistics from the Children's Department of the British Home Office
regarding the numbers and situations of children placed in the care of
local authorities in England and Wales between 1959 and 1966.

1440 Lewis, Hilda. Deprived children: the Mersham experiment: a
      social and clinical study. London: Oxford University Press, 1954.
      163p. (Bibliography).
Describes the work of the Mersham Reception Center as of 1954 in Kent,
England, in its intermediary role of caring for deprived children,
assessing their psychological and developmental needs, and recommending
healthier and more supportive long-term living arrangements. During the
post war period of 1947-1950, 500 children were admitted to the center.
Some of the children were delinquent or otherwise uncontrollable at home,
and others had lost or been deserted by their parents. One hundred and
eleven children had been neglected and another eleven cruelly treated at
home. At the center, however, all children experienced a simple and
supervised living environment. Most of the children exhibited signs of

anxiety at being separated from their parents, but the neglected children alone persisted in shunning adults and other children. Although the neglected children were often more emotionally stable and had fewer behavioral problems than their peers, they were also more likely to be mentally deficient or dull, with 44 percent of these children scoring below seventy on a standard intelligence test. After a three to four week observation period, the children were assigned to boarding schools, foster or small group homes, or returned to their parents' care. The center emphasized the importance of careful pre-placement planning in order to avoid subjecting the child to multiple and unhappy placements. In a follow-up study conducted two years after the children had left Mersham, 63 percent of all the children, and 55 percent of the neglected children, showed signs of definite improvement.

1441 Littner, Ner. Some traumatic effects of separation and placement. New York: Child Welfare League of America. 1956.
Discusses the reactions of children to separation and placement. Common emotional reactions to separation are fear, insecurity, anger at the natural parents, self-blame, and feelings that either he or his parents will die. Separation anxiety can cause physical illness and dysfunction, but some children combat the anxiety by staying hopeful that they will not be separated from their parents. In adjusting to foster parents, the child must accept his need to feel loved by them. To defend himself against this need, he will often create distance between himself and his foster parents. Repression of all anxieties is another common defense mechanism. The side effects of separation are a function of age, children under six being most vulnerable. Professionals can reduce traumatic effects through careful pre-placement procedures and by helping the child in frequent visits to adjust to the anticipated placement and then to the foster home. Professionals are cautioned about the negative consequences of hasty decisions to place the child when the situation seems, prior to any investigation, an emergency.

1442 Matthews, F. B. "Discussion on the care of children away from their parents -- Part II: Long-stay care of the homeless child." J R Sanit Inst 66(4): 331-36, August, 1946. (0 References).
Suggests improvements for the present British system of handling, care, and placement of children outside of their homes. A brief history indicates the sources of the four current methods of care which are: (1) county care of poor children; (2) court care of offenders or neglected children; (3) private placement by parents of unwanted children; and (4) voluntary agency care. Coordination of these methods is desirable and could be attained if one government body were responsible for total supervision and one local body were in charge of day-to-day administration. The system of maintaining children also needs revision. Institutions, particularly those designed for adults, are inadequate for children, yet not every child is suitable for foster placement. Group and scattered homes come closest to simulating a home life. However, the quality of the caretaker who becomes a substitute parent to the child is the most crucial element of his care. Classifying a child for a placement where he is most apt to find a nurturing caretaker should become a built-in aspect of the placement system. Receiving homes are being set up where children can be observed and matched to the most appropriate placement.

1443 Nebraska. State Department of Public Welfare. Social services
      handbook. Lincoln, Nebraska: Nebraska State Department of Public
      Welfare, 1975. 11p.
Outlines how employees of the Nebraska Department of Public Welfare are
to manage cases of adult and child abuse. For abused children, the goal
is to keep the family together and to improve relationships between the
parents and children. The handbook lists situations which indicate that
protective services are necessary or that court services are needed.
Skills, knowledge, and attitudes desirable for the staff of protective
services are also listed. Guidelines are given for determining when
children in protective custody should be returned to their homes, and
some follow-up methods are discussed.

1444 Philbrick, Elizabeth. "The Nancy Smith case: neglected child --
      unmarried mother. Denver, Colorado: The American Humane Associa-
      tion, Children's Division, 1960. 11p. (Bibliography).
Documents an actual case of child neglect as handled by the child protective services. Following a complaint filed by neighbors, a case worker
made contact with the unmarried mother of a three-year-old neglected
child. The mother had been living with an abusive and alcoholic man and
had allegedly supported herself by prostitution. The worker encouraged
the mother to better her own life and her daughter's and discussed possible foster care and adoption procedures for the child. After several
months of contact with the social worker, the mother decided to place
the child for adoption. In addition, she made plans to leave her common
law husband, but did not subsequently carry out these plans.

1445 Sandusky, Annie L. "Services to neglected children." Children
      7(1): 23-28, January-February, 1960. (5 References).
Evaluates public welfare agencies as a means of coping with the problem
of child neglect. This type of agency would not merely initiate help
but would continue to handle the problem until the child receives adequate
care. Some problems confronting the child welfare worker who attempts to
help abusing parents are considered. A crucial issue is whether or not
the child should remain at home. The worker may attempt to educate
parents who lack the ability to resolve their own problems or who do not
possess a sufficient degree of emotional maturity to properly care for
their child. A few agencies have experimented with offering homemaker
services, so that help can be provided in the child's home, and thus he
is not subjected to an unfamiliar environment. Emergency foster care
is an indispensable back-up service. Cooperative effort between the
child welfare agency and the court is necessary in order to safeguard
the rights of both the child and his parents. Legislation must empower
public welfare agencies to provide services which emphasize the
strengthening of family life, instead of the previous reliance upon law
enforcing bodies which could remove children from their homes without
the consent or involvement of their parents. Adequate training for child
welfare workers is also necessary.

1446 Smith, Austin E. "The beaten child." Hygeia 22(5): 386-88, May,
      1944. (0 References).
Describes several abused children representative of the rising incidence
of child abuse in metropolitan areas and urges community action. Children who are victims can recover from the emotional terror of maltreatment
if institutions and foster homes provide adequate warmth and affection.
Each community must establish a helping pattern for these children in
order to undo psychological damage.

1447   Smith, Selwyn M.   "The battered child syndrome -- some research
       findings." Nurs Mirror 140(22): 48-53, June 12, 1975. (44
       References).
The safety of the child should be the supreme concern of social workers
and physicians. Rehabilitation of parents and family unity are desirable
objectives but must not overshadow the immediate needs of the abused
child. Removing the children from the home if parents do not respond to
treatment is advocated. Characteristics of parents and battered children
are described. Photographs of injuries are included with captions of
the true medical diagnosis and the parents' fabrication.

1448   Taipale, V.; Moren, R.; Phila, T.; et al. "Experiences of an abused
       child." Acta Paedopsychiatr 39(3): 53-58, 1972. (12 References).
Documents a case study of the damage which can be done to an abused child
by moving him around among several institutions and foster families. The
child in question had been beaten at age three by his stepfather; by age
seven, he had lived in eight different institutions and homes. His
separation anxiety was such that the lack of stability in his life after
his removal from his parents was more damaging psychologically than the
original abuse had been. The boy's current placement in a foster home,
however, seemed to put an end to this destructive pattern.

1449   "'Transplant' some abused children, pediatrician says." Am J Nurs
       71(12): 2294-95, December, 1971. (0 References).
In many cases of child abuse, the only viable option is to transplant the
child to a radically different environment. Three groups of cases based
on family income, size of family unit, degree of child care received, and
the nature of various family crises are delineated.

2. FOSTER CARE

1450   Davoren, Elizabeth. "Foster placement of abused children." Child
       Today 4(3): 41, May-June, 1975. (0 References).
Discusses several disadvantages of foster home placement, including the
frightened reaction of the child to strange surroundings and the potentially angry response of parents to the child when he is returned home.
If separation from the parents is indicated for the child, the social
worker can help the foster parents to encourage the natural parents'
efforts to gradually reassume responsibility for the care of their child.
Allowing the parents to play with the child and to take care of some of
his basic needs, such as feeding and bathing, are steps in the direction
of reuniting the child with his family.

1451   Fanshel, David, and Shinn, Eugene B. Dollars and sense in the
       foster care of children: a look at cost factors. New York: Child
       Welfare League of America, 1972. 47p. (Bibliography).
Report on a study of the costs involved in foster care, based on the
experience of 624 children between 1966 and 1970. Factors influencing
foster care costs are itemized and given cost estimates; these include
type of care provided, size of family group, and the choice between remaining in care or returning home. In addition, costs are estimated for
those children who will remain in foster care throughout childhood. Based
on these findings, a program was established to provide incentives for the
return of these children to their parents.

1452 Ford, Donald. The deprived child and the community. London:
      Constable, 1955. 226p. (Bibliography).
Evaluates the different child care and protection services available to
the deprived child. Deprived children may have been orphaned or abandoned; most frequently, however, they have come to the attention of the
local child welfare authorities after their parents failed to provide a
healthy environment and adequate care. Parentless children are best
provided for through adoption. The pattern of interaction between the
adoptive parents, social worker, and child is outlined. Foster care can
also insure a deprived child of a warm home environment. Problems which
can arise between the foster parents and the natural, though neglectful,
parents are explored.

State supported child care institutions are evaluated. Residential children's homes are moving away from the Victorian concept of mass living,
toward the ideal of an intimate, family-like atmosphere. Nineteenth
century norms of isolation and social ostracism are being abandoned, with
institutionalized children now being encouraged to make friendly contacts
with other children and adults in the community. The importance of after
care in assisting a child to secure employment, housing, and future
happiness is stressed.

From both a human and an economic point of view, the prevention of deprivation is highly desired. The symptoms of family dysfunction and the
forewarners of deprivation include: neglect, abuse, failure to thrive,
illegitimacy, ill health, and marital problems. By providing more extensive medical, educational, and counseling services, the integrity of the
family unit can be preserved.

1453 Goldstein, Joseph; Freud, Anna; Solnit, Albert J. Beyond the best
      interests of the child. New York: Free Press, 1973. 171p.
      (Bibliography).
Psychoanalytic theory is used to develop guidelines to direct child placement decisions. Child placement is an umbrella term embracing all legislative, judicial, and executive decisions which are concerned with
establishing, administering, or rearranging parent-child relationships.
Distinguishing between biological and psychological parent-child relationships is an essential aspect of understanding the child's needs. A
child's healthy development requires that there be at least one person
whom he feels loves, values, and wants him; this person does not have to
be the biologic parent. The emotional attachments which develop between
parents and children cannot be legislated into existence, and need continuous and stable opportunities to grow.

Many laws pertaining to child placement fail to be sensitive to the complexities of parent-child relationships, and do not attend sufficiently
to the child's psychological needs. The law presently seeks to insure
the child's best interest in the settlement of custody disputes. It
should, instead, seek the least detrimental solution for the child. This
change in terminology would force recognition of the fact that the child
is already a victim of seriously damaging environmental stress, and that
his placement in a home where a psychologically stable parent-child relationship can develop is urgent. The law currently requires that biologic
parents must be proved unfit in order for custody to be withheld from
them, even if the child is already settled in a stable psychological
parent-child relationship. The disruption of such a relationship is as
destructive to the child as the death of a natural parent.

It is emphasized that the concept of a psychological, common-law adoptive
parent must be legally sanctioned. Other legal and administrative procedures, such as the existence of a year's trial period before adoption
can be legally finalized, disrupt opportunities for the development of
healthy parent-child relationships. Reasons for advocating the child's
rights over other considerations are offered, and the guidelines developed
by the authors are applied to an actual case decision involving the
placement of an eight-year-old foster child.

1454 Kreech, Florence. "Program developments: adoption outreach."
      Child Welfare 52(10): 669-75, December, 1973. (0 References).
Reviews the current changes in the field of adoption. Presently, there
are few infants available for adoption. Instead, most of the children
being placed by adoptive agencies are older and have special, often severe
problems sometimes stemming from parental abuse or deprivation. Foster
care and adoption agencies need to merge their services to meet the needs
of these children.

1455 Reeves, Christine. "Whose responsibility?" R Soc Health J 95(5):
      261-63, October, 1975. (0 References).
Examines the role of foster care in the child care delivery system.
Society fails prospective parents by not providing them with the necessary
education and financial support. When a family falls apart, foster
parents often take over the responsibility of caring for the dependent
children. But foster parents are not given adequate financial, medical,
and professional support to care for these children effectively. This
support should be the responsibility of the local authority. In addition,
the skills of foster parents could be utilized more imaginatively, for
example, to care for the handicapped child or to befriend a young troubled
family. Since foster families often undertake the care of children difficult to place, they need special education and training in these areas.
Foster parents should collaborate with the social worker in providing the
best possible environment for the child. The National Foster Care Association was established in order to accomplish some of these goals and
to expand the public knowledge of foster care so that more people would
participate in this activity.

1456 Sherman, E. A.; Neuman, R.; Shyne, A. W. Children adrift in foster
      care: a study of alternative approaches. New York: Child Welfare
      League of America, 1974. 129p. (Bibliography).
Investigates a demonstration project directed at controlling two problems
in foster care--the loss of children within the foster care system and
the elimination of natural parents from the system. Four hundred and
thirteen children in foster care were studied over an eight month period;
in the experimental group, social workers worked with natural parents.
At the conclusion of the study period, it was found that, although the
children in the experimental group ended up spending a longer time in
foster care before returning to their natural parents, none of the children in this group subsequently returned to foster care. It was also
found that the likelihood of a child's remaining in foster care increased
with time.

1457 Trasler, G. "Techniques for the care of deprived children."
      Public Health 77(6): 335-45, 1963. (5 References).
Presents insights into the foster care of children deprived of one or
both parents. Awareness of the emotional condition of the child at the

time of separation is essential. An examination of the emotional needs of the foster family is crucial as well, since these could limit their response to the child. Parents who are secure enough to support the child's loyalty to his real parents, and who do not require an immediate return of affection, prove most successful. A marked failure is the notion of the "replacement family," a family structured after the child's original one. An increased use of short-stay homes has permitted the child care officers to assess the child's long range needs within a more natural setting.

3. INSTITUTIONAL CARE

1458 Jaffe, Eliezer D. "Professional background and the utilization of institutional care of children as a solution to family crisis." Hum Relat 23(1): 15-21, February, 1970. (8 References).
Studies institutional placement of dependent children in Israel. Although institutional placement was especially popular after World War II, presently expanded day care and foster home services are gaining in popularity. An Advice to Families Scale (ATF scale) was devised from a hypothesis that better educated child care workers were less likely to prescribe an institutional setting as a viable solution to complex family problems. A coded questionnaire asking the respondent to prescribe either a home care or institutional solution to each of ten typical family problems was given to parents of institutionalized children, public health nurses, social work students, and social work faculty. It was learned that parents and public health nurses recommended institutional placement more often than the other groups.

1459 Leszczynska, C. S. F. N., Sister Mary Eunice. "A study of the effects of organizational structure on organizational climate in private institutions for dependent, neglected children." For a summary see: Diss Abstr Int 38A(2): 1025, August, 1977.

1460 Piturro, Marlene C. "The modification of behavior and self-report as a function of group contingencies in institutionalized dependent and neglected children." For a summary see: Diss Abstr Int 35B(5): 2442, November, 1974.

1461 Rosen, Alison C. "The social and emotional development of children in long-term residential care." Ther Educ 18-25, Spring, 1971.

D. PSYCHOLOGICAL TREATMENT

1. GROUP THERAPY

1462 Arvanian, Ann L. "Treatment issues in the development of an adolescent group." In: National Symposium on Child Abuse, 5th, Boston, 1974. Collected papers. Denver, Colorado: The American Humane Association, Children's Division, 1976. 135-39. (0 References).
Describes the five stages of group development occurring in a therapy group for adolescents. The group consisted of eight young girls from families with histories of abuse. The pre-affiliation stage was

characterized by the anxieties about encountering a new situation. During
the power and control stage, group members wanted defined roles for themselves in the group. In the intimacy stage, members shared common needs,
while during differentiation they recognized their individuality. The
final stage, separation, was characterized by members' awareness of their
relationship to the community and their own social needs. Upon completion
of therapy, all members voted to continue the group.

1463 Avery, Nancy. "Treatment issues in the development of a mother's
      remedial group." In: National Symposium on Child Abuse, 5th,
      Boston, 1974. Collected papers. Denver, Colorado: The American
      Humane Association, Children's Division, 1976. 128-34. (3 Refer-
      ences).

Outlines procedures and results of a therapy group for abusive and neglectful mothers. Mothers were in their thirties and forties, came from
low income families, and all had experienced rejection in their childhoods. Caseworkers provided strong encouragement for mothers to attend
the group, supplying nursery care and transportation. In sharing complaints about their lives, mothers agreed on the physical disciplining
of their children. The caseworkers tried to provide alternatives to
violence as a means of dealing with anger. Many members improved their
coping behavior by associating with family members they had previously
ignored. Termination of the group was gradual and therapeutic.

1464 Bellucci, Matilda T. "Group treatment of mothers in child protec-
      tion cases." Child Welfare 51(2): 110-16, February, 1972.
      (0 References).

Group treatment of abusing mothers is reported. Seven mothers were carefully selected for their positive attributes and potential for mothering.
Attendance was mandatory and missed sessions were taken as a signal that
the mother did not want custody of her child. This requirement elicited
anger in the mothers, creating a climate for them to examine their anger
in general. Community services were integrated into the work of the group
to make the women feel less deprived and isolated. Along with generalized
anger, the mothers were found to be fearful of authority, self-destructive,
and locked into abusive marriages. For many, the group became the family
they were lacking, and therapy helped to strengthen their assertiveness
and feelings of worth.

1465 Collins, Marilyn C. "Occupation: child abuser, a study of people
      finding careers in self-help group therapy." For a summary see:
      Diss Abstr Int 37A(7): 4646, January, 1977.

1466 Feinstein, Howard M.; Paul, Norman; Esmiol, Pattison. "Group
      therapy for mothers with infanticidal impulses." Am J Psychiatry
      120(9): 882-86, March, 1964. (4 References).

Reports the findings from the first eighty hours of group therapy with
six women at the Southard Clinic (Massachusetts Mental Health Center) in
Boston. Although the only criterion for selection to the group was the
mother's impulse to harm or kill her child, the women shared many common
characteristics in their backgrounds and psychological makeup. Shared
biographical characteristics were that all the women: (1) resented their
parents for not giving them enough attention as children; (2) had a violent or abusive parent; (3) felt hatred and rivalry toward men; and (4)
sought motherly men for husbands. Psychological characteristics were that
they: (1) felt aggressive feelings toward their children (especially

sons); (2) had many phobias; (3) were depressed; (4) had suicidal
impulses; and (5) were sometimes or always frigid. Group therapy helped
the women primarily by removing their sense of isolation, by providing
mutual support, and by offering alternative methods of adaptation.

1467   Husar, Linda K.   "Issues and case examples from a mothers' task
       group." In: National Symposium on Child Abuse, 5th, Boston, 1974.
       Collected papers. Denver, Colorado: The American Humane Associa-
       tion, Children's Division, 1976. 149-51. (0 References).
Studies the problems experienced with two members of a task group formed
by the Children's Protective Service, Boston. The purpose of the group
was to plan the agency's annual Christmas party and to give neglectful
and abusive mothers a therapeutic outlet. One mother dominated the group
with complaints about her family situation. During the party, she
threatened the children to whom she was giving free toys because they
refused to line up. Despite her disruptive behavior, she provided helpful leadership and made enthusiastic suggestions for the following year.
The other member was a very isolated woman with a history of mental disturbances. Because she had some artistic talent, social workers encouraged her to make the invitations, an activity in which she later engaged
her entire family. The success and companionship she found in the task
group motivated this mother to join the agency's remedial group.

1468   Justice, Rita, and Justice, Blair.   "TA work with child abuse."
       Trans Anal J 5(1): 38-41, January, 1975. (13 References).
The techniques of transactional analysis are successfully applied to the
treatment of ten couples charged with child abuse. The effect of the
program, as measured on Kiresuk's Goal Attainment Scale, was such that
eight of the couples regained custody of their children.

1469   McFerran, Jane.   "Parents' group in protective services." Children
       5(6): 223-28, November-December, 1958. (0 References).
Parent meetings can be helpful to neglectful parents. These meetings
provide a group setting for parents sharing similar problems and also
complement and reinforce the goals of the caseworker.

1470   Moffitt, Dorien M.   "Issues and case examples from an adolescent
       group." In: National Symposium on Child Abuse, 5th, Boston, 1974.
       Collected papers. Denver, Colorado: The American Humane Associa-
       tion, Children's Division, 1976. 140-44. (0 References).
Using specific cases, the procedures and dynamics of a therapy group for
adolescents are presented. All members were teenage girls from troubled
families. Group leaders helped the adolescents realize that anger and
other feelings can be verbalized rather than acted out. The members often
used the group leaders to set limits on their behavior or, in one case,
as protection from other group members. Because the group leaders alternated who they picked up and took home, each group member was able to
have some private, individual attention. Over the course of two years,
members progressed from angry, lonely adolescents to young girls who
possessed a higher self-esteem.

1471   O'Connell, Virginia R.   "Treatment issues in the development of a
       mothers' task force." In: National Symposium on Child Abuse, 5th,
       1974. Collected papers. Denver, Colorado: The American Humane
       Association, Children's Division, 1976. 145-48. (0 References).

Describes the purpose of a task group formed by Children's Protective Services, Boston. Ten abusive and neglectful mothers with little opportunity for social contact were invited to join a group responsible for planning the agency's annual Christmas party. Social workers felt that the task was not too intimidating and that it would give mothers a chance to use talents they could not use in their homes. Planning was organized in steps in order that mothers would have direction. Social workers provided constant, positive reinforcement to prevent members from having feelings of insecurity or failure. The group interaction allowed mothers to share problems and provide suggestions and support.

1472 Paulson, Morris J., and Chaleff, Anne. "Parents surrogate roles: a dynamic concept in understanding and treating abusive parents." J Clin Child Psychol 2(3): 38-40, Fall, 1973. (12 References).
A program of group psychotherapy for some sixty-one abuse prone parents is outlined. Since many abusive parents had been emotionally deprived as children, a therapeutic approach was tried which allowed them to experience the parental approval and support which they never knew. Older therapists acted as parent-surrogates, and the stable relationships that developed between the abusive parents and these surrogates led, in turn, to the development of better relations between the parents and their own children.

1473 Paulson, Morris J.; Savino, Anne B.; Chaleff, Anne B.; et al. "Parents of the battered child: a multidisciplinary group therapy approach to life-threatening behavior." Life-Threatening Behav 4(1): 18-31, Spring, 1974. (13 References).
Presents a case study of a three year group psychotherapy program with thirty-one child abusing families. The group was led by male and female co-therapists who came to be seen as parent surrogates by the parents. The group sessions provided acceptance, intimacy, insight, and direction to the families.

1474 Smith, R. C. "Society pushes 'monsters' like this into a corner . . . now experts are trying to draw out these battering parents." Todays Health 51(1): 57-62, 64, January, 1973. (0 References).
Examines the battering parent's problems, needs, and options for obtaining help in the community. Studies have shown that 90 percent of battering parents will respond to therapy and can be helped. Therapy must be aimed at overcoming the two immediate needs of most abusing parents, namely, bringing them out of isolation by reaching out to them with understanding and teaching them how to develop sound parenting practices. Several parents who had attended Denver's Families Anonymous program discuss their experiences and relate how the group therapy has helped them begin to make positive progress toward effective parenting.

2. PARENTS

a. General

1475 Caskey, Owen L., and Richardson, Ivanna. "Understanding and helping child-abusing parents." Elem Sch Guid Couns 9(3): 196-208, March, 1975. (30 References).

Discusses treatment for abusing parents that will meet their special
needs. In many cases parents have unrealistic expectations of their
children and make unrealistic demands on them. Many parents need the
mothering they did not receive as a child. Consequently, these parents
suffer from a lack of self confidence and isolation, for they do not find
that seeking help from family or friends is very productive. Treatment
programs for battering parents must meet these unique needs. Group
therapy techniques can help reduce the parents' anxieties in social situations and build their confidence in communicating with other individuals.
School-centered approaches are also needed for identifying abused children and abusing parents. Suggestions for implementing school programs
are provided.

1476 Hughes, Ronald C. "A clinic's parent-performance training program
      for child abusers." Hosp Community Psychiatry 25(12): 779-82,
      December, 1974. (1 Reference).
A parent performance training program, used alone or as an adjunct to
other forms of therapy, can be a means of teaching abusing parents effective techniques for dealing with their problems. A case is given of a
couple who abused their six-year-old daughter (who had been temporarily
removed from the home). The couple showed hostility toward the counselor,
and felt that they were not being clearly told what they had to do to
regain custody of their child. They were given a programmed text to read,
and agreed to take five tests on the material in the text. They were to
continue counseling appointments until they had passed all tests, and a
percentage of their counseling fees was to be returned to them if they
did 90 percent or better on the first trial of each of the five tests.
After each test, they were given feedback on the points they had missed,
and participated in a general discussion of the principles of childrearing relevant to the material. After completing the tests, they were
asked to select some undesirable behavior in one of their children, and
to change that behavior using the principles they had learned. A successful experience helped the parents to become less defensive and hostile
during counseling sessions. The training program was an effective means
of circumventing blame-placing, thereby freeing the couple to use therapy
productively.

1477 Kerr, W. C. "Lithium salts in the management of a child batterer."
      Med J Aust 2(11): 414-15, September, 1976. (3 References).
Presents a case history of a twenty-nine-year-old female with limited
intelligence who was prone to explosive rages and attacks on her children.
She served five years in prison after her son's death was connected to
physical maltreatment. The patient remarried and had another child. She
began to have fantasies about harming the child and was admitted to a
psychiatric in-patient unit where she was treated with lithium. The
treatment was successful in managing her aggressive behavior, and she
continued to take lithium for twelve months while her personality remained
stable.

1478 Polakow, Robert L., and Peabody, Dixie L. "Behavioral treatment of
      child abuse." Int J Offender Ther 19(1): 100-113, 1975. (8
      References).
Examines a successful approach to therapy in the case of a twenty-year-
old mother with abusive tendencies and her uncontrollable seven-year-old
son. The therapy was behavioral in nature, depended on assertiveness and
discrimination training, and was reinforced by contingency contracts

between mother and son. She would reward his achievement of behavioral changes which they had agreed upon; subsequently, a new goal would be set. The therapist also reinforced the mother's cooperation as each major step was passed. After forty-five weeks, the therapist withdrew. Follow-up at eighteen months found the son's behavior stabilized. The approach is recommended for other cases of child abuse.

1479   Rosenblatt, Seymour; Schaeffer, Donald; Rosenthal, Jesse S. "Effects of diphenylhydantoin on child-abusing parents: a pre-liminary report." Curr Ther Res 19(3): 332-36, March, 1976. (11 References).
Eleven women and two men suspected of physical assault on their children were seen in a series of sixteen weekly diagnostic sessions at Mount Sinai Hospital, New York City. Subjects were treated with either 200 mg. of diphenylhydantoin twice daily or an inert placebo for eight weeks, then crossed over on a random double blind basis while being evaluated weekly on one of two patient self-rating scales. The results showed that DPH significantly decreased anxiety, depression, and somatic symptoms in child abusing parents on a short-term basis. Attitudes toward children, aggressiveness, impulsiveness and hostility, however, remained uneffected.

1480   Rosten, Patricia. "Spare the rod and save the parent." McCalls 100(8): 35, August, 1973. (0 References).
Briefly describes a treatment program for battering parents at the National Center for Prevention of Child Abuse and Neglect founded by C. Henry Kempe. The treatment includes the assignment of a lay therapist to each family, the use of a self-help organization called Mothers Anony-mous, and a crisis nursery.

1481   Sanford, Donald A., and Tustin, Richard D. "Behavioral treatment of parental assault on a child." NZ Psychol 2(2): 76-82, October, 1973. (4 References).
Account of therapy which conditioned a young father to refrain from beat-ing his infant when she cried. Tolerance to loud sounds was gradually developed in the young man over a period of time.

1482   Sheridan, Mary D. "Neglectful mothers." Lancet 1(1959): 722-25, April 4, 1959. (1 Reference).
Presents a follow-up study of 100 neglectful mothers who were given spe-cial training in residential training homes. The stability and affection of a constant husband was found to be the most important factor in the successful rehabilitation of these women. Good physical and mental health of the mothers also seemed to be important factors. Many of the women came from maladjusted backgrounds and were pitifully ignorant of mother-ing and housekeeping skills. Prevention through early detection and education is sugges ted.

1483   West, Joy, and Mathers, James. "Inadequate mothers: letters to editor." Lancet 2(7894): 1451, December 14, 1974. (1 Refer-ence).
In response to a letter which advocated separation of the abused child from the mother, another alternative solution is offered. The mother's long-term inadequacy should be assessed with treatment beginning in a day hospital setting. Here, the mother can receive the mothering she needs, while staff and less disturbed mothers act as examples of healthy maternal behavior.

b. Psychotherapy

1484 Ackerman, Nathan W. Treating the troubled family. New York:
      Basic Books, 1966. 306p. (Bibliography).
The principles and practices of family psychotherapy are presented.
Treatment within the context of the family links the internal psychological problems with social and environmental considerations. Verbatim
accounts offer examples of the practical application of theoretical
formulations.

1485 Corbett, James T. "A psychiatrist reviews the battered child
      syndrome and mandatory reporting legislation." Northwest Med
      63(12): 920-22, December, 1964. (7 References).
Expresses concern that the focus of treatment for abuse is physical rather
than emotional. Emotional abuse occurs more subtly and is more psychologically damaging than physical abuse. Psychiatric help for the parent,
as well as medical help for the child, is essential. Psychological factors behind abuse are enumerated.

1486 D'Ambrosio, Richard. No language but a cry. Garden City, New York:
      Doubleday, 1970. 252p.
The simple story of a cruelly abused child who was rescued from pain,
fear, and mute silence by a young psychoanalyst and an undaunted order of
poor, but hardworking and inventive nuns. As an infant, Laura was nearly
burned alive by her alcoholic and psychotic parents. Reclaimed from
death, she spent the next three-and-one-half years of her young life in
the isolated and often unfriendly wards of city hospital. For seven
years the hunchbacked and distressedly scarred girl lived in a Catholic
institution for abandoned girls, where she never spoke or left her world
of protective fantasy.

Richard D'Ambrosio's story, in which he plays so critical a role, uncovers
sympathetically the horrors of Laura's past, while gently recounting the
psychoanalyst's growing involvement with his self-appointed, seemingly
hopeless, task of touching the heart and mind of a severely autistic
child. For months therapy consisted only of his monologues to the unresponsive adolescent labeled as retarded. But one day in the streets
of New York, she clung to him for protection and a bond of trust between
the two began. Many long months of play therapy, in which D'Ambrosio alone
participated, resulted in Laura's finally showing an interest in the
activities of the dolls. Through constructive fantasy, she recreated a
vital but absent part of her childhood: a warm and loving home life.
Risking all the progress they had achieved, D'Ambrosio manipulated the
dolls to reenact the frightening details of Laura's infancy--a child
battered by its parents; in protest Laura screamed her first words, "No!
No! No!"

As Laura gained control over words and language she reached out with
greater confidence to the nuns and the other children. Struggling against
failure, she earned a high school diploma and then met her most treasured
dream: the desire to be a baby nurse. Laura underwent four operations
to correct her deformities, operations performed gratis by surgeons
impressed with her courage and persuaded by the nuns' resoluteness. Despite what may have been permanent setbacks, including confrontations with
her still unbalanced and traitorous parents, Laura fought off the horrors
and uncertainties of her past and pressed forward. One day when she was
eighteen, pretty, and attired as a nurse, she left D'Ambrosio and the

shelter of the institution and began the new experience of life in the world.

1487 David, Charles A. "The use of the confrontation technique in the battered child syndrome." Am J Psychother 28(4): 543-52, October, 1974. (13 References).

A case history of a battering mother, outlining the dynamics of her psychopathology, and the goals of treatment are presented. The use of confrontation techniques as an effective means of helping the patient reestablish control over aggressive impulses is illustrated. The therapist tells the patient that he wants her to stop punishing her child no matter what the provocation. He, thereby, becomes a source of external control upon which she can rely, and provides a stimulus for the emergence of the patient's transference feelings which can then be worked through.

1488 Ezrine, Edwin, and Schiff, Matthew. "The pedodondist as adjunctive psychotherapist: report of a case." J Dent Child 42(3): 194-96, May-June, 1975. (6 References).

Documents a case study of an emotionally and dentally neglected sixteen-year-old girl. Due to concurrent psychiatric and dental treatment, the girl's appearance, self-concept, and oral hygiene improved. The dentist assumed the role of a father figure: he behaved consistently, addressed her directly, and supported her. The neglected child realized she was responsible for her own physical and mental development and should no longer blame her parents for their neglect.

1489 Fraiberg, Selma; Adelson, Edna; Shapiro, Vivian. "Ghosts in the nursery: a psychoanalytic approach to the problems of impaired infant-mother relationships." J Am Acad Child Psychiatry 14(3): 387-421, Summer, 1975. (1 Reference).

Two case histories of mothers who neglected and abused their infants are presented. The mothers had themselves been abused or rejected as children and the remembrances of their pasts had impaired the development of a close relationship with their own infants. The psychotherapeutic treatment of the two women involved helping them to reexperience the pain of their own childhoods so that they could identify with the injured child rather than with the abusive parents or aggressor. Once this identification had been made, the mothers were able to establish a nurturant relationship with their infants.

1490 Francis, H. W. S. "Child health -- points of concern." Public Health 81(5): 245-51, July, 1967. (11 References).

Encourages a shifting of emphasis from psychotherapy to preventive psychiatry for treating children with behavioral disorders. A brief discussion of child neglect, the important role of the physician in diagnosis, and the problems of registering and maintaining records of handicapped children is included.

1491 Fries, Charles T. "Changes in personality factors of child abusers following psychotherapy." For a summary see: Diss Abstr Int 36A(3): 1430, September, 1975.

1492 Gilbert, Marie T. "Behavioral approach to the treatment of child abuse." Nurs Times 72(4): 140-43, January 29, 1976. (6 References).

Presents a case history of a thirty-seven-year-old woman with a strong
aversion to her first child. The woman had a history of abusing the
child and had previously been hospitalized for depression. Therapy involved a behavioral approach in which the woman, the child, and a
therapist met together for treatment sessions. During the sessions, the
woman would imitate various maternal behaviors of the therapist's toward
the child. Later, the mother was placed on a self-directed and maintained
program in which she would set goals for herself such as reading, con-
versing, or playing with her daughter for a prescribed period of time.
She would record the number, length, and kind of parenting behavior she
had engaged in throughout the week, as well as the amount of enjoyment
she had experienced during each activity. The patient learned to enjoy
caring for her daughter and continued to feel more confident in her
mothering abilities. Changes in behavior often precede changes in
attitude and behavioral therapy for the abusive parent can be successful.

1493   Green, Arthur H. "A psychodynamic approach to the study and treat-
       ment of child-abusing parents." J Am Acad Child Psychiatry 15(3):
       414-29, Summer, 1976. (17 References).
In a study of the psychodynamics of child abuse, sixty mothers of abused
children were compared with thirty neglecting mothers and thirty normal
controls. A structured interview was conducted with each mother, and this
data was augmented by agency records of protective caseworkers and probation officers. Over 10 percent of the abusing mothers (and children)
participated in psychotherapy. It was found that most abusive families
had three factors in common: (1) environmental stress; (2) specific
abuse prone personality characteristics of the parents; and (3) specific
abuse provoking characteristics of the child. Environmental stress often
resulted from a breakdown in the external arrangements for child care,
physical or emotional illness of a parent, or pregnancy. Abuse prone
characteristics of the parents included impaired impulse control, poor
self-concept, a tendency to project undesirable traits onto the child,
and a tendency to turn to the child for gratification of dependency
needs. Abuse provoking characteristics of the child included physical,
emotional, intellectual, or behavioral defects which increased the burden
of caring for the child, thereby provoking parental anger, guilt, and
frustration. Treatment of the child abusing parent must be aimed at
modifying these three factors through the use of multidisciplinary
approaches and comprehensive services.

1494   In, Peter A., and McDermott, John F., Jr. "The treatment of child
       abuse: play therapy with a 4-year-old child." J Am Acad Child
       Psychiatry 15(3): 430-40, Summer, 1976. (7 References).
Focuses on a case study of an abused girl who was consequently taken from
her mother and placed in a foster home. While living with the foster
parents, the girl developed severely regressive behavior patterns and was
hospitalized for a month in a children's psychiatric treatment program.
With the intent of exploring and clarifying her past and dealing with
present issues distressful to the child, a house complete with furniture
and dolls and a pair of telephones were used in play therapy. In therapy,
the child's life experiences, including the incident of abuse, were recreated so that she could resolve her ambivalent feelings, forgive the
abusing relatives, and deal with anxiety related to her separation from
her natural mother. Resolution of these issues prevents the crystaliza-
tion of a disturbed personality structure. Removal of a child from the

abusing situation to a foster home does not always alleviate the child's psychological problems resulting from the abuse. Psychotherapy is often indicated.

1495   Kreindler, Simon. "Psychiatric treatment for the abusing parent
        and the abused child: some problems and possible solutions." Can
        Psychiatr Assoc J 21(5): 275-80, August, 1976. (14 References).
Outlines the psychological and behavioral manifestations of the abusing parent and the abused child and discusses selected themes that emerge in the psychotherapeutic treatment process. Abusing parents have a high expectation for the infant's performance, a disregard for the infant's own needs, and a lack of a sense of confidence and personal identity. Some common forms of psychopathology presented in abused children include developmental delays which are frequently functional in nature, aggressive behavior, and chronic anxiety and/or depression. If parents in treatment can become involved in a psychotherapeutic relationship, learn to reach out for help in times of crisis, acquire a more realistic view of the child's needs and capacities, and develop a better self-concept, their prognosis is good. If an abused child can be provided a loving environment--either by placement in a foster home or in an improved family situation--his/her prognosis is also good. The earlier the abused child is recognized and helped, the better are his/her chances for normal development. It is emphasized that psychotherapy is not realistically available to most families involved with child abuse and that the treatments that are offered (such as self-help groups and child protective services) are often inadequate.

1496   Lansky, Shirley B., and Erickson, Harold M., Jr. "Prevention of
        child murder: a case report." J Am Acad Child Psychiatry 13(14):
        691-98, Autumn, 1974. (9 References).
Child murder can be an expression of one person's attempt to salvage a failing marriage or punish an unloving spouse. This "Medea complex" can be treated and cured through psychotherapy, as this case study indicates, so that both the child's life and the parent's marriage can be saved.

1497   Ounsted, Christopher; Oppenheimer, Rhoda; Linsday, Janet. "Aspects
        of bonding failure: the psychopathology and psychotherapeutic
        treatment of families of battered children." Dev Med Child Neurol
        16(4): 447-56, August, 1974. (7 References).
Two systems of psychotherapeutic treatment aimed at restoring the parent-child bond are considered. Parents known to have battered their children can receive care in an in-patient facility consisting of a separate mothers' house and children's hospital. The mothers enjoy a peaceful environment and a regular routine while the children encounter affection and adults who behave predictably. In time, the family is able to build such an open environment in its own home. The second, or out-patient service, caters to potentially abusing parents. A group of mothers meet with a social worker in a home while a toddlers' play group is supervised in an adjoining room. Mutual support and professional guidance help everyone to cope with potential crisis situations.

1498   Pilisuk, Marc. "Mental health mystification and social control."
        Am J Orthopsychiatry 45(3): 414-19, April, 1975. (5 References).
Criticizes the use of jargon by mental health professionals. Mystifying language diverts attention from the crucial human needs the professionals so often fail to meet.

1499 Rhodes, Robert J., and Levinson, Martin. "Sexual deviancy. Treat-
      ment: a case study of a child molester." J Kans Med Soc 78(3):
      122-24, March, 1977. (1 Reference).
Presents a successful course of treatment for a child molester. A twenty-
eight-year-old man with a history of sexually molesting pre-adolescent
girls was concurrently provided aversive conditioning therapy and psychotherapy. Follow-up contacts up to a year after treatment indicated that
the man was functioning satisfactorily, without recurrence of sexually
deviant behavior.

1500 Shenken, L. "A child is being beaten." Aust NZ J Psychiatry 7(4):
      243-48, December, 1973. (3 References).
Psychotherapy of a patient with a child beating fantasy is presented.
Freud's paper entitled "A Child is Being Beaten," which concludes that
the beating fantasy is a function of regression to the pre-Oedipal, anal-
sadistic phase of libido development, provides the basis of discussion.

1501 Silverman, M. A., and Wolfson, E. "Early intervention and social
      class: diagnosis and treatment of preschool children in a day care
      center." J Am Acad Child Psychiatry 10(1-4): 608-18, 1971. (14
      References).
Individual psychotherapy has not been made available to the poor, largely
because of the socioeconomic and cultural gaps existing between psychiatrists and social scientists on the one hand and poor people on the other.
It is generally, and falsely, assumed that psychotherapy on an individual
basis would not be effective among the poor. Yet, observation of poor
children brought to a day care center indicated psychological problems
which could be remedied only through intensive therapy.

1502 Steele, Brandt F. "Working with abusive parents: a psychiatrist's
      view." Child Today 4(3): 3-5, 44, May-June, 1975. (0 References).
When treating abusive parents, the psychiatrist must come to grips with
his own feelings of horror and anger at the parents. The best way to do
this is to understand that abusive parents are themselves likely to have
been abused as children. Abusive parents share some common characteristics, including immaturity, dependency, low self-esteem, social isolation,
misperceptions of the infant, and an inability to emphathize with and
respond to the infant's needs. The type of treatment for abusive parents
must be matched closely to the individual. Different successful approaches
have included psychotherapy with transference, group and family therapy,
education in proper parenting techniques, or combinations of these methodologies. Ten percent of abusive parents have a severe psychiatric disorder such as schizophrenia, drug addiction, or incapacitating neurosis
or depression, which require more intensive, prolonged psychiatric care.

1503 Szasz, Thomas S. "Justice and psychiatry." Atlantic 222(4):
      127-30, October, 1968. (0 References).
The Battered Child, edited by Ray E. Helfer and C. Henry Kempe, is comprehensively reviewed. Objection is raised to the book's support of enforced
psychiatric treatment of battering parents which constitutes a denial of
a person's right to manage his own life. The book's contention that a
therapeutic, rather than a courtroom approach, is best for the child also
undermines the parent's right to a judgment by law.

c. Parents Anonymous

1504 Barnhart, Carol, ed. Eight Parents Anonymous members tell their
      stories. Detroit, Michigan: Parents Anonymous of Michigan, 1975.
      52p. (1 Reference).
Eight women who had been child abusers talk about their own unpleasant
childhood experiences, their feelings of inadequacy and self-hatred, and
their eventual turn to Parents Anonymous (PA) for help. All the women
talk of being beaten or abused by their own parents and, in some cases,
their spouses. The parents are unanimous in their appraisal of PA as a
worthwhile program, which changed their lives by teaching them new ways
to cope with problems and by offering them other outlets for their hostile
feelings.

1505 Cantoni, Lucile. The first two years: Parents Anonymous of
      Michigan. Detroit, Michigan: Parents Anonymous, 1974. 34p. (2
      References).
Comprehensively describes the history and role of the Parents Anonymous
(PA) Chapter established in Detroit in 1972. Characteristics of parents
who need the types of services PA offers are discussed, as are the procedures established by the group for handling child abuse or potential
abuse cases. The organization emphasizes acceptance, caring, understanding, and involvement among its members. In addition to handling crisis
calls, PA provides constructive advice and group counseling, offers
social activities, child care helpers, and educational information to its
members. The group differs from public social service or legal assistance
in that PA emphasizes voluntary participation and self-help for parents,
rather than protection for the child. Referrals to community resources
are given by Parents Anonymous to its members who seek individual psychiatric counseling or help for their children.

1506 Daniel, Glenda. "The child-abusers: Parents Anonymous organiza-
      tion." PTA Mag 68(1): 32-35, September, 1973. (2 References).
Parents Anonymous (PA) is a unique organization for parents who abuse
their children and who find comfort in meeting in small groups to discuss
their problems. It was started by a parent, together with a social
worker, and grew rapidly into a productive therapeutic force on a nationwide scale. Parents Anonymous stresses that assistance should be provided
to increase the parent's self-image, self-control, and self-understanding,
rather than to induce guilt by means of punitive action. Parents Anonymous members face all forms of abuse and neglect from physical to sexual
and emotional. An example illustrating how one chapter of PA learned to
cope with these problems is provided. The success of PA is well documented. The majority of those parents who seek help actually do experience an improvement in family life.

1507 "Help for child beaters." Newsweek 80(4): 66, 69, July 24, 1972.
      (0 References).
Explores the incidence of child abuse, characteristics of abusing parents,
and successful approaches to dealing with such parents. Abusing parents
were often reared in a hostile environment and have a deep suspicion of
authority. Novel approaches to helping the abusing parents include the
use of parents aides and self-help organizations such as Mothers Anonymous.

1508   Johnson, R. S. "The child-beaters: sick, but curable." <u>Natl Obs</u>
       1, March 24, 1973. (0 References).
Summarizes the success Parents Anonymous (PA) has achieved in dealing with
abuse prone parents. Important elements in this success are the fact that
most abusive parents were emotionally deprived themselves and craved
acceptance, a need which PA satisfies; the feelings of communality; the
involvement of the spouse; and the parent's opportunity to confront the
problem without shame and learn from everyone else's experience and mistakes.

1509   Parents Anonymous. <u>Chapter development manual</u>. Redondo Beach,
       California: Parents Anonymous, 1974. 18p.
Offers complete and constructive advice about how to establish a new
Parents Anonymous (PA) chapter. The procedures are outlined step-by-step
as follows: (1) read the manual; (2) locate a meeting site; (3) find a
sponsor; (4) recruit volunteer workers; (5) get a contact telephone number; (6) set up a meeting schedule; (7) begin to publicize; and (8) hold
the first meeting. Suggestions for accomplishing each step successfully
are made. PA chapters can be supported by state, county, and private
agencies, but they are excluded from initiating them. This is to avoid
any direct association between PA and the negative antiagency attitudes
common among troubled parents. Sample community information letters,
newspaper ads, radio spots, and want ads for volunteers are provided.

1510   ————. <u>Parents Anonymous chairperson-sponsor manual</u>. Redondo
       Beach, California: Parents Anonymous, 1975. 47p.
This manual describes the activities and experiences of Parents Anonymous
(PA), with particular attention to the chairperson-sponsor relationship.

1511   ————. <u>Procedures and concepts manual</u>. Redondo Beach, Cali-
       fornia: Parents Anonymous, 1972. 55p.
A handbook to assist Parents Anonymous groups to run sessions and organize
activities. Parents Anonymous (PA) is a self-help organization of parents who want help in curbing the abuse they inflict upon their children.
Redondo Beach, California is the site of the national office, which acts
to distribute information, raise money, and assist local chapters to
organize. PA groups meet routinely to discuss openly their frustrations
and difficulties and to receive help from one another. A professional
serves as an advisor but does not interfere unless a problem emerges that
the parents themselves cannot handle.

1512   ————. <u>Supplement to procedures and concepts manual</u>. <u>New
       chapters manual</u>. Redondo Beach, California: Parents Anonymous,
       1972. 8p. (Bibliography).
Offers data on aspects of organizing a chapter of Parents Anonymous.
Selecting a sponsor, publicity, and the timing and length of meetings
are discussed.

1513   "Parents Anonymous and child abuse." <u>Intellect</u> 103(2360): 76-77,
       November, 1974. (0 References).
A panel session, comprising part of a two week intensive workshop in the
Department of Child Development and Family Life at Purdue University,
aims to educate teachers and interested parents about child abuse. The
panel, consisting of a judge, a pediatrician, a therapist, and members of
Parents Anonymous, a self-help group for child abusers, is described as
attempting to de-mythologize the problem of abuse. It is emphasized that

battering parents are not "monsters" and are generally not psychotic, although they have significant difficulties with parenting, and that most adults are vulnerable to becoming child abusers themselves. On-going education for parents is seen as essential to prevention of the problem.

1514 Reed, Judith. "Working with abusive parents: a parent's view." Child Today 4(3): 6-9, May-June, 1975. (1 Reference).
Presents an interview with Jolly K., founder of Parents Anonymous (PA), Inc. Topics of discussion include the steps to be taken when founding a PA chapter, the characteristics of the membership, an account of what happens at meetings, and a review of some of the problems encountered in the operation of PA. Jolly K. states that men in PA make up too small a percentage of the groups and that she would like to see the "passive" parent attend PA meetings as well as the recognized abusive parent.

1515 Zauner, Phyllis. "Mothers Anonymous: the last resort." McCalls 99(1): 57, January, 1972. (0 References).
Describes the development and effects of Mothers Anonymous, a preventive support group for abusing mothers. A mother unable to obtain professional help with her own abuse problem eventually found treatment and subsequently developed Mothers Anonymous. Abusing mothers, often beaten themselves as children, continue this cycle. The group, however, focuses on stopping the immediate abusive behavior rather than bemoaning the parent's neglected childhood. Prevention can take the form of a phone call or even of swapping children at times of stress.

3. CHILDREN

1516 Call, Justin D. "Helping infants cope with change." Early Child Dev Care 3(3): 229-48, January, 1974.
Offers suggestions on how teachers, students, and child care workers can help infants cope with changes occurring with adoption and foster care.

1517 Gyorgy, Paul, and Burgess, Anne. Protecting the pre-school child. Philadelphia: J. B. Lippincott, 1965. 251p. (Bibliography).
Represents a collection of articles about aspects of the preschool child by various professionals ranging from nutritionists to social workers.

1518 Martin, Harold P., ed. The abused child: a multidisciplinary approach to developmental issues and treatment. Cambridge, Massachusetts: Ballinger, 1976. 304p. (Bibliography).
An examination of the psychological, developmental, and neurological wounds suffered by a child within an abusive home environment, followed by suggestions for treatment which would heal wounds within non-threatening and therapeutic environments. From the abused child's perspective, the home environment is always hostile and unpredictable. Laughter is not heard and affection is not shown. The child is under stress to perform tasks which exceed his age abilities and to meet his parents' personal needs. The child who comes from such an environment will often be withdrawn, passive, and hypervigilant. As he has not yet learned to play like most children, he displays little spontaneity or enjoyment of life.

Victims of neglect suffer the most serious neurologic impairment, due to lack of nourishment, but abused children may also exhibit the following symptoms of neurologic dysfunction: (1) serious abnormalities such as paresis; (2) deficiencies in tactile and kinesthetic perception; and (3) lack of motor coordination or delays in speech and language. In a chapter on learning and intelligence, the authors cite several factors which can handicap a child's natural development: (1) an unpredictable, non-nurturing world; (2) restriction of opportunities for learning; (3) inadequate stimulation and support, such as not being talked to or read to; and (4) a focus of the child's energies on survival.

Four distinct treatment plans for abused children and their families are discussed, ranging from the traditional foster placement to the novel residential family therapy center. Foster care is valuable on a short-term, crisis basis, yet often fails to supply the child with what he needs most: psychological parenting. Foster care can be made more therapeutic through improved family screening; a sharing of information between physician, therapist, and foster parents; and encouragement of visiting and communication between the biologic parents, the foster parents, and the child.

A young child's developmental deficiencies can most effectively be treated in a preschool for abused children which offers regular respite for the parents without removing the child from his home. In the preschool the child finds opportunities for socialization, while he is given remedial help and encouraged to grow and perform at his own pace. Crisis nurseries should be made available on a twenty-four-hour basis to parents under stress. Administrative procedures for admission should be minimized so as to encourage parents to take advantage of the facility.

Residential family therapy centers provide extensive, long-term help for abusive families. The center contains separate parent and child treatment units, with certain areas such as the dining room and recreation room shared in common by all families undergoing treatment. Parents receive individual psychotherapy and marital counseling in addition to participating in an evening therapy group for all patients. In the child care unit the children enjoy a calm and predictable environment. Staff workers meet all the children's needs at first, but gradually they instruct the parents in the mastery of each child care routine. Treatment aims at improving the bond between parent and child and at encouraging both the individual parent and child in recognizing his self-worth.

1519   Miller, Merle K., and Fay, Henry J. "Emergency child care service: the evaluation of a project." Child Welfare 48(8): 496-99, October, 1969. (7 References).
Evaluates an emergency child care service formed in Springfield, Massachusetts. The need for such a service was borne out by both the number and severity of requests made during the first year of operation. The services covered those normally provided by existing agencies during their working hours. More direct intervention was necessary than had been anticipated, and the increased use of homemakers remained an unresolved issue for the planning committee. The presence of a caseworker at the place of the emergency, however, was found calming for the children and helpful in beginning relationships with the families involved. Most requests for help came from the police; the lack of expected calls from agencies and individuals was attributed to inadequate publicity.

4. FAMILY THERAPY

1520   Bolton, F. G., Jr. A second look at the impact of family therapy in the on-going treatment of the potentially abusive and maltreat-

ing family. Phoenix, Arizona: Arizona Community Development for
Abuse and Neglect, 1977. 14p. (26 References).
Emphasizes that child abuse is a dysfunction of the entire family and
that, therefore, the form of treatment indicated is family therapy. After
an incident of child abuse has occurred, families are often unsuccessful
in aftercare treatment because: (1) they lack an understanding of the
problem; (2) they have unrealistic expectations of the abusing parent;
and (3) they lack an overall ability to communicate with each other. The
family therapist can support the family in their efforts to accomplish
realistic goals. He/she can also teach the family new communication
skills so that they can begin to deal with their problems more honestly
and effectively.

1521 Bottom, Wayne D. "The sociological phenomenon of child abuse."
Ala J Med Sci 14(2): 215-21, April, 1977. (18 References).
Suggests a sociological model for treating both abused children and abusing parents. The ultimate goal of the program, entitled PACT (Parents
and Children Together), is to preserve the family unit. Dissolving the
family is regarded as counterproductive, for it was, in many cases, a
similar severance from intimate personal relationships in the parents'
past that contributed to the development of behavior problems. The project's four major provisions for action are the following: (1) emergency
relief; (2) therapeutic relief, consisting of long-term mothering assistance and of self-help group meetings; (3) family rehabilitation and
education; and (4) public service activities to reorient the family into
the community.

1522 Colman, Wendy. "Occupational therapy and child abuse." Am J Occup
Ther 29(7): 412-17, August, 1975. (3 References).
Presents the role of occupational therapy in a community-based research
and demonstration project used to treat abusive parents and their children. Therapy was aimed at improving several problems common to abusive
parents, including social isolation, a weak ego structure, an inability
to set priorities, and a failure to perceive one's abilities and limitations accurately. Occupational therapy consisted of the following components: (1) a social skills group in which parents could learn to interact with others in an informal environment; (2) craft projects which each
parent would select and complete independently; (3) individual therapy
sessions in which the occupational therapist would meet with the parent
to discuss his/her progress; and (4) creative movement sessions in which
each parent could explore his/her own body space and its relationship to
the immediate environment. Experience with twenty-five abusive families
over a two year period demonstrates that occupational therapy can be
effective in helping abusive parents to develop a greater sense of control over his/her environment.

1523 Daniel, Jessica H., and Hyde, James N., Jr. "Working with high-
risk families." Child Today 4(6): 23-25, 36, November-December,
1975. (0 References).
Describes a dual program Family Development Study conducted over a two
year period at Children's Hospital Medical Center, Boston, Massachusetts.
Two non-traditional models of family intervention--the Parent Education
Program (PEP) and Family Advocacy--were instituted on a trial basis to
work with high risk families, with the ultimate aim of preventing abuse
and neglect of children in those families. Both programs rested on the
recognition that high risk families are often characterized by similar

stress factors: unemployment or underemployment, low parental self-esteem, unrealistic parental expectations for children, a lack of ability to effect change in the present by using available resources or a lack of knowledge of those resources and, hence, an intense feeling of isolation. PEP attempted to counteract these tensions by involving a group of twenty mothers in therapeutic teaching sessions designed to help each mother to set and achieve attainable goals apart from her mothering responsibilities and to better interact with and care for her children. Family Advocacy was designed to prepare an unprofessional member of the community, an "advocate," to work with families as a facilitator in problem-solving. The advocate might work toward solving a particular problem, such as securing legal assistance for the family, and in so doing, would familiarize that family with his methods of problem-solving and his awareness of helpful resources. Ultimately, a family would learn to solve many of its own problems, and would, thereby, function with a sense of control and higher self-esteem in a stressful environment. It was concluded after their pilot trials that both the PEP and Family Advocacy programs were promising options for expanding treatment with high risk families.

1524 Goldstein, Harriet. "Providing services to children in their own homes: an approach that can reduce foster placement." Child Today 2(4): 2-7, July-August, 1973. (2 References).
Considers the family therapy program used by the Association for Jewish Children in Philadelphia as an alternative to placement. Treatment of the parents involves "parenting" them while professionals help children understand and accept their parents. Services for children include specialized education, extra-curricular activities, psychotherapy, twenty-four-hour telephone service, and big brother and sister volunteers. Based on physical, psychological, and social evaluations, parents are rated on a continuum from adequate to inadequate, and from this, officials decide which children remain in the home and which go into placement. Statistics show that 51 percent of the families had incomes of less than $5,000 a year and most receive under $10,000. The families were plagued by the absence of at least one parent through separation, desertion, or death. Less than one-third of the parents had periods of mental illness; many of the school age children had learning difficulties. Two case histories illustrate some success with the program, but a good prognosis for most families depends on long-term treatment.

1525 Gordon, Bianca. "Battering: unfortunate backlash: letter to editor." Br Med J 2(5916): 443, May 25, 1974. (0 References).
The letter of J. W. Woodward (March 9, 1974, p. 452), cautioning against hasty investigations of parents suspected of child abuse, is endorsed. The author warns that premature or unskilled interventions into already disturbed family systems can jeopardize the goal of improving the parent-child relationship. Child abuse should not be treated as an isolated problem, but should be seen in connection with the complex web of problems of which it is a part.

1526 Halliwell, R. "Time limited work with a family at point of being prosecuted for child neglect." Case Conf 15(9): 343-48, 1968. (0 References).
Examines a case history which demonstrates the successful rehabilitation of a poor family by the British child abuse prevention team of the Family Service Unit. The success of the unit apparently stems from their rather

non-traditional approach to the problem: unit members maintain active contact with both parents, and continue these relationships well after the family situation has begun to improve, to insure the stability of the rehabilitation.

1527 Helfer, Ray E. "A plan for protection: the child abuse center."
     Child Welfare 49(9): 486-94, November, 1970. (2 References).
Outlines a systematic, family-oriented approach to the treatment of child abuse. While the optimum solution to the problem of abuse would be to cure the parent's psychiatric and personality disorders, the most realistic approach is to make the home safe for the child so that the family unit can be preserved.

Abusive parents were often the victims of inadequate mothering as children. They are unable to form close relationships with other adults or to ask for assistance when problems arise. Therefore, they must look toward their child for the satisfaction of all their needs. If the child cannot fulfill these parental demands, abuse is likely to occur.

When a physician suspects that abuse has occurred, the child should be hospitalized for diagnostic purposes. During this time, the physician should implement a treatment plan by contacting the social welfare agency. The child may have to be temporarily separated from the home while a meaningful therapeutic relationship between the parent and a parent aide is being established. The parent aides assist the abusive parents in breaking down the wall of social isolation which surrounds them. When the parents are able to ask for and accept help from others (usually between three and six months after initial contact with the parent aide), the home becomes safer for the child because the parents no longer must depend on him/her to meet their needs or solve their problems. The child is then returned home. The steps toward the development of a community center for the study and care of abused children and their families is briefly outlined.

1528 Herre, Ernest A. "Aggressive casework in a protective service
     unit." Soc Casework 46(6): 358-62, June, 1965. (0 References).
Assesses the work done by the Protective Services Unit in Milwaukee. The organization has created two major programs: the first, the coordination of protective services for children and the second, a program of family casework to prevent the disintegration of troubled families. Under the aegis of protective services, the unit provides emergency services, long-term treatment, and consultation. The program of family casework involves intensive and aggressive sessions in the family home.

1529 Isaacs, Susanna. "Physical ill-treatment of children." Lancet
     1(7532): 37-39, January 6, 1968. (3 References).
Twenty-two families in which a child was abused were treated in a child psychiatry department. Several case descriptions illustrate the nature of the psychopathology involved, its symptoms, and methods of treatment. In all but two of the cases, future abuse was prevented. It is emphasized that traditional psychotherapy is inadequate and that the severity of abuse-related problems requires frequent contact, home visits, and emergency availability from the psychiatric workers involved. It is essential that the therapist maintain a supportive rather than an accusing stance toward the parents.

1530 Kinney, Jill McCleave; Madsen, Barbara; Fleming, Thomas; et al.
      "Homebuilders: keeping families together." J Consult Clin Psychol
      45(4): 667-73, August, 1977. (10 References).
Describes a program called Homebuilders in Tacoma, Washington, which aims
at the prevention of family disintegration. Trained therapists are available at all times to families which are in such a critical state that the
removal of one or more members seems inevitable. Homebuilders therapists
remain with the family for up to six weeks, to ease the immediate crisis
and to teach family members more effective methods of dealing with their
problems and with each other. The usual approach involves talking to each
family member until the full extent of the family's trouble is known, and
then demonstrating, through role playing, how members might communicate
their feelings to one another. Techniques used include assertiveness
training, fair fight methods, and behavior modification. Preliminary results are favorable: outside placement was prevented for 97 percent of
the service's clients, at a savings to the public of over $2,300 per
client.

1531 Mathers, James. "Experts and child abuse: letter to editor." Br
      Med J 4(5937): 163, October 19, 1974. (0 References).
It is recommended that battered babies and their mothers be cared for
together in the same hospital unit in order to strengthen the mother-child
bond and insure the emotional health of the child.

1532 ————. "Inadequate mothers: letter to editor." Lancet 2(7894):
      1451, December 14, 1974. (0 References).
Recommends that mother and child be shown love and care in mutual in-
patient treatment.

1533 Newberger, Eli H., and Hyde, James N., Jr. "Child abuse: princi-
      ples and implications of current pediatric practice." Pediatr Clin
      North Am 22(3): 695-715, August, 1975. (48 References).
Emphasizes the importance of determining a family's capacity to protect
its child when diagnosing and treating child abuse and neglect. Four case
histories illustrate various unique problems within the complex spectrum
of abuse and neglect and the treatment measures employed in each situation.
Improvements in services to the abused and their families depend on improvements in the accuracy of incidence statistics. Included is an overview of current state reporting laws and a statement concerning the
effects of these laws on medical practice and social policy. Fourteen
characteristics of a model system for the management of child abuse are
outlined.

1534 Ounsted, Christopher; Oppenheimer, Rhoda; Lindsay, Janet. "The
      psychopathology and psychotherapy of the families: aspects of
      bonding failure." In: Franklin, Alfred White, ed. Concerning
      child abuse. New York: Churchill Livingstone, 1975. 30-40.
      (0 References).
Analyzes two systems of treatment for the abused child and his family--
in-patient and out-patient therapy. Approximately eighty-six families
in which abuse had occurred were admitted to the Park-Hospital Service
for Children. Here the mother and her children were provided with food,
warmth, privacy, tranquility, an undemanding routine, and the attentive
care of large varieties of mature adults. In this environment, the
parents were able to develop an open relationship with other adults, and
to relinquish their fantasies about their children and themselves. Dur-

ing the second week of treatment, the parents were often ready to admit
that they abused their child and showed hope for growth and change. The
child was treated for physical injuries and nutritional deficits, as well
as for behavioral defenses such as "frozen watchfulness." In-patient
treatment resulted in a notable improvement in intrafamilial dynamics in
most cases.

Out-patient treatment of twenty-four families consisted of individual
therapy instituted for the parents and child by the social worker in their
own home. The mothers were also introduced into a group of parents with
similar problems, and the child was introduced into a toddler's group.
The mothers were encouraged to telephone the social worker whenever a
crisis arose. The support which the parents received from out-patient
treatment helped them to cope with their problems and with their children
more effectively. Over a two year period, no battering occurred in any
of the families.

1535 "Outreach program helps eliminate child abuse." Hospitals 50(15):
        37-38, August 1, 1976. (0 References).
The objective of the outreach program at Presbyterian-University of
Pennsylvania Medical Center is to replace the lack of self-confidence and
deficient childrearing skills with positive attitudes and skills. Each
case is handled by a multidisciplinary team and begins with hospitalization of the child while the parents are assessed for child management
abilities. After discharge, the family health worker assesses the home
environment and recommends ways to correct negative behavior patterns in
the child and the parent. Out of a total of 487 children in 142 families,
only eight children in three families were untreatable and required foster
home placement.

1536 Page, Miriam O. "Cohesion, dignity, and hope for multiproblem
        families." Children 8(2): 63-68, March-April, 1961. (1 Refer-
        ence).
Reports on a demonstration project set up in Vermont to aid families suffering from economic deprivation, poor health, marital problems, or
alcoholism and whose children are not having their physical and emotional
needs fulfilled. The system of family referrals to the project differed
from the Vermont Department of Social Welfare's past procedures in that
complaints were filed before the family situation had reached the stage
where parents requested the removal of a child from the home. Methods
employed in the project included an emphasis on strengthening the role
of the problem family in community affairs, through participation in the
activities of neighborhood clubs. The project was successful and the
community, as well as the families themselves, profited from increased
involvement and cohesiveness.

1537 Paget, Norman W. "Involving protective service clients." In:
        The American Humane Association, Children's Division. Family life
        education and protection services. Denver, Colorado: The American
        Humane Association, Children's Division, 1966. 1-17. (17 Refer-
        ences).
Describes several family life education programs developed for protective
service clientele and for court ordered participants. The programs were
organized around the central idea that the function of family life is to
meet the emotional needs of its members. One such program in the United
Kingdom was based on a residential treatment plan for the multiproblem
family. A range of services were provided, including family life educa-

tion programs geared toward establishing the self-reliance of the family. A parent-education pilot program centered on the voluntary participation of parents who were currently protective service clients. Parents were divided into categories based on similarities between them and were assumed to have already established a relationship with a caseworker. They met to discuss ways of handling household problems, and especially children. Upon completion of the program, parents described an increased ability to communicate with their children and additional comfort with the parental role. A court agency parent education program followed as a result of the pilot program's success. Although court ordered partici-pation involves the problem of motivation, it does reach a population which needs parent education and which generally is not aware of services available to them. The guaranteed participation of the father is espe-cially important. These pilot programs have definitely indicated the need for family life education as an integral part of protective services.

1538   Pavenstedt, E. "An intervention program for infants from high risk homes." <u>Am J Public Health</u> 63(5): 393-95, May, 1973. (7 References).
Evaluates an experimental rehabilitative program for at risk children and their parents. A day care unit was established for fifteen children in danger of abuse; it was complimented by a training program for their mothers, who received instruction in mothering and close supervision.

1539   Roberts, Jacqueline; Beswick, Keith; Leverton, Bridget; <u>et al.</u>
"Prevention of child abuse: group therapy for mothers and chil-dren." <u>Practitioner</u> (219): 111-15, July, 1977. (7 References).
Details a project designed to assist families in potentially abusive situations. Two groups--one for mothers, one for their children--were organized to meet weekly. Criteria for selecting patients are listed. By the end of the project, the mothers showed more self-esteem and lost their sense of isolation and uselessness. The children also improved, losing their inhibitions and learning to play together. Such a program cannot help everyone. Only sound preparation, clear goals, and a careful selection of patients will assure success.

1540   Roth, Frederick. "A practice regimen for diagnosis and treatment of child abuse." <u>Child Welfare</u> 54(4): 268-73, April, 1975.
(3 References).
Describes a step-by-step system developed by the Illinois Department of Children and Family Services for identifying the severity of child abuse cases and for providing the treatment required by the troubled families and their children. Three categories of abuse (varying in severity from least to most) are described--situational, behavior-patterned, and chronic. Characteristics of abusive parents are briefly outlined. Treat-ment includes the provision of a person to work individually with the abused child as well as a social worker to deal exclusively with the parents. In treatment, the child should be encouraged to work through his ambivalent feelings toward his parents, his fear of future abuse, his need for affection and attention, and other important issues. Treat-ment of the parents involves helping them to gain behavioral control over their aggressive impulses and feelings of frustration and assisting them to meet their own needs without making inappropriate demands on their children. On-going contacts with the family must be maintained for a period of time which may amount to several years.

1541 Schmitt, Barton D., and Beezley, Patricia. "The long-term management of the child and family in child abuse and neglect." <u>Pediatr
Ann</u> 5(3): 59-78, March, 1976. (15 References).
Comprehensively reviews available long-term treatment modalities for the
abused child and his family. After a thorough diagnostic assessment of
the family is completed, the multidisciplinary child protection team makes
recommendations about what form of intervention is indicated. In most
cases, a professional (either a social worker or public health nurse) or
a paraprofessional (usually a successful parent) will visit the family
regularly and establish a one-to-one relationship with the mother. The
focus of this treatment is to help the parent to build her self-esteem,
to develop basic trust in others, and to learn about appropriate child
care methods. Additional forms of therapy for the abusive parents include marital counseling and psychotherapy which are usually provided by
psychiatrists, clinical psychologists, or psychiatric social workers;
group therapy which is provided either in Parents Anonymous organizations
or structured clinical settings; and crisis intervention hot-lines. The
abused child requires intensive, on-going pediatric care so that any
developmental lags or continued abuse can be detected. In addition, the
child needs help in learning to feel better about himself and in relating
to adults and peers in a constructive way. Therapeutic play schools,
crisis nurseries, and play therapy are treatment modes geared toward helping the child with these psychological and social adjustment problems.
The abused child and his family should be reassessed periodically to
determine if any improvements have been made or if the treatment strategy
should be revised to meet the family's needs.

1542 Schulman, Gerda L., and Leichter, Elsa. "The prevention of family
break-up." <u>Soc Casework</u> 49(3): 143-50, March, 1968. (0 References).
Studies the dynamics which can lead to the disintegration of a family when
one child departs early or is placed outside the family. In most cases,
it was found that the child was being ejected from the family unit by the
unconscious collusion of the other members; the child served as a scapegoat for family problems, and his ejection was often a covert strategy
to protect another member. Family therapy was recommended in these cases,
even though the family as a group had become accustomed to regarding the
scapegoat child as the sick or disturbed member, the one in need of
treatment. Family therapy brought out into the open the covert and often
neurotic alliances on which the family structure depended. The aim of
the therapy was to keep the family together but also, to help its members
find a healthier means of coexisting; the therapist actually challenged
the family in order to reverse longstanding tendencies. Three case
studies are presented.

1543 Steele, Brandt F. "Report from the Prevention and Rehabilitation
Work Group." <u>Clin Proc</u> 30(2): 42-45, February, 1974. (0
References).
Emphasizes the importance of dealing with the entire family unit in many
different aspects of family life in preventing and treating child abuse.
Important features of a comprehensive rehabilitation service are de-
scribed.

1544 Ten Broeck, Elsa. "The Extended Family Center: 'a home away from
home' for abused children and their parents." <u>Child Today</u> 3(2):
2-6, March-April, 1974. (1 Reference).

The Extended Family Center is a treatment facility for abused children and their parents. Its purpose is to develop the resources of an extended family for isolated parents who are acting out through violence against their children. The use of day care for the treatment of abused children is a key aspect of the Center's services. The children are given specialized attention designed to help them gain trust in their environment, learn positive ways to control their behavior, and develop their potential at their own pace. Parents feel ambivalent about these services, which relieve them from twenty-four-hour care of their children, but which also cause them to feel threatened by the possible loss of their child's love. They participate in four hours of treatment weekly and are encouraged to be active in the Center's programs. It is found that formal therapy rarely brings about changes in the parents' behavior. Rather, it is the supportive atmosphere provided by the workers and by other parents which stimulates the confidence parents need to change. They eventually accept and learn from the Center's principles of child care.

1545 Tracy, James J.; Ballard, Carolyn M.; Clark, Elizabeth H. "Child abuse project: a follow-up." Soc Work 20(5): 398-99, September, 1975. (1 Reference).
Presents a follow-up report on a project which sought to define the causes of child abuse in forty-one troubled families with abused and at risk children and to help the parents to act more effectively through a program of behavior modification. The project also aimed to make the evaluation process more objective. The follow-up study found that the families remaining in the program showed an 84 percent increase in effective behavior (measured by means of a frequency count). It is concluded that the behavior modification program can be an effective one in improving the family environment and helping to avert future child abuse.

1546 Tracy, James J., and Clark, Elizabeth H. "Treatment for child abusers." Soc Work 19(3): 338-42, May, 1974. (7 References).
Examines a program in a Philadelphia hospital aimed at helping abusive parents to manage their children more effectively by means of behavior modification. Once the cases of suspected abuse were identified, the project workers interviewed the parents (mostly single mothers) and determined the situations and the behavioral patterns which typically resulted in abuse in each family. The parent and worker then focused on altering the bad situation or the parent's pattern of response to her child's undesirable activity. A frequency count was used to assess progress more objectively. The project stressed the necessity for the staff to clearly and fully report their activities and to use specific language and objective measures. The pilot program was deemed successful and was offered as a model for dealing with other areas of behavior modification.

1547 Wayne, Julianne; Ebeling, Nancy B.; Avery, Nancy C. "Differential groupwork in a protective agency." Child Welfare 55(8): 581-91, September-October, 1976. (3 References).
Describes the development of a successful groupwork treatment program for families with a child abuse problem by the Boston District Office of Children's Protective Services. The agency views the family as a total unit which should remain intact except if the child's safety is threatened. Three models of groupwork have emerged: (1) a remedial discussion group for mothers focusing on the intrapsychic dynamics of each member; (2) a socialization group for adolescent girls of client families; and (3) a task-oriented group in which individual problems were

subordinate to the group task. It was felt that differential use of
groupwork helped to meet the individual, social, and treatment needs of
the family.

1548 Young, Leontine R. "An interim report on an experimental program
      of protective service." Child Welfare 45: 373-81, July, 1966.
      (11 References).
Considers a social welfare program directed at 125 families in which the
processes of disintegration had taken hold but were not yet irreversible.
The families were poor and managed their finances badly, the parents were
apathetic toward the children, and the children knew little discipline
or direction. The program was unusual in that it integrated casework,
education, and groupwork; workers concentrated on improving the families'
strengths and thereby compensating for the weaknesses. Early results
suggested that nearly all the families had stopped deteriorating, and 60
percent of them showed clear improvement in at least one important area--
principally finance and household management.

E. FEDERAL PROJECTS AND POLICIES

1549 Allen, Marilyn. "Child maltreatment in military communities."
      Juv Justice 26: 11-20, May, 1975. (5 References).
Evaluates the advantages and deficiencies of a military installation with
regard to the management of child abuse. The absence of state agencies
on army bases is a particular problem. A successful experiment with a
child abuse center at the Beaumont Army Medical Center near Fort Bliss
is described. The Beaumont experience has provided a model for the Army
in proposing guidelines for the handling of child abuse and child neglect
in military installations throughout the country.

1550 "Child abuse problems." Christ Today 7(20): 32, July 6, 1973.
      (0 References).
The incidence of child abuse is on the rise. Senator Walter Mondale's
sponsorship of a bill, which would allocate money to study the problem
of child abuse, is described. Research suggests that "parent-aide" projects, which send stable parents to work with child abusers, can be
successful. Volunteers are desperately needed to help solve this problem.

1551 Child Welfare League of America. Committee on Standards for Child
      Protective Services. Standards for child protective services. New
      York: Child Welfare League of America, 1973. 85p. (Bibliography).
Sets forth a proposal by the Child Welfare League of America of new guidelines for child protective services, both as child welfare agencies and
as social work agencies. The goals, priorities, organization, and administration of these services are discussed, along with the new agencies'
possible future roles in the legal and social systems.

1552 Cohn, Anne H.; Ridge, Susan S.; Collignon, Frederick C. "Evaluating
      innovative treatment programs in child abuse and neglect." Child
      Today 4(3): 10-12, May-June, 1975. (0 References).
In 1973, eleven child abuse demonstration projects located across the
United States and in Puerto Rico were initiated by the Office of Child
Development, the Social and Rehabilitation Services, and the Health
Resources Administration. The treatment focus of each program varied.
Therapeutic approaches included the use of volunteers, multidisciplinary

child protection and treatment teams, family therapy in an in-patient residential setting and in the home, day care nurseries, and others. Each project will be evaluated after a three year period of operation to determine if the project's goals have been accomplished, to analyze the quality of the services provided, to assess the cost of each treatment strategy, and to examine the project's impact in developing a more effective and coordinated community service delivery program. Based on the evaluation findings, general policy and program recommendations for the field of child abuse will be made.

1553   Ferro, Frank. "Combatting child abuse and neglect." Child Today
         4(3): inside cover, May-June, 1975. (0 References).
The goals of the National Center on Child Abuse and Neglect established in 1974 are discussed. Several points essential to the coordination and financing of a comprehensive child protective system are outlined.

1554   National Council of State Committees for Children and Youth. The
         states report on children and youth. Washington, 1960. 232p.
Presents a summary report prepared for the Golden White House Conference on Children and Youth. The States' recommendations for meeting child care needs in 1960 are listed. Suggested improvement for dependent and neglected children include the development of more protective services, closer cooperation between courts and child welfare agencies, and dissemination of child care information. Foster care programs should be statewide and should include specialized homes for the handicapped, additional supervision, and laws for controlling quality of care. The recommendations for improvement of child caring institutions included the establishment of more small, specialized institutions, increased research and experimentation, and casework services. The States also strongly recommended racial integration of institutions.

1555   Nazzaro, Jean. "Child abuse and neglect." Except Child 40(5):
         351-54, February, 1974. (10 References).
Ordinary citizens are encouraged to familiarize themselves with the different federal and community agencies available for the management of child abuse. The role of the HEW Interagency Committee on Child Abuse and Neglect in detection, prevention, treatment, and public education relative to the child abuse problem is examined.

1556   Snow, William F. "Social hygiene and the White House Conference
         on Child Health and Protection." J Soc Hyg 17(1): 36-52, January,
         1931. (0 References).
Summarizes the social hygiene program proposed by the President's White House Conference on Child Health and Protection. Its aims include the preservation of a healthy, integrated home life, particularly as this relates to the child, and sex education leading to personal development consistent with community welfare. The responsibility of parents to act as a major influence in sex education requires their on-going education also. From infancy, sex information should be presented to children according to age appropriateness; guidelines are included. Schools play an important but secondary role; sex education should be taught only in conjunction with other naturally related courses such as biology. The program emphasizes the role of the individual as a responsible member of society and the importance of achieving normalcy in sex related areas.

1557 U. S. General Accounting Office, Washington, D. C. More can be
      learned and done about the well-being of children. Social and
      Rehabilitation Service, Department of Health, Education, and Welfare:
      Report to the Congress by the Comptroller General of the United
      States. Washington, D.C.: U. S. General Accounting Office, 1976.
      84p. (Bibliography).
Discusses the status of federal child welfare programs and recommendations
for improving services on both the national and local levels. It is
suggested that the Department of Health, Education, and Welfare institute
a means of rating the effectiveness of federally funded programs and a
system which would enable the agency to explain differences in the well-
being of children among the states. "Well-being" is defined in terms of
a child's caregiving arrangement and his physical and emotional condition.
On the state level, it was found that child welfare services had expanded
and that the quality of services offered had improved in past years.
Improvements included: the institution of twenty-four-hour referral hot-
lines, an increase in trained personnel, specialization of protective
service groups, increase in availability of foster homes, and an emphasis
on cooperation with other community groups. A need for improvement of
state reporting laws is cited. A periodic compilation of data from all
federally assisted programs is viewed as the most effective means of
spotting flaws in existing programs and instituting reform or redistribu-
tion of funds. A more precise definition of "well-being" is encouraged,
and it is suggested that program effectiveness be measured in terms of
this concept. It is recommended that Congress require the Secretary of
the Department of Health, Education, and Welfare to submit biennial reports containing recent statistics and recommendations for the promotion
of child welfare services. HEW's response to GAO's study is outlined in
the report and contains many criticisms of GAO's methodology and conclusions.

1558 U. S. National Center for Child Abuse and Neglect. Federally-
      funded child abuse and neglect projects, 1975. Washington, D.C.:
      U. S. Department of Health, Education, and Welfare, 1976. 62p.
Lists projects funded in fiscal year 1975 by the National Center on Child
Abuse and Neglect and the Intradepartmental Committee on Child Abuse and
Neglect. Projects are organized first by committee and then by type.
Names and addresses for project directors are given, along with the
amount, duration, and objective of the grants. The largest percentage of
the projects are demonstration grants for family centers.

1559 U. S. Office of Child Development. Research, demonstration and
      evaluation studies, fiscal year 1975. Washington, D.C.: U. S.
      Government Printing Office, 1976. 113p.
Lists projects funded by HEW through the Office of Child Development in
fiscal year 1975. Projects are grouped by general areas, the principal
topics being child abuse and neglect, child development and the family,
children at risk and the child welfare system, day care, social policy/
information dissemination, Head Start projects, and building projects in
children's institutions. Project information includes the name and
address of the project director, amount and duration of the grant, and
a brief description of the work undertaken.

F. EVALUATIONS OF PROGRAMS

1560 Berkeley Planning Associates. Cost analysis design and pretest
      results: evaluation, national demonstration program in child abuse
      and neglect. Berkeley, California: Berkeley Planning Associates,
      1975. 57p.
Results of a cost analysis of eleven child abuse and neglect treatment
programs. The purpose of the project was to determine the allocation of
program resources (including funds, personnel, and time) and the cost
effectiveness of each service activity. Project methodology consisted
of having each program monitor its monthly expenses and the amount of
time spent on each management or service activity. Findings were statistically analyzed and presented in tabular format so as to facilitate
cross project comparisons. Service component groups evaluated include:
community activities, project operations, research, casework activities,
treatment for parents and for children, and supportive services for the
family. A detailed discussion of individual project costs, key expenditures, population served, and projected future expansion or redistribu-
tion of finances and personnel is included.

1561 ————. Second site visit report. Evaluation, demonstration
      program in child abuse and neglect. Washington, D.C.: Health
      Resources Administration, 1974. 78p.
Assesses the headway made by ten child abuse and neglect demonstration
projects located throughout the country, focusing upon community and
professional education, case management, coordination of agencies, and
legislation.

1562 Billingsley, Andrew; Streshinsky, Naomi; Gurgin, Vonnie. "Agency
      structure and the commitment to service." Public Welfare 24(3):
      246-51, July, 1966. (8 References).
Compares the services offered and procedures followed by the child welfare division and family assistance division of public social welfare
departments. The family assistance division must handle a larger caseload and work within a highly bureaucratic structure. Workers in the
child welfare division generally have graduate degrees which entitle
them to work more directly with their clients, to counsel them, and to
refer them to other professional help. The child welfare division,
obviously, is best equipped to handle such serious and complex issues
as child abuse and neglect.

1563 Class, Norris E. "Neglect, social deviance, and community action."
      Natl Probat Parole Assoc J 6(1): 17-23, January, 1960. (0
      References).
Explores reasons and solutions for community passivity in dealing with
child neglect as a factor in social deviance. Physical neglect is less
visible due to improved economic conditions and increased social mobility,
while emotional neglect is inherently difficult to detect and needs
clearer definition under the law. The hard-to-reach parents present
obstacles which demand recording, experimentation, and evaluation of
methods used in similar, previous instances. Because the use of authority
by social workers has become increasingly confused, education of police
officers and their acceptance by social workers as integral members of
the protective service field is essential and inevitable. Administrative
planning of protective services has caused inconsistent professional
leadership and could benefit from the separation of state operated protective services from public assistance offices.

1564 Cohn, Anne H. "Assessing the impact of health programs responding
to new problems: the case of child abuse and neglect." For a
summary see: Diss Abstr Int 37B(1): 162, July, 1976.

1565 Cohn, Anne H.; Collignon, Frederick C.; Armstrong, Katherine; et al.
Case management assessment working papers: evaluation, joint OCD/
SRS demonstration program in child abuse and neglect. Berkeley,
California: Berkeley Planning Associates, 1976. 72p. (Bibliography).
Consists of a preliminary report of the quality of services provided by
nine child abuse and neglect treatment programs. A quality assessment
team visited the sites and gathered data from a random selection of 274
abuse and neglect cases. The procedure used for determining the reliability of the data collection is outlined, and a sample interview checklist
and codebook are included. Tables compare data regarding the severity
of abuse, the sex and age of the client, household composition, type of
referral, placement decision, and the use of a multidisciplinary child
protection team. Characteristics of the attendant project staff, including education and experience of case workers, are also given.

1566 Costin, Lela B. "Protecting children from neglect and abuse."
In: Costin, Lela B. Child welfare: policies and practice. New
York: McGraw-Hill, 1972. 253-96. (72 References).
Assesses the current status of child protective services; some historical
background is provided.

1567 DeGraaf, Beverly J., and Ridge, Susan S. Preliminary quality
assessment design evaluation, national demonstration program in
child abuse and neglect. Berkeley, California: Berkeley Planning
Associates, 1975. 51p. (Bibliography).
Outlines a methodology for assessing the case management and services
provided at child abuse and neglect treatment projects. Criteria under
consideration include: intake of information, diagnosis of the family's
problem, quality of treatment, nature of follow-up services, and interagency cooperation. The evaluation involves a two day visit to each
project site during which time the project director and several staff
members are interviewed, numerous case records are reviewed, and two different client treatment sessions are observed. Appendices delineate the
procedures for interviewing and appraising services.

1568 Duke, R. F. N. "Battered babies: letter to editor." Br Med J
2(5964): 194, April 26, 1975. (0 References).
Raises questions about the well-intentioned, self-appointed committees
being set up in Britain to investigate complaints of child abuse. Members
have no special training, and there is potential for excessively zealous
intrusion into private life.

1569 Elmer, Elizabeth. "Abused children and community resources." Int
J Offender Ther 11(1): 16-23, January, 1967.
Analyzes and evaluates the community resources available for families with
abuse problems. The two most effective methods proved to be coordinated
community support, with the child remaining in the home, and temporary
placement of the child outside the home, with a plan for return to the
family.

1570   Ewing, Charles P. "Family crisis intervention and traditional
       child guidance: a comparison of outcomes and factors related to
       success in treatment." For a summary see: Diss Abstr Int 36B(9):
       4686, March, 1976.

1571   Gibson, Geoffrey. "Emergency medical services: the research gaps."
       Health Serv Res 9(1): 6-21, Spring, 1974. (0 References).
Discusses and evaluates research activity of the American Public Health
Association. Twenty-four papers presented to Emergency Medical Services
are viewed as being an important first step in determining proven intervention procedures so that they can be funded. One paper entitled,
"Physical Child Abuse and the Battering Parent," presented demographic
comparisons between abusive and non-battering parents.

1572   Maas, Henry S., ed. Five fields of social service: reviews of
       research. New York: National Association of Social Workers, 1966.
       208p. (Bibliography).
Summarizes research projects and publications in five areas of social
concern: family services, public welfare, child welfare, privately
operated neighborhood centers, and social planning. Public welfare programs, particularly A.F.D.C. (Aid to Families with Dependent Children),
have reported only minimal instances of child neglect or abuse associated
with families receiving public assistance. Child welfare programs handle
the bulk of child neglect cases. Each of four major child care programs--
foster home care, adoption, institutional care, and day care--must contend with its particular problem areas. Opportunities for research in
foster home care include the effect of separation upon the natural parents and siblings, and the young child's adjustment to multiple home
placements. More follow-up studies are needed to account for the adult
status of adopted children and to explore the role adjustment process
which childless adoptive couples must undergo. Prospective studies on
children reared in institutions may find a correlation between the amount
of contact maintained between parent and child and the child's emotional
development. Day care facilities which would allow more mothers to work
outside the home might alleviate the stress caused by financial difficulties and low self-esteem, pathologic symptoms of child abuse. Additional material on social planning and the role of the social worker in
the larger community are discussed.

1573   Parke, Ross D., and Collmer, Candace Whitmer. "Child abuse: an
       interdisciplinary analysis." In: Hetherington, E. Mavis; Hagen,
       John W.; Kron, Reuben; et al., eds. Review of child development
       research: Volume 5. Chicago: The University of Chicago Press,
       1975. 509-90. (209 References).
In order to facilitate useful research in the area of child abuse, evaluations of all aspects of the problem are needed. Presently, it is
impossible to assess the impact of on-going short- and long-term treatment programs, because evaluation procedures have not automatically been
incorporated into each program's structure. The definition of child
abuse is discussed. The definition should differentiate accidental from
non-accidental injuries, exclude the notion of intentionality, and, most
importantly, be constructed on a community defined basis. Three
approaches to understanding child abuse, each with its own unique treatment program, emerge as the psychiatric model, the sociological model,
and the social situation model. The underlying assumption of the psychiatric model is that the parents are ill or abnormal and have uncon-

trollable aggressive tendencies. Psychotherapy, including both group
and individual therapy, is the treatment designed to modify the problem
parent's personality. The sociological model assumes that the sociocultural environment can provide pertinent information for understanding
child abuse. Treatment measures would concentrate on eliminating poverty,
creating comprehensive family planning programs, legal abortions, and
support services for mothers. The social situation model also examines
external social factors, but focuses primarily on a detailed examination
of family interaction, where the child may, in some cases, be seen as
eliciting abuse. It assumes that both parents and child need treatment,
and introduces non-punitive disciplinary techniques as well as techniques
for controlling anger. In order to assess the effectiveness of current
innovative intervention programs, systematic field intervention experiments must be initiated. Only then will adequate research findings be
available for analysis.

1574   Purvine, Margaret, and Ryan, William. "Into and out of a child
        welfare network." Child Welfare 48(3): 126-35, March, 1969.
        (4 References).
Studies thirteen child welfare agencies located in a metropolitan area.
The agencies were under public, private, and sectarian operation. During
the five week study period, 686 inquiries were processed by the agencies.
These inquiries involved unmarried mothers, children with behavioral
problems, and parental cruelty or neglect. Charts diagram the referral
source, client's background, and disposition of the cases. Overall,
adoption services for unmarried mothers were the most efficiently run
services.

1575   Streshinsky, Naomi; Billingsley, Andrew; Gurgin, Vonnie. "A study
        of social work practice in protective services: it's not what you
    .   know, it's where you work." Child Welfare 45(8): 444-50, 471,
        October, 1966. (9 References).
Attempts to categorize the attitudes of welfare workers toward the kinds
of problems encountered in protective services. A questionnaire asking
for reactions to hypothetical cases involving child neglect and child
abuse was distributed among 170 Protective Service workers, 277 Regular
AFDC workers, and 92 Special AFDC workers in a number of different communities. The communities were generally characterized as being either
repressive or supportive in their attitude toward welfare. The responses
of the workers were characterized by their "legalism," for example, their
readiness to involve the police department in the case. It was generally
found that workers in more repressive communities tended to be more
legalistic, and that Protective Service workers tended to be more sensitive to individual client needs. It is suggested that welfare programs
might note the effect of their communities upon their workers' attitudes
and, further, that they consider restructuring their programs to emphasize service commitments.

VI

Sexual Abuse

A. PATTERNS AND CAUSES

1. INCESTUAL OFFENDERS

1576 Bethscheider, J. L.; Young, J. P.; Morris, P.; et al. "A study of father-daughter incest in the Harris County Child Welfare Unit." Crim Justice Monogr 4(4): 1-131, 1973. (19 References).
Presents case reports of thirty families in which incest occurred, along with those of seventy families judged to be negligent. Outside of the crowded conditions in which both groups typically lived, the incestuous families had little in common with the negligent families; the negligent families generally being less educated and poorer than the families in which incest occurred.

1577 Cavallin, Hector. "Incestuous fathers: a clinical report." Am J Psychiatry 122(10): 1132-38, April, 1966. (15 References).
Analyzes the prevalent psychological features of fathers who had become incestuously involved with their daughters, with reference to twelve cases evaluated at the Kansas State Reception and Diagnostic Center over a period of eighteen months. Most of the men involved had had no prior criminal history, had been married only once, and were still living with their wives at the time the incest occurred. Most had a number of children. In all cases, the wife was seen as rejecting and threatening, a tendency which repeated the pattern of the man's childhood relationship with his mother. While most of the subjects showed no signs of psychotic disorders, all indicated a certain degree of projection and paranoid thinking, with the following common psychological features: weak object relations and psychosexual identity, unconscious homosexual strivings, and projection as a major defense. It is concluded that these men were not sexual psychopaths or pedophiles, but rather that their incestuous relations were an expression of intrafamilial conflicts.

1578 Cormier, Bruno M.; Kennedy, Miriam; Sangowicz, Jadwiga. "Psychodynamics of father daughter incest." In: Bryant, Clifton D., and Wells, J. Gipson, eds. Deviancy and the family. Philadelphia: F. A. Davis, 1973. 97-116. (23 References).
Describes the psychodynamics of father-daughter incest in terms of the psychopathology of the non-deviant and non-criminal father. In a disintegrating marriage, the father turns to the daughter as the symbol of the young girl he courted and married. In doing so, his own roles are confused between husband and father, and he returns to his self as a young man. He then places the wife in the position of the disapproving mother,

and he views the daughter as the nurturing mother he lost as a child.
Prevention is difficult unless a family member suspects and reports the
possibility. Once incest is disclosed, recidivism is rare. The deep
impact of each family member prevents the denial which occurred previously, and the cycle is broken. Treatment must take into account the
maladjustment existing since the beginning of the marriage, maladjustment
of which the incest is merely a symptom.

1579 De Francis, Vincent. "Protecting the child victim of sex crimes
      committed by adults." <u>Fed Probat</u> 35(3): 15-20, September, 1971.
      (0 References).
Summarizes the results of a review of some 9,000 cases of sex crimes
against children reported in New York City during a three year period.
The most frequently reported offenses were rape, carnal abuse, sodomy,
impairment of the morals of a minor, and incest. Characteristics common
to a number of offenses and offenders are given, along with a statistical
breakdown of victims according to sex and age. Many of the crimes occurred in families with histories of prior abuse, negligence, and psychosocial disturbances, and over half of the households had had previous
contact with welfare agencies. Great concern is expressed over the
apparent failure of these agencies to remedy the situation and over the
harsh treatment of victims by the police.

1580 Fisher, Gordon, and Howell, L. M. "Psychological needs of homo-
      sexual pedophiliacs." <u>Dis Nerv Syst</u> 31(1): 623-35, September,
      1970. (12 References).
The histories of fifty men convicted of homosexual pedophilia link them
more strongly to heterosexual pedophiles than to homosexuals. Most of
the subjects were middle aged, white, unmarried, of average intelligence,
unorganized, and guilt-ridden.

1581 Fitch, J. H. "Men convicted of sexual offenses against children:
      a descriptive follow-up study." <u>Br J Criminol</u> 3(1): 18-37, July,
      1962. (10 References).
One hundred and thirty-nine men, convicted of sexual offenses against
children, were used as subjects for a follow-up study. Data comparing
the age at the time of the offense, type of offense, previous convictions,
marital status, and intelligence of homosexual and heterosexual offenders
is presented. It was found that when released, homosexual offenders
tended to repeat crimes of a sexual nature, whereas heterosexual offenders
were more likely to commit non-sexual criminal acts as well. In one-
third of the heterosexual offences under scrutiny, the victim was a family
member; however, in only two of a total of sixty-two cases was a homosexual offender related to his victim. A study of the psychological
characteristics of sex offenders yields the following five behavioral
categories: (1) immature; (2) frustrated; (3) sociopathic; (4) pathological; and (5) miscellaneous. A descriptive account of each of these
categories is provided.

1582 Gordon, Lillian. "Incest as revenge against the pre-Oedipal
      mother." <u>Psychoanal Rev</u> 42(3): 284-92, July, 1955. (5 Refer-
      ences).
Documents a case study of a young woman's incestuous activity used as a
defense against her pre-Oedipal attachment to her mother. What appears
to be an Oedipal fixation on the father is, in fact, a defense which
takes the form of masochistic revenge on the pre-Oedipal mother.

1583   Gutheil, Thomas G., and Avery, Nicholas C.   "Multiple overt incest
       as family defense against loss."   Fam Process   105-16.   (24 Refer-
       ences).
Considers a case in which father-daughter incest represented a defensive
stratagem against the departure of the mother.   The mother, conforming to
the expected pattern, had been rejected by her mother and had abdicated
her own role to her daughters.   The family was bound together by an incestuous tie between father and daughter.

\1584   Guttmacher, Manfred S.   Sex offenses: the problem, causes and pre-
       vention.   New York: W. W. Norton, 1951.   159p.   (Bibliography).
A study of 172 sex offenders, seventy-nine of whom had had sexual relations (including fondling, exhibitionism, and intercourse) with children.
It was found that pedophiles, adults who prefer children as sex partners,
were on the average older and more seriously defective mentally than
other sex criminals.   Moreover, two distinct subgroups of pedophiles were
detected: (1) passive individuals who cannot compete sexually with other
adults; and (2) elderly or senile men who reenact their childhood fantasies before children who regard them as friendly "grandfather" types.
Clinical statistics denoting the age, physical abnormalities, school and
work history, religious affiliation, and parent-child relationship of the
sex offenders are presented.   Laws dictating the handling of sex offenses
in various states are examined, and recommendations for early detection
and treatment of potential sex offenders discussed.

1585   Henderson, D. James.   "Incest: a synthesis of data."   Can Psychiatr
       Assoc J   17(4):   299-313, August, 1972.   (46 References).
Theories attempting to account for the universality of the incest taboo
are discussed, along with studies of actual cases of father-daughter
incest, their common features, and the possibility for treatment.   The
incest taboo is regarded as arising from several different human needs;
the protection of the family unit and the promotion of endogamous sexuality in order to prevent the weakening of the race are the principal
bases suggested.   Overt incest is found to occur in dysfunctional families in which the normal roles have been dramatically rearranged.   Usually
the psychodynamics involve three generations, and desertion anxiety is
a recurrent theme.   The incestuous father has usually been sexually
rejected by his wife, while the incestuous daughter, encouraged by her
mother, assumes the wife/mother role and usually does not repel the
father's advances.

1586   Kaufman, Irving; Peck, Alice L.; Tagiuri, Consuelo K.   "The family
       constellation and overt incestuous relations between father and
       daughter."   Am J Orthopsychiatry   24(2):   266-79, April, 1954.
       (0 References).
Describes the family relationships in eleven cases of incest between
father (or father figure) and daughter.   The girls all displayed depression and guilt, and frequently had learning difficulties, somatic complaints, loss of appetite, or abdominal distress as well.   Family studies
showed similar factors in the backgrounds of both the mothers and fathers.
The father's backgrounds were characterized by poverty, alcoholism,
little education, inadequate housing, and poor relationships with their
parents.   Fathers were frequently irresponsible, and all of them deserted
their children at some time.   Mothers showed common factors also: desertion by the maternal grandfather and hostile, dependent relationships
with a cold, domineering maternal grandmother.   The mother often projects

onto her own daughter her hostile relationships with the grandmother.
She abdicates her role of wife and mother by some form of desertion and
leave the daughter to look after the father and children. It is usually
at this point that incestuous relations begin. The daughter claims that
her guilt and depression result from the disruption of the home rather
than from the sexual activity which both parents have in some way condoned. However, her anxiety manifests itself by seeking forgiveness from
mother or a mother figure, by seeking punishment, or by delinquent behavior. Basic to the behavior is the craving for adequate parenting.

1587 McCaghy, Charles H. "Child molesters: a study of their careers
      as deviants." Diss Abstr 28A(2): 805, August, 1967.

1588 McGeorge, John. "Sexual assaults on children." Med Sci Law 4(4):
      245-53, October, 1964. (14 References).
Reports on the characteristics of sexual offenders of children. The data
is derived from the study of 400 first or second offenders convicted of
assaults on girls and boys. The pedophile is distinguished from depraved
sexual offenders as having probably never had normal sexual intercourse.
The results of the study show that it is the homosexual and the pedophile
who are much more likely to assault boys. The more normal appearing
offender tends to seek out girls. The average age range of the victims is
seven to fifteen years, with a peak at age ten and twelve for girls and
at age ten and fourteen for boys. Offenders most often fall in the twenty
to forty-year-old range. One-half of the perpetrators assaulting girls
were single, while 77.5 percent of those assaulting boys were not married.
Many of the offenders were laborers or tradesmen, with very few professionals involved. Most had a decided preference for one sex. The offender and victim were most often strangers, although cooperation of the
victim, boy or girl, was frequently noted to be evident. Preventive and
protective measures include sex education, proper investigative and
examination procedures which minimize stress, legal revisions, publicity,
and a realistic approach to counseling.

1589 "Sex abuse of child more common than is realized." Pediatr News
      9(3): 3, 76, March, 1975. (0 References).
Briefly discusses the problem of incest involving children. Incest between brother and sister is the most common and psychologically the least
detrimental aspect of the problem; father-daughter incest is more damaging. The physician involved should be prepared to give both physical and
psychological treatment and to watch for any lasting effects. The decision to press charges in such cases is not always a wise one, depending
upon the particular situation.

1590 "Sexual offences against children." Br Med J 2(5488): 626,
      March 12, 1966. (7 References).
The largest number of reported sex offences against children have involved relatives or friends of the family. The most typical offenders
fall into three categories: those who are mentally defective, those who
are chronically inhibited to the point that adult heterosexual behavior
has failed to develop, and those whose adult heterosexual balance is not
stable enough to endure stress. Frequently, the victims of such offences
are willing or even enticing. The effect of the sexual assault on the
child varies, but tends to be aggravated by the attitudes and questions
of members of his family concerning the assault.

1591   Tormes, Yvonne M.   Child victims of incest.   Denver, Colorado:
       The American Humane Association, Children's Division, n.d.   40p.
       (Bibliography).

Investigates the most commonly reported type of incest, that between
natural father and daughter.   Twenty cases of incest and twenty cases of
non-incestuous sexual abuse seen by the agency during the interval 1960
to 1965 were included in the study.   Characteristics common to the two
groups were as follows: (1) the victim was a female sixteen years or
younger; and (2) all study families were intact, nuclear families with
an average of four children.   Dissimilar factors included the following:
(1) incest cases were of prolonged duration and often involved more than
one daughter; (2) non-incest cases were reported promptly and the parents
showed sincere anxiety for their daughter's welfare; (3) incest victims
tended to be older than the females who were sexually abused in a single
incident; (4) outside the home, incestuous fathers were seen as passive
and ineffectual; (5) mothers in incestuous homes failed to protect their
daughters, many even encouraged incest in order to be personally free of
the burden of any sexual relationship; and (6) incestuous families had
few outside contacts.   Incestuous fathers were described as either brutal
and alcoholic or non-violent and overprotective.   Rehabilitation of the
father is difficult because the father often denies the act, charges that
the daughter was promiscuous, or finds some other fantastic justification
for his behavior.

1592   Walters, David R.   Physical and sexual abuse of children: causes
       and treatment.   Bloomington, Indiana: Indiana University Press,
       1975.   192p.   (Bibliography).

Parents who abuse their children are repeating a culturally learned pattern.   Instances in the Bible, in literature, and in history substantiate
the notion of absolute parental prerogative to discipline, sell, appren-
tice, or even kill a child.   Defining child abuse, therefore, is a com-
plicated problem.   Such factors as motivation, circumstances, ages of the
persons involved, and the degree of injury must be taken into consideration.

There is no single description of the abusive parent.   Rather, a typology
of the abusive parent distinguishing between ten distinct models, ranging
from the parentally incompetent abuser who repeats the generational
pattern of violence, to the victim-precipitated abuser who regards his
actions as justifiable punishment for the child's negative or unacceptable
behavior, is offered.   Specific treatment orientations include helping the
frustrated and displaced abuser break the sequence of behavior which has
driven him to regard his child as an object, and careful scrutiny of
juvenile and mental institutions which blatantly neglect and abuse their
charges.

The family triad of abuse is composed of an adult male, an adult female,
and a child.   Frequently, one of the adult figures is a passive accom-
plice, particularly in cases of sexual abuse.   The primary goal of treatment is to enable the parents to discover non-physical means of coping
with their children.   Priority of treatment, however, should be given to
the child, whether in the form of medical care, removal from a hostile
home, or substitute mothering.

The etiology and treatment of sexual abuse differs from that of physical
abuse.   When the myths surrounding sexual abuse are discarded, it can be
noted that the abuser is often a close friend or relative, and the sexual
involvement has taken place over a long period of time.   Choosing one's

child as a sex partner is often an expression of anger and hostility toward one's spouse. Contrary to popular opinion, sexual abuse within a family does not usually leave a child permanently damaged emotionally. Nevertheless, the stress of police investigations and court hearings can cause serious trauma.

Strategies for positive change in the management of child abuse include: (1) establishing a cabinet-level agency with the responsibility of protecting children's rights; (2) eliminating corporal punishment in schools; (3) abolishing institutional abuse; (4) forming individual state Parents' Institutions; and (5) conducting research aimed at objectifying data collection and creating new treatment options.

1593 Williams, J. E. Hall. "The neglect of incest: a criminologist's view." Med Sci Law 14(1): 64-67, January, 1974. (4 References). Studies sixty-eight cases of reported incest considered for parole by a panel in England. The offenders tended to be about forty years old; most had previous convictions for crimes; in many cases marital difficulties were noted. The victim was usually the offender's child. In most cases, the offender was not released to his home. The issue of punishment for the crime of incest is discussed, as is the need for research on the role of the victim. The environmental and social problems which often prompt incestuous relationships should be defined and, where possible, remedied.

2. OTHER CHILD MOLESTERS

1594 Frosch, Jack, and Bromberg, Walter. "The sex offender -- a psychiatric study." Am J Orthopsychiatry 9(4): 761-76, October, 1939. (12 References).
Explores the problem of 709 sex offenders from a psychiatric point of view. Findings indicate a high ratio of white offenders, especially in statutory rape cases. The rate of recidivism is low, although repeated offenses occur often within the pedophilia group. The more aggressive assaults are associated with younger men. The pedophile is commonly over forty, and the psychological and social difficulties of normal sexual contact for this age group are underrated as to their importance and impact. Maladjustment in the sex lives of homosexuals and pedophiles was much more prevalent than among other types of sex offenders. Feelings of inferiority and inadequacy have much to do with their choice of children as sex objects. Mental deficiency and alcoholism are less important factors than previously supposed. Obtaining a clinical picture of offenders is difficult given the legal surroundings of the court clinic. The legal treatment of offenders as criminals obstructs constructive rehabilitation, and individual treatment in a non-punitive atmosphere is stressed.

1595 McCaghy, Charles H. "Drinking and deviance disavowal: the case of child molesters." Soc Probl 16(1): 43-49, Summer, 1968. (10 References).
Reports the results of interviews with 158 men convicted of child molestation. The study represented an investigation of the hypothesis that those molesters who claim that their assaults had been the result of excessive drinking actually disavow their offenses as much as do those who overtly deny committing them. The hypothesis was borne out by the results of the study, which suggested that drinkers who have received a certain amount of rehabilitative therapy are more ready to assume full responsibility for their actions.

B. EFFECTS

1. INCEST

1596 Brown, Wenzell. "Murder rooted in incest [the case of Richard Loftus]." In: Masters, R. E. L. Patterns of incest. New York: Julian Press, 1963. 301-27. (0 References).
Describes the case of a young boy who murdered his mother following years of incestuous relations with her. The mother's rejection of her husband, along with her seductive treatment of her son, led to sexual relations between them. Filled with guilt, the mother withdrew from the boy, abandoning him to his confused feelings. Gradually, he also withdrew into himself, developing fetishist behaviors and obsessively spying on his mother's activities. Impotent with other women and ashamed of his activities, he became angry with his mother and finally killed her.

1597 Browning, Diane H., and Boatman, Bonny. "Incest: children at risk." Am J Psychiatry 134(1): 69-72, January, 1977. (8 References).
A study of fourteen cases of incest seen in the Child Psychiatry Clinic at the University of Oregon Health Sciences Center is presented. All of the children were girls ranging in age from four to fifteen years, except for one boy, age fifteen. The cases fell into three categories: father-daughter incest, incest with an uncle, and multiple incest. In the cases involving father-daughter incest, the mother was often away at the time of the abuse. Several fathers threatened their daughters with abandonment if they related to anyone what had happended. The father was often alcoholic and violent. The daughter was frequently the eldest girl in the family and was forced to assume many of her mother's responsibilities, resulting in role confusion. In the cases involving incest with an uncle, the man was always the mother's brother, and there were no fathers in the home. The mother often had a protective relationship with her brother and was discouraged by the family from filing criminal charges against him. There was only one instance of multiple incest involving siblings, age thirteen and fifteen, and an aunt and uncle from a chaotic fundamentalist family. Treatment of these families involved temporary placement of the child outside the home in two cases, individual counseling for the children and parents in some instances, and family therapy.

1598 Herman, Judith, and Hirschman, Lisa. "Father-daughter incest." Signs 2(4): 735-56, Summer, 1977. (22 References).
Examines incest, especially the pattern of father-daughter incest, in patriarchal societies such as ours, and reviews current knowledge concerning incest between parents and their children. Incest is strictly forbidden in human cultures, yet it continues to persist in varying forms and degrees. Its incidence is nearly impossible to determine. However, occurrences of father-daughter incest far exceed those of mother-son. One theory offered to account for this is that the incest taboo was originated by men in a patriarchal society to control the exchange of women. It is further perpetuated and enforced by men, and, therefore, it is most frequently violated by men. Consequently, the father-daughter incest taboo is somewhat weakened. Clinical reports, complete with detailed profiles of fifteen victims of father-daughter incest, are included. Psychotherapy for these victims has been largely unsuccessful.

1599   Kaplan, Stuart L., and Poznanki, Elva. "Child psychiatric patients
       who share a bed with a parent." J Am Acad Child Psychiatry 13(2):
       344-56, Spring, 1974. (9 References).
Presents a retrospective clinical study by chart review of child psychiatric patients and their parents who sleep in the same bed. Data is
given on the sleeping arrangements of 100 societies.

1600   Lukianowicz, Narcyz. "Incest. I: Paternal incest." Br J Psy-
       chiatry 120(556): 301-13, March, 1972. (53 References).
Incest was studied within the context of another culture which does not
view incest as sexually deviant behavior, but rather as the unfortunate
but inevitable result of such conditions as crowded housing, isolation,
or libidinous excess. Fifty-four cases of incest in a country in Northern
Ireland are reviewed. Over half of these involve father-daughter relationships, generally found to produce the most harmful lasting effects.
Character disorders and frigidity resulted in sixteen of the twenty-six
girls, while six showed no apparent ill effects.

1601   Rosenfeld, Alvin A.; Nadelson, Carol C.; Krieger, Marilyn; et al.
       "Incest and sexual abuse of children." J Am Acad Child Psychiatry
       16(2): 327-39, Spring, 1977. (31 References).
Reviews the literature and the problems in determining the effects of
intrafamilial sexual abuse. Incest is difficult to define because of
two factors that remain open to interpretation, i.e., which specific acts
are to be considered incestuous, and who is considered to be too close to
marry. Four case histories illustrate the family dynamics that support
and perpetuate incestuous behavior. Most studies investigating the
effects of early childhood sexual experience attempt to link incestuous
activity to later aberrant behavior such as promiscuity, frigidity, and
depression. However, this issue remains unresolved. At present the lack
of careful studies on incest prohibits any conclusions about its nature,
except that early sexual experiences may be subtle and that their effects
may surface shortly after the occurrence or much later in life.

1602   Schultz, Leroy G. "The child sex victim: social, psychological
       and legal perspectives." Child Welfare 52(3): 147-57, March,
       1973. (20 References).
Offers social work techniques for eliminating or at least lessening the
trauma suffered by child sex offense victims. Studies indicate that
trauma is caused more by the parents' overreaction to the assault and by
poorly managed legal proceedings than by the actual sexual offense. The
social worker's responsibility in such cases is to interview the victim
and parents, determine the advisability of reporting the incident, and
help the parents develop a non-damaging attitude toward the problem by
encouraging them to play down its significance. If the family decides
to prosecute, the social worker must work toward reducing the trauma of
testifying. In general, a child's personality development is not damaged
by the sexual assault itself, but by events following the assault.

1603   Seemanova, Eva. "A study of children of incestuous matings." Hum
       Hered 21(2): 108-28, 1971. (3 References).
One hundred and sixty-one children of incestuous encounters were studied
in relation to their half siblings. It was found that prenatal, natal,
and neonatal mortality rate was higher among the offspring of incestuous
unions, as was the incidence of mental retardation and congenital malformation.

1604   Sloane, Paul, and Karpinski, Eva. "Effects of incest on the par-
         ticipants." Am J Orthopsychiatry 12(4): 666-73, October, 1942.
         (7 References).
Investigates the effects of post adolescent incestuous relationship on
five girls. Feeling guilty, especially feeling guilty toward the mother
in the family, was a persistent recurrent reaction. Developing promiscuous relationships is also common. The girls tended to act out their
conflicts through promiscuity, rather than developing neurotic symptoms.
However, entering into promiscuous relationships just compounded their
guilt. Although most pre-adolescent children who have experienced incest
are not plagued with serious after effects, post adolescents are often
deeply disturbed. In fact, only one of the five girls in the study
managed to make an adequate adjustment to society.

1605   Tessman, Lora Heims, and Kaufman, Irving. "Variations on a theme
         of incest." In: Pollak, Otto, and Friedman, Alfred S., eds.
         Family dynamics and female sexual delinquency. Palo Alto, Cali-
         fornia: Science and Behavior Books, 1969. 138-50. (11 Refer-
         ences).
Discussion of instances in which an adolescent girl's resolution of her
Oedipal desires is interrupted, either by incest itself, by some thwarted
or unconscious attempt at seduction by the father, or by the father's
overt rejection of the girl in favor of another sexual partner other
than her mother. The psychosexual dynamics which operate in each of
these situations is explained and exemplified by means of case studies.
It is concluded that incestuous longings represent a healthy part of
every woman's ego development, but if these desires are not allowed to
be resolved, the woman's development may be stunted and her identity and
sense of worth damaged.

1606   Weber, Ellen. "Sexual abuse begins at home." Ms 5(10): 64-67,
         April, 1977. (10 References).
Explores the emotional and psychological conflicts experienced by victims
of incest. The average age of victims is eleven, although most girls are
trapped in the incestuous relationship for months or even years. At the
onset, many naive victims try to please their assailants and maintain
secrecy. Teenage victims are more apt to rebel against the forced relationship and confide in a responsible adult or run away from home. As
adults, childhood victims of incest suffer numerous sexual problems.
The treatment program at the Santa Clara Child Sexual Abuse Treatment
Program is described.

1607   Yorukoglu, A., and Kemph, J. P. "Children not severely damaged by
         incest with a parent." J Child Psychiatry 5: 111-24, 1966.
         (7 References).
Two separate cases of incest between a parent and a child in early
puberty are detailed. In both cases, the children suffered no apparent
psychological damage.

2. OTHER SEXUAL MOLESTATIONS

1608   Bender, Lauretta, and Blau, Abram. "The reaction of children to
         sexual relations with adults." Am J Orthopsychiatry 7(4):
         500-518, October, 1937. (24 References).

Discusses the effects of sexual relations with adults on sixteen children, aged five to twelve years. The children evidenced less trauma and anxiety over the experience than was anticipated. In fact, their exceptionally charming personalities and emotional calm indicated that perhaps they had a part in initiating the experience and had derived some pleasure from it. Guilt appeared only after they had been separated from the sex object and were under the influence of authorities. Effects noted were: (1) in the infantile stage, a tendency toward regressive behavior; (2) in early latency, a decreased educability and social adaptation; and (3) in pre-puberty, problems in adolescent adjustment. Treatment focused on discussion of sex, a promotion of normal childhood occupations, and the development of affectionate relationships with adults. Implications for theories of childhood sexuality are discussed and a survey of varying cultural norms is included.

1609   Chaneles, S. "Child victims of sexual offenses." Fed Probat
        31(2): 52-56, June, 1967. (0 References).
Surveys the results of the Child Victim Study of the American Humane Society. The study focused on the sexual abuse of children and found that sexually molested children generally sustained deep psychic damage as a result of their experience--damage which was often exacerbated by the prosecution of the molester. Most sex offenses against children, especially incest and homosexual assaults on boys, are not reported. Several characteristic traits of the adult sex offender are offered, along with a recommendation calling for special agencies to help victimized children.

1610   Freund, K.; McKnight, C. K.; Langevin, R.; et al. "The female child
        as a surrogate object." Arch Sex Behav 2(2): 119-23, December,
        1972.

1611   Gagnon, John H. "Female child victims of sex offenses." Soc Probl
        13(2): 176-92, Fall, 1965. (41 References).
Examines the literature dealing with the female victim of sex offenses against children, focusing particularly on the single study which followed the victims' progress through adulthood. It is suggested that it may be erroneous to assume that the offense will do permanent psychological damage to the victim.

1612   Hayman, Charles R.; Lanza, Charlene; Fuentes, Roberto; et al. "Rape
        in the District of Columbia." Am J Obstet Gynecol 113(1): 91-97,
        May 1, 1972. (8 References).
Summarizes statistics of 1,200 female rape victims at District of Columbia General Hospital from July, 1969 to December, 1970 and describes the Department of Public Health's assistance and follow-up.

1613   Jaffe, Arthur C.; Dynneson, Lucille; ten Bensel, Robert W. "Sexual
        abuse of children: an epidemiologic study." Am J Dis Child
        129(6): 689-92, June, 1975. (20 References).
Presents an epidemiologic study of the sexual abuse of children under sixteen. Information was gathered from the sexual offense complaint record of the Minneapolis Police Department. Research findings included the following: (1) 33 percent of all recorded sexual abuse cases involved children; (2) 88 percent of the child victims were female; (3) the mean age of the victim was 10.7 years; (4) all offenders were male with a mean age of twenty-eight years; (5) offenses termed as indecent liberties comprised 85 percent; and (6) rape comprised 15 percent of all

cases. No instances of incest were reported to the police but several
were reported to the Child Protective Services Division of the Welfare
Department. The nature of Police Department Records prevented examination of the social relationships between victims and offenders or of the
physical and emotional effects of sexual abuse.

1614 Katan, Anny. "Children who were raped." Psychoanal Study Child
      28: 208-24, 1973. (10 References).
Attempts to record the impact on adults of undetected and untreated sexual trauma suffered during childhood. In all of the six cases studied,
the subject was actually raped. Detailed analyses of two cases are provided. All of the six women had experienced similar traumas of forced
sexual overstimulation at a very early age and each was left with an
extremely low self-esteem. The subjects were found to be fixated at the
phallic development stage and experienced tremendous excitement in conjunction with phallic fantasies. However, much more serious disturbances
emerged as a result of childhood rape, namely, aggression and masochism.
While greatly encouraged by warmth and tenderness, the fusion of libido
and aggressive drives becomes extremely difficult when direct, aggressive
sexual stimulation is experienced instead. Such a fusion was completely
disrupted in these women, who at an early age had experienced more aggressive sexual stimulation than affection.

1615 Lewis, Melvin, and Sarrel, Philip M. "Some psychological aspects
      of seduction, incest, and rape in childhood." J Am Acad Child
      Psychiatry 4(4): 606-19, October, 1969. (15 References).
Sexual abuse of children and adolescents potentially ranges from mild
sexual excitement to malicious physical attack. Several case studies
illustrate the acute and long-term psychological effects which may result
from sexual assault. The family dynamics leading to sexual abuse of
children are discussed from a psychoanalytic point of view.

1616 McCaghy, Charles H. "Child molesting." Sex Behav 1: 16-24,
      August, 1971. (0 References).
A survey of 1,800 college students indicated that one-third of them had
had childhood experiences with sexual deviates, about half of them involving family members. The experiences are categorized and six types
of molesters are described. It was found that the child's response to
the experience, and its subsequent effect on him, are greatly influenced
by the parent's reaction to the incident.

1617 Miller, Patricia Y. "Blaming the victim of child molestation: an
      empirical analysis." For a summary see: Diss Abstr Int 37A(1):
      7340, May, 1977.

1618 Rothbard, Malcolm J., and Greenberg, Harvey. "Gynecologic health
      problems: socially abused adolescent female." NY State J Med
      76(9): 1483-84, September, 1976. (3 References).
A study of the gynecological problems of 117 adolescent girls who were
residents of a home for neglected and abandoned children operated by the
Bureau of Child Welfare in New York City. Approximately 31 percent were
pregnant or had been pregnant at the time of initial examination. Despite
thorough contraceptive counseling, birth control use rose to only 9.4
percent. A contrast with a previous study of a different population
suggests that the low socioeconomic background of the adolescents studied,
and the fact that many serve as prostitutes, may account for the poor

health care. Suggestions for prevention include group teaching and rap
sessions, involvement of the sexual partners, and exploration of the
subjects' need for pregnancy.

1619   Voigt, Jorgen. "Sexual offences in Copenhagen: a medicolegal
       study." Forensic Sci 1(1): 67-76, April, 1972. (6 References).
The medical and personal data regarding some 710 victims of sexual
assault over a ten year period in Denmark are analyzed. The greatest
number of offenses consisted of indecent interference with young girls
(aged ten to fourteen). Most of the victims belonged to the lower class,
and two-thirds of the perpetrators were either acquaintances or strangers
(as opposed to relatives).

C. DIAGNOSIS AND REPORTING

1620   Ackerman, A. Bernard; Goldfaden, Gary; Cosmides, James C. "Acquired
       syphilis in early childhood." Arch Dermatol 106(1): 92-93, July,
       1972. (7 References).
Documents three cases in which young children contacted syphilis through
sexual abuse of adults. Infection results from intimate skin-to-skin
contact with diseased adults, and clinical characteristics of the disease
are the same in children as in adults. Ulceronodular lesions, or
chancres, may occur in either genital or extragenital areas of the body,
genital chancres being more common in older children, and extragenital
in infants. In all three cases, the disease waned after injections of
penicillin G benzathine. Physicians should be aware that syphilis does
occur in small children and should be prepared to recognize its symptoms.

1621   Asnes, Russell S., and Grebin, Burton. "Gonococcal infection in
       children: letter to editor." J Pediatr 81: 192-93, July, 1972.
       (0 References).
Briefly discusses the examination procedure followed to ascertain whether
a gonococcal infection in a child has been transmitted through sexual
molestation.

1622   Barnes, Josephine. "Rape and other sexual offenses." Br Med J
       2(5547): 293-95, April 29, 1967. (5 References).
Describes the physical examination which a physician should conduct on
the victims of various alleged sexual offenses, including rape, incest,
and sodomy. Emphasis is placed on the particular need for a thorough
medical examination when the victims are children and may be unable to
give adequate verbal testimony.

1623   Brant, Renee S. T., and Tisza, Veronica B. "The sexually misused
       child." Am J Orthopsychiatry 47(1): 80-90, January, 1977. (9
       References).
Discusses the plight of the sexually misused child, stressing that sexual
misconduct with children too often goes undetected. After carefully reviewing hospital emergency room and pediatric gynecology clinical records
at the Children's Hospital Medical Center in Boston, a group of child
psychiatrists concludes that physicians must learn to consider a diagnosis
of sexual misuse when children are treated for genital injury, irritation,
and infection. The group also stresses that sexual misuse is a symptom
of family pathology and denounces the current tendency to call the adult
participant the "abuser" and the child the "victim." Guidelines for acute

case management of sexual misuse focusing on the advantages and disadvantages of taking legal action are included.

1624   Capraro, V. J., and Capraro, E. J.   "Vaginal aspirate studies in
       children: an atraumatic method." Obstet Gynecol 37(3): 462-64,
       March, 1971. (5 References).
A simple, homemade aspirator can be used by gynecologists to obtain
samples of vaginal secretions of children without causing pain. The device has been used in many cases in a pediatric gynecology clinic, with
good results. In cases of rape, the wet mount obtained may be studied
for the presence of spermatazoa or venereal disease and retained as permanent evidence. Other types of situations where the aspirator may be
useful are discussed.

1625   Caruso, Phillip A. "Pelvic inflammatory disease: rare sequela
       of battered child syndrome." NY State J Med 75(13): 2405-6,
       2415, November, 1975. (2 References).
Cites a case report of an eighteen-year-old girl who had been sexually
abused. The child presented with symptoms of non-specific vulvovaginitis.
Although these symptoms are more commonly caused by such problems as poor
perineal hygiene or intestinal parasites, they can also be an indication
of deliberate sexual molestation. Physicians must maintain a high index
of suspicion in such cases and not hesitate to report suspected sexual
abuse.

1626   Hartley, Albert I., and Ginn, Robert. "Reporting child abuse."
       Tex Med 71(3): 84-86, February, 1975. (6 References).
Evaluates procedures used in handling twenty-two cases of sexual abuse
to children during a period of six years at the University of Texas
Medical Branch Hospitals. One purpose of the evaluation was to determine
the impact of the reporting laws on physicians involved in the cases.
A suggested form for reporting abuse is offered.

1627   Hayman, Charles R. "Sexual assaults on women and girls." Ann
       Intern Med 72(2): 277-78, February, 1970. (8 References).
Discusses procedures and obligations of physicians examining rape victims,
and urges greater understanding of victims' emotional needs.

1628   Hayman, Charles R.; Lanza, Charlene; Fuentes, Roberto. "Sexual
       assault on women and girls in the District of Columbia." South
       Med J 62(10): 1227-31, October, 1969. (8 References).
Reports procedures and statistics for 3,000 sexual assault victims, including children, between September 15, 1965 and June 30, 1968 in the
District of Columbia. Some 1,000 referrals for reexamination are described. It is recommended that initial examinations in emergency areas
by residents in gynecology or pediatrics be eliminated.

1629   Jaffe, Arthur C.; Gershon, Anne A.; Fish, Irving; et al. "Sexual
       abuse and herpetic genital infection in children: letters to
       editor." J Pediatr 89(2): 338, August, 1976. (3 References).
Two letters respond to a previous article describing a case of a child
with genital herpes. The first complains that because genital infections
in children can signal sexual abuse, the examination should have included
a family history. The authors clarify that in this particular case,
sexual abuse is ruled out because infection was caused by a strain of
herpes not usually transmitted by sexual contact.

1630   Lipton, George L., and Roth, E. I. "Rape: a complex management
       problem in the pediatric emergency room." J Pediatr   75(5):
       859-66, November, 1969. (14 References).
A discussion of the emotional factors involved in rape, based upon the
author's experience as an emergency room consultant in rape cases. Nine
case studies are presented involving young adolescent girls primarily.
The girls' family environments and behavior patterns are related, along
with the circumstances of the alleged rape. In a number of cases, sensitive conversations with the girls revealed some conscious or unconscious
complicity in the rape. Physicians are advised to: (1) examine rape
victims sensitively and non-judgmentally, in comfortable surroundings;
(2) encourage the patient to express her feelings; and (3) advise the
parents regarding prosecution of charges.

1631   Ringrose, C. A. Douglas. "Medical assessment of the sexually
       assaulted female." Med Trial Tech Q 15: 245-47, 1969. (0 Refer-
       ences).
Reports statistics of 100 rape cases occurring in Edmonton, Canada, between July, 1965 and January, 1967. Proper examining and documenting
procedures are suggested. It is noted that most cases of child molestation occurred in the summer.

1632   Robinson, Henry A., Jr.; Sherrod, Dale B.; Malcarney, Courtney.
       "Review of child molestation and alleged rape cases." Am J Obstet
       Gynecol 110(3): 405-6, June 1, 1971. (9 References).
Describes injuries found in the medical examination of ninety-four cases
of alleged child molestation or rape at Womack Army Hospital from 1957
through 1967. Lacerations and abrasions were the most common genital
lesions.

1633   Sandes, Gladys M. "Sexual assaults on children." Br J Clin Pract
       17(3): 143-44, March, 1963. (0 References).
Outlines medical and legal procedures to follow in cases of sexually
assaulted children. A specific format for the medical examination is
included. It is advised that the child be seen as soon as possible by a
female medical specialist in the presence of a policewoman. The physician's part in obtaining medical evidence in cases of incest and homosexuality is explained.

1634   Sgroi, Suzanne M. "Sexual molestation of children: the last
       frontier in child abuse." Child Today 4(3): 18-21, 44, May-June,
       1975. (3 References).
Presents case histories of suspected sexual molestation in children age
two months through four years. Three obstacles to identifying the sexually abused child include: (1) a lack of willingness to recognize the
condition; (2) failure to obtain immediate medical collaboration--includ-
ing physical and psychological examinations; and (3) a reluctance to
report suspected cases to protective services. The reasons for these
obstacles and ways to overcome them are discussed. The presence of
venereal disease in a child under age thirteen should immediately alert
the professional to the possibility of child abuse. Theories of transmission of venereal disease through contaminated towels and sheets have
long been discarded, and, consequently, any child so infected must have
acquired the disease through some form of sexual contact.

D. LEGAL PROSECUTION

1635 "Conviction of forcible rape of a 15-year-old daughter -- reversed."
      Sex Probl Court Dig 6(1): 2, January, 1975. (0 References).
Report of the reversal by the Michigan Supreme Court of a man's conviction
for the forcible rape of his fifteen-year-old daughter. The decision was
based on purely procedural considerations.

1636 Horwitz, Elinor L. "A grieving mother fights back." McCalls
      101(3): 40, March, 1974. (0 References).
Tells of one mother's fight for legislation making molestation of children
a federal offense with harsh penalties. Her efforts followed the brutal
slaying of her own daughter.

1637 Milner, Alan. "Indecency With Children Act, 1960." Br J Criminol
      2(3): 282-91, January, 1962. (35 References).
Considers a British law which allows the conviction of a person who in-
duces a child under fourteen to engage in indecent behavior without the
use of threats or force. Coupled with harsher penalties for existing sex
crimes against children, the Indecency With Children Act is an attempt to
encourage more severe punishment of child molesters.

1638 Reifen, David. "Protection of children involved in sexual offenses:
      a new method of investigation in Israel." J Crim Law Criminol
      Police Sci 49(3): 222-29, September-October, 1958. (0 Refer-
      ences).
Describes investigative and courtroom procedures begun in 1955 in Israel
to protect children from unnecessary trauma who have been victims or witnesses to a sexual offense. Children under fourteen are kept out of the
court altogether; their testimony is taken by trained youth examiners who
then deliver the children's evidence to the court.

1639 "Sex offenses involving children." Int Juv Off Assoc Newsl 3(4):
      9-10, July-September, 1974. (0 References).
The prosecution of sex offenses against children poses a dilemma in which
medical and legal values are opposed. The welfare of the victim of a sex
offense does not always coincide with the welfare of society, and while
the physician may seek to protect the victim from the trauma of the court,
the lawyer must seek the full prosecution of the perpetrator. Both legal
and medical professions are urged to be cognizant of their areas of conflict in such cases and, above all, to be sensitive to the great vulnerability of the juvenile victim.

1640 "Sexually assaulted children." Br Med J 2(5310): 973-74, October
      13, 1962. (4 References).
The British Parliment is urged to act upon recommendations made by an ad
hoc committee of the council of the Magistrate's Association. These are
aimed at alleviating the difficulties experienced by the child sexual
offense victim during the trial of the accused. Recommendations are:
(1) one written statement of the child's evidence should be presented to
the court of trial, instead of frequent repetition of the facts; (2) the
trial should be set for the earliest possible date; (3) the public should
be excluded unless otherwise ordered by the court; and (4) the accused
should be strongly urged to accept legal representation.

1641 "Statutory rape of a 13-year-old daughter -- conviction upheld:
      discussed." Sex Probl Court Dig 6(1): 3, January, 1975. (0
      References).
Report of the denial by the Maine Supreme Court of an appeal of a man
convicted for the statutory rape of his thirteen-year-old daughter. The
decision was based on the statutory definition of rape as sexual intercourse involving a girl under the age of fourteen.

E. TREATMENT AND PREVENTION

1. CHILD CARE

1642 Breen, James L.; Greenwald, Earl; Gregori, Caterina A. "The molested
      young female: evaluation and therapy of alleged rape." Pediatr
      Clin North Am 19(3): 717-25, August, 1972. (7 References).
Outlines procedures to be followed in cases of sexual assault on minors.
Definitions of terms utilized in sexual offense cases are presented. The
general order of evaluation and treatment in alleged molestation is: (1)
immediate care of injuries and thorough examination; (2) collection of
medicolegal information, involving the signing of a consent form by a
third party witness, a statement given by the victim, evaluation of the
patient's emotional status by the physician, laboratory investigations,
and various details noted in the gynecological examination; and (3) therapy to prevent disease, pregnancy, and psychological trauma. The examining physician is responsible for an accurate and thorough collection of
evidence following sexual assault, as he may be called upon to present
his findings at a later date.

1643 De Francis, Vincent. Protecting the child victim of sex crimes
      committed by adults. Denver, Colorado: The American Humane
      Association, Children's Division, 1969. 230p. (Bibliography).
The results of a follow-up study of child victims of sexual abuse are detailed. Specific examples of abuse undergone by the 250 victims studied
include rape, sodomy, and incest. Study data was taken from the Bronx,
where no special services were provided for the victims of sexual assault,
and from Brooklyn, where protective services played a significant role in
helping the families through the investigation and court proceedings, and
during the long-term rehabilitative process.

On a projected national scale of incidence, there would be ten girl victims of sexual abuse to each male victim. In the present study, the
offender was known to the child in three-fourths of the cases, and 40
percent of the time, the sexual abuse had been prolonged over several
months or even years. The child's fear of retribution, or the wife's
fear of losing minimal economic stability, allowed the sexual abuse to go
unchecked in many families. Families where incest occurred were often
pathologic. Poor child care and a lack of supervision were evident in
one-third of the families; and in another 11 percent, the wife or children suffered physical abuse. If the offender was a father figure, he
often exploited the child's wish to please, although coercion by physical
force was evident in half of the cases. The question of whether a child
can consent to or encourage sexual abuse is discussed.

Eighty-two percent of the reports were first investigated by the police.
Victims and their families underwent repeated questionings. The standard

community response to the sexual exploitation of children is to punish
the offender; consequently, the child's emotional needs are forgotten
during the long investigative and judicial ordeal. One hundred and
seventy-three of the study cases were prosecuted, most in the adult criminal court. Half of these cases were dismissed, however, as for the most
part, the child's testimony could not be verified by other witnesses. In
Brooklyn, in an effort to diminish psychological trauma, a Child Protective Service worker of the same sex questioned the child at home and
stayed with him during court hearings and other periods of crisis.

A child, who has some understanding of the forbidden nature of what has
happened to him, will often suffer additional emotional trauma. Children
from the study population exhibited signs of fear, guilt, rejection,
anxiety, hostile-aggressive behavior, inferiority, and serious problems
in school. Because many families were themselves hostile to the victim
(17 percent of the parents blamed the child for the offense), many victims ran away from home or threatened suicide. Parents also suffered the
impact of the sexual abuse with breakdown of marriages, loss of jobs, or
harassment by neighbors occurring. To help future child victims of sexual abuse and their families, more sympathetic investigative and judicial
procedures are needed, along with supportive assistance from community
agencies.

1644   Leaman, Karen. "The sexually abused child." Nursing '77 7(5):
       68-72, May, 1977. (0 References).
Emphasizes the role of the nurse in caring for a sexually abused child.
The nurse must support all family members emotionally and help them
resolve their feelings about the abusive event and the adult offender.
The nurse's responsibility also includes: (1) explaining all medical
procedures to the parents; (2) reporting the incident when required to do
so by law; (3) recommending supportive community services; and (4) maintaining a close follow-up contact with the child and her family.

2. CORRECTIVE MEASURES FOR THE OFFENDER

1645   Davison, Gerald C., and Wilson, G. Terence. "Goals and strategies
       in behavioral treatment of homosexual pedophilia: comments on a
       case study." J Abnorm Psychol 83(2): 196-98, April, 1974. (21
       References).
Discusses and evaluates a case report by R. J. Kohlenberg concerning the
treatment of a homosexual pedophile, so that he learned to become sexually responsive to adult men. Aversive conditioning and Masters-Johnson
in vivo exposure were the techniques employed. A primary issue included
in the review of this case report is that of the social desirability of
orienting the offender toward homosexuality. Follow-up information concerning the assimilation of the client to society after treatment was
lacking in the original study. The reviews commend the mode of treatment,
but stress the need for more detailed evaluation.

1646   Giarretto, Henry. "The treatment of father-daughter incest: a
       psychosocial approach." Child Today 5(4): 2-5, 34-35, July-
       August, 1976. (5 References).
The Child Sexual Abuse Treatment Program (CSATP) in San Jose, California
is described. A father-daughter incestuous relationship is severely
damaging to the structure of the family because the roles of each member

become confused, and communication between father, daughter, and mother is hindered. The goals of the CSATP are to: (1) rehabilitate the family and marriage by providing individual and joint counseling for family members; (2) initiate self-help groups such as Parents United and Daughters United; (3) coordinate all program and community services involved in the management of incest cases; (4) inform the public of the existence of the problem; and (5) train qualified professionals to adopt similar programs in other communities. The offender must undergo the criminal justice process in order to learn that the community will not tolerate the incestuous behavior. The CSATP has been successful in treating families where father-daughter incest is present. Evaluation of the program demonstrates that no recidivism has been reported in more than 300 cases formally terminated.

1647 Halleck, S. "Treatment of the sex offender: the therapeutic encounter." Int Psychiatry Clin 8: 1-20, 1971.

1648 Harbert, T. L.; Barlow, D. H.; Hersen, M.; et al. "Measurement and modification of incestuous behavior: a case study." Psychol Rep 34(1): 79-86, February, 1974. (0 References).
Reports on the treatment regime of an incestuous father. The subject was a fifty-two-year-old male who engaged in incestuous behavior with his daughter beginning when she was twelve. His sexual history was marked by deviance at an early age, which was possibly patterned after the behavior of other family members. The subject's deviance was measured by having him rate his desire to participate in a number of normal and abnormal father-daughter situations which had been typed on cards. He was treated by covert sensitization for fifteen days with subsequent follow-up treatment. Results showed a substantial decrease in the mean penile circumference change and subject's deviant score, with only sporadic increases during the treatment process. It was noted that incestuous tendencies did not interfere with the subject's desire to perform normal father-daughter functions. It was also suggested that treatment should provide alternative behavior to deviance.

1649 Macdonald, G. J., and Di Furia, G. "A guided self-help approach to the treatment of the habitual sex offender." Hosp Community Psychiatry 22(10): 310-13, October, 1971. (0 References).
Examines a program at Western State Hospital in Washington for the rehabilitation of sex offenders. A number of the offenses had been committed against children. The program involved at least ninety days observation of the patient by a psychiatrist; the treatment seemed relatively successful, since its rate of recidivism compared favorably with that of state correctional institutions.

3. PREVENTIVE MEASURES

1650 Elonen, Anna S., and Zwarensteyn, Sara B. "Sexual trauma in young blind children." New Outlook Blind 69(10): 440-42, December, 1975. (0 References).
Cases of blind children who were sexually assaulted are described, along with measures parents and professionals should take to prevent such occurrences.

1651 Sierra, Sali. "Rx to check child molesting." <u>Ill Med J</u> 135(6): 731-32, 735, 750, June, 1969. (8 References).
Examines the problems, prevention, and treatment of child molestation. Precautions for children to follow, as developed by a nationwide Patch the Pony educational program, have already proven to be an effective preventive measure. However, if a child is molested despite self-protection, the hysterical reactions of his parents or the trauma of courtroom procedures may have a more damaging effect on the child than the actual assault. The physician can be particularly helpful at this time in calming the parents and reassuring the child. A discussion of corrective measures for offenders suggests a combination of confinement and treatment. General characteristics of offenders and victims are offered.

F. PORNOGRAPHY

1652 "Child pornography: outrage starts to stir some action." <u>US News World Rep</u> 82(23): 66, June 13, 1977. (0 References).
Explores reactions to the problem of child pornography. The trade is growing and its victims are children of broken homes, some of whom are sold into sexual slavery by their parents. Legislatures are currently proposing bills against child pornography. Some authorities feel that the cure lies in strengthening the family unit and not by law. The American Civil Liberties Union and movie producers are concerned that these laws will violate the First Amendment rights by defining films like <u>Romeo and Juliet</u> as pornographic.

1653 "Child's garden of perversity." <u>Time</u> 109(14): 55-56, April 4, 1977. (0 References).
Focuses on the widespread problem of child pornography. The types of scenes one can expect to see in pornographic literature and films involving children are described. Parents sometimes sell their children for participation in such pornography. Psychiatrists believe that these experiences will cause later sexual difficulties for the children. In an attempt to abolish child pornography, legislators are trying to avoid the touchy question of obscenity and are calling child pornography a form of abuse.

1654 Dudar, Helen. "America discovers child pornography." <u>Ms</u> 6(2): 45-47, 80, August, 1977. (0 References).
Describes the efforts of Dr. Juianne Densen-Gerber to bring child pornography to public attention as a further example of the sexual abuse of children. Otherwise healthy and attractive children are lured to pose for suggestive pictures with other children or actual sex acts with adults. Child actors are often paid for their work with trinkets as a superficial gesture of affection; teenage models are mostly runaways who can find no other means of supporting themselves. In addition to efforts aimed at instituted federal and state legislation for the prosecution of peddlers and producers of child pornography, major discussion is now focused on discovering any relationship between the greater availability of child pornography and the increase of child sex crimes, including incest.

1655 Goldstein, Michael J., and Kant, Harold S. <u>Pornography and sexual deviance: a report of the Legal and Behavioral Institute, Beverly Hills California</u>. Berkeley, California: University of California Press, 1974. 194p. (Bibliography).

Presents the findings of in-depth interviews conducted with sexually atypical males--homosexuals, rapists, pornography users. In addition, early experiences with sex and erotica were compared with a group of black and white males. The impact of pornography on society is discussed.

VII

Legal Issues

A. THE RIGHTS OF CHILDREN

1. HISTORICAL SURVEY AND PRESENT ISSUES

1656 Chandler, Christopher B. "Children and the law." Practitioner
213(1275): 335-44, September, 1974. (0 References).
Discusses and evaluates Great Britain's laws concerning children. A
description of laws involving education, employment, welfare services,
and treatment of juvenile offenders is included. The role of the courts
in child abuse cases is also outlined. Despite the reforms introduced
by the Children and Young Persons Act, 1969, unsolved problems in the
legal protection of juveniles still exist, especially in the area of
adoption.

1657 Children's Defense Fund. Report of second year activities of the
Children's Defense Fund of the Washington Research Project, Inc.
Cambridge, Massachusetts: Children's Defense Fund, 1974. 54p.
A report on the 1974 activities of the Children's Defense Fund shows that
program development had occurred in the areas of children's rights to
education, research on children, screening and diagnosis, classifying and
labeling of children, and juvenile justice.

1658 Declaration of the rights of the child adopted by the General
Assembly of the United Nations, New York, November 20, 1969.
London, England: Her Majesty's Stationery Office, 1960. 4p.
(2 References).
Outlines the rights of children as declared by the General Assembly of
the United Nations. The declaration recognizes the dependence of children on others for the guarantee of their rights. It establishes ten
principles which protect children from exploitation, discrimination, neglect and cruelty, and guarantees the right to an atmosphere of affection
and the opportunity to develop physically, mentally, spiritually, and
socially in a normal manner.

1659 Dorman, Michael. "Home and parents." In: Dorman, Michael. Under
21: a young people's guide to legal rights. New York: Delacorte,
1970. 125-41. (0 References).
Considers the legal status of child abuse and neglect, and other areas of
potential conflict between parents and minor children. Several cases of
abuse and neglect are cited to explain the necessity of reporting such
incidents. Parental custody is also discussed and several examples are
provided demonstrating the need for the representation of the child in
disposition hearings. The legal rights of runaways are also touched upon.

1660 Marker, G., and Friedman, P. R. "Rethinking children's rights."
      Child Today 2(6): 8-11, November-December, 1973. (6 References).
Presents a children's bill of rights, including the right to a supportive
environment, the right to adequate medical care, to an appropriate education, to protection from abuse and neglect, and to adequate representation
of their interests. The legal profession is urged to work for the recognition of these rights, particularly those which the law has not yet
acknowledged (for example, the rights to medical care without parental
consent, to protection from forms of abuse and neglect, and to representation).

1661 Oettinger, Katherine Brownell. "The rights of our children." Child
      Welfare 37(6): 1-6, June, 1958. (1 Reference).
Defines the rights of all children, whether poor, mentally retarded,
handicapped, or orphaned, and urges local and national efforts aimed at
securing these rights. Both rural and urban children have a right to a
home, medical treatment, an education, and opportunities for recreation.
The goal of the children's rights movement is to foster joint decision-
making between parent or adult, and child.

1662 "Parental consent requirements and privacy rights of minors: the
      contraceptive controversy." Harv Law Rev 88(5): 1001-20, March,
      1975. (103 References).
Discusses the question of whether or not the state can interfere in the
free access of contraceptives to minors. A number of decisions regarding
the rights of minors, vis à vis their parents' authority, are reviewed,
with particular reference to the recent interpretation of the equal protection clause of the Fourteenth Amendment to cover the civil liberties
of minors. It is decided that the minor's right to obtain contraceptives
outweighs the countervailing interest of the parent in controlling his
child's behavior and the state's interest in safeguarding the family.

1663 "The rights of children." Harv Educ Rev 44(1): 1-196, February,
      1974. (295 References).
Presents an assemblage of scholarly articles devoted to tracing the historical conception and present application of children's rights. Particular areas of investigation included: (1) the work of the Children's
Defense Fund in the field of child advocacy; (2) a report on major reform
in the Massachusetts juvenile correction system; (3) a study of the
application of the Constitution in recent court decisions regarding the
rights of retarded, minority, and institutionalized children; (4) a
criticism of psychological assessment procedures which stigmatize children in school and fail to recognize their multidimensionality; and (5)
a philosophical argument for children's rights which challenges the traditional paternalist view. Important books dealing with the family, the
rights of children, and the educational system are reviewed.

1664 Simpson, Keith S. "Battered babies: conviction for murder." Br
      Med J 1(5431): 393, February 6, 1965. (5 References).
Documents a case in which a nineteen-year-old father was convicted of
the murders, ten months apart, of his two young children. Both children
were apparently beaten to death; this was the first case in England in
which a child abuser was convicted of murder.

1665 Weinstein, Noah. Legal rights of children. Reno, Nevada: National
      Council of Juvenile Court Judges, 1974. 32p.

Cites the origins and history of legal rights for children, including the
cases which set the precedent for the stated law. Thirty-one legal areas,
their subdivisions, and exemplary cases from various states are listed.

2. CHILD VS. INSTITUTION

1666 "The court: don't spare the rod." Time 109(18): 58, May 2, 1977.
      (0 References).
The problem of corporal punishment in the public schools is summarized.
The Supreme Court has ruled that corporal punishment is not prohibited
by the Eighth Amendment's protection against cruel and unusual punishment
even when injury results. Punished children can sue if they feel an in-
justice has occurred. While psychiatrists feel that such punishment is
harmful and useless, the American public continues to sanction it.

1667 Farson, Richard E. "The right to freedom from physical punishment."
      In: Farson, Richard E. Birthrights. New York: Macmillan, 1974.
      113-28. (0 References).
Deplores the use of corporal punishment in schools. Corporal punishment
is defined as the infliction of unharmful, physical pain on a person for
his "wrongdoing." Its use has been accepted for centuries, endorsed in
the Bible and in the courts. The doctrine of corporal punishment in
schools operates under the assumption that parents have the right to beat
their children. Consequently, when an institution is responsible for
acting in loco parentis, it automatically has the same disciplinary rights
as parents. However, not only is the issue of parents' rights to beat
their children brought into question, but also the constitutionality of
corporal punishment in terms of violating a person's right to due process.
Furthermore, corporal punishment is charged with cruel and unusual punishment because it applies only to children. It is a violation of children's
rights as the idea that parents should exercise complete, authoritative
control over their children--a fundamental, guiding principle in our
society's conception of family life. Equally as acceptable is the practice of meeting aggression with aggression. However, bodily violence
against children should never be recognized as an appropriate response to
children under any circumstances.

1668 Ferleger, David. "The battle over children's rights." Psychol
      Today 11(2): 89-91, July, 1977. (6 References).
Questions the denial of rights to young people who are committed to mental institutions by their parents or other responsible guardians. The
decision made by the United States Supreme Court in the Bartley v. Kremens
case states that parents' powers do not extend to the waiver of their
children's constitutional rights for protection against confinement without due process. This restricts parental power and undermines the
previous erroneous assumption that parents generally act in good faith
for the benefit of their children. A discussion of further implications
of the decision in favor of children's rights is included.

1669 Freeman, C. B. "The Children's Petition of 1669 and its sequel."
      Br J Educ Stud 14(2): 216-23, May, 1966. (6 References).
Reports the use of corporal punishment in seventeenth century English
schools, and those crusaders who attempted to bring the matter to Parliment. The Children's Petition (1669) and its sequel (1698-1699) represent
major efforts protesting such cruelty. Two centuries later, the Corporal

Punishment in Schools Bill was introduced into the House of Commons, but
the bill did not receive a second reading. Subsequent attempts were also
futile, and control of this abuse was not brought about by an Act of
Parliment; it was controlled in state schools by regulations of local
education authorities or by Home Office rules.

1670   Knitzer, Jane. "Spare the rod and spoil the child revisited."
       Am J Orthopsychiatry 47(3): 372-73, July, 1977. (0 References).
Discusses the implications of the United States Supreme Court decision in
the case of Ingraham v. Wright, which supported the continued use of
corporal punishment in schools without providing due process protections
to students. This decision reflects a social attitude of indifference,
even hostility, toward children. It further illustrates that society is
not yet willing to face and prevent the institutional abuse of children.

1671   "A license to beat children." Progressive 41(6): 8, June, 1977.
       (0 References).
Agrees with the minority opinion in the Supreme Court case which denies
constitutional protection to students under the Eighth Amendment.
Majority opinion viewed the Eighth Amendment as pertaining to prisoners,
while minority opinion viewed inhumane punishment to any individual as a
violation of his constitutional rights.

1672   McDaniel, Charles-Gene. "Legalized child abuse." Progressive
       40: 12-13, January, 1976. (0 References).
Criticizes the Supreme Court decision to allow corporal punishment in the
schools. The difference between spanking and beating is sometimes small.
The fact that the United States no longer allows the beating of prisoners,
sailors, employees, and even animals, is contrasted with the fact that
Americans sanction corporal punishment for children, even for minor mistakes.

1673   McNulty, Jill K. "The right to be left alone." Am Crim Law Rev
       11(1): 141-64, Fall, 1972. (39 References).
Studies the present overreach of the juvenile court system, found to be
detrimental to the young persons subjected to its interference. The
statutory status of the "minor in need of supervision" in a number of
states is described, and the negative ramifications of the assumption of
the role of social welfare agencies by the juvenile courts are discussed.
A more appropriate social institution for the management of non-criminal
delinquency is proposed.

1674   Miller, Derek, and Burt, Robert A. "Children's rights on entering
       therapeutic institutions." Am J Psychiatry 134(2): 153-56,
       February, 1977. (14 References).
Calls attention to some of the characteristics of adolescent psychological
development which should be taken into account before new laws regarding
the placement of adolescents in psychiatric facilities are developed.
Currently, a parent or juvenile court may request placement in a facility.
New proposals include an opportunity for the adolescent to protest the
order and to receive a court review. The young adult's need for autonomy
at a particular stage of his development is stressed. If given the
opportunity to challenge his parents' or a court's decision, he might do
so, thereby depriving himself of possibly helpful treatment. It is suggested that the courts seek a compromise between "constitutional norms"
of personal freedom and parental options. It is recommended that place-

ment in residential psychiatric facilities be carried out with discretion; that the child receive effective treatment, tailored to his particular problems and needs. Purely punitive incarceration is discouraged.

1675 Paulsen, Monrad G. "Fairness to the juvenile offender." Minn Law
       Rev 41(5): 547-76, April, 1957. (206 References).
The rights and protections due the juvenile offender are detailed. Procedures used in juvenile courts are, in theory, intended to rehabilitate
and protect the child rather than to punishment him. However, the informal methods employed toward this end by the juvenile courts can
deprive the juvenile of the rights automatically granted to the adult
criminal offender. Areas in which the study examines the difference
between adult and juvenile justice are: (1) treatment before trial; (2)
specific standards of delinquency; (3) the petition for a hearing; (4)
the court hearing; (5) admission of evidence; (6) the role of the social
worker and his report; (7) the right to counsel; and (8) the appropriate
assignment of treatment.

1676 Sheils, Merrill, and Boyd, Frederick V. "Ruling on the rod."
       Newsweek 89(18): 65-66, May 2, 1977. (0 References).
Assesses the Supreme Court's decision that corporal punishment of students
is not a violation of the Eighth Amendment. The controversial case was
that of James Ingraham and Roosevelt Andrews against Drew Junior High in
Dade County, Florida. Although the majority agreed that the boys'
punishment had been extreme, they ruled that because of the openness of
the public school supervision, students do not need protection under the
Eighth Amendment. The dissenting opinion in this decision viewed the
amendment as protection for all individuals.

1677 Silbert, James D., and Sussman, Alan N. "The rights of juveniles
       confined in training schools and the experience of a training
       school ombudsman." Brooklyn Law Rev 40(2): 605-33, Fall, 1973.
       (99 References).
A negative assessment, based on personal experience, of the utility of
the ombudsman as a guardian of the rights of children in the New York
State Training School system. The first section enumerates the rights
which juveniles should be able to claim in such institutions (for example,
right to due process, to freedom of expression, the right to receive
therapy, and to reject it). However, the residents of these schools are
often not informed of their rights. The remainder of the report discusses the difficulties experienced by the authors as ombudsmen in
attempting to remedy this situation and protect the rights of juveniles
in the institution where they worked. The ombudsmen met indifference
and opposition from the other officials; their power was frustratingly
limited; the bureaucratic structure in which they operated was oppres-
sively elaborate; custodians and residents lived in an atmosphere of
mutual hostility. The current modus vivendi in the training school is,
therefore, strongly criticized as being destructive of young lives.

1678 Wheeler, Gerald R. "Children of the court: a profile of poverty."
       Crim Delinq 17(2): 152-59, April, 1971. (17 References).
Examines the tragic relationship between child neglect or delinquency and
poverty. Poor children are, by virtue of their position in society, at
risk, but the courts and social welfare agencies too often fail to consider the influence of poverty on their circumstances. Generally, these
children are automatically institutionalized with little attention to

their individual needs, and the cycle of deprivation remains unbroken.
The recent recognition of the need for procedural safeguards in the juvenile court should be accompanied by the recognition that rights even more
basic than those of due process must be preserved.

B. LEGISLATION

1. HISTORICAL SURVEY OF CHILD PROTECTION

1679   Bayne-Powell, Rosamond. "The law and the child." Bayne-Powell,
       Rosamond. The English child in the eighteenth century. New York:
       E. P. Dutton, 1939. 143-56. (0 References).
Portrays the inhuman and cruel punishments inflicted upon children under
eighteenth century English law. Petty offenses such as picking pockets
and pilfering were cause to send children to prison, from which there was
neither escape nor release unless certain fees were paid. Thievery could
result in hanging. Parents had absolute control over their offspring and
could treat them as they wished without fear of incrimination. Institutions such as workhouses exploited children of all ages. Numerous additional accounts of the brutal, often fatal, maltreatment of children by
institutions and by individuals reflect eighteenth century attitude
toward helpless children in English law.

1680   Ficarra, B. J. "Pioneer laws for child protection." Int J Law
       Sci 7(2): 68-71, April-June, 1970.
Traces the historical development of the protection of children by the
laws from the earlier precedent in 4 A.D. down to the recent burgeoning
of child abuse legislation, with particular focus upon the influence
exerted by England over Europe and the United States in this endeavor.

1681   Moore, G. Y. "The duty and necessity for child welfare work."
       J Med Assoc Ga 20(5): 168-70, May, 1931. (0 References).
Address to the Members of the Womans Auxiliary on the topic of child
welfare work. The speaker discusses President Hoover's Third White House
Conference for Child Health and Protection, results from the White House
Committee on Medical Care (indicating the presence of ten million defi-
cient children in America), and protective legislation.

1682   New Century Club, Philadelphia. Statutes of every state in the
       United States concerning dependent, neglected and delinquent chil-
       dren. Philadelphia: George F. Lasher, 1900. 368p.
A compendium of pre-1900 individual state legislation for the care and
protection of dependent, neglected, and delinquent children. Although
the majority of statutes cited were concerned with the punishment and
reformation of delinquent or vagrant youths, most states also made provisions to house and educate the blind, deaf, dumb, and orphaned. Nineteenth century definitions of neglected children often referred to children caught begging or living in the company of thieves, prostitutes, or
saloon owners. A Kentucky statute declared that abandoned or habitually
maltreated children could be discharged to a charitable reformatory by the
court. An 1899 ordinance passed in Utah stated that any parent who willfully neglected a child would be guilty of a misdemeanor. Few states had
specific provisions for interceding in behalf of abused children, although
several states did assign care of such children to the Society for the

Prevention of Cruelty to Children. An 1884 Maine statute, however, affirmed that two or more citizens in any town could file a complaint for a
child who had been willfully neglected or cruelly treated by his parents.
The parents were informed of the impending court hearing through the
county newspaper.

1683 Paulsen, Monrad; Parker, Graham; Adelman, Lynn. "Child abuse re-
      porting laws -- some legislative history." George Washington Law
      Rev 34(3): 482-506, March, 1966. (97 References).
A study undertaken at the Columbia University School of Law reviews the
legislative history of child abuse laws. Their passage in forty-seven
states since 1962 indicates the shared concern of legislators. The U.S.
Children's Bureau is cited as a major force behind the statutes, supporting mandatory reporting to protective rather than police agencies, and
providing the language used by most of the states when drafting their own
laws. Mass media, such as television and national magazines, were influential in alerting the public to the necessity for child abuse legislation, and emphasized reporting by physicians. Individual influence
came primarily from professionals working with children such as physicians, social workers, and lawyers. Voluntary organizations drafted
legislation and informed the public and legislators about issues. These
groups included organized medicine which at a national level opposed the
mandatory reporting clause and questioned to whom the report should be
made. These two issues were also a source of controversy in the legislature. State executive departments began studies, composed proposals, or
supported those groups who were directly involved. The need for expanding service to the abused child, including legislation applicable to the
deprived child, remains.

1684 Stark, Jean. "The battered child: does Britain need a reporting
      law?" Public Law 48-63, Spring, 1969. (26 References).
Compares the parallel recognition of the phenomenon of child abuse in
Britain and the United States. It is acknowledged that the problem needs
to receive more attention in Britain than it has received. The child
abuse reporting laws in the United States are examined with the purpose
of determining the efficacy of similar future legislation in Britain. It
is concluded that the United States laws have had some effect, although
more emphasis should be placed on registries and the role of social welfare agencies. Much of the work of the reporting law could be accomplished by other means in Britain, but some sort of legislation is
favored.

1685 Wilcox, D. P. "Child abuse laws: past, present, and future."
      J Forensic Sci 21(1): 71-75, January, 1976. (16 References).
While recorded incidents of child abuse date back to 2000 B.C., it was
not until Kempe described the battered child syndrome in the early
1960's that states passed legislation to define and protect abused children. Recent trends in child abuse laws have increased the number of
professionals required to report suspected abuse, expanded the definitions of abuse and neglect, and transferred the responsibility of
receiving and following up reports from law enforcement agencies to child
welfare services. Other trends provide statutory immunity for those
reporting, information centers on child abuse, and various legal provisions for the abused child. Federal legislation has provided funds for
developing treatment programs while a new model law is being developed.

2. STATUS OF PRESENT LEGISLATION

a. Model Legislation

1686 "The abused child, parents, and the law: editorial." RI Med J
      47(2): 89-90, February, 1964. (0 References).
Stresses the need for protective child abuse legislation. Statistics on
the increasing incidence of maltreatment are cited and the passage of a
model state law is urged.

1687 Besharov, Douglas J. "Model legislation -- its purpose and orienta-
      tion." In: National Symposium on Child Abuse, 5th, Boston, 1974.
      Collected papers. Denver, Colorado: The American Humane Associa-
      tion, Children's Division, 1976. 118-19. (0 References).
Questions the possibility of a national law concerning the problem of
child abuse. The success of reporting laws depends on the community's
support. Because laws must reflect the community's standards, it will
be difficult to establish a national model law which is flexible enough
to adhere to the conditions of individual communities.

1688 "Child abuse prompts plan for state legislative action." Intellect
      102(2355): 283-84, February, 1974. (0 References).
Legislative action by the Education Commission of the States (ECS) insists
that state child abuse statutes be expanded to better protect victims and
that interstate cooperation in recognizing child abusers be improved.

1689 Education Commission of the States. Child abuse and neglect: model
      legislation for the states: Report no. 71: Early childhood report
      no 9. Denver, Colorado: Education Commission of the States, 1975.
      73p. (Bibliography).
Presents model child abuse legislation drawn up by the Education Commission of the States and revised according to the guidelines set forth
in Public Law 93-247, which provides federal funds for state and local
efforts to prevent and manage child abuse and neglect. States seeking
this assistance are now required to institute regular procedures for
child abuse reporting, investigation, and treatment; in addition, a permanent multiagency professional apparatus to manage and prevent child
abuse must be maintained. The state must give priority in its distribution of federal funds to parental organizations fighting against child
abuse and neglect.

1690 Education Commission of the States. Child Abuse and Neglect Advisory
      Committee. Child abuse and neglect: model legislation for the
      states: Report no. 71: Child Abuse and Neglect Project. Denver,
      Colorado: Education Commission of the States, 1976. 64p.
      (Bibliography).
A model for state child abuse and neglect legislation which meets the
ten requirements for federal assistance specified in Public Law 93-247
is detailed. It is hoped that this precisely written legislative model
will encourage reporting, foster a non-punitive approach to working with
abusive families, and promote greater cooperation and uniformity of
policy among all child care agencies and professionals.

Each legislative proposal is spelled out and followed by commentary and
suggestions for alternative wordings. The primary purpose of a child
abuse reporting law is to protect the life and well-being of every child

while making every attempt to preserve the integrity of the family. Important terms such as "child," "abuse," and "neglect" are defined. The scope of the reporting law covers not only physical and sexual abuse and neglect, but also emotional and institutional abuse and neglect. The list of persons required to report has been expanded; moreover, medical examiners and coroners are mandated to file reports upon encountering any non-accidental deaths of children. Procedures for reporting are outlined as follows: the initial report directed to a centralized state agency (which also houses a twenty-four-hour hot-line and the central registry) can be verbal; it must be followed, however, by a written report with appropriate supporting evidence, such as color photographs or x-rays.

Provisions for initiating protective custody without the permission of the child's parents are clarified. Stipulated immunity from liability, abrogation of privileged communications, and penalty clauses are explained. The responsibilities of child protective services in coordinating both investigative and treatment programs are enumerated. Guidelines for establishing a community-wide multidisciplinary child protection team are given. The role of the guardian ad litem as protector of the child's best interests and friend of the court is defined. Additional requirements for maintaining records in the central registry and for sponsoring public and professional education programs are presented.

1691   Fraser, Brian G.   Child abuse and neglect: alternatives for state legislation: Report no. 6 of the Early Childhood Task Force.
Denver, Colorado: Education Commission of the States, 1973.   92p.
A draft of suggested legislation to focus increased attention on child abuse and neglect, bringing together some of the best provisions in existing state legislation. This proposed legislation also increases the capacity of the states to contribute to the effort against child abuse.

1692   ————.   "The tragedy of child abuse: 'Momma used to whip her.'"
Compact   8:   10-12, March-April, 1974.   (0 References).
Focuses on state and national action to combat child abuse. Three states --Idaho, Florida, and New York--have initiated advertising campaigns to educate the public. The Education Commission of the States' (ECS) proposal to standardize state legislation would insure immunity for all persons making reports in good faith, provide a central registry for tracking purposes, and expand the definition of child abuse to include non-accidental physical injury, sexual abuse, emotional abuse, and neglect.

1693   Lesermann, Sidney.   "The facts behind battered-child laws."   Med Econ   41(17):   71-75, August 24, 1964.   (0 References).
Reviews the need for laws concerning child abuse, the requirements of a physician under existing laws, and the factors influencing the effectiveness of such laws. Child abuse laws are necessary to protect the ten thousand children abused each year as well as the reporting physicians. The laws direct the physician to report the abuse to the proper agency immediately and without accusation. However, they are effective only if the agency receiving the report responds appropriately. Arguments are made for reporting to protective agencies rather than to law enforcement officers in order to emphasize protective care of the child rather than punitive action toward the parents.

1694   Oettinger, Katherine B.   "Protecting children from abuse."   Parents Mag   39(11):   12, November, 1964.   (0 References).

Notes an increase in child abuse and stresses the need for new legislation. Parents as well as children need the help which legislation,
voluntary or public agencies, and private individuals can offer.

1695 Reinhart, John B., and Elmer, Elizabeth. "The abused child."
      JAMA 188(4): 358-62, April 27, 1964. (6 References).
Presents the advantages and disadvantages of model legislation on child
abuse. The legislation proposed by the Children's Bureau (HEW) establishes procedures and expectations for dealing with maltreatment. However, the potential anger and fear aroused in the parent reported to the
police may be directed toward the child. Filing a report through protective agencies who initiate family treatment is, in many cases, more
constructive and appropriate than criminal prosecution.

1696 Theisen, William. "Implementing a child abuse law: an inquiry
      into the formulation and execution of social policy." For a
      summary see: Diss Abstr Int 33A(12): 7028, June, 1973.

1697 U.S. Children's Bureau. The abused child: principles and suggested
      language for legislation on reporting of the physically abused
      child. Washington, D.C.: U.S. Government Printing Office, 1963.
      13p.

1698 "Violent parents." Lancet 2(7732): 1017-18, November 6, 1971.
      (10 References).
Insists that new legislation is needed allowing court orders for the
removal of children at risk upon recommendation of social service workers
and the medical profession. Court trials are not the solution. This
position is preceded by an overview of child abuse in Britain.

                    b. Existing Systems: General

1699 American Humane Association, Children's Division. Child protective
      services, 1967. Denver, Colorado: The American Humane Associa-
      tion, Children's Division, 1967.
The Children's Division of the American Humane Association conducted a
nationwide survey of child protective services and child abuse reporting
legislation. The study was designed to determine the nature and extent
of existing protective services in all states, to identify their legal
bases, to assess their effectiveness, and to analyze state laws for the
reporting of child abuse. Questionnaires were submitted to state and
county departments of welfare and to community chests and welfare
councils. Responses to the questionnaire were supplemented by visits to
key communities around the nation. The report provides a succinct listing of major findings, discussion, and analysis of significant data and
a state-by-state account of services and related legislation.

Child protective services are defined as a uniquely specialized aspect of
child welfare, whose aim is to preserve the family unit and whose application requires a high degree of skill and training. Services were found
to vary greatly, both from state-to-state and within some states. The
laws authorizing the provision of services did not always clearly define
their intent or the nature of the services mandated. Some state legislation was more concerned with action against the parents than with protective services. There was a variation with regard to the age limits under

which children were deemed eligible for services and with regard to the nature of the complaints requiring investigation. No state was found to provide adequate coverage, which was defined as the capacity to respond promptly to all complaints, to explore all reports fully, to assess the damage to the child in all reported cases, to evaluate the future risk to the child in all cases, to offer remedial services without exception, and to take summary action through the courts wherever warranted. Limitations in staffing, finances, and training were responsible for inadequacies in service.

State reporting legislation was also found to vary widely. There was not complete agreement as to the definition of abuse, the need for the reporter to establish proof of abuse or to include the identity of the perpetrator in his report, the professional affiliation of the person required to report, the need for a penalty for failure to report, and the nature of the mandate to the agency designated to receive reports. There was most confusion in this last area, which was felt to be of crucial importance. The kind of action which ensued from a report of suspected child abuse was determined by the nature of the responding agency. Punitive measures were likely to be instituted by a law enforcement body; treatment measures by a public welfare agency. It is emphasized that reporting laws are not enough; adequate services must also be insured.

1700 De Francis, Vincent, and Lucht, Carroll L. Child abuse legislation
       in the 1970's. Denver, Colorado: The American Humane Association,
       Children's Division, 1974. 200p. (Bibliography)
This revision of the 1970 edition is essentially the same as the original in format and discussion. In addition to a categorical breakdown of the most recent child abuse legislation, certain newly enacted special clauses are examined. These include: (1) exclusion of children receiving spiritual healing from legislative protection; (2) authorization to hold a child in a hospital against parental wishes; (3) emergency removal and right of entry; (4) special rules of evidence; and (5) the institution of a children's guardian ad litem. Dual legislation, requiring physicians to report to law enforcement agencies and all other persons to child protective services, is criticized as being opposed to the basic non-punitive philosophy of child abuse reporting legislation.

1701 Fisher, Gordon D. "Interdisciplinary management of child abuse
       and neglect." Pediatr Ann 5(3): 114-28, March, 1976. (16
       References).
Discusses three types of laws dealing with child abuse. The purpose of criminal laws is to protect the child from physical assault and to rehabilitate the criminal parents by imposing fines or terms of imprisonment. Criminal laws are ineffective when dealing with child abuse cases because: (1) they do not provide comprehensive treatment of the child and family; (2) they have not proved to be deterrents of future abusive acts; and (3) they discourage parents from seeking help and treatment for their child and themselves when abuse occurs. Reporting laws generally come under the jurisdiction of the civil courts, although most states impose criminal sanctions against those professionals who fail to report child abuse when they are required to do so by law. While the primary purpose of reporting laws is to identify children who are abused, they are not extremely effective to this end. Reporting laws alone cannot provide community services and treatment programs, nor can they overcome the reluctance of physicians--especially those in private practice--to diagnose and report child abuse cases. An interdisciplinary team

approach for the review of suspected child abuse cases is considered to
be the most effective method of encouraging reporting by professionals.
Adoption laws provide for the termination of the rights of natural parents
if the child has been subjected to physical abuse and neglect over a long
period of time. Because the termination of parental rights is a judgment
that cannot be reversed, the courts have been reluctant to do this except
in extreme circumstances.

1702   Ganley, Paul M.   "The battered child: logic in search of law."
       San Diego Law Rev 8(2): 364-403, March, 1971. (120 References).
Attempts to clarify numerous legal questions regarding child abuse,
namely, the identification and definition of child abuse, various rationales for different child abuse laws, criminal sanctions, juvenile courts,
registries, and protective agencies.

1703   Hochhauser, Lois.   "Child abuse and the law: a mandate for change."
       Harv Law J 18(1): 200-219, 1973. (39 References).
Surveys the current legal apparatus throughout the country for handling
child abuse, including the status of reporting laws, protective services,
criminal laws, and juvenile court acts, with particular reference to New
York and the District of Columbia.

1704   Katz, Sanford N.; Howe, Ruth-Arlene W.; McGrath, Melba.   "Child
       neglect laws in America." Fam Law Q 9(1): 1-372, Spring, 1975.
       (128 References).
Surveys and analyzes the child neglect statutes in the fifty states, the
District of Columbia, Gaum, Puerto Rico, and the Virgin Islands, as
amended through August, 1974. Child neglect is often defined in physical
terms (e.g., lack of clothing or shelter, insufficient supervision, or
malnutrition), although the concept can also include the failure to ensure
the positive social and psychological development of the child. Historically, the law has been concerned with the abused and/or neglected child
in both criminal and civil contexts.

Child neglect laws have seven basic components: a statement of purpose,
definitions, procedures for neglect hearings, penalties for neglect,
reporting of neglect, termination of parental rights, and special clauses.
The statement of purpose clause that appears most frequently (thirty-
seven times) in neglect statutes in America is "to secure care, guidance,
and/or custody and discipline" of the neglected child. A large majority
of the jurisdictions (forty-five) do not have a statutory definition for
the term "neglect," and of the eight states that define neglect, five do
so in their civil code, and three in their criminal code. The typical
neglect hearing section will provide for counsel, appointed counsel, and
appeal. Only thirteen jurisdictions require the appointment of guardians
ad litem in certain circumstances for children. Usually the statutes
outline procedures for an informal hearing, closed to the public and with
no specific provision for a trial by jury. Possible dispositions and
court orders include temporary placement orders, transfers of legal
custody of the child, dismissal if neglect is not proved, protective
supervision of the child in his home by the court, and examination and
treatment of the child.

Statutory penalties for neglecting a child were found in thirty-two
jurisdictions--nineteen civil and fourteen criminal. They range from
fines of $50 to $100, and sentences of imprisonment from thirty days to
five years. Forty-three jurisdictions provide for the reporting of some

aspects of neglect under their child abuse reporting acts. All jurisdictions except Oregon have provided immunity from civil and criminal liability to the person who reports neglect in good faith. In twenty-three statutes, the termination of parental rights requires a separate proceeding from the neglect hearing. Statutory ground for termination of parental rights include abandonment (in thirty-seven statutes), neglect (in thirty-five), parental consent (in twenty-four), and parental moral unfitness (in twenty). Special clauses in neglect statutes include spiritual healing exemptions (in twenty-three jurisdictions), religious or racial placement preferences (in thirty jurisdictions), and others. A detailed digest of American statutes concerning child neglect for each jurisdiction is presented.

1705 "More of the same: editorial." Nation 198(15): 339, April 6,
      1964. (0 References).
Criticizes child abuse legislation as a verbal attack on a social problem.
Measures should be aimed at improving the poor social and economic conditions which lead to child abuse.

1706 Parker, Graham E. "The battered child syndrome (the problem in
      the United States)." Med Sci Law 5(3): 160-63, July, 1965. (5
      References).
Considers the role of legislation in alleviating the problem of child
abuse. The lack of a universally accepted child protection agency comparable to the NSPCC in Britain is felt to hamper efforts to deal effectively with the problem. Legislation can make an important contribution
but it is not a panacea. Laws which are geared to the protection of the
child are preferable to those which are interested in the prosecution of
abusers. Mandatory reporting legislation, sometimes hastily conceived,
is inadequate if it does not also delineate the responsibilities of the
agencies designated to receive reports. Sections from state child abuse
acts are quoted to illustrate the author's arguments.

1707 Paulsen, Monrad G. "The legal framework for child protection."
      Columbia Law Rev 66(4): 679-717, April, 1966. (202 References).
Reviews the legal system surrounding the problem of child abuse. Presently this legal framework is divided into four sets of provisions: (1)
criminal law invoking punishment; (2) juvenile court acts which may provide for the protective supervision of a child; (3) legislation authorizing child protective services; and (4) child abuse reporting laws.
Reporting laws are the key to initiating action, but they do not operate
effectively without community cooperation and without corrective followup action. In turn, criminal law is brought into question, not because
of any lack of legislation to handle child abuse cases, but because of
the realization that criminal punishment may not effectively correct
family problems. Legal provisions on all four levels need to be coordinated for proper functioning of the judicial process.

1708 ————. "Legal protections against child abuse." Children
      13(2): 43-48, March, 1966. (12 References).
Legal services available for child protection are reviewed. Criminal
laws established to punish abusers need little revision or attention;
increasing their severity or enforcement cannot help the child or rebuild the disintegrated family. Juvenile court acts provide supervision
of families or removal of the child from families where the goal of

rehabilitation cannot be met. The working of these acts varies, and
proof of parental misconduct is often harder to establish than improper
environment. Protective services respond to a complaint of abuse rather
than to a court order. If the family refuses aid, then court action may
be taken. However, since uninvited help is offered, the issue of privacy
is a sensitive one. Reporting laws are the springboard for services.
Their purpose is to eliminate hesitancy in reporting, especially on the
part of physicians whose medical skills are often the most reliable de-
terminers of abuse. Reporting to police versus welfare agencies is a
widely debated issue among supporters of abuse legislation. A need for
twenty-four-hour reporting services and central registries exist, although
improvement in services has occurred with increased child abuse legislation.

1709   Raisbeck, Bert L. "The legal framework." In: Borland, Marie, ed.
       Violence in the family. Atlantic Highlands, New Jersey: Humani-
       ties Press, 1976. 88-106. (0 References).
Outlines legal measures available to the battered child and the battered
wife. Legal solutions for abused children include criminal prosecution
of the abuser, civil proceedings resulting in supervision or removal of
the child, a judicial decision without court proceedings, and emergency
measures for crisis situations. Although the law encourages others to
intercede on behalf of abused children, such is not the case for battered
wives. They are assumed to be adults and capable of initiating proceedings for themselves. Many wives are not capable of such action or are
not in a position to defend themselves legally. Though legal revisions
are called for, the solution ultimately rests with social agencies alert
to family needs.

1710   "Saving battered children." Time 85(2): 43, January 8, 1965.
       (0 References).
Although cases of child beating are easily recognized, they give rise to
legal problems whose solutions cannot be separated from social concerns
about treatment for abusive families. Mandatory reporting legislation
which protects the reporter from liability does not insure effective
follow-up, and the threat of punishment may deter parents from seeking
help. The course of action for those involved in the diagnosis and treatment of child abuse is still nebulous.

1711   Shepherd, Robert E., Jr. "The abused child and the law." Va Med
       Mon 93(1): 3-6, January, 1966. (9 References).
Evaluates legislation on child abuse, particularly in Virginia. Generally,
the courts hold two views in relation to parental authority and child
abuse. The first is that the parents are the sole authority regarding
punishment of their child. The second view is that parents have the
right to punish if it is in the interest of the child's welfare; if not,
he is criminally liable to charges of assault, murder, or manslaughter.
The rights of the state surpass those of the parent where the well-being
of the child is concerned. A number of states have passed laws on that
basis and are now adopting the model act as proposed by the Children's
Bureau. Further legislation should include a provision for protective
services and de-emphasize the punitive aspects. The fact that 50 percent of maltreatment cases are subject to repeated injury underlines the
importance of effective legislation.

1712 —————. "The abused child and the law." In: Wilkerson, Albert
E. The rights of children: emergent concepts in law and society.
Philadelphia: Temple University Press, 1973. 174-89. (75 References).
Discusses the present and former laws pertaining to child abuse. Legal
limits on parental discipline are currently reflected in two different
points of view: (1) parents, or those acting in loco parentis, are
solely responsible for administering punishment and ensuring that it is
not inflicted maliciously and does not cause permanent injury; and (2)
parents can punish children as long as the punishment does not exceed the
bounds of moderation and reason. In general, the laws relating to neglect
and physical abuse are based on the idea that the interests of the state
must at times supersede the rights of parents in order to offer protection
to children. An assessment of the seriousness and extent of the problem
is given. Mandatory reporting legislation is regarded as one step toward
meeting the challenge of child abuse, and an outline of the statute suggested by the Children's Bureau (HEW) is provided. Criticism of such
legislation includes the rejection of the penalty clause because it is
unenforceable, useless, and unduly harsh. Reporting legislation alone
cannot be expected to correct abuse. Protective service programs need
to be expanded and improved. Recommendations for a statute, including
provisions for protective social service action, are offered.

1713 "State action on child abuse and neglect." Compact 10(3): 14-15,
Summer, 1976. (0 References).
Condenses federal and state legislation on child abuse and neglect into
a compact chart. Legal provisions and requirements up to January, 1976
are covered.

1714 Stoetzer, James B. "The juvenile court and emotional neglect of
children." Univ Mich J Law Reform 8(35): 351-74, Winter, 1975.
(110 References).
Discusses the feasibility of statutes protecting the emotional well-being
of the child as well as his physical safety and health. A number of
statutes make vague reference to the child's emotional welfare, but provide little in the way of standards for determining cases of emotional
neglect. Various statutes which have attempted to provide such standards
are analyzed, with New York's neglect provision appearing to be the most
satisfactory. Courts are cautioned against precipitous intervention in
cases of neglect.

1715 Sullivan, Michael F. "Child neglect: the environmental aspects."
Ohio State Law J 29(1): 85-115, Winter, 1968. (91 References).
Legal statutes dealing with five classes of parental neglect are analyzed
in terms of their clarity, objectives, and constitutional validity. Parents have a natural and constitutional right to bring up their children,
and the parens patriae power of the state allows judiciary intervention
in the family only when the parent-child relationship threatens the proper
development of the child into a responsible citizen. But neglect
statutes are vaguely written and individual judges are given too much
power, resulting in unwarranted and unconstitutional state intervention
in family life. For example, a parent can be judged to be neglectful if
he or she belongs to a non-conforming religious organization, even when
there is no evidence to suggest that the parent's involvement in the
religion will have an adverse effect on the child's development into a
responsible citizen. Or the parent can be charged with neglect if his/her

child is delinquent, even though there is no proof that the misbehavior is caused by lack of parental control rather than the child's neighborhood environment, peer group association, or other influences. The laws on child neglect threaten some of our most treasured rights and values. Alleviation of this threat depends upon careful legislation and objective judicial interpretation of the statutes.

c.   Federal Initiatives

(1)   Child Abuse Prevention and Treatment Act

1716   American Humane Association, Children's Division. Speaking out for child protection. Denver, Colorado: The American Humane Association, Children's Division, 1973.   27p.   (Bibliography).
This study is based on testimony presented at a hearing on Senator Walter Mondale's proposed child abuse legislation.   A history of the American Humane Association's involvement in securing the passage of child labor laws, providing shelter for cruelly treated or neglected children, and promoting the establishment of a separate juvenile court system is described.   The objectives, research findings, and educational role of child protective services are explained.   A discussion of federal responsibility in the management of child abuse is followed by commentary on the proposed federal legislation, S. 1191.   The strong points of the bill are: (1) the creation of a National Clearinghouse on Child Abuse and Neglect;   (2) federal authorization for funded research;   and (3) modification of the Social Security Act to provide additional protection for children.   Indicators of progress in the field of child protective services are outlined as follows: (1) the change of attitude from punitive to therapeutic;   (2) the medical discovery of the battered child syndrome in the early 60's;   (3) the passage of reporting legislation in all fifty states;   and (4) the growing cooperation between the medical profession, protective service workers, and the juvenile court.

1717   "Child abuse and neglect." Int Juv Off Assoc Newsl 3(4):   17-18, July-September, 1974.   (0 References).
Presents a notice regarding the passage of the Child Abuse Prevention and Treatment Act by the Congress.   Also discussed are the Act's ramifications for juvenile officers, who are called upon to cooperate fully with public health nurses and social service organizations in the detection and prevention of child abuse.   It is noted that child abusers have frequently been juvenile offenders.

1718   Goldman, J.   "Washington day care: editorial." Day Care Early Educ 2(1):   21-23, September, 1974.   (0 References).
Comments on the establishment by the Department of Health, Education, and Welfare of the National Center on Child Abuse and Neglect, mandated by the $85 million Child Abuse Prevention and Treatment Act of 1974.   A brief legislative history of the Act is provided, along with the purview of the new Center and the basic definition of child abuse stated in the Act.

1719   MacLeod, Celeste.   "Parent to child: legacy of battering." Nation 218(23):   719-22, June 8, 1974.   (7 References).

Discusses the Child Abuse Prevention and Treatment Act passed by Congress in January, 1974, which provides funding to state and community agencies to set up their own programs. Small community programs staffed by parents, grandparents, and other paraprofessionals are better able to break down the barriers of the nuclear family and encourage shared responsibility for childrearing.

1720 U.S. Congress. House. Committee on Education and Labor. Child Abuse Prevention and Treatment Act: Report together with dissenting views to accompany S. 1191. 93rd Congress, 1st session, 1973, H. Rept. 93-685. Washington, D.C.: U.S. Government Printing Office, 1973. 12p.

Reviews the legislation (S. 1191) devised by the Senate Select Subcommittee on Education that would provide the following: (1) the establishment of a National Center on Child Abuse and Neglect; (2) a legal definition for the phrase "child abuse and neglect;" and (3) financial assistance to demonstration child abuse team projects, as well as to states actively engaged in developing prevention and treatment programs. A section-by-section analysis of the bill's seven sections clarifies how these major provisions will be interpreted and administered. A three year projection of estimated costs shows a graduated increase of $5 million each year. Also included in the report are the dissenting views of Earl F. Langrebe on S. 1191. He questions the role of the federal government in dealing with the problem of child abuse and criticizes the Committee for neglecting to cite the source of the funds included in the projected costs. Most importantly, he charges the Committee with failing to adequately define the term "child abuse and neglect."

1721 U.S. Congress. House. Committee on Education and Labor. Select Subcommittee on Education. To establish a National Center on Child Abuse and Neglect: Hearing on H.R. 6379, H.R. 10552, and H.R. 10968. 93rd Congress, 1st session, 1974. Washington, D.C.: U.S. Government Printing Office, 1974. 292p. (Bibliography).

A record of the lengthy hearings conducted in 1973 before the Select Subcommittee on Education of the Committee on Education and Labor in the House of Representatives. Three of these hearings took place in Washington, D.C., and the fourth in New York City, New York. Prominent members of numerous public and private organizations across the country dealing with the problem of child abuse and neglect offered prepared statements and witness accounts concerning what needs to be done to more effectively detect, prevent, and treat child abuse and what they are presently doing to solve the problems. Discussed in detail are: (1) case reports illustrating the gravity of the problem; (2) reports relating the functions of various interagency systems currently in operation, some hospital-based, some rural, and some state supported; (3) reports from the June, 1973, National Conference on Child Abuse; (4) historical accounts of legislative, social, and medical action taken specifically in New York City to combat child abuse; and (5) preliminary proposals for the Parental Stress Center for Allegheny County, Pennsylvania.

Also included are the texts of three federal bills providing the following: (1) the creation of a National Center on Child Development and Abuse Prevention, that would offer financial assistance for innovative programs promising further efforts to detect, prevent, and treat child abuse and neglect (H.R. 6379, 93rd Congress, 1st session); (2) an amendment of the Elementary and Secondary Education Act of 1965 to provide grants to states for establishing programs to prevent and treat abuse (H.R. 10552, 93rd

Congress, 1st session); and (3) both the creation of a National Center
for Child Abuse and Neglect and a program of grant aid to states for prevention and treatment programs, as well as funding for research, training,
and demonstration projects. Specific sums of federal money authorized
annually for grants to aid child abuse protection programs are outlined
in each bill.

1722 U.S. Congress. Senate. Committee on Labor and Public Welfare.
      Child Abuse Prevention and Treatment Act, 1974: Public Law 93-247
      (S. 1191). Questions and answers, analysis, and text of the Act.
      93rd Congress, 2nd session, April, 1974. Washington, D.C.: U.S.
      Government Printing Office, 1974. 10p.
Includes a copy of the Child Abuse Prevention and Treatment Act enacted
by the ninety-third Congress in 1974. The Act's main purpose is to provide financial assistance to various public and private organizations,
as well as to states that engage in activities aimed at developing child
abuse and neglect prevention and treatment programs. This Act also provides for the creation of a National Center on Child Abuse and Neglect
to administer the law. The Center is contained within the Department of
Health, Education, and Welfare. Although its duties are extensive, it
is responsible primarily for administering grants, for publishing an
annual report summarizing research on child abuse and neglect, and for
conducting an authoritative study on the incidence of child abuse and
neglect. Requirements for states seeking federal grant aid for prevention and treatment programs are enumerated. Efforts to coordinate the
projects under this Act are to be made by the Secretary of the Department
of Health, Education, and Welfare.

1723 U.S. Congress. Senate. Committee on Labor and Public Welfare.
      Subcommittee on Children and Youth. Child Abuse Prevention Act,
      1973: Hearing on S. 1191. 93rd Congress, 1st session, March 26-
      31 and April 24, 1973. Washington, D.C.: U.S. Government Printing
      Office, 1973. 695p.
Hearings before the United States Senate regarding S. 1191, the Child
Abuse Prevention Act, 1973. The Act's provisions are to establish a
National Center on Child Abuse and Neglect and to provide states, as well
as public and private non-profit organizations, with grants to fund the
development of demonstration projects aimed at preventing, identifying,
and treating child abuse and neglect. Further responsibilities of the
child abuse center would include a study to estimate the national incidence of non-accidental injuries to children, an annual summary of
research conducted on child abuse and neglect, and the publication of
training materials for individuals actively involved in identifying,
preventing, or treating child abuse. Senator Walter F. Mondale, as acting chairman of the Subcommittee on Children and Youth, conducted the
hearings.

The first of the four hearings revolved around two major topics, namely,
violence to children and a discussion of the history and function of
Parents Anonymous. David Gil, Professor of Social Policy at Brandeis
University, concentrated his testimony on a definition of child abuse,
statistics reflecting its incidence, current knowledge about abusers and
their victims, and his personal reaction to the proposed legislation before the committee, including recommendations to strengthen it. Jolly
K. of Redondo Beach, California, and Gertrude Bacon of New York City,
New York, represented Parents Anonymous. More importantly, they spoke
for thousands of parents who abuse their children and, therefore, offered

the committee a dramatic and courageous testimony on the abuse problem that would have been difficult to obtain had there never been an organization like Parents Anonymous to help these parents voice their problems and receive assistance. Their comments gave the Committee a clearer sense of the needs of the abusing parent and what could be done to meet them.

The second hearing, like the first, was conducted in Washington, D.C. It opened with a panel discussion of the history of the federal government's role in child abuse and of the strengths and weaknesses of the legislation proposed. A panel of government officials, testifying against the bill, was criticized for not having sufficient information about current local and state child abuse protective programs. In fact, they had not even consulted the local Child Abuse Team at the District of Columbia's Children's Hospital for potential advice in writing up their final reactions. This fact was confirmed by representatives of the Child Abuse Team from the Children's Hospital, who then continued with a lengthy presentation describing their own operations, including medical histories, complete with slides and recommendations to strengthen the proposed bill. At the conclusion of their presentation, it was ascertained that to their knowledge, not one single individual in the federal government was currently working full-time on the question of child abuse alone.

The third hearing, conducted in Denver, Colorado, included witnesses from the well-known child abuse team located in Denver. Their reports embraced medical histories of abused children, as well as a comprehensive report on the battered child syndrome submitted by C. Henry Kempe, M.D., of the University of Colorado Medical Center. Many areas of concern were discussed. One of primary significance was a follow-up study on the development of abused children, revealing discouraging, often tragic results. Personality development problems were the most prevalent. Few of the children in the study could enjoy themselves or make friends, and many suffered from low self-esteem, learning disabilities, and behavior problems. The study points to the need for learning more about the abusive homes and about how to treat abused children to limit these disorders.

Proposals for a Child Abuse Center at the Roosevelt Hospital emerged first during the fourth hearing held in New York City, New York. Afterward, a final statement from Barbara B. Blum, Assistant Administrator/Commissioner for the Special Services for Children Program in New York City, suggested that the volunteer programs currently working in Denver would not be effective to the same extent in New York City. Such volunteer programs are presently non-existent, which helps explain the high cost of maintaining and developing efficacious child protective services in New York City. Ms. Blum maintained that the citizens of New York City were decidedly different from, and much more transient, than the residents of Denver. This transience, among other things, makes it exceptionally difficult to successfully initiate low budget abuse prevention and treatment programs operated by volunteers. Three appendices follow the text of the hearings: (I) Medical and Legal Literature, (II) Child Abuse Programs, and (III) Press Reports.

1724 U.S. Office of Child Development. <u>Child abuse and neglect activities, U.S. Department of Health, Education, and Welfare</u>. Washington, D.C.: U.S. Department of Health, Education, and Welfare, 1974. 16p. ERIC Document ED 106 002. (DHEW Publication no. (OHD) 75-4). Describes the history of federally funded child abuse programs and lists summaries of projects funded under the Child Abuse Prevention and Treatment Act of 1974. The activities of the National Center on Child Abuse and Neglect are described.

1725 U.S. Office of Human Development. <u>Report of the U.S. Department</u>
      <u>of Health, Education, and Welfare to the President and Congress of</u>
      <u>the United States on the Implementation of Public Law 93-247, the</u>
      <u>Child Abuse Prevention and Treatment Act.</u> Washington, D.C.: U.S.
      Department of Health, Education, and Welfare, Office of Human
      Development, 1975. 60p.
Lists and explains in detail the provisions of the new Child Abuse Prevention and Treatment Act. The Act was intended to provide: (1) a
definition of child abuse and neglect; (2) coordination of efforts to
identify, treat, and prevent child abuse; (3) research which will lead
to new knowledge and new methods relative to the abuse problem; (4) compilation of existing knowledge about successful methods; (5) training of
professional, paraprofessional, and volunteer workers; (6) encouragement
for agencies--state or private--to improve their services for identifying,
treating, and preventing child abuse and neglect; and (7) a comprehensive
study of the incidence of child abuse and neglect nationwide.

(2) Office of Child Development Programs; Other Programs

1726 "Child abuse." In: U.S. Department of Health, Education, and
      Welfare. <u>Promoting the health of mothers and children: FY 1973</u>.
      Washington, D.C.: U.S. Government Printing Office, 1973. 57-61.
      (0 References).
Summarizes federally funded programs dealing with child abuse in 1973.
Capsule reports included new legislation, professional and voluntary
organizations, project funds, hospital involvement, training programs,
and recent research on incidence and abuser characteristics.

1727 "The dependent and neglected." In: Golden Anniversary White House
      Conference on Children and Youth, Washington, D.C., 1960. <u>Con-</u>
      <u>ference proceedings</u>. Washington, D.C.: U.S. Government Printing
      Office, 1960. 392-93.
Proposals of the Golden Anniversary White House Conference on Children
and Youth in 1960 are outlined. The proposals generally emphasized state
and local action in the form of legislation, community services, prevention, and research, and included suggestions for care of the multiply
handicapped.

1728 National Conference on Child Abuse. Legislative Work Group.
      "Report from the Legislative Work Group." <u>Clin Proc</u> 30(2):
      39-41, 1974. (0 References).
Sets forth recommendations concerning federal legislation to combat child
abuse. It is proposed that the states receive funds to establish non-
punitive child abuse programs which follow certain federal guidelines,
including the passage of reporting legislation, the designation of a
single agency to administer the program, and the establishment of a
central registry. Additional federal projects concerning child abuse
might be the initiation of HEW training programs to foster expertise in
handling child abuse, a national information clearinghouse, and a national
registry of abused children.

1729 Thomas, Stanley B., Jr. "Federal priorities on behalf of neglected
      and abused children." In: National Symposium on Child Abuse, 4th,
      Charleston, S.C., 1973. <u>Collected papers</u>. Denver, Colorado: The
      American Humane Association, Children's Division, 1975. 34-38.

Outlines the projects of the Office of Human Development concerning child abuse and neglect. Funds were provided to state and local communities for improvement and development of protective services. Revision of the Model Child Abuse Reporting Law was expected. Other plans included a research project to determine early warning signals, the development of a model for classroom teachers for training in the detection of abuse and neglect, the establishment of Parents Anonymous, and the testing of a national clearinghouse for the collection of data on abuse and neglect.

1730   U.S. Congress. Senate. Committee on Labor and Public Welfare. Subcommittee on Children and Youth. Rights of children, 1972. Part II: Appendix: Selected readings on child abuse and day care. 92nd Congress, 2nd session, 1972. Washington, D.C.: U.S. Government Printing Office, 1972. 823p.

Consists of a collection of documents and articles for use by the Senate Select Subcommittee on Children and Youth as a reference source on the subject of child abuse. Included are reprints of a number of articles on child abuse, and the book, Child Abuse and Legislation in the 1970's, by Vincent De Francis. The final presentation in the collection is a report from the National Council of Jewish Women entitled Windows on Day Care. At that time, the Council had over 100,000 members in 176 communities, called Sections, across the nation. The majority of these Sections had day care programs. Of the 176 Sections, ninety had agreed to participate in the "Window on Day Care" project designed to examine the extent of the country's day care needs, to determine who could benefit most from such services, and to assess what was being accomplished in proprietary centers, non-profit centers, and day care homes, as well as in the day care facilities of the Council Sections. Findings indicated that millions of children were not receiving adequate developmental day care services. Many of these children had working mothers and many belonged to families living in poverty, where the mother was unemployed. Recommendations for federal subsidies and legislation are outlined by the Council. Requests for federal action in twelve areas, including federal administration and coordination, a clearinghouse of information on funding, expanding and improving services, and educating the community are emphasized.

1731   U.S. Department of Health, Education, and Welfare. Federally-funded child abuse and neglect projects: 1975. Washington, D.C.: U.S. Government Printing Office, 1975. 56p.

A directory of federally supported demonstration, resource, research, training, and technical assistance projects directly related to child abuse and neglect. Each entry lists the project director, amount of funding, the inclusive dates, and a brief description of the project. Three indices provide cross references of project directors and institutions, project titles, and a list of projects conducted in each state.

1732   U.S. Maternal and Child Health Service. Maternal and child health programs: legislative base. Rockville, Maryland: U.S. Department of Health, Education, and Welfare, 1975. 76p. (Bibliography).

Presents the verbatim legislation and regulations covering health and welfare services for mothers and children in effect on January, 1975. State maternal and child health and children's programs of Title V of the Social Security Act, the amendments to this Act in 1972, and related sections of the Public Health Service Act and Civil Rights Act are included.

1733 U.S. National Center for Education Statistics. Neglected or
      delinquent children living in state operated or supported institu-
      tions: Fiscal year 1972. Washington, D.C.: National Center for
      Education Statistics, 1974. 44p.
A statistical analysis of expenditures during the fiscal year 1972 for
supplementary services for neglected and delinquent children in state-
operated institutions, as authorized under Title One of the Elementary
and Secondary Education Act.

1734 U. S. Office of Child Development. Office of Child Development.
      Washington, D.C.: U.S. Department of Health, Education, and Wel-
      fare, 1975. 12p. (DHEW Publication no. (OHD) 76-30006).
Describes the origin, function, and organization of the Office of Child
Development (HEW).

1735 U.S. Office of Child Development. Intradepartmental Committee on
      Child Abuse and Neglect. Research, demonstration, and evaluation
      studies in child abuse and neglect. Washington, D.C.: U.S. Govern-
      ment Printing Office, 1974. 26p.
Enumerates the studies funded in fiscal year 1974 by the Office of Child
Development (HEW) through the Intradepartmental Committee on Child Abuse
and Neglect. Each entry includes the name and address of the project
director, the size and duration of the grant, and a brief description of
the project funded. Historical background is provided on the Committee.
Areas of interest covered include the prediction of child abuse, research
into maternal-child and other familial relations, and a large number of
family help projects, such as community centers and Parents Anonymous.

1736 ————. Research, demonstration, and evaluation studies on child
      abuse and neglect. Washington, D.C.: U.S. Government Printing
      Office, 1975. 32p. (DHEW Publication no. (OHD) 75-77).
Lists thirty-eight projects funded by the Intradepartmental Committee on
Child Abuse and Neglect (HEW) in fiscal year 1974. Projects are listed
according to their funding department; the principal investigator is
named, and the projects' objectives are listed. The following topics are
among those studied: demography of child abuse, community child abuse
programs, mother-child bonding, and family resource centers. Historical
background on the Committee is provided.

1737 U.S. Office of Child Development. Research and Evaluation Division.
      Research, demonstration, and evaluation studies. Washington, D.C.:
      U.S. Government Printing Office, 1973. 71p. (DHEW Publication
      no. (OHD) 74-30).
Compilation of studies funded through the Office of Child Development
(HEW) during fiscal year 1973. The information in each project is organized by subject areas and includes the name and address of the project
director, the amount and duration of the grant, and a brief synopsis of
the project.

1738 ————. Research, demonstration, and evaluation studies.
      Washington, D.C.: U.S. Government Printing Office, 1974. 89p.
      (DHEW Publication no. (OHD) 75-30).
The Office of Child Development's (HEW) Annual Report for fiscal year
1974 is detailed. The Office's role and objectives are outlined and the
projects it is currently funding are listed. Project areas include child
advocacy, child abuse and neglect, child development and the family, and
day care.

1739 Weinberger, C. W. "The oath did not make any allowance for group
      practice: editorial." Med Insight (10): 30-32, October, 1973.
      (0 References).
Summarizes recent child abuse initiatives by the Department of Health,
Education, and Welfare, including the Intradepartmental Committee on
Child Abuse, the preparation of a bibliography on the subject, the development of an improved reporting system, and the funding of several research
programs on child abuse by the National Institute of Mental Health and
the Office of Child Development. Physician reporting of child abuse
cases is urged.

                    d. Individual State Initiatives

1740 Bern, Joseph. "California law: the battered child, the family,
      and the community agency." J State Bar Calif 44(4): 557-67,
      1969. (7 References).
Focuses on the lack of clarity in California's child abuse legislation.
Members of the legislature and of the legal profession need to join with
other concerned agencies and professionals in recommending improved
legislation.

1741 "Burnt children: editorial." Br Med J 1(5646): 790, March 22,
      1969. (4 References).
A criticism of the current provision in the Young Persons Act that parents who leave children unattended near oil heaters or open grate fires
are liable for neglect only if the child is seriously injured. The
contention is that since the injury to the child is itself a greater
punishment to the parent than the penalty imposed by the law, the law
should be broadened to penalize any parent who leaves a child unattended
near an open grate oil heater, whether the child is injured or not.

1742 Burt, Marvin R. The system for neglected and abused children in
      the District of Columbia: a policy analysis. Bethesda, Maryland:
      Burt Associates, 1974. 55p. (Bibliography).
Advocates revisions in policies regarding the care of neglected and
abused children in the District of Columbia. Among other suggestions,
the study recommends widening the scope of the reporting law and mandating publicly supported child abuse treatment programs. Various options
for improving current methods of reporting, intake, and short- and long-
term care are also evaluated. These recommendations grow from experiments with model programs in selected communities. The report also
delineates existing methods of handling child abuse cases and offers
criteria for evaluating government child protection programs.

1743 Carpenter, James W. "The parent-child dilemma in the courts."
      Ohio State Law J 30(2): 292-309, Spring, 1969. (33 References).
Investigates the legal problems involved in the statutory prohibition
against child abuse and child neglect in Ohio. Certain issues serve as
the fountainheads of these problems: the mandatory reporting law, the
removal of the child from his parents' custody, and the actual prosecution of child abuse/neglect cases in court.

1744 "Child abuse." Va Health Bull 26(2, Series 2): 1-20, October-
      December, 1973. (0 References).

Reports on the current management of child abuse in Virginia. The
Virginia child abuse reporting law is described and favorably assessed.
The work of the Governor's Task Force on Child Abuse is outlined and its
recommendations enumerated. These include the establishment of child
protection committees in hospitals throughout Virginia and the integration
of all legislation pertaining to child abuse.

1745 "Child abuse: scourge of society: editorial." J Med Assoc State
      Ala 46(5): 17, November, 1976. (0 References).
Recent changes in a section of the Alabama Criminal Code relating to
child abuse are noted. The redefinition of the act of child abuse by the
Alabama Legislature in 1977 will provide the opportunity for the public
to register its opinion and to act against abuse. Legislation alone cannot be more effective than the degree to which the citizenry is informed.

1746 Coyne, Martin. "Interagency and community cooperation." In:
      National Symposium on Child Abuse, 5th, Boston, 1974. Collected
      papers. Denver, Colorado: The American Humane Association, Chil-
      dren's Division, 1976. 26-29. (0 References).
After a presentation of some data on child abuse, the problems of passing
a revised child abuse law in Minnesota are discussed. Because various
disciplines refused initially to compromise on their input, the resultant
bill was so comprehensive it was unconstitutional. Administrators fail
when they do not clarify their caseworkers' function in interagency services or do not maintain constant communication between all agencies.
Public education is needed to involve the community in providing more
effective protective services.

1747 Fotheringham, B. J. "Lesiglative aspects of the battered baby
      syndrome in the various states of Australia." Med J Aust 2(7):
      235-39, August 17, 1974. (11 References).
Reviews legislation governing the battered baby syndrome in Australia.
Although there are legal provisions in each state and territory of
Australia for handling cases of battered children, no comprehensive
nationwide legislation functions as a standard for uniform legal definitions and operating procedures. The study suggests, however, that uniformity is not essential to improve the present system. What is needed
are laws clearly stating immunity for those responsible for reporting
suspected cases of battering. Further improvements could be made in
treating detected cases by establishing multidisciplinary committees in
each state to coordinate the medical, social, and legal professionals
involved.

1748 Friel, Leo F., and Saltonstall, Margaret B. "Legal protection of
      the drug-addicted infant." Child Welfare 53(8): 493-97,
      October, 1974. (1 Reference).
Examines the plight of babies born to drug-addicted mothers. It is
recommended that Massachusetts expand its baby battering laws to include
such infants under its protection.

1749 Healey, R. O. "Legislative aspects of the battered baby syndrome
      in the various states in Australia: letter to editor." Med J Aust
      2(14): 540, October 5, 1974. (0 References).
Points out that the writing of child protective legislation in New South
Wales, Australia will be dependent upon the findings of five investigative
project teams.

1750 "Indiana's statutory protection for the abused child." Valparaiso
      Univ Law Rev 9(1): 89-133, Fall, 1974. (92 References).
Reviews Indiana's statutes regarding child abuse and neglect. Four statutory areas are focused upon: (1) the mandatory reporting act, which
requires all people to report suspected cases of child abuse; (2) the
provision in the criminal law for the punishment of acts of child abuse;
(3) provisions in the juvenile law empowering the state to remove abused
children from their homes; and (4) the establishment of a program of
child welfare services to deal with neglected children. The current
statutory apparatus is found to be basically adequate, but it is strongly
urged that the separate provisions for child abuse and neglect be coordinated and amplified into a comprehensive Child Protection Act, since the
current system contains many areas of overlap and confusion.

1751 Isaacs, Jacob L. "The law and the abused and neglected child."
      Pediatrics 51(4, Part II): 783-92, April, 1973. (0 References).
Describes the four branches of law related to child abuse in New York,
namely, reporting laws, penal law, legal procedures for processing civil
cases of abuse, and provisions for assigning various protective services
to the appropriate public and private agencies. Attempts have also been
made to develop laws effectively relating drug abuse to child abuse and
neglect, but such laws have been quite difficult to work with. Laws pertaining to dispositional alternatives, once an abuse case has been determined, are flexible. Many courses of action, from suspending judgment to
removing the child from the home, are possible alternatives to protecting
the child and rehabilitating the family. Community services take responsibility for carrying out the court decision.

1752 James, Joseph, Jr. "Child neglect and abuse." Md State Med J
      21(7): 64-65, July, 1972. (0 References).
Considers the legal aspects of child abuse in Maryland. The intent of a
recently passed law is to preserve the family structure whenever possible
in child abuse cases. The protective services social worker assesses the
incident and the extent of the damage to the child, reports the facts to
the Juvenile Court, if necessary, and initiates rehabilitative services
to the parents. In addition to social and medical aid, the Department of
Social Services provides a Homemaker Service which offers adult supervision for a child in a high risk situation.

1753 Jones, James L. "Montana's child neglect law -- a need for revi-
      sion." Mont Law Rev 31(2): 201-19, Spring, 1970. (30 Refer-
      ences).
Analyzes Montana's current statutory provisions regarding procedures in
child abuse and neglect hearings. The current laws are found to be inadequate in a number of areas--principally the handling of cases involving children over seventeen, and the recognition and control of the conferences leading to the disposition of the case. Revisions to correct
these deficiencies in the law are proposed.

1754 Kinney, B. D. "Child neglect." Manitoba Law J 3(1): 31-46,
      1968. (7 References).
Reviews the Manitoba Child Welfare Acts of 1902 and 1954. Since the
problem of child abuse is a newly recognized one, the application of the
earlier legislation has not been clear-cut; the definition of child
abuse has particularly been a flexible matter, usually depending upon the
personal experiences of the welfare workers involved. Although no com-

plaint is expressed against the attitudes of those currently responsible for the administration of the Act, there is some concern that "reactionary" officials may at some future date reverse the current pattern of progress.

1755 Lamb, Robert L. "New child abuse law explained." Pa Med 79(2): 30, February, 1976. (0 References).
Explains the Pennsylvania Child Protective Services Law of 1975. The law: (1) supersedes all previous child abuse statutes; (2) requires all professionals to report suspected cases of child abuse; (3) provides those reporting such cases with immunity; (4) allows professionals to order protective custody for up to twenty-four hours for an abused child; and (5) mandates every county to establish a Child Protective Service.

1756 Levi, Stuart, and Schuh, Sara. "Issues on child abuse and neglect in South Carolina." J SC Med Assoc 72(4): 119-23, April, 1976. (7 References).
Discusses controversial issues involved in updating South Carolina's child abuse laws. Parents' rights groups insist on maintaining the absolute right of parents to discipline their children without interferences, while child advocacy groups believe that serious physical battering may be occurring under the guise of "discipline." The groups disagree on how abuse should be defined, whether reporters should be granted immunity from civil suit if their report is proven to be incorrect, and when reporting of abuse should be mandatory. It is recommended that: (1) definitions of abuse and neglect should be specific enough so that very little is left up to the interpretation of the reporter; (2) penalties for making a report of abuse out of spite or to harrass a family should be written into the law in order to discourage this activity; (3) funds should be provided for the establishment of rehabilitative programs for abusing families; and (4) mandatory reporting should be instituted in cases of physical and sexual abuse.

1757 Montana. State Department of Social and Rehabilitative Services. Montana laws relating to abused, neglected and dependent children and youth. (Section 10.1330-.1322). Helena, Montana: Montana State Department of Social and Rehabilitative Services, n.d. 9p.
The laws of Montana relating to child abuse define "child" as any person under eighteen years old, and "abuse" as acts which have some deleterious impact on the physical or emotional development of the person. Neglect, and failure to seek outside the home provision of services not rendered by the parent, are also viewed as constituting abuse. Reporting policy, including its legal implications, is outlined. This collection of statutes is extremely thorough. An addendum, referring to the protective services available in Montana, is included.

1758 Robbins, Jerry H. The legal status of child abuse and neglect in Mississippi. Jackson, Mississippi: Governor's Office of Education and Training, 1974. 101p. ERIC Document ED 089 436.
Includes the text of the Mississippi law on child abuse, along with a discussion of other states' statutory provisions and model acts. Recommendations for improving the Mississippi law are included.

1759 Smith, Jack L. "New York's child abuse laws: inadequacies in the present statutory structure." Cornell Law Rev 55(2): 298-305, 1969-1970. (11 References).

Evaluates the 1969 addition of Article 10 to New York's Family Court Act. The new article narrowly defines procedures for handling physical abuse, which the article distinguishes from child neglect in general. Problems arise, however, in the overlap which exists between the original act which allowed the court broader options for dealing with child abuse, and the new act, which requires the removal of the child from the family whenever serious physical abuse has occurred. It is concluded that the new article is too restrictive and raises too many problems of interpretation to represent a wholly effective addition to the statutory provisions for child neglect.

1760   ten Bensel, Robert W., and Raile, Richard B. "The battered child syndrome." Minn Med 46(10): 977-82, October, 1963. (6 References).

Reviews the characteristics of the battered child syndrome and outlines the responsibilities of physicians under two new laws passed by the 1963 Minnesota State Legislature. The text of these laws is provided. Two medically detailed case studies, including pictured x-rays of injuries, are presented as representative examples of this syndrome. Demographic incidence information is briefly reported, along with general sociological and psychological characteristics.

1761   Tocchio, O. J. "Legislation and law enforcement in California for the protection of the physically battered child." For a summary see: Diss Abstr 28(4): 1509-10, October, 1967.

1762   U.S. Congress. House. Committee on the District of Columbia. Subcommittee on Labor, Social Services and the International Community. Child abuse prevention: Hearing on H.R. 15779 and H.R. 15918. 93rd Congress, 2nd session, 1974. Washington, D.C.: U.S. Government Printing Office, 1974. 155p. (Bibliography).

A complete record is provided of the Congressional hearings on two House bills to establish an agency for the prevention of child abuse in the District of Columbia. Included are: the text of the two bills, a transcript of the hearing testimony, and documents submitted for the record. An index accompanies the materials.

1763   Wooster, Kelly C. "The California legislative approach to problems of willful child abuse." Calif Law Rev 54(4): 1805-31, October, 1966. (52 References).

Reviews the legislative history of two child abuse statutes in California --the 1966 statute mandating the reporting of suspected cases, and the 1965 law providing for the criminal prosecution of the perpetrators. Previous versions of these statutes are discussed, along with the current means of implementing them, and several suggestions for improving both the legislation and the response of the legal system to child abuse cases. The increased utilization of social casework as a tool for dealing with child abuse is urged.

C. REPORTING AND ENFORCEMENT

1. REPORTING LAWS

a. Model Reporting Laws

1764   American Academy of Pediatrics. Committee on Infant and Preschool
       Child. "Maltreament of children: the physically abused child."
       Pediatrics 37(2): 377-82, February, 1966. (24 References).
A review of the major problems attending the recent recognition of child
abuse as a problem includes the diagnosis, reporting, and treatment of
child abuse, the role of the physician, the role of community agencies,
and the utility of the central registry. The Committee on Infant and
Preschool Child sets forth several major recommendations for reporting
legislation: (1) the reporting be mandatory and apply to physicians;
(2) the reports be made to welfare or law enforcement agencies, which
would be equipped and staffed to handle the responsibility; (3) the report
and investigation be managed promptly; and (4) provision be made for the
child's safety and the reporter's immunity.

1765   "The child-abuse problem in Iowa: the extent of the problem, and
       a proposal for remedying it." J Iowa Med Soc 53(10): 692-94,
       October, 1963. (2 References).
Lists the results of a study by the Iowa State Department of Social Welfare, revealing an alarming incidence of child abuse. Suspected or
established causes include emotionally immature parents who know little
about parenting. Medical care for the children and counseling for the
parents are strongly suggested. A proposed act, written by the Children's Bureau (HEW), for the mandatory reporting of abuse by physicians
and institutions, is printed in full. The act includes a provision protecting physicians from liability.

1766   De Francis, Vincent. "Laws for mandatory reporting of child abuse
       cases." State Gov 106-11, Winter, 1966. (1 Reference).
Argues for the passage of mandatory child abuse reporting laws in all
fifty states. The purpose of reporting legislation is to treat the
child's present injuries while protecting him from possible repeated injuries or even death. Mandatory reporting should encourage a supportive
community response toward abusive families instead of a punitive attitude.
Such measures as immunity clauses and waivers of privileged communications may bring about more extensive reporting by physicians.

1767   Education Commission of the States. State services in child
       development: regional conference highlights, spring, 1975: Report
       no. 75: Early childhood report no. 14. Denver, Colorado: Educa-
       tion Commission of the States, 1975. 45p.
Summarizes the proceedings of three regional Education Commission of the
States conferences, focusing particularly on need assessment, child abuse,
and day care centers. The discussion of child abuse centered on the need
for and language of a model reporting statute and on the various techniques for identifying and managing child abuse problems.

1768   "Legislation as protection for the battered child -- I: The prob-
       lem and its history." Villanova Law Rev 12(2): 313-23, Winter,
       1967. (43 References).

A general discussion of the management of child abuse, focusing upon the
reporting statute. The model statute devised by the Children's Bureau
(HEW) is assessed provision-by-provision, and the adaptations of the
model's provisions by the states are generally reviewed. The least helpful portions of the model are judged to be the limitation of the class
of reporting persons to physicians and the recommendation in the earlier
form of the model that cases of abuse be reported to the police, rather
than to a non-punitive agency.

1769   Marer, Jack W. "Development of the law of 'the battered child
       syndrome.'" Nebr Med J 51(9): 368-72, September, 1966. (0
       References).
Reviews the development of a model law for reporting child abuse and includes a survey of the literature from 1946 to 1962. The legislation,
proposed by the Children's Bureau (HEW) in 1962, focused on the issue of
mandatory reporting, which the American Medical Association opposed. The
law, as it was adopted, differed from state to state except for the
immunity it universally granted to reporting physicians. A study of 557
families, conducted by the Children's Division of the American Humane
Association of Denver, was the catalyst in the passage of the law in many
states. The physician is placed squarely between the family and the
law, a position which requires careful investigation and discretion on
his part.

1770   Sussman, Alan. "Model legislation for reporting child abuse."
       In: National Symposium on Child Abuse, 5th, Boston, 1974.
       Collected papers. Denver, Colorado: The American Humane Associa-
       tion, Children's Division, 1976. 120-24. (0 References).
The types of abuse and neglect reporting which should be required include
all incidences of physical harm. Reports of neglect and emotional abuse
should be permissive, but not required, in order to avoid excessive reporting of cases that agencies are not equipped to treat and to prevent
unnecessary labeling of children.

       b.   Comparisons and Surveys of Reporting Legislation

1771   American Medical Association. Office of the General Council.
       "Battered child legislation." JAMA 188(4): 386, April 27, 1964.
       (0 References).
Agrees there is a need for child abuse legislation, but does not approve
of compulsory reporting laws for physicians. This social problem should
have its emphasis on detection prior to need for medical treatment and
should involve other professions such as nursing, teaching, counseling.

1772   Bechtold, Mary Lee. "Silent partner to a parent's brutality."
       Sch Community 52(3): 33, November, 1965. (0 References).
Documents a case study in which legal snarls, such as the threat of a
liability suit, prevent a school psychologist from intervening to protect a child he believed to be abused. The need for legislative and
procedural reforms is stressed.

1773   Birrell, J. H. W. "'Where death delights to help the living.'
       Forensic medicine -- Cinderella?" Med J Aust 1: 253-61,
       February 7, 1970. (31 References).

Discusses the various aspects of forensic medicine in Australia. One
topic is the role of forensic medicine in child maltreatment, which is
regarded as a major problem. Reporting legislation is called for, along
with an increase in the number of health workers.

1774 Brown, Rowine H. "Child abuse: attempts to solve the problem by
      reporting laws." Women Lawyers J 60(2): 73-78, Spring, 1974.
      (43 References).
An exposition of the burden placed upon social agencies and protective
services as a result of the recent spread of the mandatory reporting of
child abuse cases. The requirement to report all known incidents of child
abuse--now in effect in forty-four states--was intended to facilitate the
treatment and ultimate prevention of the problem. However, because of
mandatory reporting, the number of incidents reported has increased at a
rate which has exceeded the capacity of existing agencies to meet the
demand for preventive, protective and rehabilitative services. The study
recommends increasing the appropriations to agencies providing these
services. It also discusses various technicalities of mandatory reporting, including the methods for identifying, reporting, and tabulating
incidents of child abuse and the liabilities for the failure to report.

1775 ————. "Controlling child abuse: reporting laws." Case Comment
      80(1): 10-16, January-February, 1975. (4 References).
An analysis, from a physician-attorney's point of view, of the child abuse
reporting statutes throughout the country. Points of reference are the
issues of mandatory/permissive reporting, the class of persons required
to report, the injuries to be reported, the official channel for reports,
immunity, liability for failure to report, and central registries. The
general increase in child abuse reporting resulting from these statutes
is described. The current legislation is deemed to be adequate.

1776 "Child abuse reporting laws: editorial." J Am Dent Assoc 75(5):
      1070, November, 1967. (0 References).
Summarizes several types of child abuse reporting laws and where these
are operative. In twenty-two states, dentists are required to report
battered or neglected children. The Nebraska law covers reporting of
helpless adults as well as children. All states have child abuse reporting laws, with hospitals filing the major number of reports.

1777 De Francis, Vincent. Child abuse legislation in the 1970's.
      Denver, Colorado: The American Humane Association, Children's
      Division, 1970. 134p. (Bibliography).
Child abuse reporting legislation in the fifty states, the District of
Columbia, Gaum, and the Virgin Islands is surveyed. The thirteen major
components of reporting legislation, including the definition of abuse,
persons mandated to report, procedures for reporting, and immunity and
penalty clauses, are discussed. A state-by-state breakdown of legislation cites the appropriate reporting statutes and elucidates the significant passages. An analysis of recent state amendments explores the problem areas of child abuse legislation. A broadening of persons required
to report is advised, in addition to simplified procedures for reporting.
The practice of allowing several community agencies to accept and process
reports of suspected abuse is criticized because it encourages an unequal
handling of abuse cases. A model, and optimally protective, child abuse
reporting law with selected phrases drawn from existing state statutes
is presented with commentary.

1778 ————. "Child abuse: the legislative response." <u>Denver Law J</u>
44(1): 3-41, Winter, 1967. (59 References).
Comprehensively reviews the child abuse reporting statutes in all the
states. The following topics are discussed: age and injury of the victim, identity of the perpetrator, source and recipient of the report,
mandatory or permissive nature of the report, form of the report, the
responsibility of the recipient, immunity for the reporter, penalty for
failing to report, waiver of testimonial privilege, and central registries. It is concluded that much of the reporting legislation has been
too hastily seized upon as the answer to the problem of child abuse,
whereas reporting represents only the beginning of the question. Immediate attention to the neglected area of child protective services is urged.

1779 Donovan, Thomas J. "The legal response to child abuse." <u>William
Mary Law Rev</u> 11(4): 960-87, Summer, 1970. (77 References).
Surveys the legal apparatus which has grown up around the problem of
child abuse, with very detailed attention to the reporting laws. A
lengthy chart is included which compares the reporting statutes in all
the states with respect to classes of reporting persons, age limit of
victims, receiver of the report, mandatory or permissive nature of the
law, penalty for failure to report, immunity extended to reporters,
abrogation of privilege not to testify, and the form prescribed for reports. Recommendations are made concerning the most effective construction and implementation of reporting laws.

1780 Education Commission of the States. <u>Child abuse and neglect in
states: a digest of critical elements of reporting and central
registries: Report no. 83</u>. Denver, Colorado: Education Commission of the States, 1976. 26p.
Compares child abuse state legislation relative to who reports to whom,
what form the report should take, penalties for not reporting, and
immunities for those reporting. In addition, state central registries
are examined. Data presented on the registries included whether a central
registry existed, who had access to it, and penalties for inappropriate
use.

1781 ————. <u>A comparison of the states' child abuse and neglect
reporting statutes: Report no. 84</u>. Denver, Colorado: Education
Commission of the States, 1976. 9p.
Tabulates the child abuse reporting laws for all the states. Information
presented includes year enacted, requirement for mandatory reporting,
definitions of abuse, offer of immunity penalty, requirement for appointment of guardian <u>ad litem</u>, and the nature of the relationships with the
courts and state agencies.

1782 ————. <u>Trends in child abuse and neglect reporting statutes:
Report no. 95 from the ECS child abuse project</u>. Denver, Colorado:
Education Commission of the States, 1977. 28p.
Describes the current status of the child abuse reporting legislation.
The reporting statutes of all the states are listed, along with the
actions against child abuse and neglect taken by the various states.

1783 Fraser, Brian G. "A pragmatic alternative to current legislative
approaches to child abuse." <u>Am Crim Law Rev</u> 12(1): 103-24,
Summer, 1974. (127 References).

Discusses the issue of mandatory reporting of child abuse cases, pointing out the rather broad areas in which the statutes for reporting such cases differ from state to state. Legislative trends in mandatory reporting are indicated, most of them tending to widen the requirement to report; it is suggested that the definition of child abuse is generally being broadened to cover neglect and sexual and emotional abuse, that the requirement to report is being extended to more classes of persons, and that immunity for reporting persons is increasing. Privileged communication is being restricted more and more to lawyer-client relationships, and more and more states are using a central registry. Various other changes in child abuse law are proposed, including the provision for a temporary hold allowing a hospital or physician to retain temporary custody of an abused child without court order if the child is perceived to be in danger. Despite the emphasis on the legal aspects of the problem, the essay recommends that those concerned should explore the areas of therapy for parents and rehabilitation, rather than seeking criminal prosecution of offenders.

1784 Goldney, R. D. "Abusing parents: legal and therapeutic aspects."
      Med J Aust 2(11): 597-600, September 9, 1972. (18 References).
Suggests several means of easing the reluctance of physicians to co-operate with child abuse reporting laws. One proposal would make reporting voluntary if the parents agree to undergo therapy; the other would establish a special court, more rehabilitative than punitive in its orientation, to handle cases of child abuse.

1785 Hansen, Richard H. "Child abuse legislation and the interdiscipli-
      nary approach." Am Bar Assoc J 52(8): 734-36, August, 1966. (16
      References).
An overview of the current status of child abuse reporting laws, recommending that all persons be required to report acts of child abuse, that a penalty be imposed on those failing to report, and that reports be made to the state department of child welfare. Child abuse statutes in effect as of May 1, 1966, are listed. References made to the application of child abuse statutes to non-children, as in the case of handicapped or mentally defective persons.

1786 ————. "Doctors, lawyers and the battered child law." J Trauma
      5(6): 826-30, November, 1965. (0 References).
A discussion of mandatory reporting legislation advocates broadening the scope of such laws so as to reach the largest number of abuse victims. The class of reporters should not be restricted to physicians, but should include teachers, social workers, and other relevant professionals. Disabled and incompetent patients as well as children should be entitled to the law's protection. An efficient reporting system requires that immunity from liability be granted, that the husband-wife and doctor-patient privilege be waived, and that a penalty be attached for failure to report. The children's division of the state department of public welfare is the agency best equipped to receive reports, as it can investigate a complaint and offer services or involve law enforcement officials as needed.

1787 "Legislation and litigation: editorial." J Am Dent Assoc 75(5):
      1081-82, November, 1967. (6 References).
Discusses the issue of mandatory reporting of suspected child abuse, with particular reference to the problems inherent in the requirement in

twenty-two states that dentists as well as physicians report suspected cases. Some information about this method of reporting is included.

1788 Lehto, Neil J. "Civil liability for failing to report child abuse." Detroit Coll Law Rev 1: 135-66, Spring, 1977. (167 References). Analyzes the ineffectiveness of much child abuse reporting legislation, with particular emphasis on the extent of liability for non-compliance. The California case, Landeros v. Flood, is treated in detail, as an example of the lack of clarity on the questions of liability in most states' reporting laws. The applicability of criminal as opposed to civil liability for the failure to report is discussed. It is concluded that criminal liability would be so difficult to enforce that the purpose of the law would be defeated. State legislators are urged to explore other enforcement mechanisms--for example, professional or administrative enforcement. The Model Act prepared by the National Center for Child Abuse and Neglect is held up as a model for those states which acknowledge the need for reform in the reporting legislation.

1789 Lucht, Carroll L. "Providing a legislative base for reporting child abuse." In: National Symposium on Child Abuse, 4th, Charleston, S.C., 1973. Collected papers. Denver, Colorado: The American Humane Association, Children's Division, 1975. 49-60. Evaluates current child abuse reporting laws. A brief history of reporting laws indicate that the number of professional groups required to report has increased. Definitions of reportable abuse should be broad enough in order to relieve the informant of the responsibility of making legal judgment and to allow for the reporting of various abuses, such as psychological or moral, which are hard to define. Most reports are currently being made to social services. Some state laws exclude the reporting of children receiving religious healing. These laws, along with those which allow medical professionals to hold abused children without consent and provide emergency removal and right of entry, are questioned.

1790 McCoid, Allan H. "The battered child and other assaults upon the family: Part I." Minn Law Rev 50(1): 1-58, November, 1965. (148 References). Part I of a three part study of child abuse is detailed. The development of awareness and medical expertise regarding child abuse is traced, and a survey of the medical literature concerning the identification and etiology of child abuse is supplied. The issue of reporting becomes the major focus for the discussion; the reporting statutes in all of the states are compared to one another and to the model statute devised by the Children's Bureau (HEW). The points of comparison concern the identity of the reporter, immunity, statutory encouragement of breaches in physician-patient confidentiality, nature of injuries to be reported, recipient of the report, and the effectiveness of the reporting law.

1791 Paulsen, Monrad G. "Child abuse reporting laws: the shape of the legislation." Columbia Law Rev 67(1): 1-49, January, 1967. (110 References). Comprehensively surveys the child abuse reporting laws which were in effect in 1966 throughout the states. Existing reporting legislation is analyzed from a number of different perspectives, including the persons required to report, the mandatory or permissive nature of the injunction to report, the injuries warranting the report, and the prescribed governmental channels for the report. Particular attention is devoted to the function of central registries in the reporting system, and to the issues of liability and immunity in the light of the concern of many physicians over the legal and professional consequences of reporting cases of suspected child abuse among their patients. The various statutory patterns in relation to these issues are presented and evaluated with a view toward their practicable and effective enactment.

1792   Paulsen, Monrad G.; Parker, Graham; Adelman, Lynn. "Child abuse
         reporting laws -- some legislative history." George Washington
         Law Rev 34(3): 482-506, March, 1966. (102 References).
Discusses the role of the Children's Bureau (HEW), Children's Division of the American Humane Society, and the mass media in developing an awareness of child abuse and in encouraging legislation. While acknowledging the slow process of expanding services, the significant progress made by the medical, legal, and social work professions is illustrated. It commends the work of volunteer organizations which aid families and strive for legislation that demands mandatory reporting of suspected child abuse.

1793   Ramsey, Jerry A., and Lawler, Byron J. "The battered child syn-
         drome." Pepperdine Law Rev 1(3): 372-81, 1974. (9 References).
An account is given of a case in which several physicians failed to report symptoms of the battered child syndrome in a child who subsequently suffered brain damage. The much revised California statute mandating such reporting by physicians and other professionals under pain of criminal sanctions is discussed in terms of its apparent ineffectiveness. It is proposed that civil liability be added to the statute, to impose a monetary incentive for reporting. The physicians who fail to report symptoms of child abuse could then be sued for the damages which their negligence incurs.

1794   Russell, Donald Hayes. "Law, medicine and minors: Part IV." N
         Engl J Med 279(1): 31-32, July 4, 1968. (4 References).
Outlines reforms in the area of child abuse reporting laws. Complainants were formerly obliged to assume the burden of proof and, hence, were liable to countersuits. Reporting is encouraged by new laws which offer immunity from liability, but in some states the reporter is required to name the offender or to state his belief that the injury was willfully inflicted. Such accusations should be left to the investigating officers so as not to discourage prospective reporters. Reporting laws can achieve maximum effectiveness if they also specify the responsibilities of the receiving agency.

1795   Shepherd, Robert E., Jr. "The abused child and the law." Wash
         Lee Law Rev 22(2): 182-95, Fall, 1965. (142 References).
Surveys the magnitude of the problem of child abuse, with some discussion of the development of child abuse reporting laws, and recommendations concerning these. Penalties for not reporting are criticized as being unfair; recommendations include provisions for the immunity for the reporter from civil or criminal liability and the abrogation of evidenciary privilege.

1796   Sussman, Alan. "Reporting child abuse: a review of the litera-
         ture." Fam Law Q 8(3): 245-313, Fall, 1974. (399 References).
Trends in the reporting of child abuse are surveyed. Definitions of abuse and neglect are considered problematic because they are so elusive. Legally viable definitions of these terms must be found if there are to

be clear guidelines for those who are required to report abuse. An examination of both the literature and the state legislation enacted after the 1963 Department of Health, Education, and Welfare model child abuse reporting law reveals the following trends: (1) there has been a general enlargement of the scope of those required to report and of those reported; (2) there has been an increasing emphasis upon treatment rather than punishment, which directs reporting to social rather than to law enforcement agencies; (3) there has been increasing interest in the establishment of central registers for the purpose of coordinating reporting. Serious investigations into the demand for enlarged, mandatory reporting and non-punitive, non-judicial intervention are recommended. New child abuse literature should critically examine the nature of the services so eagerly recommended by previous literature, as some writers have already begun to do.

1797   Sussman, Alan, and Cohen, Stephan J.   Reporting child abuse and
       neglect: guidelines for legislation. Cambridge, Massachusetts:
       Ballinger, 1975. 255p. (Bibliography).
Comprehensively examines state and national child abuse reporting and management legislation. At the request of the Office of Child Development (HEW), the authors researched and drafted a revised version of the 1963 Department of Health, Education, and Welfare's model child abuse reporting act. This book represents their finalized draft of the statute with extensive commentary and summaries of additional research studies.

The statute is preceded by a statement of purpose which offers protective services to the child and appropriate services to the family to promote a state of well-being for the child. It is emphasized that no legislative act can be effective unless there is assurance of sufficient resources to actually protect the children. Section 2 defines abuse as serious physical harm or sexual molestation, and neglect as failure to provide adequate food, shelter, clothing, physical protection, or medical care necessary to sustain the life or health of the child.

The statute expands the list of those required to report cases of suspected abuse to include all professionals in the health field, social workers, teachers, law enforcement officers, and even religious healers. No one is required under penalty of law to report his suspicions of child neglect, as the signs of neglect are more difficult to define and to detect. Reports should be directed to the state department of social services rather than to law enforcement officials due to the non-punitive nature of the statute. Immunity from liability for persons reporting in good faith is assured.

Duties of state and local protective service agencies are outlined. The statute recommends that each state establish a central register for reporting cases of abuse, classifying them after investigation as unfounded, suspected, or indicated abuse. The standardization of practices allowing access to records and expungement of records is urged. In cases of judicial action, the statute assures children of legal counsel appointed by the court at public expense. Parents are entitled to separate legal representation.

Legal precedents and the trends of reporting abuse legislation in the fifty states are examined. Certain legal problems such as whether to include emotional neglect in the statute are evaluated. Results of a 1974 nationwide survey of 1,439 persons working in state and local social service departments, hospitals, schools, and law enforcement agencies are

reported. The study found that the survey population was generally well-
informed of reporting legislation, though many persons thought they were
required to report when actually they were not. A significant 92 percent
felt that cases of neglect should be subject to the reporting law.

A second study of child abuse reporting in four states--California,
Colorado, New York, and West Virginia--focuses on one urban and one rural
county in each state. Persons were questioned about their knowledge of
reporting laws, the quality of treatment furnished by their agency, and
the reciprocity of information between agencies. Lastly, appendices
evaluate the operation of child abuse laws in California and the recognition of abuse in military communities.

1798 U.S. Children's Bureau. The child abuse reporting laws: a tabular
      review. Washington, D.C.: U.S. Government Printing Office, 1966.
      47p. (Bibliography).
Furnishes precise information arranged in tabular form of the child abuse
reporting statutes in each of the fifty states as of 1966. In addition
to citing each state's specific child abuse reporting statute, the following information is diagramed: (1) the age of the child covered by the
statute; (2) persons who are required to report; (3) the nature of injuries to be reported; (4) the person or agency to whom the report is
directed; (5) provisions for follow-up action; (6) the presence of an
immunity clause or penalty for failing to report; (7) the possible abrogation of the physician-patient, husband-wife privilege; and (8) whether
or not a statewide central registry has been established.

c. Individual State Laws

1799 "The abused child." Wis Med J 68(1): 31-32, January, 1969.
      (0 References).
An explanation of Wisconsin's mandatory child abuse reporting law. The
law is quoted in full, guidelines to be followed in submitting a report
are offered, and the steps which are usually taken by the receiving
agency are outlined.

1800 "The abused child law." Wis Med J 69(1): 25-26, January, 1970.
      (0 References).
Outlines the Wisconsin State statute on child abuse. The 1965 and 1967
additions to the original legislation provide for much wider mandatory
reporting by professionals to the city police department as well as to
the sheriff and grant civil and criminal immunity to those who report in
good faith. Recommended procedures for filing a report and the responsibility of agencies and individuals in insuring the safety of the child
are included.

1801 "The abused child law: how it affects you." Wis Med J 66(1):
      23-24, January, 1967. (0 References).
Explains and elucidates the new (1965) Child Abuse reporting legislation
in Wisconsin. The classes of persons required to report are identified,
and suggestions are made regarding the form and content of the report.
The responsibilities and courses of action of the county welfare department or county children's board receiving the report are outlined.

1802 Allen, Hugh D.; ten Bensel, Robert W.; Raile, Richard B. "The bat-
      tered child syndrome -- Part III: Legal aspects." Minn Med
      52(2): 345-47, February, 1969. (11 References).

The history of child abuse legislation in Minnesota is discussed. It is
pointed out that anyone who makes a report of suspected abuse is immune
from criminal or civil liability. The Minnesota State Child Abuse Reporting Law is presented verbatim.

1803 "The battered baby syndrome: some practical aspects." Med J Aust
      2(7): 231-32, August 17, 1974. (12 References).
Discusses the feasibility of a nationwide system of child abuse notifica-
tion and management in Australia. Possible legislation to make reporting
by physicians compulsory and to increase legal representation for child
victims are discussed. The need for an educational program about child
abuse is stressed.

1804 "Battered child law takes effect July 1." Ill Med J 127(5):
      570-71, May, 1965. (0 References).
Presents a report to the medical community on the new Illinois battered
child law. Mandatory reporting of suspected cases of abuse and immunity
from civil or criminal liability for the reporter are the main principles
affirmed by this law.

1805 "Better program for the defenseless: Tennessee's revised Mandatory
      Child Abuse Reporting Statute." Memphis State Univ Law Rev 4(3):
      585-93, Spring, 1974. (32 References).
Compares the 1973 revision of Tennessee's Child Abuse Reporting Law and
its 1965 predecessor. The revision is found to be superior in the
matters of immunity, waiver of testimonial privileges, abolition of
accusatory reporting, and establishment of central registries. Despite
the new law's merits, a caveat is issued to the effect that the reporting
law will not be effective without the cooperation of a concerned public.

1806 Bevan, Hugh. "Should reporting be mandatory?" In: Franklin,
      Alfred White, ed. Concerning child abuse. New York: Churchill
      Livingstone, 1975. 133-35. (0 References).
Summarizes a paper presented by Bevan proposing a child abuse reporting
law for the United Kingdom. The law must include guidelines for determining the extent of injury necessary before a report is made and provide
for legal immunity. Because children need an advocate who is solely concerned with their protection, a new position of "children's guardian" is
suggested. A note by an official prefers voluntary reporting. In a
discussion of the paper, professionals were ambivalent about mandatory
reporting.

1807 Bynum, Alvin S. "A report on the battered child: Indiana, 1966."
      J Indiana State Med Assoc 60(4): 469, April, 1967. (1 Refer-
      ence).
Legislation in Indiana paved the way for protecting individuals who identify and report cases of battered children to authorities. After the
legislation passed, records of the incidence of abuse were kept in each
county. In all, 242 instances were reported and 117 of the children
became public wards. Not only physicians, but also school social workers
and nurses, were responsible for many reports. Information concerning
battered children must be distributed on a broader basis so that more
persons can report abuse when it occurs.

1808 Ciano, Mario C. "Ohio's mandatory reporting statute for cases of
      child abuse." West Reserve Law Rev 18(4): 1405-13, May, 1967.
      (33 References).

Discusses the 1965 amendments to the child abuse reporting law in Ohio. The major changes included a broadening of the class of persons required to report, the extension of immunity to reporting persons, and the suspension of the physician-patient privilege.

1809   Daly, Barbara. "Willful child abuse and state reporting statutes."
       Univ Miami Law Rev   23(2-3):   283-346, Winter-Spring, 1969. (44
       References).
Consists of a survey of some general aspects of child abuse, a discussion of the legal issues involved, and a set of recommendations directed specifically at the State of Florida's reporting statute. The recommendations tend to broaden the domain of the statute in the areas of reporting persons and reported injuries, and to amplify the methods of recording reported cases. Suggestions are also made regarding changes in the judicial handling of cases of child abuse.

1810   Governor's Task Force on Child Abuse. Proceedings: Child abuse.
       Richmond, Virginia: Governor's Task Force on Child Abuse, 1973.
       14p.
Report of a Task Force assigned to research Virginia's child abuse reporting law and to make recommendations for its improvement. The study group favored repeal of the law and its replacement by a law containing detailed provisions for: (1) the identification of abused children; (2) the provision of protective services to families in need of assistance; and (3) the preservation of family life by promoting, whenever possible, satisfactory parental care. The proposed law also includes: (1) definitions of abuse, report, complaint, and other terms referred to in the law; (2) duties of the public service groups involved; (3) a description of a State Registry; (4) discussion of the roles of hospitals, physicians, the court, and law enforcement agencies; and (5) policy for the appropriation of necessary funds.

1811   Green, Donald W., III. "Parent and child -- child beating -- recent
       legislation requiring reporting of physical abuse." Oreg Law Rev
       45(2):   114-23, February, 1966. (13 References).
General overview of various aspects of the child abuse problem, including a historical perspective on the development of information concerning the phenomenon. The evolution of Oregon's 1965 Child Abuse Reporting Act is traced; it is compared with its 1963 predecessor and found superior, particularly in its provisions regarding immunity and the definition of injuries to be reported.

1812   Hall, Marian. "The right to live." Nurs Outlook 15(8):   63-65,
       August, 1967. (11 References).
Discusses the recent measures taken by state legislatures to encourage and support the reporting of suspected cases of child abuse. Legislation requiring medical personnel to report abuse offers them immunity from liability. Several states also provide immunity to school teachers, social workers, and nurses who report suspected abuse. This facilitates the early detection of abuse before the case becomes serious enough to warrant a physician's attention. Most nurses are in an excellent position to detect, treat, and often prevent abuse by recognizing behavioral and emotional signs in parents and future parents that might be indicative of violent tendencies.

1813   Hansen, Richard H. "Legal implications of the battered child syn-
       drome." Nebr Med J 50(1): 595-97, December, 1965. (0 Refer-
       ences).
Reviews a Nebraska Committee for Children and Youth study and the child
abuse legislation which resulted from its recommendations. The intent of
the legislation is to require the reporting of battered child cases and
to authorize whatever steps are necessary to insure the child's protection. The implications of specific sections of the law and the rationale
behind them are discussed.

1814   Hart, Walter Moore. "The law concerning abuse of children." J SC
       Med Assoc 61(12): 391, December, 1965. (0 References).
Presents a verbatim account of South Carolina's mandatory child abuse
reporting law. Criticisms have been leveled against the act because it
does not provide for the punishment or rehabilitation of the perpetrator
or for the treatment of the child.

1815   Hawaii. Department of Social Services and Housing. Public Welfare
       Division. Hawaii's children need your protection. Honolulu,
       Hawaii: Department of Social Services and Housing, Public Welfare
       Division, n.d. 8p.
Explains Hawaii's reporting procedures for child abuse. Abuse and neglect are briefly defined. Many professionals must report, but anyone may
report suspected abuse. Hawaii's law provides immunity from prosecution
for those who report in good faith. Reports are made to the Public Welfare Department which then sends a social worker to the family's home.
The Child Protective Service Center in Honolulu is the most organized of
all services in Hawaii, although the neighboring islands have welfare
departments and access to team consultation. A list of conditions which
may signal abuse and neglect are included.

1816   "Helping physicians protect children." Christ Century 82(17):
       516, April 28, 1965. (0 References).
New Illinois legislation requires physicians to report cases of child
abuse to the Illinois Department of Children and Family Services. Physicians will be exempt from libel suits and thus may be less apprehensive
about reporting their findings. The aim of the Department is to protect
children and not to punish parents.

1817   Hendriksen, Douglas G. "The battered child: Florida's mandatory
       reporting statute." Univ Fla Law Rev 18(3): 503-11, Winter, 1965.
       (33 References).
Provides general background for the problem of child abuse. An evaluation
of Florida's mandatory reporting act suggests that the statute is not
ambitious enough in that it says nothing about the treatment of the cases
reported and thus further taxes the resources of the juvenile court system.
Revisions are proposed to shift the management of child abuse cases to
the Child Welfare Units.

1818   Hoel, Hans W. "The battered child: editorial." Minn Med 46(10):
       1001, October, 1963. (0 References).
Expresses dissatisfaction with Minnesota's mandatory reporting law because
it is a criminal law with primitive emphasis rather than a child welfare
statute. Because a child abuse case is an individual judgment, penalties
for failure to report are not approved.

1819   Hoshino, George, and Yoder, George H.   "Administrative discretion
       in the implementation of child abuse legislation."   Child Welfare
       52(7):   414-24, July, 1973.   (6 References).
Discusses an amendment passed in Pennsylvania requiring that county child
welfare administrators report all suspected cases of child abuse to law
enforcement authorities.   This "police clause" was a reaction to the
sensational newspaper reporting of an abuse case and was passed in the
legislature without consulting the agencies involved in its implementation.   Administrators responsible for carrying out the legislation should
have been exposed to the amendment first, public hearings should have
been held to seek advice from authorities, and the legislature should
have debated the bill before taking a final vote.   The entire matter was
so poorly handled that the impact of the amendment suffered and its
implementation had made few changes in the former non-punitive procedures
for dealing with suspected abuse cases on the local level.

1820   Kansas.   State Department of Health.   Division of Maternal and
       Child Health.   Child abuse.   Topeka, Kansas: Kansas State Depart-
       ment of Health, Division of Maternal and Child Health, 1971.   9p.
Discusses child abuse data and the reporting law in Kansas.   Since the
law went into effect in 1967, reporting has increased.   The 1970 revision raised the age for reporting from sixteen to eighteen years and made
reporting mandatory for school personnel.   The Health Department has
worked to educate the public on the problem of child abuse and feels that
it is the public's responsibility that all new and expectant mothers and
their children receive health care.   Statistics show that the most serious
injuries occur in children under six years of age.   Abusers are usually
natural parents between the ages of nineteen and twenty-four.   Some cases
of abuse involve babysitters and day care services.   The need exists for
funding of protective, counseling, and health care services.

1821   Kansas.   State Department of Health and Environment.   Bureau of
       Maternal and Child Health.   Child abuse and the law.   Topeka,
       Kansas: Kansas State Department of Health and Environment, Bureau
       of Maternal and Child Health, 1975.   5p.
Defines the reporting law in Kansas.   Citizens are encouraged to report
suspected abuse to the Department of Social and Rehabilitation Services
or a juvenile court.   Reporting is mandatory for a wide range of professional personnel.   The law also defines abuse and provides immunity from
prosecution for those who report in good faith.

1822   Krywulak, W., and Elias, J. C.   "The physically abused child."
       Manitoba Med Rev   47(1):   472-75, October, 1967.   (15 References).
Examines existing legislation governing child abuse and concludes that
laws presently in effect in Manitoba adequately protect the child.   The
five major procedures applied in reporting and treating the problem are
outlined.   Legislative provisions for mandatory reporting are suggested
but may not prove to be necessary.   There is general agreement that
voluntary reporting, possibly with minor amendments protecting physicians,
would be more effective.

1823   Leibsker, Donald.   "Patient privilege to protect the battered
       child."   DePaul Law Rev   15(1):   453-61, Autumn-Winter, 1966.
       (58 References).
Discusses the terms of the Illinois child abuse reporting statute, with
particular reference to the provisions regarding immunity.   Comparisons

are drawn between portions of the Illinois statute and relevant clauses in the statutes of other states. It is recommended that Illinois extend the obligation to report (and the concomitant immunity) beyond physicians to teachers and social workers, who may encounter cases of child abuse for which parents might not seek medical attention.

1824 "Mandatory reporting of injuries inflicted by other than accidental means upon children under the age of eighteen years." RI Med J 47(8): 398-400, August, 1964. (0 References).
Reports legislation concerning child abuse passed by the Rhode Island General Assembly in 1964. The passage makes reporting of such cases mandatory for physicians and provides for their protection from liability. The roles of community protective services and of the law enforcement agency are also indicated.

1825 Merrill, Edgar J. "Reporting of abused or battered children." J Maine Med Assoc 56(1): 119-20, May, 1965. (0 References).
Summarizes child abuse legislation in Maine. Both physicians and institutions are required to report suspected cases of abuse and are granted immunity from liability. The Department of Health and Welfare's Division of Child Welfare is designated as the recipient of abuse reports, and the medical, legal, and social work professions are held responsible for child protection. A brief case summary is illustrative of the law's intent.

1826 "Mississippi child abuse law covers reporting nurses." Am J Nurs 67(1): 15, January, 1967. (0 References).
Due to a recent battered child amendment to the Mississippi Youth Court Act, the reporting of child abuse is mandatory. Immunity from civil and criminal liability is provided for those required to report cases of abuse, namely, registered nurses, physicians, dentists, interns, and residents.

1827 Moore, John L., Jr. "Reporting of child abuse." J Med Assoc Ga 55(7): 328-29, July, 1966. (0 References).
Reports on legislation of the 1965 Session of the General Assembly of Georgia regarding required reports of child abuse. Although the law protects the physician from liability, the parents may still file suit indicating that the report was not made in "good faith." The physician is urged to note findings and to seek additional witnesses to corroborate his findings in court. The disadvantages of mandatory reporting include: (1) focus on the reported child and not the siblings; (2) fear instilled in parents which may prevent their seeking treatment for the child; and (3) use of the police which, unlike a social agency, immediately suggests criminal activities.

1828 "New law on child abuse and neglect." Va Med Mon 102(7): 568, July, 1975. (0 References).
Reviews the significant features of a new child abuse and neglect statute in Virginia. The law is meant to simplify reporting procedures and requires that one social agency receive reports, undertake investigations, and deliver protective services for all suspected cases. It is believed that these measures will contribute greatly to improving the management of child abuse.

1829 "A new Missouri approach to the agony of child abuse: editorial." Mo Med 67(1): 56, January, 1970. (0 References).

A 1969 revision to the 1965 child abuse reporting law in Missouri is analyzed. The revised law makes the reporting of suspected cases of child abuse mandatory, and it requires any individual dealing with children for pay (such as physicians, teachers, school nurses) to report any suspected cases of child abuse under threat of imprisonment or a fine. Reporters are granted immunity, and a central registry is instituted to cross-check repeated offenders.

1830 Ocampo, T. P. "The battered child syndrome." J SC Med Assoc
      70(11): 356-58, November, 1974. (7 References).
Considers the problem of child abuse in South Carolina with particular emphasis on the statistical breakdown of cases and on the legislation passed by that state.

1831 "Physicians required to report child beatings." Minn Med 46(9):
      876, September, 1963. (0 References).
Presents the text of the amended Minnesota State Law which requires that wounds inflicted by firearms, beatings, or similar treatment of minors under age sixteen be reported to the proper authorities. Enacted June 30, 1963, the law provides protection from suits involving slander or libel.

1832 Rayford, Linwood; McCall, Frances; Miller, Morris, et al. "The
      social and legal aspects of the battered child in the District of
      Columbia: panel discussion." Clin Proc Child Hosp 24(11):
      375-93, December, 1968. (0 References).
The legal procedure for reporting and protecting battered children in the District of Columbia is detailed. Several cases illustrate the problems of intervention. Separate sets of procedures are described for emergency life and death cases where some form of intervention has already taken place and where it has become apparent that the child needs to be removed from his parents. Legal action must, in the first place, be designed to protect and help the child and secondly, assist the family member who is responsible for the injury.

1833 "Report suspected child abuse." Ill Med J 141(6): 587, June,
      1972. (0 References).
The newly added amendment to the Illinois Child Abuse Law is described briefly. It requires physicians to report all cases of suspected child abuse, including child deaths. The Department of Children and Family Services is charged with the responsibility of investigating each case and providing the necessary treatment services to the abused child and his family.

1834 Sheeley, Jo Ann. "Use and control of abuse of a central child
      abuse registry." In: National Symposium on Child Abuse, 5th,
      Boston, 1975. Collected papers. Denver, Colorado: The American
      Humane Association, Children's Division, 1976. 115-16. (3
      References).
Presents the purpose of revisions in the Iowa Child Abuse Law which pertain to data obtained from the central registry. The revisions clarify reporting procedures, increase the number of professionals required to report, and delegate the monetary responsibility for photographs and x-rays to the public. The most important revision provides for the protection of the rights of registry families by defining who may have access to the files and by establishing procedures for handling erroneous reports or information submitted to the registry.

1835 Silver, Larry B.; Barton, William; Dublin, Christina C. "Mandatory
reporting of physical abuse of children in the District of Columbia:
community procedures and new legislation." Med Ann DC 36(2):
127-30, February, 1967. (10 References).
Discusses the key issues of the six sections outlined in the Mandatory
Reporting Law for the District of Columbia. Questions are raised as to
its effectiveness and its limitations. The responsibilities of each
agency handling different aspects of child abuse cases are outlined in
detail. Action by the various agencies is initiated by the Woman's Bureau
of the District of Columbia Metropolitan Police Department, the agency
that receives reports directly from physicians. In order to become more
effective, the lines of communication between physicians and agencies
must be improved.

1836 Smith, H. A. "The legal aspects of child abuse." South Med Bull
58(3): 19-21, June, 1970. (2 References).
The Oklahoma statute mandating the reporting of suspected cases of child
abuse is discussed. The various avenues for reporting are outlined,
along with the options available to the court in the disposition of the
child.

1837 Snedeker, Lendon. "Notes on childhood trauma." N Engl J Med
275(19): 1061-62, November 10, 1966. (1 Reference).
Evaluates child abuse laws, with an emphasis on Massachusetts legislation.
It is noted that since the 1964 passage of the Massachusetts statute requiring the reporting of physical injury in children, a high number of
cases have been reported; yet, this number includes only physically
abused children. The law needs to be broadened to encompass those who
are neglected and deprived. Various state laws are compared, highlighting
the point that in Massachusetts, physicians, not administrators, are
required to make the report. The physicians' reluctance to report is
discussed, along with the tendency of the courts to uphold parental
rights.

1838 Teague, Russell E. "Kentucky legislation concerning reporting of
abused children." J Ky Med Assoc 64(7): 584, July, 1966. (0
References).
Reviews the child abuse law passed by the 1964 Kentucky General Assembly
and expresses concern about its non-enforcement. The legislation provides for mandatory written reports of abuse and protection from liability for reporting physicians. Questions directed to the Child Welfare
Department, as well as the low number of cases reported, indicate that
the law has not been understood or adhered to. The Department plans a
central file of all battered child cases to improve coverage. Physicians are instructed to cooperate with the law.

1839 U.S. Congress. Conference Committees, 1966. Requiring reporting
by physicians of physical abuse of children: Conference Report to
accompany H.R. 10304. 89th Congress, 2nd session, 1966, H. Rept.
2230. Washington, D.C.: U.S. Government Printing Office, 1966.
2p.
Statements of the bill's managers on the part of the House in response
to nine Senate amendments submitted on H.R. 10304, a bill providing for
mandatory reporting of physical abuse of children by physicians and institutions in the District of Columbia. The statements clarify the House
position in relation to each Senate amendment.

1840   U.S. Congress. House. Committee on the District of Columbia.
       Reporting physical abuse of children: Hearing on H.R. 3394, H.R.
       3411, and H.R. 3814. 89th Congress, 1st session, June 10, 1965.
       Washington, D.C.: U.S. Government Printing Office, 1965. 36p.
Includes the texts of several identical bills (H.R. 3394, H.R. 3411, H.R.
3814) requiring physicians and institutions to report child abuse in the
District of Columbia. The goal of mandatory reporting legislation is to
protect abused and neglected children. Physicians and institutions are
to report suspected instances of abuse and neglect to the Metropolitan
Police Department in order to engage the services of the city's protective service agencies. The required contents of the reports are specified, as well as the form. Immunity from liability is granted to anyone
making a required report in good faith. The application of certain
privileges, namely, physician-patient and husband-wife privileges, is
excluded in judicial proceedings. Penalties for violating the bill's
provisions are suggested. Also included in the report is a document entitled "The Abused Child: Principles and Suggested Language for Legislation on Reporting of the Physically Abused Child," submitted by the
Children's Bureau of the U.S. Department of Health, Education, and Welfare
intended for use as a legislative guide by states preparing legislation
to protect abused children.

Numerous witnesses provided statements accentuating the urgency of the
need for legislation. All statements offered support for the proposed
bill, although some suggested minor revisions or amendments. David J.
Sharpe, Secretary of the Committee on Medical and Legal Problems of the
Bar Association in Washington, D.C., endorsed the bill but at the same
time called for a fundamental legal change. He recommended omitting
section six entirely, thereby removing the criminal penalty for failing
to report.

1841   —————. Require reporting by physicians of physical abuse of
       children: Report to accompany H.R. 10304. 89th Congress, 1st
       session, 1965, H. Rept. 744. Washington, D.C.: U.S. Government
       Printing Office, 1965. 6p.
Describes the purpose of mandatory reporting legislation (H.R. 10304) as
a measure to protect children in the District of Columbia who have suffered non-accidental injuries. Reports by physicians are to be made to
the Metropolitan Police Department in order to initiate action by the
city's protective services. The bill requires that physicians immediately
report suspected cases of physical abuse. It provides immunity from
civil and criminal liability for those who make reports and renounces
both the physician-patient confidentiality privilege and the husband-wife
privilege as grounds for excluding evidence required in judicial proceedings. A discussion of the need for such legislation is included.

1842   Warren, Eugene R. "Battered child syndrome." J Arkansas Med Soc
       62(10): 413, March, 1966. (0 References).
Outlines the child abuse bill passed by the Arkansas General Assembly in
1965. Act 25 requires the physician to make an oral and written report
of abuse to police while releasing him from liable and from the physician-
patient privilege. The statute also suspends the husband-wife privilege.
It is noted that the act not yet been legally tested.

1843   White, Desbert J., Jr. "Protecting the abused child in Georgia:
       identifying and reporting." J Med Assoc Ga 60(3): 86-88, March,
       1971. (3 References).

Summarizes the Georgia framework for reporting and treating child abuse. Georgia law requires mandatory reporting by medical and social professionals and grants them immunity from civic or criminal liability, as well as any other person responsible for reporting a suspected case. The Department of Family and Children Services receives the reports and initiates treatment procedures. Protecting the child is the primary concern. Involvement with the parents is also carried out in order to assist them and help prevent the threat of further abuse.

1844 "Who cares for New York's abused children?" NY Med 30(4): 120-23, 137, April, 1974. (0 References).
Outlines the provisions of the 1973 New York Child Protective Services Act, which mandated reporting of child abuse cases and authorized the maintenance of a central registry. New federal legislation calling for the establishment of a National Center on Child Abuse is also described. The act authorized and $85 million expenditure on research and community projects. Both pieces of legislation are heralded as enlightened.

1845 Winking, Cyril H. "Coping with child abuse: one state's experience." Public Welfare 26(3): 189-92, July, 1968. (0 References).
Features of a three-year-old Illinois child abuse law are summarized. The law requires that reports of suspected abuse be filed by physicians, surgeons, dentists, and other practitioners with the Department of Children and Family Services. The law provides immunity from criminal and civil liability to those who report suspected abuse. The law is non-punitive in intent and is focused on the discovery of abuse cases, protection of the children involved, and rehabilitation of the family if possible. Problems with providing adequate follow-up treatment include a shortage of qualified staff and insufficient resources such as day care, temporary placement facilities for children, and homemaker services. It is concluded that the Illinois Child Abuse Law is good, but that more money is needed to strengthen and extend diagnostic, treatment, and preventive services.

2. ENFORCEMENT

a. Role of Physician

(1) Responsibilities

1846 "'Battered-child' cases: editorial." America 110(17): 559-60, April 25, 1964. (0 References).
Indicates a need for legislation requiring physicians to report cases of suspected child abuse.

1847 "Battered child law (LSA RS 14:403)." J La State Med Soc 122(8): 247-50, August, 1970. (0 References).
Reprint of the Louisiana statutes regarding various issues of interest to physicians, including mandatory reporting of child abuse cases, the limitation on the physician's liability for gratuitous service in an emergency ("Good Samaritan Law"), and the grounds for commitment. The absence of statutory provision regarding the handling of rape cases by the physician is noted.

1848 "Battered child law reporting procedure places moral obligation on
      physician." Tex Med 63(5): 120, May, 1967. (0 References).
The responsibility of a physician to report his suspicions regarding child
abuse is emphasized. The 1965 Texas reporting law is reviewed, and the
speedy compliance of physicians is urged.

1849 Bernstein, Arthur H. "Hospital liability for battered children."
      Hospitals 50(5): 95-97, March 1, 1976. (0 References).
Cites several cases in which criminal prosecutions of battering parents
have resulted in guilty verdicts. This trend should convince physicians
that they are not wasting their time when reporting abuse. Because state
law provides immunity from civil suit to those who report suspected
abuse, the reporting physician should not fear legal harrassment. In
fact, the physician that does not report a suspected case of abuse can be
sued on behalf of the child whose beatings, injuries, or death might have
been prevented if the abuser had been reported earlier.

1850 "Confidentiality for informants." Br Med J 1(6023): 1476-77,
      June 12, 1976. (6 References).
Presents the proceedings of a lawsuit in which a mother won disclosure of
an informant's identity when he had mistakenly reported her child as
abused. Since it is believed that this situation will arise infrequently,
it would be a tragedy if it led physicians to exaggerate the perils of
making a report of suspected abuse. It is pointed out that if a parent
brings charges of slander against a reporting physician, he/she must prove
that the physician made the report out of malice or with knowledge that
it was untrue.

1851 Courter, Eileen M. "Physicians must cooperate in child abuse
      cases." Mich Med 72(15): 361-62, May, 1973. (0 References).
Emphasizes the importance of the role of the physician in reporting suspected cases of child abuse. Michigan has a mandatory child abuse reporting law which provides immunity from criminal liability.

1852 "Doctors and hospitals must report child abuse: recent Supreme
      Court ruling doesn't invalidate state law." Ill Med J 140(1):
      41, July, 1971. (0 References).
Affirms that the 1965 Illinois State Child Abuse Law requiring medical
personnel to report suspected child abuse cases is not invalidated by a
recent Supreme Court decision to reverse the conviction of a man found
guilty of endangering the life of a child after a jury trial.

1853 Ferguson, William M. "Battered child syndrome." J Kans Med Soc
      65(2): 67-69, February, 1964. (0 References).
Reports the opinion of the Attorney General of Kansas supporting physician's legal obligation and privilege in reporting child abuse cases.
The opinion, directed to physicians, results from a high incidence of
child abuse cases in Kansas.

1854 ————. "The reporting of child abuse." Bull Menninger Clin
      28(5): 269-70, September, 1964. (1 Reference).
Cites excerpts from the opinion given by the Kansas Attorney General regarding the reporting of child abuse. These include his claim that a
physician is not breaking the physician-patient privilege when he is
acting for the patient's safety and that he is not liable for giving his
medical opinion. Also noted in the article is a recommendation made by

the Kansas Medical Society to the Kansas Legislature regarding the mandatory reporting of child abuse and the protection from liability for doing so.

1855 George, James E., ed. "Child abuse reporting." Emerg Physician Leg Bull 3(2): 5-10, Spring, 1977. (0 References).
Explores two major legal questions involved in the reporting of suspected cases of child abuse by emergency room physicians: (1) can a physician be held in violation of child abuse reporting statutes when he/she is negligent in diagnosing the battered child syndrome and, therefore, fails to report it, or only when the physician intentionally does not report a suspected case of child abuse; and (2) can a physician be sued by a parent for defamation of character, slander or libel if he/she erroneously diagnoses a child as abused when this, in fact, is not the case? Several lawsuits and court judgments are reviewed to carefully answer these questions.

1856 Goodpaster, Gary S., and Angel, Karen. "Child abuse and the law: the California system." Hastings Law J 26(5): 1081-1125, March, 1975. (38 References).
A detailed account of the actual operation of the medicolegal apparatus for reporting and dealing with child abuse cases in Los Angeles is presented. The statutes regarding the reporting, processing, and disposition of child abuse cases are analyzed in conjunction with the actual implementation of the laws by hospitals, schools, agencies, and courts. The activities of all these organizations are found to be badly coordinated, and this lack of coordination results in the underreporting of cases. Also, the lack of flexibility in the disposition of cases makes school and medical personnel reluctant to report cases for fear of needlessly inflicting great damage on families. Recommendations are made to remedy these problems.

1857 Gunn, Alexander D. G. "Wounds of violence." Nurs Times 63(18): 590-92, May 5, 1967. (0 References).
Although physicians and nurses may view "injury" and "wound" as synonymous, criminal law distinguishes clearly between the two. Legal definitions for the following types of wounds are listed: abrasions, bruises, lacerations, incised wounds, stab wounds, and bullet wounds. When they are initially treated, descriptions of wounds must be recorded precisely by medical personnel. This is especially important in the case of battered children, where accurate diagnoses and reporting are essential for preventing the recurrence of the problem.

1858 Harper, Fowler V. "The physician, the battered child, and the law." Pediatrics 31(6): 899-902, June, 1963. (0 References).
Outlines the role of the physician in relation to the battered child. Since the physician is often the first person to suspect abuse, it is his duty to initiate legal proceedings. Proposed state legislation, drafted by the Children's Bureau (HEW), provides for mandatory reporting by physicians, protection from liability suits, and release from the physician-patient privilege. The meaning of various legal phrasing is discussed.

1859 Hays, Richard. "Child abuse and our responsibility." Nebr Nurse 3(3): 24, May, 1970. (0 References).

Urges medical personnel throughout Nebraska to assume their responsibility of reporting suspected child abuse cases to the local Protective Service Unit, the County Public Welfare Office, or the County Attorney.

1860   "The health professions and child abuse and neglect: a guide to fulfilling the legal responsibilities of the medical profession in cases of suspected child abuse or neglect." J Med Soc NJ 72(7): 605-9, July, 1975. (5 References).
Examines the New Jersey statutes dealing with the role and responsibility of the physician in handling and reporting cases of suspected child abuse and neglect. According to the Child Abuse and Neglect Law which became effective in January, 1975, the physician is required to report cases of suspected child abuse and neglect to the Division of Youth and Family Services and to make any records on the child and his family available to the agency for purposes of investigation. The Protective Custody Law which became effective in May, 1973, empowers any physician or hospital to maintain a child in protective custody for up to three days without a court order in cases of suspected abuse and neglect. Findings which may indicate a diagnosis of suspected abuse/neglect are reviewed. Social services available to families of abused children include day care, homemaker assistance, family planning, medical care, job and personal counseling, periodic home visits, community mental health centers, and others.

1861   Jaso, Hector. "The Battered and Abused Children Act of the State of Rhode Island: report of suspected battery or abuse of any child is mandated by the law." RI Med J 58(11): 474-75, November, 1975. (2 References).
The Battered and Abused Children Act of Rhode Island is considered. The physician's responsibility to report suspected cases to the Department of Social and Rehabilitative Services and to the local police is stressed.

1862   Ludwig, S.; Heiser, A.; Cullen, T.; et al. "You are subpoenaed." Clin Proc 30(6): 133-47, June, 1974. (0 References).
A description of the activity involved in a grand rounds devoted to child abuse at the Children's Hospital, and of the functioning of a multiagency child abuse team made up of members from the Departments of Police, Social Work, and Psychiatry, a public health nurse, a Child Life worker, and a pediatrician. Special attention was given to the role of the pediatrician in responding to cases of suspected child abuse, both in the hospital at the time of admission and in the courtroom later on.

1863   Mant, A. K., and Williams, A. D. "The battered baby syndrome." Med Leg Bull 17(12): 1-8, December, 1968. (0 References).
Investigates the medical and legal aspects of fatalities resulting from child abuse as exemplified by some thirty-seven cases at Guy's Hospital in London.

1864   Maxwell, I. D. "Assault and battery of children and others." NS Med Bull 45(4): 105-7, April, 1966. (5 References).
Presents the legal and moral responsibilities of physicians reporting child abuse. Typical fears associated with reporting are discounted; physicians are infrequently requested to be in court or to make charges against specific individuals. The principles ascribed to by The Advisory Committee to the Children's Division of the American Humane Association are recounted in full. It is suggested that police be called in only when investigation is necessary or where severe injury is evident. Hospitals

need a clearly established system of reporting since several professionals
are likely to be involved. Recommended regulations for hospital staffs
are noted.

1865 Paull, Dorothy; Lawrence, Robert J.; Schimel, Beverly. "A new
      approach to reporting child abuse." Hospitals 41(2): 62-64,
      January 16, 1967. (7 References).
Introduces a plan for reporting child abuse more effectively than the
reporting procedures outlined by law. At the Milwaukee Children's Hospital, it was decided that a standing committee of one or more physicians,
a psychiatrist, a social service administrator, and a social worker
should review all suspected abuse cases, report them to the proper legal
authorities, and propose treatment measures. It was found that simplify-
ing committee procedures made it possible to accumulate information
swiftly, to retain family records, to initiate treatment quickly, and
even to recommend removing the child when the situation mandated it. An
increase in reporting and a decrease in subsequent injuries resulted after
the formation of the committee. This plan is offered as a model for
action in other communities.

1866 Riley, Nancy M. "The abused child." Rocky Mt Med J 68(9): 33-
      36, September, 1971. (4 References).
Discusses responsibility of medical personnel, particularly physicians,
to report suspected child abuse and suggests techniques to assist the
physician in interviewing parents suspected of abuse. The 1962 Model Act
for the Mandatory Reporting by Physicians and Institutions of Certain
Physical Abuse of Children is discussed as a statement of principles for
all state legislation on the reporting of child battery incidents. It
states that failure to report should result in a misdemeanor and protects
the reporter from personal liability stemming from either criminal or
civil suits. Nearly all jurisdictions in the country have enacted a
mandatory reporting statute based on the Model Act.

1867 Ryan, James H. Suffer the little ones. Nashville, Tennessee:
      Aurora Publishers, 1972. 176p.
A fictionalized account of a small midwestern town's reaction to the
death of a battered child in its midst. Patrick Brennan, a pediatrician
and expert in the area of child abuse, is called in to advise the judge
in reaching a just decision in the trial of the dead child's mother. As
Brennan examines the scene of the battering, questions neighbors and
police, and interviews the mother, typical attitudes toward child abuse
surface and are answered by Brennan's clear and pointed knowledge of the
subject. The book's simple narrative is freely interspersed with medical
and legal jargon. In addition to its main plot, the novel is also involved with a bribery scheme, charges of sexual assault, and the physician's own struggle with his demanding and frustrating career.

1868 Schrotel, S. R. "Responsibilities of physicians in suspected cases
      of brutality." Cincinnati J Med 42(10): 408, October, 1961.
      (0 References).
The author, Chief of Police of Cincinnati, urges local physicians to report three types of cases to the police: (1) all malnutrition cases
where neglect is evident; (2) all injury cases where parents' stories do
not coincide with the nature of the injury; and (3) all assault cases
where violence is indicated.

1869 Stone, Alan A. Mental health and law: a system in transition.
      Rockville, Maryland: U.S. National Institute for Mental Health,
      Center for Studies of Crime and Delinquency, 1975. 266p. (Bibli-
      ography). (DHEW Publication no. (ADM) 75-176).
Interactions between medical and legal systems are applied to the field
of child abuse and neglect.

1870 Woodward, J. W. "Battering: unfortunate backlash: letter to
      editor." Br Med J 1(5905): 452, March 9, 1974. (0 References).
Closer laison between general practitioners and the staff of the National
Society for the Prevention of Cruelty to Children is recommended. It is
suggested that a family's physician be consulted before investigations
into complaints of child abuse are conducted. The distressing effects on
a non-battering parent of a NSPCC investigation is given as an example.

1871 Young, Harold A. "The battered child." J Iowa Med Soc 64(10):
      438-39, October, 1974. (0 References).
Asserts the need for reporting of child abuse cases by physicians.
According to Iowa law, physicians are not liable for reporting in good
faith, but they are liable if they fail to report abuse.

                    (2) Reluctance, Failure to Report

1872 Braun, Ida G.; Braun, Edgar J.; Simonds, Charlotte. "The mistreated
      child." Calif Med 99(2): 98-103, August, 1963. (9 References).
Reviews cases of parental neglect or abuse and outlines an approach for
physicians to follow. Physicians, for varying reasons, including a lack
of knowledge about what should be done, may hesitate to report their
findings. The hospital social worker familiar with proper procedures
should be consulted. Legal steps can be taken to help the child without
initiating criminal proceedings against the parents, although legal safeguards are better defined for the battered child than for the emotionally
abused or physically neglected child. A reliable means of reporting and
recording child abuse information has yet to be developed. However, laws
are being established to protect physicians or institutions reporting
such cases. Several systems described for handling child abuse cases
effectively include the coordination of medical, social, and legal efforts.

1873 Brown, Rowine H. "Physician/hospital liability and responsibility
      in case of child abuse." Hosp Med Staff 6(5): 10-14, May, 1977.
      (2 References).
Reports on mandatory child abuse reporting laws and advises medical staff
about the consequences of failure to report. Increased litigation is
expected in the future as a result of the California Supreme Court's
decision (in the Landeros v. Flood case) that a physician and a hospital
may be held liable for failure to diagnose and report child abuse. The
article discusses court proceedings and the kinds of information and
proof needed in such cases. Appropriate steps are also listed for hospitals and physicians to take to protect both themselves and the abused
children.

1874 Child Abuse and Neglect Committee. "Child abuse and neglect."
      J Indiana State Med Assoc 69(8): 580-81, August, 1976. (0
      References).

Child abuse is a self-perpetuating cycle: abused children often grow up to be abusive parents. This cycle must be stopped, but many physicians are reluctant to report suspected abuse because they feel the medical evidence will not stand up in court or they distrust the capacity of protective services to treat the problem. A proposed child abuse law in Indiana would alleviate some of these concerns by defining abuse and neglect more clearly, establishing interdisciplinary child protection units for the management of child abuse, appointing an attorney to represent the child in legal proceedings, and requiring the reporting of neglect as well as abuse.

1875 Clymer, James N. "Torts: the battered child -- a doctor's civil
     liability for failure to diagnose and report." Washburn Law J
     16(2): 543-51, Winter, 1977. (62 References).
Evaluates the legal ramifications of the Landeros v. Flood case, in which a physician was sued for failure to diagnose and report the battered child syndrome in a patient. The child, treated and released by the physician, was permanently injured by her parents three months later. The court has difficult problems in such cases: (1) specialized knowledge is necessary to decide whether the physician should have recognized that the child's injuries were not accidental; (2) proximate cause is difficult to decide because of the intervening force (the parents' continued abuse) and because of the question of foreseeability; (3) proof is difficult because many mandatory reporting laws are ambiguous about whether a physician is liable only if he actually suspected abuse and did not report it or if he should have suspected abuse and did not. If a state agency decides an abused child should be released to its parents, a question arises about the state's liability if the child is subsequently battered again. Many people are legally required to report suspected child abuse, but the physicians remain liable for failure to report because they possess the most training in diagnosis of the battered child syndrome. An increase in failure to report suits against physicians is predicted.

1876 Dewees, Phillip E. "The role of the family doctor in the social
     problem of child abuse." NC Med J 27(8): 385-88, August, 1966.
     (0 References).
Examines new legislation which should diminish physicians' concerns about reporting child abuse. Although medical practitioners are the logical persons to report abuse, many have been reluctant for the following reasons: (1) fear of the law; (2) fear of violating a confidential relationship; (3) low level of suspicion regarding abuse cases; and (4) a feeling that a report would have no constructive results. However, North Carolina passed legislation in 1965 granting physicians legal immunity. The wording "may report" rather than "shall report" imposes no new legal restrictions on the practitioner. Although the method by which the report must be made is not indicated, the department of welfare is mandated to be the reporting agency. This restriction is praised since the welfare department has a knowledgeable social perspective, and their aim will be to work with the family to avoid legal action or removal of the child. Many kinds of abuse are noted, ranging from battering to neglect. The Good Samaritan Law, protecting physicians from liability when assisting in accident cases, is linked to the passage of the child abuse law since the fear motivating their enactment is so similar.

1877 Finberg, Laurence. "A pediatrician's view of the abused child:
     letter to editor." Child Welfare 44(1): 41-43, January, 1965.
     (0 References).

The purported reluctance of physicians to report cases of child abuse stems not from the difficulty of identifying them nor from the reporting law. The rising number of cases reported by physicians in recent years is due to the publicity given the symptoms and improvement in diagnostic techniques. But many physicians have met frustration and incompetence in the handling of the cases they have reported. Joint efforts to correct this situation must be made by the medical, judicial, and social work communities.

1878   Foster, Henry H., Jr., and Freed, Doris J. "Battered child legislation and professional immunity." Am Bar Assoc J 52(11): 1071-73, November, 1966. (19 References).
Focuses principally on the provision of immunity in child abuse statutes and, to a lesser extent, on Good Samaritan laws which exempt a physician from liability in the charitable performance of medical arts at the scene of an accident, crime, and others. Such statutes are found to be superfluous, but are regrettably approved of as necessary spurs to the physician's conscience. There is some brief discussion of other legal aspects of child abuse, including the misguided emphasis upon the punishment of perpetrators as opposed to their rehabilitation.

1879   Fuller, Marjorie G. "Child abuse: the physician's responsibility." J Leg Med 3(5): 24-29, May, 1975. (20 References).
Although physicians should be the primary source of referral, they are negligent in reporting cases of child abuse. They may be ignorant of the physical manifestations of abuse but more likely, they want to avoid the legal involvement, do not know the proper referral process, fear the wrath of parents, and the possibility of a mistaken diagnosis. The legal, medical, and social responsibilities of the physician are emphasized. The safety of the child must be the physician's major concern.

1880   George, James E. "Battered child revisited." J Emerg Nurs 3(2): 53, March-April, 1977. (0 References).
Recapitulates action taken by the California Supreme Court to reverse a lower court's decision in the case, Landeros v. Flood. The higher court declared that the physician, who upon examining a battered child failed to take protective action, was guilty of negligence. The plaintiff, a minor represented by her guardian, received monetary compensation for both physical and mental trauma suffered at her parents' hands subsequent to the physician's examination.

1881   Hall, Douglas A. "Protecting the abused child in Maine." J Maine Med Assoc 65(6): 148-49, June, 1974. (0 References).
The reasons for the significantly low reporting of child abuse in Maine, despite the mandatory reporting law for physicians, are explored. Physician reluctance to report is thought to be due, in part, to lack of familiarity with the bureaucracy responsible for investigating families. The article explains the procedures and aims of Maine's Department of Health and Welfare, the agency mandated to investigate reports of abuse, in an effort to familiarize physicians with the likely outcome of a report. Also suggested is a specific format for reporting abuse and the actual addresses of Department of Health and Welfare offices designated to receive reports.

1882   Helpern, Milton. "Fatalities from child abuse and neglect: responsibility of the medical examiner and coroner." Pediatr Ann 5(3): 42-57, March, 1976. (0 References).

Although state laws require the reporting of all violent or suspicious sudden and unexpected deaths to the coroner for investigation by the medical examiner, infant deaths are often not consistently reported. Many deaths in infants are automatically labeled "sudden death syndrome" or "cot deaths" when a thorough investigation could have revealed other causes, such as disease or non-accidental injury. The reporting physician, coroner, medical examiner, and police should coordinate their efforts to determine the circumstances surrounding the death and the probable cause. The medical examiner or pathologist who performs the autopsy should notice and document the pattern and age of any lesions. An injury inflicted upon an infant in two days or even two or three weeks prior to death can be considered the cause—injuries do not have to be "fresh" to cause death. All attempts at resuscitation and procedures performed on the body postmortem should be carefully charted so that injuries sustained antemortem can be distinguished from them. The medical examiner must inform the prosecutor, the police, and the appropriate social-service agencies if there is an indication or suspicion that non-accidental injury or neglect contributed to the death. The medical examiner's report must be carefully prepared so that it can be used as clear cut evidence if a case of infant death is taken to criminal court.

1883 Holder, Angela R. "Child abuse and the physician." JAMA 222(4): 517-18, October, 1972. (0 References).
Outlines the role of the physician in reporting child abuse. It is stressed that a physician can report suspected abuse without the fear of being sued for defamation of character. In fact, if a physician fails to report a case of suspected abuse, he can be considered legally negligent in the administration of his duties.

1884 Johnson, Norma. Child abuse in North Dakota. Grand Forks, North Dakota: University of North Dakota, Bureau of Governmental Affairs, 1974.
Reports on the survey of 234 physicians regarding child abuse. The responses indicated that reports were not always made to the proper authorities and that a lack of evidence prevented reporting. Physicians were unfamiliar with reporting laws and would have liked to see them broadened. Recommendations based on the recorded information were: (1) to increase available information on child abuse laws, procedures, and roles of other involved professionals; (2) to increase mandatory reporting by other professionals in addition to physicians; (3) to broaden the definition of child abuse; (4) to eliminate required written report; (5) to investigate cases through police agencies, not social service agencies; and (6) to make the information in the Central Registry available to physicians.

1885 Kempe, C. Henry. "Duty to report child abuse: editorial." West J Med 121(3): 229, September, 1974. (0 References).
Although laws require physicians to report all cases of suspected child abuse, a physician should not feel that in doing so he is acting "against the parent" but "for the family," since the majority of families respond positively to sympathetic treatment and therapy.

1886 Kohlman, Richard J. "Malpractice liability for failing to report child abuse." West J Med 121(3): 244-48, September, 1974. (18 References).

Despite the threat of civil liability, many physicians are not complying with the child abuse statutes recently enacted in all fifty states. Malpractice suits against non-complying physicians and hospitals may eventually encourage other physicians and hospitals to cooperate and report suspected cases. In California, child abuse has been judicially recognized as "an accepted medical diagnosis," an action which will finally bring the syndrome into medical indices and lexicons.

1887 Ledakowich, Ann. "Child abuse decision reversed by Supreme Court of California." Med Times 104(12): 47-48, December, 1976. (0 References).
Cites a reversal by the Supreme Court on a malpractice suit involving a physician who failed to report a case of child abuse. The complaint claimed that the child suffered permanent damage as a result of the practitioner's negligence. The trial court dismissed the case, and the Court of Appeals sustained the action, claiming that a lack of definition of the battered child syndrome made it impossible to hold the physician legally responsible for recognizing it. The Supreme Court, however, indicated that there is sufficient literature available on child abuse to make it medically recognizable. The particular suit remained to be decided on the basis of testimony.

1888 ————. "Malpractice decisions you should know about." Med Times 104(8): 91-92, August, 1976. (2 References).
Concerns a medical malpractice lawsuit against a physician and hospital for failure to detect and report a case of child abuse. The California Court of Appeals held that the physician was under no legal obligation to undertake investigative efforts to determine the actual cause of injuries. However, the Court did hold the physician responsible for damages to the infant due to breach of his statutory duty to report suspected non-accidental injury to the authorities.

1889 Lesermann, Sidney. "There's a murderer in my waiting room." Med Econ 41(17): 62-71, August 24, 1964. (0 References).
A physician relates his discovery and treatment of a severely abused child and his difficulty in prosecuting the mother or saving the child from murder due to a loophole in state laws.

1890 "More on the battered child: editorial." N Engl J Med 269(26): 1437, December 26, 1963. (2 References).
Disapproves of physician's reporting of child abuse to the police. Instead, it is suggested that laws be passed protecting physicians from legal complications and an agency for child guardianship be established promoting therapeutic treatment of these families rather than legal prosecution. Massachusetts is cited as having made progress in this area.

1891 O'Neill, James A., Jr. "Deliberate childhood trauma: surgical perspectives." J Trauma 13(4): 399-400, April, 1973. (0 References).
Physicians must overcome their reluctance to report their suspicions regarding child abuse cases, and legal authorities are urged to build rehabilitative apparatus into child abuse legislation.

1893 "Reporting child abuse." Pediatr Curr 16(10): 37-40, November-December, 1967. (12 References).

Expresses concern over the startling extent to which physicians are either unaware of their obligation to report suspected cases of child abuse, or reluctant to make the report. A survey of national statistics indicated that nearly half of the reports of child abuse in the country came from either California or Texas, and that less than one-third of the reported cases involved children younger than three years. These distorted proportions suggest that a very high percentage of physicians, particularly those in private practice, are ignoring the reporting laws. Improved communication is called for, on the order of a system used in Illinois to inform physicians of their responsibilities and of the procedures they should follow in reporting.

1893 Rosenberg, A. H. "Compulsory-disclosure statutes." N Engl J Med
      280(14): 1287-88, April 3, 1969. (4 References).
Criticizes the compulsory reporting laws as they apply to the physician. Such laws are seen as interfering with the physician's discretion in the treatment of his patient.

1894 Silver, Larry B.; Barton, William; Dublin, Christina C. "Child
      abuse laws -- are they enough?" JAMA 199(2): 65-68, January 9,
      1967. (10 References).
Discusses the reluctance of physicians to report suspected cases of child abuse and the need for legislation requiring them to do so. The principal features of the 1963 model legislation introduced by the Children's Bureau (HEW) are given, as well as many of the questions and doubts concerning its effectiveness. In order to determine the physician's role in reporting, a study was conducted by sending 450 questionnaires to physicians in Washington, D.C. who have contact with children. Results showed that many were unaware of the battered child syndrome and were not familiar with community procedures for reporting it. Communication should be facilitated and legal protection made available to physicians to encourage them to report cases of child abuse.

1895 Silver, Larry B.; Dublin, Christina C.; Lourie, Reginald S. "Child
      abuse syndrome: the 'gray areas' in establishing a diagnosis."
      Pediatrics 44(4): 594-600, October, 1969. (11 References).
Analyzes the major reasons why it is difficult to diagnose and report suspected child abuse. Many physicians admit that they cannot believe a parent could abuse his/her child. Some have difficulties in drawing the line between a parent's privilege to punish and child abuse. If a sibling caused another child's injury, is the parent responsible for the abuse? If abuse occurred while a parent was under the influence of alcohol, is that parent responsible for his actions? Will a report of abuse cause suffering to the family or hurt the physician's medical practice? While these are understandable concerns, there is a legal and moral obligation to report suspected abuse. It is the function of other special agencies to determine whether abuse actually occurred, who was responsible for the abuse, and what should be done about it.

1896 Stamm, Mortimer J. "Battered children: doctors, parents, and the
      law." J Ky Med Assoc 74(2): 89-93, February, 1976. (19 Refer-
      ences).
The definition of child abuse has evolved into one which now includes mental abuse. This, in fact, may be basis for legal action. Child abuse is not restricted to one particular socioeconomic group, but there is a somewhat classic clinical profile for an abusive parent. The legislation

of the 1960's made reporting of suspected cases mandatory; however, in
a 1967 survey of 450 physicians, over one-half of them were not familiar
with the reporting procedures. The reluctance of the physicians to believe that parents are potential child abusers is matched with reluctance
on the part of lawyers to prosecute abusing parents.

1897 Weinbach, Robert W. "Case management of child abuse." Soc Work
      20(5): 396-97, September, 1975. (8 References).
The sources of the medical community's difficulty in managing child abuse
cases efficiently are enumerated. They include the lack of awareness on
the part of practitioners and hospital administrators of the characteristic symptoms of abuse. Ignorance of the precise terms of the reporting
of child abuse cases is another problem: many medical personnel are unaware of the provisions granting immunity to reporters, and are confused
about the procedures reporters should follow. There is also widespread
pessimism regarding the ultimate disposition of the case and the availability of effective treatment.

                        b.   Role of Police

1898 Collie, James. "Notes on education: the police." In: Franklin,
      Alfred White, ed. Concerning child abuse. New York: Churchill
      Livingstone, 1975.   p. 152. (0 References).
The policeman's education regarding child abuse is outlined. Basic training includes an introduction to sociological problems but no attention is
given to child abuse. An officer learns about the problem mainly through
experience, although seminars and special courses during his career supplement on-the-job education.

1899 ————. "The police role." In: Franklin, Alfred White, ed.
      Concerning child abuse. New York: Churchill Livingstone, 1975.
      123-26. (0 References).
Discusses the problem of child abuse from a law enforcer's perspective.
A short definition of the battered child syndrome introduces the reluctance to involve criminal authorities in a child abuse case. Although
the police are not opposed to family management, they are obligated to
protect and must investigate assaults. Investigations can serve to dis-
prove abuse allegations as well as confirm them. Delay in reporting can
result in subsequent injury or the unavailability of sufficient evidence,
should court intervention be necessary. A closing discussion stresses
interagency cooperation.

1900 Flammang, C. J. The police and the underprotected child. Spring-
      field: Charles C. Thomas, 1970. 310p. (Bibliography).
Intended to provide law enforcement officers and agencies with the most
current information regarding the unprotected child, this study encompasses several aspects of the role of the police in child protection.
Included in this wide-ranging presentation are discussions of the relationship between the police and other professionals concerned with child
protection--lawyers, judges, teachers, physicians, and social workers.
The present inadequacies and areas for improvement in these relationships
are analyzed. Child neglect and child abuse are discussed at length,
with particular criticism for what is seen as the community's failure to
protect the neglected child.

1901   Knapp, Vrinda S. "The role of the juvenile police in the protec-
       tion of neglected and abused children." For a summary see: Diss
       Abstr 22(9): 3289, March, 1962.

1902   Mounsey, Joseph. "Offenses of criminal violence, cruelty and neg-
       lect against children in Lancashire." In: Franklin, Alfred White,
       ed. Concerning child abuse. New York: Churchill Livingstone,
       1975. 127-30. (0 References).
Although law enforcers appreciate the efforts of medical and social work
professionals, the police must concern themselves with the victim of
child abuse. Currently, the police are the last to receive a report,
which usually occurs in the event of the child's death. Some child abuse
statistics show that in Lancashire the incidence of child deaths by non-
accidental injury has increased drastically since 1962, indicating that
methods of management are failing. Cooperation between police and other
protective agencies is stressed, followed by a discussion of the possibility of a compulsory reporting law in the United Kingdom.

1903   Sokoloff, Burton. "The battered child: letter to editor." West
       J Med 121(6): 509, December, 1974. (1 Reference).
Despite the physician's liability to report cases of suspected child
abuse, the police follow-up of such children has often been remiss. Many
of these same children later return to the physician's office, often in
a worsened condition.

1904   Swanson, Lynn D. "Role of the police in the protection of children
       from neglect and abuse." Fed Probat 25(1): 43-48, March, 1961.
       (8 References).
Explores the role of the police in child neglect and abuse cases. The
most useful role of the law enforcement officer is to provide emergency
service, particularly during the non-working hours of community agencies.
Once the police have responded, they must verify and evaluate the complaint through investigation and then decide whether to close the case
with a warning to the parents or refer the case to a community agency or
to the police unit handling the children's cases. If the child is removed from his home, the removing officer must refer him to juvenile or
family court. Cooperative planning between law enforcement and community
agencies is strongly recommended, as is the standardization of police
agency involvement.

                    c. Role of Other Professionals

1905   Badner, George. "Child abuse cases increase." Pa Sch J 124(2):
       20-22, October, 1975. (0 References).
Proposed Senate Bill 25 from Pennsylvania's General Assembly, making
school officials and school teachers legally responsible for reporting
suspected cases of child abuse, is discussed.

1906   Baker, Helen. "A question of witness." Nurs Times 67(23): 691-
       94, June 10, 1971. (12 References).
An increasing number of British nurse health visitors assigned to child
abuse cases are having to testify in court. The author discusses the
problems which derive from this professional responsibility, including
the possible effects upon the health visitor-family relationship. Her
report includes a brief survey of literature on the problem, as well as

findings from a questionnaire distributed to health visitors, all of whom
had appeared in court in a professional capacity. The majority of nurses
who took part in the inquiry felt they were not sufficiently prepared for
their responsibility in legal proceedings.

1907 "Child abuse." Bull Cleveland Dent Soc 25(1): 18-19, October,
      1969. (0 References).
Attempts to alert dentists to their professional responsibility to report
suspected child abuse. Portions of the 1965 Ohio Child Abuse Law are
highlighted, including a definition of the abused child, a list of professionals responsible for reporting suspected abuse or neglect, names of
agencies which receive and investigate abuse reports, and a statement of
the immunity regulation.

1908 Clark, Jane H., and Sawyer, Janet A. "I solemnly swear . . . a
      nurse testifies to child neglect." Nurs Outlook 16(4): 35-37,
      April, 1968. (2 References).
Consists of personal accounts of the experiences of two public health
nurses who testified in court about child neglect. To be a competent
witness, a nurse should understand local legal systems, cooperate with
assisting agencies, and report the facts of the case as accurately and
completely as possible. After testifying at a court hearing, a nurse
will often be apprehensive about how the family will respond to her. The
nurse should attempt to clarify her role as a professional interested in
helping, not punishing, the parents and family.

1909 "Dentists required to report cases of abused and maltreated chil-
      dren." NY State Dent J 39(10): 629, December, 1973. (0 Refer-
      ences).
Cites mandatory reporting law applicable to dentists treating abused
children. Under Section 413 of the Social Security Law in New York State,
dentists are required to report cases of abuse to the person or agency
in charge. Failure to comply comprises a Class A Misdemeanor and liability for damages which result from this negligence. Procedures for filing
oral and written reports in New York City are listed.

1910 Divoky, Diane. "Child abuse -- mandate for teacher intervention."
      Learning 4(8): 14-22, April, 1976. (0 References).
Indicates how state laws encourage the schools to protect suspected victims of child abuse. The conflicting opinions about various acts and
laws related to abuse and neglect of children are discussed.

1911 "From the states: legislation & litigation." J Am Dent Assoc
      75(5): 1081-82, November, 1967. (6 References).
Reviews legislation mandating dentists to report child abuse. Only
twenty-two states require dentists to report maltreatment, despite laws
in every state making that requirement of physicians. Dentists are unlikely to be involved in the initial treatment of these children. In a
study made of the Illinois Department of Child and Family Services involving 934 reports, only one came from a dentist. Most of the statutes
involving dentists waive the doctor-patient privilege, as well as providing for civil and criminal immunity.

1912 Martin, David L. "The growing horror of child abuse and the un-
      deniable role of the schools in putting an end to it." Am Sch
      Board J 160(11): 51-55, November, 1973. (0 References).

Studies the potential role of school personnel in reporting child abuse
cases. Teachers, principals, and administrators have the greatest opportunity to observe suspected maltreatment of children between the ages of
five and eighteen years. Specific school board policies (reminding
personnel about state laws requiring them to report abuse cases, teaching
school employees how to recognize child abuse and neglect, and outlining
specific procedures for reporting such cases) are necessary if schools
are to take more responsibility for the protection of abused children.
All fifty states have child abuse reporting laws, so more legislation is
probably not needed. What is needed are social agencies with programs
for management of the reporting, investigation, and treatment of child
abuse.

1913 Murdock, C. George. "The abused child and the school system." Am
      J Public Health 60(1): 105-9, January, 1970. (6 References).
Describes a school program developed in Syracuse, New York in compliance
with the mandatory child abuse reporting law. Despite the initial reluctance of school personnel to report, the program identified abused children not normally seen by a physician. School reports filed with the
Department of Social Welfare's central registry accounted for 20 to 30
percent of all reported incidents. Children ranged in age from five to
fourteen, most of whom received injury from a disturbed parent or guardian. Recommendations for the program stressed expediency in reporting
suspected abuse cases and in protecting the child.

1914 Sherman, Gilbert. "The abused child -- New York State." NY State
      Dent J 36(2): 109, February, 1970. (0 References).
Acquaints dentists with the provisions of Article X of the Family Court
Act in New York State and urges them to report suspected abuse cases.
Lists pertinent information about how and to whom to report.

D. THE COURTS

1. BASES FOR JUDICIAL INTERVENTION

1915 Baker, James A. "Court ordered non-emergency medical care for
      infants." Cleveland-Marshall Law Rev 18(2): 296-307, May, 1969.
      (63 References).
Reviews the legal arguments for and against invocation of the state's
discretionary privilege to require medical care for a child against the
parent's wishes. It is concluded that, although no clear-cut standard
for judgment exists, the legal validity of any action in the matter will
probably be influenced by a number of factors--for example, the child's
need of the treatment, the danger posed by the projected treatment, and
the degree to which the child's own cooperation is available.

1916 Bergman, Norma W. "Family law -- termination of parental rights --
      a new standard for balancing the rights of parents, children, and
      society." Emory Law J 24(1): 183-94, 1975. (42 References).
Cites a case study which documents the recent tendency of child custody
and adoption proceedings to deemphasize the once prevalent right of the
natural parents to the custody of the child. A case (In re Levi) in
which a Georgia court denied a negligent mother the custody of her child
is used to trace the implementation of Georgia's new statute regarding

the termination of parental rights. The new law is characterized as a
progressive improvement over its predecessor, in its expansion of the
grounds for termination to include deprivation as well as the narrower
and more traditional ground of abandonment. The court's cautiously progressive attitude in distinguishing between this termination of the parent's rights and other cases in which the parent's rights were upheld is
recommended as a model for the judicious revision by other courts in
other states of traditional assumptions regarding the most suitable disposition of the child.

1917 Bialestock, Dora. "Custody of children." Med J Aust 2(25): 1128,
      December 22, 1973. (2 References).
Argues that the only way children can be ensured of normal growth and
protected from physical abuse is if the society sets aside some of the
adult's rights to privacy and opens up the home to a visiting nurse or
other protective community services.

1918 Burt, Robert A. "Forcing protection on children and their parents:
      the impact of Wyman vs. James." Mich Law Rev 69(7): 1259-1310,
      June, 1971. (73 References).
Assesses the Supreme Court's decision in the case of Wyman v. James in
favor of the state's right to force assistance upon a welfare mother in
the interest of her child's well-being. The attitude of the Court in
this matter is contrasted with the more libertarian In re Gault decision
which had upheld the application of judicial safeguards to delinquency
cases. Although neither case is directly concerned with the issues of
child abuse or neglect, each implies a different attitude in one part of
the Court regarding the constitutionality of the state's intervention in
the family. The Wyman decision is criticized on the grounds that the
Court interpreted the case in too narrow a context, thus disregarding the
broader implications which would be drawn from its opinion.

1919 "Cager court disallows existence of illegitimates as sole basis
      for neglect removals." Welfare Law Bull 16: 8-9, March, 1969.
      (0 References).
Report of a four-to-one ruling by the Maryland Court of Appeals which
found that an illegitimate child cannot be officially declared neglected
simply because he lives with his mother who has had other illegitimate
offspring. The Court's decision was based on the finding that the
presence of illegitimate children is not in itself sufficient evidence
of an unstable moral environment. The Court also held that the State's
attorney, in using information on the mother's welfare application, had
violated the confidentiality of those records.

1920 "Child neglect: due process for the parent." Columbia Law Rev
      70(3): 465-85, March, 1970. (140 References).
Considers the implications of the due process clause of the Fourteenth
Amendment on the abrogation of the substantial and procedural rights of
parents in child neglect proceedings. Although the powers of the state
in the matter are conceded, it is emphasized that the rights of parents
to raise their children must be safeguarded. Specifically, the rights
of parents in neglect proceedings are too often overlooked in the court's
concern with the protection of the child.

1921 Cobin, Herbert L. "Legal opinion on child abuse." Del Med J
      49(4): 209-19, April, 1977. (0 References).

Reports a legal opinion on a child abuse case handed down by the Family
Court of the State of Delaware for New Castle County. The two defendants
in the case were charged with conduct that endangered the welfare of the
twin girls in their care. Medical findings did not confirm the defendants
testimony concerning the history of the children's injuries. In addition
to the conflicting testimonies, further evidence of willful neglect on
the part of the defendants was presented. Despite the obvious severity
of the burns suffered by both girls, the defendants failed to seek immediate attention for them until the day after the injury. As a result, the
court's opinion stated that the defendants were guilty of neglect and
endangering the welfare of their children. Numerous other abuse cases
and decisions are cited to support the court's opinion.

1922 "Constitutionality of the Illinois Child Abuse Statute." North-
      western Univ Law Rev 67(5): 765-72, November-December, 1972.
      (23 References).
Assesses a decision by the Illinois Supreme Court which maintained that
the language of the Illinois statute making child abuse a criminal offense
was not unconstitutionally vague. It is argued that the Court did not
adequately lay to rest the charge of vagueness, and that, by basing its
decision upon the implied definition of the term "child" (a word the
defense had focused on), it had ignored the potential for vagueness in
the remainder of the statute, and avoided the opportunity to clarify what
could become a troublesome issue.

1923 Crary, Ralph W. "Neglect, red tape, and adoption." Natl Probat
      Parole Assoc J 6(1): 33-39, January, 1960. (7 References).
Illustrates the importance of facilitating adoptions of abandoned children. Long-term institutionalization can have devastating effects on a
child's cognitive and emotional development, which justifies the release
of the child for adoption without parental consent by means of an Iowa
abandonment law.

1924 "Criminal liability of parents for failure to control their chil-
      dren." Valparaiso Univ Law Rev 6(4): 332-52, Summer, 1972.
      (101 References).
An assessment of the extent to which a parent can be liable for the
delinquent action of his child, in the light of the popular assumption
that the parent actually is the responsible party in cases of juvenile
delinquency. The concern here is with those statutes which hold a parent liable for his child's behavior if he (the parent) failed to do his
duty and prevent the child's misdeed. It is contended that a broad
interpretation of this provision endangers a parent's civil rights, unless parental liability is narrowly restricted to cases in which the
parent either clearly could have prevented the misdeed, or failed to
inform himself of his child's activity when such investigation was possible and clearly called for, or when the parent is negligently uncon-
cerned about his child's welfare. It is concluded that, even with these
restrictions, prosecution of parents under such provisions will do little
to deter delinquency.

1925 "The custody question and child neglect rehearings." Univ Chic
      Law Rev 35(3): 478-92, Spring, 1968. (83 References).
Focuses on the particular problem in cases of child neglect wherein
parents at one time judged negligent later petition for the restoration
of their custody. No guideline currently exists to aid the courts in

determining the long-term disposition of the child in such cases, and the only rule which is applied to the situation is the general custody rule, used in all custody disputes. Neither of the current standards for determining neglect--the best interests of the child and the unfitness of the parent--is an adequate solution to the problem of long-term custody. A custody rule should be designed which makes it incumbent upon the original complainant to prove that the child should remain outside of the custody of his parents.

1926   "The death of a child." New Soc 39(752): 434, March 3, 1977.
        (0 References).
Outlines mistakes which led to Wayne Brewer's death. Against the recommendation of social workers, the courts returned Wayne to his parents with required supervision. Even though social workers noticed more injury to the boy during their visits, there was not enough evidence for another court hearing. Had the police been informed, the court hearing may have been possible. The fact that injuries did occur indicated that supervision was not constant and proved that courts must be cautious in ordering family management when social services cannot provide it effectively.

1927   DeCourcy, Peter, and DeCourcy, Judith. A silent tragedy: child
        abuse in the community. Port Washington, New York: Alfred Publishing Company, 1973. 231p. (Bibliography).
Twelve representative case histories of children beaten, neglected, or killed by their parents in comfortable middle class communities are documented. Because these children were afraid to testify against their parents, or because their testimony and that of court psychiatrists and psychologists was not taken into consideration by the presiding juvenile court judge, most were systematically returned home only to be beaten or sexually assaulted again. Major reforms in the juvenile court system are strongly advocated. The court should be under state rather than county jurisdiction, and judges should be appointed and required to have a knowledge of the behavioral sciences and a familiarity with public welfare proceedings. In closed, informal hearings, abusive parents have always been the protected party. Only in an open court and before a jury will an abused child, represented by his own court-appointed attorney, receive due process of law. Most importantly, the court must act to terminate parental rights in instances when parents either refuse or do not respond to rehabilitation and therapy. It is both false and dangerous to assume that anyone can be a good parent.

1928   De Francis, Vincent. Termination of parental rights -- balancing
        the equities. Denver, Colorado: The American Humane Association,
        Children's Division, 1971. 20p. (Bibliography).
Discusses court responsibility in the termination of parental rights based on a survey of the fifty states. Parents' rights include custody and guardianship, while children are guaranteed the right to be with their natural family, the right to education, emotional security, health care, and protection from harm. Although parental rights can be terminated by marriage, legislation, the age of the child, and voluntary relinquishment, court orders can also terminate these rights. Because lack of time and money often prevents agencies from keeping an abuse family intact, it is more convenient to terminate the parents' rights even when such action may not be best for the child. In some states, the evidence need only show that the child is neglected, whereupon, the judge

can arbitrarily decide to remove the child from his home without any
guidelines for such a decision. A fairer procedure operating in a majority of states requires the courts to prove that parents have acted in a
manner which fits the clearly defined, statutory requirements for termination.

1929 Dembitz, Nanette. "The good of the child versus the rights of the
      parent: the Supreme Court upholds the welfare home-visit." Polit
      Sci Q 86(3): 389-405, September, 1971. (39 References).
Reports on the Supreme Court's decision to uphold the home-visit requirement for welfare recipients. The New York courts had upheld Mrs. James'
position that a required home visit violated the Fourth Amendment against
unreasonable search. A New York State Family Court judge felt that home
visits were essential in detecting abuse and neglect. In support of home
visits, the Supreme Court argued that the AFDC program was set up for the
child's protection and that the required visits were necessary in the
interests of the child. Mrs. James' claim that her "entitlement" to
public assistance should not be subject to conditions of home visits was
overruled by the Supreme Court because "entitlement" is not a legal right,
merely compensation for the inequality of the distribution of wealth.
The impetus behind the Work Incentive Act, which required welfare mothers
to seek employment, was to give mothers a sense of independence as working members of society so that they might set an example for their children. It was hoped that increased day care would reduce the need for
home visits for determining the welfare of the child.

1930 ─────. "Welfare home visits: child versus parent." Am Bar
      Assoc J 57: 871-74, September, 1971. (16 References).
Supports the Supreme Court's decision in Wyman v. James that a welfare
worker is entitled to visit an A.F.D.C. mother at home against the
mother's will. The child's interest in the matter is seen as opposing
and outweighing that of the mother (since the welfare worker's visit was
made to determine the well-being of the child). Criticism is expressed
of the dissenting opinions on the ground that they ignore the child's
interest altogether and that they are unfounded in the law.

1931 Derdeyn, Andre P. "Child abuse and neglect: the rights of par-
      ents and the needs of their children." Am J Orthopsychiatry
      47(3): 377-87, July, 1977. (67 References).
Delineates recent developments in legal decisions regarding the custody
and placement of abused and neglected children. Traditionally, the
parental right to custody of children, regardless of the circumstances,
has remained largely unquestioned. However, recently the rights of
biological parents have begun to change to reflect the needs of their
children. It is the state's responsibility in questions of removal to
prove that parents are incapable of providing for their children. When
it is deemed necessary to remove a child, parents will now find it somewhat more difficult to reclaim possession of their children simply by
asserting their hitherto unquestioned parental rights to custody.

1932 Dobson, M. V. "The juvenile court and parental rights." Fam Law Q
      4(4): 393-408, December, 1970. (0 References).
A consideration of the detrimental aspects of legal intervention in cases
of suspected neglect is related. Both parents and children are seen as
suffering irreparable damage as the result of agencys' and courts'
attempt to protect the child by removing him from a supposedly harmful
environment.

1933   Edgar, W. M. "Battered baby syndrome: letter to editor." Br Med J
       1(5439): 924, April 3, 1965. (1 Reference).
Documents an incident in which a twenty-one-year-old man received a five
year sentence for manslaughter as a result of the fatal beating of an
eighteen-month-old boy.

1934   "First degree murder indictment of parents: child neglected."
       Soc Welfare Court Dig 16(12): 1, December, 1971. (1 Reference).
Report of the Oregon Court of Appeals' action concerning the lower court's
dismissal of an indictment of a husband and wife for the first degree
murder of their young child. The child had apparently died of deprivation. The Appellate Court sustained the lower court's dismissal of the
indictment on the grounds that the indictment had not clearly stated the
duration of the child's deprivation, and furthermore, that the terms of
the actual charge were imprecise.

1935   Fischer, Michael S. "Neglected children and their parents in
       Indiana." Indiana Law Rev 7(6): 1048-63, 1974. (68 References).
Examines the implications for Indiana for the landmark case In re Gault
which maintained the necessity for judicial safeguards in delinquency
cases. Indiscriminate use of the parens patriae justification for state
intervention in family affairs is warned against, and the potential for
abrogating fundamental and substantive rights is emphasized. These
rights, which have been neglected in child abuse and neglect proceedings,
include the parent's right to raise his child and the child's right to
his parent's care.

1936   Gill, Thomas D. "The legal nature of neglect." Natl Probat Parole
       Assoc J 6(1): 1-16, January, 1960. (0 References).
Describes the historical foundation of legal doctrines involving neglect
and examines their role in establishing current legal theories, debates,
and practices. The rights of the individual and the rights of society
are at odds in a neglect case, and what is best for the child should
determine the outcome. However, the finding of neglect must be determined
solely by evidence and by the statutory definitions of neglect. The
criteria defining neglect must be flexible to be responsive to individual
cases and to cultural and social changes. Moral, medical, emotional, and
educational neglect and the legal problems inherent in each particular
type of neglect case are discussed. Once a finding of neglect is made,
the court makes whatever disposition seems best to assure the welfare of
the child.

1937   Graham-Hill, Jean. "Court proceedings." In: Franklin, Alfred
       White, ed. Concerning child abuse. New York: Churchill Living-
       stone, 1975. 136-39. (0 References).
Investigates the court system in the United Kingdom as it relates to
child abuse. An analysis of pre-court decisions concludes that when
physicians and social workers refrain from using the courts, they deprive
the child of his legal rights to protection. An investigation of a
child abuse report can lead simultaneously to criminal proceedings against
the parents in the adult courts and care proceedings for the child in
the juvenile courts. Lack of coordination between the two courts often
results in confusion, particularly with disposition. Consequently,
family court is needed.

1938 Grumet, Barbara R. "The plaintive plaintiffs: victims of the
      battered child syndrome." Fam Law Q 4(3): 296-317, 1970. (70
      References).
The battered child syndrome is discussed, with attention to its incidence,
the rehabilitation of the parents, and prevention. Difficulties in
implementing the reporting laws are presented, and revisions suggested,
among them being the immediate assumption of jurisdiction by the juvenile
or family court in cases of child abuse. An attorney should be appointed
to speak for the child's interests.

1939 Hansen, Richard H. "Suggested guidelines for child abuse laws."
      J Fam Law 7(1): 61-65, Spring, 1967. (8 References).
Guidelines for a revision of child abuse laws in Nebraska are suggested.
The principal recommendation is that one judge in a case of child abuse
be empowered to order a study into the family's fitness to care for the
child, and, upon the recurrence of abusive treatment, remove the child
from the family environment.

1940 Hicks, Graham M. "State v. McMaster: Due process in termination
      of parental rights." Williamette Law J 8(2): 284-93, June, 1972.
      (54 References).
A negative evaluation of a decision by the Oregon Supreme Court regarding
the constitutionality of the Oregon statute providing for the termination
of parental rights. The Supreme Court reversed a termination order by a
lower court, not on the grounds that the authorizing statute was unconstitutionally vague, as the defense had contended, but rather because the
parents, though of questionable stability, did not strictly endanger the
well-being of their child. It is argued that the Supreme Court erroneously imposed a narrow interpretation on the statute in order to dispel
its vagueness and find it constitutional. Revision of the statute is
called for, since in its present state it endangers both the procedural
rights of the parents and the fundamental right of the child to an intel-
ligently determined disposition.

1941 Katz, Sanford N. When parents fail: the law's response to family
      breakdown. Boston, Massachusetts: Beacon Press, 1971. 251p.
      (Bibliography).
Examines the concept of parens patriae, or the legal process of state
intervention into the parent-child relationship under circumstances in
which the parent has neglected or abandoned a child, or otherwise failed
to meet his parental responsibilities. An introductory chapter discusses
the role of the family within the community and the responsibilities which
the community expects of its parents, such as: to provide a stable and
healthy home environment, to provide financial support, medical care, and
the opportunity for education, and to instruct the child in the moral
values of the community.

Although the family has no specific constitutional right to privacy and
autonomy, the process of public intervention into the family circle is
complex. After a neighbor, relative, or agency has filed a report of
child neglect, the child welfare agency investigates the report and determines whether or not any legal action should be taken. If the agency
decides to dispute the parents' right of custody, a judicial challenge
occurs at which parents and agency argue for custody of the child before
the court. A petition initiates the legal process of removing the child
from his home and is followed by a court investigation into the alleged
neglect. Finally, an informal and private hearing in the judge's chambers

determines the disposition of the case. Since the hearing does not take place before a jury, the judge's position is often based upon his personal interpretation of vague legal definitions of neglect.

The theoretical bases of both foster care and adoption, in addition to difficulties which arise in both, are examined. Foster care is designed to provide temporary care and protection for a neglected child with the goal of returning the child to his natural parents after problems at home have been resolved. The rights and duties of the foster parents are set forth in a placement contract. Adoption, on the other hand, can only occur after the termination of the natural parents' rights to custody of the child. In most states, grounds for termination include: abandonment, mental illness, life imprisonment, and death of natural parents. Such factors as differences in religion and race between the natural and the adoptive parents may stall the selection process so that the final decision for adoption is often reached only after court intervention. Appendices include transcripts of judicial action taken in neglect cases and adoption hearings mentioned in the body of the text.

1942   Kelley, Florence M. "Role of the courts." Pediatrics 51(4, Part
       II): 796-98, April, 1973. (0 References).
Presents a practical discourse on judicial limitations and responsibil- ities when dealing with child abuse. Under present law, there are serious restrictions on the courts. For example, it is impossible to punish a parent who has deliberately harmed his child unless he has been previously found guilty of the same crime and is consequently violating a formerly issued court order. At the same time, the discussion seriously questions the effectiveness of punitive court action in helping the abusive parent solve his problem. Community action programs that could intervene before a case ever reaches the courts would be more effective for actually treat- ing problem families. Nevertheless, the final decision as to whether a child should stay in his home or be removed is the sole responsibility of the judge.

1943   Knudsen, Stephen T. "The education of the Amish child." Calif Law
       Rev 62(5): 1506-31, December, 1974. (57 References).
Comments on the problems of striking a legal balance among the interests of parent, child, and state on the issue of education. Particular refer- ence is made to the Wisconsin v. Yoder Supreme Court decision which held that the right of Amish parents to control the education of their chil- dren took precedence over the state's mandatory education statute. A number of references are made to other court decisions bearing on neglect statutes, including findings which favor the child's rights (usually cases of medical care).

1944   Lewis, Hilda N. "Adoption." Br Med J 2(5461): 577-80, September
       4, 1965. (5 References).
Current practices in Great Britain with respect to adoption are examined. The legal requirements are set forth for the benefit of the family physi- cian who may be called upon by his patients for advice, and whose assess- ment of the parents' suitability may be required. Physicians are also advised to watch adopted children for signs of rejection; the procedures for the redisposition of such children are explained.

1945   Lipton, George L. "Mother is a bad word: the rights of children
       in law in two custody cases." Aust NZ J Psychiatry 11(1): 19-23,
       March, 1977. (10 References).

Focuses on the right of children to have a stable and continuing relationship with a caring individual who may or may not be a child's natural
parent. Gradually, the quality of care is being regarded as more important than who administers the care. Parents can no longer be afforded the
luxury of having absolute rights to the custody of their children at the
expense of their children's right to protection. Included is an examination of two judicial decisions analyzing whether or not the rights of
the children were upheld. In both cases the arguments centered on the
legal equivalent of psychological as opposed to biological parenthood.
Communities must begin to apply pressure to influence court decisions,
so they will consistently reflect the best interests of the child.

1946 LoPresti, Joseph M. "The abused 'battered child': editorial."
      Clin Proc Child Hosp 24(11): 351-52, December, 1968. (0 Refer-
      ences).
Legal reform in the area of child abuse is imperative. The present judicial system is oriented toward the protection of the legal rights of the
defendant, so that in the majority of cases the deciding judge is obliged
to return the child to his home. Almost half of the abused infants returned to their parents are murdered. Despite increased public awareness
of the problem, the child's rights have not yet been legally recognized.

1947 McCloskey, Kenneth D. "Torts: parental liability to a minor child
      for injuries caused by excessive punishment." Hastings Law J
      11(3): 335-40, February, 1960. (32 References).
Discusses the controversial doctrine of immunity and its relation to a
California case. The basic, conflicting arguments are presented: the
family is a self-governing unit, the courts have no right to interfere
with parental discipline, a child suing a parent may create friction, a
suit against parents may encourage collusion, yet everyone has the right
to voice his complaints and have his situation remedied. Clarification
of the terms "willfulness," "excessiveness," and "reasonableness" are
recommended. Therefore, the jury will not establish subjective standards
for disciplining a child, and children will not abuse the role of the
courts in family disagreements.

1948 "Mother incarcerated held not to have abandoned or neglected chil-
      dren." Soc Welfare Court Dig 20(3): 4, March, 1975. (0 Refer-
      ences).
Reports on the decision of a California appeals court that a woman jailed
on a marijuana charge did not abandon or neglect her children.

1949 National Symposium on Child Abuse, 2nd, Denver, 1972. Collected
      papers . . . to explore on an interdisciplinary basis the problems
      of child abuse and sexual exploitation of children. Denver,
      Colorado: The American Humane Association, Children's Division,
      1973. 60p. (Bibliography).
A collection of papers, presented at a national meeting in Denver,
Colorado, on October 11, 1972, defines court and community responsibility
to neglected children and the problems of sexual abuse. Child abuse
cases are handled best in juvenile courts where rulings can be flexible
to fit the needs of the family. To fully respect the rights of both
parents and child, the adjudicatory process, involving legal counsel and
testimony, first determines whether the court should intervene. Should
intervention be necessary, the process of disposition determines what to
do with the child, a decision which should include recommendations from

several professional disciplines. Lack of specific definitions of child
neglect and the short notice often given to accused parents concerning
the hearing are present infringements on parental rights in some states.
Courts should be the last resort. One paper noted that, historically,
child protective services have sought to remedy the situation after the
damage has been done, whereas preventive measures should be employed.
The community of Honolulu, Hawaii recognized a need for more services to
families in crisis. The William Beaumont General Hospital in El Paso,
Texas set up a multidisciplinary abuse team for families in the military,
believing that martial law is inadequate and too punitive to deal effectively with child abuse. The symposium gives specific attention to
sexual abuse and its effects on the family.

1950 "Physically abused child held 'deprived.'" Soc Welfare Court Dig
      17(4): 2, April, 1972. (1 Reference).
Report on a North Dakota Supreme Court's decision to sustain a lower
court's termination of parental rights in a case involving both child
abuse and parental neglect. The ruling was based on the evidence of the
child's injuries and the probability that the abuse would continue.

1951 Polier, Justine Wise. "Parents arraigned." In: Polier, Justine
      Wise. Everyone's children, nobody's child: a judge looks at
      underprivileged children in the United States. New York: Charles
      Scribner's Sons, 1941. 106-23. (0 References).
Examines the responsibilities of the courts in deciding questions of
child protection and removal in cases of neglect. One primary obstruction to the effectiveness of court action is parental resistance and indifference to any guidance or assistance by societal agencies. Another
problem the courts face is determining the impact of removal on a child's
emotional stability and development, for in many cases the emotional
damage by destroying his world far exceeds any threat to the child from
poverty or substandard living conditions. Courts must remember that their
first concern is always the welfare of the child.

1952 ————. "Parents complain." In: Polier, Justine Wise. Every-
      one's children, nobody's child: a judge looks at underprivileged
      children in the United States. New York: Charles Scribner's Sons,
      1941. 124-29. (0 References).
Studies parental attempts to invoke authority in order to affect a change
in their child's behavior. Several case histories describing parents who
felt they could no longer control their children are included. The use
of court authority in such instances must be calculated carefully to conform to the child's needs and drives and to improve intrafamilial relationships.

1953 Raffalli, Henri C. "The battered child: an overview of a medical,
      legal, and social problem." Crime Delinq 16(2): 139-50, April,
      1970. (23 References).
The legal problems peculiar to child abuse, especially in the apparent
conflict between the rights of parents and children in child abuse cases,
are analyzed. The early identification of potentially severe conflicts
between parents and children as a means of preventing child abuse is
recommended.

1954 "Refusal of parental consent to blood transfusion." Br Med J
      2(5476): 1494, December 18, 1965. (1 Reference).

Documents a court case in which a woman who had refused a transfusion for her child on religious grounds was denied parental powers. The woman was not charged with neglect upon the child's death, however, because she had acted as a result of religious convictions.

1955   Rowe, Daniel S. "Rights of parents and children." N Engl J Med
       283(3): 156-57, July 16, 1970. (2 References).
Response to a letter stressing the importance of a precise definition of "abuse" in order to protect parents. Attention should be aimed at ensuring the well-being of the child and not toward prosecution of abusers. If this rule is followed, children will be spared further harm, and innocent parties will not be adversely effected.

1956   Rubenstein, I. H. "Custody of infant children in medical neglect
       cases." J Am Med Wom Assoc 16(10): 771-74, October, 1961. (26
       References).
Calls attention to the legal duty of parents to provide medical care to their infants and young children. The court's right to order the immediate custody of the child in cases of neglect, regardless of religious affiliation, is considered essential. Case studies, several involving practicing Christian Scientists, illustrate the physician's legal responsibility where parents are negligent in obtaining medical care.

1957   Schuchter, Arnold. Child abuse intervention: prescriptive pack-
       age. Washington, D.C.: U.S. Government Printing Office, 1976.
       157p. (Bibliography).
From a criminal justice point of view, a model system of child abuse intervention is offered. Recommendations included are that medical treatment be prompt, that children and parents receive due process, and that court action take place as civil proceedings. A review of child abuse literature provides a framework for the prescriptive package. The second part offers information on the operation of the model system dealing with discussions on emergency intake and examination, law enforcement, civil adjudication strategy, accountability, and performance monitoring. A detailed comparison of existing and proposed model systems is offered.

1958   Thomas, Ellen K. "Child neglect proceedings -- a new focus."
       Indiana Law J 50(1): 60-81, Fall, 1974. (104 References).
Reviews the traditional roles of child, parent, and state in neglect proceedings, taking issue with the prevalent assumption that the best interest of the child lies either with the state or with the parent. The "best interest" standard, as traditionally interpreted, is shown to be lacking in sensitivity to the special nature of child neglect cases, which involve a greater number of factors and options than are usually considered. Among these, one in great need of attention is the proposition, based on state and federal statutes, that parents charged with neglect have a right to obtain remedial and support services. Greater consideration is also urged for the post dispositional treatment of the child who is removed from his family.

1959   Thurston, Gavin. "Problems of consent." Br Med J 2(5500):
       1405-7, June, 1966. (3 References).
Studies the problem of obtaining consent from subjects for medical examination and treatment and of the additional difficulties encountered when parental consent must be obtained, especially in situations in which the child requires treatment, and the parent refuses permission on religious grounds.

1960   Wadlington, Walter. "A new look at the courts and children's
       rights." <u>Children</u> 16(4): 138-42, July-August, 1969. (24 Refer-
       ences).
The recent movement by the judicial system to protect the legal rights of
children is outlined. Several cases in which the courts have intervened
in the family for the purpose of protecting the rights or well-being of a
child are presented. Future areas where court action may be taken are
discussed.

1961   Wilson, Reginald A. "Legal action and the 'battered child': letter
       to editor." <u>Pediatrics</u> 33(5): 1003, May, 1964. (0 References).
Response to an article in <u>Pediatrics</u> (Harper, 1963) concerning the battered child. A case is cited in which a social welfare agency removed
a child from his home, despite protestations of the parents that they
were not responsible for the child's injury. The parents sued, the court
failed to prove child abuse, and custody was returned to the couple. The
need for safeguards to protect innocent parents from overaggressive social
agencies is discussed.

2. JUDICIAL PROCEDURES FOR INTERVENTION

1962   Betzendorfer, Joseph Q., Jr. "For the respondents -- counsel for
       the parents." In: National Symposium on Child Abuse, 5th, Boston,
       1974. <u>Collected papers</u>. Denver, Colorado: The American Humane
       Association, Children's Division, 1976. 79-82. (0 References).
Explores various problems and practices for the parents' counsel in child
abuse cases. The attorney must know the facts and be able to stabilize
the emotions of his clients. Initial contact with the caseworker should
explore the possibilities of a workable solution without going to court.
Once in court, the attorney must present the parents' position as best
he can. Because his responsibility is to protect the parents' rights,
the attorney must ask for a dismissal when the state has produced insufficient evidence even though he may not believe it the best action for
the child.

1963   Bottoms, A. E.; McLean, J. D.; Patchett, K. W. "Children, young
       persons, and the courts: a survey of the new law." <u>Crim Law Rev</u>
       368-95, July, 1970. (38 References).
Details the role of juvenile courts, police, and children's departments
in implementing Britain's Children and Young Persons Act of 1969. In
this Act, care proceedings replace criminal proceedings against children
under fourteen.

1964   Bowers, William C. "Does due process require clear and convincing
       proof before life's liberties may be lost?" <u>Emory Law J</u> 24(1):
       105-50, Winter, 1975. (205 References).
Examines the question of what constitutes proof in non-criminal proceedings brought by the state against an individual and resulting in that
person's loss of liberty or property. It is contended that the standard
of proof should be explicitly stated in all such cases, and that proof
stronger than the preponderance of the evidence be the standard in cases
involving the loss of liberty. One of the cases used in illustration
concerns the termination of parental rights by the state. Because of the
operation of the countervailing interests in such cases, preponderance
of the evidence is regarded as sufficient proof.

1965   Brown, Rowine H.; Fox, Elaine S.; Hubbard, Elizabeth L. "Medical
       and legal aspects of the battered child syndrome." Chic Kent Law
       Rev 50(1): 45-84, Summer, 1973. (110 References).
Comprehensively discusses the medical and legal aspects of child abuse,
and includes a historical perspective on both. The Illinois Child Abuse
Law is explained and evaluated. The courtroom management of child abuse
cases is also discussed, with the suggestion that the state's attorney
assign more lawyers to represent the children in these hearings. In this
vein, a Bill of Rights for children is proposed.

1966   Burt, Robert A. "Protecting children from families and themselves:
       state laws and the Constitution." J Youth Adolesc 1(1): 91-111,
       March, 1972. (19 References).
Criticizes the tendency of the courts to apply procedural safeguards
across the board to child protective legislation. It is concluded that
the indiscriminate application of criminal safeguards to protective
legislation restricts these laws unnecessarily.

1967   Campbell, Catherine E. "The neglected child: his and his family's
       treatment under Massachusetts law and practice and their rights
       under the due process clause." Suffolk Univ Law Rev 4(3): 632-88,
       Spring, 1970. (95 References).
Analyzes the procedures by which Massachusetts currently determines the
best interests of the child in neglect cases. Many cases are handled
outside the court system, by the Division of Child Guardianship, whose
staff of underpaid and inadequately prepared social workers are often
responsible for deciding the disposition of a child. The procedural
rights of children and parents in neglect hearings are also discussed
with reference to the implication of the Supreme Court's landmark decision, In re Gault. In the light of Gault's application of the equal
protection clause to juvenile delinquency hearings, the procedural rights
of children in neglect hearings in Massachusetts are virtually ignored,
most particularly the child's right to counsel.

1968   Cavenagh, Winifred. "Battered children cases in the courts." In:
       Franklin, Alfred White, ed. Concerning child abuse. New York:
       Churchill Livingstone, 1975. 140-46. (0 References).
Discusses procedures and problems of the court system as it relates to
child abuse. The present judicial system in the United Kingdom provides
for separate hearings for the offending parents and the abused child.
Criminal proceedings against parents often are of little value due to
lack of evidence. Care proceedings for the child are usually held pending until adult court outcome is determined, despite the risk of emotional
damage to the child. Because evidence in care proceedings is frequently
inadmissable or insufficient and because expert witnesses have little or
no court experience, dispositional decisions are not always optimal.
Orders of the juvenile court can authorize supervision of the child in
the home or removal of the child. Under the present judicial system,
all the variables of the case cannot be considered, and the possibility
of a family court is suggested.

1969   Curran, W. J. "The revolution in American criminal law: its
       significance for psychiatric diagnosis and treatment." J Public
       Health 58(7): 2209-16, July, 1968. (30 References).
Calls attention to the shift which has occurred in the relationship between psychiatrist and court as a result of recent landmark judicial

decisions establishing the procedural guarantees of a full-blown criminal hearing in cases of child abuse. These moves have tended to formalize the role of the psychiatrist and to restrict freedom to question and diagnose parents charged with abuse.

1970 "Disputes over children: editorial." Br Med J 4(5677): 182-83, October 25, 1969. (0 References).
Offers suggestions for guaranteeing the objectivity of psychiatric testimony in child custody cases and thus rendering such testimony more acceptable to the court.

1971 Fairlie, Chester. "Post-commitment custody of neglected children." Conn Law Rev 4(1): 143-53, Summer, 1971. (25 References).
Procedures recommended to protect the rights of children and, more particularly, their parents, in the permanent disposition of the child are outlined. A child should not be removed once he is returned to his parents without a formal hearing, at which the parents can be fully informed of the case against them, and can offer a rebuttal to it. The state must also present evidence of attempts to help the parents improve their situation. The voluntary relinquishment of parental rights should only occur within procedures guaranteeing that the parents are informed of their right to a hearing.

1972 Ford, Donald. "The battered child syndrome -- the law." Nurs Mirror 140(22): 58, June 12, 1975. (0 References).
The author, chairman of the Inner London Juvenile Court, describes the procedure for bringing cases of child battering or neglect before a juvenile court. In such cases, though parents are party to the proceedings, they are not on trial. The court's focus is on the future well-being of the child. In order to ensure well-being, evidence gathered must be first hand, thorough, and relevant to the case. When neglect or battering has been proven, the court may issue a Supervision Order or a Care Order. The first authorizes local social service agents to supervise (up to three years) the care a child receives by his parents in the home. The second option is more likely to be taken if actual battering has occurred. The child is removed from the home and cared for by local authorities until a time when the home is determined to be safe.

1973 Fraser, Brian G. "Independent representation of the abused and neglected child: the guardian ad litem." Calif West Law Rev 13(1): 16-45, 1976-1977. (179 References).
Argues that the guardian ad litem can most effectively represent the child in child abuse hearings, with explanations of the historical and current manifestations of the role. The guardian ad litem should not treat the hearing as an adversary proceeding, but he must recognize that the interests of parents and children in such hearings do not always coincide. He must be able to investigate the charges, and then serve as an advocate and guardian of the child's interest, offering counsel on the issues at hand. Rather than legislate specific guidelines for the function, it is recommended that a general spectrum of responsibilities for the guardian ad litem be described, thus allowing individual guardians to adapt the role to the demands of the case.

1974 "Infanticide cases before magistrates." Br Med J 2(5453): 118, July 10, 1965. (0 References).

Report of a Parliamentary debate on a bill altering the prosecution of infanticide so that the crime could be tried by magistrates and would not be punishable by imprisonment.

1975 Kaplan, Eugene N. "Appointment of counsel for the abused child --
       statutory schemes and the New York approach. New York State
       Assembly Select Committee on Child Abuse, report (1972)." Cornell
       Law Rev 58(1): 177-90, November, 1972. (90 References).
Reviews the statutory provisions regarding the abused child's right to counsel throughout the country, and a discussion of recent attempts at reforming New York's approach to this issue. The traditional--and still prevailing--attitude that the court will informally safeguard the child's rights is criticized. In New York, the system of law guardians--attorneys who represented children without counsel--was found to be ineffective by the New York Assembly Select Committee on Child Abuse, which proposed the establishment of a Children's Attorney, a specialized public prosecutor, who would be a necessary party to all abuse proceedings. The bill was vetoed in 1972 by Governor Rockefeller.

1976 Knight, Bernard. "Perinatal deaths and the law." Nurs Mirror
       Midwives J 140(6): 74-75, 1975. (0 References).
Surveys the difficulties involved in prosecuting cases of infanticide, the principal problem being the proof of a live birth. Some historical background is included.

1977 Landau, Hortense. "Preparation and presentation for the juvenile
       court." In: National Symposium on Child Abuse, 5th, Boston, 1974.
       Collected papers. Denver, Colorado: The American Humane Associa-
       tion, Children's Division, 1976. 74-78. (0 References).
Describes the fundamentals of a typical child abuse case. The attorney for the state prepares and presents the results of the investigation, which should include a complete inquiry into each allegation, interviews with the parents and the child, accurate observations by the caseworker, and interviews with witnesses. Parents are given a timely notice concerning the allegations prior to the court summons. The evidence is derived from several sources, such as direct evidence from the caseworker, the presentation of the injured child, circumstantial evidence, testimony from health care professionals, and, in some states, hearsay. All witnesses undergo direct and cross examination. If the courts assume jurisdiction of the child, a dispositional hearing follows.

1978 Levy, Nathan, Jr. "Neglected children in Mississippi." Miss Law J
       29(2): 165-91, March, 1958. (96 References).
Presents the development of those aspects of the Mississippi State Civil Judicial System which ensure the welfare of neglected and delinquent children. As early as 1807, the Legislature made some material provisions for children whose parents could not care for them. The establishment of a Juvenile Court Department in 1940 became the forerunner of the present day Youth Court created in 1946, now a part of each county court in the state, which provides for the care of any neglected or delinquent child. Flexibility in ruling distinguishes between neglected and delinquent children so that each case can receive the individual disposition best for the child. Counselors appointed by the Youth Court or by the County Department of Public Welfare carry out the provisions of the Youth Court Act. The court may file a formal petition declaring neglect or delinquency or may make an informal arrangement concerning the welfare

of the child. Dispositions range from supervision in the home to removal
of the child. Questions are raised regarding the increased incidence of
reported cases in larger towns, the relation of race to handling and disposition of cases, the distribution by age of neglected and delinquent
children, and the wide fluctuation in the disposition of neglect cases.

1979 Low, Colin. "The battering parent, the community, and the law."
      Appl Soc Stud 3(2): 65-80, May, 1971. (38 References).
Classifies the legal charges which may be brought against a parent accused
of child abuse. The terms defined and discussed are: murder, attempted
murder, infanticide, manslaughter, various offenses under sections eighteen and twenty of the Offenses Against the Person Act, 1861, and assault
occasioning bodily harm, and statutory offenses of cruelty and neglect.
Some possible defenses (accident, provocation, and diminished responsibility) are cited and discussed. The ultimate processing of a child
abuse case is largely dependent on the choice of prosecution, while
sentencing is affected by the type of court, type and seriousness of
offense, and age and history of the abusing parent. The attitude of
social workers and physicians toward reporting suspected cases of child
abuse to the police is seen as an ambivalent one, as feelings of responsibility to their own professions may come into conflict with the results
of reporting. The need for such reporting is emphasized.

1980 McKenna, James J. "A case study of child abuse: a former prose-
      cutor's view." Am Crim Law Rev 12(1): 165-78, Summer, 1974.
      (72 References).
The prosecution of two parents for murder in the fatal abuse of their
daughter is detailed. The difficulties in prosecuting child abuse cases
in general are elaborated with reference to this case, some of them being
the reluctance of family members to testify, the sensationalist attention given such cases by the media, and the reliance upon circumstantial
evidence to prove causality. A particularly interesting aspect of the
case was the charge--first degree murder which resulted from a felony
(mayhem). Given this charge, the prosecution does not need to prove
intent to kill in order to obtain a conviction. The general role of the
prosecutor in the matter of child abuse is discussed, including the
opportunity for encouraging abusive parents to obtain treatment.

1981 Mallard, Robert. "Due process -- guidelines for fair play and
      protection of rights." In: National Symposium on Child Abuse,
      4th, Charleston, S.C., 1973. Collected papers. Denver, Colorado:
      The American Humane Association, Children's Division, 1975.
      70-74.
Defines the role of the court in cases of child abuse and neglect in
Charleston, South Carolina. The primary consideration is the protection
of the rights of both parents and child. Restraining orders are issued
immediately in order to protect the child, but parents are given as much
time as possible to prepare action on their behalf. The court requires
evidence of neglect and abuse from a number of sources before termination and invites recommendations from other disciplines. When possible,
reunification of the family is the ultimate aim.

1982 "Matter of Ella B." Hofstra Law Rev 1: 324-31, Spring, 1973.
      (15 References).
Presents a history of the case Mother of Ella B., in which an indigent
mother charged with neglect was not informed of her right to free counsel.

After losing custody of her child, the mother appealed the decision on
the grounds that she was denied the fundamental right of equal protection
under the laws as guaranteed by the Fourteenth Amendment. The Appellate
Court rejected the state's argument that the injunction to inform indigent
parties of their right to free counsel applies exclusively to <u>criminal</u>
proceedings, contending rather that the potential removal of a child from
the parent represented a loss of liberty to the parent and that the civil
neglect proceeding was, therefore, subject to the same due process injunction as a criminal proceeding would be. The New York Family Court
Act was found to be unconstitutional for its failure to take this into
account.

1983　"Mother did not abandon children even if she failed to support
　　　　them." <u>Soc Welfare Court Dig</u>　20(3):　3, March, 1975.　(0 Refer-
　　　　ences).
Report of a trial in which a breach of procedural rights resulted in a
court decision against the termination of parental rights, despite evidence which supported the charge of abandonment.

1984　Plaine, Lloyd L.　"Evidentiary problems in criminal child abuse
　　　　prosecutions." <u>Georgetown Law J</u>　63(1):　256-73, October, 1974.
　　　　(94 References).
Examines the problems in presenting evidence in child abuse hearings.
Since most cases of child abuse occur in the privacy of the home, and
involve victims and witnesses (children, spouses) likely to be influenced
by the perpetrators (parents), evidence giving is particularly difficult.
The prosecution must base its case largely on circumstantial, character,
and hearsay evidence. Rulings which abrogate the traditional provisions
against these forms of evidence are discussed in terms of the situations
which justify them.

1985　Polier, Justine Wise.　"Problems involving family and child."　In:
　　　　National Conference on Law and Poverty, Washington, D.C., 1965.
　　　　<u>Conference proceedings</u>. Washington, D.C.:　U.S. Government
　　　　Printing Office, 1966.　14-29.　(20 References).
States that civil law reforms for the poor have been neglected in modern
day affluent society. The development of the juvenile court system over
the past sixty-five years has been slow and ill-planned. In fact, less
has been done by the courts to provide care for dependent and neglected
children than has been done to rehabilitate delinquents. A first step
toward improvement would be to provide legal counsel for children faced
with a juvenile court appearance. Further improvements must be focused
on eliminating the pervasive denial of legal rights to poor children and
their families. Such illegal practices include:　(1) transferring persons to prisons without the protections guaranteed under criminal law;
(2) administering unequal justice to unmarried mothers and their children; (3) terminating parental rights, indiscriminately; and (4) providing inadequate financial benefits for children who remain with their
families, while, at the same time, providing far greater financial support to children placed in institutions. Additional violations of the
rights of poor children are included. The judicial system must revise
and intensify its efforts to strengthen, rather than to undermine, family
life among the poor.

1986　Prince, Russell C.　"Evidence:　child abuse. Expert medical testi-
　　　　mony concerning 'battered child syndrome' held admissable. <u>Ford-
　　　　ham Law Rev</u>　42(4):　935-43, May, 1974.　(42 References).

A discussion of what constitutes admissable evidence in child abuse proceedings. Background is supplied for the first court use of the diagnosis
battered child syndrome and the gradual admission of various kinds of
testimony and evidence in such proceedings is traced. The indiscriminate
admission of previously excluded evidence is warned against as endangering
parental rights.

1987 "Representation of child-neglect cases: are parents neglected?"
      Columbia J Law Soc Probl 4(2): 230-54, July, 1968. (33 Refer-
      ences).
Calls attention to the problem of the lack of parental representation in
cases of child neglect heard by the King's County Family Court in New
York. In such proceedings, the court looks after the interests of the
child, but the parents do not have ready access to counsel. An amendment
to the Family Court Act is recommended on an experimental basis which
would allow a member of the law guardian staff to represent the parents
in neglect proceedings.

1988 Schrekinger, Frederick. "Counsel for the child in neglect and
      dependency hearings." In: National Symposium on Child Abuse, 5th,
      Boston, 1974. Collected papers. Denver, Colorado: The American
      Humane Association, Children's Division, 1976. 83-87. (0 Refer-
      ences).
Stresses the need for separate counsel for the child. The processes of
adjudication and disposition are defined. The attorney's duties are to
present the facts, understand the objectives of child protection, and
in cases of disposition, follow-up on the child in order to assess the
effectiveness of the dispositional decision.

1989 Weaver, Colin. "Legal procedures in cases of non-accidental
      injury to children: letter to editor." Br Med J 2(6028): 180-81,
      July 17, 1976. (0 References).
Three legal difficulties in securing care orders for battered children
from civil courts are presented by a social services officer.

3. COURTS AND WELFARE AGENCIES

1990 Cavenagh, Winifred. "A report on the teaching of legal studies on
      social work courses." In: Franklin, Alfred White, ed. Concerning
      child abuse. New York: Churchill Livingstone, 1975. 153-54.
      (0 References).
Outlines the necessary legal training for social workers. Social workers
should receive a minimum amount of legal training in the form of active
participation, such as mock courts or seminars. Training should cover
the common problems of social work clients and the court procedures for
abuse and neglect cases. Because probation officers can expect to appear
in court regularly, their legal training should be more intensive than
for the less specialized social worker.

1991 Coffey, Carol. "Invoking the court's authority -- a diagnostic
      approach." In: National Symposium on Child Abuse, 5th, Boston,
      1974. Collected papers. Denver, Colorado: The American Humane
      Association, Children's Division, 1976. 70-73. (0 References).
Identifies the ills of the legal system as it relates to child abuse.
Frustrations on the part of social workers due to unsatisfactory deci-

sions occur when the state fails to produce enough evidence or because
legal professionals misunderstand the nature of the child abuse problem.
Rather than using state attorneys, child protective services need private
attorneys who are motivated to learn and care about child protection.
The confidentiality of juvenile courts prevents the public from knowing
whether the court functions coincide with community beliefs.

1992 Delaney, James J. "The legal process -- a positive force in the
     interest of children." In: National Symposium on Child Abuse,
     4th, Charleston, S.C., 1973. Collected papers. Denver, Colorado:
     The American Humane Association, Children's Division, 1975. 62-69.
Suggests how professionals can most effectively use the courts in child
abuse cases. Social workers often avoid the courts because of past
failures or in an effort to protect their relationship with the family.
In order to best protect the child, social workers need to learn what
legally constitutes a solid case just as legal professionals need education about the dimensions of the child abuse problem. If the case is
well-prepared, a pre-trial conference will often prevent an actual trial.
The recommendations of the social worker weighs heavily in court decisions.

1993 Driscoll, Margaret C. "The buck stops here -- the judge." In:
     National Symposium on Child Abuse, 5th, Boston, 1974. Collected
     papers. Denver, Colorado: The American Humane Association, Chil-
     dren's Division, 1976. 88-91. (0 References).
Reveals a judge's perspective on the problems of court intervention. The
remedy for dissatisfied social workers is for them to educate the judge
during the hearing about the nature of abuse and neglect, particularly
in the dispositional phase. There is a clear shifting of roles in child
abuse hearings as to who has the burden of proof, a problem which makes
presentation difficult and confusing. Disposition which seeks to maintain
the family unit depends on the availability of resources.

1994 Kahn, Jack H., and Nursten, Jean P. "Child guidance procedure in
     relation to the juvenile court." Br J Criminol 3(3): 294-301,
     January, 1963. (5 References).
Explains the procedures and findings of the Child Guidance Clinic upon
conducting a psychiatric evaluation of several dependent or delinquent
children. The juvenile court sought the assistance of the clinic for
reasons such as the following: (1) to understand the causes of the
child's behavior; (2) to aid in deciding whether or not to remove a child
from his home; and (3) to aid in prescribing a therapeutic treatment
program for the child. Recommendations from the clinic were honored in
84 percent of the cases.

1995 Rosenheim, Margaret K. "The child and his day in court." Child
     Welfare 45(1): 17-27, January, 1966. (46 References).
Concerns recent developments in juvenile courts which have focused on
constitutional, legal, and procedural questions, tending to formalize
the workings of the court. The place of the social welfare agency within
this pattern is discussed, particularly in terms of the relationship
between social worker and lawyer. What has become increasingly an
adversary relationship need not remain one. It is recommended that
several agencies collaborate on the hiring of a lawyer/social worker team
to represent them in juvenile court. Besides advising in procedural
matters, the lawyer can bring much that is valuable to agency recommendations regarding the child's best interests.

1996   Tamilia, Patrick R.   "Neglect proceedings and the conflict between
        law and social work."   <u>Duquesne Law Rev</u> 9:   579-89, 1970-1971.
        (22 References).
Discusses the impact of the recent concern for the rights of the child
upon the relationship between the legal and social work communities,
particularly in terms of the conflicts occurring between the two groups
over the institution of neglect proceedings. Social workers tend to
focus on the best interests of the individuals concerned, as they interpret it. This concern is sometimes seen by lawyers as an overly emotional
response to the problem, ignoring the role of the legal system as the
protector of society. The conflict, which occurs on both the ideological
and procedural levels, is seen as an ultimately beneficial force in its
potential for balancing the interests of the individual and the system.

1997   Weinberger, Paul E., and Smith, Peggy J.   "The disposition of child
        neglect cases referred by caseworkers to a juvenile court."   <u>Child</u>
        <u>Welfare</u> 45(8):   457-63, 471, October, 1966.   (14 References).
Investigates the criteria influencing welfare workers' petitions for the
placement of neglected children outside the home, and of the relationship
between these criteria and the factors influencing the judicial disposition of the case. In the sample studied, fewer than one-third of the
petitions for removal were sustained. It was found that the welfare
workers tended to support their petitions with discussions of the emotional damage likely to result from the child's continued presence in an
unsatisfactory environment, while the court seemed more likely to be
impressed by hard evidence of unfitness--such as alcoholism or the involvement of the police. It is suggested that welfare agencies seek legal
counsel in preparing such petitions in the future, and, more fundamentally,
that the juvenile court and welfare agency join forces with other agencies
concerned with child welfare to formulate a clearer definition of child
neglect criteria and one with a higher degree of consensus.

E. PROTECTIVE SERVICES

1998   Alabama.   State Department of Pensions and Security.   Bureau of
        Family and Children's Services.   <u>Protective services manual for</u>
        <u>administration of services for children and their families.</u>   Chapter
        <u>V.</u>   Montgomery, Alabama: Alabama State Department of Pensions and
        Security, 1974.   15p.
The protective services provided by statute under the Alabama Department
of Pensions and Security are detailed. This chapter from the state
administrative manual sets forth the protective services mandated by the
statute, along with the criteria and procedures for their provision.
The statute is chiefly concerned with the protection of the child; the
agency is empowered to correct any abuse of the child's rights to adequate
care and nurture, including physical and emotional neglect, physical
abuse, denial of medical care, failure to provide education, exploita-
tions, and exposure to demoralizing circumstances. In addition, the
chapter outlines the procedures for receiving, evaluating, and investigating complaints; coordinating educational, health and rehabilitative
services; using the courts, law enforcement agencies and substitute care
facilities; and reporting child abuse. It also includes legal forms for
court petition and summons, foster care agreement, and child abuse
reports.

1999 Askwith, Gordon K. "Authority, prevention, and a new child welfare
      act." Child Welfare 46(6): 407-9, July, 1967. (4 References).
Studies the provision in Ontario's 1965 Child Welfare Act which mandates
the authority to protect children to all child welfare agencies. Concern
is expressed that the Act will not be interpreted literally and that the
mandated extension of authority will not be actualized.

2000 Becker, Thomas T. Child protective services and the law. Denver,
      Colorado: The American Humane Association, Children's Division,
      1968. 23p. (Bibliography).
Because it is the responsibility of child protective agencies to initiate
legal proceedings for the protection of neglected children, any innovations in juvenile court procedures may have a great impact upon the operations of these agencies. The first juvenile court was established in
1899 in Chicago for the handling of charges of parental misconduct against
their children. The atmosphere of the early juvenile courts was informal
and many of the legal safeguards and technical procedures were dropped
from the proceedings. About a decade ago, however, concern over the
rights of children and parents in the juvenile court began to increase.
Judges declared that the parent had a right to know the nature of the
charges against him and a right to legal counsel. The famous Gault decision of 1967 suggested that children in juvenile courts possessed these
rights as well. Today the juvenile court must consider the welfare of
the child as well as safeguard the rights of all persons involved in legal
proceedings. The social worker may view formal legal procedures as inappropriate obstacles to the diagnosis and treatment of a social disorder.
The lawyer will be ineffective if he is unfamiliar with the purpose of
child protection and the respective roles of the child protective agency
and the court. Therefore, professionals in the fields of social work
and law should work together to overcome their differences so that
effective disposition of cases of neglect can be made.

2001 Cheney, Kimberly B. "Safeguarding legal rights in providing pro-
      tective services." Children 13(3): 86-92, May-June, 1966. (28
      References).
Points out several situations in which the legal rights of families may
be violated by protective service agencies involved in treating cases of
child neglect. Well defined legal guidelines for defining physical,
psychological, and social neglect are essential. Most importantly, however, states must articulate the values they hope to promote when taking
intervention measures. Providing such a protective statute could then
serve to coordinate the values upheld in social agencies with those of
the state. In any case, the parent's right to due process of law and
the right to counsel must be honored.

2002 De Francis, Vincent. The court and protective services: their
      respective roles. Denver, Colorado: The American Humane Associa-
      tion, Children's Division, n.d. 19p. (Bibliography).
Successful prevention of child abuse and neglect depends on cooperation
and mutual respect between the court and the protective service agencies.
The responsibilities of protective service agencies are to prevent neglect, abuse, and exploitation of children; to help parents to change
harmful patterns of living; and to help strengthen family life so that
all members can develop. Protective agencies have the responsibility
and the authority to initiate service in neglect cases, to gather evidence, and to invoke judicial authority if the neglect continues. The

duties of juvenile court are to dispense individualized justice to children--justice which focuses on treatment and help rather than on punishment. A strictly judicial agency, the court is not an investigative agency, nor should it administer the child protective services. It should enter the case only after a neglect petition has been filed. It must be bound by the statutory definitions of neglect, and its right to respond to the needs of neglected children depends on sufficient evidence to prove statutory neglect. The court alone has the responsibility for determining the issues, for evaluating evidence, for applying legal principles, and for reaching a decision. The court can and should call upon the protective services to lend their skills and special knowledge to help the judge make sound dispositions for the best interest of the child.

2003   ————. Guidelines for legislation to protect the battered
        child: basic principles and concepts. Denver, Colorado: The
        American Humane Association, Children's Division, 1962. (Bibliog-
        raphy).
Promotes the preliminary handling of all child abuse cases by child protective services rather than by police or juvenile courts. Physicians should be required to report cases of suspected abuse to the child protective services, which would take steps to protect the child while helping the parents solve their problems. The aid of the juvenile court would only be sought if the child's life were in danger, and the involvement of the police or public prosecutor would only be necessary in obvious felony cases.

2004   Eads, William E. "Observations on the establishment of a child-
        protective service system in California." Stanford Law Rev 21:
        1129-55, May, 1969. (20 References).
Considers the difficulties involved in implementing the Child Protective Service Units mandated by California's Veneman Act. The major problem lies in the fact that child abuse cases have long been the province of the juvenile probation departments around the state. The non-punitive, rehabilitative CPS units must compete for the recognition and cooperation of individuals and agencies accustomed to associating child abuse cases with the more established law enforcement agencies. Not only are the CPS units better equipped to handle the complex range of psychosocial problems which occur in child abuse cases, but the action of the CPS unit does not bear the stigma of "police trouble." It is suggested that the current elaborate and oppressive system for reporting and registering child abuse cases in California be dismantled, and that the funding instead be concentrated upon building up an effective system of CPS units.

2005   Felder, Samuel. "A lawyer's view of child abuse." Public Welfare
        29(2): 181-88, Spring, 1971. (19 References).
Calls attention to the role of the attorney as a protector of the rights of the child, parent, and community in child abuse cases. A historical review of child abuse legislation is presented with discussion of the corresponding medical findings and public outbursts which precipitated the legislative action. Because criminal prosecutions are difficult to obtain and emotionally trying to all persons involved, child protective and rehabilitative services can best cure abusive behavior in a family and better provide for the prevention of abuse.

2006   Hagenbuch, John J., Jr. "Preserving the state's mandate to deliver
        protective services." In: National Symposium on Child Abuse, 5th,
        Boston, 1974. Collected papers. Denver, Colorado: The American
        Humane Association, Children's Division, 1976. 47-52. (5 Refer-
        ences).
Identifies the problem of implementing a Massachusetts law mandating the
protection of the family. Case reports are increasing while services are
unprepared to handle them. The state does provide some services, but
these treat only the symptoms of abuse and not the cause, which is family
dysfunction. Lack of funds have prevented the state from developing
programs comprehensive enough to protect the family. Coordination and
knowledge of resources in the community can help alleviate the problem.

2007   New York (State). Department of Social Services. Child protective
        services in New York State, 1976: annual report for the provision
        of child protective services in New York State. Albany, New York:
        New York State Department of Social Services, 1977. 43p. Publica-
        tion No. 1200.
The 1976 annual report on the operations of state and local child protective services in New York contains information about financing, recommendations for legislation, and statistical analyses of various aspects
of the child abuse problem.

2008   "Non-accidental injury to children: editorial." Med J Aust   1(26):
        986, June 26, 1976. (1 Reference).
Calls for the adoption of increased legal protective measures in
Australia. Citing the recommendations of a Community Welfare Advisory
Committee, it is suggested that hospitals' custodial capacities be in-
creased, legal protection be provided for all wishing to report abuse,
and the child's rights as an individual be increased.

2009   Philbrick, Elizabeth. The Masterson case: neglected children --
        constructive use of the juvenile court. Denver, Colorado: The
        American Humane Association, Children's Division, 1960. 30p.
        (Bibliography).
Documents a child neglect case handled by the child protective services
with the assistance of the juvenile court. The mother was unable to
plan, budget, or provide for her own and her children's clothing and
medical needs. Her two sons were constantly absent from school due to
chronic illnesses. The social worker visited the family frequently and
made arrangements for housing and medical care. Under pressure from
school authorities, the agency filed a neglect petition in the juvenile
court. Observing positive adjustments and improvements in the mother
and children, the judge decided to keep the family intact but to put the
two sons under supervisory probation.

APPENDIX A:

Basic Bibliographic Tools

1. Bibliographic Index

2. Book Review Digest

3. Books in Print

4. British Education Index

5. Child Development Abstracts

6. Cumulative Book Index

7. Cumulative Index to Nursing Literature

8. Current Index to Journals in Education

9. Developmental Disabilities and Mental Retardation Abstracts

10. Developmental Medicine and Child Neurology Bibliography

11. Dissertation Abstracts International

12. Education Index

13. Exceptional Child Education Abstracts

14. Excerpta Medica

15. Hospital Literature

16. Index Medicus

17. International Index to Nursing Literature

18. Monthly Catalog of U. S. Government Publications

19. National Union Catalog

20. Popular Periodicals Index

21. Psychological Abstracts

22. Psychopharmacology Abstracts

23. Public Affairs Information Service

24. Readers' Guide to Periodical Literature

25. Rehabilitation Literature

26. Research Relating to Children

27. Resources in Education (ERIC)

28. Science Citation Index

29. Social Sciences Citation Index

30. Social Sciences Index

31. Sociological Abstracts

32. Subject Guide to Books in Print

APPENDIX B:

Selected Organizations Interested
in Child Abuse and Neglect

American Academy of Pediatrics
1801 Hinman Avenue
Evanston, Illinois   60204
(312) 869-4255

American Humane Association
Children's Division
5351 Roslyn
Denver, Colorado   80201
(303) 771-1300

Association for the Care of
  Children in Hospitals
Box H
Union, West Virginia   24983
(304) 772-5201

Child Abuse Listening
  Mediation (CALM)
P. O. Box 718
Santa Barbara, California   93102
(805) 963-1115

Child Welfare League of America
67 Irving Place
New York, New York   10003
(212) 254-7410

Children's Rights, Inc.
3443 17th Street, N.W.
Washington, D.C.   20010
(202) 462-7573

End Violence Against the Next
  Generation
977 Keeler Avenue
Berkeley, California   94708
(415) 527-0454

Foundation for Child Development
345 East 46th Street
New York, New York   10017
(212) 697-3150

International Union for Child
  Welfare
International Centre
Rue De Varembe, 1
Geneva 20, Switzerland
CH-1211

National Center for the Prevention
  and Treatment of Child Abuse
  and Neglect
1205 Oneida Street
Denver, Colorado   80220
(303) 321-3963

National Center on Child Abuse
  and Neglect
Office of Child Development
Children's Bureau
330 Independence Avenue, S.W.
Washington, D.C.   20201

National Clearinghouse on Child
  Neglect and Abuse
P. O. Box 1266
Denver, Colorado   80202

National Committee for Prevention
  of Child Abuse
111 East Wacker Drive -- Suite 510
Chicago, Illinois   60601
(312) 565-1100

New York State Child Abuse and
  Maltreatment Register
1450 Western Avenue
Albany, New York   12203
1-800-342-3720

Parents Anonymous (Self-help)
2810 Artesia Boulevard
Suite F
Redondo Beach, California   90278
(213) 371-3501

APPENDIX C:

Child Abuse Prevention and Treatment Act
(Text of Public Law 93-247)

AN ACT

To provide financial assistance for a demonstration program for the prevention, identification, and treatment of child abuse and neglect, to establish a National Center on Child Abuse and Neglect, and for other purposes.

Be it enacted by the Senate and House of Representatives of the United States of America in Congress assembled, That this Act may be cited as the "Child Abuse Prevention and Treatment Act".

THE NATIONAL CENTER ON
CHILD ABUSE

SEC 2. (a) The Secretary of Health, Education, and Welfare (hereinafter referred to in this Act as the "Secretary") shall establish an office to be known as the National Center on Child Abuse and Neglect (hereinafter referred to in this Act as the "Center").

(b) The Secretary, through the Center, shall --

(1) compile, analyze, and publish a summary annually of recently conducted and currently conducted research on child abuse and neglect;

(2) develop and maintain an information clearinghouse on all programs, including private programs, showing promise of success, for the prevention, identification, and treatment of child abuse and neglect;

(3) compile and publish training materials for personnel who are engaged or intend to engage in the prevention, identification, and treatment of child abuse and neglect;

(4) provide technical assistance (directly or through grant or contract) to public and nonprofit private agencies and organizations to assist them in planning, improving, developing, and carrying out programs and activities relating to the prevention, identification, and treatment of child abuse and neglect;

(5) conduct research into the causes of child abuse and neglect and into the prevention, identification, and treatment thereof; and

(6) make a complete and full study and investigation of the national incidence of child abuse and neglect, including a determination of the extent to which incidents of child abuse and neglect are increasing in number or severity.

DEFINITION

SEC. 3. For purposes of this Act the term "child abuse and neglect" means the physical or mental injury, sexual abuse, negligent treatment, or maltreatment of a child under the age of eighteen by a person who is responsible for the child's welfare under circumstances which indicate that the child's health or welfare is harmed or threatened thereby, as determined in accordance with regulations prescribed by the Secretary.

DEMONSTRATION PROGRAMS AND PROJECTS

SEC. 4. (a) The Secretary, through the Center, is authorized to make grants to, and enter into contracts with, public agencies or nonprofit private organizations (or combinations thereof) for demonstration programs and projects designed to prevent, identify, and treat child abuse and neglect. Grants or contracts under this subsection may be --

(1) for the development and establishment of training programs for professional and paraprofessional personnel in the fields of medicine, law, education, social work, and other relevant fields who are engaged in, or intend to work in, the field of prevention, identification, and treatment of child abuse and neglect; and training programs for children, and for persons responsible for the welfare of children, in methods of protecting children from child abuse and neglect;

(2) for the establishment and maintenance of centers, serving defined geographic areas, staffed by multidisciplinary teams of personnel trained in the prevention, identification, and treatment of child abuse and neglect cases, to provide a broad range of services related to child abuse and neglect, including direct support and supervision of satellite centers and attention homes, as well as providing advice and consultation to individuals, agencies, and organizations which request such services;

(3) for furnishing services of teams of professional and paraprofessional personnel who are trained in the prevention, identification, and treatment of child abuse and neglect cases, on a consulting basis to small communities where such services are not available; and

(4) for such other innovative programs and projects, including programs and projects for parent self-help, and for prevention and treatment of drug-related child abuse and neglect, that show promise of successfully preventing or treating cases of child abuse and neglect as the Secretary may approve.

Not less than 50 per centum of the funds appropriated under this Act for any fiscal year shall be used only for carrying out the provisions of this subsection.

(b)(1) Of the sums appropriated under this Act for any fiscal year, not less than 5 per centum and not more than 20 per centum may be used by the Secretary for making grants to the States for the payment of reasonable and necessary expenses for the purpose of assisting the States in developing, strengthening, and carrying out child abuse and neglect prevention and treatment programs.

(2) In order for a State to qualify for assistance under this subsection, such State shall --

(A) have in effect a State child abuse and neglect law which shall include provisions for immunity for persons reporting instances of child abuse and neglect from prosecution, under any State or local law, arising out of such reporting;

(B) provide for the reporting of known and suspected instances of child abuse and neglect;

(C) provide that upon receipt of a report of known or suspected instances of child abuse or neglect an investigation shall be initiated promptly to substantiate the accuracy of the report, and, upon a finding of abuse or neglect, immediate steps shall be taken to protect the health and welfare of the abused or neglected child, as well as that of any other child under the same care who may be in danger of abuse or neglect;

(D) demonstrate that there are in effect throughout the State, in connection with the enforcement of child abuse and neglect laws and with the reporting of suspected instances of child abuse and neglect, such administrative procedures, such personnel trained in child abuse and neglect prevention and treatment, such training procedures, such institutional and other facilities (public and private), and such related multidisciplinary programs and services as may be necessary or appropriate to assure that the State will deal effectively with child abuse and neglect cases in the State;

(E) provide for methods to preserve the confidentiality of all records in order to protect the rights of the child, his parents or guardians;

(F) provide for the cooperation of law enforcement officials, courts of competent jurisdiction, and appropriate State agencies providing human services;

(G) provide that in every case involving an abused or neglected child which results in a judicial proceeding a guardian ad litem shall be appointed to represent the child in such proceedings;

(H) provide that the aggregate of support for programs or projects related to child abuse and neglect assisted by State funds shall not be reduced below the level provided during fiscal year 1973, and set forth policies and procedures designed to assure that Federal funds made available under this Act for any fiscal year will be so used to supplement and, to the extent practicable, increase the level of State funds which would, in the absence of Federal funds, be available for such programs and projects;

(I) provide for dissemination of information to the general public with respect to the problem of child abuse and neglect and the facilities and prevention and treatment methods available to combat instances of child abuse and neglect; and

(J) to the extent feasible, insure that parental organizations combating child abuse and neglect receive preferential treatment.

(3) Programs or projects related to child abuse and neglect assisted under part A or B of title IV of the Social Security Act shall comply with the requirements set forth in clauses (B), (C), (E), and (F) of paragraph (2).

(c) Assistance provided pursuant to this section shall not be available for construction of facilities; however, the Secretary is authorized to supply such assistance for the lease or rental of facilities where adequate facilities are not otherwise available, and for repair or minor remodeling or alteration of existing facilities.

(d) The Secretary shall establish criteria designed to achieve equitable distribution of assistance under this section among the States, among geographic areas of the Nation, and among rural and urban areas. To the extent possible, citizens of each State shall receive assistance from at least one project under this section.

AUTHORIZATION

SEC. 5. There are hereby authorized to be appropriated for the purposes of this Act $15,000,000 for the fiscal year ending June 30, 1974, $20,000,000 for the fiscal year ending June 30, 1975, and $25,000,000 for the fiscal year ending June 30, 1976, and for the succeeding fiscal year.

ADVISORY BOARD ON CHILD ABUSE AND NEGLECT

SEC. 6. (a) The Secretary shall, within sixty days after the date of enactment of this Act, appoint an Advisory Board on Child Abuse and Neglect (hereinafter referred to as the "Advisory Board"), which shall be composed of representatives from Federal agencies with responsibility for programs and activities related to child abuse and neglect, including the Office of Child Development, the Office of Education, the National Institute of Education, the National Institute of Mental Health, the National Institute of Child Health and Human Development, the Social and Rehabilitation Service, and the Health Services Administration. The Advisory Board shall assist the Secretary in coordinating programs and activities related to child abuse and neglect administered or assisted under this Act with such programs and activities administered or assisted by the Federal agencies whose representatives are members of the Advisory Board. The Advisory Board shall also assist the Secretary in the development of Federal standards for child abuse and neglect prevention and treatment programs and projects.

(b) The Advisory Board shall prepare and submit, within eighteen months after the date of enactment of this Act, to the President and to the Congress a report on the programs assisted under this Act and the programs, projects, and activities related to child abuse and neglect administered or assisted by the Federal agencies whose representatives are members of the Advisory Board. Such report shall include a study of the relationship between drug addiction and child abuse and neglect.

(c) Of the funds appropriated under section 5, one-half of 1 per centum, or $1,000,000, whichever is the lesser, may be used by the Secretary only for purposes of the report under subsection (b).

COORDINATION

SEC. 7. The Secretary shall promulgate regulations and make such arrangements as may be necessary or appropriate to ensure that there is effective coordination between programs related to child abuse and neglect under this Act and other such programs which are assisted by Federal funds.

Approved January 31, 1974.

AUTHOR INDEX

In the list below, the numbers after each name

refer to item numbers in the Bibliography

A

Ackerman, A. Bernard, 1620
Ackerman, Nathan W., 1484
Ackley, Dana C., 1379
Adams, P. L., 666
Adams, Patricia C., 853
Adelman, Lynn, 1683, 1792
Adelson, Edna, 1489
Adelson, Lester, 269, 486, 817, 954
Afifi, Abdelmonem A., 265, 266, 522, 523
Agostino, Paul A. d'
  See D'Agostino, Paul A.
Agrest, Susan, 75
Ahmed, S., 910
Aine, Joseph C. Schutt-
  See Schutt-Aine, Joseph C.
Akbarnia, Behrooz A., 854, 855
Akbarnia, Nasrin O., 854
Alabama. State Department of
  Pensions and Security. Bureau
  of Family & Children's Services,
  1998
Alberts, M. E., 1120
Alexander, Betty, 1359
Alexander, Doris, 454
Alexander, Jerry, 164
Alimohammadi, A., 818
Allen, Ann F., 39
Allen, Anne, 336
Allen, Hugh D., 40, 201, 742, 1802
Allen, John E., 1054
Allen, Marilyn, 1549
Allison, Patricia K., 337
Altman, Donald H., 856
Alvy, Kerby T., 149, 338
Ambrosio, Richard d'
  See D'Ambrosio, Richard

Ambuel, J. Phillip, 1352
Ameli, N. O., 818
Ament, Marvin E., 946
American Academy of Pediatrics, 339, 1282, 1764
American Humane Association.
  Children's Division, 289, 1121, 1699, 1716
American Medical Association.
  Office of the General Council, 1771
Amiel, Shirley, 150
Anderson, C. Wilson, 340
Anderson, Charles, 976
Anderson, George M., 657
Anderson, John P., 240, 290
Anderson, Lee R., 861
Anderson, William R., 955
Andrews, John P., 125
Andrews, Roberta G., 628
Angel, Karen, 1856
Annecillo, C., 1039
Anthony, E. James, 544
Aptekar, Herbert, 90
Arboleda-Florez, Julio, 605
Armstrong, Katherine, 1565
Arnold, Mildred, 461
Arthur, L. J. H., 1259
Arvanian, Ann L., 1462
Asch, Stuart S., 248, 606
Askwith, Gordon K., 624, 1999
Asnes, Russell S., 1621
Astley, Roy, 857
Avery, Jane C., 1165
Avery, Nancy C., 1463, 1547
Avery, Nicholas C., 1583
Ayoub, Catherine, 341, 371

B

Babow, Irving, 990
Babow, Robin, 990
Bach-y-Rita, George, 487
Badner, George, 1905
Baher, Edwina, 1
Bain, Katherine, 1300, 1301
Baizerman, Michael, 166
Bakan, David, 126, 426
Baker, David H., 858
Baker, Helen, 1906
Baker, James A., 1915
Bakwin, Harry, 859, 860, 1058
Baldwin, J. A., 237
Ball, Margaret, 1206
Ballantine, Thomas V. N., 779
Ballard, Carolyn M., 1545
Balyeat, Ralph, 1263
Bamford, Frank N., 743
Banagale, Raul C., 202
Bandman, Rosalyn, 1352
Bandoli, Larry R., 1380
Bandura, Albert, 678
Banks, Henry H., 890
Barbero, Guilio J., 270, 1022
Bard, M., 342
Bardon, D., 545
Barlow, D. H., 1648
Barlow, Matthew J., 989
Barmeyer, George H., 861
Barnard, Martha U., 1353
Barnes, Geoffrey B., 1283, 1286
Barnes, George R., Jr., 879
Barnes, Josephine, 1622
Barness, Lewis A., 862
Barnett, Bernard, 249, 250,
  1166, 1302
Barnhart, Carol, 1399, 1504
Baron, Michael A., 744
Barta, Rudolph A., 956
Barton, William, 1183, 1835, 1894
Bassett, Louise B., 1354
Bates, Doris, W., 1279
Bates, Talcott, 1167
Batinich, M. E. Mancina, 1417
Baxter, S. J., 747
Bayne-Powell, Rosamond, 1679
Bean, S., 1233
Bean, Shirley L., 1260
Bechtold, Mary Lee, 1418, 1772
Becker, Elisabeth Trube-
  See Trube-Becker, Elisabeth
Becker, Thomas T., 2000
Becker, Wesley C., 679
Beer, Sally, 1381

Beezley, Patricia, 1013, 1014,
  1096, 1541
Bejar, Rafael L., 744
Bell, Gwyneth, 2
Bell, William E., 849
Bellucci, Matilda T., 1464
Benady, D. Roger, 1114
Bendel, Robert B., 524
Bender, Barbara, 991
Bender, Lauretta, 1608
Bendix, S., 658
Bennett, A. N., 625
Bennett, Arletha, 407
Bennett, Robert F., 1122
Bennie, Ernest H., 489, 490
Bensel, Robert W. ten
  See ten Bensel, Robert W.
Benson, Irene, 295
Benstead, J. G., 819
Benton, Joseph G., 1100
Bentovim, Arnon, 953
Berant, Moshe, 957
Berdie, Jane, 33, 166
Berdon, Walter E., 858, 922
Berenberg, W., 820
Berg, Pamela I., 723
Berger, Deborah, 1236
Bergman, Norma W., 1916
Berkeley Planning Associates,
  1241, 1560, 1561
Berkowitz, Leonard, 491
Berlow, Leonard, 317
Bern, Joseph, 1740
Bernstein, Arthur H., 1849
Besdine, Matthew, 583
Besharov, Douglas J., 318, 1169,
  1687
Beswick, Keith, 1261, 1539
Bethscheider, J. L., 1576
Betzendorfer, Joseph Q., Jr.,
  1962
Bevan, Hugh, 1806
Bezzeg, E. D., 1382
Bhat, Usha S., 837
Bhattacharya, A. K., 863, 958
Bialestock, Dora, 1917
Bierman, Jessie M., 1087
Bilainkin, George, 343
Billingsley, Andrew, 472, 1171,
  1383, 1562, 1575
Binion, Rudolph, 659
Bird, Harmony, 1356
Birrell, J. H. W., 428, 748,
  1773
Birrell, R. G., 428, 1772
Bishop, Frank, 251, 546, 1123

Bishop, Julia A., 1124
Blair, Louis H., 1208
Blake, Phillip R., 26, 230
Blau, Abram, 1608
Bleiberg, Nina, 167
Blizzard, R. M., 1045
Bloch, Dorothy, 607, 992
Bloch, Harry, 151, 152
Block, Myrna, 492
Blockney, N. J., 864
Blomgren, Paul G., 453
Bloom, Lawrence A., 993
Blount, June G., 749
Blue, M. T., 1125
Blumberg, Marvin L., 493, 1170
Boardman, Helen E., 270, 1284
Boatman, Bonny, 1597
Boisvert, Maurice J., 494
Bolton, F. G., Jr., 1520
Bolz, W. Scott, 750
Bongiovi, Joseph J., 906
Booz-Allen and Hamilton, Inc., 1126
Borgman, Robert D., 478, 479, 660, 672, 673, 1410
Boriskin, Jerry A., 724, 725
Bosanquet, Nicholas, 429
Bossard, James H. S., 626
Bottom, Wayne D., 1521
Bottoms, A. E., 1963
Bourke, William A., 1384
Bowden, M. L., 1288
Bowen, D. A. L., 751
Bowers, William C., 1964
Bowley, Agatha H., 43, 1059
Boyd, Frederick V., 1676
Boyer, A., 594
Boysen, Bette E., 959
Bradford, Kirk A., 1385
Braen, B. B., 647
Brandon, Sydney, 680
Brandwein, Harold, 1089
Brant, Renee S. T., 1623
Brasel, J. A., 1045
Bratrude, Amos P., 984
Bratu, Marcel, 907
Braun, Edgar J., 1872
Braun, Ida G., 1872
Breen, James L., 1642
Brem, Jacob, 1262
Bremner, Robert H., 112, 113
Brenneman, George, 44
Breslow, Lester, 1304
Bresnan, Michael J., 853
Brett, Dawn I., 3
Brewster, Thomas, 1285

Brieland, Donald, 1127, 1207
Brings, E. G., 943
Broadhurst, Diane D., 291, 344, 1419, 1420
Brodeur, Armand E., 404, 752
Brody, Howard, 252
Brody, Sylvia, 547
Broeck, Elsa ten
  See Ten Broeck, Elsa
Bromberg, Walter, 1594
Brooks, A. L., 888
Brosseau, B. E., 563
Browder, J. Albert, 430
Brown, Edward M., 984
Brown, George W., 153
Brown, John A., 495
Brown, Richard J., 154
Brown, Rowine H., 4, 203, 1774, 1775, 1873, 1965
Brown, Staurt L., 590
Brown, Wenzell, 1596
Browne, Kenneth M., 292
Browne, William J., 608
Browning, Diane H., 1597
Brozovsky, Morris, 609
Bryant, Clifton D., 627
Bryant, Harold D., 1171
Buchan, A. R., 968
Buglass, Robert, 661
Buist, Neil R. M., 127, 994
Bullard, Dexter M., Jr., 1023, 1024, 1027
Burgess, Anne, 1517
Burland, J. Alexis, 628
Burn, J. L., 345
Burne, Brien H., 346
Burns, Kevin, 240, 290
Burt, Marvin R., 199, 200, 1208, 1263, 1742
Burt, Robert A., 1674, 1918, 1966
Bush, Sherida, 431
Bussey, Kenneth L., 753
Butler, Karen O., 960
Butler, Raymond V., 1386
Button, A., 681
Button, J. H., 610
Bwibo, N. O., 432, 462
Byassee, J. E., 629
Bylinsky, Gene, 584
Bynum, Alvin S., 1807
Bysshe, Janette, 821

C

Cable, Mary, 102

Cadol, Roger V., 1028
Caffey, John, 433, 754, 822, 823,
  865, 866, 867, 868, 869
Caldwell, Bettye M., 1060
Calef, Victor, 496, 611
Call, Justin D., 1516
Callaghan, K. A., 1305
Cameron, Alan, 926
Cameron, J. Malcolm, 612, 755,
  756, 757, 758, 759, 981
Cameron, James S., 1264
Campbell, Catherine E., 1967
Camps, F. E., 271, 758
Cantoni, Lucile, 1399, 1505
Capraro, E. J., 1624
Capraro, V. J., 1624
Carpenter, James W., 1743
Carr, Corinne H., 1298
Carr, J. N., 734
Carrington, William L., 347
Carter, Bryan D., 1357
Carter, Jan, 5
Cartlidge, N. E., 825
Caruso, Phillip A., 1625
Cary, Ara C., 348
Caskey, Owen L., 1475
Cassert, Hilda P., 1242
Cassidy, Richard K., 1209
Castle, Raymond L., 6, 245
Caulfield, Ernest, 103
Cavallin, Hector, 1577
Cavenagh, Winifred, 1968, 1990
Ceresnie, Steven J., 434
Chabon, Robert S., 1283, 1286
Chadwick, David L., 1306
Chaleff, Anne, 265, 522, 1472,
  1473
Challenor, B., 349
Chamberlain, Nancy, 253
Chambers, Douglas R., 168
Chan, Chee-Khoon, 1044
Chance, William, 114
Chandler, Christopher B., 1656
Chandler, James E., 262
Chandra, R. K., 497
Chaneles, S., 1609
Chang, Albert, 293
Char, Donald, 229, 1340
Chase, Naomi F., 7
Cheney, Kimberly B., 2001
Cherry, Barbara J., 1210
Chesley, Joan, 592
Chesser, Eustace, 435
Child Abuse and Neglect Committee,
  1874

Child Welfare League of America.
  Committee on Standards for Child
  Protective Service, 1551
Children's Defense Fund, 155,
  1657
Chin, Carmel, 784
Christiansen, James L., 995, 1008
Christy, Duane W., 351, 1212
Chung, George K., 918
Ciano, Mario C., 1808
Clark, Elizabeth H., 1545, 1546
Clark, Jane H., 1908
Clark, Karen N., 586
Clarke, A. D. B., 1090
Class, Norris E., 1563
Clemons, Donald, 1243
Clifford, John H., 909
Climent, Carlos E., 1105
Clymer, James N., 1875
Clyne, Max B., 996
Cobe, P., 47
Cobin, Herbert L., 1921
Cochintu, A., 1233
Cochrane, W. A., 762, 801
Coffey, Carol, 1265, 1991
Cohen, Michael I., 498
Cohen, Stephan J., 169, 1797
Cohn, Anne H., 1243, 1552, 1564,
  1565
Colbach, Edward M., 630
Colclough, I. R., 284
Coleman, Rose W., 1025
Coles, Robert, 1307
Coll, Blanche D., 464
Collie, James, 1898, 1899
Collignon, Frederick C., 1552,
  1565
Collins, Camilla, 824
Collins, Gary G., 499
Collins, Marilyn C., 1465
Collins, Seymour, 143
Collipp, P. J., 1047
Collmer, Candace W., 1573
Colman, Wendy, 1522
Colucci, N. D., Jr., 294
Connecticut Child Welfare
  Association, 400, 416, 417,
  418, 419
Connell, John R., 763
Conway, Esther F., 1096
Cooper, Carol, 1296
Cooper, Christine, 1308
Cooper, Elizabeth, 1266
Coppolillo, H. P., 735
Corbett, James T., 1485
Cordell, Chris, 631

Corey, Eleanor J. B., 205
Cormier, Bruno M., 1578
Corry, Peter C., 564
Cosgrove, John G., 206
Cosmides, James C., 1620
Costin, Lela B., 1566
Cottle, Thomas J., 465
Council for Exceptional Children.
  Information Services and
  Publication, 84, 85
Courcy, Judith de
  See DeCourcy, Judith
Courcy, Peter de
  See DeCourcy, Peter
Court, Donald, 1173
Court, Joan, 352, 500, 565, 566,
  587
Courter, Eileen M., 1851
Cox, Jane, 713
Cox, Walter B., 861
Coyle, J. Terrence, 932
Coyne, Martin, 1746
Cozen, Lewis, 870
Craft, A. W., 825
Crary, Ralph W., 1923
Creaghan, Sidney, 302, 1435
Cremin, B. J., 764
Criswell, Howard D., Jr., 501
Crown, Barry, 295
Cullen, John C., 871
Cullen, T., 1862
Cullinan, T. R., 320
Cupoli, J. Michael, 1174
Curphey, Theodore J., 1309
Curran, W. J., 1969
Currie, J. R. B., 49
Curtis, George C., 1106
Cutts, Norma E., 682

D

Daeschner, C. W., Jr., 902
D'Agostino, Paul A., 1267
Dailey, Timothy B., 502
Dalton, K., 548
Daly, Barbara, 1809
D'Ambrosio, Richard, 1091, 1486
Danckwerth, Edward T., 321
Daniel, Glenda, 1506
Daniel, Jessica H., 1129, 1523
Daniels, Robert, 495
Dargan, E. L., 908
David, Charles A., 1487
David, Lester, 50, 503
Davies, Jean M., 383, 1358
Davies, Joann F., 1388, 1389

Davis, Gwendolyn, 86
Davis, Joseph H., 883
Davis, Roger W., 688
Davis, Thomas S., 970
Davison, Gerald C., 1645
Davoren, Elizabeth, 1390, 1450
Dawe, Kathleen E., 51, 1175
Dawson, K. P., 1052
Deasy, Patrick, 196, 676, 1158
Debenham, Arthur E., 961
DeCourcy, Judith, 1927
DeCourcy, Peter, 1927
De Francis, Vincent, 207, 254,
  353, 1130, 1131, 1132, 1133,
  1176, 1177, 1213, 1391, 1392,
  1579, 1643, 1700, 1766, 1777,
  1778, 1928, 2002, 2003
DeGraaf, Beverly J., 1243, 1567
De L. White, G.
  See White, G. de L
Delaney, Donald W., 8
Delaney, James J., 1167, 1992
de Lesseps, Suzanne, 53
Delsordo, James D., 128
Delta, Basil G., 909
deMause, Lloyd, 91, 92, 704
Dembitz, Nanette, 1929, 1930
Dennis, James L., 296
Densen-Gerber, Judianne, 334, 736
Denzin, Norman K., 156
Derdeyn, Andre P., 1931
Dershewitz, Robert, 944
DeSaix, Christine, 478, 479,
  480, 559, 672, 673, 674, 1410
Dewees, Phillip E., 1876
Dewhurst, K. E., 714
Di Furia, G., 1649
Diggle, Geoffrey, 322
DiMascio, Alberto, 1069
Dine, Mark S., 663, 945
Disbrow, Mildred A., 504
Divoky, Diane, 1910
Dobson, M. V., 1932
Dodge, Philip R., 20
Dolder, Suzy J., 683
Dolins, David, 1296
Donnan, S. P. B., 765
Donnison, David V., 1214
Donovan, Denis, 772
Donovan, Thomas J., 1779
Donovan, Woodrow M., 967
Doris, John L., 1244
Dorman, Michael, 1659
Dowell, A. C., 643
Dower, John C., 907
Downs, Elinor, F., 232, 313

Drake, Frances M., 1135
Drash, Allan L., 1050
Driscoll, Margaret C., 1993
Dublin, Christina C., 719, 1276,
  1835, 1894, 1895
Duckworth, P. M., 765
Dudar, Helen, 1654
Dudding, Burton, 1179
Duke, R. F. N., 297, 1568
Duncan, C., 157
Duncan, David F., 446, 1329
Duncan, Glen M., 1107, 1108
Duncan, Jane W., 1108
Dyke, Vicki van
  See Van Dyke, Vicki
Dynneson, Lucille, 1613

E

Eads, William E., 2004
Earl, Howard G., 54
Earle, Alice, 104
Ebbin, Allan J., 208
Ebeling, Nancy B., 354, 1178,
  1297, 1547
Eckert, William G., 826
Eddy, Evelyn, 1046
Edgar, W. M., 1933
Education Commission of the States,
  401, 1689, 1690, 1767, 1780,
  1781, 1782
Education Professions Development
  Consortium, 298
Ehrlich, Frank E., 921
Eichler, Aviva W., 1044
Eickhoff, Louise F. W., 402
Eisen, Peter, 1310
Eisenstein, Elliot M., 909
Elias, J. C., 1822
Ellinger, A. J., 1179
Ellis, Mary A., 1434
Elmer, Elizabeth, 55, 281, 436,
  466, 632, 633, 766, 767, 768,
  778, 887, 997, 998, 1167, 1569,
  1695
Elmore, Joyce, 1359
Elonen, Anna S., 1650
Emery, John, 355
Emmerson, Roma, 107
Endler, N. S., 999
Erickson, Harold M., Jr., 1496
Erickson, Marilyn T., 1092
Erikson, Erik H., 1062
Erlanger, Howard S., 684
Ervin, Frank R., 1105
Erwin, Donald T., 1311

Esmiol, Pattison, 1466
Etches, P. C., 952
Evans, Alan Lee, 549
Evans, Philip, 613
Evans, S. L., 550
Evans, William A., Jr., 904
Everett, M. G., 1268
Ewing, Charles P., 1570
Ezrine, Edwin, 1488

F

Fagan, C. J., 884
Fairburn, Anthony C., 356, 872
Fairlie, Chester, 1971
Falit, Harvey, 609
Fanaroff, Avroy, 567
Fanshel, David, 1451
Farley, F. H., 551
Farn, Kenneth T., 170
Farson, Richard E., 1667
Fasman, Jean, 1069
Fatteh, A. V., 769
Fay, Henry J., 1519
Feinstein, Howard M., 1466
Felder, Samuel, 2005
Felman, A. H., 925
Fenby, T. Pitts, 357
Ferguson, Charles A., 242
Ferguson, William M., 1853, 1854
Fergusson, David M., 239
Ferleger, David, 1668
Ferro, Frank, 358, 1553
Feshbach, N. D., 403, 685
Feshbach, S., 403
Ficarra, B. J., 1680
Field, Jack G., 1109
Finberg, Laurence, 1196, 1877
Finch, A. T., 1312
Fine, Rubin, 659
Finkelstein, Marcia, 1051
Fischer, Michael S., 1935
Fischhoff, Joseph, 588, 686,
  1057
Fiser, Robert H., 873
Fish, Irving, 1629
Fisher, Gordon D., 1580, 1701
Fisher, Samuel H., 874
Fitch, J. H., 1581
Fitch, Michael J., 1028
Flammáng, C. J., 1900
Flato, Charles, 56
Fleck, Stephen, 437
Fleisher, David, 946
Fleming, G. M., 57
Fleming, Joan, 239

Fleming, Thomas, 1530
Florez, Julio Arboleda-
  See Arboleda-Florez, Julio
Floyd, Linda M., 552
Flynn, William R., 505
Foley, Frank W., 1275
Folks, Homer, 115
Follis, Peggy, 770
Fomufod, Antoine K., 568, 569
Fontana, Vincent J., 9, 58, 59,
  60, 129, 171, 172, 272, 299, 438,
  439, 506, 634, 687, 705, 728,
  771, 772, 1181, 1269, 1313, 1314,
  1315, 1373
Forbis, Oriel L., 803
Forbush, J. B., 647
Ford, Donald, 1452, 1972
Forrer, Stephen E., 1424
Forrest, Tess, 553
Foster, Henry H., Jr., 1878
Fotheringham, B. J., 1305, 1747
Fox, Elaine S., 1965
Fraiberg, Selma, 1489
Francis, H. W. S., 467, 1490
Francis, Jo, 1393
Francis, Vincent de
  See De Francis, Vincent
Frank, George H., 507
Franklin, Alfred W., 173, 1136,
  1173
Fraser, A., 739
Fraser, Brian G., 323, 1691,
  1692, 1783, 1973
Fraser, F. Murray, 240, 290
Fraser, William, 589
Fratianne, R. B., 1382
Frauenberger, George S., 836,
  875
Frazier, Claude A., 93
Frazier, Shervert H., 1107
Freed, Doris J., 1878
Freedman, Alan R., 1348
Freedman, David A., 590, 706
Freeman, C. B., 1669
Freud, Anna, 591, 1063, 1453
Freud, K., 1610
Friedman, Allison L., 1361
Friedman, F. G. A., 199, 200
Friedman, Morris S., 876
Friedman, P. R., 1660
Friedman, Robert M., 10
Friedman, Stanford B., 255, 638,
  782, 1097, 1185
Friedrich, William N., 209, 724,
  725
Friel, Leo F., 1748

Friendly, David S., 933
Fries, Charles T., 1491
Frosch, Jack, 1594
Fruchtl, Gertrude F., 404
Fuentes, Roberto, 1612, 1628
Fulk, Delores L., 1362
Fuller, Marjorie G., 1879
Furia, G. di
  See Di Furia, G.
Furst, William D., 1182, 1316

G

Gagnon, John H., 1611
Gaines, Richard W., 707, 1101
Gaiss, Betty, 252
Galdston, Richard, 359, 962,
  1000, 1246
Gale, Patricia, 300
Gambino, Vincent, 1001
Gane, E. Marguerite, 116
Ganley, Paul M., 1702
Gans, Bruno, 773, 774
Gants, Robert, 1111
Garbarino, James, 468
Garber, Clark M., 469
Garber, Michael, 1247
Gardiner, Muriel, 635
Gardner, John W., 61
Gardner, Lytt I., 1042, 1043
Gardner, Thomas G., 1430
Gay, James R., 1002
Gayford, J. J., 648
Gaylin, Jody, 360
Geddis, D. C., 285
Geha, Richard, 1110
Gelles, Richard J., 62, 130, 440
George, James E., 11, 1855, 1880
Gerber, Judianne Densen-
  See Densen-Gerber, Judianne
Gershenson, Charles P., 636
Gershon, Anne A., 1629
Giarretto, Henry, 1646
Gibbens, T. C. N., 554
Gibbs, Charles E., 1189
Gibson, Christine H., 174
Gibson, Geoffrey, 1571
Gil, David G., 158, 172, 175,
  176, 177, 178, 179, 180, 210,
  405, 441, 470, 471
Gilbert, Marie T., 1492
Gilden, Jerome J., 895
Giles, Rosalind, 1215
Gill, Thomas D., 1936
Gillespie, Robert W., 963
Gilman, Merritt C., 1394

Ginn, Robert, 1626
Giovannoni, Jeanne M., 144, 472
Girdany, Bertram R., 887
Gittens, John, 1425
Gjenvick, Benjamin A., 1395
Glaser, Helen H., 1023, 1024, 1027
Glaser, Y. I. M., 545
Glockner, Mary, 87
Gluckman, L. K., 508
Goldacre, Patricia, 324
Goldberg, Gale, 1396
Goldfaden, Gary, 1620
Goldfarb, William, 1064
Goldman, J., 1718
Goldney, R. D., 1784
Goldson, Edward, 1028
Goldstein, Harriet, 1524
Goldstein, Jeffrey H., 88, 688
Goldstein, Joseph, 1453
Goldstein, Michael J., 1655
Gollub, Michael H., 208
Golub, Sharon, 1363
Gonzalez-Pardo, Lillian, 211
Goode, William J., 689
Goodman, Sharon T., 87
Goodpaster, Gary S., 1856
Gordon, A., 63
Gordon, Bianca, 1525
Gordon, Henrietta, 1397
Gordon, Lillian, 1582
Gordon, R. R., 256
Gordon, Thomas, 406
Gornall, P., 910
Gottlieb, David H., 442
Gould, Robert W., 710, 711
Governor's Task Force on Child
   Abuse, 1810
Gower, M. D., 1364
Graaf, Beverly J. de
   See DeGraaf, Beverly J.
Graham-Hall, Jean, 1937
Grant, Francis C., 827
Grantmyre, Edward B., 12
Gray, Jane, 1287
Grebin, Burton, 1621
Green, Arthur H., 707, 1003,
   1101, 1493
Green, Donald W., III, 1811
Green, Frederick C., 361, 1317
Green, Karl M., 64, 775
Green, M. A., 105
Green, Morris, 1046
Green, Orville C., 1029
Green, Phillip E., 498
Greenberg, Harvey, 1618
Greengard, Joseph, 776

Greenwald, Earl, 1642
Gregg, Grace S., 768, 777, 778,
   998, 1318
Gregori, Caterina A., 1642
Gretton, John, 1216
Griffin, Paul P., 799
Griffiths, Alan L., 877
Griffiths, D. L., 878
Griggs, Shirley A., 300
Gritz, Francine S., 1137
Groff, Robert A., 827
Grosfeld, Jay L., 779
Gross, Seymour Z., 1004
Grossman, Moses, 224
Grumet, Barbara R., 1938
Grygier T., 592
Guandolo, Vincent, 1183
Guarnaschelli, John, 828
Guin, Grace H., 791
Gunn, Alexander D. G., 388, 1857
Gurgin, Vonnie, 1562, 1575
Gurry, D. L., 273
Gutheil, Thomas G., 1583
Guthkelch, A. N., 829
Guttmacher, Alan F., 570
Guttmacher, Manfred S., 1584
Gwinn, John L., 879, 880
Gyorgy, Paul, 1517

                    H

Haas, G., 1223
Haas, L., 830
Hagebak, R. W., 1005
Hagenbuch, John J., 1297, 2006
Haka-Ikse, Katerina, 1065
Hall, Douglas A., 1881
Hall, Jean Graham-
   See Graham-Hall, Jean
Hall, Malcolm H., 780
Hall, Marian, 1812
Halleck, S., 1647
Haller, J. Alex, Jr., 1319
Halliwell, R., 1526
Hally, Carolyn, 146
Halpern, S. R., 1320
Hamlin, Hannibal, 911
Hammell, Charlotte L., 1217
Hanks, Susan E., 708
Hansen, Christian M., Jr., 1321,
   1322
Hansen, Richard H., 1785, 1786,
   1813, 1939
Hanson, Ruth, 509, 533, 534, 561,
   580, 655, 675
Harawitz, Alan, 923

Harbert, T. L., 1648
Harcourt, Brian, 934, 935
Harder, Thøger, 614
Hardin, Garrett, 389
Harlow, Robert G., 1077
Harper, Fowler V., 1858
Harriman, Robert L., 301
Harrington, J. A., 510
Harris, M. J., 274
Harris, Susan B., 13
Harrison, Stanley L., 1138
Harrison-Ross, Phyllis, 690
Harrston, M. A., Jr., 977
Hart, Walter M., 1814
Hartley, Albert I., 212, 1626
Hartman, Mary S., 106
Have, Ralph ten
  See Ten Have, Ralph
Havens, Leston L., 691
Hawaii. State Department of Social
  Services and Housing. Division
  of Public Welfare, 213, 214,
  215, 216, 1815
Hawkes, C. D., 831
Hayden, John W., 881
Hayman, Charles R., 1612, 1627,
  1628
Haynes, Edythe, 1430
Hays, Janice, 100
Hays, Richard, 1859
Hayward, M. A., 243
Hazlewood, Arthur I., 781
Headsten, Sally J., 628
Heagarty, Margaret C., 1024, 1027
Healey, R. O., 1749
Hedges, Wallace, H. V., 571
Heins, Marilyn, 65
Heiser, A., 1862
Heiskanen, O., 832
Helfer, Ray E., 14, 15, 66, 181,
  257, 275, 362, 637, 947, 1143,
  1184, 1248, 1249, 1323, 1324,
  1325, 1527
Hellsten, Penetti, 649
Helpern, Milton, 1882
Henderson, D. James, 1585
Henderson, J. G., 833
Hendriksen, Douglas G., 1817
Henke, Lorraine J., 1426
Henley, Arthur, 145
Hepner R., 1030
Hepworth, H. P., 363
Herman, Bernice J., 1270
Herman, Dennis, 688
Herman, Judith, 1598
Herre, Ernest A., 1528

Hersen, M., 1648
Hertzberg, Leonard J., 1283, 1286
Hessel, Samuel J., 325
Hewitt, Lester, 1006
Heyl, Henry L., 1327
Hick, John F., 1326
Hicks, Graham M., 1940
Higgins, Edward, 1398
Higgins, Judith, 86
Hildebrandt, H. M., 1288
Hill, Deborah, A., 1178, 1271
Hill, Dorothy M., 1427
Hiller, H. G., 882
Hiller, R. B., 1365
Hinton, Cornelia, 1250
Hirksyj, Peter, 1066
Hirschenfang, Samuel, 1100
Hirschman, Lisa, 1598
Hochhauser, Lois, 1703
Hock, Yeoh O., 1031
Hodge, P. R., 979
Hoel, Hans W., 1818
Hoffman, Mary, 324
Hoffmeister, James K., 257
Holder, Angela R., 1883
Holder, John C., 873
Holler, Jack O., 922
Holliday, Malcolm A., 976
Holman, R. R., 572
Holmes, Sally A., 1399
Holter, Joan C., 638, 782, 1185
Honigsberger, Leo, 535, 536
Hood, Catriona, 1067
Hopkins, David, 934, 935
Hopkins, Joan, 1366, 1371
Hopper, Mark A., 89, 131, 134
Horenstein, David, 593
Horn, Pat, 511
Hornbein, Ruth, 1400
Horner, Gerald, 1401
Horovitz, M., 623
Horrobin, R., 579
Horwitz, Elinor L., 1636
Hoshino, George, 1819
Housden, Leslie G., 364
Househam, K. C., 733
Houston Child Care Council, 67
Howard, Maxwell C., 1420
Howe, J. G., 182
Howe, Ruth-Arlene W., 1704
Howell, L. M., 1580
Howells, John G., 182, 355, 639,
  1068, 1402
Hubbard, Elizabeth L., 1965
Hudson, Bob, 443
Hudson, Phoebe, 276, 326

Hudson, R. Page, 955
Hughes, A. F., 512
Hughes, Ronald C., 1476
Humphrey, Charles R., 982
Hunt, Anthony C., 872
Hurd, Jeanne M., 258
Hurley, Anitra, 420
Hurley, John R., 557
Hurster, Madeline M., 232
Hurt, Maure, Jr., 16
Husain, S. A., 100
Husar, Linda K., 1467
Hussey, Hugh H., 783
Hwang, Woon T., 784, 1031
Hyde, James N., Jr., 1403, 1523, 1533
Hyman, Clare A., 1, 513
Hyman, Irwin, 1428

I

Ikse, Katerina Haka-
  See Haka-Ikse, Katerina
In, Peter A., 1494
Ingraham, Franc D., 834, 1327
Ingram, Eben M., 1095
Ireland, William H., 327, 328
Ironside, Wallace, 1032
Irwin, Clare, 1289
Irwin, Theodore, 1139
Isaacs, Jacob L., 1751
Isaacs, Susanna, 514, 1529
Isaacson, E. K., 785

J

Jackson, Graham, 322, 786
Jackson, R. H., 1186
Jacobs, J., 957
Jacobson, Shirley, 1069
Jacobucci, Louis, 1404
Jacobziner, Harold, 183
Jaffe, Arthur C., 1613, 1629
Jaffe, Eliezer D., 1458
Jaffe, Peggy E., 1272
Jaisinghani, Vijay Taneja-
  See Taneja-Jaisinghani, Vijay
James, Hector E., 787
James, Howard, 159
James, Joseph, Jr., 1752
Jarvella, Robert, 1099
Jaso, Hector, 1861
Jayaratne, Srinika, 664
Jeffress, J. Elizabeth, 1328
Jenkins, Melvin E., 913
Jenkins, Richard L., 594, 1006, 1111

Jennett, Bryan, 835
Jobling, Megan, 191
Johnson, Adelaide M., 640
Johnson, Betty, 218, 219, 1235
Johnson, Charles F., 665
Johnson, Clara L., 220
Johnson, H. R. M., 758
Johnson, Mildred, 1367
Johnson, Norma, 1884
Johnson, R. S., 1508
Johnson, Sylvia, 407
Johnston, C., 421
Jolleys, A., 910
Jones, Carolyn, 1
Jones, Henry H., 883
Jones, James L., 1753
Jones, John W., 94
Jones, M. Douglas, Jr., 947
Joos, Thad H., 964
Jordan, June B., 1429
Jorgensen, James D., 1389
Joseph, Michael, 920
Josten, Lavohn, 1368
Joyce, Walter C., 1430
Joyner, Edmund N., III, 184, 1290
Judge, Cliff, 107
Juntti, M. Jeanette, 1361
Justice, Blair, 445, 446, 641, 692, 1329, 1468
Justice, Rita, 641, 692, 1468
Juvenile Protective Association, 1218

K

Kade, Harold, 1309
Kadushin, Alfred, 1140
Kagan, Jerome, 604
Kahn, Jack H., 1994
Kalisch, Beatrice J., 1330, 1369, 1370
Kaltwasser, Cari, 425
Kamerman, Sheila B., 17
Kane, Robert L., 476
Kansas. State Department of Health. Division of Maternal and Child Health, 1820
Kansas. State Department of Health and Environment. Bureau of Maternal and Child Health, 1821
Kant, Harold S., 1655
Kanwar, S., 572
Kaplan, Eugene N., 1975
Kaplan, Joseph, 873

Kaplan, Stuart L., 1599
Kaplun, David, 221
Karnasiewicz, S. Q., 1382
Karpinski, Eva, 1604
Kaste, M., 832
Kastel, Jean, 709
Katan, Anny, 1614
Katila, Olavi, 649
Katz, Julian, 1007
Katz, Morton L., 555
Katz, Sanford N., 1704, 1941
Kaufman, Irving, 20, 525, 1586, 1605
Kaul, Mohan L., 132
Keen, J. H., 965
Keeney, Ronald E., 912
Kelley, Florence M., 1942
Kelly, George A., 1171
Kempe, C. Henry, 14, 15, 133, 365, 384, 788, 807, 966, 1141, 1142, 1143, 1291, 1331, 1371, 1885
Kemph, J. P., 1607
Kenel, Mary E., 556
Kennedy, Miriam, 1578
Kennell, John H., 567, 595, 596, 1099
Kenny, Frederic M., 1050
Kentucky. Department for Human Resources. Bureau of Social Services. Family and Children's Services Branch, 222, 223
Kerr, Anna, 587
Kerr, W. C., 1477
Kety, Seymour S., 601
Keys, Marshall P., 940
Khan, Hammid A., 390
Kibby, Robert W., 302, 1435
Kiel, Frank W., 95
Kiffney, G. T., Jr., 936
Kim, Taek, 913
King, Charles H., 1112
King, Kurt J., 34
King-Meese, Ruth E., 1070
Kinney, B. D., 1754
Kinney, Jill McCleave, 1530
Kirchner, Sandra G., 1033
Kirkpatrick, Francine K., 650
Kirkpatrick, John, 855
Kittrell, Ed, 447
Klaus, Marshall H., 567, 595, 596
Klein, Michael, 573
Klerman, Lorraine V., 391
Klibanoff, Elton B., 1187
Kline, Donald F., 89, 134, 1008
Klotz, Donald, Jr., 924
Knapp, Richard E., 896

Knapp, Vrinda S., 1901
Knight, Bernard, 615, 1976
Knitzer, Jane, 1670
Knudsen, Stephen T., 1943
Koch, Charles, 967
Koel, Bertram S., 277
Kogelschatz, J. L., 666
Kogutt, M. S., 884
Kohlman, Richard J., 1886
Koluchova, Jarmila, 1093, 1094
Komisaruk, Richard, 515
Kosciolek, Edward J., 201
Koski, Marvin A., 1095
Kottmeier, Peter K., 924
Kraft, Irvin A., 692
Kreech, Florence, 1454
Kreindler, Simon, 1495
Kreitman, Norman, 544
Kretchmer, Helen, 1179
Krieger, Ingeborg, 1034
Krieger, Marilyn, 1601
Krige, H. N., 789
Kristal, Helen F., 1292
Krywulak, W., 1822
Kuby, Alma M., 1210
Kunstadter, Ralph H., 914
Kushnick, Judith B., 1332
Kushnick, Theodore, 1332

L

L. White, G. de
   See White, G. de L.
Laing, S. A., 968
Lalonde, Claire, 25
Lamb, Robert L., 1755
Lampard, F. Gillian, 1035
Landau, Hortense, 1977
Landsmann, Leanna, 667
Landwirth, J., 1047
Lange, Gus B., 1219
Langer, William L., 659
Langevin, R., 1610
Langmeier, Josef, 160
Langshaw, W. C., 241
Lansky, Lester L., 948
Lansky, Shirley B., 1496
Lanza, Charlene, 1612, 1628
Lascari, Andre D., 516
Laskin, Daniel M., 790
Lauer, Brian, 224
Laupus, William E., 1333
Laury, Gabriel V., 726, 1009, 1010
Lawler, Byron J., 1793
Lawrence, Robert J., 1865

Lawton, Henry, 68
Layton, J. J., 1334
Leach, Robert E., 890
Leaman, Karen, 1644
Learoyd, Sandra, 1372
Leaverton, David R., 597
Leavitt, Jerome E., 18, 1431
Lebensohn, Zigmond M., 392
LeBourdais, Eleanor, 69
Ledakowich, Ann, 1887, 1888
Lederman, R. S., 242
Lee, John, 828
Lee, Ying T., 1033
Leese, Stephanie M., 1188
Lehto, Neil J., 1788
Leibsker, Donald, 1823
Leichter, Elsa, 1542
Leikin, Sanford L., 791
Leivesley, S., 1293
Lelchuck, Louis, 1054
Lendrum, J., 965
Leng, Lam K., 784
Lentle, B. C., 885
Leonard, Martha F., 315, 332
Lesermann, Sidney, 1693, 1889
Lesseps, Suzanne de
  See de Lesseps, Suzanne
Lester, David, 1011
Leszcznska, C. S. F. N., Sister
  Mary Eunice, 1459
Leuchter, H. J., 1432
Leverton, Bridgett, 1539
Levi, Stuart, 1756
Levin, Daniel B., 941
Levine, Lowell J., 969
Levine, Milton I., 792, 793
Levinson, Martin, 1499
Levy, Nathan, Jr., 1978
Lewin, Kenneth W., 880
Lewis, Harold, 1144
Lewis, Hilda, 668, 1440, 1944
Lewis, Hylan, 474
Lewis, I. C., 1268
Lewis, Melvin, 1615
Light, Richard J., 185
Lindenthal, Jacob J., 407
Lindsay, Janet, 738, 1497, 1534
Lipton, George L., 1630, 1945
Lis, Edward F., 836, 875
Lister, James, 1173
Lister, John, 1294
Litin, Edward M., 1107
Little, Ruby, 1394
Littner, Ner, 1441
Lloyd-Roberts, G., 886
Lloyd-Still, John D., 225

Lo, Nerissa, 1019
Lobsenz, Norman, 1251
Logosso, Ronald D., 906
Lohner, CDR Thomas, 186
Loomis, W. G., 1012
Looney, John, 1113
LoPresti, Joseph M., 1946
Lorber, John, 837
Lorence, Bogna W., 96
Lourie, Ira S., 166
Lourie, Reginald S., 693, 719,
  727, 1276, 1895
Louy, Vicki E., 569
Loveland, Robert John, 694
Lovens, Herbert D., 329
Low, Colin, 1979
Lowry, Anthea, 393
Lowry, Thomas P., 393
Lucht, Carroll L., 1700, 1789
Ludwig, S., 1862
Lukianowicz, Nancy, 517, 616,
  617, 1600
Lund, Susan J. N., 518
Lung, Richard J., 970
Lyman, Laura, 1359
Lynch, Annette, 187
Lynch, Margaret A., 259, 375,
  574, 598, 738, 1261, 1295
Lyons, Michael M., 226
Lystad, Mary H., 695

                    M

Maas, Henry S., 1572
McAfee, Oralie, 408
McAnarney, Elizabeth, 1433
McAnulty, Elizabeth H., 798
McCaghy, Charles H., 1587, 1595,
  1616
McCall, Frances, 1832
MacCarthy, Dermod, 1036
McCloskey, Kenneth D., 1947
McCoid, Allan H., 1790
McCort, James, 915
McCoy, W. T., 905
McDaniel, Charles-Gene, 1672
McDermott, John F., Jr., 1494
McDonald, D. I., 117
Macdonald, G. J., 1649
McFerran, Jane, 1469
McGeorge, John, 1588
McGowan, Brenda G., 1405
McGrath, Melba, 1704
McHenry, Thomas, 887
McIntire, Matilda S., 202
McKay, Cathy, 599

MacKeith, Ronald, 838, 839, 1335
McKenna, James J., 1980
McKenzie, Michael W., 260
Mackler, S. F., 888
McKnight, C. K., 1610
McLaren, Noel K., 944
McLean, J. D., 1963
MacLeod, Celeste, 1719
McLoughlin, William G., 108
McNulty, Jill K., 1673
McQuarrie, Howard G., 1189
McRae, Kenneth N., 242
Madsen, Barbara, 1530
Maginnis, Elizabeth, 575
Maiden, N. C., 1030
Maier, Frank, 75
Mair, Catherine H., 1268
Makepeace, Dorothy, 1145
Malcarney, Courtney, 1632
Malee, Thomas J., 949
Mallard, Robert, 1981
Mandal, J. N., 958
Mangold, George B., 118
Mann, G. T., 769
Mant, A. K., 1863
Marer, Jack W., 1769
Margrain, Susan A., 19
Marker, G., 1660
Martin, Barbara, 225
Martin, David L., 1912
Martin, Harold P., 1013, 1014, 1096, 1518
Martin, Helen L., 651
Mascio, Alberto di
  See DiMascio, Alberto
Massachusetts Society for the Prevention of Cruelty to Children, 1220
Matejcek, Z., 160
Mathers, James, 1483, 1531, 1532
Matson, Donald D., 834
Matthews, F. B., 1442
Matthews, Patricia J., 711
Maurer, Adah, 135, 448
Mause, Lloyd de
  See deMause, Lloyd
Maxwell, I. D., 1864
Mayer, J., 367
Mayhew, Henry, 109
Meacham, William F., 799, 840
Meadow, Roy, 796
Medovy, Harry, 919
Meerloo, Joost A. M., 1009, 1010
Meese, Ruth E. King-
  See King-Meese, Ruth E.
Melli, Marygold S., 1197

Melnick, Barry, 557
Melson, Elwood F., 1408
Menninger, Karl, 527
Merrill, Edgar J., 20, 1825
Meyer, Hermann, 1189
Meyer, Roger J., 172
Meyers, Alan, 1296
Michael, Marianne K., 227, 286
Michell, Guy, 1072
Milburn, W., 1259
Miles, A. E., 971
Miller, Carol L., 205
Miller, Derek, 1113, 1674
Miller, Donald S., 889
Miller, John K., 451
Miller, Mary B., 1221
Miller, Merle K., 1519
Miller, Morris, 1832
Miller, Patricia Y., 1617
Miller, Stephen H., 970
Milner, Alan, 1637
Milowe, Irvin D., 727, 1301
Mindlin, Rowland L., 119, 304
Mintz, A. A., 696
Minuchin, Salvator, 967
Mitchell, Betsy, 1406
Mitchell, Ross G., 261
Mitchiner, Myra J., 1407
Moffitt, Dorien M., 1470
Mogielnicki, Nancy P., 262
Mogielnicki, R. Peter, 262
Moncrieff, Martin W., 952, 1259
Money, John, 1037, 1038, 1039
Montana. State Department of Social and Rehabilitative Services, 1757
Mooney, Eileen, 1258
Moore, G. Y., 1681
Moore, Jean G., 652, 653
Moore, John L., Jr., 1827
Moore, Pamela, 449
Moorehead, Caroline, 1273
Moren, R., 1448
Morgan, Dorothy, 394
Morgan, Gwyn, 937, 939
Morris, Larry A., 541
Morris, Marian G., 270, 710, 711
Morris, Naomi M., 396
Morris, P., 1576
Morris, T. M. O., 916
Morris, Vivian G., 1190
Morse, Carol W., 255, 1097
Morse, Harold A., 218, 219
Morse, Thomas S., 305
Morton, Arthur, 120, 336
Moseley, Nicholas, 682

Moss, Miriam S., 1073
Moss, Sidney Z., 1073
Mounsey, Joseph, 1902
Mowat, Alex P., 797
Moyes, Peter D., 841
Moynihan, F. J., 878
Mukundarao, Kathirisetti, 1252
Mulford, Robert M., 70, 120, 1074, 1146, 1223, 1408
Mundie, Gene E., 1373
Murdock, C. George, 1913
Murrell, S. A., 629
Mushin, Alan S., 937, 938, 939
Myers, Steven A., 558

N

Nadelson, Carol C., 1601
Nagi, Saad Z., 21, 368, 1147
National Conference on Child Abuse. Legislative Work Group, 1728
National Conference on Child Abuse, Washington, D.C., 1973, 22
National Council of State Committees for Children and Youth, 1554
National Symposium on Child Abuse, 1st, Rochester, N.Y., 1971, 1149
National Symposium on Child Abuse, 2nd, Denver, 1972, 1949
National Symposium on Child Abuse, 4th, Charleston, S.C., 1973, 23
National Symposium on Child Abuse, 5th, Boston, 1974, 24
Nazzaro, Jean, 1555
Nebraska. State Department of Public Welfare, 1443
Nedler, Shari, 408
Neill, Alexander S., 712
Nelson, Gerald D., 972
Nelson, James H., 247
Nesi, William A., 1222
Neuberg, R., 739
Neuman, R., 1456
New Century Club, 1682
New York (City). Department of Health, Health Services Administration, 1337
New York (State). Board of Social Welfare, 1223
New York (State). Department of Social Services, 1224, 2007
New York (State). Legislature, Assembly, 1225
Newberger, Carolyn M., 669

Newberger, Eli H., 136, 369, 450, 475, 669, 798, 1150, 1174, 1226, 1297, 1338, 1533
Ngomane, D., 733
Nichamin, Samuel J., 728
Nichtern, S., 740
Nixon, H. H., 1191
Nixon, James, 973
Noble, John H., 179, 180
Noble, Sheila, 246, 533, 534, 655
Noguchi, Thomas T., 1309
Nomura, Fred M., 71
Nong the Anh, 974
Nordstrom, Jerry L., 1274
Norman, Mari, 385
North Dakota. Social Service Board, 1227
Novick, Jack, 519
Novick, Kerry K., 519
Noyes, Mona K., 1344
Nurse, Shirley N., 642
Nursten, Jean P., 1994
Nwako, Festus, 188
Nyden, Paul V., 330
Nye, Ivan F., 1075
Nyswander, Dorothy B., 413

O

Oakland, Lynne, 476
Oates, R. K., 1041
Ocampo, T. P., 1830
O'Connell, Virginia R., 1471
Odlum, Doris M., 520
O'Doherty, N. J., 842
Oettinger, Katherine B., 120, 1151, 1661, 1694
Oglesby, Allan C., 293
Oglov, Linda, 25
O'Hearn, Thomas P., 521
O'Keefe, Edward J., 1015
Oliver, J. E., 237, 395, 670, 713, 714, 715, 843
Olson, Robert J., 263
O'Neill, David P., 239
O'Neill, James A., Jr., 799, 1891
Onyeani, L., 349
Oppe, Thomas E., 1194
Oppenheimer, Rhoda, 1497, 1534
Orriss, Harry D., 414
Orton, Clive I., 917
Ostow, M., 716
O'Toole, Thomas J., 278
Ott, John F., 228

Ounsted, Christopher,   279, 598,
    738, 1295, 1497, 1534
Overton, Alice,   1409
Owens, Mark P.,   918

P

Page, Miriam O.,   1536
Paget, Norman W.,   1212, 1229,
    1279, 1537
Paletta, F. X.,   972
Palmer, Anthony J.,   608
Palmer, C. H.,   975
Paneth, J.,   1230
Pardo, Lillian Gonzalez-
    See Gonzalez-Pardo, Lillian
Parents Anonymous,   1509, 1510,
    1511, 1512
Parfit, Jessie,   1153
Parke, Ross D.,   1573
Parker, Barbara,   717
Parker, Graham E.,   1683, 1706,
    1792
Parry, Wilfrid H.,   280, 800
Parsons, Elsie C.,   97
Pasamanick, Benjamin,   477, 576
Pashayan, H.,   801
Patchett, K. W.,   1963
Patterson, Peter H.,   229, 1340
Patti, Rino J.,   121
Patton, Robert G.,   1042, 1043
Paul, Norman,   1466
Paul, Shashi D.,   190
Paull, Dorothy,   1865
Paulsen, Monrad G.,   1675, 1683,
    1707, 1708, 1791, 1792
Paulson, Morris J.,   26, 230, 265,
    266, 370, 522, 523, 524, 1472,
    1473
Pavenstedt, E.,   1538
Paxson, Charles L., Jr.,   603
Payne, E. E.,   844
Payne, George H.,   98
Peabody, Dixie L.,   1478
Pearn, John,   973
Peck, Alice L.,   1586
Peckham, Catherine S.,   191
Pemberton, David A.,   1114
Pena, Sergio D. J.,   919
Penner, G. Lewis,   1231
Pessirilo, Gloria,   1236
Peterson, Herbert G., Jr.,   880
Peterson, Karen,   718
Pettit, Marvin G.,   588, 1057
Pfeifer, Donald R.,   341, 371
Pfohl, Stephen J.,   122

Pfundt, Theodore R.,   27
Phila, T.,   1448
Philbrick, Elizabeth,   254, 1444,
    2009
Pickel, Stuart,   976
Pickering, Douglas,   950, 951, 952
Pickett, John,   1232
Pickett, Lawrence K.,   306
Pietrucha, Dorothy M.,   1332
Pike, E. L.,   423
Pilisuk, Marc,   1498
Pinkerton, P.,   671
Pitts, Frederick W.,   828
Piturro, Marlene C.,   1460
Pivchik, Elizabeth,   575
Pizzo, P. D.,   1233
Plaine, Lloyd L.,   1984
Plank, Esther L.,   161
Polakow, Robert L.,   1478
Polansky, Nancy F.,   146
Polansky, Norman A.,   146, 267,
    478, 479, 480, 559, 672, 673,
    674, 1103, 1410
Polier, Justine W.,   1195, 1951,
    1952, 1985
Pollane, Leonard,   267
Pollitt, Ernesto,   1044
Pollock, Carl B.,   1184
Polomeque, F. E.,   977
Popplestone, Ruth,   1411
Postel, Kenneth L.,   1285
Potts, William E.,   803
Powell, G. F.,   1045
Powell, Rosamond Bayne-
    See Bayne-Powell, Rosamond
Poznanki, Elva,   1599
Prescott, James W.,   599, 1076,
    1115
Priestley, B. L.,   978
Prince, Russell C.,   1986
Pringle, Mia K.,   372, 386
Prothero, D.,   545
Provence, Sally,   1025
Prugh, Dane G.,   1077
Pugh, R. J.,   192
Purvine, Margaret,   1574

Q

Quigley, Thomas B.,   890

R

Rae, L. J.,   759
Raffalli, Henri C.,   1953
Raile, Richard B.,   40, 742,
    1760, 1802

Raisbeck, Bert L., 1709
Raju, V. Balagopala, 310
Rako, Jules, 329
Rall, Mary E., 1412
Ramanujam, B. K., 1098
Ramsey, Jerry A., 1793
Randall, Dolores, 247
Raphling, David L., 498
Rapp, George F., 753
Rappaport, Mazie F., 1196
Rascovsky, Arnaldo, 618
Rascovsky, Matilde, 618
Ratner, Herbert, 137
Rausen, Aaron R., 28
Rayford, Linwood, 1832
Reay, H. A. J., 916
Redlener, Irwin, 295
Reeb, Kenneth G., 1197
Reed, Judith, 1514
Reed, Ruth, 1357
Rees, Alan, 920
Rees, B., 747
Reeves, Christine, 1455
Reh, Ceil G., 1357
Reich, Robert, 221
Reid, Dorothy A., 1035
Reidy, Thomas J., 1016
Reifen, David, 1638
Reiner, Beatrice S., 525
Reinhart, John B., 281, 550, 1695
Reinitz, Freda G., 331
Reivich, Ronald S., 610
Renvoize, Jean, 409
Resnick, Phillip J., 619, 620
Reveal, Mary T., 348
Rhodes, Robert J., 1499
Ribble, Margaret A., 600
Rice, Mary P., 99
Richardson, Ivanna, 1475
Richette, Lisa A., 1116, 1254
Richmond, Julius B., 1046
Ricketson, Mary A., 1257
Ridge, Susan S., 1552, 1567
Rigler, David, 537
Riley, H. D., 804
Riley, Nancy, 1866
Riley, R. L., 1047
Rinaldo, Lucille, 982
Ringler, Norma M., 1099
Ringrose, C. A. Douglas, 1631
Rita, George Bach-y-
  See Bach-y-Rita, George
Roaf, Robert, 891
Robbins, Jerry H., 1758
Roberts, Albert R., 1078
Roberts, G. Lloyd-
  See Lloyd-Roberts, G.

Roberts, Jacqueline, 259, 375,
  598, 1261, 1539
Roberts, Robert W., 1413
Robertson, B. A., 243
Robertson, I., 979
Robertson, Isobel, 1048
Robins, Eli, 140
Robinson, Henry A., Jr., 1632
Robinson, W., 566
Robison, Esther, 1269
Rochester, D. E., 1434
Rodenburg, Martin, 526
Rogers, David, 953
Rohner, Ronald P., 1079
Rohrs, C. C., 736
Rolston, Richard H., 1117
Rose, Cassie B., 892
Rosen, Alison C., 1461
Rosen, Irwin, 527
Rosen, Shirley R., 1100
Rosenbaum, C. Peter, 708
Rosenberg, A. H., 1893
Rosenblatt, Seymour, 1479
Rosenbloom, L., 455
Rosenblum, Herman, 1341
Rosenfeld, Alvin A., 1154, 1601
Rosenheim, Margaret K., 1995
Rosenthal, David, 601
Rosenthal, Jesse S., 1479
Rosman, N. Paul, 927
Ross, Phyllis Harrison-
  See Harrison-Ross, Phyllis
Rosten, Patricia, 1480
Roth, E. I., 1630
Roth, Frederick, 1540
Roth, Sally S., 260
Rothbard, Malcolm J., 1618
Rowe, Daniel S., 325, 332, 1955
Rubenstein, I. H., 1956
Rubin, Jean, 729
Rubin, Lowell J., 248
Russell, Donald H., 1794
Russell, Patricia A., 845
Rutter, Michael, 1049
Ryan, James H., 194, 309, 1867
Ryan, Jamice, 1155
Ryan, William, 1574
Ryken, Virginia, 425

S

Sadoff, Robert L., 1118
Sage, Wayne, 73
Sahler, Olle J. Z., 1097
Saix, Christine de
  See DeSaix, Christine

Salk, Lee, 1080
Salmon, James H., 846
Salmon, M. A., 138
Saltonstall, Margaret B., 1748
Sampson, Paul, 1156
San Filippo, J. Anthony, 923
Sanders, Lola, 302, 1435
Sanders, R. Wyman, 1342, 1374
Sandes, Gladys M., 1633
Sandford, Donald A., 1481
Sandgrund, Alice, 707, 1101
Sandusky, Annie L., 1445
Sangowicz, Jadwiga, 1578
Santhanakrishnan, B. R., 310
Sarrel, Philip M., 1615
Sarsfield, James K., 643, 805, 847
Satten, Joseph, 527
Sattin, Dana B., 451
Sauer, Louis W., 577, 654
Savage, S. W., 244
Savino, Anne B., 1374, 1473
Sawyer, Janet A., 1908
Sayles, Mary B., 697
Sayre, James W., 1275
Schaeffer, Donald, 1479
Schechner, Stephen A., 921
Scherer, Lorena, 1234
Schermerhorn, W., 1081
Schiff, Matthew, 1488
Schimel, Beverly, 1865
Schlieper, Anne, 481
Schloesser, Patricia T., 231
Schmidt, Dolores M., 1198, 1235, 1414
Schmidt, Wilfred H. O., 1102
Schmitt, Barton D., 311, 806, 807, 1541
Schneider, Carol, 257
Schorr, Alvin L., 162
Schreiber, Karen, 1428
Schrekinger, Frederick, 1988
Schrotel, S. R., 1868
Schuchter, Arnold, 1957
Schuh, Sara, 1756
Schulman, Gerda L., 1542
Schulman, K., 848
Schultz, Leroy G., 1602
Schumacher, Dale N., 717
Schut, Luis, 787
Schutt-Aine, Joseph C., 1050
Schwartz, E. K., 528
Schwemer, Gregory T., 266, 524
Sciortino, Sam C., 1434
Sclare, A. B., 490
Scoblic, Mary A., 1361
Scott, Pena D., 374, 529, 621, 622

Scott, Winifred J., 452
Scoville, A. B., 74
Seaberg, James R., 139
Seashore, Margretta R., 332
Seed, Philip, 123
Seemanova, Eva, 1603
Segal, Rose S., 530
Sendi, Ismail B., 453
Senn, Milton J. E., 1082
Severo, Richard, 578
Seville, R. H., 980
Seymour, Margaret W., 280, 800
Sgroi, Suzanne M., 312, 1634
Shade, Dolores A., 1375
Shaffer, Helen B., 30
Shaheen, Eleanor, 100, 454, 1022
Shanas, Bert, 1436
Shapiro, Vivian, 1489
Sharlin, Shlomo A., 480, 559, 1103
Shashi, Paul D., 190
Shaw, Anthony, 808, 1298, 1343
Shaw, Constance, 989
Shaw, D. A., 825
Sheaff, Peter J., 744
Sheeley, Jo Ann, 1834
Sheils, Merrill, 75, 1676
Shengold, Leonard, 1017
Shenken, L., 1500
Shepherd, Robert E., Jr., 1711, 1712, 1795
Sheridan, Mary D., 333, 560, 1482
Sheriff, Hilla, 531
Sherman, E. A., 1456
Sherman, Gilbert, 1914
Sherrod, Dale B., 1632
Shetty, M. Vasanthakumar, 310
Shinn, Eugene B., 1451
Shoji, Takeshi, 1111
Shydro, Joanne, 1344
Shyne, A. W., 1456
Siegel, Bernard, 907
Siegel, E., 396
Sierra, Sali, 1651
Silber, David L., 849
Silbert, James D., 1677
Sills, J. A., 455
Silver, Henry K., 365, 1051
Silver, Larry B., 31, 532, 719, 1183, 1276, 1835, 1894, 1895
Silverman, Frederic N., 788, 809, 893, 894, 895
Silverman, M. A., 1501
Simonds, Charlotte, 1872
Simonian, Kenneth, 1087

Simons, Betty, 232, 313
Simpson, D. W., 1157
Simpson, Keith S., 76, 77, 1664
Sims, B. G., 981
Singer, Myron H., 914
Singh, Rev. J. A. L., 482
Singleton, Edward B., 902
Sinkford, Stanley M., 569
Skinner, Angela E., 245
Slack, Georgia, 1437
Slack, Patricia, 1376
Sloan, R. E. G., 579
Sloane, Paul, 1604
Slovis, Thomas L., 922
Smith, Austin E., 1446
Smith, Carol A., 535, 536
Smith, Clement A., 387
Smith, E. Ide, 810
Smith, H. A., 1836
Smith, Jack L., 1759
Smith, Marcus J., 850
Smith, Nancy, 575
Smith, Nathan J., 956
Smith, Peggy J., 1997
Smith, R. C., 1474
Smith, Richard L., 856
Smith, Ronald E., 932
Smith, Selwyn M., 195, 246, 314,
   509, 533, 534, 535, 536, 561,
   580, 644, 655, 675, 800, 1447
Smith, Sona, 196, 676, 1158
Snedecor, Spencer T., 896, 897
Snedeker, Lendon, 1345, 1837
Snow, William F., 1556
Soeffing, Marylane, 730
Sokoloff, Burton, 1903
Solnit, Albert J., 1453
Solomon, Theo, 233, 1236
Soman, Shirley C., 78
Sourkes, Barbara M., 698
Spargo, John, 110
Spinetta, John J., 537
Spitz, Rene A., 1083
Stainton, M. Colleen, 1377
Stamm, Mortimer J., 1896
Starbuck, George W., 811
Stark, Jean, 1684
Stark, Stanley N., 663
Steele, Brandt F., 699, 731, 788,
   1018, 1502, 1543
Stein, Arthur M., 208
Steinberg, Derek, 1295
Steinberg, Rose, 914
Steinmetz, Suzanne K., 700, 701
Steinschneider, Alfred, 1326
Stephenson, P. Susan, 1019

Sterling, Joanne W., 1250
Stern, Leo, 573, 581
Stevenson, W. J., 174
Stewart, Ronald B., 260
Still, John D. Lloyd-
   See Lloyd-Still, John D.
Stillman, Angeliki K., 197
Stoenner, Herb, 32
Stoetzer, James B., 1714
Stolk, Mary van
   See Van Stolk, Mary
Stone, Alan A., 1869
Stone, Frederick, H., 602
Stone, J. S., 898
Stone, Nelson H., 982
Stone, Richard K., 375, 923
Storey, Bruce, 812
Stott, D. H., 1104
Stover, William H., Jr., 483
Strand, Roy D., 853
Straus, Murray A., 701
Streshinsky, Naomi, 1562, 1575
Streshinsky, Shirley, 424
Stringer, Elizabeth A., 1256
Stroud, John, 1415
Stultz, Sylvia L., 677
Suarez, Mary L., 1257
Succop, R. A., 550
Suchara, Helen T., 1438
Sullivan, Michael F., 1715
Sumpter, E. E., 1346
Surdock, Pete W., Jr., 234, 1278
Suson, Eduardo M., 924
Sussman, Alan N., 169, 1677,
   1770, 1796, 1797
Sussman, Sidney J., 656, 983
Sutherland, Dorothy, 147
Sutton, Andrew, 1393
Swanson, David W., 984
Swanson, Lynn D., 1904
Swischuk, Leonard E., 884, 899,
   900, 901
Symonds, Percival M., 732
Symons, John, 920
Szasz, Thomas S., 1503
Szurek, S. A., 640

T

Tagg, Peggy I., 1378
Tagiuri, Consuelo K., 1586
Taipale, V., 1448
Talbert, J. L., 925
Talukder, M. Q., 1052
Tamilia, Patrick R., 1996
Tanay, Emanuel, 1119

Taneja-Jaisinghani, Vijay, 1190
Tapp, Jack T., 425
Tate, R. J., 985
Taylor, Audrey, 715
Taylor, Craig, 456
Teague, Russell E., 1838
ten Bensel, Robert W., 33, 34, 40, 124, 201, 410, 603, 742, 1613, 1760, 1802
Ten Broeck, Elsa, 224, 1544
Teng, Ching Tseng, 902
Ten Have, Ralph, 397
Terr, Lenore C., 645, 1199
Tessman, Lora H., 1605
Teuscher, G. W., 813
Texas. State Department of Public Welfare, 79
Thatcher, Aileen A., 538
Theisen, William, 1696
Thomas, Ellen K., 1958
Thomas, L. J., 455
Thomas, Mary, 211
Thomas, Mason P., Jr., 101
Thomas, Meirion, 926
Thomas, P. S., 285
Thomas, Stanley B., Jr., 1729
Thomason, Mary L., 523
Thomson, Ellen M., 1279
Thurston, Gavin, 1959
Till, Kenneth, 851, 1347
Tisza, Veronica B., 1623
Tizard, Jack, 457
Toby, Jackson, 283
Tocchio, Octavio J., 1237, 1761
Togut, Myra R., 1054
Toland, Marjorie, 376
Tomasi, Lawrence G., 927
Tompkins, Kevin J., 582
Tooley, Kay M., 1020
Torg, Joseph S., 855
Tormes, Yvonne M., 1591
Touloukian, Robert J., 928, 929, 930
Tracy, James J., 1545, 1546
Trasler, G., 1457
Trend, John B. G. Trouern-
See Trouern-Trend, John B. G.
Trexler, Richard G., 111
Tripp, John, 953
Trouern-Trend, John B. G., 315
Trube-Becker, Elisabeth, 1055
Truskowisky, Marie, 454
Tseng, Stanley S., 940
Tucker, D. M., 666
Tucker, Ford, 1292
Tulkin, Steven R., 484, 604

Tustin, Richard D., 1481
Tuters, Elizabeth W., 592

U

U.S. Children's Bureau, 1697 1798
U.S. Congress. Conference Committee, 1839
U.S. Congress. House. Committee on Education and Labor, 1720
U.S. Congress. House. Committee on Education and Labor. Select Subcommittee on Education, 1721
U.S. Congress. House. Committee on the District of Columbia, 1840, 1841
U.S. Congress. House. Committee on the District of Columbia. Subcommittee on Labor, Social Services, and the International Community, 1762
U.S. Congress. Senate. Committee on Labor and Public Welfare, 1722
U.S. Congress. Senate. Committee on Labor and Public Welfare. Subcommittee on Children and Youth, 287, 1723, 1730
U.S. Congress. Senate. Committee on the Judiciary. Subcommittee on Constitutional Amendments, 398
U.S. Department of Health, Education, and Welfare, 1159, 1731
U.S. General Accounting Office, 1557
U.S. Maternal and Child Health Service, 1732
U.S. National Center for Child Abuse and Neglect, 35, 1160, 1201, 1558
U.S. National Center for Child Advocacy, 1161
U.S. National Center for Education Statistics, 1733
U.S. National Institute of Mental Health. Office of Program Planning and Evaluation, 458
U.S. Office of Child Development, 1559, 1724, 1734
U.S. Office of Child Development. Intradepartmental Committee on Child Abuse and Neglect, 1735, 1736

U.S. Office of Child Development,
  Research and Evaluation Division,
  288, 1737, 1738
U.S. Office of Human Development,
  1725

                    V

Van Dyke, Vicki, 80
Van Stolk, Mary, 539, 720, 721
Varon, Edith, 1238
Vaudagna, James, 915
Vaughn, Mark, 1084
Venkatadri, P. C., 81
Veno, Arthur, 487
Venters, Maurine, 410
Vestal, Bonita, 944
Virginia. Department of Welfare.
  Bureau of Child Protective
  Services, 235
Voigt, Jorgen, 1619

                    W

Wadlington, Walter, 1960
Wagner, Marsden, 415
Wagner, Mary, 415
Wald, Max, 1085, 1197
Wall, Charles M., 1162
Wallace, Helen M., 293
Walters, David R., 1592
Walters, Richard, 678
Ward, David M., 1239
Warren, Eugene R., 1842
Wasserman, Harry, 1416
Wasserman, Sidney, 540
Wathey, Richard, 334
Watson, Andrew S., 1199
Watson, Jacqueline, 174
Watt, J. M., 1056
Wayne, Julianne, 1547
Weaver, Colin, 1989
Weaver, Edward T., 1203
Webb, K. W., 199, 200
Weber, Ellen, 1606
Webster, T., 411
Wei, Stephen H., 986
Weidenthal, Daniel T., 941
Weinbach, R. W., 1897
Weinberger, C. W., 1739
Weinberger, Paul E., 1997
Weinstein, Noah, 1665
Weir, J. G., 739, 741
Weller, Carolyn M. R., 814
Welner, Amos, 140
Welner, Zila, 140

Wender, Paul H., 601
Wenger, Don S., 1301
Werkman, Sidney L., 1086
Werner, Emmy, 1087
Wertham, Frederic, 141
West, Joy, 1483
West, S., 987
Weston, J. T., 975
Weston, W. J., 903
Wheeler, Gerald R., 1678
Wheeler, John S., 1249, 1344
White, Desbert J., Jr., 1843
White, G. de L., 733
White House Conference on
  Children, Washington, D.C.,
  1970, 380
Whiting, Leila, 148, 335, 1280
Whitten, Charles F., 588, 1057
Wichlacz, Casimer R., 247
Wick, Emil C., Jr., 1021
Wickes, Ian G., 988
Widlak, Frederic W., 205
Wiffin, E. M., 579
Wight, Byron W., 236
Wilcox, D. P., 1685
Wild, D., 268
Williams, A. D., 1863
Williams, J. E. Hall, 1593
Williamson, Ann, 1372
Willner, Florence, 1258
Willner, Milton, 1258
Wilson, G. Terence, 1645
Wilson, Harrison B., 896, 897
Wilson, Reginald A., 1961
Wing, Mary Lou, 674
Winking, Cyril H., 1845
Winnik, H., 623
Winston, Ellen, 1240
Wisner, Joan Jones, 562
Wittels, Fritz, 702
Wolf, Lorraine, 1353
Wolff, Georg, 1038, 1039
Wolff, Howard, 316
Wolff, Wirt M., 541
Wolfman, Earl F., Jr., 918
Wolfson, E., 1501
Wolkenstein, Alan S., 381,
  1281, 1299
Wolman, B., 965
Wolman, Irving J., 1348
Wong, Raymond J., 772
Wooden, Kenneth, 163
Woods, Merilyn B., 459
Woods, Walter, 816
Woodward, J. W., 1870
Woodworth, Robert M., 646

Woolley, Paul V., Jr., 904, 1349
Wooster, Kelly C., 1763
Wright, Byron, 768
Wright, Logan, 36, 542
Wright, Walter, Jr., 1163
Wurfel, Lois J., 905
Wyden, Barbara, 690
Wylegala, Victor B., 1408

XYZ

Yates, Patricia K., 1204
Yeatman, Gentry W., 989
Yelaja, S. A., 485
Yoder, George H., 1819
Yorukoglu, A., 1607
Young, H. Boutourline, 1088
Young, Harold A., 1871
Young, J. P., 1576
Young, Leontine R., 37, 543, 1548
Young, Marjorie, 1350
Yudkin, S., 142

Zacker, J., 342
Zadik, Donna, 942
Zaidi, Zafar H., 988
Zalba, Serapio R., 38, 382, 460,
  1205
Zaphiris, Alexander G., 254
Zauner, Phyllis, 1515
Ziering, William, 1351
Zilboorg, Gregory, 722
Zingarella, Leonor S., 1275
Zingg, Robert M., 482
Zuckerman, Kenneth, 1352
Zwarensteyn, Sara B., 1650

SELECTIVE KEY WORD SUBJECT INDEX

In the list below, the numbers after each word

refer to item numbers in the Bibliography

A

Abandon, -ed, 145, 1067, 1332, 1948, 1983
Abdominal, 928, 929
Abortion, -s, 90, 137, 389, 392, 393, 496
Act (Law), 1637, 1720, 1722, 1723, 1725, 1839, 1840, 1841, 1861, 1960, 1999
Addict, 741
Adequacy, 472, 672
Adjustment, 1064, 1075
Adolescent, -s, 154, 391, 453, 1108, 1113, 1119, 1462, 1470, 1618
Adoption, 1454, 1923, 1944
Advocacy, -te, 153, 186, 1161, 1187, 1405, 1428
After-care, 114
Aftermath, 1100
Agency, -ies, 373, 1171, 1223, 1240, 1258, 1276, 1388, 1407, 1416, 1562, 1740
Aggression, -ive, 556, 688, 738, 1117
Alcohol, -ic, 708, 984, 1126
America, -n, 7, 155, 159, 163, 185, 217, 415, 1654, 1704, 1969
Amish, 1943
Anger, 50, 503
Animal Abuse, 718
Anjea, 90
Anorexia Nervosa, 561
Antagonism, 722
Antecedents, 651, 681
Antenatal, 579
Anthropological, 599
Antisocial, 640, 686
Appalachia, 480, 672
Army, 247, 630

Assessing, -ment, 49, 436, 551, 814, 1126, 1353, 1565, 1567, 1631
At Risk, 1, 43, 107, 251, 265, 320, 333, 341, 356, 564, 1597
Attitude, -s, 179, 180, 290, 293, 295, 297, 626, 677, 683, 723
Attributes, 557
Australia, 117, 1747, 1749
Authority, -ies, 330, 1135, 1152, 1400, 1402, 1999
Autistic, 541, 629

B

BAPS, 1191
BPA, 1191
Background, 119
Battered and Abused Children Act (Rhode Island), 1861
Battered Wife, 717
Battered Women, 708
Bayley Scale, 1095
Beaten Women, 720
Behavior, -al, 543, 586, 658, 681, 686, 735, 1002, 1003, 1013, 1037, 1044, 1070, 1076, 1117, 1460, 1473, 1478, 1481, 1492, 1645, 1648
Bibliography, 83, 84, 85, 86, 87, 88, 89
Birth Order, 551
Bite, 955, 981
Black, -s, 194, 690, 733
Blind, 1650
Bond, -ing, 259, 1497, 1534
Bone, -s, 857, 860, 866, 867, 869, 886, 897
Book Review, 58, 66, 68, 70, 367, 465, 589, 1188
Bowen Center Demonstration Project, 1218

Brain, 1076
Brain Damage, -ed, 154, 822, 823
Brain Disorder, 838
Brain Dysfunction, 272, 728
Brain Injury, 832, 844
Britain, 1401, 1684 See also:
  Great Britain
Burn, -ed, -ing, -s, -t, 638, 651,
  962, 965, 970, 972, 982, 1382,
  1741

C

CALM (Child Abuse Listening and
  Mediating), 423
CEC (Council for Exceptional
  Children), 1429
Caffey, 872
Caffey-Kempe, 433
California, 121, 1655, 1740,
  1761, 1763, 1856, 1887, 2004
Canada, 539
Care, 123, 1210, 1263, 1304,
  1359, 1367, 1372, 1382, 1439,
  1442, 1451, 1456, 1457, 1458,
  1461, 1916 See also: Child
  Care; Day Care; Medical Care
Care-group, 1387
Care-line, 416, 418, 419
Case, -s, 105, 106, 202, 220,
  232, 255, 323, 545, 597, 610,
  782, 786, 818, 879, 885, 913,
  921, 937, 939, 948, 975, 1037,
  1047, 1050, 1066, 1090, 1094,
  1185, 1199, 1201, 1208, 1252,
  1256, 1276, 1292, 1324, 1352,
  1399, 1405, 1408, 1413, 1444,
  1464, 1467, 1470, 1488, 1496,
  1499, 1565, 1596, 1632, 1648,
  1766, 1808, 1851, 1860, 1868,
  1873, 1897, 1905, 1909, 1945,
  1956, 1968, 1974, 1980, 1987,
  1989, 1997, 2009
Casework, 128, 1206, 1242, 1257,
  1384, 1389, 1395, 1400, 1404,
  1409, 1412, 1528
Caseworker, -s, 1406, 1408, 1413,
  1997
Causative, 889
Causes, 584, 687, 1188, 1584,
  1592
Celiac Syndrome, 914
Center, -s, 358, 1138, 1262,
  1432, 1527, 1721
Character Disorders, 525

Characteristic, -s, 237, 247,
  499, 530, 541, 549, 552, 694,
  789, 998
Child Abuse Prevention and Treat-
  ment Act, 1720, 1722, 1723,
  1725, 1839, 1840, 1841 See
  also: Public Law 93-247
Child Care, -ing, 415, 1153,
  1223, 1519 See also: Care
Child Care Worker, 1382
Child Find (Program), 1437
Child Guidance, 1570, 1994
Child Welfare Act (Ontario),
  1999
Children's Defense Fund, 1657
Children's Petition of 1669,
  1669
China, 95
Chorio-retinal, 935
Chylous Ascites, 959
City, 445, 1232
Classification, 382, 1002
Classroom, 161
Cleveland, 1222
Clinic, -s, 798, 1006, 1476
Clinical, 266, 510, 515, 524,
  609, 726, 791, 867, 1022, 1100,
  1118, 1348, 1440, 1577
Coenesthetic Stimulation, 590
Cognitive, 556, 1001, 1016
Collaboration, -tive, 1196, 1271
Columbus Children's Hospital
  (Ohio), 1352
Columella, 917
Colwell, Maria, 366, 374
Committee on Child Abuse (New
  York), 1275, 1975
Communication, 993, 1194, 1271,
  1396
Community, -ies, 15, 329, 342,
  349, 351, 370, 1133, 1144, 1153,
  1169, 1177, 1182, 1201, 1204,
  1221, 1237, 1238, 1241, 1252,
  1275, 1278, 1279, 1280, 1286,
  1432, 1452, 1563, 1569, 1740,
  1746, 1835, 1927, 1979
Conference (Health), 167, 1179,
  1197
Conference (Meeting), 25, 1197,
  1767
Confidentiality, 1850
Confines, 1040
Conflict, 650, 700
Confrontation Technique, 1487
Congenital, 1104
Connecticut, 315

Consent, 1662, 1954, 1959
Consequences, 679, 1014
Constitution, -ality, 1922, 1966
Contraception, -tive, 90, 1662
Control, -ling, 1436, 1775, 1834
Cooperate, -tion, 1177, 1231, 1275, 1746, 1851
Coordinated, -tion, 1176, 1194
Copenhagen, 1619
Coroner, 168, 1882
Cortical Hyperostosis, 865
Counsel (Attorney), 1962, 1975, 1988
Counseling, 347, 425
Counselor, -s, 300, 1424
Court, -s, 1666, 1678, 1714, 1743, 1915, 1919, 1932, 1937, 1942, 1960, 1963, 1968, 1977, 1991, 1994, 1995, 1997, 2002
Coxa Vara, 864
Crib Death, 606
Criminal, 1902, 1984
Criminologist, 1593
Crisis, 446, 632, 1229, 1272, 1296, 1458, 1570
Cross-cultural, 17, 599
Cultural, 484, 1129
Curriculum, 1422
Custody, 1917, 1925, 1945, 1956, 1971

D

Dallas, 1005
Danish, 415
Daughter, 1586, 1635, 1641 See also: Father-daughter
Day Care, 1233, 1501, 1718, 1730 See also: Care
Death, -s, 170, 182, 191, 271, 334, 615, 943, 1055, 1294, 1773, 1926, 1976
Death Rates, 97
Definition, 1154
Dehydration, 976
Delinquent, -s, 115, 525, 592, 681, 1682, 1733
Demography, 233
Demonstration (Study), 288, 1218, 1241, 1243, 1272, 1559, 1560, 1561, 1565, 1567, 1735, 1736, 1737, 1738
Dental, 969
Dentist, -s, 781, 1909
Denver, 1028, 1235
Dependency, 1988

Dependent, 118, 1208, 1222, 1459, 1460, 1682, 1727, 1757
Depressed, -ion, 526, 606, 1007, 1069
Deprivation, -ed, 160, 386, 464, 484, 709, 1004, 1034, 1045, 1048, 1051, 1058, 1060, 1069, 1077, 1078, 1087, 1088, 1090, 1092, 1093, 1094, 1100, 1102, 1440, 1950 See also: Maternal Deprivation; Maternally Deprived; Parental Deprivation
Derby, 1259
Dermatological, 977
Deserted, 347
Destitute, 115, 117
Detect, -tion, 291, 332, 348, 363, 383, 1435
Determining, -mination, 199, 200, 997
Developmental, 998, 1060, 1518
Deviance, 1595, 1563
Deviant, -s, 502, 1587
Diagnose, -ing, -sis, -tic, 743, 754, 775, 837, 846, 886, 888, 1314, 1323, 1501, 1540, 1875, 1895, 1969, 1991
Die, -s, 54, 463, 1228
Diphenylhydantoin, 947, 1479
Directory, 1148, 1223
Disadvantage, -ed, 349, 463, 1030
Discipline, -ary, 104, 678, 679, 682, 694, 1005
Disclosure, 1893
Discriminant Function, 522
District of Columbia, 1612, 1628, 1742, 1832, 1835
Disturbed, 629, 996, 1001
Doctor, -s, 276, 316, 1308, 1335, 1786, 1852, 1875, 1876, 1896
Dominance-submission, 650
Douglas County (Nebraska), 202
Drinking, 1595
Drug, 658, 735
Drug Abuse, 949
Drug-addicted, -tion, 736, 737, 739, 978, 1748
Drug Use, -users, 734, 740
Due Process, 1920, 1940, 1964, 1967, 1981
Dwarfism, 1034, 1037, 1038, 1039, 1051

E

EEG, 535, 536
ERIC/ECE, 87
Early, 255, 283, 337, 572, 597,
  602, 692, 693, 706, 782, 811,
  868, 1076, 1083, 1099, 1501,
  1620
Early Childhood Task Force, 1691
Ecology, -ical, 451, 468, 636
Economic, 473
Education, -al, 89, 114, 134,
  401, 408, 410, 995, 1008, 1162,
  1335, 1398, 1898, 1943
Education Work Group, 411
Effects, 822, 839
Ego, 555, 583, 1062, 1112
Eighteenth-century, 96, 103 See
  also: Federal
Emergency, 255, 765, 780, 1207,
  1229, 1519, 1571, 1630
Emotional, -ly, 148, 348, 661,
  785, 1012, 1016, 1045, 1058,
  1074, 1085, 1714
Environment, -al, 372, 457, 967,
  1022, 1025, 1043, 1087, 1715
Epidemiologic, -al, -y, 197, 209,
  232, 237, 1150, 1613
Epiphyseal, -ial, 878, 898
Eskimo, 469, 1035
Ethical, -s, 252, 1115, 1129
Ethnic, 472
Etiology, -ical, 637, 638, 1107
Europe, 96, 247
Evangelical, 108
Evidence, -tiary, 275, 969, 1984,
  1986
Exceptional Children, 730
Expectations, 723
Experimental, 688
Experts, 355, 1173, 1180, 1531
Extended Family Center, 1544
Eye, 936

F

Facilities, 1215, 1219, 1222,
  1234, 1235
Factor, -s, 97, 205, 243, 430,
  434, 502, 518, 535, 546, 562,
  568, 569, 581, 1089, 1104, 1107,
  1181, 1385, 1491
Failure to Thrive, 277, 454, 550,
  561, 575, 1022, 1023, 1024,
  1027, 1028, 1041, 1044, 1047,
  1054, 1353

Familial Patterns, 642
Family, -ies, 15, 244, 381, 472,
  474, 507, 515, 550, 585, 629,
  633, 641, 645, 680, 689, 701,
  712, 713, 715, 717, 723, 967,
  987, 1025, 1111, 1122, 1143,
  1155, 1250, 1267, 1283, 1360,
  1368, 1378, 1384, 1412, 1484,
  1497, 1523, 1526, 1530, 1534,
  1536, 1541, 1542, 1570, 1583,
  1584, 1740, 1790, 1966, 1967,
  1985
Family Brutality, 456
Family Casework, 1206
Family Characteristics, 237
Family Conflict, 700
Family Crisis, 632, 1272, 1458,
  1570
Family Dynamics, 553
Family Environment, 1043
Family Factors, 434
Family Interaction, 707
Family Intervention, 798
Family Law, 1916
Family Life, 340, 691, 1217
Family Life Development Center
  (Cornell University), 1244
Family Planning, 392, 394, 395,
  396
Family Relationships, 996
Family Stress, 636
Family Styles, 666
Family Therapy, 1520
Family Unit, 1295
Family Violence, 342, 370
Fantasy, -ies, 519, 611, 992,
  1117
Fatal, -ities, 277, 529, 844,
  1882
Father, -ing, -s, 521, 594,
  1577, 1586
Father-daughter, 1576, 1578,
  1598, 1646 See also: Daughter
Fatherless, 666
Fear, 992
Federal, -ly, 1558, 1729, 1731
Federal (18th Century), 102
  See also: Eighteenth Century
Felson's Sign, 907
Feral, 482
Fibula, 877
Filicidal, -e, 555, 558, 618,
  619
Finland, 649
Florence, 111
Florida, 1817

Follow-up, 206, 255, 286, 466, 567, 624, 1048, 1097, 1545, 1581
Fontanel, -le, -s, 818, 828
Food, 1034
Forensic, 95, 226, 615, 769, 971, 1773
Forum 23, 380
Foster, 1004, 1048, 1402, 1450, 1451, 1456, 1524
Fracture, -s, 836, 850, 857, 863, 866, 867, 875, 877, 881, 884, 889, 890, 903

G

General Practice, 1261
Generations, 714, 715
Genital, 1629
Georgia, 1843
Glaucoma, 931, 940
Gonococcal, 1621
Government, 1208
Great Britain, 443 See also: Britain
Greeks, 94
Group, 1374, 1460, 1462, 1463, 1464, 1469, 1470, 1543, 1739
Group Therapy, 1374, 1465, 1466, 1473, 1539 See also: Therapy
Groupwork, 1547
Growth, 1038, 1043, 1045
Growth Failure, 588, 1042, 1057
Growth Rate, 1030
Guardian, 1973
Gynecocide, 1110
Gynecologic, 1618

H

Handicapped, 134
Hawaii, 213, 214, 215, 216, 229, 1340, 1815
Health Educator, 1426
Health Professions, 1860
Hearing, -s, 287, 398, 1840
Hearing (Sense), 1721, 1723, 1762, 1840
Hepatomegaly, 944
High-risk, 595, 1523, 1538
Hip, 862, 870
Histopathology, 979
History, -ical, 34, 101, 233, 754, 1105, 1683, 1768, 1792
Holistic, 158
Home, -s, 345, 413, 481, 695, 697, 1053, 1075, 1202, 1246, 1374,

1412, 1430, 1524, 1538, 1544, 1659
Home Economists, 1198
Home Visit, -s, 1929, 1930
Homeless, 1442
Homemaker, 1242, 1256
Homicide, -s, -al, 269, 453, 486, 649, 954, 969, 1108, 1112, 1113
Homosexual, 1580, 1645
Hospital, -s, 55, 208, 259, 286, 332, 428, 765, 784, 1067, 1285, 1286, 1287, 1289, 1290, 1291, 1295, 1296, 1297, 1299, 1330, 1849, 1852, 1873
Hospitalism, 1025, 1083
Hostility, 491, 496, 716, 732
Houston, 67
Huntington's Pedigree, 714
Hydrocephalus, 837
Hypoglycemia, 944, 950, 1050
Hypopituitarism, 1045
Hyposomatotropism, 1037, 1038

I

IQ, 509, 513
Identification, -fying, 34, 212, 265, 283, 285, 362, 386, 522, 744, 751, 767, 925, 1843
Identification Work Group, 133
Ill-health, 574, 576, 639, 724
Illegitimates, 1914
Illinois, 1207
Illinois Child Abuse Statute, 1922
Immaturity, 673
Immorality, 113
Impulse, -s, 1015, 1466
Impulsivity-reflectivity, 556
Inadequacy, -quate, 372, 402, 594, 660, 669, 1483, 1532
Incarcerated, 163
Incest, -ual, -uous, 618, 1576, 1578, 1582, 1583, 1585, 1586, 1591, 1593, 1596, 1597, 1598, 1600, 1601, 1603, 1604, 1605, 1607, 1615, 1646, 1648
Incidence, 169, 199, 200, 261, 763
Indecency with Children Act 1960, 1637
India, 190, 1098
Indian (Native American), 430, 984
Indiana, 1750, 1807, 1935

Indicators, 452
Infant Development Distress
  Syndrome, 1032
Infant-mother, 1489 See also:
  Mother
Infanticide, -al, 90, 111, 469,
  605, 606, 607, 610, 611, 612,
  613, 614, 616, 617, 623, 747,
  818, 992, 1466, 1974
Infantilization, 1103
Infertility, 496
Influence, -s, 457, 502
Informants, 1850
Institution, -al, -s, -alized,
  448, 627, 1223, 1458, 1459,
  1460, 1674, 1733
Insulin, 944
Intellectual, 541, 1087, 1096
Intelligence, 244, 560, 660
Interaction, -s, 236, 337, 481,
  586, 604, 629, 671, 707, 999,
  1276
Interagency, 1267, 1746
Interdisciplinary, 23, 369, 410,
  1265, 1573, 1701, 1785
Interpersonal, 675
Intervene, 1388
Intervention, -tive, 282, 337,
  342, 370, 729, 798, 1146, 1178,
  1272, 1353, 1357, 1378, 1405,
  1501, 1538, 1570, 1910, 1957
Interview, -s, 667, 678, 1396
Intra-abdominal, 910
Investigation, -s, 321, 1638
Iowa, 1765
Ireland, 196, 676, 1158
Israel, 1638
Issues, 24, 1462, 1463, 1467,
  1470, 1471, 1518

                J

Jejunal Hematoma, 907, 909
Joints, 886
Judge (Noun), 1408, 1951, 1952,
  1993
Justice, 1503
Juvenile, -s, 1675, 1677, 1714

                K

Kentucky, 1838
Kill, 420, 621, 635, 1119
Koluchova, 1071, 1090

                L

Lancashire, 1902
Language, 1091
Law, -s, 94, 1318, 1656, 1679,
  1680, 1683, 1684, 1685, 1686,
  1693, 1696, 1702, 1703, 1704,
  1711, 1712, 1740, 1751, 1753,
  1755, 1757, 1759, 1766, 1769,
  1774, 1775, 1776, 1786, 1791,
  1792, 1794, 1795, 1800, 1801,
  1804, 1814, 1821, 1826, 1828,
  1847, 1848, 1852, 1856, 1858,
  1861, 1869, 1894, 1896, 1916,
  1939, 1941, 1963, 1966, 1967,
  1972, 1976, 1979, 1996, 2000
Law Enforcement, 1272, 1761
Lawyer, -s, 1786, 2005
Legal, -ized, 94, 101, 349,
  1602, 1665, 1672, 1707, 1708,
  1709, 1748, 1758, 1779, 1784,
  1802, 1813, 1832, 1836, 1860,
  1921, 1936, 1953, 1961, 1965,
  1989, 1990, 1992, 2001
Legal and Behavior Institute,
  1655
Legislation, -tive, 1485, 1683,
  1687, 1688, 1689, 1690, 1691,
  1697, 1700, 1732, 1747, 1749,
  1763, 1768, 1770, 1771, 1777,
  1778, 1783, 1784, 1787, 1789,
  1791, 1792, 1797, 1811, 1819,
  1826, 1835, 1838, 1878, 1911,
  2003
Legislative Work Group, 1728
Lesions, 859, 871, 883, 895,
  904, 935
Liability, 1788, 1849, 1873,
  1875, 1886, 1924, 1947
Lithium, 1477
Litigation, 1787, 1911
Liver, 918, 923, 924
Liverpool, 455
Loftus, Richard, 1596
London, 109
Los Angeles, 1266
Los Angeles County, 208
Low Birth Weight, 567, 568, 573
Low-income, 474

                M

MD, 795
MMPI See: Minnesota Multiphasic
  Personality Inventory

MSPP, 257
Magistrates, 1974
Maine, 1881
Maladaptive, 698
Malaysian, 784
Malnourished, 1048
Malnutrition, 457, 1030
Malpractice, 1886, 1888
Management, 34, 35, 206, 247,
  369, 638, 811, 846, 890, 918,
  1012, 1158, 1160, 1185, 1196,
  1201, 1232, 1281, 1297, 1305,
  1336, 1338, 1348, 1477, 1541,
  1565, 1630, 1701, 1897
Managing, 1285, 1292
Manchester (England), 1232
Manifestation, -s, 744, 783, 855,
  874, 880, 894, 909, 913, 933,
  951, 959, 963, 966, 977, 983
Maramus, 1052
Maryland, 1419
Massachusetts, 1187, 1226, 1967
Massachusetts Society for the
  Prevention of Cruelty to
  Children, 1238
Masterson Case, 2009
Maternal, 258, 553, 558, 567,
  660, 672, 673, 734, 1065, 1088,
  1732
Maternal Deprivation, 588, 589,
  597, 1042, 1043, 1049, 1050,
  1057, 1072, 1082, 1104, 1109,
  See also: Deprivation
Maternally Deprived, 240
Medical, -ly, 100, 136, 232,
  580, 742, 743, 804, 942, 1156,
  1210, 1315, 1316, 1336, 1338,
  1356, 1631, 1860, 1953, 1956,
  1965, 1986
Medical Care, 1210, 1915
Medical Examiner, 1882
Medical-legal, 1199
Medical Profession, 1316
Medical Students, 1322
Medicine (profession), 1794
Medicolegal, 105, 605, 1619
Medico-social, 936
Memory, 546
Men, 487, 708
Mental, 1104
Mental Cruelty, 1009, 1010
Mental Health, 392, 458, 570,
  1272, 1498, 1869
Mental Illness, 1065
Mersham, 1440
Metaphyseal, -ses, 857, 869,
  882, 903

Michigan, 1505
Michigan Screening Profile of
  Parenting, 257
Microcephaly, 843
Military, 451, 1549
Minnesota Multiphasic Personality
  Inventory, 265, 523, 524
Mississippi, 1758, 1826, 1978
Missouri, 1234, 1829
Molestation, 1617, 1632
Molested, -ing, 1430, 1616,
  1642, 1651
Molester, -s, 1499, 1587, 1595
Monitoring, 314, 322
Montana, 234, 1753, 1757
Moral, -ity, 1115, 1848
Mortality, 244
Mother, -ing, -s, 266, 402, 431
  452, 468, 544, 545, 547, 549,
  552, 557, 560, 562, 586, 588,
  591, 594, 595, 596, 600, 677,
  694, 709, 735, 1030, 1040,
  1044, 1104, 1357, 1404, 1444,
  1463, 1464, 1466, 1467, 1471,
  1482, 1483, 1532, 1539, 1582,
  1636, 1726, 1945, 1948, 1983
  See also: Infant-mother;
  Working Mother
Mother-child, 481, 569, 604,
  1073
Mother-infant, 602
Mothers Anonymous, 1515
Motivation, 726
Motor, 1015
Multidisciplinary, 352, 512,
  1231, 1269, 1280, 1285, 1473,
  1518
Multiservice, 1260
Munchausen, 796
Murder, -er, -ous, 221, 431,
  526, 527, 544, 608, 620, 649,
  1107, 1108, 1496, 1596, 1664,
  1889, 1934

N

NSPCC See: National Society for
  the Prevention of Cruelty to
  Children
Narcotic, 741
National, 368, 377, 415, 1148,
  1567
National Center on Child Abuse
  and Neglect, 358, 1721
National Society for the Prevention of Cruelty to Children,
  1, 336, 357

Navajo, 476
Naval, 1285
Naval Regional Medical Center,
  186
Needs, 43, 1126, 1580, 1931
Neighborhood-based, 1247
Neonatal, 568, 950
Neonaticide, 609, 620
Network, 1574
Neurologic, -al, 744, 840, 847,
  895, 1096
Neurologist, 849
Neuromotor, 820
Neuro-pediatrics, 1179
Neurosurgeon, 787, 851
New South Wales, 117
New York (State), 1224, 1759,
  1844, 1914, 1975, 2007
New Zealand, 239, 1157
Newborn, 596, 620, 896, 978
Nigeria, 188
Nineteenth-century, 105, 107
North Dakota, 1884
Nova Scotia, 240, 290, 1175
Nurse, -s, 253, 1355, 1359, 1363,
  1366, 1371, 1826, 1908
Nursing, 1066, 1353, 1357, 1361,
  1367, 1370, 1372, 1378
Nurture, -ing, 565, 583
Nutrient, 1030
Nutritional, 1052

                    O

OCD/SRS Demonstration Program,
  1565
Observations, 1000, 1013
Obstetrical, 897
Occupational Therapy, 1522
Ocular, 933, 937, 938, 939
Offender, -s, 554, 1675
Offenses, 1902
Office of Child Development (U.S.),
  1734
Ohio, 1209, 1808
Oklahoma, 646, 1350
Ontogenic, 1076
Ophthalmic, 934
Opinions, 179, 180
Oregon, 1219
Organizational, 21, 147
Orthopedist, 854
Outcome, -s, 1096, 1570
Overprotection, 732
Overstimulation, 1017
Overview, 101, 647, 680, 1379,
  1953

                    P

PITS See: Parent-Infant
  Traumatic Stress
Paediatric See: Pediatric
Pain, 895, 1039
Pancreas, -tic, 906, 908, 913,
  919
Pancreatitis, 922
Papers, 23, 318, 1136, 1149,
  1949
Paramenstrual, 548
Paraprofessionals, 1272
Parent Attitude Research
  Instrument, 266
Parent-child, 601, 671, 697,
  722
Parent-infant, 337
Parent-Infant Traumatic Stress,
  310, 433
Parental Deprivation, 592 See
  also: Deprivation; Maternal
  Deprivation
Parental Stress Service, 421
Parenthood, 408, 647
Parents Anonymous, 1504, 1505,
  1506, 1510, 1513
Parents' Center Project, 1260
Parents' Center Project for the
  Study and Prevention of Child
  Abuse, 359
Parricide, 1118, 1119
Paternal, 1600
Pathologic, -al, -y, 226, 546,
  707, 769, 791, 881
Pathologist, 1309
Patterns, 642, 799, 884, 1004
Pediatric, -s, 226, 1058, 1182,
  1328, 1331, 1533, 1630
Pediatrician, 304, 597, 792,
  793, 807, 1249, 1308, 1349,
  1449, 1877
Pedodonist, 1488
Pedophilia, -iacs, 1580, 1645
Pelvic, 1625
Pepper, 954
Perception, 546, 1081
Perforation, 921, 923
Perinatal, 1087, 1976
Periosteal, 898, 987
Periostitis, 861, 876, 892, 896
Personality, 518, 527, 535, 536,
  538, 541, 542, 549, 551, 552,
  557, 694, 1004, 1006, 1491
Perversity, 1653
Pharmacist, 260

Pharyngeal Atresia, 916
Phenomenological, 990
Physician, -s, 124, 137, 290, 293, 296, 312, 646, 802, 956, 1290, 1317, 1318, 1321, 1325, 1333, 1337, 1350, 1395, 1816, 1831, 1839, 1840, 1848, 1851, 1858, 1868, 1873, 1879, 1883
Placement, 1441, 1450, 1524
Play Therapy, 1494 See also: Therapy
Poisoning, 361, 945, 948, 950, 951, 952, 953
Police, 1898, 1899, 1900, 1901, 1904
Policies, -y, 121, 185, 344, 391, 401, 475, 1163, 1696, 1742
Poor, 472
Poor Law, 114
Population, 390
Pornography, 1652, 1654, 1655
Portsmouth (England), 1084
Post Mortem, 751
Postnatal, 1099
Postpartum, 248, 603, 606
Poverty, 464, 1678
Predelinquent, -s, 283
Predict, -ing, -ive, -or, 256, 259, 375, 453, 567, 1032, 1113
Predisposition, 453
Pregnancy, -t, 391, 563, 570, 582, 739, 741
Prematurity, 581
Preschool, 348, 367, 1087, 1157, 1501, 1517
Prevent, -able, -tion, -tive, 19, 129, 132, 158, 230, 258, 268, 291, 299, 315, 319, 329, 337, 338, 341, 342, 348, 351, 353, 359, 361, 362, 364, 372, 373, 377, 379, 383, 384, 393, 397, 408, 413, 423, 587, 687, 711, 820, 986, 1014, 1080, 1181, 1188, 1201, 1260, 1271, 1371, 1407, 1435, 1496, 1539, 1542, 1543, 1584, 1999
Primate, 593
Principal, 1417
Privacy, 1662
Privation, 1064
Professional, -s, 1129, 1160, 1195, 1416, 1458
Prognosis, 832
Program, -s, 291, 326, 332, 337, 341, 368, 372, 391, 1139, 1159, 1161, 1167, 1208, 1241, 1243,

1248, 1272, 1281, 1282, 1322, 1323, 1419, 1454, 1476, 1535, 1538, 1548, 1552, 1560, 1561, 1564, 1565, 1732
Project, -s, 331, 1138, 1245, 1262, 1284, 1387, 1519, 1545, 1731
Project Protection, 291, 1419, 1420
Prosecuted, -tions, 1526, 1984
Prosecutor, 1980
Protect, -ing, -tion, -tive, 20, 112, 113, 116, 121, 128, 136, 164, 307, 358, 367, 377, 1131, 1142, 1163, 1176, 1177, 1203, 1231, 1252, 1265, 1280, 1417, 1464, 1517, 1527, 1558, 1566, 1579, 1638, 1643, 1680, 1694, 1707, 1708, 1716, 1748, 1750, 1761, 1768, 1805, 1815, 1823, 1843, 1881, 1901, 1904, 1918, 1966, 2003
Protective Agency, 1238, 1383, 1547
Protective Organization, 1264
Protective Service, -s, 202, 254, 354, 1085, 1127, 1130, 1133, 1137, 1140, 1144, 1207, 1211, 1212, 1213, 1224, 1227, 1229, 1235, 1239, 1257, 1266, 1380, 1391, 1392, 1397, 1403, 1407, 1469, 1528, 1537, 1548, 1551, 1575, 1699, 1998, 2001, 2002, 2004, 2006, 2007
Protective Services Workers, 1385
Pseudo-battered, -ing, 974, 989
Pseudocyst, -s, 906, 908, 913, 919
Psychiatrist, 741, 1485, 1502
Psychiatry, -tric, 49, 201, 545, 588, 619, 620, 630, 671, 1083, 1098, 1495, 1503, 1594, 1599, 1969
Psychoanalytic, 1110, 1489
Psychodynamic, -s, 609, 1493, 1578
Psychohistory, 704
Psychologic, -al, -y, 36, 88, 160, 498, 532, 537, 580, 602, 668, 995, 1001, 1004, 1008, 1027, 1039, 1054, 1058, 1059, 1064, 1328, 1580, 1602, 1615
Psychopathological, -y, 440, 493, 507, 523, 601, 614, 1497, 1534

Psycho-social, 499, 1001, 1034,
1037, 1038, 1044, 1060, 1353,
1646
Psychosomatic, 262, 1046
Psychotherapist, 1488
Psychotherapy, -peutic, 704,
1491, 1497, 1534
Puberty, 1026, 1038
Public Assistance, 1209
Public Law 93-247, 1722, 1725
See also: Child Abuse Prevention
and Treatment Act
Punishment, 135, 403, 683, 684,
1667, 1947
Purtscher Retinopathy, 927
Pycnodysostosis, 885

Q-R

Radiographic, 905
Radiologic, -y, 749, 751, 769,
853, 867, 879, 899
Rape, -ed, 1612, 1614, 1615, 1622,
1630, 1632, 1635, 1641, 1642
Rat People, 1017
Recidivist, 1109
Recognition, -zing, 190, 299,
317, 597, 811, 970, 1158, 1196
Registration, 331, 332
Registries, -y, 318, 319, 323,
327, 328, 335, 1780, 1834
Rehabilitation, 154, 1142, 1543
Rejected, -tion, 591, 732, 1036,
1079, 1114, 1394
Relationship, -s, 601, 602, 697,
996, 1073, 1489
Report, -ed, -ing, 193, 202, 232,
308, 313, 1318, 1485, 1626,
1683, 1684, 1766, 1770, 1774,
1775, 1776, 1780, 1781, 1782,
1788, 1789, 1791, 1792, 1796,
1797, 1798, 1805, 1806, 1808,
1811, 1817, 1824, 1825, 1827,
1831, 1833, 1835, 1838, 1839,
1840, 1841, 1843, 1848, 1852,
1854, 1855, 1861, 1865, 1875,
1885, 1886, 1892, 1909
Report (noun), 16, 22, 67, 133,
134, 199, 200, 213, 214, 215,
216, 222, 234, 235, 334, 380,
416, 418, 419, 1220, 1224, 1225,
1236, 1241, 1243, 1319, 1330,
1548, 1554, 1561, 1577, 1655,
1657, 1692, 1720, 1725, 1728,
1839, 2007

Research, 10, 16, 89, 134, 240,
288, 1447, 1559, 1571, 1572,
1735, 1736, 1737, 1738
Research Work Group, 450
Residential, 1461
Responsibility, -ties, 376, 443,
816, 1144, 1160, 1195, 1239,
1240, 1274, 1309, 1321, 1361,
1367, 1373, 1402, 1424, 1455,
1859, 1868, 1873, 1879, 1882
Retardation, 822, 823, 1025,
1089, 1101
Retinal, 941
Retinopathy, 932
Review, 19, 26, 31, 224, 537,
610, 619, 664, 695, 725, 827,
958, 1096, 1150, 1632, 1796,
1798
Rhode Island, 1861
Rickety, 987
Right, -s, 161, 287, 325, 600,
1658, 1660, 1661, 1662, 1663,
1665, 1667, 1668, 1673, 1674,
1677, 1730, 1812, 1916, 1928,
1929, 1931, 1932, 1940, 1945,
1955, 1960, 1967, 1981, 2001
Roentgen, -ographic, -ologic,
860, 868, 880, 894
Role, -s, 33, 124, 298, 306, 507,
650, 686, 725, 727, 781, 795,
807, 854, 1160, 1264, 1290,
1359, 1371, 1382, 1383, 1417,
1426, 1876, 1899, 1901, 1904,
1912, 1942, 2002
Role Reversal, 710
Rumination, 1046
Rural, 225, 672, 674, 733

S

SCAN, 1288
Sadistic, 702
Salicylate, 950, 951
Scapegoating, 991
Scattergood (Thomas), 105
Schizophrenia, -ic, 607, 608,
1003, 1080
School, -s, 33, 150, 153, 155,
289, 291, 294, 301, 308, 344,
405, 996, 1005, 1081, 1274,
1417, 1419, 1432, 1434, 1912,
1913
School Age, 187, 647
School Psychology, 1428
Screening, 252, 257, 263
Seduction, 1615

Self-abuse, 106
Self-concept, 1021, 1070
Self-help, 1465, 1649
Self-injury, 1039
Self-instructional, 1248
Self-mutilating, 1011
Self-report, 1460
Separated, -tion, 568, 569, 596, 603, 1441
Sequelae, 847, 1625
Service, -s, 6, 1148, 1195, 1203, 1209, 1215, 1222, 1234, 1235, 1242, 1256, 1375, 1445, 1519, 1524, 1562, 1571, 1767
Sex Abuse, 1589
Sex Crimes, 1579, 1643
Sex Offender, 1594, 1647, 1649
Sex Victim, 1602
Sexual, 1650
Sexual Abuse, 1592, 1601, 1606, 1613, 1629
Sexual Assault, -s, 1588, 1627, 1628, 1633
Sexual Deviance, -cy, 1499, 1655
Sexual Molestation, 1634
Sexual Offenses, 1581, 1584, 1590, 1609, 1611, 1619, 1622, 1638, 1639
Sexual Relations, 1608
Sexually Abused, 1644
Sexually Assaulted, 1631, 1640
Sexually Misused, 1623
Sexually-molested, 1348
Shaking, 822, 823, 824, 843
Sibling, -s, 958, 1020, 1048
Site Visit, 1241, 1243, 1561
Skeletal, -ton, 859, 868, 874, 883, 887, 888, 894, 895, 902, 904, 922
Smith, Nancy, 1444
Social, -ly, 88, 97, 101, 130, 201, 395, 434, 452, 463, 585, 655, 705, 813, 942, 1016, 1055, 1063, 1087, 1092, 1230, 1277, 1356, 1440, 1461, 1498, 1602, 1618, 1696, 1832, 1876, 1953
Social Class, 684, 1129, 1501
Social Hygiene, 1556
Social Service, -s, 1155, 1214, 1443, 1572
Social Work, 1125, 1575, 1990, 1996
Social Worker, -s, 436, 575, 1265, 1381, 1383, 1390, 1398, 1400, 1401, 1415, 1416
Societal, 1162

Society, 90, 93, 217, 1018, 1052, 1474, 1745, 1916
Sociocultural, 441, 618
Socioeconomic, 468
Sociological, 440, 1521
Sociological Autopsy, 334
Sociomedical, 1028
Somatic, 967
Somatosensory, 1076
Somatotropin, 1039
South Carolina, 1756
Southeast (U.S.), 220
Speech, 1099
Speech Clinician, 278
Spinal, -e, 871, 901
Standards, 1163, 1551
Starvation, -ed, 54, 269
State, -s, 1240, 1554, 1682, 1688, 1689, 1690, 1691, 1713, 1733, 1767, 1780, 1781, 1809, 1845, 1852, 1911, 1966, 2006
Statistical, -s, 173, 213, 214, 215, 216, 266
Statute, -s, -tory, 1682, 1750, 1759, 1781, 1782, 1805, 1808, 1809, 1817, 1893, 1922, 1975
Stress, 93, 436, 468, 625, 636, 967, 1122
Subdural Effusions, 841
Subdural Hematoma, 819, 827, 829, 833, 834, 836, 842, 845, 846, 850, 866, 875, 1327, 1347
Subgaleal Hematoma, 911
Sudden Infant Death, 287, 1326
Support Groups, 1380
Supreme Court, 1852, 1887, 1929
Surgeon, 306, 1343
Surgical, 779, 1891
Surrogate, 1472, 1619
Survey, 11, 38, 146, 175, 207, 209, 239, 428, 545, 1130, 1330, 1963
Symposium, 28, 1367
Syphilis, 868, 873, 1620

T

TA (Transactional Analysis), 1468
Tardieu, Ambroise, 809
Task Force, 1471
Task Force on Child Abuse and Neglect, 1236
Tasmanian, 1268
Teacher, -s, 298, 311, 806, 1436, 1910

Team, 282, 1201, 1273, 1278, 1280, 1283, 1287, 1288, 1298
Teen-age, 577, 654
Teeth, -ing, 947, 987
Telephone, 425
Temper Tantrums, 273
Tennessee, 1805
Tennessee Home Community Program, 1070
Testifies, 1908
Testimony, 1986
Texas, 1215, 1316
Theory, 1200
Therapeutic, 24, 1784
Therapy, 1541, 1642 See also: Family Therapy; Group Therapy; Occupational Therapy; Play Therapy
Thompson, Ellen M., 667
Thoracoabdominal, 925
Torts, 1875, 1947
Training Schools, 1677
Trains, -ing, 114, 254, 378, 403, 1376, 1387, 1476
Tranquilizer, -s, 738, 945
Transcultural, 243
Transfusion, 1954
Treating, -ment, 19, 283, 363, 382, 593, 837, 870, 888, 925, 1146, 1170, 1178, 1250, 1269, 1271, 1283, 1323, 1368, 1382, 1394, 1404, 1410, 1462, 1463, 1464, 1471, 1472, 1478, 1481, 1484, 1492, 1493, 1494, 1495, 1497, 1499, 1501, 1518, 1520, 1546, 1552, 1570, 1592, 1645, 1646, 1649, 1967, 1969
Tunbridge Wells Study Group, 1136
Typology, 382

U

Underprivileged, 1951, 1952
United Nations, 1658
United States, 21, 169, 178, 179, 180, 210, 646, 1130, 1147, 1682, 1706, 1951, 1952
U.S. Department of Health, Education, and Welfare, 1724
Unmarried, 1444
Unwanted, 563, 570, 571, 582, 1059
Urban, 458, 1098, 1219

V

Vaginal, 1624
Values, 149
Ventricular Septal Defect, 920
Verbal Conditioning, 1092
Vertebra, 900
Victorian, 106, 107, 284
Vietnamese, 989
Virginia, 186
Visceral, 915, 928, 930
Vision, 942
Visitor, -s, 384, 1358, 1364, 1365
Visits, 1374 See also: Home Visit; Site Visit
Volunteers, 1250, 1257

W

Washington Research Project, 1657
Wayland, 108
Welfare, 103, 1127, 1240, 1247, 1312, 1395, 1407, 1416, 1574, 1576, 1681, 1929, 1930
Whiplash, 823, 829, 852
White House Conference on Child Health and Protection, 1556
Wife Battering, 648
Witness, 1906
Women, 608, 708, 1069
Working Mother, 430, 459, 476 See also: Mother
Workshop, 166, 254, 1245, 1319
Wyman vs. James, 1918

X-Y-Z

X-ray, -s, 774, 789, 1033
Youth, 33, 166, 1112, 1304, 1554, 1757

LIST OF JOURNAL
ABBREVIATIONS

Abbreviation	Title
A	A
Acta Paedopsychiatr	Acta Paedopsychiatrica
Acta Psychiatr Scand	Acta Psychiatrica Scandinavica
Addict Dis	Addictive Diseases
Adolescence	Adolescence
Adv Pediatr	Advances in Pediatrics
Ala J Med Sci	Alabama Journal of Medical Sciences
Alaska Med	Alaska Medicine
Am Acad Psychiatry J	American Academy of Psychiatry Journal
Am Bar Assoc J	American Bar Association Journal
Am Crim Law Rev	American Criminal Law Review
Am Educ	American Education
Am Fam Physician	American Family Physician
Am J Dis Child	American Journal of Diseases of Children
Am J Ment Defic	American Journal of Mental Deficiency
Am J Nurs	American Journal of Nursing
Am J Obstet Gynecol	American Journal of Obstetrics and Gynecology
Am J Occup Ther	American Journal of Occupational Therapy
Am J Ophthalmol	American Journal of Ophthalmology
Am J Orthop	American Journal of Orthopedics
Am J Orthopsychiatry	American Journal of Orthopsychiatry
Am J Psychiatry	American Journal of Psychiatry
Am J Psychoanal	American Journal of Psychoanalysis
Am J Psychother	American Journal of Psychotherapy
Am J Public Health	American Journal of Public Health
Am J Roentgenol Radium Ther Nucl Med	American Journal of Roentgenology, Radium Therapy and Nuclear Medicine
Am Psychol	American Psychologist
Am Sch Board J	American School Board Journal
Am Sociol Rev	American Sociological Review
AMA J Dis Child	American Medical Association Journal of Diseases of Children
America	America
Ann Am Acad Polit Soc Sci	Annals of the American Academy of Political and Social Science
Ann Intern Med	Annals of Internal Medicine
Annu Prog Child Psychiatry Child Dev	Annual Progress in Child Psychiatry and Child Development

Abbreviation	Title
Appl Soc Stud	Applied Social Studies
Arch Dermatol	Archives of Dermatology
Arch Dis Child	Archives of Disease in Childhood
Arch Gen Psychiatry	Archives of General Psychiatry
Arch Ophthalmol	Archives of Ophthalmology
Arch Sex Behav	Archives of Sexual Behavior
Arch Surg	Archives of Surgery
Atlantic	Atlantic
Aust J Forensic Sci	Australian Journal of Forensic Sciences
Aust NZ J Psychiatry	Australian and New Zealand Journal of Psychiatry
Aust Paediatr J	Australian Paediatric Journal

B

Abbreviation	Title
Boston Med Surg J	Boston Medical and Surgical Journal
Br J Clin Pract	British Journal of Clinical Practice
Br J Criminol	British Journal of Criminology
Br J Educ Stud	British Journal of Educational Studies
Br J Hosp Med	British Journal of Hospital Medicine
Br J Med Psychol	British Journal of Medical Psychology
Br J Ophthalmol	British Journal of Ophthalmology
Br J Oral Surg	British Journal of Oral Surgery
Br J Prev Soc Med	British Journal of Preventive and Social Medicine
Br J Psychiatry	British Journal of Psychiatry
Br J Radiol	British Journal of Radiology
Br J Soc Work	British Journal of Social Work
Br Med J	British Medical Journal
Brooklyn Law Rev	Brooklyn Law Review
Bull Calcutta Sch Trop Med	Bulletin of the Calcutta School of Tropical Medicine
Bull Cleveland Dent Soc	Bulletin of the Cleveland Dental Society
Bull Menninger Clin	Bulletin of the Menninger Clinic
Bull NY Acad Med	Bulletin of the New York Academy of Medicine

C

Abbreviation	Title
Calif Health	California's Health
Calif Law Rev	California Law Review
Calif Med	California Medicine
Calif West Law Rev	California Western Law Review
Can Hosp	Canadian Hospital
Can J Public Health	Canadian Journal of Public Health
Can Med Assoc J	Canadian Medical Association Journal
Can Ment Health	Canada's Mental Health
Can Nurse	Canadian Nurse
Can Psychiatr Assoc J	Canadian Psychiatric Association Journal
Can Psychol Rev	Canadian Psychological Review

Abbreviation	Title
Can Welfare	Canadian Welfare
Case Comment	Case and Comment
Case Conf	Case Conference
Cat Sel Doc Psychol	Catalog of Selected Documents in Psychology
Cathol World	The Catholic World
Chic Kent Law Rev	Chicago-Kent Law Review
Chic Sch J	Chicago Schools Journal
Chic Theol Semin Regist	The Chicago Theological Seminary Register
Child Care Health Dev	Child: Care, Health and Development
Child Dev	Child Development
Child Educ	Childhood Education
Child Fam	Child and Family
Child Today	Children Today
Child Welfare	Child Welfare
Children	Children
Christ Century	Christian Century
Christ Today	Christianity Today
Cincinnati J Med	Cincinnati Journal of Medicine
Cleveland-Marshall Law Rev	Cleveland-Marshall Law Review
Clin Neurosurg	Clinical Neurosurgery
Clin Obstet Gynecol	Clinical Obstetrics and Gynecology
Clin Pediatr	Clinical Pediatrics
Clin Proc	Clinical Proceedings
Clin Proc Child Hosp	Clinical Proceedings of the Children's Hospital
Clin Psychol	Clinical Psychologist
Clinician	Clinician
Columbia Law Rev	Columbia Law Review
Community Health	Community Health
Community Top	Community Topics
Compact	Compact
Compr Psychiatry	Comprehensive Psychiatry
Conn Law Rev	Connecticut Law Review
Conn Med	Connecticut Medicine
Contemp Educ	Contemporary Education
Contemp Rev	Contemporary Review
Cornell Law Rev	Cornell Law Review
Crim Justice Monogr	Criminal Justice Monograph
Crim Law Rev	Criminal Law Review
Crime Delinq	Crime and Delinquency
Crisis Intervention	Crisis Intervention
Curr Med Dialog	Current Medical Dialog
Curr Probl Pediatr	Current Problems in Pediatrics
Curr Public Health	Currents in Public Health
Curr Ther Res	Current Therapeutic Research

D

Day Care Early Educ	Day Care and Early Education
Del Med J	Delaware Medical Journal
Denver Law J	Denver Law Journal
DePaul Law Rev	DePaul Law Review

Abbreviation	Title
Detroit Coll Law Rev	Detroit College of Law Review
Dev Med Child Neurol	Developmental Medicine and Child Neurology
Dev Psychol	Developmental Psychology
Dis Nerv Syst	Diseases of the Nervous System
Diss Abstr	Dissertation Abstracts
Diss Abstr Int	Dissertation Abstracts International
Dist Nurs	District Nursing
Duquesne Law Rev	Duquesne Law Review

E   E

Early Child Dev Care	Early Childhood Development and Care
East Afr Med J	East African Medical Journal
Economist	Economist
Ed Res Rep	Editorial Research Reports
Educ Dig	Education Digest
Educ Train Ment Retarded	Education and Training of the Mentally Retarded
Elem Sch Guid Couns	Elementary School Guidance and Counseling
Emerg Med	Emergency Medicine
Emerg Med Serv	Emergency Medical Services
Emerg Physician Leg Bull	Emergency Physician Legal Bulletin
Emory Law J	Emory Law Journal
Eugen Rev	Eugenics Review
Except Child	Exceptional Children
Expository Times	Expository Times

F   F

Fam Coord	Family Coordinator
Fam Law Q	Family Law Quarterly
Fam Process	Family Process
Fed Probat	Federal Probation
Feelings Their Med Significance	Feelings and Their Medical Significance
Fordham Law Rev	Fordham Law Review
Forecast Home Econ	Forecast for Home Economics
Forensic Sci	Forensic Science
Fortune	Fortune

G   G

George Washington Law Rev	George Washington Law Review
Georgetown Law J	Georgetown Law Journal
Good Housekeeping	Good Housekeeping
GP	GP
Guys Hosp Rep	Guy's Hospital Reports

H   H

Harv Educ Rev	Harvard Educational Review
Harv Law Rev	Harvard Law Review

Abbreviation	Title
Hastings Law J	Hastings Law Journal
Hawaii Med J	Hawaii Medical Journal
Health Educ	Health Education
Health Serv Res	Health Services Research
Henry Ford Hosp Med Bull	Henry Ford Hospital Medical Bulletin
Hist Child Q	History of Childhood Quarterly
Hofstra Law Rev	Hofstra Law Review
Hosp Community Psychiatry	Hospital and Community Psychiatry
Hosp Med Staff	The Hospital Medical Staff
Hosp Physician	Hospital Physician
Hosp Pract	Hospital Practice
Hosp Top	Hospital Topics
Hospitals	Hospitals
Hum Behav	Human Behavior
Hum Context	Human Context
Hum Ecol Forum	Human Ecology Forum
Hum Hered	Human Heredity
Hum Needs	Human Needs
Hum Relat	Human Relations
Humanist	Humanist
Hygeia	Hygeia

I

Ill Med J	Illinois Medical Journal
Ill Soc Serv Outlook	Illustrated Social Service Outlook
Imprint	Imprint
Indian J Pediatr	Indian Journal of Pediatrics
Indian Pediatr	Indian Pediatrics
Indiana Law J	Indiana Law Journal
Indiana Law Rev	Indiana Law Review
Injury	Injury: British Journal of Accident Surgery
Instructor	Instructor
Int Dent J	International Dental Journal
Int J Law Sci	International Journal of Law and Science
Int J Offender Ther	International Journal of Offender Therapy
Int J Psychoanal	International Journal of Psycho-Analysis
Int J Psychoanal Psychother	International Journal of Psychoanalytic Psychotherapy
Int J Soc Psychiatry	International Journal of Social Psychiatry
Int Juv Off Assoc Newsl	International Juvenile Officer's Association Newsletter
Int Rev Psychoanal	International Review of Psycho-Analysis
Int Surg	International Surgery
Intellect	Intellect
Iowa J Soc Work	Iowa Journal of Social Work
Isr Ann Psychiatry	Israel Annals of Psychiatry and Related Disciplines

Abbreviation	Title
J	J
J Abnorm Child Psychol	Journal of Abnormal Child Psychology
J Abnorm Psychol	Journal of Abnormal Psychology
J Am Acad Child Psychiatry	Journal of the American Academy of Child Psychiatry
J Am Acad Psychoanal	Journal of the American Academy of Psychoanalysis
J Am Dent Assoc	Journal of the American Dental Association
J Am Med Wom Assoc	Journal of the American Medical Women's Association
J Am Pharm Assoc	Journal of the American Pharmaceutical Association
J Am Psychoanal Assoc	Journal of the American Psychoanalytic Association
J Arkansas Med Soc	Journal of the Arkansas Medical Society
J Autism Child Schizo	Journal of Autism and Childhood Schizophrenia
J Bone Joint Surg (Am)	Journal of Bone and Joint Surgery: American Volume
J Bone Joint Surg (Br)	Journal of Bone and Joint Surgery: British Volume
J Can Assoc Radiol	Journal of the Canadian Association of Radiologists
J Can Dent Assoc	Journal of the Canadian Dental Association
J Child Psychiatry	Journal of Child Psychiatry
J Child Psychol Psychiatry	Journal of Child Psychology and Psychiatry and Allied Disciplines
J Clin Child Psychol	Journal of Clinical Child Psychology
J Clin Psychol	Journal of Clinical Psychology
J Coll Radiol Aust	Journal of the College of Radiologists of Australia
J Comp Physiol Psychol	Journal of Comparative and Physiological Psychology
J Consult Clin Psychol	Journal of Consulting and Clinical Psychology
J Crim Law Criminol Police Sci	Journal of Criminal Law, Criminology, and Police Science
J Dent Child	Journal of Dentistry for Children
J Emerg Nurs	Journal of Emergency Nursing
J Fam Law	Journal of Family Law
J Fla Med Assoc	Journal of the Florida Medical Association
J Forensic Sci	Journal of Forensic Sciences
J Forensic Sci Soc	Journal of the Forensic Science Society
J Home Econ	Journal of Home Economics
J Indiana State Med Assoc	Journal of the Indiana State Medical Association
J Int Coll Surg	Journal of the International College of Surgeons
J Iowa Med Soc	Journal of the Iowa Medical Society

Abbreviation	Title
J Ir Med Assoc	Journal of the Irish Medical Association
J Kans Med Soc	Journal of the Kansas Medical Society
J Ky Med Assoc	Journal of the Kentucky Medical Association
J La State Med Soc	Journal of the Louisiana State Medical Society
J Laryngol Otol	Journal of Laryngology and Otology
J Leg Med	Journal of Legal Medicine
J Maine Med Assoc	Journal of the Maine Medical Association
J Marriage Fam	Journal of Marriage and the Family
J Med Assoc Ga	Journal of the Medical Association of Georgia
J Med Assoc State Ala	Journal of the Medical Association of the State of Alabama
J Med Educ	Journal of Medical Education
J Med Soc NJ	Journal of the Medical Society of New Jersey
J Miss State Med Assoc	Journal of the Mississippi State Medical Association
J Mount Sinai Hosp	Journal of the Mount Sinai Hospital
J Natl Med Assoc	Journal of the National Medical Association
J Neurosurg	Journal of Neurosurgery
J Newark Beth Israel Hosp	Journal of Newark Beth Israel Hospital
J NY State Sch Nurse Teach Assoc	Journal of the New York State School Nurse & Teachers Association
J Okla State Med Assoc	Journal of the Oklahoma State Medical Association
J Oper Psychiatry	Journal of Operational Psychiatry
J Oral Surg	Journal of Oral Surgery
J Pediatr	Journal of Pediatrics
J Pediatr Surg	Journal of Pediatric Surgery
J Pers Assess	Journal of Personality Assessment
J Pers Soc Psychol	Journal of Personality and Social Psychology
J Pract Nurs	Journal of Practical Nursing
J Psychiatr Nurs	Journal of Psychiatric Nursing and Mental Health Services
J Psychoanal	Journal of Psychoanalysis
J Psychosom Res	Journal of Psychosomatic Research
J Public Health	Journal of Public Health
J R Nav Med Serv	Journal of the Royal Naval Medical Service
J R Sanit Inst	Journal of the Royal Sanitary Institute
J SC Med Assoc	Journal of the South Carolina Medical Association
J Sch Health	Journal of School Health
J Soc Hist	Journal of Social History
J Soc Hyg	Journal of Social Hygiene
J Sociol Soc Welfare	Journal of Sociology and Social Welfare

Abbreviation	Title
J State Bar Calif	Journal of the State Bar of California
J Tenn Med Assoc	Journal of the Tennessee Medical Association
J Trauma	Journal of Trauma
J Youth Adolesc	Journal of Youth and Adolescence
JAMA	Journal of the American Medical Association
JOGN Nurs	JOGN Nursing
Juv Court Judges J	Juvenile Court Judges Journal
Juv Justice	Juvenile Justice

K-L	K-L
Lancet	Lancet
Lang Speech Hear Serv Sch	Language, Speech and Hearing Services in Schools
Learning	Learning
Leg Med Annu	Legal Medicine Annual
Life	Life
Life-Threatening Behav	Life-Threatening Behavior

M	M
McCalls	McCalls
Manitoba Law J	Manitoba Law Journal
Manitoba Med Rev	Manitoba Medical Review
Marriage Fam Living	Marriage and Family Living
Mass Physician	Massachusetts Physician
Matern Child Nurs J	Maternal Child Nursing Journal
Md State Med J	Maryland State Medical Journal
Med Ann DC	Medical Annals of the District of Columbia
Med Dimens	Medical Dimensions
Med Econ	Medical Economics
Med Insight	Medical Insight
Med J Aust	Medical Journal of Australia
Med J Malaysia	Medical Journal of Malaysia
Med Leg Bull	Medico-Legal Bulletin
Med Sci Law	Medicine, Science, and the Law
Med Times	Medical Times
Med Trial Tech Q	Medical Trial Technique Quarterly
Med World News	Medical World News
Memphis State Univ Law Rev	Memphis State University Law Review
Ment Health Program Rep	Mental Health Program Reports
Ment Hyg	Mental Hygiene
Ment Retard	Mental Retardation
Merrill-Palmer Q	Merrill-Palmer Quarterly of Behavior and Development
MH	MH: Mental Hygiene
Mich Law Rev	Michigan Law Review
Mich Med	Michigan Medicine
Midwives Chron Nurs Notes	Midwives Chronicle and Nursing Notes
Milit Med	Military Medicine

Abbreviation	Title
Minn Law Rev	Minnesota Law Review
Minn Med	Minnesota Medicine
Miss Law J	Mississippi Law Journal
Mo Med	Missouri Medicine
Mod Med	Modern Medicine
Mont Law Rev	Montana Law Review
MS	MS: The New Magazine for Women
Munic Public Serv J	Municipal and Public Services Journal

N

Abbreviation	Title
N Engl J Med	New England Journal of Medicine
Nation	Nation
Natl Assoc Soc Workers News	National Association of Social Workers News
Natl Obs	National Observer
Natl Probat Parole Assoc J	National Probation and Parole Association Journal
NC Law Rev	North Carolina Law Review
NC Med J	North Carolina Medical Journal
Nebr Med J	Nebraska Medical Journal
Nebr Nurse	Nebraska Nurse
Neurology (Minneap)	Neurology (Minneapolis)
New Outlook Blind	New Outlook for the Blind
New Repub	New Republic
New Soc	New Society
New Yorker	The New Yorker
Newsweek	Newsweek
Northwest Med	Northwest Medicine
Northwestern Univ Law Rev	Northwestern University Law Review
NS Med Bull	Nova Scotia Medical Bulletin
Nurs Care	Nursing Care
Nurs Clin North Am	Nursing Clinics of North America
Nurs Forum	Nursing Forum
Nurs Mirror	Nursing Mirror
Nurs Mirror Midwives J	Nursing Mirror and Midwives' Journal
Nurs Outlook	Nursing Outlook
Nurs Res	Nursing Research
Nurs Times	Nursing Times
Nursing '72	Nursing '72
Nursing '74	Nursing '74
Nursing '77	Nursing '77
Nutr Rev	Nutrition Reviews
NY Med	New York Medicine
NY State Dent J	New York State Dental Journal
NY State J Med	New York State Journal of Medicine
NZ Med J	New Zealand Medical Journal
NZ Psychol	New Zealand Psychologist

O

Abbreviation	Title
Obstet Gynecol	Obstetrics and Gynecology
Ohio State Law J	Ohio State Law Journal

Abbreviation	Title
Ohio State Med J	Ohio State Medical Journal
Oreg Law Rev	Oregon Law Review
Orthop Clin North Am	Orthopedic Clinics of North America

P

Abbreviation	Title
Pa Med	Pennsylvania Medicine
Pa Sch J	Pennsylvania School Journal
Parents Mag	Parents Magazine
Peabody J Educ	Peabody Journal of Education
Pediatr Ann	Pediatric Annals
Pediatr Clin North Am	Pediatric Clinics of North America
Pediatr Curr	Pediatric Currents
Pediatr News	Pediatric News
Pediatr Nurs	Pediatric Nursing
Pediatrician	Pediatrician
Pediatrics	Pediatrics
Pepperdine Law Rev	Pepperdine Law Review
Percept Mot Skills	Perceptual and Motor Skills
Pharos Alpha Omega Alpha	Pharos of Alpha Omega Alpha
Phi Delta Kappan	Phi Delta Kappan
Physicians Manage	Physician's Management
Plast Reconstr Surg	Plastic and Reconstructive Surgery
Police	Police
Police Chief	Police Chief
Polit Sci Q	Political Science Quarterly
Popular Gov	Popular Government
Postgrad Med	Postgraduate Medicine
Postgrad Med J	Postgraduate Medical Journal
Practitioner	Practitioner
Prism	Prism
Proc R Soc Med	Proceedings of the Royal Society of Medicine
Progressive	Progressive
Psychiatr Ann	Psychiatric Annals
Psychiatr Clin (Basel)	Psychiatria Clinica (Basel)
Psychiatr Opin	Psychiatric Opinion
Psychiatr Q	Psychiatric Quarterly
Psychiatry	Psychiatry
Psychoanal Q	Psychoanalytic Quarterly
Psychoanal Rev	Psychoanalytic Review
Psychoanal Study Child	Psychoanalytic Study of the Child
Psychol Bull	Psychological Bulletin
Psychol Rep	Psychological Reports
Psychol Sch	Psychology in the Schools
Psychol Today	Psychology Today
PTA Mag	PTA Magazine
Public Health	Public Health
Public Health Curr	Public Health Currents
Public Health Nurs	Public Health Nursing
Public Health Rep	Public Health Reports
Public Health Rev	Public Health Review
Public Law	Public Law
Public Welfare	Public Welfare

Abbreviation	Title
Q-R	**Q-R**
R Soc Health J	Royal Society of Health Journal
Radiol Clin North Am	Radiologic Clinics of North America
Radiology	Radiology
Read Dig	Reader's Digest
Redbook	Redbook
Res Relat Child	Research Relating to Children
Resid Staff Physician	Resident and Staff Physician
RI Med J	Rhode Island Medical Journal
RN	RN: National Magazine for Nurses
Roche Med Image	Roche Medical Image
Rocky Mt Med J	Rocky Mountain Medical Journal
S	**S**
S Afr Med J	South African Medical Journal
San Diego Law Rev	San Diego Law Review
Saturday Evening Post	Saturday Evening Post
Sch Community	School and Community
Sch Couns	School Counselor
Sci Dig	Science Digest
Sci Mon	Scientific Monthly
Sci News	Science News
SD J Med Pharm	South Dakota Journal of Medicine and Pharmacy
Senior Scholastic	Senior Scholastic
Sepia	Sepia
Sex Behav	Sexual Behavior
Sex Probl Court Dig	Sex Problems Court Digest
Signs	Signs: Journal of Women in Culture and Society
SLJ Sch Libr J	SLJ School Library Journal
Smith Coll Stud Soc Work	Smith College Studies in Social Work
Soc Casework	Social Casework
Soc Probl	Social Problems
Soc Rehabil Rec	Social and Rehabilitation Record
Soc Serv Rev	Social Service Review
Soc Welfare Court Dig	Social Welfare Court Digest
Soc Work	Social Work
Soc Work Today	Social Work Today
South Med Bull	Southern Medical Bulletin
South Med J	Southern Medical Journal
Spec Educ	Special Education
Stanford Law Rev	Stanford Law Review
Stanford Med Bull	Stanford Medical Bulletin
State Gov	State Government
Suffolk Univ Law Rev	Suffolk University Law Review
Suicide	Suicide
Surg Clin North Am	Surgical Clinics of North America
Surg Gynecol Obstet	Surgery, Gynecology and Obstetrics
Surg Neurol	Surgical Neurology

Abbreviation	Title
T	**T**
Tex Med	Texas Medicine or Texas State Journal of Medicine
Ther Educ	Therapeutic Education
Thrust Educ Leadersh	Thrust for Education Leadership
Time	Time
Times Educ Suppl	Times Educational Supplement
Todays Educ	Today's Education
Todays Health	Today's Health
Trans Am Acad Ophthalmol Otolaryngol	Transactions of the American Academy of Ophthalmology and Otolaryngology
Trans Anal J	Transactional Analysis Journal
Trans Ophthalmol Soc UK	Transactions of the Ophthalmological Societies of the United Kingdom
Trans Stud Coll Physicians Phila	Transactions and Studies of the College of Physicians of Philadelphia
Transaction	Trans-action: Social Science and Modern Society
Trauma	Trauma
Trial	Trial
U	**U**
Univ Chic Law Rev	University of Chicago Law Review
Univ Fla Law Rev	University of Florida Law Review
Univ Miami Law Rev	University of Miami Law Review
Univ Mich J Law Reform	University of Michigan Journal of Law Reform
US Med	U. S. Medicine
US Navy Med	U. S. Navy Medicine
US News World Rep	U. S. News and World Report
V	**V**
Va Health Bull	Virginia Health Bulletin
Va Med Mon	Virginia Medical Monthly
Valparaiso Univ Law Rev	Valparaiso University Law Review
Villanova Law Rev	Villanova Law Review
Voice Child	Voice for Children
W	**W**
Wash Lee Law Rev	Washington and Lee Law Review
Wash State J Nurs	Washington State Journal of Nursing
Washburn Law J	Washburn Law Journal
Welfare Law Bull	Welfare Law Bulletin
Welfare Rev	Welfare in Review
West J Med	Western Journal of Medicine
West Reserve Law Rev	Western Reserve Law Review
Whats New	What's New
William Mary Law Rev	William and Mary Law Review
Williamette Law J	Williamette Law Journal
Wis Med J	Wisconsin Medical Journal

Abbreviation	Title
Women Lawyers J	Women Lawyers Journal
World Med J	World Medical Journal

XYZ

Young Child	Young Children